*When should I travel to get the best airfare?*
*Where do I go for answers to my travel questions?*
*What's the best and easiest way to plan and book my trip?*

# www.frommers.travelocity.com

**Frommer's**, the travel guide leader, has teamed up with **Travelocity.com**, the leader in online travel, to bring you an in-depth, easy-to-use resource designed to help you plan and book your trip online.

At **www.frommers.travelocity.com**, you'll find free online updates about your destination from the experts at Frommer's plus the outstanding travel planning and purchasing features of Travelocity.com. Travelocity.com provides reservations capabilities for 95 percent of all airline seats sold, more than 47,000 hotels, and over 50 car rental companies. In addition, Travelocity.com offers more than 2,000 exciting vacation and cruise packages. Travelocity.com puts you in complete control of your travel planning with these and other great features:

**Expert travel guidance from Frommer's** - over 150 writers reporting from around the world!

**Best Fare Finder** - an interactive calendar tells you when to travel to get the best airfare

**Fare Watcher** - we'll track airfare changes to your favorite destinations

**Dream Maps** - a mapping feature that suggests travel opportunities based on your budget

**Shop Safe Guarantee** - 24 hours a day / 7 days a week live customer service, and more!

Whether traveling on a tight budget, looking for a quick weekend getaway, or planning the trip of a lifetime, Frommer's guides and Travelocity.com will make your travel dreams a reality. You've bought the book, now book the trip!

D0049988

## Here's what the critics say about Frommer's:

"Amazingly easy to use. Very portable, very complete."
—*Booklist*

♦

"The only mainstream guide to list specific prices. The Walter Cronkite of guidebooks—with all that implies."
—*Travel & Leisure*

♦

"Complete, concise, and filled with useful information."
—*New York Daily News*

♦

"Hotel information is close to encyclopedic."
—*Des Moines Sunday Register*

♦

"Detailed, accurate and easy-to-read information for all price ranges."
—*Glamour Magazine*

## Other Great Guides for Your Trip:

*Frommer's Boston*

*Frommer's Portable Maine Coast*

*Frommer's New England*

*Frommer's Great Outdoor Guide to New England*

*Frommer's USA*

# Frommer's®

2nd
Edition

# Vermont, New Hampshire & Maine

by Wayne Curtis

IDG Books Worldwide, Inc.
An International Data Group Company
Foster City, CA • Chicago, IL • Indianapolis, IN • New York, NY

## ABOUT THE AUTHOR

**Wayne Curtis** is the author of *Maine: Off the Beaten Path* (Globe Pequot) and numerous travel articles in newspapers and magazines, including the *New York Times, National Geographic Traveler,* and *Outside.* He lives in Portland, Maine, where he endeavors to support local microbreweries and minor-league baseball.

## IDG BOOKS WORLDWIDE, INC.

An International Data Group Company
919 E. Hillsdale Blvd.
Suite 400
Foster City, CA 94404

Find us online at **www.frommers.com**

ISBN 0-02-863782-8
ISSN 1098-9463

Editor: Nicole Daro
*Special thanks to Christopher George and Rob Andrejewski*
Production Editor: Jenaffer Brandt
Photo Editor: Richard Fox
Design by Michele Laseau
Staff Cartographers: John Decamillis, Roberta Stockwell, Elizabeth Puhl
Page Creation by: IDG Books Indianapolis Production Department

## SPECIAL SALES

For general information on IDG Books Worldwide's books in the U.S., please call our Consumer Customer Service department at 1-800-762-2974. For reseller information, including discounts, bulk sales, customized editions, and premium sales, please call our Reseller Customer Service department at 1-800-434-3422.

Manufactured in the United States of America

5   4   3   2   1

# Contents

# List of Maps

## AN INVITATION TO THE READER

In researching this book, we discovered many wonderful places—hotels, restaurants, shops, and more. We're sure you'll find others. Please tell us about them, so we can share the information with your fellow travelers in upcoming editions. If you were disappointed with a recommendation, we'd love to know that, too. Please write to:

*Frommer's Vermont, New Hampshire & Maine,* 2nd Edition
IDG Books Worldwide, Inc.
909 Third Avenue
New York, NY 10022

## AN ADDITIONAL NOTE

Please be advised that travel information is subject to change at any time—and this is especially true of prices. We therefore suggest that you write or call ahead for confirmation when making your travel plans. The authors, editors, and publisher cannot be held responsible for the experiences of readers while traveling. Your safety is important to us, however, so we encourage you to stay alert and be aware of your surroundings. Keep a close eye on cameras, purses, and wallets, all favorite targets of thieves and pickpockets.

## WHAT THE SYMBOLS MEAN

### ✪ Frommer's Favorites

Our favorite places and experiences—outstanding for quality, value, or both.

The following abbreviations are used for credit cards:

| | | | |
|---|---|---|---|
| AE | American Express | EURO | Eurocard |
| CB | Carte Blanche | JCB | Japan Credit Bank |
| DC | Diners Club | MC | MasterCard |
| DISC | Discover | V | Visa |
| ER | enRoute | | |

## FIND FROMMER'S ONLINE

**www.frommers.com** offers up-to-the-minute listings on almost 200 cities around the globe—including the latest bargains and candid, personal articles updated daily by Arthur Frommer himself. No other Web site offers such comprehensive and timely coverage of the world of travel.

# The Best of Vermont, New Hampshire & Maine

In Northern New England, you'll find an often overwhelming choice of destinations—you can head to the mountains or the beach, stay at upscale inns or retro motels, and dine with a linen napkin in your lap or a plastic bib around your neck. If you're inclined toward outdoor activities, there's hiking, canoeing, sea kayaking, and mountain biking to choose from. The region is especially appealing for anyone the least interested in American history, especially 19th-century history, with almost every village seemingly boasting a historic home or museum. One of the greatest challenges of planning a vacation here is narrowing down the options.

So, where to start? Here's an entirely biased list of destinations, the places I enjoy returning to time and again. Over years of traveling through the region, I've discovered that these places are worth more than just a quick stop when I'm in the area. They're worth a major detour.

## 1 The Seven Wonders of Northern New England

- **The Appalachian Trail:** The 2,100-mile Appalachian Trail runs from Georgia to Maine, stitching together some of the most spectacular scenery in northern New England. The trail enters the region in southwest Vermont, and winds through the southern Green Mountains before angling toward the rugged White Mountains of New Hampshire. From here, it passes by remote Maine lakes and through hilly timberlands before finishing up on the summit of Mt. Katahdin. See chapters 4, 7, and 9.
- **Lake Champlain** (Vermont): "New England's West Coast" is lapped by the waves of Lake Champlain, that vast, shimmering sheet of water between Vermont and New York. You can't help but enjoy good views when you're on this lake—to the west are the stern Adirondacks; to the east are the distant, rolling ridges of the Green Mountains. Sign up for a lake cruise, or just hop the ferry from Burlington for a low-budget excursion across the lake and back. See chapter 5.
- **Connecticut River** (Vermont & New Hampshire): The broad, lazy Connecticut River forms the border between New Hampshire and Vermont, and it's a joy to travel along. You'll find wonderful

# Northern New England

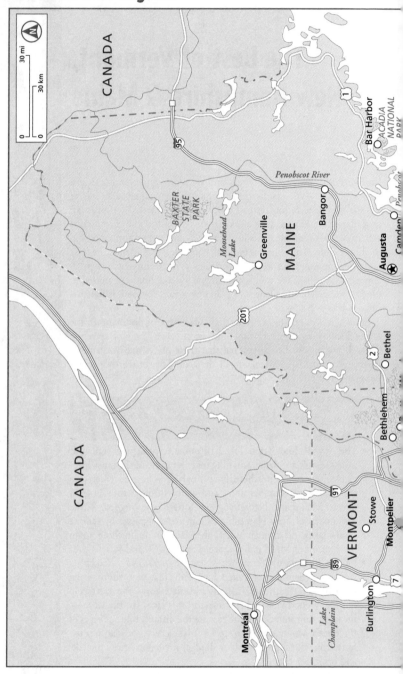

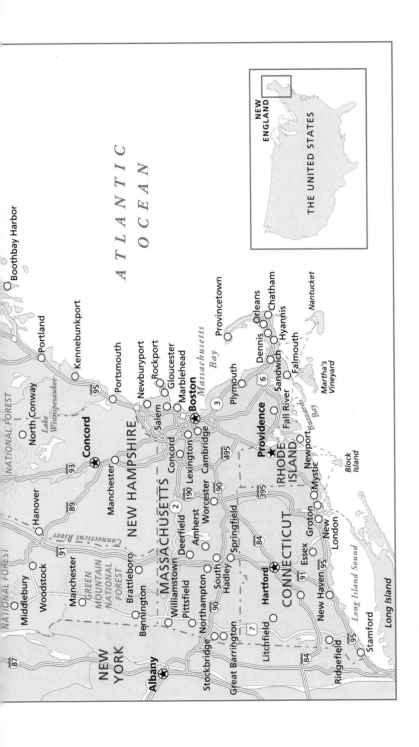

Boothbay Harbor

ATLANTIC
OCEAN

NEW ENGLAND

THE UNITED STATES

Portland
Kennebunkport

NATIONAL FOREST

North Conway
Lake Winnipesaukee

Portsmouth
Newburyport
Rockport
Gloucester
Marblehead
Salem
Boston
Cambridge
Lexington
Concord

Massachusetts Bay
Provincetown

Plymouth
Dennis
Orleans
Chatham
Hyannis
Sandwich
Falmouth
Nantucket

Martha's Vineyard

Concord

Manchester

NEW HAMPSHIRE

Hanover

Connecticut River

Woodstock
Middlebury
Manchester

GREEN MOUNTAIN NATIONAL FOREST

Brattleboro
Bennington

MASSACHUSETTS

Williamstown
Pittsfield
Deerfield
Amherst
Worcester
South Hadley
Northampton
Springfield

Providence

RHODE ISLAND

Fall River
Newport
Mystic

Block Island

Buzzards Bay

CONNECTICUT

Hartford
Essex
Groton
New London

New Haven

Long Island Sound

Stamford
Ridgefield

Litchfield

Stockbridge
Great Barrington

NEW YORK

Albany

Long Island

3

vistas, peaceful villages, and evidence of the region's rich history when the river served as the superhighway of northern New England. Today, it's often overlooked as a destination. See chapters 4, 6, and 7.

- **Franconia Notch** (New Hampshire): This rocky defile through the craggiest part of the White Mountains is spectacular to drive through, but it's even more wondrous if you stop and explore on foot or bike. Hike the flanking ridges, bike the pathway along the valley floor, or just lounge in the sun at the edge of Echo Lake. New Hampshire's famous Old Man of the Mountains lives here. See chapter 7.
- **Tuckerman Ravine** (New Hampshire): This glacial cirque high on the flanks of Mt. Washington (New England's highest peak) seems part medieval, part Alps, and entirely other worldly. Snows blown across the upper lip throughout the winter accumulate to depths of 70 feet or more. In spring, skiers trek here from throughout the country to challenge this sheer face, and hikers will find snow in this vast and dramatic bowl well into summer. See chapter 7.
- **Acadia National Park** (Maine): New England's only national park happens to be one of the nation's most popular; and it's no wonder why. The fractured, rocky coastline pounded by surf is the main attraction here, but don't overlook the quiet boreal forests and open summits of low mountains that afford spectacular coastal views. See chapter 8.
- **Mount Katahdin** (Maine): Rising abruptly from a thick blanket of North Woods forest, the nearly mile-high Mt. Katahdin has an ineffable spiritual quality to it. It's the centerpiece of equally inspiring Baxter State Park, one of the last, best wildernesses of the eastern states. See chapter 9.

## 2  The Best Small Towns

- **Grafton** (Vermont): Just a handful of decades ago Grafton was a down-at-the-heels mountain town slowly being reclaimed by termites and the elements. A wealthy family took it on as a pet project and has lovingly restored the village to the way it once was—even burying the electric lines to reclaim the landscape. It doesn't feel like a living history museum; it just feels *right*. See chapter 4.
- **Woodstock** (Vermont): Woodstock has a stunning village green, a whole range of 19th-century homes, woodland walks just out of town, and a settled, old-money air. This is a good place to explore by foot or bike, or to just sit on a porch and watch summer unfold. See chapter 4.
- **Montpelier** (Vermont): This is the way all state capitals should be—slow-paced, small enough that you can walk everywhere, and with shops that sell wrenches and strapping tape. Montpelier also shows a more sophisticated edge, with its Culinary Institute, a theater showing art-house films and several fine-book shops; but at heart it's a small town, where you just might run into the governor buying duct tape at the corner store. See chapter 5.
- **Hancock** (New Hampshire): This quiet hamlet—a sort of satellite of the commercial center of Peterborough—has an historic and settled white-clapboard grace that's been utterly unperturbed by the centuries since it was founded. See chapter 6.
- **Castine** (Maine): Soaring elm trees, a peaceful harborside setting, plenty of grand historic homes, and a selection of good inns make this a great spot to soak up some of Maine's coastal ambience off the beaten path. See chapter 8.

## 3  The Best Places to See Fall Foliage

- **Route 100** (Vermont): Route 100 winds the length of the Vermont from Readsboro to Newport. It's the major north–south route through the center of the Green Mountains, yet it's surprisingly undeveloped for most of its length. It can be crowded along the southern stretches on autumn weekends, but head further north and you'll leave the crowds behind. See chapter 4.

- **I-91** (Vermont): An interstate? Don't scoff. If you like your foliage viewing big and fast, cruise I-91 from White River Junction to Newport. You'll be overwhelmed with gorgeous terrain, from the gentle Connecticut River Valley to the rolling hills of the Northeast Kingdom. The traffic isn't as bad as on state roads, either. See chapter 4.

- **Aboard the M/S *Mount Washington*** (New Hampshire): One of the more majestic views of the White Mountains is from Lake Winnipesaukee to the south. The vista is especially appealing in fall from the deck of the *Mount Washington,* an uncommonly handsome 230-foot long vessel that offers a variety of tours on the lake through mid-October. The fringe of fall color along the lake's shoreline is a welcome bonus. See chapter 6.

- **Crawford Notch** (New Hampshire): Route 302 passes through this scenic valley, where you can see the brilliant red maples and yellow birches high on the hillsides. Mt. Washington stands guard in the background and, in fall, is likely to be dusted with an early snow. See chapter 7.

- **Blueberry barrens of Downeast Maine:** Maine's wild blueberry barrens turn a brilliant cranberry-red in fall, setting the fields ablaze. Wander the dirt roads northeast of Cherryfield through the upland barrens, or just drive on Route 1 between Harrington and Machias past the experimental farm atop aptly named Blueberry Hill. See chapter 8.

## 4  The Best Ways to View Coastal Scenery

- **Bicycle Route 1A from Hampton Beach to Portsmouth** (New Hampshire): You'll get a sampling of all sorts of coastal scenery along New Hampshire's minuscule coastline. You'll begin with sandy beaches, then pass rocky headlands and handsome mansions before coasting into Portsmouth, the region's most scenic seaside city. See chapter 6.

- **Drive the Park Loop Road at Acadia National Park** (Maine): This is the region's premier ocean drive. You'll start high along a ridge with views of Frenchman Bay and the Porcupine Islands, then dip down along the rocky shores to watch the surf crash against the dark rocks. Plan to do this 20-mile loop at least twice to get the most out of it. See chapter 8.

- **Sea kayak Merchant's Row** (Maine): The islands between Stonington and Isle au Haut, rimmed with pink granite and capped with the stark spires of spruce trees, are among the most spectacular anywhere. A wonderful way to explore them is by sea kayak, which will get you to islands inaccessible by motorboat. Outfitters offer overnight camping trips on the islands. See "Sea Kayaking & Boating Along 'Merchant's Row'" in chapter 8.

- **Hike Monhegan Island** (Maine): The village of Monhegan is clustered around the harbor of this island far off the Maine coast. The rest of this 700-acre island is comprised of picturesque wildlands, with miles of trails crossing open meadows and along rocky bluffs. See chapter 8.

- **Sit in a rocking chair** (Maine): The views are never better than when you're caught unaware—such as suddenly looking up from an engrossing book on the front porch of an oceanside inn. Throughout the Maine chapters, look for mention of hotels and inns right on the water. Some of the better porches: Beachmere Inn (Ogunquit), Black Point Inn (Scarborough), Grey Havens (Georgetown Island), East Wind Inn (Tenant's Harbor), Samoset Resort (Rockport), Inn on the Harbor (Stonington), Inn at Canoe Point (Bar Harbor), and the Claremont (Southwest Harbor).

## 5  The Best Active Vacations

- **Biking inn-to-inn** (Vermont): Vermont is a biker's paradise. Serpentine roads wind through the verdant hills and along tumbling streams. Several organizations will ferry your baggage from inn to inn; you provide the pedal power to get yourself from one point to the next. See "Enjoying the Great Outdoors" in chapter 4.
- **Skiing in the Green Mountains:** Vermont has nearly two dozen ski areas, offering everything from the cozy friendliness of Bolton Valley to the high-impact skiing of sprawling Killington. Vermont has long been New England's ski capital, and they've learned how to do it right. My favorite? The village of Stowe, where great skiing is combined with fine lodging and dining. See chapter 4.
- **Hiking the White Mountains** (New Hampshire): These rugged peaks draw hikers from all over the globe, attracted by the history, the beautiful vistas, and the exceptional landscapes from the craggy ridgelines. You can undertake day-hike forays and retreat to comfortable inns at night, or stay in the hills at the Appalachian Mountain Club's historic high huts. See chapter 7.
- **Mountain biking at Acadia** (Maine): John D. Rockefeller, Jr. built the carriage roads of Mount Desert Island so the gentry could enjoy rambles in the woods with their horses and away from pesky cars. Today, this extensive network makes for some of the most enjoyable, aesthetically pleasing mountain biking anywhere. See chapter 8.
- **Canoeing the North Woods** (Maine): Maine has thousands of miles of flowing rivers and streams, and hundreds of miles of shoreline along remote ponds and lakes. Bring your tent, sleeping bag, and cooking gear, and come prepared to spend a night under the stars listening to the sounds of the loons. See chapter 9.

## 6  The Best Destinations for Families

- **Montshire Museum of Science** (Norwich, Vermont): This new children's museum in a soaring, modern space on the Vermont–New Hampshire border is a treat, with wonderful interactive exhibits inside and nature trails along the Connecticut River on the outside. See chapter 4.
- **Weirs Beach** (New Hampshire): Did somebody say cheesy? You bet. This is the trip your kids would plan if you weren't so meddlesome. Weirs Beach on Lake Winnipesaukee offers passive amusements like train and boat rides that appeal to younger kids, and plenty of active adventures for young teens like go-kart racing, water slides, and video arcades. The parents can recuperate on the lakeside beach. See chapter 6.
- **Cog Railroad** (Crawford Notch, New Hampshire): It's fun. It's terrifying. It's a great glimpse into history. Kids love this ratchety climb to the top of New England's highest peak aboard trains specially designed to scale the mountain in

1869. As a technological marvel, the railroad attracted tourists by the thousands a century ago. They still come to marvel at its sheer audacity. See chapter 7.

- **Monhegan Island** (Maine): Kids from 8 to 12 years old especially enjoy overnight excursions to Monhegan Island. The mail boat from Port Clyde is rustic and intriguing, the hotels are an adventure, and the 700-acre island's scale is perfect for kids to explore. See chapter 8.

## 7  The Most Intriguing Historic Homes

- **Hildene** (Manchester, Vermont): This lavish summer home was built by Abraham and Mary Todd Lincoln's son, Robert. A prosperous businessman, the younger Lincoln built this summer retreat complete with a 1,000-pipe organ and extensive formal gardens. If you're curious about how the other half lived late in America's gilded age, this is the destination. See chapter 4.
- **Canterbury Shaker Village** (Canterbury, New Hampshire): This historic village outside Concord nicely captures the Shaker way of life, which stressed simplicity and industry. See the massive laundry room, or enjoy a Shaker-inspired meal at the restaurant, followed by an evening candlelight tour of the village at its most peaceful. See chapter 6.
- **Drisco House** (Portsmouth, New Hampshire): The Drisco House is the most fascinating of any at Strawbery Banke, the region's premier historic attraction. Half of this house was restored to its 1790s grandeur, and half was left as it appeared in the 1950s. You'll learn plenty about how a house adapts to the technology and culture of each era. See chapter 6.
- **Saint-Gaudens National Historic Site** (Cornish, New Hampshire): Sculptor Augustus Saint-Gaudens has been overshadowed somewhat by his contemporary, Daniel Chester French, but his works were extraordinary and prolific. You'll learn all about the man and the artistic culture of the late 19th and early 20th centuries during tours of his studio and house, located in the peaceful Connecticut River Valley of southwest New Hampshire. See chapter 6.
- **Zimmerman House** (Manchester, New Hampshire): Designed in 1950 by Frank Lloyd Wright, the Zimmerman house is so, well, *last century*. Mid-century modern, to be specific. It's a great example of a Wright Usonian home and offers lessons in how to live right in any age. See chapter 6.
- **Victoria Mansion** (Portland, Maine): Donald Trump had nothing on the Victorians when it came to material excess. You'll see Victorian decorative arts at their zenith in this elaborate Italianate mansion built during the Civil War years by a prosperous hotelier. It's open to the public for tours throughout the summer. See chapter 8.
- **Parson Fisher House** (Blue Hill, Maine): Parson Jonathan Fisher, who served as minister to the quiet town of Blue Hill in the late 18th century, was a man of extraordinary talents, from designing his own house to building his own clocks to preaching sermons in five languages (including Aramaic). As if that wasn't enough, his primitive landscapes of the region are widely regarded as among the best to come from the area. See chapter 8.

## 8  The Best Places to Rediscover America's Past

- **Plymouth** (Vermont): President Calvin Coolidge was born in this high, upland valley, and the state has done a superb job preserving his hometown village. You'll get a good sense of the president's roots but also gain a greater understanding of how a New England village once worked. Don't miss the excellent cheese shop, until recently owned by the Coolidge family. See chapter 4.

- **Shelburne Museum** (Shelburne, Vermont): Think of this sprawling museum as New England's attic. Located on 45 acres on the shores of Lake Champlain, the Shelburne Museum not only features the usual exhibits of quilts and early glass, but whole buildings preserved like specimens in formaldehyde. Look for the lighthouse, railroad station, and stagecoach inn. This is one of northern New England's "don't miss" destinations. See chapter 5.
- **Portsmouth** (New Hampshire): Portsmouth is a salty coastal city that just happens to have some of the most impressive historic homes in New England. Start at Strawbery Banke, a 10-acre compound of 42 historic buildings. Then visit the many other grand homes in nearby neighborhoods, including the house John Paul Jones lived in while building his warship during the Revolution. See chapter 6.
- **Sabbathday Lake Shaker Community** (New Gloucester, Maine): This is the last of the active Shaker communities in the nation and the only one that voted to accept new converts rather than die out. The 1,900-acre farm about 45 minutes outside of Portland has a number of exceptional buildings, including some dating back to the 18th century. Visitors come to view examples of historic Shaker craftsmanship and buy locally grown Shaker herbs to bring home. See chapter 8.
- **Mount Desert Island & Bar Harbor** (Maine): In the mid-19th century, America launched a love affair with sublime nature and never looked back. See where it started amid the surf-wracked rocks, and where some of the nation's most affluent families ventured to erect vacation "cottages" that counted bedrooms by the dozen. The area can still teach lessons on how to design with nature as an accomplice rather than an adversary. See chapter 8.

## 9  The Best Resorts

- **Woodstock Inn & Resort** (Woodstock, Vermont; ☎ **800/448-7900** or 802/457-1100): The 140-room inn was built in the 1960s with a strong Colonial Revival accent. Located right on the green in picturesque Woodstock, the inn offers easy access to the village, along with plenty of other activities, including golf on a course designed by Robert Trent Jones, indoor and outdoor pools, hiking, and skiing (both downhill and cross-country) in winter. See chapter 4.
- **Basin Harbor Club** (Vergennes, Vermont: ☎ **800/622-4000** or 802/475-2311): This classic lakeside resort on 700 acres was founded in 1886, and is still run by the same family. The resort's icon, fittingly, is an Adirondack chair, dozens of which are arrayed for slouching and enjoying views across the lake to New York. Most guests occupy cottages, which are more elemental than swank. See chapter 5.
- **Balsams Grand Resort Hotel** (Dixville Notch, New Hampshire; ☎ **800/255-0600** or 603/255-3400, or 800/255-0800 in NH): It's like having your own castle on your own private estate. Set on 15,000 acres in far northern New Hampshire, The Balsams has been offering superb hospitality and gracious comfort since 1866. It has two golf courses, miles of hiking trails, and, in winter, its own downhill and cross-country ski areas. See chapter 7.
- **Mount Washington Hotel** (Bretton Woods, New Hampshire; ☎ **800/258-0330** or 603/278-1000): The last of the grand Edwardian resorts, the Mount Washington has come back from the brink of bankruptcy with its famed flair intact.

This is the place to play golf, climb Mt. Washington, or just sit on the broad porch and feel important. See chapter 7.

- **The Colony Hotel** (Kennebunkport, Maine; ☎ **800/552-2363** or 207/967-3331): This rambling, gleaming white resort dates back to 1914 and has been nicely upgraded over the years without losing any of its charm. You can play shuffleboard, putt on the green, or lounge in the ocean-view pool. More vigorous souls cross the street to brave the cold Atlantic waters. See chapter 8.
- **Black Point Inn** (Scarborough, Maine; ☎ **800/258-0003** or 207/883-2500): This compound of shingled buildings near two beaches dates back to 1973 but has been impeccably maintained ever since. New owners have brought back the luster without obscuring the old-fashioned charm. See chapter 8.
- **Quisisana** (Center Lovell, Maine; ☎ **207/925-3500**, or 914/833-0293 in winter): It's a rustic Maine vacation with a musical twist. The waiters, chambermaids, and other staff are recruited from conservatories around the nation, and they perform everything from light opera to chamber music for guests at this pine-filled lakeside resort. Between performances, there's ample opportunity for canoeing and hiking. See chapter 9.

## 10  The Best Country Inns

- **Blueberry Hill Inn** (Goshen, Vermont; ☎ **800/448-0707** or 802/247-6735): In search of the perfect Vermont getaway? This remote, casual inn on a quiet byway surrounded by national forest is a great retreat for those who love the natural world. There's hiking and swimming in summer, skiing in the winter. See chapter 4.
- **Jackson House Inn** (Woodstock, Vermont; ☎ **800/448-1890** or 802/457-2065): The constant improvements and the meticulous attention to service have made this longtime favorite a solid addition to our "best of" list for this edition. The meals are stunning, and the guest rooms are the very picture of antique elegance. The only downside? It fronts a sometimes noisy road. See chapter 4.
- **Twin Farms** (Woodstock, Vermont; ☎ **800/894-6327** or 802/234-9999): Just north of Woodstock is the most elegant inn in New England. The prices will appall many readers (rooms start at $800 for two, including all meals and liquor), but you'll certainly be pampered here. Novelist Sinclair Lewis once lived on this 300-acre farm, and today it's an aesthetic retreat that offers serenity and exceptional food. See chapter 4.
- **Windham Hill Inn** (West Townshend, Vermont; ☎ **800/944-4080** or 802/874-4080): New innkeepers have skillfully upgraded this historic inn, adding welcome amenities like soaking tubs while still preserving the antique charm of this 1823 farmhouse. It's at the end of a remote dirt road in a high upland valley, and guests are welcome to explore 160 private acres on a network of walking trails. See chapter 4.
- **The Pitcher Inn** (Warren, Vermont; ☎ **888-867-8424** or 802/496-6350): Innkeepers who try to meld whimsy with class often end up with disaster. That's not the case here in a brand-new New England–village building that somehow feels more historic than many old places. The dining room is top-notch. See chapter 5.
- **Adair** (Bethlehem, New Hampshire; ☎ **800/441-2606**): This is one of the newer country mansions in the White Mountains (it dates from 1927), but innkeepers Judy and Bill Whitman have done a stellar job of infusing this Georgian

Revival with a time-honored elegance. This inn, tucked away in a little-tracked corner of the White Mountains, boasts a superb dining room on the first floor and easy access to mountain activities and golf. See chapter 7.

- **Claremont** (Southwest Harbor, Maine; ☎ **800/244-5036**): The 1884 Claremont is a Maine classic. This waterside lodge has everything a Victorian resort should, including sparely decorated rooms, creaky floorboards in the halls, great views of water and mountains, and a croquet pitch. The dining room's only so-so, but Southwest Harbor has other dining options. See chapter 8.
- **The White Barn Inn** (Kennebunkport, Maine; ☎ **207/967-2321**): Much of the White Barn staff hails from Europe, and guests are treated graciously. The rooms are a delight, and the meals (served in a gloriously restored barn) may be the best in Maine. See chapter 8.

## 11  The Best Bed & Breakfasts

- **1811 House** (Manchester Village, Vermont; ☎ **800/432-1811** or 802/362-1811): The 1811 House is one of the best historic inns around. If you prefer your room decor to match the architectural era, you'll be content here. Everything is steeped in austere early American elegance, nicely avoiding the kitschy look that often afflicts places less adept at re-creating an historical sensibility. See chapter 4.
- **Hickory Ridge House** (Putney, Vermont; ☎ **800/380-9218** or 802/387-5709): Set in a classic New England landscape of open fields edged by narrow lanes and shady trees, Hickory Ridge occupies an 1808 home with high ceilings and gorgeous natural light. It's an ideal destination for a quiet retreat. Bring books, or enjoy the video library on premises. See chapter 4.
- **Inn at Round Barn Farm** (Waitsfield, Vermont; ☎ **802/496-2276**): The beautiful lap pool hidden beneath the monumental former barn is only one of the secrets concealed at this charming inn. The rooms are romantic, the surrounding hillsides the very picture of pastoral Vermont, and small touches everywhere make guests feel very welcome. See chapter 5.
- **Captain Lord** (Kennebunkport, Maine; ☎ **207/967-3141**): You'll transcend the "wannaB&Bs" at this genuine article, with grandfather clocks, Chippendale highboys, and other wonderful antiques. This uncommonly handsome mansion is set right in the village of Kennebunkport, perfectly situated for relaxed strolls. See chapter 8.
- **Pomegranate Inn** (Portland, Maine; ☎ **800/356-0408** or 207/772-1006): Whimsy and history combine with good effect at this fine B&B in one of Portland's most stately neighborhoods. The Italianate mansion is stern on the outside yet alive on the inside with creative wall paintings and an eclectic collection of unique antiques. See chapter 8.
- **Grey Havens** (Georgetown Island, Maine ☎ **207/371-2616**): This graceful, 1904 shingled home with prominent turrets sits on a high, rocky bluff overlooking the sea. Inside, it's all richly mellowed pine paneling, with a spacious common room where you can relax in cozy chairs in front of the cobblestone fireplace while listening to classical music. See chapter 8.
- **Inn at Canoe Point** (Bar Harbor, Maine; ☎ **207/288-9511**): It's got just five rooms, but what rooms! The magical 1889 home is tucked over a quiet cove with a deck right on the waters of Frenchman Bay. The architecture manages the neat trick of being both intimate and heroic. See chapter 8.

## 12  The Best Moderately Priced Accommodations

- **Inn at the Mad River Barn** (Waitsfield, Vermont; ☎ **802/496-3310**): It takes a few minutes to adapt to the spartan rooms and no-frills accommodations here, but you'll soon discover that the real action takes place in the living room and dining room, where skiers relax and chat after a day on the slopes and share heaping helpings at mealtime. Rooms with breakfast are $74 for two in summer, and $110 in winter. See chapter 5.
- **Birchwood Inn** (Temple, New Hampshire; ☎ **603/878-3285**): Simple comfort is the watchword at this quiet village inn, once visited by Henry David Thoreau. Veteran innkeepers Judy and Bill Wolfe have been running this inn and dining room with considerable graciousness since 1980. Rooms with breakfast are under $70. See chapter 6.
- **Philbrook Farm Inn** (Shelburne, New Hampshire; ☎ **603/466-3831**): Go here if you're looking for a complete getaway. The inn has been hosting travelers since the 1850s, and they know how to do it right. The farmhouse sits on 1,000 acres between the Mahoosuc Mountains and the Androscoggin River, and guests can take vigorous hikes or relax in leisure. Rooms for two are $150 and under for two, including breakfast and dinner. Ask about discounts for longer stays. See chapter 7.
- **Thayers Inn** (Littleton, New Hampshire; ☎ **800/634-8179** or 603/444-6469): This old-fashioned downtown inn has 42 eclectic rooms and a whole lot of relaxed charm. Ulysses S. Grant and Richard Nixon slept here, among others. Rooms from $39 if you're willing to share a bath; from $49 for private bath. See chapter 7.
- **Driftwood Inn & Cottages** (Bailey Island, Maine; ☎ **207/833-5461**): Where else can you find rooms at the edge of the rocky Maine coast for $70 and up? This classic shingled compound dates from 1910 and offers mostly rooms with a shared bath; but the views alone are worth that inconvenience. See chapter 8.
- **Maine Idyll Motor Court** (Freeport, Maine; ☎ **207/865-4201**): The 1932 Maine Idyll Motor Court is a Maine classic—a cluster of 20 cottages scattered about a grove of beech and oak trees. Each has a tiny porch, wood-burning fireplace (birch logs provided), TV, modest kitchen facilities (no ovens), and time-worn furniture. The downside? Highway noise. Cottages are $44 to $70 for two. See chapter 8.

## 13  The Best Alternative Accommodations

- **Camping in the Green Mountains** (Vermont): Whether your preferred mode of travel is foot, car, canoe, or bike, you'll find plenty of good campsites in the verdant hills of Vermont. The state parks are well-regarded, with many dating from the Civilian Conservation Corps days. The national forest, aided by the Green Mountain Club, maintains dozens of backcountry sites and lean-tos offering secluded getaways far from the noise of everyday life. See chapters 4 and 5.
- **Appalachian Mountain Club Huts** (New Hampshire): For more than a century, the AMC has been putting up weary hikers at its huts high in the White Mountains. Today, the club still manages eight of them (each about a day's hike apart), serving up filling, family-style meals and offering sturdy bunks stacked three high in rustic bunk rooms. See chapter 7.

- **Windjammers** (Maine): Maine has the East Coast's largest fleet of windjammers, offering travelers adventure on the high seas throughout the summer. You can explore offshore islands and inland estuaries, and learn how sailors once made the best of the wind. Accommodations in private cabins are typically spartan, but you'll spend most of your time on the deck luxuriating in the stunning views. See chapter 8.
- **Maine Island Trail:** About 70 remote islands along the Maine Coast are open to camping, and from these remote, salty wildernesses, you'll see some of the best sunsets imaginable. See "Sea Kayaking" in the "Enjoying the Great Outdoors" section of chapter 8.

## 14  The Best Restaurants

- **Chantecleer** (Manchester Center, Vermont; ☎ 802/362-1616): Swiss chef Michel Baumann has been turning out dazzling dinners here since 1981, and the kitchen hasn't gotten stale in the least. The dining room in an old barn is magical; the waitstaff helpful and friendly. It's a great spot for those who demand top-notch continental fare but don't like the fuss of a fancy restaurant. See chapter 4.
- **Hemingway's** (Killington, Vermont; ☎ 802/422-3886): Killington seems an unlikely place for serious culinary adventure, yet Hemingway's will meet the loftiest expectations. The menu changes frequently to ensure only the freshest of ingredients. If it's available, be sure to order the wild mushroom and truffle soup. See chapter 4.
- **Jackson House Inn** (Woodstock, Vermont; ☎ 800/448-1890 or 802/457-2065): Situated in a modern addition to an upscale country inn, the meals here are ingeniously conceived, deftly prepared and artfully arranged. The three-course meals cost around $50 per person and offer excellent value at that price. See chapter 4.
- **White Barn Inn** (Kennebunkport, Maine; ☎ 207/967-2321): The setting, in an ancient, rustic barn, is magical. The tables are draped with floor-length table-cloths, and the chairs feature imported Italian upholstery. The food is to die for. Enjoy entrees such as grilled duckling breast with ginger and sun-dried cherry sauce, or a roast rack of lamb with pecans and homemade barbecue sauce. See chapter 8.
- **Back Bay Grill** (Portland, Maine; ☎ 207/772-8833): Back Bay Grill has been serving up some of Maine's most innovative meals for more than a decade. The fresh pastas are notable and include fettuccini with smoked tomatoes and oyster mushrooms, and ravioli filled with maple-butternut squash and served with a tangy cranberry, orange, and ginger sauce. The service is top-rate, and the decor is modern edged with humor. See chapter 8.
- **Robinhood Free Meetinghouse** (Robinhood, Maine; ☎ 207/371-2188): The menu features between 30 and 40 entrees, and they're wildly eclectic—from Thai-grilled vegetables to Wiener schnitzel to salmon en papiollote; but you just can't go wrong here—even the sorbet served between courses is homemade and delicious. See chapter 8.

## 15  The Best Local Dining Experiences

- **Blue Benn Diner** (Bennington, Vermont; ☎ 802/442-5140): This Bennington favorite, housed in a classic 1945 Silk City diner, has a barrel ceiling, acres of stainless steel, and a vast menu. Make sure you don't overlook specials scrawled on paper and taped all over the walls; and leave room for a slice of delicious pie, like blackberry, pumpkin, or chocolate cream. See chapter 4.

- **Common Ground** (Brattleboro, Vermont; ☎ **802/257-0855**): There's no finer memorial to Brattleboro's Woodstock-era heritage than this vegetarian and whole-foods cooperative, where you can get everything from a simple meal of beans and tortillas to the more creative marinated sea-vegetable salad. See chapter 4.
- **Bove's** (Burlington, Vermont; ☎ **802/864-6651**): A Burlington landmark since 1941, Bove's is a classic red-sauce-on-spaghetti joint that's a throwback to a lost era. The red sauce is rich and tangy; the garlic sauce packs enough garlic to knock you clear out of your booth. See chapter 5.
- **Lou's** (Hanover, New Hampshire; ☎ **603/643-3321**): Huge crowds flock to Lou's, just down the block from the Dartmouth campus in Hanover, for breakfast on weekends. Fortunately breakfast is served all day here; the sandwiches served on fresh-baked bread are huge and delicious. See chapter 6.
- **Becky's** (Portland, Maine; ☎ **207/773-7070**): Five different kinds of homefries on the menu? It's breakfast nirvana at this local institution on the working waterfront. It's a favored hangout of fishermen, high school kids, businessmen, and just about everyone else. See chapter 8.
- **Silly's** (Portland, Maine; ☎ **207/772-0360**): Hectic and fun, this tiny, informal, kitschy restaurant serves up delicious finger food, like pita-wraps, hamburgers, and pizza. The milkshakes alone are worth the detour. See chapter 8.
- **Keenan's** (Bass Harbor, Maine; ☎ **207/244-3403**): This informal seafood shack is one of those local secrets most travelers zip right by. Inside you'll find some of the best seafood value for your money, from fried clams to a spicy gumbo. See chapter 8.

## 16  The Best Destinations for Serious Shoppers

- **Manchester** (Vermont): The dozens of outlet stores clustered in this handsome village include the usual high-fashion suspects, along with some notable individual shops. Head to Orvis, the maker of noted fly-fishing equipment, for a selection of outdoor gear and clothing. See chapter 4.
- **Portsmouth** (New Hampshire): Downtown Portsmouth offers a grab-bag of small, manageable, eclectic shops, ranging from funky shoe stores to classy art galleries. The downtown district is small enough to browse leisurely on foot, but you'll find a broad assortment of stuff for sale that will appeal to almost any taste. See chapter 6.
- **North Conway** (New Hampshire): Combine outdoor adventure with serious shopping along the 3-mile stretch of discount outlet stores that makes up most of North Conway. Look for Anne Klein, American Tourister, Izod, Dansk, Donna Karan, Levi's, Polo/Ralph Lauren, Reebok/Rockport, J. Crew, and Eddie Bauer in town, along with dozens of others. See chapter 7.
- **Freeport** (Maine): L.L. Bean is the anchor store for this thriving town of outlets, but you'll also find Patagonia, J. Crew, Dansk, Brooks Brothers, Levi's, and about 100 others. This is the most aesthetically pleasing of the several outlet centers in northern New England. See chapter 8.

# 2 Planning a Trip to Northern New England

This chapter is designed to provide most of the nuts-and-bolts travel information you'll need before setting off for northern New England. A good strategy is to browse through this section before you hit the road to ensure you've touched all the bases.

## 1 Visitor Information

New England's leading cash crop sometimes seems to be the brochure. Shops, hotels, and restaurants often feature racks of colorful pamphlets touting local sights and accommodations. These mini-centers can be helpful in turning up unexpected attractions, but for a more comprehensive overview, you should head for the state information centers or the local chambers of commerce. Chamber addresses and phone numbers are provided for each region in the chapters that follow. If you're a highly organized traveler, you'll call in advance and ask for information to be mailed to you long before you depart. If you're like the rest of us, you'll swing by when you reach town and hope the office is still open.

All three states are pleased to send out general visitor information packets and maps to travelers who call or write ahead. Here's the contact information:

- **Maine Tourism Association,** P.O. Box 2300, Hallowell, ME 04347. (☎ **800/533-9595** outside Maine, or 207/623-0363; www.visitmaine.com.)
- **New Hampshire Office of Travel and Tourism,** P.O. Box 1856, Concord, NH 03302. (☎ **800/386-4664** or 603/271-2343; www.visitnh.gov.)
- **Vermont Travel and Tourism,** 134 State St., Montpelier, VT 05602. (☎ **800/837-6668** or 802/828-3237 for general information, or 800/833-9756 to receive information by fax; www. travel-vermont.com.)

## 2 Money

Here's a scene I've seen repeated more than once. A young couple stands at a tourist information center looking despondent. "Isn't there *anything* cheaper?" one asks. "No, and that's a good price," responds the staff person behind the desk. "You won't find anything better."

Budget travelers are in for a bit of sticker shock in northern New England, at least during peak travel seasons. In midsummer, there's simply no such thing as a cheap motel in the most popular areas, like Winnipesaukee, southwest Vermont, Camden, or Bar Harbor. Even no-frills chain motels on the commercial strips outside of some cities can and do get $90 to $100 a night. (To be fair, many innkeepers in these northern latitudes need to reap all their profit in what amounts to a 2- or 3-month season.) To save money on accommodations, consider these alternatives:

- **Travel in the off-season.** Inexpensive rooms are often available in April or May, and November and early December. Granted, it's a bit bleak then (winter may be out the door in April, but it still hasn't left the driveway), but you can find good deals if you're just looking for a quiet retreat. If you'd like to spend more time exploring, consider the period between Memorial Day and July 4, when you can still often find discounts or budget packages as innkeepers ready themselves for the crowds of high summer. The best "off-season" period to my mind is September. The weather is great, and many inns and hotels cut their prices for 2 or 3 weeks between the summer and foliage periods. Early fall is growing more popular with travelers each year, however, and it may be harder to find discounts than it was in the past.

- **Commute from lower-priced areas.** If you're willing to drive a half-hour to an hour to reach prime destinations, you can often find cheaper lodging in less glamorous settings. Rutland isn't far from Killington, and Bangor is within striking distance of Acadia National Park. Study a map and be creative.

- **Camp out.** All three states offer ample camping opportunities at both public and private campgrounds, with prices ranging from about $9 to $25 per night. Because the region is relatively undeveloped, you can often find camping within a short drive of even major cities. Camping out for a few nights should also free up some cash for a much-earned splurge at a nicer spot.

## ATMS

ATMs are easy to find in the more populated areas and regions that cater to tourists. The machines are even making their way to the smaller villages, but don't count on finding machines in the more remote parts of the region. Stock up on greenbacks when you can. As in many locales these days, most ATM machines assess a fee of about $1 or $1.50 for each transaction.

Most ATMs are linked to a national network that most likely includes your bank at home. **Cirrus** (☎ 800/424-7787; www.mastercard.com/atm/) and **Plus** (☎ 800/843-7587; www.visa.com/atms) are the two most popular networks; check the back of your ATM card to see which network your bank belongs to. Use the 800 numbers to locate ATMs in your destination. Be sure to check the daily withdrawal limit before you depart.

## TRAVELER'S CHECKS

Traveler's checks are commonly accepted everywhere, although some smaller shops may balk at cashing larger checks. Traveler's checks are a good alternative to carrying around large amounts of cash—they are as reliable as currency, unlike personal checks, but could be replaced if lost or stolen, unlike cash.

You can get **American Express** by calling ☎ 800/221-7282; by using this number, Amex gold and platinum cardholders are exempt from the 1% fee. **AAA** members can obtain checks without a fee at most AAA offices.

**Visa** offers traveler's checks at Citibank locations nationwide, as well as several other banks. The service charge ranges between 1.5% and 2%. **MasterCard** travelers checks are available—call ☎ 800/223-9920 for a location near you.

If you opt to carry traveler's checks, be sure to keep a record of their serial numbers, separately from the checks of course, so you're ensured a refund in just such an emergency.

## CREDIT CARDS

Credit cards are a safe way to carry money when you travel, and they provide a convenient record of all your expenses. You can also withdraw cash advances from your credit cards at any bank (though you'll start paying hefty interest on the advance the moment you receive the cash). Call your credit card company and ask them to send you your PIN number for cash advances.

**THEFT**    Almost every credit card company has an emergency 800 number that you can call if your wallet or purse is stolen. The toll-free information directory will provide the number if you dial ☎ **800/555-1212.** Citicorp Visa's U.S. emergency number is ☎ **800/336-8472.** American Express cardholders and traveler's check holders should call ☎ **800/221-7282** for all money emergencies. MasterCard holders should call ☎ **800/307-7309.**

## 3  When to Go

## THE SEASONS

The well-worn joke about the climate in northern New England is that it has just two seasons—winter and August. There's a kernel of truth in it, but it's mostly a canard to keep outsiders from moving here, the same way the Pacific Northwest "celebrates" its 11-month "rain festival." In fact, the ever-shifting seasons are one of those elements that make New England so distinctive, and with one exception, the seasons are long and well-defined.

**SUMMER**    The peak summer season runs from July 4 to Labor Day. Vast crowds surge into northern New England during these two holiday weekends, and the level of activity remains high throughout July and August.

This should be no surprise: Summers are exquisite here. The forests are verdant and lush; the sky can be an almost lurid blue and the cumulus clouds painfully white. In the mountains, warm (rarely hot) days are the rule, followed by cool nights. Along the coast, ocean breezes keep the temperatures down and often produces vichyssoise fogs that linger for days. (In Portland, it tops 90 degrees only 4 or 5 days a year on average.)

Local weather is determined by the winds. Southwest winds bring haze, heat, and humidity. The northwest winds bring cool weather and knife-sharp vistas. These systems tend to alternate during the summer, with the heat arriving stealthily and slowly, then getting exiled by stiff, cool winds rising from the north a few days later. (The change from hot to cool will sometimes occur in a matter of minutes.) Rain is rarely far away—some days it's an afternoon thunderstorm, sometimes it's a steady drizzle that brings a 4-day soaking. On average, about 1 day in 3 will bring some rain. Travelers should come prepared for it.

For most of the region, midsummer is the prime season. Expect to pay premium prices at hotels and restaurants. The exception is around the empty ski resorts where you can often find bargains. Also be aware that early summer brings out the blackflies and the mosquitoes in great multitude, a state of affairs that has spoiled many north-country camping trips. Outdoorspeople are best off waiting until after July 4 if they want to avoid becoming human pincushions.

**AUTUMN**    Don't be surprised to smell the tang of fall approaching as early as mid-August, a time when you'll also notice a few leaves turned blaze-orange on the lush maples at the edges of wetlands. Fall comes early to northern New England, puts its feet up on the couch, and stays for some time. The foliage season begins in earnest in the northern part of the region by the third week in September; in the south, it reaches its peak by the middle of October.

Fall is to New England what the Grand Canyon is to the Southwest. It's one of the great natural spectacles of the United States, and with its rolling hills tarted up in brilliant reds and stunning oranges, fall is garish in a way that seems determined to embarrass understated New England. Just keep in mind that this is the most popular time of year to travel—bus tours flock to New England in early October like migrating geese. As a result, hotels are invariably booked solid. Some years local radio stations put out calls for residents to open their doors to stranded travelers who otherwise would have to sleep in their cars. Reservations are essential. Don't be surprised if you're assessed a foliage surcharge of $10 or $20 per room at some inns.

All three states maintain recorded **foliage hot lines** to let you know when the leaves are at their peak: call **Maine** (☎ 800/777-0317), **New Hampshire** (☎ 800/258-3608), or **Vermont** (☎ 802/828-3239).

**WINTER**   New England winters are like wine—some years are good, some are lousy. During a good season, mounds of light, fluffy snow blanket the deep woods and fill the ski slopes. A good New England winter offers a profound peace and tranquillity. The muffling qualities of fresh snow bring a thunderous silence to the region, and the hiss and pop of a wood fire at a country inn can sound like an overwrought symphony. During these winters, exploring the forest on snowshoes or cross-country skis is an experience that borders on the magical.

During the *other* winters, the lousy ones, the weather brings a nasty melange of rain, freezing rain, and sleet. The woods are filled with nasty, crusty snow, the cold is damp and numbing, and it's bleak, bleak, bleak. Look into the eyes of residents on the street during this time. They're all longing for the Caribbean.

The higher you go in the mountains, and the further north you head, the better your odds of finding snow and avoiding rain. Winter coastal vacations can be spectacular (not much beats cross-country skiing at the edge of the pounding surf), but it's a high-risk venture that could well yield rain rather than snow.

Naturally, ski areas are crowded during the winter months. They're especially so during school vacations, when most ski resorts take the rather mercenary tactic of jacking up rates at hotels and on the slopes.

**SPRING**   Spring lasts only a weekend or so, often around mid-May, but sometimes as late as June. One day the ground is muddy, the trees barren, and gritty snow is still collected in shady hollows. The next day, it's in the 80s, trees are blooming, and kids are swimming in the lakes. Travelers must be very crafty and alert if they want to experience spring in northern New England. This is also known as mud season, and it's a time many innkeepers and restaurateurs close up for a few weeks for repairs or to venture someplace warm.

### Burlington, Vermont's Average Temperatures (°F)

|           | Jan | Feb | Mar | Apr | May | Jun | July | Aug | Sep | Oct | Nov | Dec |
|-----------|-----|-----|-----|-----|-----|-----|------|-----|-----|-----|-----|-----|
| Avg. High | 25  | 27  | 38  | 53  | 66  | 76  | 80   | 78  | 69  | 57  | 44  | 30  |
| Avg. Low  | 8   | 9   | 21  | 33  | 44  | 54  | 59   | 57  | 49  | 39  | 30  | 15  |

### Portland, Maine's Average Temperatures (°F)

|           | Jan | Feb | Mar | Apr | May | Jun | July | Aug | Sep | Oct | Nov | Dec |
|-----------|-----|-----|-----|-----|-----|-----|------|-----|-----|-----|-----|-----|
| Avg. High | 31  | 32  | 40  | 50  | 61  | 72  | 76   | 74  | 68  | 58  | 45  | 34  |
| Avg. Low  | 16  | 16  | 27  | 36  | 47  | 54  | 61   | 59  | 52  | 43  | 32  | 22  |

# Northern New England Calendar of Events

## January

⭐ **New Year's and First Night Celebrations,** regionwide. Portland, Portsmouth, and Burlington, among others, all celebrate the coming of the New Year with plenty of activities for families and friends at venues spread across each city. Greet January with fireworks at midnight. Check with local chambers for details.

## February

- **U.S. National Toboggan Championships,** Camden, Maine. Raucous and lively athletic event where being overweight is an advantage. Held at the toboggan chute of the Camden Snow Bowl. Call ☎ **207/236-3438.** Early February.
- **Dartmouth Winter Carnival,** Hanover, New Hampshire. Huge and elaborate ice sculptures grace the Green during this festive celebration of winter, which includes numerous sporting events and other winter-related activities. Call ☎ **603/646-1110.** Mid-February.
- **Stowe Derby,** Stowe, Vermont. The oldest downhill/cross-country ski race in the nation pits racers who scramble from the wintry summit of Mt. Mansfield into the village on the Stowe Recreation path. Call ☎ **802/253-3423.** Late February.

## March

- **Maine Boatbuilders' Show,** Portland, Maine. More than 200 exhibitors and 9,000 boat aficionados gather as winter fades to make plans for the coming summer. A great place to meet boatbuilders and get ideas for your dream craft. Call ☎ **207/774-1067.** Late March.

## April

- **Sugarbush Spring Fling,** Waitsfield, Vermont. Ski-related events like pond skimming and big-air contests herald the coming of spring. Reggae provides the soundtrack. Call ☎ **802/583-2381.** Early April.

## May

- **Annual Basketry Festival,** Stowe, Vermont. A weeklong event with displays and workshops by talented weavers. ☎ **800/344-1546** or 802/253-7223. Mid-May.
- **Lilac Festival,** Shelburne, Vermont. See the famed lilacs at the renowned Shelburne Museum when they're at their most beautiful. More than 400 bushes. Call ☎ **802/985-3346.** Mid- to late May.
- **Annual Spring Farm Festival,** Woodstock, Vermont. Both a celebration of spring and an educational event, here you can learn all about what happens on a traditional farm, from sowing to shearing. Billings Farm Museum, ☎ **802/457-2355.**

## June

- **Old Port Festival,** Portland, Maine. A daylong block party in the heart of Portland's historic district with live music, food vendors, and activities for kids. Call ☎ **207/772-2249.** Early June.
- **Market Square Weekend,** Portsmouth, New Hampshire. This lively street fair attracts hordes from throughout southern New Hampshire and Maine into downtown Portsmouth to dance, listen to music, sample food, and enjoy summer's arrival. Call ☎ **603/436-2848.** Early June.
- **Motorcycle Week,** Loudon and Weirs Beach, New Hampshire. Tens of thousands of bikers descend on the Lake Winnipesaukee region early each summer to compare their machines and cruise the strip at Weirs Beach. The Gunstock Hill

Climb and the Loudon Classic race are the centerpieces of the week's activities. Call ☎ **603/783-4931.** Mid-June.

- **Annual Windjammer Days,** Boothbay Harbor, Maine. For nearly four decades, windjammers have gathered in Boothbay Harbor to kick off the summer sailing season. Expect music, food, and a parade of magnificent sailboats. Call ☎ **207/ 633-2353.** Late June.

- **Whatever Family Festival.** Augusta, Maine. A community celebration to mark the cleaning up of the Kennebec River, culminating in a wacky race involving all manner of watercraft, some more seaworthy than others. Call ☎ **207/623-4559.** Late June–early July.

## July

- ✪ **Independence Day,** regionwide. Communities throughout all three states celebrate July 4 with parades, greased-pole climbs, cakewalks, cookouts, road races, and fireworks. The bigger the town, the bigger the fireworks. Contact local chambers of commerce for details.

- **Moxie Festival,** Lisbon Falls, Maine. A quirky community festival celebrating a soft drink that once outsold Coca-Cola. Call ☎ **207/783-2249.** Early July.

- **Vermont Quilt Festival,** Northfield, Vermont. Displays are only part of the allure of New England's largest quilt festival. You can also attend classes and have your heirlooms appraised. See class and event descriptions at www.vqf.org or call ☎ **802/485-7092.** Mid-July.

- **Revolutionary War Days,** Exeter, New Hampshire. Learn all you need to know about the War of Independence during this historic community festival, which features a Revolutionary War encampment and dozens of re-enactors. Call ☎ **603/772-2622.** Mid-July.

- **Marlboro Music Festival,** Marlboro, Vermont. This is a popular 6-week series of classical concerts featuring talented student musicians performing in the peaceful hills outside of Brattleboro. Concerts are held weekends from July through mid-August. Call ☎ **802/254-2394.**

- **Maine Lobster Festival,** Rockland, Maine. Fill up on the local harvest at this event marking the importance and delectability of Maine's favorite crustacean. Enjoy a boiled lobster or two, and take in the ample entertainment during this informal waterfront gala. Call ☎ **800/562-2529** or 207/596-0376. Late July–early August.

## August

- **Maine Festival,** Brunswick, Maine. A 3-day festival showcasing Maine-made crafts, music, foods, and performers. Boisterous, fun, and filling. Call ☎ **207/ 772-9012.** Early August.

- **Southern Vermont Crafts Fair,** Manchester. More than 200 artisans show off their fine work at this popular festival, which also features creative food and good music. Held at Hildene in early August. ☎ **802/362-1788.**

- **Annual Star Party,** St. Johnsbury, Vermont. The historic Fairbanks Museum and Planetarium hosts special events and shows, including night-viewing sessions, during the lovely Perseid meteor shower. ☎ **802/748-2372.** Mid-August.

- **Blueberry Festival,** Machias, Maine. A festival marking the harvest of the region's wild blueberries. Eat to your heart's content. Call ☎ **207/794-3543.** Mid-August.

- **Blue Hill Fair,** Blue Hill, Maine. A classic country fair just outside one of Maine's most elegant villages. Call ☎ **207/374-9976.** Late August.

## September

- **Vermont State Fair,** Rutland, Vermont. All of Vermont seems to show up for this grand event, with a midway, live music, and plenty of agricultural exhibits. Call ☎ **802/775-5200.** Early September.
- **Windjammer Weekend,** Camden, Maine. Come visit Maine's impressive fleet of old-time sailing ships, which host open houses throughout the weekend at this scenic harbor. Call ☎ **207/236-4404.** Early September.
- ✪ **Common Ground Fair,** Windsor, Maine. An old-time state fair with a twist: the emphasis is on organic foods, recycling, and wholesome living. Call ☎ **207/ 623-5115.** Late September.

## October

- **Northeast Kingdom Fall Foliage Festival,** Northeast Vermont. A cornucopia of events staged in towns and villages throughout Vermont's northeast corner heralds the arrival of the fall foliage season. Be the first to see colors at their peak. Call ☎ **802/748-3678.** Early October.
- ✪ **Fryeburg Fair,** Fryeburg, Maine. Cotton candy, tractor pulls, live music, huge vegetables, and barnyard animals at Maine's largest agricultural fair. There's also harness racing in the evening. Call ☎ **207/985-3278.** Runs for a week in early October.
- **Harvest Day,** Canterbury, New Hampshire. A celebration of the harvest season, Shaker-style. Lots of autumnal exhibits and children's games. Call ☎ **603/ 783-9511.** Mid-October.

## November

- **Victorian Holiday,** Portland. From late November until Christmas, Portland decorates its Old Port in a Victorian Christmas theme. Enjoy the window displays, take a free hayride, and listen to costumed carolers sing. ☎ **207/772-6828.**
- **Country Craftsmen of New Hampshire Show,** Bedford, New Hampshire. Quality crafts from a wide range of artisans is displayed and sold at this annual pre-holiday get together. Call ☎ **603/224-0060.**

## December

- **Chester Greenwood Day,** Farmington, Maine. Come help this Maine town celebrate Chester Greenwood! Who? Why, the inventor of the earmuff! The daylong festival includes a parade and lots of earmuff-related fun. Call ☎ **207/ 778-4215.** Early December.
- **Christmas Prelude,** Kennebunkport, Maine. This scenic coastal village greets Santa's arrival in a lobster boat, and marks the coming of Christmas with street shows, pancake breakfasts, and tours of the town's inns. Call ☎ **207/967-3286.** Early December.
- ✪ **Candlelight Stroll,** Portsmouth, New Hampshire. Historic Strawbery Banke gets in a Christmas way with old-time decorations and more than 1,000 candles lighting the 10-acre grounds. Call ☎ **603/433-1100.** Takes place during the first 2 weekends of December.
- **Woodstock Wassail Celebration,** Woodstock, Vermont. Enjoy classic English grog, along with parades and dances, at this annual event. Call ☎ **802/457-3555.** Early December.

# 4 The Active Vacation Planner

Northern New England is a superb destination for those who don't consider it a vacation unless they incorporate some sweating and fretting into their itinerary. Hiking, canoeing, and skiing are among the most popular activities, but there's also rock climbing, sea kayaking, mountain biking, road biking, sailing, winter mountaineering, and snowmobiling. In general, the further north you go in the region, the more remote and wild the terrain becomes. For pointers on where to head, see the "Enjoying the Great Outdoors" section in subsequent chapters. More detailed information on local services is included in each regional section.

## GENERAL ADVICE

The best way to enjoy the outdoors is to head to public lands where the natural landscape is preserved. Wilderness areas in northern New England include Green Mountain National Forest in Vermont, White Mountain National Forest in New Hampshire, and Baxter State Park and Acadia National Park in Maine. Adventure-travel outfitters and suppliers can often be found in towns at the perimeter of these areas.

A bit of added advice: To find real adventure, plan to stay put. I've run across too many gung-ho travelers who try to bite off too much—some biking in Vermont, some hiking in the White Mountains, then maybe a little kayaking off Acadia in Maine. All in a week. That's only a good formula for developing a close, personal relationship with your car. I'd advise prospective adventurers to pick just one area, then settle in for a few days or a week, spending the long summer days exploring locally by foot, canoe, or kayak. This will give you the time to enjoy an extra hour lounging at a remote backcountry lake, or to spend an extra day camped in the backcountry. You'll also learn a lot more about the area. Few travelers ever regret planning to do too little on their vacations. A lot of travelers regret attempting to do too much.

## FINDING YOUR WAY

Travelers used to hire guides to ensure they could find their way out of the woods. With development encroaching on many once-pristine areas, it's now helpful to have guides to find your way *into* the woods and away from civilization and its long reach. Clear-cuts, second-home developments, and trails teeming with weekend hikers are all obstacles to be avoided. Local knowledge is the best way to find the most alluring, least congested spots.

Travelers have three choices: Hire a guide; Sign up for a guided trip; or dig up the essential information yourself.

**HIRING A GUIDE**    Guides of all kinds may be hired throughout the region, from grizzled fishing hands who know local rivers like their own homes to young canoe guides attracted to the field because of their interest in the environment. Alexandra and Garrett Conover of Maine's **North Woods Ways,** RR#2, Box 159A, Guilford, ME 04443 (☎ 207/997-3723) are among the most experienced in the region. The couple offers canoe trips on northern Maine rivers (and as far north as Labrador), and are well-versed in North Woods lore.

Maine has a centuries-old tradition of guides leading "sports" into the backwoods for hunting and fishing, although many now have branched out to include recreational canoeing and more specialized interests, such as bird-watching. Professional guides are certified by the state; you can learn more about hiring Maine guides by contacting the **Maine Professional Guides Association,** P.O. Box 847, Augusta, ME 04332 (☎ 207/549-5631). The association's Web site (www.maineguides.com) features links to many of its members.

In Vermont, contact the **Vermont Outdoor Guide Association,** ☎ 802/425-6211 (www.voga.org), whose members can help arrange adventure-travel tours, instruction, and lodging. The Web site is a great place to get ideas for an outdoor vacation, with links to numerous outfitters and outdoor-oriented inns.

Elsewhere, contact the appropriate chambers of commerce for suggestions on local guides.

**GUIDED TOURS**    Guided tours have boomed in recent years, both in number and variety. These range from 2-night guided inn-to-inn hiking trips to weeklong canoe and kayak expeditions, camping each night along the way. A few reputable outfitters to start with:

- **Allagash Canoe Trips,** P.O. Box 713, Greenville, Maine 04441 (☎ **207/ 695-3668;** www.allagashcanoetrips.com), leads 5- to 7-day canoe trips down Maine's noted and wild Allagash River. You provide a sleeping bag and clothing; everything else is taken care of.
- **Battenkill Canoe Ltd.,** 6328 Historic Rte. 7A, Arlington, VT 05250 (☎ **800/ 421-5268** or 802/362-2800; www.battenkill.com), runs guided canoeing and walking excursions of between 2 and 6 nights' duration in Vermont (as well as abroad). Nights are spent at quiet inns.
- **Bike the Whites,** P.O. Box 37, Intervale, NH 03845 (☎ **800/448-3534;** www.bikethewhites.com), offers self-guided biking tours between three inns in the White Mountains, with each day requiring about 20 miles of biking. Luggage is shuttled from inn to inn.
- **Country Walkers,** P.O. Box 180, Waterbury, VT 05676 (☎ **800/464-9255** or 802/244-1387; www.countrywalkers.com), has a glorious color catalog (more like a "wishbook") outlining supported walking trips around the world. Among them: walking tours in coastal Maine and north-central Vermont. Trips run 4 or 5 nights and include all meals and lodging at appealing inns.
- **Machias Adventures,** 4 Whitney Ave. Extension, Westport, CT 06880 (☎ **888/427-3497** or 203/227-7337; www.adventuretravel.to), offers an annual weeklong camping trip down the St. John River, which forms the northern border between Maine and Vermont. River levels are high enough to run the river only during the spring runoff.
- **Maine Island Kayak Co.,** 70 Luther St., Peaks Island, ME 04108 (☎ **207/ 766-2373;** www.sea-kayak.com), has a fleet of seaworthy kayaks, which it takes on camping trips up and down the Maine Coast, as well as to Canada and Belize. The firm has a number of 2- and 3-night expeditions each summer and has plenty of experience training novices.
- **New England Hiking Holidays,** P.O. Box 1648, North Conway, NH 03860 (☎ **800/869-0949;** www.nehikingholidays.com), has an extensive inventory of trips, including weekend trips in the White Mountains as well as more extended excursions to the Maine Coast, Vermont, and overseas. Trips typically involve moderate day hiking coupled with nights at comfortable lodges.
- **Vermont Bicycle Touring,** P.O. Box 711, Bristol, VT 05442 (☎ **802/453-4811;** www.vbt.com), is one of the more established and well-organized touring operations, with an extensive bike tour schedule in North America, Europe, and New Zealand. VBT offers five trips in Vermont, and three in Maine, including a 6-day Acadia trip with some overnights at the grand Claremont Hotel.

**GETTING MORE INFORMATION**    Guidebooks to the region's backcountry are plentiful and diverse. L.L. Bean in Freeport, Maine, and the Green Mountain Club headquarters in Waterbury, Vermont, both have an excellent selection of guidebooks for sale, as do many local bookshops throughout the region. An exhaustive collection of New England outdoor guidebooks for sale may be found on the Web at www.mountainwanderer.com. The **Appalachian Mountain Club,** 5 Joy St., Boston,

MA 02108 (☎ 617/523-0636), publishes a number of definitive guides to hiking and boating in the region; call for a catalog or visit their Web site: www.outdoors.org.

**Map Adventures,** 846 Cottage Club Rd., Stowe, VT 05762, is a small firm that publishes a growing line of recreational maps covering popular northern New England areas, including the Stowe and Mad River Valley areas and the White Mountains. See what they offer on the Web at www.gorp.com/mapadventures.

Local outdoor clubs are also a good source of information, and most open trips to non-members. The largest of the bunch is the **Appalachian Mountain Club** (see address above), whose chapters run group trips almost every weekend throughout the region, with northern New Hampshire especially well-represented. Another active group is the **Green Mountain Club,** RR#1, Box 650, Rte. 100, Waterbury Center, VT 05677 (☎ 802/244-7037).

A good source of online information on New England–area parks and recreational activities is **Gorp.com.** Head for www.gorp.com/gorp/location/us/us.htm, then choose from among the New England states.

## LEARNING & SPECIAL-INTEREST VACATIONS

A richly rewarding way to spend a vacation is to learn a new outdoor skill or add to your knowledge while on holiday. There are plenty of options in northern New England, ranging from formal weeklong classes to 1-day workshops.

Among the better choices:

- **Learn to fly-fish on New England's fabled rivers.** Among the region's most respected schools are those offered by **Orvis** (☎ 800/548-9548) in Manchester, Vermont, and **L.L. Bean** (☎ 800/341-4341) in Freeport, Maine. (L.L. Bean also offers a number of shorter workshops on various outdoor skills through its **Outdoor Discovery Program;** call ☎ 888/552-3261.)

- **Learn about birds and coast ecosystems in Maine.** Budding and experienced naturalists can expand their understanding of marine wildlife while residing on 333-acre Hog Island in Maine's wild and scenic Muscongus Bay. Famed birder Roger Tory Peterson taught birding classes here in the past, and the program has a stellar reputation. Contact the **Maine Audubon Society,** 20 Gilsland Farm Rd., Falmouth ME 04105 (☎ 207/781-2330).

- **Sharpen your outdoor skills.** The **Appalachian Mountain Club,** 5 Joy St., Boston, MA 02108 (☎ 617/523-0636) has a full roster of outdoor adventure classes, many of which are taught at the club's Pinkham Notch Camp at the base of Mount Washington in the heart of the White Mountains. You can learn outdoor photography, wild mushroom identification, or backcountry orienteering for starters. In winter, there are ice-climbing and telemark-skiing lessons held on the slopes of the rugged White Mountains. Classes often include accommodations, and most are reasonably priced. Call or write for a course catalog.

## 5 Choosing an Inn or B&B

"The more we travel," said an unhappy couple next to me one morning at a New Hampshire inn, "the more we realize why we go back to our old favorites time and again." The reason for their disgruntlement? They were up and switching rooms at 2am when rain began dripping on them through the ceiling.

Northern New England's inns and bed-and-breakfasts (B&Bs) offer a wonderful alternative to the homogenized, cookie-cutter chain-hotel rooms that line U.S. highways coast-to-coast; but as that unhappy couple learned, there are good reasons why some people prefer cookie-cutter sameness. Predictability isn't always a bad thing. In a chain hotel, you can be reasonably certain water won't come dripping in through your ceiling at night. Likewise, you can bet that beds will be firm, that the sink will be relatively new and lacking in interesting sepia-toned stains, and that you'll have a TV, telephone, and a lot of counter space next to the bathroom sink.

Happily, the great majority of smaller, family-run inns and B&Bs offer hospitable places to rest your head. Maine, New Hampshire, and Vermont are home to a great profusion of inns a century or two old, places with creaky floors, narrow staircases, and intricate woodwork that have captured a piece of the region's past and kept it nicely preserved. You can sleep in rustic country-inn rooms (where you prop up the window with a well-worn piece of wood to let in the sounds of crickets and owls, or rooms furnished to a high gloss with stunning mahogany antiques and Persian carpets.

I've personally visited every inn and B&B mentioned in this guide, and I'm confident all will yield a quality experience. Just keep in mind that every place is different, and you still need to match the personality of a place with your own personality. Some are more polished and fussier than others. Many lack the amenities travelers have grown accustomed to in chain hotels. (In-room phones and air-conditioning lead the list.) Note that a great number of places I've visited are not included in this guide because, for one reason or another, they're not quite ready for prime time.

The difference between an inn and a B&B may be confusing for some travelers, since the gap between the two narrows by the day. A couple of decades ago, inns were full-service affairs, whereas B&Bs consisted of private homes with an extra bedroom or two and a homeowner looking for a little extra income. These old-style B&Bs still exist around the region. I've occupied a few evenings sitting in a well-used living room watching Tom Brokaw with the owner, as if visiting with an aunt I forgot I had.

Today, B&Bs are more commonly professionally run affairs, where guests have private baths, a separate common area, and attentive service. The owners have apartments tucked away in the back, prepare sumptuous breakfasts in the morning (some B&Bs offer "candlelight breakfasts"), and offer a high level of service. All of the B&Bs in this guide are of the more professionally run variety (although several or more still have shared bathrooms). Other guidebooks are available for those searching for homestay lodging.

The sole difference between inns and B&Bs—at least as defined by this guide—is that inns serve dinner (and sometimes lunch). B&Bs provide breakfast only. Readers shouldn't infer that B&Bs are necessarily more informal or in any way inferior to a full-service inn. Indeed, the places listed in "The Best Bed-&-Breakfasts" section in the prior chapter all have the air of gracious inns that just happened to have overlooked serving dinner. That's true for many of the other B&Bs listed in this guide; and with a little luck, you'll stumble into Ralph Waldo Emerson's idea of simple contentment: "Hospitality consists in a little fire, a little food, and an immense quiet," he wrote in his journal.

As innkeeping evolves into the more complex and demanding "hospitality industry," you're bound to bump up against more restrictions, rules, and regulations at places you're staying. It's always best to ask in advance to avoid unpleasant surprises.

A few notes on recent trends:

**SMOKING**    Smokers looking to light up are being edged out the door to smoke on front lawns and porches. It's no different in the region's inns and B&Bs than in other public spaces. Ten years ago only a handful of places prohibited smoking. Today, I'd wager that the majority of inns and B&Bs have banned smoking within their buildings entirely, and some have even exiled smokers from their property,—front lawn included.

Frommer's has stopped mentioning whether smoking is allowed or not in inns because it has rapidly become a non-issue—almost everyone has banned it. Assume that no smoking is allowed at any of the accommodations listed in this guide. (As in other regions, the larger, more modern hotels—say a Radisson or Holiday Inn—will have guest rooms set aside for smokers.) If being able to smoke in your room or the lobby is paramount to your vacation happiness, be sure to inquire first. Likewise, if you're a non-smoker who finds the smell of cigarette smoke obnoxious in the extreme, it also wouldn't hurt to ask and make sure you're at a fully non-smoking establishment.

**ADDITIONAL GUESTS**    The room rates published in this guide are for two people sharing a room. Many places charge $10 or more for each extra guest sharing the room. Don't assume that children traveling with you are free; ask first about extra charges; and don't assume that all places are able to accommodate children or extra guests. The guest rooms at some inns are quite cozy and lack space for a cot. Ask first if you don't want to end up four to a bed.

**MINIMUM STAY**    It's become increasingly common for inns to require guests to book a minimum of 2 nights or more during busy times. These times typically include weekends in the summer (or in the winter near ski areas), holiday periods, and the fall foliage season. These policies are mentioned in the following pages when known, but they're in constant flux, so don't be surprised if you're told you need to reserve an extra day when you make reservations.

Note that minimum-stay policies typically apply only to those making advance reservations. If you stop by an inn on a Saturday night and find a room available, innkeepers won't make you stay a second night. Also, thanks to erratic travel planning, the occasional stray night sometimes becomes available during minimum-stay periods. Don't hesitate to call and ask if a single night is available when planning your itinerary.

**DEPOSITS**    Many establishments now require guests to provide a credit card number to hold a room. What happens if you cancel? The policies are Byzantine at best. Some places have a graduated refund—cancel a week in advance, and you'll be charged for one night's stay; cancel one day in advance, and you're charged for your whole reserved stay—unless they can fill the room. Then you'll be charged for half. Other places are quite generous about refunding your deposit. It's more than a bit tedious to figure it all out if you're booking a half dozen places over the course of your trip, and the policies can often seem irrational. One Frommer's reader wrote to say that she made a reservation at a Vermont motel 3 days before her arrival, then called to cancel the next day because a hurricane had veered to hit her home state and she wanted to stay home. Sorry, she was told, cancellations must be made a week in advance; she was billed for the room. Go figure.

Most hotels and inns are fair and will scrupulously spell out their cancellation policy when you make reservations, but always ask about it before you divulge your credit card number, and if possible, ask to have it e-mailed, faxed, or mailed to you before you agree to anything. Most travelers experience no unpleasant surprises on their credit card bills, but it's always better to err on the side of caution.

**PETS**    No surprise: Some places allow pets, some don't. We've noted inns that allow pets, but even here we don't recommend showing up with a pet in tow unless you've cleared it over the phone with the innkeeper. Note that many establishments have only one or two rooms (often a cottage or room with exterior entrance) set aside for guests traveling with pets, and they won't be happy to meet Fido if the pet rooms are already occupied. Also, it's increasingly common for a surcharge of $10 or $20 to be charged to pet owners to pay for the extra cleaning.

Some innkeepers informed me they will accept pets but didn't want to have "Pets allowed" mentioned in this guide. Their policy is to have travelers ask them first so they can explain the ground rules and ascertain that the pet in question isn't a hyperactive terrier with unresolved barking issues. It doesn't hurt to inquire, even if the pet policy isn't mentioned in these pages.

**SERVICE CHARGES** Rather than increase room rates in the face of rising competition, hotels, inns, and B&Bs are increasingly tacking on unpublicized fees to guests' bills. Most innkeepers will tell you about these when you reserve or check in; the less scrupulous will surprise you at check-out. In my opinion, this is not a welcome trend.

The most common surcharge is an involuntary "service charge" of 10% or 15%. Coupled with state lodging taxes (even "sales-tax-free" New Hampshire hits tourists with an 8% levy), that bumps the cost of a bed up by nearly 25 percent. (The rates listed in this guide don't include service charges or sales tax.)

Other charges might include a pet fee (as much as $10 per day extra), a foliage-season surcharge ($10 or more per room), or a "resort fee" (there's a 15% levy at Waterville Valley, New Hampshire, hotels to pay for guest access to the local athletic club). Other fees are more irksome than financially burdensome. One example: The Radisson Hotel in Burlington has in-room safes, for which guests are billed an additional $1 per day at check-out whether they use them or not.

## 6 Health & Insurance

**STAYING HEALTHY** New Englanders by and large consider themselves a healthy bunch, which they ascribe to clean living, brisk northern air, vigorous exercise (leaf raking, snow shoveling, and so on), and a sensible diet. Other than picking up a germ or two that might lead to colds or flu, you shouldn't face any serious health risks when traveling the region.

Exceptions? Well, yes—you may find yourself at higher risk when exploring the outdoors, particularly in the backcountry. A few things to watch for when venturing off the beaten track:

**Poison ivy:** The shiny, three-leafed plant is common throughout the region. If touched, you may develop a nasty, itchy rash that will seriously erode the enjoyment of your vacation. The reaction tends to be worse in some people than others. It's safest to simply avoid it. If you're unfamiliar with what it looks like, ask at a ranger station or visitor information booth for more information. Many have posters or books to help with identification.

**Giardia:** That crystal-clear stream coursing down a high backcountry peak may seem as pure as it gets, but consider the possibility that it may be contaminated with animal feces. Gross, yes, and also dangerous. Giardia cysts may be present in some streams and rivers. When ingested by humans, the cysts can result in copious diarrhea and weight loss. Symptoms may not surface until well after you've left the backcountry and returned home. Carry your own water for day trips, or bring a small filter (available at most camping and sporting goods shops) to treat backcountry water. Failing that, at least boil water or treat it with iodine before using it for cooking, drinking, or washing. If you detect symptoms, see a doctor immediately.

**Lyme Disease:** Lyme Disease has been a growing problem in New England since 1975 when the disease was identified in the town of Lyme, Connecticut. In1997, some 14,000 cases were reported nationwide. The disease is transmitted by tiny deer ticks—smaller than the more common, relatively harmless wood ticks. Look for a bull's-eye shaped rash (3 to 8 inches in diameter); it may feel warm but usually doesn't itch. Symptoms include muscle and joint pain, fever, and fatigue. If left untreated, heart damage may occur. It's more easily treated in early phases than later, so it's best to seek medical attention as soon as any symptoms are noted.

**Rabies:** Since 1989, rabies have been spreading northward from New Jersey into New England. The disease is spread by animal saliva and is especially prevalent in skunks, raccoons, bats, and foxes. It is always fatal if left untreated in humans. Infected animals tend to display erratic and aggressive behavior. The best advice is to keep a safe distance between yourself and any wild animal you may encounter. If bitten, wash the wound as soon as you can and immediately seek medical attention. Treatment is no longer as painful as it once was but still involves a series of shots.

**INSURANCE**    There are three kinds of travel insurance: trip-cancellation; medical; and lost-luggage coverage. Trip-cancellation insurance is a good idea if you have paid a large portion of your vacation expenses up front. Check your existing policies before you buy any additional coverage. For independent travel health-insurance providers, see below. Your homeowner's insurance should cover stolen luggage. For information on car-renter's insurance, see "By Car," below.

Some credit cards (American Express and certain gold and platinum Visas and Master-Cards, for example) offer automatic flight insurance against death or dismemberment in case of an airplane crash.

Among the reputable issuers of travel insurance are:

- **Access America,** 6600 W. Broad St., Richmond, VA 23230 (☎ 800/284-8300)
- **Travel Guard International,** 1145 Clark St., Stevens Point, WI 54481 (☎ 800/826-1300)
- **Travel Insured International, Inc.,** P.O. Box 280568, East Hartford, CT 06128 (☎ 800/243-3174)
- **Travelex Insurance Services,** P.O. Box 9408, Garden City, NY 11530-9408 (☎ 800/228-9792)

## 7 Tips for Travelers with Special Needs

**FOR TRAVELERS WITH DISABILITIES**    Prodded by the Americans with Disabilities Act, a growing number of inns and hotels are retrofitting some of their rooms for people with special needs. Most innkeepers are quite proud of their improvements—when I arrive for a site visit, they're invariably quick to show me their new rooms with barrier-free entrances, wheelchair-accessible showers, and fire alarms equipped with strobe lights. Outdoor-recreation areas, especially on state and federal lands, are also providing more trails and facilities for those who've been effectively barred in the past. Accessibility is improving regionwide, but improvements are far from universal. When in doubt, call ahead to ensure that you'll be accommodated.

Travelers with disabilities may also want to consider joining a tour that caters specifically to them. One of the best operators is **Flying Wheels Travel,** 143 W. Bridge, P.O. Box 382, Owatonna, MN 55060 (☎ **800/525-6790;** www.flyingwheels.com). They offer various escorted tours and cruises, as well as private tours in minivans with lifts. **Wilderness Inquiry,** 1313 Fifth St. SE, Box 84, Minneapolis, MN 55414 (☎ **800/728-0719** or 612/379-3858; www.wildernessinquiry.org) offers adventure-travel packages for travelers with disabilities nationwide, including three lake and river canoe trips in Maine.

Other resources include *A World of Options,* a 658-page book of resources for travelers with disabilities that covers everything from biking trips to scuba outfitters. It costs $35 and is available from **Mobility International USA,** P.O. Box 10767, Eugene, OR 97440 (☎ **541/343-1284,** voice and TDD; www.miusa.org). For more personal assistance, Moss Rehab in Philadelphia offers a free **Travel Information Service** for people with disabilities. Call ☎ **215/456-5995.**

Many of the major car-rental companies now offer hand-controlled cars for disabled drivers. **Avis** (☎ **800/331-1212**) can provide such a vehicle at any of its locations in the U.S. with 48-hour advance notice; **Hertz** (☎ **800/654-3131**) requires between 24 and 72 hours of advance reservation at most of its locations. **Wheelchair Getaways** (☎ **800/873-4973;** www.wheelchair-getaways.com) rents specialized vans with wheelchair lifts and other features for the disabled in more than 100 cities across the U.S. Delivery can be arranged to all three northern New England states.

Vision-impaired travelers should contact the **American Foundation for the Blind,** 11 Penn Plaza, Suite 300, New York, NY 10001 (☎ **800/232-5463;** www.afb.org), for information on traveling with seeing-eye dogs.

**FOR SENIORS**　New England is well-suited to older travelers, with a wide array of activities for seniors and discounts commonly available. It's wise to request a discount at hotels or motels when booking the room, not when you arrive. An identification card from the American Association of Retired Persons (**AARP**), 601 E St., NW, Washington, DC 20049 (☎ **202/434-2277;** www.aarp.org) can be invaluable in obtaining discounts.

Excellent programs for seniors are offered by Elderhostel, which is based in Boston. These educational programs for people over 55 years old are reasonably priced and include lodging and meals. Participants can study everything from the art of downhill skiing to the art of autobiography. The locations for these classes are often intriguing and dramatic. For more information, contact **Elderhostel,** 75 Federal St., Boston, MA 02110 (☎ **617/426-7788;** www.elderhostel.org).

Most of the major domestic airlines, including **American, United, Continental, US Airways,** and **TWA,** all offer discount programs for senior travelers—be sure to ask whenever you book a flight. In most cities, people over the age of 60 get reduced admission at theaters, museums, and other attractions, and they can often get discount fares on public transportation. Carrying identification with proof of age can pay off in all these situations.

**FOR FAMILIES**　Families will have little trouble finding things to do with kids in northern New England. The natural world seems to hold tremendous wonder for the younger set—an afternoon exploring the mossy banks and rocky streambeds can be a huge adventure. Older kids often like the challenge of climbing a high mountain peak or learning to paddle a canoe in a straight line; and there's always the beach, which is good for hours of afternoon diversion.

Be sure to ask about family discounts when visiting attractions. Many places offer a flat family rate that is less than paying for each ticket individually. Some parks and beaches charge by the car rather than the head.

When planning your trip, be aware that a number of inns cater to couples and prefer that children are over a certain age. We note in this guide the recommended age for children where restrictions apply, but it's still best to ask first just to be safe. At any rate, if you mention that you're traveling with kids when making reservations, often you'll get accommodations nearer the game room or the pool, making everyone's life a bit easier.

Recommended destinations for families include Weirs Beach and Hampton Beach in New Hampshire, and York Beach and Acadia National Park in Maine. North Conway,

New Hampshire, also makes a good base for exploring with younger kids. The town has lots of motels with pools, and there are nearby train rides, streams suitable for splashing around, easy hikes, and the wonderful distraction known as Story Land.

Several specialized guides offer more detailed information for families on the go. Try *Best Hikes with Children in Vermont, New Hampshire & Maine* by Cynthia and Thomas Lewis (Mountaineers, 2000), *Fun Places to Go With Children in New England* by Pamela Wright and Diane Bair (Chronicle Books, 1998), and *Great Family Vacations North East* by Candyce Stapen (Globe Pequot, 1999).

**FOR GAY & LESBIAN TRAVELERS**   In general, Northern New England isn't exactly a hotbed of gay culture, especially compared to Cape Cod's Provincetown; but many gays and lesbians live and travel here, and have found these three states accepting if not always welcoming. As elsewhere in the country, the larger cities tend to be more accommodating to an alternative lifestyle than smaller towns. Vermont is the most welcoming of the three states; it has been in the news lately for passing a law recognizing civil unions between gay and lesbian couples.

**Portland, Maine,** has the most substantial gay population, attracting many refugees who've fled the crime and congestion of Boston and New York. Portland hosts a sizable gay pride festival early each summer that includes a riotous parade and a dance on the city pier, among other events. In early 1998, Maine narrowly repealed a statewide gay-rights law that had been passed earlier by the state legislature. In Portland, however, the vote was nearly four to one against the repeal and in support of equal rights. Portland also has a municipal ordinance that prohibits discrimination in jobs and housing based on sexual orientation.

**Ogunquit** on the southern Maine coast is a hugely popular destination among gay travelers and features a lively beach and bar scene in the summer. In the winter, it's still active but decidedly more mellow. A well-designed Web site, www.gayogunquit.com, is a great place to start to find information on gay-owned inns, restaurants, and nightclubs in the town.

For a more detailed directory of gay-oriented enterprises in New England, track down a copy of *The Pink Pages,* published by KP Media (66 Charles St., #283, Boston, MA 02114; e-mail: kpmedia@aol.com). The price is $8.95 plus $1.10 shipping and handling. Call ☎ **800/338-6550** or visit the firm's Web site at www.pinkweb.com, which also contains much of the information in the published version.

More adventurous souls should consider linking up with the **Chiltern Mountain Club,** P.O. Box 407, Boston, MA 02117 (☎ **617/859-2843;** www.chiltern. org/chiltern/). This is an outdoor-adventure club for gays and lesbians; about two-thirds of its 1,200 members are men. The club organizes trips to northern New England throughout the year.

## 8 Getting There

### BY PLANE

Airlines serving northern New England include **American** (☎ 800/433-7300), **Business Express** (☎ 800/345-3400), **Comair** (☎ 800/354-9822), **Continental** (☎ 800/525-0280), **Delta** (☎ 800/221-1212), **Northeast Airlines** (☎ 800/983-3247), **Northwest** (☎ 800/225-2525), **United** (☎ 800/241-6522), and **US Airways** (☎ 800/247-8786).

Major commercial carriers serve Burlington, Vermont; Manchester, New Hampshire; and Portland and Bangor, Maine. Airlines most commonly fly to these airports from New York or Boston, although direct connections from other cities, such as

# CyberDeals for Net Surfers

It's possible to get some great deals on airfare, hotels, and car rentals via the Internet. Grab your mouse and surf before you take off—you could save a bundle on your trip. Always check the lowest published fare, however, before you shop for flights online.

## AIRLINE WEB SITES

All **major airlines** have their own Web sites and often offer incentives, such as bonus frequent flyer miles or Net-only discounts, for buying online. Here's a list of Web sites for the major airlines that fly into northern New England:

- **American Airlines:** www.aa.com
- **Continental Airlines:** www.flycontinental.com
- **Delta Airlines:** www.delta-air.com
- **Northwest Airlines:** www.nwa.com
- **TWA:** www.twa.com
- **United Airlines:** www.ual.com
- **US Airways:** www.usairways.com

## THE TOP TRAVEL-PLANNING WEB SITES

If you don't have a favorite airline and want to survey the fare wars without consulting each carrier's Web site, try one of these travelagent–type Web sites that scavenge the airlines' databases for you and divine the cheapest fares available at a given moment:

- **Cheap Tickets:** www.cheaptickets.com
- **Microsoft Expedia:** www.expedia.com
- **Preview Travel:** www.previewtravel.com
- **Smarter Living:** www.smarterliving.com
- **Travelocity:** www.travelocity.com
- **WebFlyer:** www.webflyer.com

Chicago, Cincinnati, and Philadelphia, are also available. Many of the scheduled flights to northern New England from Boston are aboard smaller prop planes; ask the airline or your travel agent if this is an issue of concern for you.

Several smaller airports in the region are served by feeder airlines and charter companies, including Rutland, Vermont; Rockport, Maine; and Trenton, Maine (near Bar Harbor).

Visitors to northern New England can sometimes pay less and have a wider choice of flight times by flying into Boston's Logan Airport, then renting a car or connecting by bus to their final destination. Boston is about 2 hours by car from Portland, less than 3 hours from the White Mountains. If you're heading to the Bennington or Manchester area of Vermont, Albany, New York, is the closest major airport.

## FLYING FOR LESS: TIPS FOR GETTING THE BEST AIRFARES

Passengers who can book their ticket long in advance, who don't mind staying over a Saturday night, or who are willing to travel on a Tuesday, Wednesday, or Thursday after 7pm, will pay a fraction of the full fare. Here are a few other easy ways to save:

- Check your newspaper for advertised discounts or call the airlines directly and ask if any **promotional rates** or special fares are available.
- **Consolidators,** also known as bucket shops, are a good place to find low fares. Their small ads usually run in the Sunday travel section at the bottom of the page. Before you pay, however, ask for a confirmation number from the consolidator and then call the airline itself to confirm your seat.

    Reliable consolidators include: **Council Travel** ☎ 800/226-8624, www.counciltravel.com; **STA Travel** ☎ 800/781-4040, www.sta.travel.com; **Travel Bargains** ☎ 800/AIR-FARE, www.1800airfare.com; **1-800-FLY-CHEAP** www.1800flycheap.com; and **TFI Tours International** ☎ 800-745-8000 or 212/736-1140.
- Book a seat on a **charter flight.** Discounted fares have pared the number available, but they can still be found. Most charter operators advertise and sell their seats through travel agents, thus making these local professionals your best source of information for available flights.
- Join a travel club such as **Moment's Notice** (☎ 718/234-6295) or **Sears Discount Travel Club** (☎ 800/433-9383, or 800/255-1487 to join), which supply unsold tickets at discounted prices. You pay an annual membership fee to get the club's hotline number. Of course, you're limited to what's available, so you have to be flexible.

## BY CAR

Coming from the New York area, there are two main interstate highway corridors. I-91 heads more or less due north from Hartford, Connecticut, through Massachusetts and along the Vermont–New Hampshire border. I-95 parallels the Atlantic coast through Boston, after which it strikes northeast across New Hampshire and along the southern Maine coast before heading north for the Canadian border.

From Boston, you can head north on I-95 for Maine, or take I-93 for New Hampshire and the White Mountains. In Concord, New Hampshire, I-89 departs from I-93 northwestward toward Burlington, Vermont.

If scenery is your priority, the most picturesque way to enter northern New England is from the west. Drive through New York's scenic Adirondack Mountains to Port Kent, New York, on Lake Champlain, then catch the memorable car ferry across the lake to Burlington.

## BY BUS

Express bus service is well-run if a bit spotty in northern New England. You'll be able to reach the major cities and tourist destinations by bus, but few of the smaller towns or villages. Tickets range from $20 one-way for Boston to Portland, to $45 for Boston to Burlington. Taking the bus requires no advance planning or reservations.

Two major bus lines serve northern New England. **Vermont Transit Lines** (☎ 800/451-3292 or 800/642-3133) is affiliated with Greyhound and serves all three states with frequent departures from Boston. **Concord Trailways** (☎ 800/639-3317) serves New Hampshire and Maine, including some smaller towns in the Lake Winnipesaukee and White Mountains area. Concord Trailways buses are a bit more luxurious (and a few dollars more expensive) than Vermont Transit, and often entertain travelers with movies and music (piped through headphones) en route.

## BY TRAIN

Unless you're traveling to Vermont, train service is very limited in northern New England. Amtrak's **Vermonter** departs Washington, D.C., with stops in Baltimore, Philadelphia, and New York before following the Connecticut River northward. Stops

# Your Car: Leave Home Without It

Options exist for those who don't own a car or those who don't consider it a real vacation unless they leave their car at home. Here are a few suggestions:

- Take Amtrak to Brattleboro, Vermont, and stay at the downtown **Latchis Hotel** (☎ 802/254-6300), just a 2-minute walk from the train station. From this base, you can explore this small town of brick architecture, good restaurants, and quirky shops. Cross the river to hike Wantastiquet Mountain one afternoon. Another day, rent a canoe and explore the Connecticut River, or get a bike and head off into the hilly countryside. Canoes are available for rent at **Vermont Canoe Touring Center** just north of town (☎ 802/257-5008 or 802/254-3908). For bike rentals, try **Brattleboro Bicycle Shop** at 165 Main St. (☎ 800/272-8245 or 802/254-8644).

- From Boston take the Concord Trailways bus directly to the **Appalachian Mountain Club's Pinkham Notch Camp** (☎ 603/466-2725), high in the White Mountains. Spend a night or two, then backpack for 2 days across demanding, rugged mountains, staying at AMC's backcountry huts (all meals provided). At the end of your sojourn, catch the AMC shuttle back to North Conway or Pinkham Notch, then hail the return bus back to Boston.

- Bus or fly to Portland, Maine, where you can sign up for a guided sea-kayak excursion. **Maine Island Kayak Co.** (☎ 207/766-2373) is just 20 minutes outside of the city by ferry (the terminal is at the corner of Commercial and Franklin streets) on Peaks Island, and offers trips throughout the state all summer long. You can camp within the city limits on remote Jewell Island at the edge of Casco Bay, or head out for a few days along more remote parts of the coast. Spend an extra day or two in Portland to visit museums and sample from the excellent restaurants.

in Vermont include Brattleboro, Bellows Falls, Claremont (New Hampshire), White River Junction, Randolph, Montpelier, Waterbury, Burlington/Essex Junction, and St. Albans. A bus connection takes passengers on to Montreal. The **Ethan Allen Express** departs New York and travels northward up the Hudson River Valley and into the Adirondacks before veering over to Vermont and terminating at Rutland. Buses continue on to Killington and northward to Middlebury and Burlington.

At press time, it was uncertain if both Vermont lines would continue to operate into 2001. For more information or reservations on either of these trains, contact **Amtrak** at ☎ 800/872-7245 or www.amtrak.com.

Rail service from Boston to Portland also serving seacoast New Hampshire, was slated to begin in 1994, but wrangling over track upgrades, funding, and other issues has severely delayed the process. At press time, it was looking reasonably certain that service would resume by late 2000. Contact Amtrak for more information.

## 9 Getting Around

One of my most fervent wishes is that someday I'll be able to travel around northern New England without a car, as my ancestors did. I'd love to see a reversion to historic times, when travelers could venture to the White Mountains or Maine's Mount Desert Island or Vermont's Lake Champlain via luxurious rail car or steamship. Early in this

- Bus or fly to Bar Harbor, Maine, then settle into one of the numerous inns or B&Bs downtown. (There's a free shuttle bus from the airport to downtown.) Rent a mountain bike and explore the elaborate network of carriage roads at Acadia National Park, then cruise along picturesque Park Loop Road. Another day, sign up for a sea-kayak tour or whale-watching excursion. By night, enjoy lobster and other fine meals at Bar Harbor's fine restaurants. Mountain bikes may be easily rented along Cottage Street in Bar Harbor. Try **Bar Harbor Bicycle Shop** (☎ 207/288-3886) at 141 Cottage St.; **Acadia Outfitters** (☎ 207/288-8118) at 106 Cottage St.; or Acadia Bike & Canoe (☎ 207/288-9605) at 48 Cottage St. For sea kayaking, the following outfitters offer half- and full-day tours: **Acadia Outfitters** (☎ 207/288-8118) at 106 Cottage St.; **Coastal Kayaking Tours** (☎ 207/288-9605) at 48 Cottage St.; and **National Park Sea Kayak Tours** (☎ 207/288-0342) at 137 Cottage St.

- Fly to Bangor, Maine, on a commercial flight. **KT Aviation** (☎ 207/945-5087) can meet you at the airport and take you by van to a nearby lake for a seaplane flight to a remote sporting camp. Here you can spend a week or so hiking, dubbing around in canoes, or reading and relaxing. Among the better sporting camps is **Bradford Camps** (☎ 207/746-7777; www.bradfordcamps.com), a compound of rustic log cabins on an unpopulated lake right out of an L.L. Bean catalog. Meals are served in a handsome 1940s-style dining room. Also of interest is the tiny fishing community of Grand Lake Stream, which has several sporting camps (try **Weatherby's Fisherman's Resort,** ☎ 207/796-5558, or **Grand Lake Lodge** ☎ 207-796-5584). Link up with **Grand Lake Outfitters** (☎ 207/796-5561) for kayak or rafting tours of area lakes and rivers.

century, visitors could even link one trolley line with the next to travel great distances between seaboard cities and inland towns.

Alas, the rise of the motorcar doomed New England's once-extraordinary mass-transit system (visit the Trolley Museum in Kennebunkport, Maine, for a glimpse of this golden era), and today you pretty much need a car to do any serious exploring in the area. Yes, you can explore by canoe, bike, foot, or sea kayak—all of which beats staring dully through a bug-streaked windshield during a 10-hour touring day—but getting to areas where biking is best, from one end of the river to the other, or to remote trailheads, will likely require that car. There are some other options (see "Your Car: Leave Home Without It" on p. 32 for suggestions), or you can sign up for a guided bike tour or other adventure trip; but for the most part, attempting to sightsee without the convenience of a car will mostly yield frustration and considerable wasted time.

## BY CAR

The four major airports in northern New England (see "Getting There," above) all host national car-rental chains. Some handy phone numbers are **Avis** (☎ 800/331-1212), **Budget** (☎ 800/527-0700), **Enterprise** (☎ 800/325-8007), **Hertz** (☎ 800/654-3131), **National** (☎ 800/227-7368), **Rent-A-Wreck** (☎ 800/535-1391), and **Thrifty** (☎ 800/367-2277). You might also find independent car-rental firms in the bigger towns, sometimes at better rates than those offered by the chains. Look in the Yellow Pages under "Automobile–Renting."

## Moose X-ing

Driving across the northern tier of Maine, New Hampshire, and Vermont, you'll often see "Moose Crossing" signs, complete with silhouettes of the gangly herbivores. These are not placed here to amuse the tourists. In Maine, the state with the most moose (an estimated 30,000 at last count), crashes between moose and cars are increasingly common.

These encounters are usually more dramatic than deer-car collisions. For starters, the large eyes of moose don't reflect in headlights like those of deer, so you often come upon them with less warning when driving late at night. Moose can weigh up to 1,000 pounds, with almost all of that weight placed high atop spindly legs. When a car strikes a moose broadside in the road, it usually knocks the legs out and sends a half ton of hapless beast right through the windshield. Need we dwell on the results of such an encounter? I thought not. In 1998, the state of Maine recorded 859 crashes involving moose, with 247 injuries and five fatalities. When in moose country, drive slowly, and drive carefully.

A noted New England joke ends with the punch line "You can't get there from here," but you may conclude it's no joke as you try to navigate through the region. Travel can be convoluted and often confusing; it's handy to have someone adept at map reading in the car with you if you veer off the main routes for country-road exploring. North–south travel is fairly straightforward, thanks to the four major interstates in the region. Traveling east to west (or vice versa) across the region is a more vexing proposition and will likely involve stitching together a route of several state or county roads. Don't fight it; just relax and understand that this is part of the New England experience. It's like rain in the northwest or rattlesnakes in the southwest.

On the other hand, New England is of a size that touring by car can be done quite comfortably, at least in New Hampshire and Vermont. You can drive from Portland to Burlington quite easily in a day across the heart of the region. Note that Maine is much larger than the other two states; when making travel plans, beware of two-sided maps that alter the scale from one side to the other. Remember when budgeting your time that Portland is closer to New York City than it is to Madawaska at the state's extreme northern tip.

Here are some representative distances between points:

| Boston, Massachusetts to: | |
| --- | --- |
| Bar Harbor, Maine | 281 miles |
| Portland, Maine | 107 miles |
| North Conway, New Hampshire | 138 miles |
| Burlington, Vermont | 214 miles |

| Portland, Maine to: | |
| --- | --- |
| Bar Harbor, Maine | 174 miles |
| Greenville, Maine | 153 miles |
| Rangeley, Maine | 118 miles |
| Manchester, New Hampshire | 95 miles |

| Burlington, Vermont to: | |
|---|---|
| Brattleboro, Vermont | 148 miles |
| Killington, Vermont | 92 miles |
| Stowe, Vermont | 37 miles |
| Portland, Maine | 232 miles |

| North Conway, New Hampshire to: | |
|---|---|
| Concord, New Hampshire | 80 miles |
| Bar Harbor, Maine | 216 miles |
| Portland, Maine | 65 miles |
| Burlington, Vermont | 141 miles |

**Traffic** is generally light compared to most urban and suburban areas along the East Coast, but there are exceptions. Traffic on the interstates leading from Boston can be sluggish on Friday afternoons and evenings in the summer. A handful of choke points, particularly on Route 1 along the Maine Coast, can back up for miles as tourists seek to cross two-lane bridges spanning tidal rivers. North Conway in New Hampshire is famed for its hellish traffic, especially during the foliage season. To avoid the worst of the tourist traffic, try to avoid being on the road during big summer holidays; if your schedule allows it, travel on weekdays rather than weekends and hit the road early or late in the day to avoid the midday crunch.

If you're a connoisseur of backroads and off-the-beaten-track exploring, **DeLorme Atlases** are invaluable. These are produced for each of the three states, and offer an extraordinary level of detail, right down to logging roads and public boat launches on small ponds. DeLorme's headquarters and map store (☎ **888/227-1656**) is in Yarmouth, Maine, but their products are available widely at book- and convenience stores throughout the region.

Travelers who are organized to a degree that sometimes alarms their family and close friends probably already know about **MapQuest** (www.mapquest.com). This handy Web site calculates distances and driving directions from any point in the country to any other point. Type in where you want to start and where you want to go, and the online software calculates the total distance and provides detailed driving instructions, along with maps if you want them. Before departing, you can plot your route and print out a daily driving itinerary.

## BY BUS

As mentioned above in section 7, "Getting There," above, express bus service into the region is quite good, but beware of trying to travel *within* the region by bus. Quirky schedules and routes may send you well out of your way, and what may seem a simple trip could take hours. One example: A clerk at Vermont Transit explained that the 65-mile trip from Portland to North Conway was necessarily via Boston and, with lay-overs, would require approximately 9 hours—somewhat longer than it would require a moderately fit person to travel between these points by bicycle.

Traveling north–south between towns along a single bus route (for example, Concord to North Conway, or Portland to Bangor) is feasible, but east–west travel across northern New England is by and large impractical. For information on travel within northern New England, call **Vermont Transit Lines** (☎ **800/451-3292** or 800/642-3133) or **Concord Trailways** (☎ **800/639-3317**) for service in New Hampshire and Maine.

## BY PLANE

Service between airports within the region is sketchy at best. You can find limited direct flights between some cities (such as Portland to Bangor), but for the most part, you'll have to backtrack to Boston and fly out again to your final destination. Convenient it's not. See section 7, "Getting There," above.

## BY TRAIN

Amtrak provides limited rail travel within the region, and is mostly confined to a few stops in Vermont. See "Getting There," above. Long-term plans call for resuming train service from Boston to Portland and beyond, with stops in New Hampshire and along the southern Maine coast. Call **Amtrak** at ☎ **800/872-7245** for more information.

# Fast Facts: Northern New England

**AAA**  The Maine and Vermont AAA services are jointly managed from the club's headquarters in Portland, Maine, but the national auto club has branch offices throughout northern New England to help members with trip planning, road service in the event of a breakdown, and discount tickets to events and attractions. Call ☎ **800/222-4357** for more information on membership.

**American Express**  American Express offers travel services, including check cashing and trip planning, through several affiliated agencies in the region. The office in Portland, Maine, is located at 480 Congress St. (☎ **207/772-8450**); in West Lebanon, New Hampshire, at 24 Airport Rd. (☎ **603/298-5997**); and in Barre, Vermont, at 325 N. Main St. (☎ **802/479-0541**).

**Emergencies**  In the event of fire, crime, or medical emergency, dial ☎ **911.**

**Liquor Laws**  The legal age to consume alcohol is 21, and all three states sell hard liquor through state-run stores. Beer and wine is available in grocery and convenience stores. Restaurants that don't have liquor licenses sometimes allow patrons to bring their own alcoholic beverages. Always ask first. Tolerance for drunk driving is nil in northern New England. Don't do it. In all three states the legal blood alcohol level is .08 percent, which is lower than most other states. If you plan to imbibe with abandon, allow plenty of time for the effects to wear off before getting behind the wheel, or make sure you've booked a room within walking distance of your watering hole. Punishment for drunk driving is swift and severe.

**Maps**  Maps of the region and individual states are commonly available at convenience stores and supermarkets for $2 or $3. Some states also offer free road maps at their official tourist-information centers (they're $1 in Maine). For more detailed coverage of the region, consider purchasing DeLorme atlases, which are available individually for Maine, New Hampshire, and Vermont. These are sold at DeLorme's map store in Yarmouth, Maine, and at most book- and outdoor stores around the region.

**Newspapers/Magazines**  Almost every small town seems to have a daily or weekly newspaper covering the events and happenings of the area. These are good sources of information for small-town events and specials at local restaurants— the day-to-day things that slip through the cracks at the tourist bureaus. The largest papers in each state are the *Portland Press Herald* (Maine), *Manchester Union–Leader* (New Hampshire), and the *Burlington Free-Press* (Vermont).

Burlington and Portland have free alternative weeklies that are handy sources of information on concerts and shows at local clubs. The *New York Times* and *Wall Street Journal* are by now often available same-day in many shops around the region, except in the smallest towns and at the farthest fringes of the region.

**Seat Belts**   Drivers and all passengers are required to wear seat belts in both Maine and Vermont. New Hampshire requires only that children under 12 be restrained.

**Speed Limits**   The speed limit on interstate highways in the region is generally 65 m.p.h., although this is reduced to 55 m.p.h. near cities. State highways are a less formal network, and the speed limits (and road conditions) vary widely. Watch for speed limits to drop in one or two stages as you approach a settlement. *Be alert:* This is often where the local constabulary lurks.

**Taxes**   The current state sales taxes are: Maine, 5.5% (7% on lodging); New Hampshire, no general sales tax, but 8% tax on lodging and dining; and Vermont, 6% (9% on lodging).

**Time**   All three states are in the Eastern Time Zone, as is the Canadian province of Quebec to the north. The provinces of New Brunswick, Nova Scotia, and Prince Edward Island are in the Atlantic Time Zone, which is 1 hour later.

# 3 For Foreign Visitors

Most of the general information to ensure a pleasant trip can be found in the preceding introductory chapters. Some aspects of U.S. laws, customs, and culture that might be perplexing to guests from overseas are covered in this chapter.

## 1 Preparing for Your Trip

### ENTRY REQUIREMENTS

Immigration laws are a hot issue right now, and the following requirements may have changed by the time you plan to take your trip. For the most up-to-date information on requirements for visiting the U.S., go to the State Department's Web site at **http://state.gov**.

**VISAS** Canadian citizens have it easiest to visit the United States. Canadians need only present some form of identification at the border; a passport isn't necessary unless one plans to stay more than 90 days, although it may be helpful as identification for certain transactions, especially financial.

A number of countries participate in the **visa waiver pilot program,** which allows travelers from selected countries to enter the U.S. with just a valid passport and a visa waiver form. In recent years, the visa waiver program has been renewed routinely with little comment. Check with your travel agency for its current status or visit the Web at http://travel.state.gov. The countries in this program are currently Andorra, Argentina, Australia, Austria, Belgium, Brunei, Denmark, Finland, France, Germany, Iceland, Ireland, Italy, Japan, Liechtenstein, Luxembourg, Monaco, the Netherlands, New Zealand, Norway, San Marino, Slovenia, Spain, Sweden, Switzerland, and the United Kingdom.

Other foreign visitors should apply for a U.S. visa at the embassy or consulate with jurisdiction over their permanent residence. One can apply for a visa in any country, but it's generally easier to get a visa in one's own. Applicants must have a passport that's valid for at least 6 months beyond the dates they propose to visit, a passport-sized photo (1.5 inches square), and some indication that they have a residence outside the U.S. to which they plan to return. Applicants must also fill out a Form OF-156 (available free at all U.S. embassies and consulates). If you have a letter of invitation from a U.S. resident, that's sometimes helpful.

Once in the country, foreign visitors come under the jurisdiction of the Immigration and Naturalization Service (INS). If you'd like to change the length or the status of your visa (for instance, from non-immigrant to immigrant), call the INS Customer Information Center at ☎ **800/375-5283.**

Be sure to carefully check the valid dates on your visa. If you overstay 1 or 2 days, it's probably no big deal. If it's more than that, you may be on the receiving end of an interrogation by customs officials on your way out of the country, and it may hinder efforts to get another visa the next time you apply.

**MEDICAL REQUIREMENTS**    Unless you've recently been in an area suffering from an epidemic (such as yellow fever or cholera), no inoculations are needed to enter the United States. Not all prescription drugs that are sold overseas are necessarily available in the United States. If you bring your own supplies of prescription drugs (and especially syringes), it's wise to carry a physician's prescription in case you need to convince customs officials that you're not a smuggler or drug addict.

HIV-positive visitors should call the **National Center for HIV** (☎ 404/332-4559; www.hivatis.org) or the **Gay Men's Health Crisis** (☎ 212/367-1000; www.gmhc.org) for up-to-date information on traveling to the U.S.

**CUSTOMS**    Jet and ship passengers will be asked to fill out a customs form declaring what goods you are bringing into the country just prior to entering the United States. Visitors planning to spend at least 72 hours in the United States may bring 1 liter of alcohol, 200 cigarettes *or* 4.4 pounds of smoking tobacco *or* 50 cigars (but no Cuban cigars), and $100 worth of gifts without paying any duties. Anything over these amounts will be taxed. No food may be brought into the country (this includes canned goods); live plants are also prohibited. Up to US$10,000 in cash may be brought in or out of the country without any formal notification. If you are carrying more than that amount, you must notify customs officials when either entering or departing the country. For more detailed information, visit the official Web site of the U.S. Customs Service at www.customs.gov/travel/travel.htm and look for the section "customs regulations for non-residents."

## MONEY

The basic unit of U.S. currency is the dollar, which is about enough to buy a cup of coffee. The dollar consists of 100 cents. Common coins include penny (1¢), nickel (5¢), dime (10¢), and quarter (25¢), 1-dollar coins that are tinted gold were introduced in 2000 and may be common by the time you read this. Bills and coins are accepted everywhere, but some smaller shops won't accept larger bills ($50 or $100) because they lack sufficient change or are fearful of counterfeit bills. It's easiest to travel with a plentiful supply of $10 and $20 bills.

**CURRENCY EXCHANGE**    Many banks will exchange foreign currency for dollars, but it's often a time-consuming and expensive process. It's best to plan ahead and obtain dollars or dollar-based traveler's checks in your own country before departure.

Canadian dollars are commonly accepted in Maine, New Hampshire, and Vermont (all of which border Canada), although it's generally easier to use Canadian currency the closer to the border you are. Most hotels and many restaurants will accept Canadian currency at a discount close to its current trading value. Increasingly common in

**Travel Tip**

Be sure to keep a copy of all your travel papers separate from your wallet or purse, and leave a copy with someone at home should you need it faxed to you in an emergency.

border towns on the Canadian side are ATM machines that dispense US dollars from your Canadian account.

**TRAVELER'S CHECKS**    Traveler's checks are considered as good as cash in most U.S. shops and banks. Widely recognized brands include American Express, Barclay's, and Thomas Cook. With other types of checks, you might meet with some resistance, particularly in smaller towns. Some small shops may not be willing to cash checks of $100 or more if they have insufficient change; it's best to cash these at hotels or banks. Many banks will cash traveler's checks denominated in U.S. dollars without charge.

**CREDIT CARDS**    Credit cards are the most common form of payment throughout the United States for everything from expensive hotel rooms to inexpensive gifts. It's not impractical to travel the country with no cash, just a credit card in your back pocket. Among the most commonly accepted credit cards are American Express, Discover, MasterCard, and Visa. Because American Express charges a higher rate for processing its transactions, some hotels and restaurants refuse to accept this card.

It's highly recommended to have at least one credit card (fully paid up) when you travel in the United States. Credit cards are commonly accepted in lieu of deposits when renting a car or a hotel room. Many ATM (automatic teller machines) will debit your credit card and provide cash on the spot. Don't ever give your card to anyone as a deposit; they should always record the information on it and return it to you. Also be careful with your credit card receipts, as the information on them may be used by the unscrupulous to make purchases.

## INSURANCE

Foreign visitors who are not insured are strongly urged to take out a traveler's insurance policy to cover any emergencies that may arise during their stay here. The United States does not offer national medical coverage for its residents; medical services are paid for either in cash or, more commonly, by an individual's insurance company. Be aware that hospital and doctors' costs are extremely high in the United States, and even a minor medical emergency could result in a huge extra expense for those traveling without insurance.

Comprehensive policies available in your country may also cover other problems, including bail (in the event you are arrested), automobile accidents, theft or loss of baggage, and emergency evacuation to your country in the event of a dire medical situation. Check with your local automobile association (if there is one) or insurance company for detailed information on travelers' insurance.

Packages such as "Worldwide Assistance" in Europe are sold by automobile clubs and travel agencies at attractive rates. **Travel Assistance International (TAI)** (☎ **800/ 821-2828** or 202/347-2025) is the agent for Worldwide Assistance, so holders of this company's policies can contact TAI for assistance while in the United States.

Canadians should check with their provincial health offices or call **HealthCanada** (☎ **613/957-2991**) to find out the extent of their coverage and what documentation and receipts they must take home in case they are treated in the United States.

## SAFETY

Maine, New Hampshire, and Vermont have among the lowest crime rates in the country, and the odds of being a victim of a crime during your visit here are very slight, but all travelers are advised to take the usual precautions against theft, robbery, and assault.

**ON THE STREETS**    Travelers should avoid any unnecessary displays of wealth when in public. Don't bring out big wads of cash from your pocket, and save your best jewelry for private occasions. If you are approached by someone who demands money, jewelry, or anything else from you, do what most Americans do: Hand over what the mugger requests. Don't argue. Don't negotiate. Just do what they say. Then immediately contact police; in most locales, this is done by dialing ☎ **911** from any telephone (no coin needed at pay phones).

**IN YOUR CAR**    The crime you're statistically most likely to encounter is theft from your automobile. Break-ins can occur any time of the day or night. Don't leave any items of value in plain view—that provides a tempting target for even the casual miscreant. At the least, keep your valuables locked securely in your trunk. Better still, have them with you at all times.

There are very few neighborhoods in northern New England where you're likely to feel threatened. (This isn't the case in the bigger cities of southern New England.) Still, late at night you should look for a well-lighted area to get gas or if you need to step out of your car for any reason. Also, it's not advisable to sleep in your car at night at highway rest areas, which can leave you vulnerable to robbers passing through the area.

**IN YOUR HOTEL OR INN**    Take the usual precautions against leaving cash or valuables in your room when you're not present. Larger hotels have safe-deposit boxes. Smaller inns and hotels will not, although it can't hurt to ask to leave small items in the house safe. A good number of small inns don't even have locks on guest-room doors. Don't be alarmed; if anything, this is a good sign, indicating that there have been no problems here in the past. If you're feeling at all nervous about this, lock your valuables in your car trunk.

One personal note: I've traveled for many years in northern New England, often leaving my inn room door unlocked, and can't report a single unpleasant experience.

## 2  Getting to & Around Northern New England

There are few international flights into Maine, New Hampshire, or Vermont (those that exist are mostly from Canada), so the odds are you'll arrive by way of Boston or New York; and the odds are better still that you'll arrive by car. Bus and train service reaches parts of Maine, New Hampshire, and Vermont, but it tends to be quite spotty and relatively expensive, especially if two or more are traveling together (it's often much cheaper to rent a car than to pay for two tickets). Note also that these states are best seen by exploring the countryside, which is virtually inaccessible by mass transportation. If you're dead set against renting a car, look for "Your Car: Leave Home Without It" in chapter 2. For information on renting a car, see "Getting Around" in chapter 2.

Many international travelers come to northern New England via Boston's Logan Airport or one of the three New York City–area airports. Boston offers the easiest access to northern New England: Portland, Maine; New Hampshire's White Mountains; and the southern Green Mountains are 2 to 3 hours away by car. Figure on about 6 to 8 hours of driving time to most attractions if you're coming from New York airports. For information on getting to northern New England from within the U.S., see "Getting There" in chapter 2.

Dozens of airlines serve New York and Boston airports from overseas, although New York gets far more overseas traffic. Some helpful numbers include (all numbers in London): **American Airlines** (☎ 0181/572-5555); **British Airways** (☎ 0345/222-111); **Continental** (☎ 4412/9377-6464); **Delta** (☎ 0800/414-767); **United** (☎ 0181/990-9900); and **Virgin Atlantic** (☎ 0293/747-747).

Those coming from Latin American, Asia, Australia, or New Zealand will probably arrive in New England through gateway cities like Miami, Los Angeles, or San Francisco, clearing customs there before connecting onward. From here, you can fly directly to northern New England. Bus service is available from Boston's Logan Airport to several cities in northern New England. Limited train service is also offered. See "Getting Around" in the previous chapter.

Airports with regularly scheduled flights in the region include Portland and Bangor, Maine; Manchester, New Hampshire; and Burlington, Vermont. Albany, New York, is another option, especially if your destination is southern Vermont.

## Fast Facts: For the Foreign Traveler

**Abbreviations**   On highway signs and publications you'll see the states of northern New England abbreviated. Maine is "Me.," New Hampshire is "N.H.," and Vermont is "Vt." All capital letters are used when addressing mail for the U.S. Postal Service.

**Automobile Organizations**   Becoming a member of an automobile club is handy for obtaining maps and route suggestions, and can be helpful should an emergency arise with your automobile. The nation's largest automobile club is the American Automobile Association (AAA), which has nearly 1,000 offices nationwide. AAA offers reciprocal arrangements with many overseas automobile clubs; if you're a member of an automobile club at home, find out whether your privileges extend to the United States. For more information on AAA, call ☎ **800/222-4357.**

**Business Hours**   Most offices are open from 8 or 9am to 5 or 6pm. Shops usually open around 9:30 or 10am. Banks typically close at 3 or 4pm, but many have cash-card machines available 24 hours. Post offices in larger cities may be open past 5pm, but it's best to call ahead before going out of your way. A few supermarkets are open 24 hours a day, but they're not terribly common in this part of the world. If you need quick provisions, look for one of the brightly lit convenience stores, which are usually open until at least 10 or 11pm.

**Climate**   See "When to Go" in the previous chapter.

**Currency**   See "Money" in section 1, above.

**Drinking Laws**   You must be 21 years old to legally drink alcohol in the U.S. No matter what your age, state laws in New England are notoriously harsh on those who drive drunk. Know your tolerance. If you plan to exceed that in an evening, allow enough time for the effects to wear off, or imbibe within walking distance of your hotel or inn.

**Driving**   A current overseas license is valid on U.S. roads. If your license is in a language other than English, it's recommended that you obtain an International Drivers Permit from the American Automobile Association affiliate or other automobile organization in your own country prior to departure (see "Automobile Organizations," above).

Drivers may make a right turn at a red light, provided that they first stop fully and confirm that no other driver is approaching from the left. At some intersections, signs prohibit such a turn.

**Electricity**   Electrical incompatibility makes it tricky to use appliances manufactured for Europe in the United States. The current here is 110 to 120 volts,

60 cycles, compared to the 220 to 240 volts, 50 cycles used in much of Europe. If you're bringing an electric camera flash, portable computer, or other gadget that requires electricity, be sure to bring the appropriate converter and plug adapter.

**Embassies/Consulates**   Embassies for countries with which the United States maintains diplomatic relations are located in Washington, D.C. Call directory assistance (☎ **202/555-1212**) and request the phone number.

A handful of countries maintain consulates in Boston, including **Canada,** 3 Copley Place, Suite 400, Boston, MA 02116 (☎ 617/262-3760); **Great Britain,** Federal Reserve Plaza, 600 Atlantic Ave. (25th floor), Boston, MA 02210 (☎ 617/248-9555); **Ireland,** 535 Boylston St., Boston, MA 02116 (☎ 617/267-9330); and **Israel,** 1020 Statler Office Building, 20 Park Plaza, Boston, MA 02116 (☎ 617/535-0200). For other countries, contact directory assistance (☎ 617/555-1212).

**Emergencies**   In the event of any type of emergency—whether medical, fire, or if you've been the victim of a crime—simply dial ☎ **911** from any phone. You do not need a coin to make this call. A dispatcher will immediately send medics, the police, or the fire department to assist you. If 911 doesn't work (some of the more remote areas haven't yet been connected to the network), dial "0" (zero) and report your situation to the operator. If a hospital is nearby when a medical emergency arises, look for the "Emergency" entrance, where you will be quickly attended to.

**Gasoline**   Gasoline is widely available throughout the region, with the exception of the North Woods region of Maine where you can travel many miles without seeing a filling station. Gas tends to be cheaper farther to the south and in larger town and cities, where the competition is a bit stiffer; you're better off filling up before setting off into remote or rural areas. Gas is available in several different grades at each station; the higher the octane, the more expensive it is.

Many of the filling stations in New England have both "self-serve" and "full-service" pumps; look for signs as you pull up. The full service pumps are slightly more expensive per gallon, but an attendant will pump your gas and check your oil (you might have to ask for this). The self-serve pumps often have simple directions posted on them. If you're at all confused, ask anyone who happens to be around for instructions.

**Holidays**   With some important exceptions, national holidays usually fall on Mondays to allow workers to enjoy a 3-day holiday. The exceptions are New Year's Day (January 1), Independence Day (July 4), Veterans Day (November 11), Thanksgiving (last Thursday in November), and Christmas (December 25). Other holidays include Martin Luther King, Jr. Day (third Monday in January), President's Day (third Monday in February), Easter (first Sunday following a full moon occurring March 21 or later), Memorial Day (last Monday in May), Labor Day (first Monday in September), and Columbus Day (second Monday in October). In Maine and Massachusetts, Patriot's Day is celebrated on the third Monday in April.

On these holidays, banks, government offices, and post offices are closed. Shops are sometimes open and sometimes not on holidays, but assume almost all will be closed on Thanksgiving and Christmas Day.

**Languages**   Some of the larger hotels may have multilingual employees, but don't count on it. Outside of the cities, English is the only language spoken. The exception is along the Canadian border and in some Maine locales (including Old Orchard Beach, Biddeford, Lewiston, and Van Buren), where French is commonly spoken or at least understood.

**Legal Aid**    If a foreign tourist accidentally breaks a law, it's most likely to be for exceeding the posted speed limit on a road (it's the law U.S. residents frequently run afoul of). If you are pulled over by a policeman, don't attempt to pay the fine directly—that may be interpreted as a bribe, and you may find yourself in graver trouble. If pulled over, your best bet is to put on a display of confusion or ignorance of local laws (this may be feigned or legitimate), combined with a respect for authority. You may be let off with a warning. Failing that, you'll be issued a summons with a court date and a fine listed on it; if you pay the fine by mail, you don't have to appear in court. If you are arrested for a more serious infraction, you'll be allowed one phone call from jail. It's advisable to contact your embassy or consulate for further instruction.

**Mail**    Virtually every small town and village has a post office; ask anyone on the street where it is and you'll be directed there. Mail within the United States costs 33¢ for a 1-ounce letter, and 22¢ for each additional ounce; postcards are 20¢. Overseas mail to Europe, Australia, New Zealand, Asia, and South America is 60¢ for a half ounce, 55¢ for a postcard. A half-ounce letter to Mexico is 40¢; a half-ounce letter to Canada is 48¢. If in doubt about weight or costs, ask the postal clerk. Mail may also be deposited at blue mailboxes with the inscription "U.S. MAIL" or "United States Postal Service" located on many streets.

If you need to receive mail during your travels, have your correspondents address it to your name, "[c/o] General Delivery" at the city you are visiting. Go in person to the main post office to collect it; you'll be asked for identification (a passport is ideal) before it's given to you.

**Newspapers/Magazines**    Foreign newspapers and magazines are commonly found in Boston and Cambridge to the south, but are harder to track down in northern New England. Your best bet is to go to Borders Books & Music (Portland and Bangor, Maine or Burlington, Vermont), or Barnes & Noble (Augusta, Maine; Salem, Nashua, and Manchester, New Hampshire; and South Burlington, Vermont). Both chains have large stores and offer a limited selection of overseas newspapers and magazines.

**Taxes**    Visitors to the United States are assessed a $10 Customs tax upon entering the country and a $6 tax on departure. The United States does not have a value-added tax (VAT). The tax you most commonly come across is a sales tax (usually 5% to 6%) added on to the price of goods and some services. New Hampshire does not have a sales tax on goods but does levy an 8% tax on hotel rooms and meals at restaurants.

**Telephone and Fax**    Pay phones are not hard to find except in the more remote regions. Shops that have public phones inside usually display a blue sign featuring a bell inside a circle outside the store.

Telephone numbers beginning with "800," "877," "888" are toll-free. Press "1" before dialing a toll-free number.

Phone directories are divided between Yellow Pages (stores and services, listed by category) and the White Pages (names, listed alphabetically). Some White Pages are sometimes further split between commercial and residential listings. Phone books are sometimes found at pay phones; failing that, ask to see one at a friendly shop or restaurant. To find a specific local phone number, dial "411" and an operator will take your request. Sometimes this is a free call from a pay phone, sometimes it's not. The Yellow Pages section often features maps of the local area and other information of interest to travelers.

Local calls usually cost 35¢ for an unlimited amount of time; the price of a local call will appear on the phone. How far you can call on a local call varies from place to place, and the boundaries will often seem arbitrary. If you're uncertain whether a call is long distance or not, try it as a local call. If a recorded voice comes on telling you to deposit more money for the first 3 minutes, that means it's a long-distance call.

Long-distance calls at pay phones tend to be very expensive, and you'll need a lot of coins. There are other options. At some phones you can use your credit card. Prepaid phone cards are available at many convenience stores and other outlets, typically for $5 or $10. Follow the instructions on the card (you'll call a toll-free number first, then punch in a code and the number you wish to call). Long-distance charges using the cards are typically about 25¢ per minute. The cards are less expensive and more convenient than feeding coins into a pay phone.

Be aware that many hotels (notably the more expensive chain hotels) tack on a surcharge for local and long-distance calls made from your room. Even toll-free calls can cost you $1 or more. Ask about phone charges when you check in. If your hotel does add a high surcharge and you plan to make a number of local phone calls, you're better off using a pay phone.

To charge the phone call to the person receiving your call, dial "0," then the area code, and the number you're calling. An operator (or computer) will come on and ask your name, and will then call the number to ask permission to reverse the charges. If the person you're calling accepts, the call will be put through.

If you need to send or receive a fax (facsimile), ask at your hotel, or look in the Yellow Pages under "Fax Transmission Service."

**Time**    All of northern New England is in the Eastern Time Zone—the same as Boston, New York, and the rest of the eastern seaboard. All states shift to Daylight Savings Time in summer, setting clocks ahead 1 hour in the spring (the first Sunday in April), and back again in the fall (the last Sunday in October).

**Tipping**    Tipping is commonly practiced in the United States to recognize good service. Be aware that in restaurants, servers are typically paid a bare minimum and depend on tips for their wage. Tipping isn't considered optional, unless the service is unspeakably bad. For decent to good service, tip 15%; for outstanding service 20%. Other suggestions for tipping include: bartenders 10% to 15%; bellhops $1 per bag; cab drivers 10% of fare; chambermaids $1 to $2 per day; checkroom attendants $1 per garment; and parking attendants $1. No tipping is expected at gas stations, or at fast-food or other self-service restaurants.

**Toilets**    Public toilets (often called "rest rooms") are increasingly scarce in the United States, and where they do exist, they're often not fit for use. Restaurants have rest rooms for their customers; some will let people off the street use them, but many have signs indicating "For Patrons Only." This is remedied by buying a pack of gum or a cup of coffee. Fast food restaurants (like McDonald's or Burger King) are a good bet for reasonably clean toilets when traveling on the highways.

# 4 Southern & Central Vermont

A pair of East Coast academics raised some dust some years back with a proposal to turn much of the Great Plains into a national park and let the buffalo roam free again.

With all due respect, if there's any place that should be turned wholesale into a national park, it's Vermont. Such a move would preserve a classic American landscape of rolling hills punctuated with slender white church spires and covered bridges (Vermont has more than 100). It would preserve the perfectly scaled main streets in towns like Woodstock, Bennington, Middlebury, and Montpelier. It would save the dairy farms that sprawl across the shoulders of verdant ridges, but most of all, it would preserve a way of life that, one day, America will wish it had done much more to save.

Without feeling in the least like a theme park, Vermont captures a sense of America as it once was. Vermonters still share a strong sense of community, and they still respect the ideals of thrift and parsimony. They prize their small villages and towns, and they understand what makes them special. Governor Howard Dean once said that one of Vermont's special traits was in knowing "where our towns begin and end." It seems a simple notion, but that speaks volumes when one considers the erosion of identity that has afflicted many small towns swallowed up by one creeping megalopolis or another.

Of course, it's not likely that Vermont residents would greet a national-park proposal with much enthusiasm. Meddlesome outsiders and federal bureaucrats don't rank high on their list of folks to invite to Sunday supper. At any rate, such a preservation effort would ultimately be doomed to failure: Vermont's impeccable sense of place is tied to its autonomy and independence, and any effort to control it from above would certainly cause the state as we know it to perish.

Happily for travelers exploring the state, it's not hard to get a taste of Vermont's way of life. You'll find it in almost all of the small towns and villages, and they are small—let the numbers tell the story: Burlington, Vermont's largest city, has just 39,127 residents; Montpelier, the state capital, 8,247; Brattleboro, 8,612; Bennington, 9,532; Woodstock, 1,037; Newfane, 164. (All these figures are from the 1990 census.) The state's entire population is just 560,000—making it one of a handful of states with more senators than representatives in Congress.

Of course, numbers don't tell the whole story. You have to let the people do that. One of Vermont's better-known former residents, Nobel Prize–winning author Sinclair Lewis, wrote 70 years ago: "I like

# Vermont

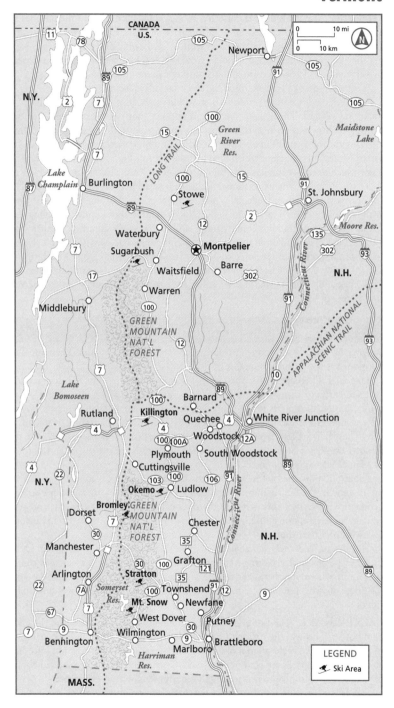

Vermont because it is quiet, because you have a population that is solid and not driven mad by the American mania—that mania which considers a town of four thousand twice as good as a town of two thousand. . . . Following that reasoning, one would get the charming paradox that Chicago would be 10 times better than the entire state of Vermont, but I have been in Chicago and not found it so."

With all respect to readers from Chicago, that still holds true today.

Southern and Central Vermont is a region of rolling hills, shady valleys, and charming villages. Throughout you'll find antique shops and handsome inns, fast-flowing streams and inviting restaurants. It's anchored at each corner by the towns of Bennington and Brattleboro; between them and running northward is the spine of the Green Mountains, much of which is part of the Green Mountain National Forest, and all of which rewards explorers who find dirt roads an irresistible temptation. Here and there you'll find remnants of former industries—marble quarrying around Rutland, the convergence of train tracks at White River Junction—but mostly it's rural living, with cow pastures high on the hills, old clapboard farmhouses under spreading trees, maple-sugaring operations come spring, and the distant sound of timber being twitched out of a woodlot on the far side of a high ridge. The steep-sided hills also host many of the state's most popular ski resorts, like Okemo, Killington, Sugarbush, and Mount Snow. Much of southern Vermont is within reasonable striking distance of New York and environs, and it's becoming an increasingly popular spot for the vacation homes of harried urbanites.

## 1 Enjoying the Great Outdoors

Arizona has the Grand Canyon; Florida has the Everglades. And Vermont? Well, Vermont has the Green Mountains.

The chief difference is that the Green Mountains aren't so much a destination as part and parcel of Vermont itself. These rolling mountains, which form a north–south spine from Massachusetts to the Canadian border, not only define Vermont, but also offer wonderful recreational opportunities, especially for those attracted to soft adventure. These hills are less dramatic and more forgiving than the harsh White Mountains of northern New Hampshire, and more friendly than the bristly spruce and fir forests of Maine. These are mountains where you can feel at home.

About 500,000 acres are included in the Green Mountains National Forest, which offers some of the best hiking and mountain biking in the Northeast, but outdoorspeople needn't restrict themselves to the national forest land. State forests and parks contain some exceptional hiking trails, and even many privately owned lands are open to low-impact recreation.

This mix of wilderness and civilization gives Vermont much of its character. One of the great pleasures of exploring Vermont, whether by foot, bike, or canoe, is coming over a hill or around a bend and spying a graceful white steeple or a sturdy wooden silo, both of which are as integral to the landscape here as maple trees and rolling ridges.

**BACKPACKING**    The **Long Trail** runs 270 miles from Massachusetts to the Canadian border. This was the nation's first long-distance hiking path, and it remains one of the best. This high-elevation trail follows Vermont's gusty ridges and dips into shady cols, crossing federal, state, and private lands. Open-sided shelters are located about a day's hike apart. To hike the entire length requires stamina and experience.

The best source of information about backcountry opportunities is the **Green Mountain Club** (4711 Waterbury-Stowe Rd., Waterbury Center, VT 05677 ☎ 802/244-7037; www.greenmountainclub.org; e-mail: gmc@sover.net), which publishes the *Long Trail Guide*. Club headquarters is on Route 100 between Waterbury and Stowe, and the information center and bookstore is open weekdays usually until about 4:30pm. Annual membership dues, which will get you a newsletter and discounts on guides, are $27 for an individual, or $35 for a family.

**BIKING**    Vermont's backroads offer some of the most appealing biking in the Northeast. Even Route 100—the main north–south thoroughfare up the middle of the state—is inviting along many stretches, especially from Killington to Sugarbush. While steep hills on some backroads can be excruciating for those who've spent too much time behind a desk, close scrutiny of a map should reveal routes that follow rivers and offer less grueling pedaling.

Vermont also lends itself to superb mountain biking. Abandoned county and town roads offer superior backcountry cruising. Most Green Mountain National Forest trails are also open to mountain bikers (but not the Appalachian or Long trails). Mountain bikes are prohibited from state-park and state-forest hiking trails, but they are allowed on gravel roads. Mount Snow and Jay Peak ski areas, among others, will bring you and your bike to blustery ridges via lift or gondola, allowing you to work with gravity on your way down. The Craftsbury Center is your best bet if you're looking for backroad cruising through farmland rather than forest.

Organized inn-to-inn bike tours are a great way to see the countryside by day while relaxing in luxury at night. Tours are typically self-guided, with luggage transferred for you each day by vehicle. Try **Vermont Bicycle Touring** (☎ **800/245-3868**) or **Bike Vermont** (☎ **800/257-2226;** e-mail: bikevermont@bikevermont.com).

**CANOEING**    Good paddling rivers include the Battenkill in southwest Vermont, the Lamoille near Jeffersonville, the Winooski near Waterbury, and the Missisquoi from Highgate Center to Swanton Dam. The whole of the historic Connecticut River, while frequently interrupted by dams, offers uncommonly scenic paddling through rural farmlands. Especially beautiful is the 7-mile stretch between Moore and Comerford dams near Waterford. Rentals are easy to come by near Vermont's major waterways; just check the local Yellow Pages.

For inn-to-inn canoe-touring packages (2 to 6 days), contact **Battenkill Canoe Ltd.,** Rte. 7A, Arlington, VT 05250 (☎ **800/421-5268** or 802/362-2800).

In recent years the **Upper Valley Land Trust** (19 Buck Rd., Hanover, NH 03755; ☎ **603/643-6626**) set up a network of primitive campsites along the Connecticut River; canoeists can paddle and portage its length and camp along the riverbanks. Two of the campsites are accessible by car. Call for a brochure or visit the group's Web site at www.uvlt.org.

A helpful general guide is Roioli Schweiker's *Canoe Camping Vermont & New Hampshire Rivers,* published by Countryman Press (1999, $15.95).

**FISHING**    Both lake and river fishing can be excellent—if you know what you're doing. Vermont has 288 lakes of 20 acres or larger, hundreds of smaller bodies of water, and countless miles of rivers and streams.

Novice fly-fishermen would do well to stop by the famed **Orvis Catalog Store** (☎ **802/362-3750**) in Manchester to ask for some friendly advice, then perhaps try out some tackle on the store's small ponds. If time permits, sign up for one of the Orvis fly-fishing classes and have an expert critique your technique and offer some pointers.

Vermont's rivers and lakes are home to 14 major species of sportsfish, including landlocked salmon, four varieties of trout (rainbow, brown, brook, and lake), and large- and smallmouth bass. The 100-mile-long Lake Champlain attracts its share of enthusiasts angling for bass, landlocked salmon, and lake trout. In the south, the

Battenkill is perhaps the most famed trout river (thanks in part to the proximity of Orvis), although veteran anglers contend that it's lost its luster. The Walloomsac and West rivers have also been rumored to give up a decent-size trout or two; and don't overlook the Connecticut River, which the Fish and Wildlife Department calls "probably the best-kept fishing secret in the Northeast."

Fishing licenses are required and are available by mail from the state or in person at many sporting-goods and general stores. License requirements and fees change from time to time, so write or call for a complete list: **Vermont Fish & Wildlife Dept.,** 103 S. Main St., #10 South, Waterbury, VT 05671 (☎ **802/241-3700**). Current license information is on the Web at www.anr.state.vt.us/fw/fwhome/html/fees.htm.

**HIKING**    A spectacular range of hiking trails are here, from undemanding woodland strolls to rugged treks. The two premier long-distance pathways in Vermont are the Appalachian and Long trails (see "Backpacking," above); day hikes are easily carved out of these longer treks. The Green Mountain National Forest offers 500 miles of hiking trails. Any of the four Green Mountain offices will make a good stop for picking up maps and requesting hiking advice from rangers. The **main office** is in Rutland (☎ **802/747-6700**). District **ranger offices** are in Middlebury (☎ **802/ 388-6688**), Rochester (☎ **802/767-4261**), and Manchester (☎ **802/362-2307**).

Vermont also has some 80 state forests and parks. Guides to hiking trails are essential to getting the most out of a hiking vacation. Recommended guides include the Green Mountain Club's *Day Hiker's Guide to Vermont* and *50 Hikes in Vermont* published by Countryman Press, both widely available in bookstores throughout the state.

**SKIING**    Vermont has been eclipsed by upscale Western and Canadian ski resorts in the past few decades, but to many, it's *still* the capital of downhill skiing in the United States. The nation's first ski lift—a rope tow—was rigged up off a Buick engine in 1934 near Woodstock. The first lodge built specifically to accommodate skiers was at Sherburne Pass.

For the allure of big mountains, steep faces, and a lively ski scene, there's Killington, Sugarbush, Stratton, Mount Snow, and Stowe. Families and intermediates find their way to Okemo, Bolton Valley, and Smuggler's Notch. For old-fashioned New England ski-mountain charm, there's Mad River Glen, Ascutney, Burke, and Jay Peak. Finally, those who prefer a small mountain with a smaller price tag, make tracks for Middlebury Snow Bowl, Bromley, Maple Valley, and Suicide Six. Information on **ski conditions** is available by calling ☎ **800/837-6668** or visiting the Web at **www. skivermont.com**.

Vermont is also blessed with about 50 cross-country ski areas. These range from modest mom-and-pop operations to elaborate destination resorts with snowmaking. Many of these are connected by the 200-mile Catamount Trail, which runs the length of the state parallel to, but at lower elevations than the Long Trail. For more information, contact the **Catamount Trail Association,** P.O. Box 1235, Burlington, VT 05402 (☎ **802/864-5794;** www.catamounttrail.together.com). For a free brochure listing all the cross-country facilities, contact the **Vermont Department of Travel and Tourism** (☎ **800/837-6668**). The state updates a recorded cross-country ski report every Thursday (☎ **802/828-3239**).

The best general advice for cross-country skiers is to head north, and to higher elevations, where the most persistent snow is usually found. Among the snowiest, best-managed destinations are the Trapp Family Lodge in Stowe, the Craftsbury Nordic Center in the Northeast Kingdom, and Mountain Top near Killington.

Inn-to-inn ski touring is growing in popularity. **Country Inns Along the Trail** (☎ **802/247-3300;** www.inntoinn.com) offers a self-guided 4-night trip along the

Catamount Trail that connects three inns in central Vermont. This runs $520 per person, double occupancy, and includes lodging and all meals. Customized trips may also be arranged.

**SNOWMOBILING**   Vermont boasts a lengthy, well-developed network of snowmobile trails throughout the state. The best source of information on snowmobiling in Vermont is **VAST,** P.O. Box 839, Montpelier, VT 05601 (☎ **802/229-0005;** www.snowmobilevt.com), which produces a helpful newsletter and can help point you and your machine in the right direction.

Snowmobile rentals are still somewhat hard to come by in Vermont, although guided tours are common. In southern Vermont, **High Country Snowmobile Tours,** located 8¹/₂ miles west of Wilmington (☎ **800/627-7533** or 802/464-2108) offers tours in the Green Mountain National Forest lasting between 1 hour ($55) and a full day ($275). If you've never been on a snowmobile before but want to give it a whirl, rides around a 1¹/₂-mile track are offered just south of Stowe at **Nichols Snowmobile Rentals** (☎ **802/253-7239**).

## 2  Bennington, Manchester & Southwestern Vermont

Bennington is 143 miles northwest of Boston and 126 miles south of Burlington. Manchester is 24 miles north of Bennington.

Southwestern Vermont is the turf of Ethan Allen, Robert Frost, Grandma Moses, and Norman Rockwell. As such, it may seem familiar even if you've never been here before. Over the decades, it has subtly managed to work itself into America's cultural consciousness.

The region is sandwiched between the Green Mountains to the east and the rolling hills along the Vermont–New York border to the west. If you're coming from Albany or the southwest, the first town you're likely to hit is Bennington—a commercial center that offers up low-key diversions for residents and tourists alike. Northward toward Rutland, the terrain is more intimate than intimidating, with towns clustered in broad and gentle valleys along rivers and streams. Former 19th-century summer colonies and erstwhile lumber and marble towns exist side by side, offering pleasant accommodations, delightful food, and—in the case of Manchester Center—world-class shopping.

These outposts of sophisticated culture are within easy striking distance of the Green Mountains, allowing you to enjoy the outdoors by day and goose-down duvets by night. The region also attracts its share of weekend celebrities, as well as shoppers, gourmands, and those simply looking for a brief and relaxing detour to the elegant inns and B&Bs for which the region is widely known.

Keep in mind when exploring the area that two Route 7s exist. Running high along the foothills is the new Route 7, which offers limited access and higher speeds, resulting in a speedy trip up the valley toward Rutland. Meandering along the valley floor is Historic Route 7A, a more languorous road with plenty of diversions (antiques shops and wonderful views). If you've got the time, take the slow road from Bennington north.

### BENNINGTON

Bennington owes its fame (such as it is) to a handful of eponymous moments, places, and things: Like the Battle of Bennington, fought in 1777 during the American War of Independence; Bennington College, a small but prestigious liberal arts school; and Bennington pottery, which traces its ancestry back to the first factory here in 1793, and is today prized by collectors for its superb quality.

# Southern Vermont

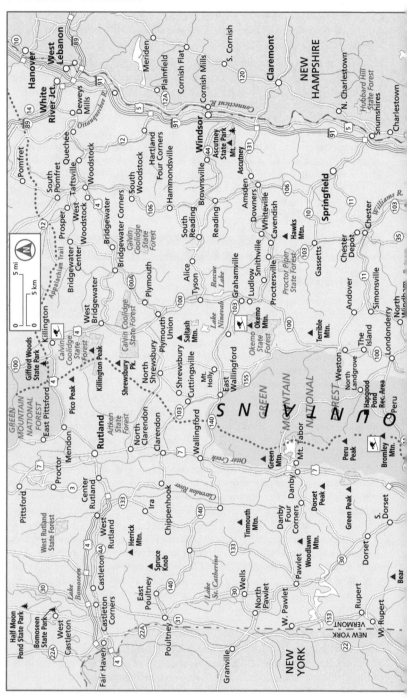

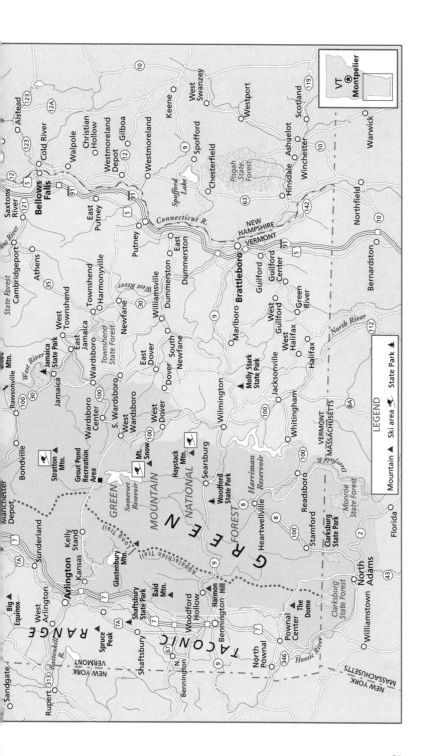

Today, visitors will find two Benningtons. Historic Bennington with its white clapboard homes sits atop a hill just west of town off Route 9. (Look for the mini–Washington Monument.) Modern downtown Bennington is a pleasant if no-frills commercial center with restaurants and stores that still sell things that people actually need. It's not so much a tourist destination as a handy supply depot. (It's actually Vermont's third largest city.) The downtown is compact, low, and handsome, and boasts a fair number of architecturally striking buildings. In particular, don't miss the stern marble Federal building (formerly the post office) with its six fluted columns, at 118 South St. The surrounding countryside, while defined by rolling hills, is afflicted with fewer abrupt inclines and slopes than many of Vermont's towns.

## ESSENTIALS

**GETTING THERE**    Bennington is located at the intersection of Routes 9 and 7. If you're coming from the south, the nearest interstate access is via the New York Thruway at Albany, New York, about 35 miles away. From the east, I-91 is about 40 miles away at Brattleboro.

**Vermont Transit** (☎ **800/451-3292** or 802/442-4808) offers bus service to Bennington from Albany, Burlington, and other points. Buses arrive and depart from 126 Washington St.

**VISITOR INFORMATION**    The **Bennington Area Chamber of Commerce,** Veterans Memorial Dr., Bennington, VT 05201 (☎ **802/447-3311**), maintains an information office on Route 7 north near the veterans complex. The office is open Monday to Friday from 8:30am to 4:30pm year-round; in summer and fall, it's also open weekends from 9am to 4pm. Information is also available on the Internet at www.bennington.com.

## EXPLORING THE TOWN

One of Bennington's claims to history is the fabled Battle of Bennington, which took place August 16, 1777. A relatively minor skirmish, it had major implications for the outcome of the American Revolution.

The British had devised a grand strategy to defeat the impudent colonists: divide the colonies from the Hudson River through Lake Champlain, then concentrate forces to defeat first one half and then the other. As part of the strategy, British Gen. John Burgoyne was ordered to attack the settlement of Bennington and capture the military supplies that had been squirreled away by the Continental militias. There he came upon colonial forces led by Gen. John Stark, a veteran of Bunker Hill. After a couple of days playing cat and mouse, Stark ordered the attack on the afternoon of August 16, proclaiming, "There are the redcoats, and they are ours, or this night Molly Stark sleeps a widow!" (Or so the story goes.)

The battle was over in less than 2 hours—the British and their Hessian mercenaries were defeated, with more than 200 enemy troops killed; the colonials lost but 30 men. This cleared the way for another vital colonial victory at the Battle of Saratoga, that ended the British strategy of divide and conquer, and set the stage for colonial victory.

That battle is commemorated by northern New England's most imposing monument. You can't miss the **Bennington Battle Monument** if you're passing through the surrounding countryside. This 306-foot obelisk of blue limestone atop a low rise was dedicated in 1891. It resembles a shorter, paunchier Washington Monument. Note also that it's actually about 6 miles from the site of the actual battle; the monument marks the spot where the munitions were stored. The monument's viewing platform, which is reached by elevator, is open from 9am to 5pm daily from April through October. A fee of $1 is charged.

Near the monument you'll find distinguished old homes lushly overarched with ancient trees. Be sure to spend a few moments exploring the old burying ground, where several Vermont governors and the poet Robert Frost are buried. The chamber of commerce (see above) offers a walking tour brochure that will help you make sense of the neighborhood's vibrant past.

**Bennington College** was founded as an experimental women's college in the 1930s. It's since gone co-ed and has garnered a national reputation as a leading liberal arts school. Bennington has a great reputation for the teaching of writing; W. H. Auden, Bernard Malamud, and John Gardner have all taught here. In the 1980s, Bennington produced a number of prominent young authors, including Donna Tartt, Bret Easton Ellis, and Jill Eisenstadt. The pleasant campus north of town is worth wandering about.

**Bennington Museum.** W. Main St. (Rte. 9 between Old Bennington and the current town center). ☎ **802/447-1571.** www.benningtonmuseum.com. $6 adults, $5 students and seniors, free for children under 12, $13 family (with children under 18). Daily 9am–6pm (until 5pm Nov 1–May 31).

This eclectic and intriguing collection traces its roots back to 1875, although the museum has occupied the current stone-and-column building overlooking the valley only since 1928. The expansive galleries feature a wide range of exhibits on local arts and industry, including early Vermont furniture, glass, paintings, and Bennington pottery. Of special interest are the colorful primitive landscapes by Grandma Moses (1860–1961), who lived much of her life nearby. (The museum has the largest collection of Moses paintings in the world.) Look also for the glorious 1925 luxury car called the Wasp, 16 of which were handcrafted in Bennington between 1920 and 1925. A $2 million expansion of the museum, including new galleries and an expanded gift shop, was completed in 1999.

## WHERE TO STAY

**Four Chimneys.** 21 West Rd., Bennington, VT 05201. ☎ **802/447-3500.** Fax 802/447-3692. www.fourchimneys.com. E-mail: innkeeper@fourchimneys.com. 11 units. A/C TV. Weekends, holidays and summer midweek $125–$205 double; winter midweek $100–$180. Rates include breakfast. 2-night minimum stay foliage and holiday weekends. AE, CB, DC, DISC, MC, V. No children under 12.

This striking Colonial Revival building will be among the first to catch your eye as you arrive in Bennington from the west. Set off Route 7 on an 11-acre, nicely landscaped lot, it's an imposing white, three-story structure with—no surprise—four prominent chimneys. (Local secret: The third chimney's a fake, added for the purpose of symmetry.) The inn, built in 1912, is at the edge of Historic Bennington; the towering Bennington Monument looms over the backyard. The carpeted guest rooms are inviting and homey. The inn is still searching for its niche; three innkeepers have owned the place since 1996, with the newest coming on board as of March 1999.

**Dining:** The dining room has long been a destination for Benningtonians looking for a big night out; the chef offers meals with a continental flair. It's open Tuesday to Sunday for lunch and dinner; dinner is fixed-price at $33.50.

**South Shire Inn.** 124 Elm St., Bennington, VT 05201. ☎ **802/447-3839.** Fax 802/442-3547. www.southshire.com. E-mail: sshire@sover.net. 9 units. A/C TEL. Foliage season $125–$180 double; off-season $105–$160 double. Rates include full breakfast. AE, MC, V. No children under 12.

A locally prominent banking family hired architect William Bull to design and build this impressive Victorian home in 1880. The downstairs is spacious and open, with detailing including leaded glass on the bookshelves and intricate plasterwork in the dining room. The guest rooms are richly hued, and most have canopied beds and working fireplaces (Duraflame-style logs only). The best of the bunch is the old master bedroom, which has a king-size canopied bed, a tile-hearth fireplace, and a beautiful bathroom with hand-painted tile. Four more modern guest rooms are in the carriage house. The carriage house's downstairs rooms are slightly more formal; the upstairs rooms are more intimate with low eaves and skylights over the tubs.

## WHERE TO DINE

**Alldays & Onions.** 519 Main St. ☎ **802/447-0043.** Reservations accepted for dinner but not often needed. Breakfast and lunch $2–$7, dinner $10.95–$19.95. AE, DISC, MC, V. Mon–Tues 7:30am–5pm; Wed–Sat 7:30am–8pm. ECLECTIC.

First off, the name: This eminently casual place is named after an early 20th-century British automobile manufacturer. Locals flock here to enjoy the wholesome, tasty sandwiches, the filling deli salads, and tasty soups. More ambitious dinners are served later in the week, with entrees changing frequently but including the likes of Southwest cowboy steak with skillet corn sauce and soba and stir-fried vegetables. The atmosphere is that of a small-town restaurant gussied up for a big night out—the fluorescent lights are a bit bright, but the dark hues of the walls knock down the intensity a notch, and folk-rock background music mellows it further still.

✪ **Blue Benn Diner.** North St. (Rte. 7). ☎ **802/442-5140.** Breakfast and lunch $1.50–$5.95; dinner $7.95. No credit cards. Mon–Tues 6am–5pm; Wed–Fri 6am–8pm; Sat 6am–4pm; Sun 7am–4pm. DINER.

Diner aficionados make pilgrimages here to enjoy the ambience of this 1945 Silk City classic, with barrel ceiling and copious amounts of stainless steel. Blue stools line the laminate counter, on which you see plain evidence that more people are right-handed than left-handed by the wear marks; but even folks who don't give a fig for diners flock here for the tremendous value on food. The printed menu is vast, but don't overlook the specials scrawled on paper and taped all over the walls. Blue-plate dinner specials are $7.95 or $8.95 and include vegetables, rice, soup or salad, rolls, and rice pudding for dessert. A bit incongruously, fancier and vegetarian fare is also available; especially good is the grilled portobello on sourdough. There's also a great selection of pies, like blackberry, pumpkin, and chocolate cream, which start at $2.75 a slice.

# ARLINGTON, MANCHESTER & DORSET

The rolling Green Mountains are rarely out of view from this cluster of hamlets; in midsummer the lush green hereabouts gives Ireland a good run for its money—verdant hues are found in the forests blanketing the hills, the valley meadows, and the mosses along the tumbling streams, making it obvious how these mountains earned their name.

These quintessential Vermont villages make ideal destinations for romantic getaways, aggressive antiquing, and serious outlet shopping. Each of the towns is worth visiting, and each has its own peculiar charm. Arlington has a town center that borders on microscopic; with its auto-body shops and redemption center (remnants of a time when the main arterial passed through town), it gleams a bit less than its sibling towns to the north, and has a slightly less refined character.

To the north, Manchester and Manchester Center share a blurred town line but maintain distinct characters. The more southerly Manchester has an old-world, old-money elegance with a campus-like town centered around the resplendently columned Equinox Hotel. Just to the north, Manchester Center is a major mercantile center with dozens of national outlets offering discounts on brand-name clothing, accessories, and housewares. A worthy detour off the beaten track is Dorset, an exquisitely preserved town of white clapboard architecture and marble sidewalks.

One caveat: With its proximity to the New York Thruway just 40 miles east at Albany, the area attracts a disproportionate number of affluent weekenders from New York City—so the prices for inns and restaurants tend to be higher throughout the region. Those looking for a budget vacation will find better values to the north and east.

## ESSENTIALS

**GETTING THERE**   Arlington, Manchester, and Manchester Center are located north of Bennington on Historic Route 7A, which runs parallel to and west of the more modern, less scenic Route 7. Dorset is north of Manchester Center on Route 30, which departs from Route 7A in Manchester Center. Vermont Transit bus lines (☎ **800/451-3292** or 802/362-1226) offers service to Manchester.

**VISITOR INFORMATION**   The **Manchester and the Mountains Chamber of Commerce,** 5046 Main St., Suite 1, Manchester Center, VT 05255 (☎ **802/ 362-2100**), maintains a year-round information center in Manchester Center. Hours are 9am to 5pm Monday to Saturday (from Memorial Day weekend through October, it's also open Sunday 9am to 5pm). You can also get information on the Web at www.manchesterandmtns.com.

For information about outdoor recreation, the Green Mountain National Forest maintains a district **ranger office** (☎ **802/362-2307**) in Manchester on Routes 11 and 30 east of Route 7. It's open from 8am to 4:30pm Monday to Friday.

## EXPLORING THE AREA

Arlington has long been associated with painter and illustrator Norman Rockwell, who resided here from 1939 to 1953. Arlington residents were regularly featured in Rockwell covers for the *Saturday Evening Post.* "Moving to Arlington had given my work a terrific boost. I'd met one or two hundred people I wanted to paint . . . the sincere, honest, homespun types that I love to paint," Rockwell wrote in his autobiography.

Visitors can catch a glimpse of this long relationship in a 19th-century Carpenter Gothic–style church in the middle of town, called **The Norman Rockwell Exhibition** (☎ **802/375-6423**). This small museum features a variety of displays, including many of those famous covers, along with photographs of the original models. Sometimes you'll find the models working as volunteers. Reproductions are available at the gift shop. It's open from 9am to 5pm daily in summer; open in the off-season from 10am to 4pm weekdays and 10am to 5pm weekends (closed January). Admission is $2, children under 12 free.

**Manchester** has long been one of Vermont's more moneyed resorts, attracting prominent summer residents like Mary Todd Lincoln and Julia Boggs Dent, the wife of Ulysses S. Grant. This town is well worth visiting just to wander its quiet streets, bordered with distinguished homes dating from the early Federal period. It feels a bit like you've entered a time warp here, and the cars driving past the green seem strangely out of place. Be sure to note the sidewalks made of irregular marble slabs. The town is said to have 17 miles of such sidewalks, made from the castoffs of Vermont's marble quarries.

On Route 30, 7 miles north of Manchester is the village of **Dorset.** Fans of American architecture owe themselves a visit. While not as grand as Manchester, this quiet town of white clapboard and black-and-green shutters has a quiet and appealing grace. The elliptical green is fronted by early homes that are modest by Manchester standards, but nonetheless are imbued with a subtle elegance. In the right light, Dorset feels more like a Norman Rockwell painting than many Norman Rockwell paintings.

## Museums & Historic Homes

**American Museum of Fly Fishing.** Rte. 7A (a block north of the Equinox Hotel), Manchester. ☎ **802/362-3300.** Admission $3 adults; free for children under 12 and students. Daily 10am–4pm. Closed major holidays.

This is the place for serious anglers interested in the rich history and delicate art of fly-fishing. The museum includes exhibits on the evolution of the fly-fishing reel, paintings and sculptures of fish and anglers, displays of creels, and dioramas depicting fishing at its best. You can see the fly-fishing tackle of some of the nation's more notable anglers, including Herbert Hoover, Andrew Carnegie, and Ernest Hemingway; and, naturally, there are extensive exhibits of beautifully tied flies displayed in oak and glass cases.

✪ **Hildene.** Rte. 7A, Manchester. ☎ **802/362-1788.** www.hildene.org. Admission $8 adults, $4 children 6–14, free for children under 6. Tours given daily mid-May through Oct 9:30am–4pm; grounds close at 5:30pm. Special holiday tours Dec 27–29.

Robert Todd Lincoln was the only son of Abraham and Mary Todd Lincoln to survive to maturity, but he's also noted for his own achievements: He earned millions as a prominent corporate attorney, and he served as Secretary of War and ambassador to Britain under three presidents. He also was president of the Pullman Company (makers of deluxe train cars) from 1897 to 1911, stepping in after the death of company founder George Pullman.

What did one do with millions of dollars in an era when a million bucks was more than chump change? Build lavish summer homes, for the most part. Lincoln was no exception. He summered in this stately, 24-room Georgian Revival mansion between 1905 and 1926 and delighted in showing off its remarkable features, including a sweeping staircase and a 1908 Aeolian organ with its 1,000 pipes (you'll hear it played on the tour). It's more regal than ostentatious and made with an eye to quality; and what summer home would be complete without formal gardens? Lincoln had gardens designed after the patterns in a stained-glass window and planted on a gentle promontory with outstanding views of the flanking mountains. The home is viewed on group tours that start at an informative visitor's center; allow time following the tour to explore the grounds.

**Southern Vermont Art Center.** West Rd. (P.O. Box 617), Manchester. ☎ **802/362-1405.** www.svac.org. Summer and fall: $3 adult, 50¢ student; off-season: $2 adult, 50¢ student. Summer and fall: Tues 10am–8:30pm, Wed–Sat 10am–5pm, Sun noon–5pm; off-season: Mon–Sat 10am–5pm.

This fine-art center is well worth the short detour from town. Located in a striking Georgian Revival home surrounded by more than 400 pastoral hillside acres (it overlooks land that once belonged to Charles Orvis of fly-fishing fame), the center features a series of galleries displaying works from its well-regarded collection, as well as frequently changing exhibits of contemporary Vermont artists. The Elizabeth deC. Wilson Museum, located facing the original building, opened in July 2000. This contemporary addition was designed to display more of the 800-piece permanent collection and allow for more traveling exhibitions. Check the schedule before you arrive via phone or Internet; you may be able to take in a concert or sign up for a class while you're in town. At least leave time to enjoy a light lunch at the Garden Cafe, and to wander the grounds, exploring both the sculpture garden and the fields and woods beyond.

## AREA SKIING

**Bromley Mountain Ski Resort.** P.O. Box 1130, Manchester Center, VT 05255. ☎ **800/865-4786** for lodging or 802/824-5522. www.bromley.com. Vertical drop: 1,334 ft. Lifts: 6

chairlifts (including 1 high-speed detachable quad), 3 surface lifts. Skiable acreage: 175. Lift tickets: $47 weekends, $36 weekdays.

Bromley is a great place to learn to ski. Gentle and forgiving, the mountain also features long, looping intermediate runs that are tremendously popular with families. The slopes are mostly south-facing, which means the warmth of the sun and some protection from the harshest winter winds. (It also means the snow may melt quicker than at other ski resorts.) The base lodge scene is more mellow than at many resorts, and your experience is almost guaranteed to be relaxing.

**Stratton.** Stratton Mountain, VT 05155. ☎ **800/843-6867** for lodging or 802/297-2200. www.stratton.com. Vertical drop: 2,003 ft. Lifts: 1 gondola, 9 chairlifts (including 1 6-person high-speed), 2 surface lifts. Skiable acreage: 583. Lift tickets: $59 weekends and holidays, $55 weekdays.

Founded in the 1960s, Stratton labored in its early days under the belief that Vermont ski areas had to be Tyrolean to be successful. Hence Swiss chalet–nightmare architecture, and the overall feel of being Vail's younger, less affluent sibling. In recent years, Stratton has worked to leave the image of Alpine quaintness behind in a bid to attract a younger, edgier set. New owners added $25 million in improvements, mostly in snowmaking, with coverage now up over 80 percent The slopes are especially popular with snowboarders, a sport that was invented here when bartender Jake Burton slapped a big plank on his feet and aimed down the mountain. Expert skiers should seek out Upper Middlebrook, a fine, twisting run off the summit.

## OTHER OUTDOOR PURSUITS

**HIKING & BIKING**    Scenic hiking trails ranging from challenging to relaxing can be found in the hills a short drive from town. At the Green Mountain District Ranger Station (see "Visitor Information," above), ask for the free brochure *Day Hikes on the Manchester Ranger District.*

The Long Trail and Appalachian Trail overlap in southern Vermont. They run just east of Manchester; a popular day trek is along these trails to **Spruce Peak.** Five miles east of Manchester Center on Routes 11 and 30, look for parking where the two trails cross the road. Strike out southward on foot over rocky terrain for 2.2 miles to the peak, looking for the blue-blazed sidetrail to the open summit with its breathtaking views of the Manchester Valley.

A scenic drive northwest of Manchester Center will bring you to the **Delaware and Hudson Rail-Trail,** approximately 20 miles of which have been built in two sections in Vermont. (Another 14 miles will eventually be developed across the state line in New York.) The southern section of the trail runs about 10 miles from West Pawlet to the state line at West Rupert, over trestles and past vestiges of former industry, such as the old Vermont Milk and Cream Co. Like most rail-trails, this is perfect for exploring by mountain bike. You'll bike sometimes on the original ballast, other times through grassy growth. To reach the trailhead, drive north on Route 30 from Manchester Center to Route 315, then continue north on Route 153. In West Pawlet, park across from Duchie's General Store (a good place for refreshments), then set off on the trail southward from the old D&H freight depot across the street.

**ON THE WATER**    For a duck's-eye view of the rolling hills, stop by **Battenkill Canoe Ltd.** in Arlington (☎ **800/421-5268** or 802/362-2800; www.battenkill.com; e-mail: info@battenkill.com). This friendly outfit offers daily canoe rentals on the scenic Battenkill and surrounding areas. Trips range from 2 hours to a whole day ($45 per canoe including shuttle), but the firm specializes in multiday inn-to-inn canoe packages. The shop is open daily in season (May through October) from 9am to 5:30pm; limited hours the remainder of the year.

Aspiring anglers can sign up for fly-fishing classes taught by skilled instructors affiliated with **Orvis** (☎ **800/548-9548**), the noted fly-fishing supplier and manufacturer. The 2¹/₂-day classes include instruction in knot-tying and casting; students practice catch-and-release fishing on the company pond and the Battenkill River. Classes are held from mid-April to Labor Day.

## WHERE TO STAY

**Arlington Inn.** Rte. 7A (P.O. Box 369), Arlington, VT 05250. ☎ **800/443-9442** or 802/375-6532. Fax 802/375-6534. www.arlingtoninn.com. E-mail: stay@arlingtoninn.com. 17 units. A/C TV. $115–$265 double, discounts in off-season. Rates include breakfast. 2-night minimum stay most weekends. AE, DC, DISC, MC, V.

This stout, cream-colored, multicolumned Greek Revival home, built in 1848, would be perfectly at home in the Virginia countryside, but it anchors this village well, set back from the Historic Route 7A on a lawn bordered with sturdy maples. Inside, the inn boasts a similarly courtly feel, with unique wooden ceilings adorning the first-floor rooms and a tavern that borrows its atmosphere from an English hunt club. If you prefer modern comforts, ask for a room in the 1830 parsonage next door, where you'll find telephones and TVs. The quietest rooms are in the detached carriage house, which is most removed from the sound of Route 7A. Innkeepers Sherrie and Bill Noonan have recently taken steps to upgrade the inn (they turned three rooms into two suites), and give it a more Victorian feel.

**Dining:** The chef strives to use local produce and other Vermont products wherever possible. Depending on the season, options may include rack of lamb with a roasted garlic sauce, or grilled salmon with a crabmeat and sweet potato hash. Entrees are priced from $14.95 to $26.95.

**Amenities:** Tennis court, municipal golf course nearby, and baby-sitting.

**Barrows House.** Rte. 30, Dorset, VT 05251. ☎ **800/639-1620** or 802/867-4455. Fax 802/867-0132. www.barrowshouse.com. E-mail: innkeepers@barrowshouse.com. 28 units. A/C. $185–$255 double, including breakfast and dinner. Discounts available in the off-season and midweek. 2-night minimum on weekends and some holidays. AE, DISC, MC, V. Pets are allowed in 2 cottages.

Within easy strolling distance of the village of Dorset stands this compound of eight early American buildings set on 12 nicely landscaped acres studded with birches, firs, and maples. The main house was built in 1784, and it's been an inn since 1900. The rooms are more comfortable than elegant; some have gas or wood fireplaces. A few rooms have telephones—ask in advance if that's important. Innkeepers Linda and Jim McGinnis are very cordial and helpful, especially in planning day trips around the region.

**Dining:** Enjoy a before-dinner drink in the casual and cozy tavern with the trompe l'oeil bookshelves. The main dining area offers a choice: a traditional country-inn room or a modern greenhouse addition. The cuisine is contemporary New England, with entrees like Chesapeake-style Maine crab cakes, or strip steak with caramelized onions and roasted shiitake mushrooms. Entrees range from $10.95 to $23.95.

**Amenities:** Outdoor heated pool, bicycle rental, game room, sauna, and two tennis courts.

**Dorset Inn.** Church and Main sts., Dorset, VT 05251. ☎ **802/867-5500.** Fax 802/867-5542. www.dorsetinn.com. 31 units. Foliage season $200 double, $220–$260 suite; off-season $150 double, $200–$240 suite. Rates include breakfast. AE, MC, V. Children over 5 are welcome.

Set in the center of genteel Dorset, this former stagecoach stop was built in 1796 and claims to be the oldest continuously operating inn in Vermont. With 31 rooms, the

Dorset Inn is fairly large by Vermont standards but feels far more intimate than comparably sized places. The carpeted guest rooms, some of which are in a well-crafted addition built in the 1940s, are furnished in an upscale country style, with a mix of reproductions and antiques, including canopied and sleigh beds. All but two rooms have air-conditioning (innkeepers hope to have it in all rooms by summer 2000), and only the two suites have TVs and telephones.

**Dining:** The tavern is wonderfully casual and pubby, paneled in dark wood with a stamped-tin ceiling. The dining room is a bit more formal, although the menu is anything but stuffy. Dinner options range from an oversize burger with red wine sauce to blackened tuna with a mango-papaya salsa. Entrees range from $12.50 to $22.

✪ **1811 House.** Rte. 7A, Manchester Village, VT 05254. ☎ **800/432-1811** or 802/362-1811. Fax 802/362-2443. www.1811house.com. E-mail: stay1811@vermontel.com. 14 units. A/C. $180–$230 double. Rates include full breakfast. AE, DISC, MC, V.

This historic Manchester Village home, the first part of which was built in the mid-1770s, started taking in guests in 1811 (hence the name). And it often seems that not much has changed here in the intervening centuries. The cozy, warren-like downstairs common rooms are rich in history—the pine floors are uneven, the doors out of true, and everything is painted in earthy, Colonial tones. Even the exterior is painted a pheasant-brown color. The antique furniture re-creates the feel of the house during the Federal period, and a delightful English-style pub lies off the entryway, complete with tankards hanging from the beams. The rooms are comfortably sized—you won't feel that you're lost in them, but neither will you feel cramped. Among my favorites: the Robinson Room, with a private deck, great view, and unique tub-shower combo. The chocolate chip cookies offered each afternoon are quite memorable.

**The Equinox.** Rte. 7A (P.O. Box 46), Manchester Village, VT 05245. ☎ **800/362-4747** or 802/362-4700. Fax 802/362-1595. www.equinoxresort.com. E-mail: reservations@equinoxresort.com. 183 units. A/C TV TEL. $179–$329 double; $489–$589 suite. Ask about package rates. AE, DC, DISC, MC, V.

A blue-blood favorite, the Equinox faces the village green and dominates Manchester Village with its gleaming white clapboard and trim rows of columns. The resort's roots extend back to 1769, when the Marsh Tavern was established (today the structure serves as an informal restaurant within the resort), but make no mistake, this is a full-blown modern resort, its historic lineage notwithstanding. You'll find extensive sports facilities spread about its 2,300 acres, four dining rooms, and all the expected in-room amenities. Guest rooms are by and large decorated similarly in a country pine motif, although the suites are a bit more richly hued. Room prices vary based on size, but in truth, there's not a huge difference between the largest and smallest rooms. In any event, guests are likely to spend much of their time living large around the resort, both within the buildings and when availing themselves of the numerous amenities, which includes falconry lessons and a Land Rover off-road driving school.

Next door to the inn is the grand **Charles Orvis Inn,** an 1812 home renovated and managed by the Equinox. It offers nine elegantly appointed suites for $589 to $899 per night, including breakfast. It's perfectly nice, but not worth the super-premium price.

**Dining:** Choose the dining room to fit your mood: There's the continental elegance of the Colonnade, where it's suggested that men wear jackets at dinner, or the more relaxed, clubby comfort of Marsh Tavern.

**Amenities:** Golf course, indoor and outdoor pools, 3 tennis courts, nature trails, croquet court, health club, sauna, sundeck, limited room service, concierge, valet parking, baby-sitting, dry-cleaning and laundry, express check-out, safe-deposit boxes, valet parking, nightly turndown, beauty salon, boutiques, and a falconry school. In winter, there's ice-skating on the grounds and cross-country skiing and snowshoeing nearby.

**✪ Inn at Ormsby Hill.** Rte. 7A (near Hildene, south of Manchester Village), Manchester Center, VT 05255. ☎ **800/670-2841** or 802/362-1163. Fax 802/362-5176. www.ormsbyhill. com. E-mail: ormsby@vermontel.com. 10 units. A/C TEL. Foliage season $275–$335 double; off-season $215–$255 double weekends; $175–$215 double weekdays. Rates include full breakfast. 2-night minimum stay on weekends. DISC, MC, V. Closed briefly in Apr. No children under 14.

The oldest part of the striking Inn at Ormsby Hill dates to 1764 (the revolutionary, Ethan Allen, was rumored to have hidden out here). Today, it's a harmonious medley of eras and styles, with inspiring views out toward the Green Mountains, and wonderful hospitality offered by veteran innkeepers Chris and Ted Sprague. The common rooms are comfortable and spacious; the most intriguing is the dining room, built by prominent 19th-century attorney Edward Isham to resemble the interior of a sumptuous steamship. This is now the inn's dining room, where guests enjoy Chris's otherworldly breakfasts as they admire the views. Among the best guest rooms are the Taft Room, with its vaulted wood ceiling, and the first-floor Library, with many of Isham's books still lining the shelves. The Tower Room (added in 1998) features an extraordinary Jacuzzi–steam shower combination on the top floor of the home's compact tower. Nine of the ten rooms feature two-person Jacuzzis and fireplaces.

**The Reluctant Panther.** 39 West Rd. (P.O. Box 678), Manchester Village, VT 05254. ☎ **800/822-2331** or 802/362-2568. Fax 802/362-2586. www.reluctantpanther.com. E-mail: panther@sover.net. 22 units, 1 with detached private bathroom. A/C TV TEL. Foliage season and holiday weekends $235–$450; off-season weekends $198–$395 double; $168–$298 midweek (summer). Rates include breakfast and dinner. Winter midweek rates ($120–$250) include breakfast only. AE, MC, V. No children under 14.

The Reluctant Panther, located a short walk from the Equinox, is easy to spot: It's painted a pale eggplant color and has faded yellow shutters, making it stand out in this staid village of white clapboard. It's run with couples in mind. This 1850s home is elegantly furnished throughout (as are guest rooms in an adjacent building, built in 1910) and features nice touches, including goose-down duvets in every room. Twelve of the rooms have fireplaces (some more than one), and the Mark Skinner suite even features a wood-burning fireplace and a double Jacuzzi in the bathroom.

**Dining:** The first-floor dining room, decorated with floral prints, manages the feat of being intimate without feeling crowded. (There's also a greenhouse with a slate floor, which is pleasant on summer evenings.) The cuisine is European, prepared by Swiss-German chef Robert Bachofen, a former director at the Plaza Hotel in New York. The menu changes frequently, but expect entrees like veal sautéed with mushrooms in a chardonnay cream. Entree prices range from $21 to $27.

**West Mountain Inn.** River Rd., Arlington, VT 05250. ☎ **802/375-6516.** Fax 802/375-6553. www.westmountaininn.com. E-mail: info@westmountaininn.com. 18 units (including 6 suites). A/C. Foliage season $196–$244 double; spring and winter weekends, summer, $176–$224 double; winter midweek $155 double. Rates include breakfast and dinner. 2-night minimum stay on weekends. AE, DISC, MC, V.

Sitting atop a grassy bluff at the end of a dirt road a half mile from Arlington center, the West Mountain Inn's rambling, white-clapboard building dates back a century and a half. It's a perfect place for travelers seeking to get away from the irksome hum of modern life. The guest rooms, named after famous Vermonters, are nicely furnished with country antiques and Victorian reproductions. The rooms vary widely in size and shape, but even the smallest has plenty of charm and character. Several rooms in outlying cottages feature kitchenettes. These are popular among attendees of family reunions, who also use the 100-year-old post-and-beam barn for gatherings.

**Dining:** Dinners feature regional fare and are prepared and served with flair; seasonal menus are augmented with nightly specials. Typical entrees might include filet mignon and shrimp on smoked morel ragout, and citrus poached halibut with grilled eggplant. Dinner for non-guests is $35 fixed-price; reservations requested.

**Amenities:** Conference rooms, nature trails, and nearby health club; in-room massage and baby-sitting by prior arrangement.

**Wilburton Inn.** River Rd., Manchester Village, VT 05254. ☎ **800/648-4944** or 802/ 362-2500. www.wilburton.com. E-mail: wilbuinn@sover.net. 36 units (1 with private hall bath). A/C TV TEL. Holidays and foliage $170–$265; weekends $140–$225 double, midweek $125–$180. Rates include full breakfast. 2-night minimum weekends; 3-night holidays. AE, MC, V.

This is the sort of inn where you find yourself involuntarily muttering, "My, my!" You arrive at this vast Victorian estate built in 1902 via a driveway that ascends a knoll theatrically up a broad curve and under spreading maples. The brick Tudor-style manor is sumptuously appointed, the common spaces filled with European antiques, Persian carpets, and even a baby grand.

Throughout the manor you'll find works from the eclectic modern art collection amassed by the inn's owners, Albert and Georgette Levis (he's a Greek psychiatrist; she's sister of playwright Wendy Wasserstein). The guest rooms, which aren't as lavishly appointed as the common rooms, are divided between the main house (11 rooms) and several outbuildings of various vintages. They vary in size and style. Room No. 15 is the smallest and would be suitable for one person. The second floor contains mostly spacious suites, some with great valley views. In the outbuildings, my favorite is No. 24, with plenty of room and a private deck with views of Mt. Equinox and quirky outdoor sculptures. Three rooms have fireplaces. One note: The inn hosts weddings virtually every weekend in summer, so travelers looking for quiet may be best off booking midweek.

**Dining:** The two dining rooms—the dusky Billiard Room and the formal Dining Room—are wonderful settings for elegant meals. Entrees change seasonally; look for dishes along the lines of pumpkin-seed-crusted pheasant with a wild mushroom jus, or grilled salmon with a lemongrass butter. Main courses are priced $17.50 to $24. Dinner is served nightly except Tuesday; outside diners should call for reservations.

**Amenities:** Access to the lush 20-acre estate studded with superb modern sculpture is almost worth the price of the room. Other amenities include three tennis courts and an outdoor pool. Golf is nearby.

## WHERE TO DINE

Note that most of the inns listed above offer excellent dining, often in romantic settings.

✪ **Chantecleer.** Rte. 7A (3¹/₂ miles north of Manchester Center). ☎ **802/362-1616.** Reservations recommended. Main courses $26–$35. AE, CB, DC, MC, V. Wed–Mon 6–9:30pm. Closed Mon in winter and for 2–3 weeks in Nov and Apr. CONTINENTAL.

If you like superbly prepared continental fare but are put off by the stuffiness of high-brow Euro–wanna-be restaurants, this is your place. Rustic elegance is the best description for the dining experience in this century-old dairy barn. The oddly tidy exterior, which looks as if it could house a chain restaurant, doesn't offer a clue to the pleasantly romantic interior. Heavy beams define the soaring space overhead, the walls are appropriately of barn board, and the small bar is crafted of a slab of pine. A rooster motif predominates (of course, you remembered that *chantecleer* is French for rooster), fresh flowers decorate the tables, and when the weather's right, a fire blazes in the arched fieldstone fireplace. Swiss-born chef Michel Baumann, who's owned and operated the inn since 1981, changes his menu every 3 weeks, but his selections might feature roasted veal with a roasted garlic, sage and balsamic demi-glaze, or slow-roasted duck with sesame seeds and hoisin sauce. Arrive expecting an excellent meal; you're not likely to be disappointed.

**Little Rooster Café.** Rte 7A South, Manchester Center. ☎ **802/362-3496.** Entrees $4.95–$8.95. No credit cards. Daily 7am–2:30pm (closed Weds in off-season). CREATIVE BREAKFAST/LUNCH.

This appealing spot near the outlets is partly owned by the same folks at the decidedly creative Chantecleer (see above), and their inclination to serve good food creatively applies even at budget prices. The place has more of a feel of a restaurant than a diner, with cloth napkins and jams served nobly in ramekins rather than ignobly in vexing plastic tubs with peel-off tops. Breakfasts include smoked salmon and bagels, Belgian waffles, and a luscious corned beef hash (go ahead—your doctor won't know). Lunches feature a creative sandwich selection, like roast beef with pickled red cabbage and a horseradish-dill sauce.

**Mistral's at Toll Gate.** Toll Gate Rd. (east of Manchester off Rte. 11). ☎ **802/362-1779.** Reservations recommended. Main courses $19–$30. AE, MC, V. Thurs–Tues 6–9pm (from May–Nov also closed Tues). FRENCH.

The best tables at Mistral's are along the windows, which overlook a lovely New England bedrock creek that's spotlit at night. Located in a tollhouse of a long-since-bypassed byway, the restaurant is a mix of modern and old, blended together in a way that invites romance. The menu changes seasonally and is exceptionally inviting, with dishes like salmon cannelloni stuffed with lobster, or grilled filet mignon with Roquefort ravioli. The kitchen is run with great aplomb by chef-owner Dana Markey, who does an admirable job ensuring consistent quality. (That's his wife, Cheryl, who seated you.) The couple has been in business here since 1988, and they understand both food and hospitality. The service is just right, neither too aloof nor too folksy.

## SHOPPING

Manchester Center is one of several upscale factory-outlet meccas in New England, and it's the most upscale of the bunch. Retailers include (take a deep breath) Calvin Klein, Donna Karan, Tommy Hilfiger, Liz Claiborne, Polo/Ralpha Lauren, Dockers, Levi's, Brooks Brothers, Joan & David, Nine West, Coach, Cole-Haan, Anne Klein, Seiko, Movado, Giorgio Armani, and Bennington Potters. The shops conveniently cluster along a T intersection in the heart of Manchester Center. Most are readily accessible on foot, while others are a bit farther afield, requiring scuttling from one to the next by car.

One hometown favorite is worth seeking out if your interests include fishing or rustic, outdoorsy fashion: Orvis, which has crafted a worldwide reputation for manufacturing topflight fly-fishing equipment, happens to be based in Manchester. The **Orvis Catalog Store** (☎ **802/362-3750**) is located between Manchester and Manchester Center and offers housewares, sturdy outdoor clothing, and—of course—fly-fishing equipment. Two small ponds just outside the shop allow prospective customers to try before they buy.

Near the middle of Manchester Center, at the intersection of Route 7A and Route 30, is the **Northshire Bookstore** (☎ **802/362-2200;** www.northshire.com), one of the best bookshops in a state where reading is a popular pastime. In addition to great browsing, the store sponsors frequent readings by prominent authors, both local and from elsewhere.

## 3  Brattleboro & the Southern Green Mountains

Brattleboro is 105 miles northwest of Boston and 148 miles southeast of Burlington.

The southern Green Mountains are New England writ large. If you've developed a notion in your head of what New England looks like but haven't ever been there, this may be the place you're thinking of. You half expect to walk into an inn and bump into Bob Newhart, the innkeeper.

The hills and valleys around the bustling town of Brattleboro in Vermont's southeast corner contain some of the state's best-hidden treasures. Driving along the main valley floors—on roads along the West or the Connecticut rivers, or on Route 100— tends to be fast and only moderately interesting. To really soak up the region's flavor, turn off the main roads and wander up and over rolling ridges into the narrow folds in the mountains that hide peaceful villages. If it seems to you that the landscape hasn't changed all that much in the past 2 centuries, well, you're right. It hasn't.

This region is well-known for its pristine and historic villages. You can't help but stumble across them as you explore, and no matter how many other people have found them before you, there's almost always a sense that these are your own private discoveries. A good strategy is to stop for a spell in Brattleboro to stock up on supplies or sample some local food or music. Then set off for the southern Green Mountains, settle into a remote inn, and continue your explorations by foot or bike. In winter, you can plumb the snowy white hills by cross-country ski or snowshoe.

The single best source of travel information on the region is the **State Visitor Center** (☎ **802/254-4593**) on I-91 in Guilford, south of Brattleboro.

## BRATTLEBORO

Deeply set in a scenic river valley, Brattleboro is not only a good spot for last-minute provisioning, but it also has a funky, slightly dated charm that's part 19th century, part 1960s. The rough brick texture of this compact, hilly city has aged nicely, its flavor only enhanced since it was adopted by "feral hippies" (as a friend of mine calls them), who live in and around town and operate many of the best local enterprises.

While Brattleboro is very much part of the 20th century, its heritage runs much deeper. In fact, Brattleboro was Vermont's first permanent settlement. (The first actual settlement, which was short-lived, was at Isle La Motte on Lake Champlain in 1666.) Soldiers protecting the Massachusetts town of Northfield built an outpost here in 1724 at Fort Dummer, about a mile and a half south of the current downtown. The site of the fort is now a small state park with a campground. In later years, Brattleboro became a center of trade and manufacturing, and was the home of the Estey Organ Co., which once supplied countless home organs carved in ornate Victorian-style to families across the nation.

Brattleboro is the commercial hub of southeastern Vermont, located at the junction of I-89, Routes 5 and 9, and the Connecticut River. It's also the most convenient jumping-off point for those arriving from the south via the interstate. If you're looking for basic travel supplies, a strip-mall area with grocery and department stores is just north of town on Route 5. For a more interesting selection of items, take the time to explore downtown.

Brattleboro has long seemed immune from the vexations of modern life, but one modern inconvenience has made a belated appearance: traffic jams. Lower Main St. (near the bridge from New Hampshire) can back up heading into town, leading to horns and frustration. It's the source of considerable local grousing.

## ESSENTIALS

**GETTING THERE**    From the north or south, Brattleboro is easily accessible by car via Exit 1 or 2 on I-91. From the east or west, Brattleboro is best reached via Route 9. Brattleboro is also a stop on the **Amtrak** (☎ **800/872-7245**) line from Boston to northern Vermont.

**VISITOR INFORMATION**    The **Brattleboro Chamber of Commerce,** 180 Main St., Brattleboro, VT 05301 (☎ **802/254-4565**) dispenses travel information year-round between 8:30am and 5pm weekdays. You can request information via e-mail at bratchmb@sover.net; the Web address is www.brattleboro.com.

## EXPLORING THE TOWN

Here's a simple, straightforward strategy for exploring Brattleboro: Park and walk.

The commercially vibrant downtown is blessedly compact, and strolling around on foot is the best way to appreciate its human scale and handsome commercial architecture. It's a town of cafes, bookstores, antiques stores, and outdoor-recreation shops, and it invites browsing. Even if you're en route to a destination up north, it's well worth a stop for a bite to eat and some light shopping. Shops of note include **Sam's Outdoor Outfitters,** 74 Main St., ☎ **802/254-2933,** an easy-to-get-lost-in store filled to the eaves with outdoor camping and fishing gear, along with a selection of casual, durable clothing; and **Tom and Sally's Handmade Chocolates,** 6 Harmony Place, ☎ **800/827-0800,** a boutique chocolate shop that features delicous handmade chocolates. They also sell a chocolate body-paint kit, complete with two brushes, which I hesitate to mention only for fear of incurring the wrath of area innkeeepers.

Enjoyable for kids and curious adults is the **Brattleboro Museum & Art Center** (☎ **802/257-0124**) at the Union Railroad Station. Founded in 1972, the center offers wonderful exhibits highlighting the history of the town and the Connecticut River valley, along with paintings and sculpture by artists of local and international repute. The museum is open Tuesday to Sunday from noon to 6pm, mid-May through October. It's located downtown near the bridge to New Hampshire. Admission is $3 for adults, $2 for seniors and college students, free for children under 18.

## OUTDOOR PURSUITS

A soaring aerial view of Brattleboro can be found atop **Wantastiquet Mountain,** which is just across the Connecticut River in New Hampshire (figure on a round-trip of about 3 hours). To reach the base of the "mountain" (a term that's just slightly grandiose), cross the river on the two green steel bridges, then turn left on the first dirt road; go two-tenths of a mile to a parking area on your right. The trail begins here via a carriage road (stick to the main trail and avoid the sidetrails) that winds about 2 miles through forest and past open ledges to the summit, which is marked by a monument dating from 1908. From here, you'll be rewarded with sweeping views of the river, the town, and the landscape beyond.

Serious canoeists and dabbling paddlers alike will find contentment at **Vermont Canoe Touring Center** (☎ **802/257-5008**), where Route 5 spans the West River north of town. Located in a shady riverside glen, this is a fine spot to rent a canoe or kayak to poke around for a couple of hours ($10 for two people), a half day ($15), or a full day ($20). Explore locally, or arrange for a shuttle upriver or down. The owners are exceedingly helpful about providing information and maps to keep you on track. Among the best spots, especially for birders, are the marshy areas along the lower West River and a detour off the Connecticut River locally called "the Everglades." Get a lunch to go at the Brattleboro Food Co-Op (see below) and make a day of it.

Bike rentals and good advice on day-trip destinations are both available at the **Brattleboro Bicycle Shop,** at 165 Main St. (☎ **800/272-8245** or 802/254-8644). Hybrid bikes ideal for exploring area backroads can be rented by the day ($20) or week ($100).

## WHERE TO STAY

The Artist's Loft (103 Main St., ☎ **802/257-5181,** www.theartistsloft.com) features one—count it—one guest room, but if it's available, it makes a good base. It's a spacious and bright third-floor suite with two rooms in an historic building smack in the middle of downtown. It faces east, away from traffic and toward the river. It's run by Patricia Long and William Hays, who also operate the art gallery next door. (Hays' paintings adorn the guest room). One funky thing: the bathroom is in the Hays' adjacent apartment. Midweek rates are $98 double without breakfast ($118 with breakfast), and $145 on weekends with breakfast. Midweek rates are higher during foliage season. If traveling with family or a group, ask about the additional room that can be rented in conjuction with the suite.

**Chesterfield Inn.** Rte. 9, Chesterfield, NH 03443. ☎ **800/365-5515** or 603/256-3211. Fax 603/256-6131. www.chesterfieldinn.com. E-mail: chstinn@sover.net. 15 units (includes 2 suites). MINIBAR TV TEL. $105–$200 double. 2 night minimum holiday and foliage season. Pets allowed with advance permission. AE, DC, DISC, MC, V.

Located a 10-minute drive east of Brattleboro, the attractive Chesterfield Inn sits in a field just off a busy state highway, but inside it's more quiet and refined than you'd imagine. The original farmhouse dates back to the 1780s, but it's been expanded and modernized and today has a casual contemporary sensibility (some high ceilings and oversize windows) augmented with antique touches. Nine guest rooms are located in the main inn, and six in cottages nearby. All are uncommonly spacious and comfortably appointed with a mix of modern and antique furniture. Eight have wood-burning fireplaces, and two have gas fireplaces. The priciest rooms have fireplaces, double jacuzzis, and a private deck.

**Dining:** Dinner is served nightly except Sunday in the bright, carpeted dining room. New American main courses might include salmon in puff pastry, lime-coconut chicken, or beef tenderloin with wild mushrooms ($17 to $23).

**40 Putney Road.** 40 Putney Rd., Brattleboro, VT 05301. ☎ **800/941-2413** or 802/254-6268. Fax 802/258-2673. www.putney.net/40putneyrd/. E-mail: frtyptny@sover.net. 4 units. A/C TV TEL. $120–$160 double. Rates include breakfast. AE, DISC, MC, V. Pets allowed with advance permission; $10 per pet.

Built in the early 1930s, this compact French château–style home features four guest rooms that are attractively appointed with a mix of modern country furnishings and reproductions. (Plans call for adding several rooms within the next 5 years). Two feature gas fireplaces; all rooms have VCRs (free videos from downstairs), bathrobes, hair dryers and modem hookups. The best of the bunch is Room 4, a spacious mini-suite with built-in bureaus and an old-fashioned tiled bathroom. The inn is close enough to town that you can stroll there within a few minutes. The one downside: it's situated along a busy road, which diminishes the pastoral qualities somewhat. The innkeepers are Gwen and Dan Pasco, who added a cozy pub in 1999 offering more than 30 wines and a dozen brands of beers.

**Latchis Hotel.** 50 Main St., Brattleboro, VT 05301. ☎ **802/254-6300.** Fax 802/254-6304. www.brattleboro.com/latchis. 30 units. A/C TV TEL. $75–$115 double. AE, MC, V.

This downtown hotel fairly leaps out in Victorian-brick Brattleboro. Built in 1938 in an understated art-deco style, the Latchis was once the cornerstone for a small chain of hotels and theaters. It no longer has its own orchestra or commanding dining room (although the theater remains), but it's still owned by the Latchis family and has an authentic if funky and slightly outdated flair. For the most part, the guest rooms are compact and comfortable, but not luxurious, with simple maple furniture and old-time radiators that keep the place toasty in winter. About two-thirds of the rooms have limited views of the river, but those come with the sounds of cars on Main Street. If you want quiet, you can sacrifice a view and ask for a room in the back. From the hotel, it's easy to explore the town on foot, or you can wander the first-floor hallways to take in a first-run movie at the historic Latchis Theatre (the main section was renovated from 1999 to 2000) or quaff a fresh pint at the Windham Brewery.

**Dining:** See Latchis Grille & Windham Brewery, below.

**Naulakha.** Landmark Trust, RR#1 Box 510, Brattleboro, VT 05301. ☎ **802/254-6868.** Fax 802/257-7783. www.landmarktrust.co.uk. 1 4-bdrm house; accommodates up to 8 people. Summer–fall $2,150–$2,700 per week; winter–spring $1,300–$2,230 per week, shorter stays (min. 3 nights) in off-season $285 per night. Rates are estimated; billing is in English pounds. MC, V.

This unique property, owned and managed by the British-based Landmark Trust, is available for rent only by the week during peak season. (It can be rented for shorter stays in winter.) What makes this forthright, two-story shingled home in the hills outside of Brattleboro so extraordinary is its rich literary heritage. The home was built for British writer Rudyard Kipling, who lived here for several years in the mid-1890s while working on *The Jungle Book* and *Captains Courageous*. Kipling never quite fit in rural Vermont. A local newspaper reported, "Neighbors say he is strange; never carries money, wears shabby clothes and often says Begad; drives shaggy horses and plays with the baby." He left somewhat abruptly, selling the home with much of its furniture in place.

It's a superb place to unwind in summer, strolling the 55-acre grounds, admiring the views from the porches, or just knocking a ball around on Kipling's clay tennis court. The price may cause the faint-hearted to blanche, but note that even during the prime summer season the rate works out to about $80 per night per room . . . assuming you can find three compatible companions with whom to share your vacation.

## WHERE TO DINE

**Brattleboro Food Co-Op.** Brookside Plaza, 2 Main St. ☎ **802/257-0236.** Sandwiches $3.50–$5.50, prepared foods around $4–$5/pound. Mon–Wed, Sat 9am–8pm, Thurs–Fri 9am–9pm, Sun 10am–6pm. DELI.

The Co-op has been selling wholesome foods since 1975, and its location, downtown near the New Hampshire bridge with plenty of parking, features a deli counter and seating area. It's a great spot for a quick, filling lunch. The emphasis is on natural foods, although it's not all tofu and sprouts—you can get a smoked turkey and Swiss cheese sandwich, or opt for a crunchy salad (priced by the pound) or something like a plate of steamed cold broccoli with a garlic black-bean sauce. Before you leave, check out the eclectic wine selection and the cheeses, especially the award-winning Vermont Shepherd cheeses, made nearby in Putney.

**✪ The Common Ground.** 25 Eliot St. ☎ **802/257-0855.** Reservations not accepted. Lunch $3–$7.50; dinner $3.50–$8. No credit cards. Summer: Mon–Thurs 11:30am–8pm; Fri–Sat 11:30am–9pm; Sun 11am–2pm and 5–8pm; fall–spring: Thurs–Sun 5–8pm, plus Sun 11am–2pm. VEGETARIAN.

The Common Ground opened 2 years after the Woodstock Music Festival, which establishes it both chronologically and spiritually. This culinary landmark occupies a funky, sometimes chaotic space on the second floor of a downtown building. At the top of the stairs, diners choose from a well-worn dining room with flea-market tables or a pleasant greenhouse addition overlooking the street. The Common Ground is operated as a worker-owned cooperative, and service is cordial if not always brisk. A meal might include grilled tofu with tahini, brown rice with tamari ginger sauce, or a marinated sea-vegetable salad. There's often live music on the weekends, usually of the folk variety. (Don't confuse this restaurant with one by the same name a little further north in Bellows Falls, with which it has no connection.)

**Latchis Grille & Windham Brewery.** 6 Flat St., Brattleboro. ☎ **802/254-4747.** Reservations for parties of 6 or more only. Cafe items $6–$12; main courses $14–$19. AE, DISC, MC, V. June–Dec Wed–Mon 5–9pm, Jan–May Wed–Sun 5–9pm; also open for lunch Fri–Sun 11:30am–3pm year-round. INTERNATIONAL.

The Latchis Grille is situated beneath the Latchis Theatre and Latchis Hotel, and is worth venturing downstairs to sample the excellent homemade ales, stouts, and lagers made on-site by the Windham Brewery, and to range through their menu of global foods. The Latchis Grille, while subterranean, is comfortably decorated with paintings and old lithographs. The rectangular dining room has soft lighting and upbeat jazz; enclosed at one end is an informal, tile-floored bar great for sipping the local stuff. Appetizers include tasty Tibetan momos (steamed lamb and pork dumplings); entrees feature chicken breast stuffed with cheese, pears, and watercress, and grilled filet mignon with sherried wild mushrooms. The "Vermont Favorites" section of the menu offers cheaper, more basic fare, like baked scrod and grilled pork chops.

**Peter Havens.** 32 Eliot St., Brattleboro. ☎ **802/257-3333.** Reservations strongly recommended. Main courses $17–$22. MC, V. Tues–Sat 6–9pm. REGIONAL/AMERICAN.

Chef-owned Peter Havens has been serving up consistently reliable fare since his restaurant opened in 1989. Situated downtown in an upscale, contemporary building, Peter Havens may not bowl you over with its menu, but you will be impressed by what you're served. You're likely to feel instantly at home in this friendly spot, which has just ten tables and never advertises. (You'll still need reservations.) The meals are prepared with choice ingredients, and are served with panache and flair. Seafood is the speciality of the house, with preparations including salmon with a chipolte peper remoulade, and scallops sautéed with roasted red peppers and crabment. Non-seafood entres might include something like tenderloin or duck. Wines are limited, the selection decent.

**Shin La.** 57 Main St. ☎ **802/257-5226.** Entrees $5–$9.50. No credit cards. Mon–Sat 11am–9pm. AMERICAN/KOREAN.

This is your best bet in Brattleboro for spicy food. With wooden booths and mismatched furniture it has the character of a pizza shop but is usually teeming with locals who come for the consistently good food. One side of the laminated menu features sandwiches (Reubens, Dagwoods, and so on), but you're best advised to head for the other side, which offers simple Korean country fare, like bool ko ki (sliced sirloin) and shu mai (steamed dumplings). The fare is tasty and light on the wallet. Service can be pokey on busy nights.

**✪ T. J. Buckley's.** 132 Eliot St. ☎ **802/257-4922.** Reservations usually essential. Main courses $25–$30. No credit cards. Spring–fall Weds–Sun 6–9pm (sometimes open later on busy nights), winter Thurs–Sun 6–9pm. NEW AMERICAN.

This is Brattleboro's best restaurant. The lilliputian T. J. Buckley's is housed in a classic old diner on a dim side street. It's been renovated with slate floors and golden lighting into an intimate restaurant that seats about 20. There are no secrets between you, the chef, the sous chef, and the server, all of whom remain within a couple dozen feet of one another throughout the meal. The entire restaurant is smaller than the kitchen alone at many other restaurants. The menu is limited, with just four entrees each night—beef, poultry, shellfish, and fish—but the food has absolutely nothing in common with simple diner fare. The ingredients are fresh and select; the preparation more concerned with melding the tastes just right rather than dazzling with architectural flourishes. The beef is typically left alone in all its goodness; if you want to sample chef Michael Fuller's inventiveness, try the fish or shellfish. Vegetarians can ask for the special veggie platter.

## THE WILMINGTON/MOUNT SNOW REGION

Set high in the hills on the winding mountain highway midway between Bennington and Brattleboro, Wilmington has managed to retain its charm as an attractive crossroads village despite its location on two busy roads. It's definitely a town for tourists—if you want to get a lightbulb or haircut, you're better off in Bennington or Brattleboro, but Wilmington has a nice selection of antiques shops, boutiques, and pizza joints. Except on busy holiday weekends, when it's inundated by visitors driving frightfully large SUVs (especially from the New York metro area), Wilmington still manages to feel like a gracious mountain village untroubled by the times.

From Wilmington, the ski resort of Mount Snow/Haystack is easily accessible to the north via Route 100, which is brisk, busy, and close to impassable on sunny weekends in early October. Heading north, you'll first pass through West Dover, an attractive, classically New England town with a prominent steeple and acres of white clapboard.

Between West Dover and Mount Snow, it becomes increasingly evident that developers and entrepreneurs discovered the area in the years following the founding of Mount Snow in 1954. Some regard this stretch of highway as a monument to lack of planning. While development isn't dense (this is no North Conway, New Hampshire), the buildings represent a not-entirely-savory melange of architectural styles, the most prominent of which is Tyrolean Chicken Coop. Many of these buildings began their lives as ski lodges and have since been reincarnated as boutiques, inns, and restaurants. The silver lining is this: The development along here prompted Vermont to later pass a progressive and restrictive environmental law called Act 250, which has preserved many other areas from being blighted by too-fast growth. Remember that you're not restricted to Route 100, no matter what the locals tell you. The area is packed with smaller roads, both paved and dirt, that make for excellent exploring.

### ESSENTIALS

**GETTING THERE**    Wilmington is located at the junction of Routes 9 and 100. Route 9 offers the most direct access. The Mount Snow area is located north of Wilmington on Route 100. No buses connect to Wilmington, although plans are underway to establish a connection.

**VISITOR INFORMATION**    The **Mount Snow/Haystack Region Chamber of Commerce,** P.O. Box 3, Wilmington, VT 05363 (☎ **802/464-8092**), maintains a visitor center at 21 West Main Street in Wilmington. It's open year-round from 10am to 5pm daily. Information may also be requested via e-mail at **info@visitvermont.com**. The chamber offers a room-booking service, which is especially helpful for smaller inns and B&Bs; call ☎ **877/887-6884.** For on-mountain accommodations, check with **Mount Snow Lodging Bureau and Vacation Service** (☎ **800/245-7669**).

### THE MARLBORO MUSIC FESTIVAL

The renowned Marlboro Music Festival offers classical concerts performed by accomplished masters as well as highly talented younger musicians on weekends from mid-July to mid-August in the agreeable town of Marlboro, east of Wilmington on Route 9. The retreat was founded in 1951 and has hosted countless noted musicians, including Pablo Casals, who participated between 1960 and 1973. Concerts take place in the 700-seat auditorium at Marlboro College, and advance ticket purchases are strongly recommended. Call or write for a schedule and a ticket order form. Ticket prices range from $5 to $25. Between September and June, contact the festival's winter office at **Marlboro Music,** 135 S. 18th St., Philadelphia, PA 19103 (☎ **215/ 569-4690**). In summer, write Marlboro Music, Marlboro, VT 05344, or call the box office (☎ **802/254-2394**).

## MOUNTAIN BIKING

Mount Snow was among the first resorts to foresee the growing appeal of mountain biking, and the region remains one of the leading destinations for those whose vehicle of choice has knobby tires. Mount Snow established the first mountain-bike school in the country in 1988. Clinics and guided tours are also available.

The **Mountain Bike Center** (call Crisports at ☎ **802/464-4040**) is open late May through mid-October at the base of the mountain and offers equipment rentals, maps, and advice. Independent mountain bikers can also explore some 140 miles of trails and abandoned roads that lace the region. For a fee, you can take your bike to the mountaintop by chairlift and coast your way down along marked trails or earn the ride by pumping out the vertical rise to the top. Fanning out from the mountain are numerous abandoned town roads that make for less challenging but no less pleasant excursions.

## DOWNHILL SKIING

**Mount Snow/Haystack.** Mount Snow, VT 05356. ☎ **800/245-7669** for lodging or 802/464-3333. www.mountsnow.com. E-mail: info@mountsnow.com. Vertical drop: 1,700 ft. Lifts: 21 chairlifts (3 high-speed), 5 surface lifts. Skiable acreage: 769. Lift tickets: $53 weekends/ holidays, $49 midweek. Haystack only: $49 daily.

Mount Snow and Haystak were once competitors, now both owned by American Skiing Company, which also owns Killington and numerous other ski resorts. The main mountain is noted for its widely cut runs on the front face (disparaged by some as "vertical golf courses"), yet remains an excellent destination for intermediates and advanced intermediates. More advanced skiers can migrate to the North Face, which is its own little world of bumps and glades.

Because it's the closest Vermont ski area to Boston and New York (it's a 4-hour drive from Manhattan), the mountain can get crowded, especially on weekends. The third high-speed quad added in 1997 helped put a dent in some of those lines, but don't overlook Haystack, which is 10 miles distant by car (it's much closer if you're a crow), a classic older New England ski mountain, with challenging, narrow runs. Lift lines are typically much shorter at Haystack.

Mount Snow's village is attractively arrayed along the base of the mountain. The most imposing structure is the balconied hotel overlooking a small pond, but the overall character is shaped more by the unobtrusive smaller lodges and homes. Once famed for its groovy singles scene, Mount Snow's post-skiing activities have mellowed somewhat and embraced the family market, although 20-somethings will still find a good selection of apres-ski activities.

## CROSS-COUNTRY SKIING

The Mount Snow area offers excellent cross-country ski centers. The 9 miles of groomed trail at **Timber Creek Cross-Country Touring Center** (☎ **802/464-0999**) in West Dover near the Mount Snow access road is a popular area with beginners and holds snow nicely thanks to its high elevation. Ticket price is $15. The **Hermitage Ski Touring Center** (☎ 802/464-3511) attracts more advanced skiers to its varied terrain and 30 miles of trails. A trail pass is $14. The **White House Ski Touring Center** (☎ 800/541-2135 or 802/464-2135), at the inn by the same name on Route 100, has the easiest access to the Vermont woods, a good range of terrain, and 25 miles of trails ($12). The center also maintains snowshoe trails and offers rentals.

## WHERE TO STAY

The Mount Snow area has a surfeit of lodging options, ranging from basic motels to luxury inns to slopeside condos. Rates drop quite a bit in the summer when the region slips into a pleasant lethargy. In the winter, the higher prices reflect relatively easy access to skiers from New York and Boston. The best phone call to make first is to Mount Snow's lodging line (☎ 800/245-7669) to ask about vacation packages and condo accommodations.

**Deerhill Inn and Restaurant.** Valley View Rd., West Dover, VT 05356. ☎ **800/993-3379** or 802/464-3100. Fax 802/464-5474. www.deerhill.com. E-mail: deerhill@sover.net. 15 units. $95–$265 double, including breakfast ($120–$320 holidays and foliage). 2-night minimum on weekends. Children over age 8 are welcome. AE, MC, V.

The Deerhill Inn, located on a hillside above Route 100 with views of the rolling mountains, was built as a ski lodge in 1954, but always-helpful innkeepers Linda and Michael Anelli have given it a more gracious country look. In summer, there are attractive gardens and a stonework pool; in winter, the slopes are a short drive away. Guests have access to two comfortable sitting areas upstairs stocked with a television and books. The guest rooms vary from very cozy to reasaonably spacious, and most are decorated with a light country flair; four are located in a motel-like addition with balconies. The best of the lot are Rooms L1 and L2, both of which have cathedral ceilings; L2 has spare Asian decor, bamboo wallpaper, and an outside terrace; L1 features Laura Ashley–country styling. Five rooms have gas fireplaces, seven have balconies or terraces, and five have televisions.

**Dining:** Dinners are served most nights (sometimes closed Tuesday or Wednesday in the slower seasons) in the country dining room on the first floor. Dishes are mostly Continental and beyond. Look for venison chops with lingonberry sauce, weiner-schnitzel, and macademia-encrusted chicken with a pineapple garnish. Entrees are priced $21 to $32, and reservations are suggested for outside diners.

**The Hermitage.** Coldbrook Rd. (P.O. Box 457), Wilmington, VT 05363. ☎ **802/464-3511.** Fax 802/464-2688. www.hermitageinn.com. E-mail: hermitage@sover.net. 15 units. TV TEL. $225–$250 double, including breakfast and dinner. 2–3-night minimum on weekends/ holidays in winter. AE, DC, MC, V.

I love this place not so much for its unpretentious sense of style—the 19th century as interpreted by the 1940s—but for the way it combines the stately with the quirky. The inn is located on 25 acres of meadow and woodland, and feels a bit like one of those British summer estates that P.G. Wodehouse wrote about. Out back are cages filled with game birds, some quite exotic, that are raised for eating, hunting, and show. There's the new 15-station sporting-clays area for shotgun enthusiasts. The walls are obsessively covered with the busy, happy lithographs of Michael Delacroix, and you'll find an extensive wine shop in the basement, where Californian and French wines are well-represented, especially burgundies. The guest rooms are designed for comfort more than for elegance, and some may seem a bit past their prime, but that's part of the charm—it's still far from shabby.

I prefer the four older rooms in the main inn to seven rooms in the Wine House, which I found a bit lacking in character. The main inn rooms are also nicer than the four more modern rooms in the nearby carriage house.

**Dining:** The two handsome dining rooms are best known for their wines (some 40,000 bottles age quietly in the cellar), but the continental cuisine carries its own quite nicely. For a special treat, opt for one of the game birds raised on the premises. Entrees for outside guests are $15 to $26.

**Amenities:** Cross-country ski center on premises; sporting clays, stocked trout pond, private hunting preserve, and access to clay tennis court and pool (1 mile away).

**Inn at Quail Run.** 106 Smith Rd., Wilmington, VT 05363. ☎ **800/343-7227.** E-mail: quailrunvt@aol.com. 13 units. TV. Summer $120–$160 double, foliage $165–$200, ski season $135–$180. Rates include full breakfast. 3-night minimum holiday weekends; 2-night minimum foliage season. AE, DISC, MC, V. Pets allowed in some rooms, $15 per night.

Quail Run is a hybrid of the sort New England could use more of: an intimate B&B that welcomes families (and even pets). Set on 13 acres in the hills east of Route 100, the converted ski lodge was renovated and expanded in 1997, with guest rooms done up in a contemporary country style. Family accommodations include king and bunk beds; the standard rooms are motel-size, and four have gas fireplaces. Other amenities include a kid's playroom with Ping-Pong and video games, a heated pool, sauna, and a 9-person Jacuzzi.

**Inn at Sawmill Farm.** Crosstown Rd. & Rte. 100, (P.O. Box 367), W. Dover, Vt 05356. ☎ **800/493-1133** or 802/464-8131. Fax 802/464-1130. 20 units (including 10 suites). A/C. $340–$470 double. Rates include breakfast and dinner. AE, MC, V. Closed Apr–May.

Willing to pay for luxury? The Inn at Sawmill Farm is an exclusive Relais and Chateaux property on 28 acres, and one of the first inns in New England to cater to affluent travelers. Guest rooms in this old farmhouse, parts of which date back to 1797, are each different, but all share a similar contemporary country styling and Colonial reproduction furniture. Most are spacious; among the best are Cider House #2, with its rustic beams and oversize canopy bed, and the Woodshed, a quiet cottage with a beautiful brick fireplace and a cozy loft. Some guests report that the inn has lost a bit of its burnish and its edge as a bastion of service in recent years.

**Dining:** See "Where to Dine, below.

**Trail's End.** 5 Trail's End Lane (look for turn between Haystack and Mt. Snow), Wilmington, VT 05363. ☎ **800/859-2585** or 802/464-2727. Fax 802/464-5532. www.trailsendvt.com. E-mail: trailsend@together.net. 15 units. Summer $105–$155 double; fall $115–$175 double; winter $125–$185 double. Rates include full breakfast. 2-night minimum stay on weekends, 3 nights on holidays. AE, DISC, MC, V. Children over 7 are welcome.

Trail's End, located a short drive off Route 100 on 10 nicely tended acres, is located in an updated vintage 1960s ski lodge with attractive rooms and plenty of common space. The carpeted guest rooms are spotlessly clean, styled in a modern country fashion with pine and wicker furniture. Six feature fireplaces, and two have Jacuzzis. The two suites are fit for midwinter cocoooning, with microwaves, refrigerators, and VCRs. My favorite? Number 6, with a lovely fireplace and nice oak accents. Other good places to hang out include the main common room with 22-foot stone fireplace, the stone-floored library and game room, and the informal second-floor loft.

**Amenities:** Heated outdoor pool (summer only), clay tennis court, Jacuzzi, game rooms, sundeck, and free videos.

**White House of Wilmington.** 178 Rte. 9, East Wilmington, VT 05363. ☎ **800/541-2135** or 802/464-2135. Fax 802/464-5222. www.whitehouseinn.com. E-mail: whitehse@sover.net.

23 units. $128–$178 double. Rates include full breakfast. Fireplace rooms are $30 less in summer. 2-night minimum reservation on weekends. AE, MC, V. Children age 8 and older welcome in main lodge; all ages in the guest house.

The White House of Wilmington, a fanciful Greek Revival–style home with two prominent porticos (built in 1915 by a wealthy lumber baron), sits impressively on the crest of an open hill just east of Wilmington. The interior is spacious and open, with hardwood floors, arched doorways, and superb detailing throughout. The guest rooms are comfortably furnished; nine have wood fireplaces, and four feature whirlpools. Formal without being stuffy, the inn has an especially appealing bar on its enclosed porch, which can't be beat as a spot to sip something soothing while watching the sun sink over the Vermont hills. An adjacent guest house is less fancy but still comfortable, with seven guest rooms.

**Dining:** The inn's restaurant is well-regarded for its continental cuisine, served in an attractive dining room with hardwood floors, dark wood trim, pink tablecloths, and an intricate fireplace mantel. Entrees include duck stuffed with walnuts, apples, and grapes (the chef's specialty); veal piccatta; and filet mignon au poivre ($15.95 to $19.95).

**Amenities:** Outdoor heated swimming pool, tennis courts, Jacuzzi, nature trails, conference rooms, sauna, snowshoe rentals, and 25 miles of groomed cross-country ski trails. The inn is also popular with snowmobilers in winter.

## WHERE TO DINE

**Dot's.** 3 W. Main St., Wilmington. ☎ **802/464-7284.** Breakfast and lunch $2.95–$7.50, dinner $2.75–$10.95. DISC, MC, V. Daily 5:30am–8pm (until 9pm Fri and Sat). DINER.

Wilmington is justly proud of Dot's, an institution that has stubbornly remained loyal to its longtime clientele, offering good, cheap food in the face of creeping boutique-ification elsewhere in town.(There's a second, more modern Dot's in Dover.) Located right in the village, Dot's is a classic, with pine paneling, swivel stools at the counter, and checkerboard linoleum tile. It's famous for its chili and pancakes, but don't over-look other breakfast fare, like the Cajun skillet—a medley of sausage, peppers, onions, and homefries sautéed and served with eggs and melted jack cheese (although they certainly don't call it a medley here). The budget-priced blue-plate specials include New England fare like roast turkey and gravy served with fries and coleslaw.

✪ **Inn at Sawmill Farm.** Crosstown Rd. & Rte. 100, W. Dover. ☎ **802/464-8131.** Reser-vations recommended. Main courses $27–$38. AE, DC, MC, V. Daily 6–9:30pm. Closed mid-Apr–Memorial Day weekend. CONTINENTAL.

More than 30,000 bottles of wine lurk in the inn's custom-made wine cellar, and in part that's what garnered it a coveted "Grand Award" from *Wine Spectator* magazine. You can order uncommonly excellent wines by the glass, and if you feel like splurging on a $400 bottle of wine, this is your place, but the wine is only one of the reasons the inn consistently attracts well-heeled diners. The food is deftly prepared, with entrees ranging from pheasant breast and roasted salmon, to Delmonico steak with bordelaise sauce, and potato-crusted sea bass with wild mushrooms. The converted barn-and-farmhouse atmosphere is romantic and the service superb, although the for-mality of the servers (one waiter will lavish grated cheese on your salad while another simultaneously proffers pepper) puts some folks on edge.

**Le Petit Chef.** 840 Rte. 100, Wilmington. ☎ **802/464-8437.** Reservations recommended. Main courses $17–$30. AE, MC, V. Wed–Thurs and Sun–Mon 6–9pm; Fri–Sat 6–10pm. Closed late fall and early spring. FRENCH.

Situated in an old Cape Cod–style farmhouse on Route 100, Le Petit Chef has attract-ed legions of satisfied customers who flock here to sample Betty Hillman's creative fare. The interior has been updated and modernized at the expense of some historic character, but the quality of the food usually makes diners overlook the made-for-ski-crowds ambience. By all means, start with the signature "Bird's Nest," an innovative melange of shiitake mushrooms and onions cooked in a cream sauce and served in a basket of deep-fried potato. The main courses are equally appealing, with selections like a fillet of salmon baked in a horseradish crust, loin of venison with a fruit marmalade, and fillet of beef with merlot sauce and morels.

**Piero's Trattoria.** Rte. 100, Wilmington. ☎ **802/464-7147.** Reservations recommended. Main courses $13.95–$16.95. AE, MC, V. Thurs–Sun 5:30–9:30pm. ITALIAN.

This spot, located at the Orchard Inn, is easy to miss as you speed by on Route 100, but it's worth slowing down to seek out. The oddly styleless dining room is small and dim, with just seven tables, located off the lobby of the upstairs B&B. Not a promising appearance, but note that both chefs come from the central Italian province of Le Marche. The pastas are homemade, and include a fine smoked salmon and caper tagliatelle. The other entrees include a good selection of chicken and veal dishes, which range from chicken with homemade polenta and a chianti sauce, to thinly sliced veal stuffed with prosciutto and mozarella and served with a Sambuca-sage sauce.

**Skyline Restaurant.** Rte. 9, Hogback Mt., Marlboro. ☎ **802/464-5535.** Reservations recommended for window seats. Lunch $4.95–$16.25; dinner $10.95–$16.95. Summer daily 7:30am–9pm; winter Fri–Sun 7:30am–9pm, Mon 7:30am–3pm, closed Tues–Thurs. MC, V.

The Skyline is a classic knotty-pine, stone-fireplace, tourist-stop restaurant atop a 2,350-foot ridge between Brattleboro and Wilmington. It's the sort of place that seems not to have changed a whit since it opened in 1950—and it really hasn't, except that one young waitress was sporting a nose ring on a recent visit. The restaurant claims a 100-mile southerly view through its massive plate-glass window; the maps on the paper place mats help you identify the mountains in sight, from Grand Monadnock in New Hampshire to the Berkshires in Massachusetts. One problem: The restaurant is often in the clouds, which knocks the view down to 100 feet or so. ("Then I'm your view," the waitresses tell customers.) The menu offers basic New England fare (waffles for breakfast, club sandwiches for lunch, baked sugar-cured ham for dinner) at reasonable prices. Opt for the rich and tasty Indian pudding for dessert.

## PUTNEY

The sleepy village of Putney is like Brattleboro, only more so. It's infused with a sort of pleasant ennui, and you're likely to see more dreadlocks here than in any other comparably sized New England village. (Much of this is thanks to the Putney School, an alternative boarding school founded in 1935 where students attend to farm chores along with their classes.) The village is home to an uncommonly high number of artists and healers of various stripes (for example, New Age physical therapists, writing counselors, and freelance social workers).

Putney's free-spirited character has a long history. In the early 19th century, the son of a congressman (and cousin of President Rutherford B. Hayes) named John Humphrey Noyes settled here with a band of followers, called Perfectionists. For several years, they quietly practiced not only communism of household and property, but also communism of love (called "complex marriage" by Noyes). "In a holy community there is no more reason why sexual intercourse should be restrained by the law than why eating and drinking should be," Noyes wrote. When discovered, this did not go over well among the townfolks. Noyes was arrested in 1847, and it took decades for Putney to recover from the great indiscretions that had been taking place under their noses.

## ESSENTIALS

**GETTING THERE**   Putney is approximately 12 miles north of Brattleboro on Route 5. Take Exit 4 off I-91.

**VISITOR INFORMATION**   There's no formal information center in Putney, but the Discovery Putney Council maintains a serviceable Web site at www.putney.net.

## EXPLORING THE TOWN

The compact village center has several intriguing restaurants and shops, the latter featuring global imports, antiques, and used books. **Everyone's Drumming,** 4 Christian Sq. (☎ **800/326-0726** or 802/387-2249), specializes in handmade drums and accessories, and the staff is happy to talk with beginning or advanced drummers. The **Putney Hearth Bakery and Coffee House** (☎ **802/387-2708**), is located next to town hall and is the perfect spot for a coffee, cookie, or something more elaborate (cinnamon roll, seven-grain organic bread). There's an adjoining bookstore.

**Basketville,** 2 Bellows Falls Rd. (☎ **802/387-5509**), has roots back to 1842, and been owned and operated by Vermonters ever since. (It adopted its current, recherché name in the 1940s.) There are currently eight Basketville stores between Florida and Vermont, but the Putney store is the original. It's a sprawling shop, with Shaker-style baskets, Native American–style ash baskets, pine buckets, and a lot more. It's located just north of the village center on Route 5.

Savory, award-winning cheese (the *New York Times* has raved about it) is made in Putney at **Vermont Shepherd Cheese,** 875 Patch Rd. (☎ **802/387-4473**). The creamy and rich cheeses have a brown rind and are aged 4 to 8 months in a cave on the property. The cheese may be easiest to find in better food shops along the eastern seaboard (check the Brattleboro Food Co-op, or Balducci's or Zabar's in New York City), but tours of the cave with cheese tastings are offered in August, September, and October Thursday and Saturday mornings from 10am to noon. There's no charge, no reservations are needed, and cheese may be purchased afterwards (MasterCard and Visa accepted). Call for directions.

## WHERE TO STAY

✪ **Hickory Ridge House.** 53 Hickory Ridge Rd. S., Putney, VT 05346. ☎ **800/380-9218** or 802/387-5709. Fax 802/387-4328. www.hickoryridgehouse.com. E-mail: mail@ hickoryridgehouse.com. 7 units (includes 2-bdrm cottage); 2 with private hall bath. A/C TV TEL. $95–$145 double; $310 for cottage. Rates include full breakfast. 2-night minimum on holiday and foliage weekends. AE, MC, V.

This historic brick Federal home dating from 1808 has high ceilings, large windows, wide pine floors and an eclectic mix of furniture (ranging from Colonial to Mission) that blends very well. The decor is simple rather than cluttered, common rooms are upstairs and down, the grounds are a lovely combination of fields, gardens, and handsome trees, and the innkeepers put cookies and flowers in the rooms. In all, it's a splendid retreat. Room 6 is larger than most and my favorite, with an oak bed, mix of antiques, gas woodstove, and a great bathroom with a sink made of an old dresser (alas, only a stall shower). Room 2 is a corner room and has old wooden floors, a four-poster bed, periwinkle blue walls, and braided rugs. You can save a few dollars with Room 3, which gets great morning light (it reflects luridly off the yellow walls) but requires a short walk to the private bath down the hall. Rooms all have VCRs and there's a library of videos to select from. Breakfasts feature homemade baked goods and hand-squeezed orange juice.

## WHERE TO DINE

**Curtis Bar-B-Q.** Rte. 5, Putney. ☎ **802/387-5474.** Main courses $4–$20. No credit cards. Tues–Sun 10am–dark. Closed Nov–spring. BARBECUE.

Just uphill from Exit 4 off I-91, you suddenly smell the delicious aroma of barbecue sizzling over flaming pits. Do not pass this place by, because you *will* change your mind later and waste a lot of time and gasoline backtracking. This classic roadside food joint, situated on a more or less empty lot next to a gas station, has a heap of charm despite itself. This self-serve restaurant consists of two blue school buses and a newer open-sided shed for dining; guests take their plunder to a smattering of picnic tables scattered about the lot. Place your order, grab a seat, dig in, and enjoy. The wide price range is explained simply: small order of ribs: $4. Slab: $20. Sizes in between also available.

# NEWFANE & TOWNSHEND

These two villages, about 5 miles apart on Route 30, are the picture-perfect epitome of Vermont. Both are set deeply within the serpentine West River Valley, and both are built around open town greens. Both towns consist of impressive white-clapboard homes and public buildings that share the grace and scale of the surrounding homes. Both boast striking examples of Early American architecture, notably Greek Revival.

Don't bother looking for strip malls, McDonald's, or garish video outlets hereabouts. Newfane and Townshend have a feel of having been idled on a sidetrack for decades while the rest of American society steamed blithely ahead, but these villages certainly don't have the somber feel of a mausoleum. On one visit during a breezy autumn afternoon, a swarm of teenagers skateboarded off the steps of the courthouse in Newfane, and a lively basketball game was underway at the edge of the green in Townshend. There is life here.

For visitors, inactivity is often the activity of choice. Guests find an inn or lodge that suits their temperament, then spend the days strolling the towns, undertaking aimless backroad driving tours, soaking in a mountain stream, hunting up antiques at the many shops, or striking off on foot for one of the rounded, wooded peaks that overlook villages and valleys.

## ESSENTIALS

**GETTING THERE**   Newfane and Townshend are located on Route 30 northwest of Brattleboro. The nearest interstate access is off Exit 3 from I-91.

**VISITOR INFORMATION**   There's no formal information center serving these towns. Brochures are available at the **State Visitor Center** (☎ **802/254-4593**) on I-91 in Guilford, south of Brattleboro.

## EXPLORING THE AREA

Newfane was originally founded in 1774 on a hill a few miles from the current village; in 1825, it was moved to its present location on a valley floor. Some of the original buildings were dismantled and rebuilt, but most date from the early to mid-19th century. The **National Historic District** is comprised of some 60 buildings around the green and on nearby side streets. You'll find styles ranging from Federal through Colonial Revival, although Greek Revival appears to carry the day. A strikingly handsome courthouse—where cases are still heard, as they have been for nearly 2 centuries—dominates the shady green. This structure was originally built in 1825; the imposing portico was added in 1853. For more detailed information on area buildings, obtain a copy of the free walking-tour brochure at the Moore Free Library on West Street or the Historical Society, below.

Newfane's history is explored at the engaging **Historical Society of Windham County,** located on Route 30 across from the village common. It's housed in in a handsome "fireproof" brick building constructed for the collection in Colonial Revival–style in the 1930s. There's an eclectic collection of local artifacts (dolls, melodeons, and rail ephemera), along with changing exhibits that feature intriguing snippets of local history. ("Many potions such as Mrs. Winslow's Soothing Syrup 'worked' because of the high alcohol or opium content.") It's open from late May to mid-October Wednesday to Sunday noon to 5pm; admission by donation.

More than two dozen **antiques shops** are located on or near Route 30 in the West River Valley. They provide good grazing on lazy afternoons and are a fine resource for serious collectors. At any of the shops, look for the free brochure "Antiquing in the West River Valley," which provides a good overview of what's out there. Among them: the **Riverdale Antiques Center** (☎ 802/365-4616) is a group shop with some country furniture but mostly smaller collectibles, and **Schommer Antiques** (☎ 802/365-7777) on Route 30 in Newfane Village, which carries a good selection of 19th-century furniture and accessories in a shop that's listed on the National Register of Historic Places.

Treasure hunters should time their visit to hit the **Newfane Flea Market** (☎ 802/365-4000), which features 100-plus tables of assorted stuff, much of it the 12-tube-socks-for-$5 variety. The flea market is held Sunday from May through October on Route 30 just north of Newfane village.

## OUTDOOR PURSUITS

Townshend State Park (☎ 802/365-7500) and **Townshend State Forest** are located at the foot of Bald Mountain, 3 miles outside Townshend. The park consists of a solidly built campground constructed by the Civilian Conservation Corps in the 1930s. You can park here to hike **Bald Mountain,** one of the better short hikes in the region. A 3.1-mile loop trail begins behind the ranger station, following a bridle path along a brook. The ascent soon steepens, and at 1.7 miles, you'll arrive at the 1,680-foot summit, that turns out not to be bald at all. Open ledges afford views toward Mount Monadnock to the east and Bromley and Stratton mountains to the west. The descent is via a steeper 1.4-mile trail that ends behind the campground. The park is open early May to Columbus Day; a small day-use fee is charged. Ask for trail maps at the park office. The park is reached by crossing the Townshend Dam (off Route 30), then turning left and continuing to the park sign.

## WHERE TO STAY & DINE

**Four Columns Inn.** West St. (P.O. Box 278), Newfane, VT 05345. ☎ **800/767-6633** or 802/365-7713. Fax 802/365-0022. www.fourcolumnsinn.com. E-mail: frcolinn@sover.net. 15 units. A/C TEL. Peak season $140–$195 double ($270 suite); off-season $110–$165 double. Rates include continental breakfast. AE, CB, DC, DISC, MC, V. Pets accepted with prior permission; $10 per pet per night.

You can't help but notice the Four Columns Inn in Newfane: It's the regal white-clapboard building with four Ionic columns just off the green. This perfect village setting hides a near-perfect inn within. Pam and Gorton Baldwin, who bought the inn in 1996, have retained the best parts of the inn (the chef, for instance, who has been here for more than 2 decades), while improving those areas where quality had slipped over the years. Rooms in the Main House and Garden Wing are larger (and more expensive) than those above the restaurant. Four of the 15 rooms have been made over as luxury suites, with double Jacuzzis. The best room in the house is Room 12, with a 2-person Jacuzzi, skylight, double-sided gas fireplace, small sitting area, and a private deck with a view to a small pond. Room 8 is the least expensive and lacks a view, but it is still appealing with its low eaves and understated country styling.

**Dining:** There's a pleasing atmosphere with low beams and white damask tablecloths, but the place isn't quite as romantic as other dining rooms in the region (Windham Hill and the Old Tavern both come to mind). On the other hand, the meals are excellent, featuring New American cooking with entrees like mixed seafood with Chinese black beans, bok choy, and lemongrass broth; and venison loin with a spicy Zinfandel glaze and sundried cherries. Entree prices range from $21 to $26.

**Amenities:** Outdoor pool, hiking trails on 150 private acres, sundeck, and baby-sitting.

**Old Newfane Inn.** Rte. 30, Newfane, VT 05345. ☎ **802/365-4427.** 8 units. (2 rooms share 1 bathroom). $125–$155 double, including continental breakfast. 2-night minimum stay on weekends, 3 nights some holidays. No credit cards.

The old-fashioned Old Newfane Inn dates back to 1797 and sits squarely, perhaps a little sternly, on the Newfane village common. It's been run for 3 decades by the Weindl family, and will appeal to those whose tastes tend toward a dim and dusky sort of faded charm. There's nothing fancy or overly elegant here. That the lobby features yellowing articles about the inn dating from the Jimmy Carter administration speaks volumes. The guest rooms are simply furnished in a traditional Colonial style (two have shared bath). The largest and best is Room 23, which features a pleasant sitting area.

**Dining:** Dinner is served daily except Mondays in the air-conditioned dining room with pewter lamps. The menu features continental and classic French-Swiss cuisine, with entrees priced $17 to $27.

**✪ Windham Hill Inn.** 311 Lawrence Dr., West Townshend, VT 05359. ☎ **800/944-4080** or 802/874-4080. Fax 802/874-4702. www.windhamhill.com. E-mail: windham@sover.net. 21 units. A/C TEL. $270–$395 double (add $50 during foliage). Rates include breakfast and dinner. 2-night minimum stay on weekends, 3 nights some holidays. AE, DISC, MC, V. Closed the week prior to Dec 27. Children over age 12 are welcome. Directions: Turn uphill across from the country store in W. Townshend and climb 1 1/4 miles to a marked dirt road; turn right and continue to the end.

The Windham Hill Inn is about as good as it gets, especially if you're looking for a romantic getaway. Situated on 160 acres at the end of a dirt road in a high upland valley, the inn was originally built in 1823 as a farmhouse and remained in the same family until the 1950s, when it was converted to an inn. Under the ownership of innkeepers Pat and Grigs Markham, the Windham Hill has ratcheted up several notches in quality as extensive renovations have managed to meld the best of the old and the new. The guest rooms are wonderfully appointed in an elegant country style and refrain from being too cluttered or cute; a half dozen have Jacuzzis or soaking tubs, nine have balconies or decks, 13 have gas fireplaces, and all feature views. Especially nice is Jesse's Room on the third floor, with soaking tub, gas woodstove, a large bathroom, and lustrous pine floors; and Forget-Me-Not, with soaking tub and four-poster bed. The common areas, like the guest rooms, are appointed in a restrained country fashion that's more refined than rustic.

**Dining:** The dining room, which is open to the public, features exceptionally creative cooking with a strong emphasis on local and seasonal ingredients. The menu changes seasonally; recent entrees have included maple-glazed boneless breast of duck with cranberry-balsamic sauce, and beer tenderloin fillet with roasted and caramelized onion chutney. The fixed-price five-course dinner is $40 and provides good value.

**Amenities:** Hiking trails, outdoor heated pool, clay tennis court, game alcove, conference rooms, and 6 miles of groomed cross-country ski trails.

# GRAFTON & CHESTER

When I first visited **Grafton**, I was fully prepared to dislike it. I'd heard from others that it was pristine and quaint, the result of an ambitious preservation plan by wealthy benefactors. I figured it would be too precious, too fussy, too much an overwrought picture-book re-creation of New England, as envisioned by the Daughters of the American Revolution; but it only took me about half an hour of aimless wandering to come away a serious fan of the place. It's not a museum like Sturbridge Village or Colonial Williamsburg, but an active town with around 600 residents. It just happens to have dozens of museum-quality homes and buildings.

Grafton was founded in 1763 and soon grew into a thriving settlement. By 1850, the town was home to some 10,000 sheep and boasted a handsome hotel that provided shelter for guests on the stagecoach between Boston and Montreal. A cheese cooperative was organized in 1890. The soapstone industry flourished., but as agriculture and commerce shifted west and to the cities, Grafton became a mere shadow of a town—by the Depression, many of the buildings were derelict; for 3 decades afterwards, much of the town could be purchased for a song.

In 1963, Hall and Dean Mathey of New Jersey created the Windham Foundation. These two brothers had been entrusted by a wealthy relative, who had recently died, to come up with a worthy cause for her fortune. It took a few years, but they eventually hit on Grafton, where their family had summered, and began purchasing and restoring the dilapidated center of town, including the old hotel. The foundation eventually came to own some 55 buildings and 2,000 acres around the town—even the cheese cooperative was revived. Within time, the village again came to life, although it's now teeming with history buffs and tourists rather than farmers and merchants. The Windham Foundation has taken great care in preserving this gem of a village, even to the point of burying utility lines so as not to mar the landscape with wires.

To the north, more commercial **Chester** is less pristine and more lived in. The downtown area has a pleasant neighborly feel to it, along with a handful of boutiques and shops along the main road. Chester is a great destination for antiquing, with several good dealers in the area. When heading north of town on Route 103, be sure to slow through the Stone Village, a neighborhood of well-spaced, austere stone homes that line the roadway. Many of these are rumored to have been stopping points on the Underground Railroad.

## ESSENTIALS

**GETTING THERE**    Take I-91 to Bellows Falls (Exit 5 or 6), and follow signs to town via Route 5. From there, take Route 121 west for 12 miles to Grafton. For a more scenic route, take Route 35 north from Townshend.

**VISITOR INFORMATION**    The **Grafton Information Center,** Grafton, VT 05146 (☎ 802/843-2255), is located in the Daniels House on Townshend Road, behind the Grafton Inn. For information about Chester, contact the **Chester Area Chamber of Commerce,** P.O. Box 623, Chester, VT 05143 (☎ 802/875-2939).

## EXPLORING THE TOWN

Grafton is best seen at a languorous pace, on foot, when the weather is welcoming. A picnic is a good idea, especially if it involves the excellent local cheddar. There are no grand historical homes open for tours; it's more a village to be enjoyed with aimless walks outdoors. Don't expect to be overwhelmed with grandeur. Instead, keep a keen eye out for telling historical details.

Start at the **Grafton Village Cheese Co.** (☎ 800/472-3866), a small, modern building where you can buy a snack of award-winning cheese and peer through plate-glass windows to observe the cheese-making process. (To the casual observer, cheese-making may be neither very complicated nor interesting.) It's open Monday to Friday 8am to 4pm, weekends 10am to 4pm.

From here you can follow the trail over the nearby covered bridge, then bear right on the footpath along the cow pasture to the **Kidder Covered Bridge.** Head into town via Water Street, continuing on to Main Street. Toward the village center, white-clapboard homes and shade trees abound. This is about as New England as New England gets.

On Main Street, stop by the **Grafton Historical Society Museum** (☎ 802/843-2344; open weekends only) to peruse photographs, artifacts, and memorabilia of Grafton. Afterwards, stop by the **Old Tavern at Grafton,** the impressive building that anchors the town and has served as a social center since 1801, and partake of a beverage at the rustic Phelps Barn Lounge or a meal in one of the dining rooms (see below). From here, you can make your way back to the cheese company by wandering on pleasant side streets. If you'd like to see Grafton from a different perspective, ask at the inn about horse-and-buggy rides.

Also in town is **The Nature Museum at Grafton** (☎ 802/843-2111; open 1 to 4pm weekends and holidays) which offers exhibits about Vermont flora and fauna, a wildlife garden, and short walking trails on the property. The museum is located on Townshend Road ¹/₄ mile south of Grafton center.

More active travelers, whether visiting in winter or summer, should head for the **Grafton Ponds Nordic Ski and Mountain Bike Center** (☎ 802/843-2400), located just south of the cheese factory on Route 35. Managed by the Old Tavern, Grafton Ponds offers mountain-bike rentals and access to a hillside trail system summer and fall. Come winter, it grooms 18 miles of trails and maintains a warming hut near the ponds, where you can sit by a wood stove and enjoy a steaming bowl of soup. The Big Bear loop runs high up the flanks of a hill and is especially appealing; travel counter-clockwise so that you walk up the steep hill and enjoy the rolling descent. Ski and snowshoe rentals are available; a trail pass costs $15 for adults and $10 for children 12 and under (6 and under ski free).

## WHERE TO STAY & DINE

**Fullerton Inn.** Rte. 11 (P.O. Box 589), Chester, VT 05143. ☎ **802/875-2444.** Fax 802/875-6414. www.fullertoninn.com. E-mail: getaway@fullertoninn.com. 21 units. $99–$149 double, including continental breakfast. 2-night minimum foliage weekends. AE, DISC, MC, V. Children over age 12 are welcome.

The Fullerton Inn is more of a hotel than a country inn, located in a tall building (well, relatively speaking) smack in the middle of Chester's one-street downtown. Downstairs the lobby has the feel of an informal old roadhouse (you half expect to see Willy Loman trudging through with his weary bags), but with polished maple floors, handsome fieldstone fireplace, and piano, it's a welcoming spot. The eclectically furnished guest rooms on the two upstairs floors vary in size in decor, although most have small bathrooms and there's little soundproofing, so noises from neighbors can carry. Several rooms have recently been combined by the innkeepers to create more spacious suites; Room 17 is quiet, faces the rear of the property, and has a separate sitting area. For the more socially inclined, Rooms 8 and 10 have doors onto a balcony that overlooks the street. Some rooms can be combined to serve as suites, which is handy for couples traveling together.

**Dining:** The dining room has a relaxed, old-world setting, reminiscent of older hotels that once catered to business travelers. The menu is small but appealing—expect chicken stuffed with spinach and tomato, shrimp scampi, Mediterranean pizza, and grilled filet mignon ("with a touch of worcestershire and onion"), entrees are priced $10.95 to $18.95.

**Hugging Bear Inn.** 244 Main St., Chester, VT 05143. ☎ **800/325-0519** or 802/ 875-2412. Fax 802/875-3823. www.huggingbear.com. E-mail: georgette@huggingbear.com. 6 units. A/C. $85–$125 double. Rates include full breakfast. AE, DISC, MC, V. Closed midweek in winter.

Young kids love this place. It's an old Queen Anne–style home on Chester's Main Street that's filled with teddy bears., and I mean filled. There's a 5-foot teddy in the living room and some 250 of them scattered about the inn ("A teddy bear in every bed.") , and that's just the tip of the iceberg. In the attached barn, there's another about, oh, *9,000* teddy bears for sale at the Hugging Bear Shoppe, which attracts serious collectors from around the world. The guest rooms are themed around—no surprise here—teddy bears. Expect bear sheets, bear light-switch plates, bear shower curtains, and so on. "Pandamonium" has a panda theme; the "Winnie the Pooh Room" is all Winnie all the time.

✪ **The Old Tavern at Grafton.** Rtes. 35 and 121, Grafton, VT 05146. ☎ **800/843-1801** or 802/843-2231. Fax 802/843-2245. www.old-tavern.com. E-mail: tavern@sover.net. 63 units. $145–$280 double year-round. Rates include full breakfast. 2- or 3-night minimum stay on winter weekends, some holidays, and during foliage season. MC, V. Closed Apr.

Countless New England inns seek to replicate the service and gracious style of a far larger resort but fall short because of understaffing and a lack of capital, but the Old Tavern at Grafton succeeds wildly. It should be noted that this is called Old Tavern, not "Ye Olde Taverne," a good reflection of the understated quality and professional service that has long pervaded the establishment. The inn, the main part of which was built in 1801, seems much more intimate than its 63 guest rooms would suggest, since the rooms are spread throughout the town. Fourteen rooms are in the handsome colonnaded main inn building, 22 are across the street in the Homestead Cottage, and the remaining rooms are scattered among seven historic guest houses in and around the village. All are decorated with antiques and an upscale country sensibility; the rooms in the Homestead Cottage (which is actually two historic homes joined together) have a more modern, hotel-like character.

**Dining:** "Appropriate dinner attire" is requested, but there's still a fairly relaxed air to the three dining rooms in the evening. Dinner features adaptations of traditional New England fare, including gulf shrimp with a Ritz cracker stuffing, and double lamb chops with a rosemary and roasted garlic sauce; dinner prices range from $14 to $26. Live music is offered some evenings in a rustic pub.

**Amenities:** Sand-bottomed pond, bicycle rentals (half and whole day), game room, nature trails, laundry facility, Jacuzzi, two tennis courts, platform tennis (night-lit in winter), cross-country skiing, and conference rooms.

## LUDLOW & OKEMO

Centered around a former mill that produced fabrics and, later, aircraft parts, Ludlow has an unpretentious made-in-mill-town-Vermont character that seems quite distant from the prim grace of white-clapboard Grafton. Low-key and unassuming, it draws skiers by the busload in winter (it's especially popular with travelers from the N.Y. area); in summer, it's a good place to slouch down in a comfortable chair and watch the clouds float over the mountaintops.

Ludlow is home to Okemo Mountain, a once-sleepy ski resort that's come to life in recent years. Ludlow is also notable as one of the few ski towns that didn't go through an unfortunate Tyrolean identity crisis, as did many winter resorts in New England.

## ESSENTIALS

**GETTING THERE**   Ludlow is situated at the intersection of Routes 193 and 100. The most direct route from an interstate is Exit 6 off I-91; follow Route 103 west to Ludlow. **Vermont Transit** (☎ **800/451-3292**) bus lines offers service to Ludlow.

**VISITOR INFORMATION**   The **Ludlow Area Chamber of Commerce,** P.O. Box 333, Ludlow, VT 05149 (☎ **802/228-5830**), staffs a helpful information booth at the Okemo Marketplace, at the foot of Mountain Road. It's generally open 10am to 4pm daily except Monday, with some seasonal variations. Information can be found online from **www.vacationinvermont.com**, or by e-mailing heartovt@tds.net.

## EXPLORING THE AREA

The intriguing history of Ludlow and the surrounding region is the subject of the **Black River Academy Museum** (☎ **802/228-5050**), located on High Street near the village green. Open during summer and early fall, the museum includes an exhibit on Pres. Calvin Coolidge, who graduated from the Academy in 1892. Other exhibits explore the role of industry and farming in the Black River Valley and offer a look at life in a Finnish community. It's open Memorial Day to Columbus Day, Tuesday to Saturday, 1 to 4pm. Free admission.

## SKIING

**Okemo.** Ludlow, VT 05149. ☎ **800/786-5366** for lodging or 802/228-4041. www.okemo.com. E-mail: info@okemo.com. Vertical drop: 2,150 ft. Lifts: 10 chairlifts (3 high-speed), 3 surface lifts. Skiable acreage: 500. Lift tickets: $54 weekend, $49 weekday.

Okemo fans like to point out a couple of things. First, this is one of the few family-owned mountains remaining in Vermont (it's been owned by Tim and Diane Mueller since 1982). Second, it now features a more varied and challenging terrain. It's also put considerable effort into making it more welcoming and challenging for young snow-boarders. Fans also point out that Okemo doesn't attract as many yahoos as does Killington to the north. As such, it's first and foremost a mountain for families, who not only like the welcoming terrain but also the friendly base area built on a scale that isn't too intimidating for kids. Well-maintained halfpipes with music are popular with younger snowboarders. Okemo has plans to expand its slopes on to adjacent Jackson Gore Peak in the next couple of years, a move that will also include a new base development. Dining on the mountain has taken a significant turn for the better following its 1999 affiliation with the New England Culinary Institute, which now manages Gables Restaurant. Families should note that the mountain offers three levels of ticket prices, with discounts for young adults (ages 13 to 18) and juniors (7 to 12). Children 6 and under ski free.

## A ROAD TRIP TO BELLOWS FALLS

A trip southeast through the ravine of Proctorsville Gulf to the riverside village of Bellows Falls is a recommended activity for an idle day, or to schedule into your travel in or out of the Ludlow area.

Bellows Falls has a rough-edged industrial charm. Set in a deep valley at the edge of the Connecticut River, Bellows Falls went through several booms, each time riding the wave of a new technology. America's first canal was constructed here in 1802, offering a way for boats carrying freight to bypass the tumultuous falls, which are still dramatic during spring runoff. After the train eclipsed the canal, Bellows Falls was the junction of three train lines in the 19th century, which provided another infusion of cash. Advances in paper, farm machinery manufacturing, and hydroelectric power also led to a rise in the town's economic fortunes.

Today, Bellows Falls isn't riding much of any economic wave but offers a glimpse of these earlier times through the varied architecture around town. The compact downtown is Victorian brick and is overlorded by town hall's crenelated clock tower, which, on a foggy day, looks as if it could rise above a square in Venice. Handsome commercial architecture attests to an earlier affluence. Note especially the handsome Romanesque brick post office, which is near the site of the early canal.

An uncommonly well-written brochure guides visitors on a walking tour of Bellows Falls, offering a quick tour of the centuries from the remains of the early canal to examples of Craftsman-style homes dating from the 1920s.

The brochure is available at the **Great Falls Regional Chamber of Commerce,** 55 Village Sq., Bellows Falls, VT 05101 (☎ 802/463-4280). Be sure also to stop by the visitor's center at the hydroelectric dam for a tour of the clever fish ladder with its canal-like locks. This allowed the reintroduction of salmon to the upper Connecticut River when it opened in 1982.

Before leaving town, swing by the classic **Miss Bellows Falls Diner** (☎ 802/ 463-9800), at the north edge of downtown. This 1920s diner has been a Bellows Falls fixture since 1942, when it was towed here from Massachusetts. Today, it features the original marble countertop along with the good home cooking. As of early 2000, the diner was for sale. The owners attempted to sell it on eBay in 1999, but no one came forward with the $135,000 minimum bid.

## WHERE TO STAY

During ski season, contact the **Okemo Mountain Lodging Service** (☎ 800/786-5366 or 802/228-5571) for reservations in slopeside condos. More information is also available at www.okemo.com.

**The Governor's Inn.** 86 Main St., Ludlow, VT 05149. ☎ 800/468-3766 or 802/228-8830. Fax 802/228-2961. www.thegovernorsinn.com. E-mail: kubec@thegovernorsinn.com. 8 units. $95–$170 double; $230 suite. Add $25 during peak periods. Rates include full breakfast. MC, V.

This regal village home was built in 1890 by Vermont governor William W. Stickney (hence the name) and is the very picture of Victorian elegance. The downstairs lobby and common room (both with gas fireplaces) are richly hued with time-worn hardwood. The rooms vary in size (some are quite small), but all are comfortably appointed with antiques. Three new gas fireplaces were added to rooms in 1999 by new innkeepers Cathy and Jim Kubec.

**Dining:** Chef-innkeeper Cathy Kubec was trained in classic French cooking, which she enlivens with New Orleans elements. (Visitors to the inn when run by chef-owner Deedy Marble with also recognize some of the traditional New England recipes.) Dinner in the cozy Victorian dining rooms is by reservation only, served Thursday to Sunday; the fixed-price dinner $50, with a discount for inn guests.

**The Inn at Water's Edge.** 45 Kingdom Rd, Ludlow, VT 05149. ☎ 888/706/9736 or 802/228-8143. Fax 802/228-8443. www.innatwatersedge.com. 11 units (includes 2 suites). A/C. $175–$250 double, including breakfast and dinner. AE, MC, V. Children over age 12 are welcome.

Located a 10-minute drive north of Okemo Mountain, this newly opened (1999) inn occupies a 150-year-old house on the banks of the Black River, just off Route 100. It's been thoroughly renovated and updated in a floral Victorian style, and innkeepers Tina and Bruce Verdrager have focused on making this a destination for romantic get-aways. The attached barn features a lounge and bar perfect for relaxing, with an oak pool table, chess set, leather couches, TV, and a great mahogany bar imported from England. The guest rooms in the barn over the bar tend toward the cozy and dark (even the two-room suite). Room #11 upstairs in the main house would be my choice—bright and appealingly furnished, with corner windows, maple bed, and wood floors.

**Dining:** The first-floor dining room serves four-course meals nightly, usually with a choice of two entrees, along the lines of broiled fish or rack of lamb. Dinner is available to outside guests for $25 complete; reservations requested.

## WHERE TO DINE

See also The Governor's Inn, above.

**Archie's Prime Time Steak House.** 57 Pond Rd. (Rte. 103, across from Okemo access road), Ludlow. ☎ **802/228-3003.** Main courses $10–$23. AE, MC, V. Sun 4:30–9pm, Mon–Thurs 4:30–10pm, Fri–Sat 4:30–11pm. PUB/STEAKHOUSE.

Archie's is located in a modest strip mall at the base of the ski mountain's access road, and features a dining room and an adjacent bar with five TVs (almost always tuned to sports). It's casual and comfortable, and the steaks are better than you might expect—succulent, tender, and generously cut. (The kitchen is also willing to cook them very rare, legal liability be damned.) Prime rib, filet mignon, strip and top sirloin can be ordered variously sized; there's also pork chops, chicken teriyaki, and salmon encrusted with horseradish. Pub fare includes burgers and chicken wings. The salad bar is pale and tired, but at least it's cheap when ordered with a meal.

**Harry's Café.** Rte. 103 (5 miles north of Ludlow), Mount Holly. ☎ **802/259-2996.** Reservations recommended on weekends. Main courses $10.95–$16.95. AE, MC, V. Wed–Sun 5–10pm. ECLECTIC.

Along a dark stretch of road north of Ludlow, you'll pass a brightly lit roadside cafe with a red neon "Harry's" over the door. At 50 m.p.h., it looks like a hamburger joint, It's not. It's an appealing family restaurant with a menu that spans the globe. Entrees are a veritable culinary United Nations, with New York sirloin, jerk pork, flautas, spicy Thai curry, fish-and-chips, and chicken breast stuffed with ricotta cheese, basil, and sun-dried tomatoes. ("An oasis for the passionate appetite" is their slogan.) Thai fare is the house specialty and your best bet. On the downside, the interior is more blandly efficient than cozy, and the service can bog down on busy nights.

**Nikki's.** Rte. 103, Ludlow. ☎ **802/228-7797.** www.nikkisrestaurant.com. Reservations not accepted. Main courses $12.95–$28.95 (most under $20). AE, DC, MC, V. Daily, spring and summer 5:30–9:30pm, fall and winter 5–9pm (until 10pm weekends). REGIONAL.

Nikki's is the best choice in town for a nice dinner out. It's a popular and friendly local spot that's been serving up great meals since 1976 and is divided between an older section with a crackling fireplace and a new addition that's bright and sleekly modern. Think of the fare as updated comfort food, with familiar favorites like grilled salmon and Black Angus steak, along with more adventurous dishes like sesame-crusted red snapper with wasabi, or pork tenderloin with an apple cider demi-glace. The wine selection is several notches above the usual ski-resort fare (*Wine Spectator* Award of Excellence winner) and well-priced.

## 4  Woodstock & Environs

Woodstock is 16 miles west of White River Junction, 140 miles northwest of Boston, and 98 miles southeast of Burlington.

For more than a century, the resort community of Woodstock has been considered one of New England's most exquisite villages, and its attractiveness has benefitted from the largess of some of the country's affluent citizens. Even the surrounding countryside is by and large unsullied—you simply can't drive to Woodstock on a route that *isn't* pastoral and scenic, putting one in mind of an earlier, more peaceful era. Few other New England villages can top Woodstock for sheer grace and elegance. The tidy downtown is compact and neat, populated largely by galleries and boutiques. The superb village green is surrounded by handsome homes, creating what amounts to a comprehensive review of architectural styles of the 19th and early 20th centuries.

In addition to Woodstock, there's White River Junction and Norwich, two towns of distinctly different lineage located along the Connecticut River on the New Hampshire border.

## WOODSTOCK

Much of the town of ✪ **Woodstock** is on the National Register of Historic Places and 500 acres surrounding Mt. Tom (see below) have been deeded to the National Park Service by the Rockefeller family. In fact, locals sometimes joke that downtown Woodstock could be renamed Rockefeller National Park, given the attention and cash the Rockefeller family have lavished upon the town in the interest of preservation. (For starters, Rockefeller money built the faux-historic Woodstock Inn and paid to bury the unsightly utility lines around town.)

Woodstock, which sits on the banks of the gentle Ottauquechee River, was first settled in 1765, rose to some prominence as a publishing center in the mid-19th century (no fewer than five newspapers were published here in 1830), and began to attract wealthy families who summered here in the late 19th century. To this day, Woodstock feels as if it should have a prestigious prep school just off the Green, and it comes as some surprise that it doesn't. A Vermont senator in the late 19th century noted that "the good people of Woodstock have less incentive than others to yearn for heaven," and that still holds today.

Wealthy summer rusticators were instrumental in establishing and preserving the character of the village, and today the very wealthy have turned their attention to the handsome farms outside of town. Few of these former dairy farms still produce milk; barns that haven't been converted to architectural showcase homes more than likely house valuable collections of cars or antiques.

Woodstock is also notable as an historic center of winter outdoor recreation. The nation's first ski tow (a rope tow powered by an old Buick motor) was built in 1933 at the Woodstock Ski Hill near today's Suicide Six ski area. While no longer the skiing center of Vermont, Woodstock remains a worthy destination during the winter months for skating, cross-country skiing, and snowshoeing.

One caveat: Woodstock's excellent state of preservation hasn't gone unnoticed, and it draws hordes of travelers. During the peak foliage season, the town green is perpetually obscured by tour buses slowly circling around it.

### ESSENTIALS

**GETTING THERE**  Woodstock is 13 miles west of White River Junction on Route 4 (take Exit 1 off I-89). From the west, Woodstock is 20 miles east of Killington on

Route 4. Vermont Transit (☎ 800/451-3292) offers daily bus service to Woodstock, with connections to Boston and Burlington.

**VISITOR INFORMATION**    The **Woodstock Area Chamber of Commerce,** 18 Central St., Woodstock, VT 05091 (☎ **888/496-6378** or 802/457-3555), staffs an information booth daily from 9:30am to 5:30pm on the green from June through October. On the Web: **www.woodstockvt.com.**

## EXPLORING THE TOWN

The heart of the town is the shady, elliptical Woodstock Green. The noted Admiral George Dewey spent his later years in Woodstock, and locals may tell you that the Green was laid out in the shape of Dewey's flagship. This is such a fine and believable explanation for the odd, cigar-shaped green that it causes me a small amount of distress to note that the Green was in place by 1830, 7 years before Dewey was born.

To put local history in perspective, stop by the **Woodstock Historical Society,** 26 Elm St. (☎ **802/457-1822**). Housed in the 1807 Charles Dana House, this beautiful home has rooms furnished in Federal, Empire, and Victorian styles, and offers displays of dolls, costumes, and examples of early silver and glass. The Dana House and adjoining buildings, featuring more exhibits, are open from late May through October, plus weekends in December. Hours are 10am to 5pm Monday to Saturday and Sunday from noon to 4pm. Admission is $1.

**Billings Farm and Museum.** Elm St. (about ¹/₂ mile north of town on Rte. 12). ☎ **802/ 457-2355.** www.billingsfarm.org. $8 adult, $7 senior, $6 children 13–17, $4 children 5–12, $1 children 3–4, free for children under 3. Daily May through October 10am–5pm.

You needn't be a farm or history buff to enjoy a trip to the nearby Billings Farm and Museum, a working farm worth visiting for a glimpse of life in a grander era as well as an introduction to the history of scientific farming techniques. This extraordinary spot, now operated by a non-profit foundation, was the creation of Frederick Billings, who is credited with completing the Northern Pacific Railroad. (Billings, Montana, is named after him.) This 19th-century state-of-the-art dairy farm was once renowned for its scientific breeding of Jersey cows and its fine architecture, especially the gabled 1890 Victorian farmhouse. A tour of the farm includes hands-on demonstrations of farm activities, exhibits of farm life, a look at an heirloom kitchen garden, and a visit to active milking barns.

**Marsh-Billings-Rockefeller National Historic Park.** P.O. Box 178, Woodstock, VT 05091. ☎ **802/457-3368.** www.nps.gov/mabi. Free admission to grounds; mansion tour $6 adult, $3 for 16 and under. Daily late May–October 10am–5pm.

The Billings Farm and the National Park Service have teamed up to manage the new Marsh-Billings-Rockefeller National Historic Park. This is the first and only national park that focuses on the history of conservation. You'll learn about the life of George Perkins Marsh, the author of *Man and Nature* (1864), which is considered one of the first and most influential books in the history of the environmental movement. You'll also learn how Woodstock native and rail tycoon Frederick Billings, who read *Man and Nature,* eventually returned and purchased Marsh's boyhood farm, putting into practice many of the principles of good stewardship that Marsh espoused. The property was subsequently purchased by Mary and Laurance Rockefeller, who in 1982 established the non-profit farm; a decade later they donated more than 500 acres of forest land and their mansion, filled with exceptional 19th-century landscape art, to the National Park Service. Visitors can tour the elaborate Victorian mansion, walk the graceful carriage roads surrounding Mount Tom, and view one of the oldest

# Central Vermont & the Champlain Valley

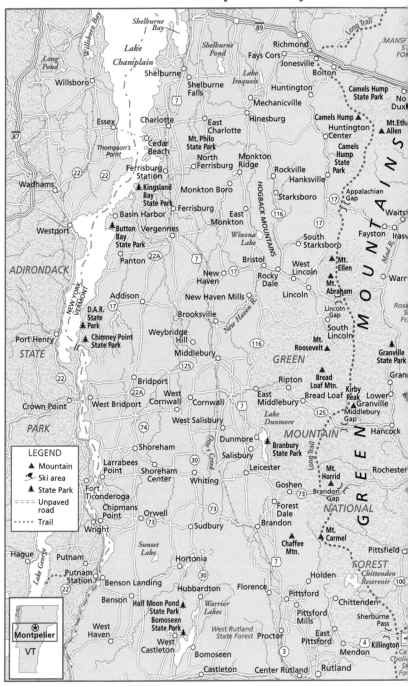

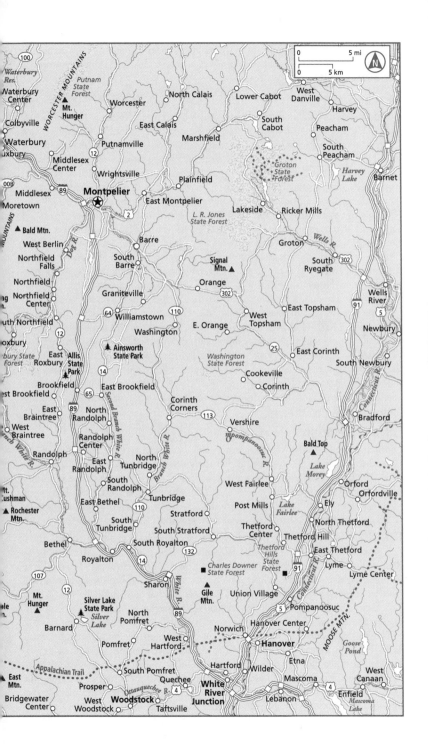

professionally managed woodlands in the nation. Tours of the mansion can accommodate only a limited number of people; advance reservations are highly recommended (☎ 802/457-3368).

## NEARBY SIGHTS

Birders and other wildlife aficionados will enjoy a trip to the **Vermont Raptor Center** (☎ 802/457-2779). The center is home to 25 species of birds of prey that have been injured and can no longer survive in the wild. (About one-third of the birds come here after being hit by a car.) The winged residents change from time to time, but its denizens typically include bald eagles, great horned owls, peregrine falcons, saw-whet owls (cute!), and an array of hawks, like red-shouldered, rough-legged, and red-tailed. The birds are located in spacious cages along a horseshoe-shaped trail set on hillside. (Friendly tip: Start at the top and work down.) Serious birders might choose to spend some time afterwards at the institute's Pettingill Ornithological Library. Other attractions include an herbarium and nature trails in the Bragdon Nature Preserve. The institute is located 1 1/2 miles southwest of the village on Church Hill Road. (Look for the turn at the west end of the green.) From May through October it's open daily from 9am to 5pm; November through April open Monday to Saturday 10am to 4pm. Admission is $6 adult, $3 student 12 to 18, $2 children 5 to 11, under 5 free.

About 5 miles east of Woodstock is the riverside village of **Quechee.** The small village, with a handful of boutiques and restaurants, still revolves spiritually and economically around the restored brick mill building along the falls. **Simon Pearce Glass** (☎ 802/295-2711), which makes exceptionally fine glassware and pottery, occupies the former Downer's Mill, where it houses a glassmaking operation, retail store, and well-regarded restaurant (see "Where to Dine," below). Visitors can watch glassblowing take place weekdays and on summer weekends from a downstairs viewing gallery. It's open daily from 9am to 9pm.

## OUTDOOR PURSUITS

Outdoor activities in the Woodstock area aren't as rugged as those you'll find in the Green Mountains to the west, but they'll easily occupy travelers for an afternoon or two. One-stop shopping for low-key exploration is available at **Quechee Outdoor Adventures,** Rte. 4, Quechee Gorge Village (☎ 800/438-5565, ext. 114). The group offers canoe and kayak rentals (shuttles available), as well as guided hiking, fly-fishing, and boating trips. Visit their Web site at www.vtoutdooradventures.com.

**HIKING MOUNT TOM** Don't leave the village without climbing Mount Tom, the prominent hill that overlooks Woodstock. (It's part of the Marsh-Billings-Rockefeller National Historic Park; see above.) Start your ascent from Faulkner Park, named after Mrs. Edward Faulkner, who created the park and had the mountain trail built to encourage healthful exercise. (To reach the trailhead from the Woodstock Green, cross Middle Covered Bridge and continue straight on Mountain Avenue. The road bends left and soon arrives at the grassy park at the base of Mount Tom.)

The trail winds up the hill, employing one of the most lugubrious sets of switchbacks I've ever experienced. Designed after the once-popular "cardiac walks" in Europe, the trail appears to require you to walk miles only to gain a few feet in elevation, but persevere. This gentle trail eventually arrives at a clearing overlooking the town. A steeper, rockier, and more demanding trail continues 100 yards or so to the summit. At the top, a carriage path encircles the summit like a friar's fringe of hair, offering fine views of the town and the Green Mountains to the west. You can follow the carriage path down to Billings Farm or retrace your steps back to the park.

**HORSEBACK RIDING**   Experienced and aspiring equestrians should head to the **Kedron Valley Stables** (☎ 802/457-1480; www.kedron.com.), about 4¹/₂ miles south of Woodstock on Route 106. A full menu of riding options is available, ranging from a 1-hour beginner ride ($35, or $30 per person for parties of two or more) to a 5-night inn-to-inn excursion ($1,450 per person including all meals and lodging, double occupancy). Ask also about weekend riding programs. The stables rent horses to experienced riders for local trail rides, offer sleigh and carriage rides, and have an indoor riding ring for inclement weather. It's open every day except Thanksgiving and Christmas.

**BIKING**   The rolling hilly terrain around Woodstock is ideal for exploring by road bike for those in reasonably good shape. Mountain bikes are available for rent ($20 per day) in town from **Woodstock Sports,** 30 Central St. (☎ **802/457-1568**).

**QUECHEE GORGE**   Five miles east of town, Route 4 crosses Quechee Gorge, a venerable if somewhat overrated tourist attraction. The sheer power of the glacial runoff that carved the gorge some 13,000 years ago must have been dramatic, but the 165-foot gorge itself isn't all that impressive today. More impressive is its engineering history. This chasm was first spanned in 1875 by a wooden rail trestle, when 3,000 people gathered along the gorge to celebrate the achievement. The current steel bridge was constructed in 1911 for the railroad, but the tracks were torn up in 1933 and replaced by Route 4.

   The best view of the bridge is from the bottom of the gorge, which is accessible by a well-graded gravel path that descends south from the parking area on the gorge's east rim. The round-trip requires no more than a half hour. If the day is warm enough, you might also follow the path northward, then descend to the river to splash around in the rocky swimming hole near the spillway.

**SKIING**   The area's best cross-country skiing is at the **Woodstock Ski Touring Center** (☎ 800/448-7900 or 802/457-6674) at the Woodstock Country Club, just south of town on Route 106. The center maintains 36 miles of trails, including 12 miles of trails groomed for skate-skiing, and it's not all flat; the high and low points along the trail system vary by 750 feet in elevation. There's a lounge and restaurant at the ski center and a large health and fitness center accessible via ski trail. Lessons and picnic tours are available. The full-day trail fee is $12.50 for adults and $8.25 for children under 14.

   **Suicide Six ski area** (☎ 802/457-6661) has an intimidating name, but at just 650 vertical feet, it doesn't pose much of a threat to either life or limb. Owned and operated by the Woodstock Inn, this venerable family-oriented ski resort (it first opened in 1934) has two double chairs, a complimentary J-bar for beginners, and a modern base lodge. Beginners, intermediates, and families with young children will be content here. Weekend lift tickets are $40 for adults, $25 for seniors and children under 14; midweek it's $22 and $18, respectively. The ski area is located 2 miles north of Woodstock on Pomfret Road.

## WHERE TO STAY

✪ **Jackson House Inn.** 37 Old Rte. 4 W., Woodstock, VT 05091. ☎ **800/448-1890** or 802/457-2065. Fax 802/457-9290. www.jacksonhouse.com. E-mail: innkeepers@jacksonhouse.com. 15 units. A/C. $180–$340 double. Rates include full breakfast. 2-night minimum stay most weekends. AE, MC, V. No children under 14.

Antiques buffs will be at home in the Jackson House Inn, located just west of Woodstock en route to Killington. The furnishings in this yellow 1890 Victorian are perfectly chosen, from the Oriental rugs to the antique chests. The home was built by a lumber baron who hoarded the best wood for himself; the cherry-and-maple floors are so beautiful you'll feel guilty for not taking off your shoes. The guest rooms are equally well-appointed, although some of the older rooms are rather small. A well-conceived 1997 addition added four "one-room suites" with fireplaces and Jacuzzis. The inn welcomes guests with a series of nice surprises, including complimentary evening hors d'oeuvres and champagne, a small basement fitness room with steam room, and a 3-acre backyard with formal English gardens. This inn deserves the Frommer's star for its overall elegance and attentive service; only its location, a stone's throw off a busy stretch of Route 4, detracts from the graceful tranquillity the innkeepers have succeeded in creating.

**Dining:** There's superb dining—see "Where to Dine," below.

**Kedron Valley Inn.** Rte. 106, South Woodstock, VT 05071. ☎ **800/836-1193** or 802/457-1473. Fax 802/457-4469. E-mail: kedroninn@aol.com. 28 units. TV. $120–$230 double; foliage season and Christmas week $150–$260 double. Rates include full breakfast. Discounts available spring and midweek. AE, DISC, MC, V. Closed Apr and briefly prior to Thanksgiving. Pets permitted with advance approval.

Located in a complex of Greek Revival buildings at a country crossroads about 5 miles south of Woodstock, the inn is run by Max and Merrily Comins, a cordial couple who offer their guests a mix of history and country style. The attractive guest rooms in three buildings are furnished with both antiques and reproductions, and all have heirloom quilts from Merrily's collection; 15 feature wood-burning fireplaces, and two have double Jacuzzis. The rooms in the newer, motel-like log building by the river are equally well-furnished, with canopied beds, custom oak woodwork, and fireplaces (and they're less expensive). Room 37 even has a private streamside terrace. Among the most popular rooms: #12 and #17; both are suites with fireplaces and double jacuzzis. Some Frommer's readers have noted that the inn's rooms can be on the cool side in deep winter, and that the inn's service is not as crisp and attentive as it once was.

**Dining:** The menu is contemporary American cooking built on a classical French foundation. You might start with fresh tomatoes and chèvre, or shrimp cocktail with anchos and lime. Then it's on to sea scallops with a shiitake and sherry sauce, or sautéed chicken with asparagus and tomato. There are also vegetarian courses and a lighter tavern menu. The main entrees are priced from $18.50 to $26.

**Amenities:** Baby-sitting (extra charge), safe, private swimming pond with two beaches, and health club nearby ($10 extra).

**Shire Motel.** 46 Pleasant St., Woodstock, VT 05091. ☎ **802/457-2211.** www.shiremotel. com. 36 units (includes 3 suites). A/C TV TEL. $145–$165 double holidays and foliage, $68–$125 summer, $48–$95 off-season; suites $200–$300. Rates include continental breakfast. AE, MC, V.

The convenient Shire Motel is located within walking distance of The Green and the rest of Woodstock Village, and with its attractive Colonial decor is much better appointed than your average motel. The rooms are bright and have more windows than you might expect, with most facing the river that runs behind the property. (The downside: thin sheets and some scuffed walls.) At the end of the second-floor porch is an outdoor kitchen where you can get a cup of coffee in the morning and sit on rockers overlooking the river. The yellow-clapboard house next door was recently made into three spacious and modern suites (one or two bedrooms), and all with gas fireplaces and Jacuzzis.

**Three Church St.** 3 Church St., Woodstock, VT 05091. ☎ **802/457-1925.** Fax 802/457-9181. E-mail: threechrch@aol.com. 11 units, including 5 that share 2 bathrooms. $80–$115 double. Rates include full breakfast. Rates $10 higher during foliage season and Christmas week. MC, V. Closed Apr. Pets allowed.

This sturdy brick Greek Revival B&B with a white-clapboard ell is located just off the west end of the Woodstock Green, and is well-situated for launching an exploration of the village. It offers excellent value, especially if you don't mind sharing a bathroom and can overlook small imperfections like the occasional water stain seeping through on the ceiling. The inn's main foyer is stylish in a fusty, old-fashioned sort of way, with an elegant staircase sweeping upward to the second floor. There's a lovely porch in the back for breakfast or sitting quietly. Guest rooms are furnished eclectically and comfortably with country antiques. Room 3 (shared bath) is among the brightest and most pleasant of the bunch, very bright with painted floors and a fireplace (non-working). A stay here is more like visiting a relative than a fancy inn.

**Amenities:** The inn is situated on 3 acres that border on the river and has a tennis court and swimming pool.

✪ **Twin Farms.** Stage Rd., Barnard, VT 05031. ☎ **800/894-6327** or 802/234-9999. Fax 802/234-9990. www.twinfarms.com. 14 units and cottages. A/C MINIBAR TV TEL. $800–$950 double; $950–$1,500 cottage. Rates include all meals, liquor, and many amenities. AE, MC, V. Closed Apr. No children under 18.

Twin Farms offers uncommon luxury at an uncommon price. Housed on a 300-acre farm that was once home to Nobel Prize–winning novelist Sinclair Lewis and his wife, journalist Dorothy Thompson, Twin Farms has carved out an international reputation as a very private, exceptionally tasteful small resort. The clientele includes royalty and corporate chieftains looking for quiet and simplicity, and willing to pay for it. The compound consists of the main inn with four guest rooms, and ten outlying cottages. The inn is owned by the Twigg-Smith family, who are noted art collectors in Hawaii. Some of the work on display at the inn and in guest rooms includes originals by David Hockney, Roy Lichtenstein, Milton Avery, and William Wegman. Rates include everything, including open bar and use of all recreational equipment.

**Dining:** Meals are understatedly sumptuous affairs served at locations of your choosing—at your cottage, along a stream, or in one of the dining areas around the estate. Don't bother looking for a menu; the gourmet chefs serve what's fresh, and your meal is likely to include ingredients from the organic vegetable and herb gardens on the property. If you have any special requests, don't hesitate to make them.

**Amenities:** Lake swimming, bicycle and car rentals, game rooms, Jacuzzi, two tennis courts, nature trails, conference rooms, fitness center, canoes, fishing pond, croquet, concierge, limited room service, newspaper delivery, in-room massage, stocked minibar, hair dryers, irons and ironing boards, twice-daily maid service, valet parking, free shuttle to rail or plane, and guest safe.

✪ **Woodstock Inn & Resort.** 14 The Green, Woodstock, VT 05091. ☎ **800/448-7900** or 802/457-1100. Fax 802/457-6699. www.woodstockinn.com. E-mail: email@woodstockinn. com. 141 units, 3 townhouses. A/C TV TEL. $165–$325 double; $425–$535 suite. Ask about packages and off-season rates. AE, MC, V.

The Woodstock Inn, an imposing brick structure set behind a garden off the Woodstock Green, appears a venerable and long-established institution at first glance, but it's not—at least not *this* building; it wasn't built until 1969. Happily, the inn shunned the unfortunate trends in 1960s architecture for the more dignified look suitable for Woodstock. Everyone's the better for it. Inside, guests are greeted by a broad stone fireplace, and sitting areas are tucked throughout the lobby in the manner of a 1940s-era resort. Guest rooms are tastefully decorated in either country pine or a Shaker-inspired style. The best rooms are in the new wing (built 1991) and feature lush carpeting, refrigerators, fireplaces, and built-in bookshelves. All but a few rooms were renovated between 1997 and early 2000.

**Dining:** The dining room is classy and semiformal, with continental and American dishes served on elegant green-bordered custom china. Entrees are in the $19-to-$29 price range. The more casual Eagle Cafe is open for three meals, with dinner priced from $9 to $18.

**Amenities:** Robert Trent Jones–designed golf course (at the inn-owned Woodstock Country Club), two swimming pools (indoor and outdoor), nature trails, putting greens, shuttle to fitness center with tennis, squash, racquetball, and steam rooms. Also: bike rentals, dry cleaning, laundry service, baby-sitting, in-room safes, irons and ironing boards, valet parking, concierge, and room service (7am to 9pm). In winter, the resort grooms 36 miles of cross-country ski trails.

## WHERE TO DINE

Right in the village center is **Pane Salute,** 61 Central St. (☎ **802/457-4882**), a bakery that specializes in delectable Italian breads. It's worth a stop to pick up a loaf for snacking or to enjoy with a rustic mustard and cheese on a picnic atop Mt. Tom.

**Bentley's.** 3 Elm St. ☎ **802/457-3232.** www.bentleysrestaurant.com. Reservations recommended for parties of 4 or more. Lunch items $6.95–$9.95; main dinner courses $15.95–$19.50. AE, CB, DC, DISC, MC, V. Mon–Thurs 11am–9:30pm, Fri–Sat 11am–10pm, Sun 11am–9:30pm. Open later for drinks and dancing on weekends. AMERICAN.

Bentley' adopts an affluent English gentleman's club feel and offers Woodstock's best choice for lunch. The dining room, located beyond an Anglophilic bar, affects a Victorian elegance, but not ostentatiously so. Lunch is the time for one of their juicy burgers or creative sandwiches (grilled chicken in mango sauce with almonds, anyone?). The dinner menu leans more toward resort standards like chicken and shrimp pescatore or steak flambéed with Jack Daniels, but also cracks its doors to slightly more ambitious fare, like maple mustard chicken with pecans. There's a fine brunch on Sunday; put your doctor out of mind and order the New England corned beef hash with poached eggs and hollandaise sauce. Stick around late enough on weekend evenings and witness a transformation: the tables get swept off a dance floor, the ceiling rolls back to reveal high-tech lighting, and Bentley's becomes the place to dance the night away.

✪ **Jackson House Inn.** 37 Old Rte. 4 W. ☎ **800/448-1890** or 802/457-2065. Reservations highly recommended. Three course fixed-price $49 (chef's tasting menu $58). AE, MC, V. Thurs–Mon 6–9pm. CONTINENTAL.

The Jackson House dining room is a modern addition to the original, classic country inn (see "Where to Stay," above). Its centerpiece is a 16-foot-high stone fireplace, and it boasts soaring windows offering views to the gardens in back. Gentlemen might feel most comfortable in a sports coat, although it's not required. Once settled, you'll sample some of the most exquisite meals in New England, ingeniously conceived, deftly prepared and artfully arranged. (The service is top-notch, as well.) The three course meals begin with offerings like Maine crabmeat and field green salad with shaved fennel, or a red-wine and port poached foie gras, served with French lentils and roasted parsley root. The main courses do an equally good job combining the earthy with the celestial. Expect dishes like crispy-skin salmon with a shiitake compote, or an Angus fillet with creamy white corn polenta and a three onion marmalade. May I interest you in dessert? (Hint: Say "yes!") The banana-walnut souflee is surprisingly delicate, and the crème brûlée with a cranberry compote is striking. Expect a meal that lingers in your memory.

**The Prince and the Pauper.** 24 Elm St. ☎ **802/457-1818.** Reservations recommended. 3-course dinner $36. AE, DISC, MC, V. Sun 11am–1:30pm; Sun–Thurs 6–9pm; Fri–Sat 6–9:30pm. Lounge opens at 5pm. NEW AMERICAN/CONTINENTAL.

It takes a bit of sleuthing to find the Prince and the Pauper, located down Dana Alley (next to the Woodstock Historical Society's Dana House), but it's worth the effort. This is one of Woodstock's most inviting restaurants, with an intimate but informal setting. Ease into the evening with a libation in the taproom (it's open an hour before the restaurant), then move over to the rustic-but-elegant dining room. The menu changes daily, but you might start with an appetizer of smoked salmon or ravioli with roasted artichoke, then move on to filet mignon with a Jack Daniels sauce, or yellow-fin tuna with a thyme-flavored beurre rouge. The fixed-price dinner menu offers good value (although desserts are extra at $4 to $5.50); those on a tighter budget should linger in the lounge and order from the bistro menu ($12 to $16), with selections like barbecue pork, Maryland crab cakes, and Indonesian curried lamb. There's also a selection of tasty pizzas.

**Simon Pearce Restaurant.** The Mill, Quechee. ☎ **802/295-1470.** Reservations recommended for dinner. Lunch items $8.50–$11.50; dinner main courses $18–$25. AE, CB, DC, DISC, MC, V. Daily 11:30am–2:45pm and 6–9pm. AMERICAN/CONTINENTAL.

The setting can't be beat. Housed in a restored 19th-century woolen mill with wonderful views of a waterfall (it's spotlit at night), Simon Pearce is a collage of exposed brick, buttery-yellow pine floorboards, and handsome wooden tables and chairs. Meals are served on Simon Pearce pottery and glassware—if you like your setting, you can buy it afterwards at the sprawling retail shop in the mill. The restaurant atmosphere is a wonderful concoction of formal and informal, ensuring that everybody feels comfortable here whether in white shirt and tie or (neatly laundered) jeans. Lunches feature dishes like crispy calamari with field greens and crab and cod cakes with a red pepper coulis. At dinner, look for dishes like crispy roast duck with mango chutney, or salmon baked in phyllo with roast shiitakes and spinach.

**Wild Grass.** Rte. 4 (east of the village), Woodstock. ☎ **802/457-1917.** Reservations recommended during peak season. Main courses $14.25–$19.25. DISC, MC, V. Tues–Sat 6–9pm; occasionally open Sunday. ECLECTIC.

Wild Grass is located east of town on Route 4 in a small business complex that includes a cyber-auction hall. While it lacks the quaintness of much of the rest of Woodstock, the food rises above the prosaic surroundings with a menu that contains genuinely creative offerings. Especially appealing are the unique crispy sage leaves with tangy dipping sauces, served as as an appetizer. Fish is grilled to perfection here, and sauces are pleasantly zesty and piquant. Other entrees include roast duckling with a shallot port sauce, Caribbean pork with a black-bean corn salsa, and for vegetarians, marinated tempeh served with fried vegetables and a spicy peanut sauce.

## WHITE RIVER JUNCTION & NORWICH

White River Junction is a Vermont rarity: an industrial-era town that was built on the fruits of industry rather than wrenched from the earth on hardscrabble farmlands or in deep quarries. Industry, in this case, was the railroad. In 1847, White River Junction had only one farmhouse. Within 15 years, five different rail lines had established terminals here, and the town was bustling, noisy, and full of grit. Rail has suffered a well-documented decline since that golden era, and White River Junction has slipped from prominence along with the mighty steam trains and the lonesome whistle, but it retains a shopworn grace.

To the north, Norwich is a peaceful New England town slightly off the beaten track. The town has a fine selection of woodframe and brick homes, and boasts a superb restaurant and an excellent science museum for kids. First settled in 1761, Norwich has long-established ties with Hanover across the river. Many Dartmouth faculty and staff commute from Norwich, and the two towns even share a school district.

## ESSENTIALS

**GETTING THERE**   White River Junction is easily reached via either I-89 or I-91, which converge just south of town. Norwich may be reached from Exit 13 on I-91, or by driving north from White River Junction on Route 5. White River Junction is also served by daily **Amtrak** service (☎ **800/872-7245**) originating in Washington, D.C.

**VISITOR INFORMATION**   The **Upper Valley Chamber of Commerce,** P.O. Box 697, White River Junction, VT 05001 (☎ **802/295-6200**), staffs a seasonal information booth near the railroad station in downtown White River Junction. (The exact address was being ironed out at press time.) It's open 9:30am to 4:30pm daily during the peak season (summer and foliage season). For more information, call or visit the chamber's Web site at www.uppervalleyvt.com.

## EXPLORING THE REGION

White River Junction's compact old downtown is clustered near the river and a confusion of old train tracks. Downtown was never particularly cheerful or quaint—the bustle of the railyards always overpowered it—but today it manages to retain a rugged, historic character in the face of strip-mall sprawl that keeps expanding on the ridge above town. With an exception or two, downtown rolls up the sidewalk at dusk. It's easy to get a glimpse of the town's sooty history with a brief excursion by foot or car. A monument of sorts to its rail heritage may be found near the Amtrak station (built in 1911), where an 1892 Boston & Maine locomotive, along with a caboose, are on display.

A few miles south of White River Junction in the historic town of Windsor is the **American Precision Museum,** 196 Main St. (☎ **802/674-5781**), a narrowly focused but broadly informative museum. The collections in part commemorate Windsor's role as the birthplace of the state's machine tool industry, and as home to countless inventors and inventions. The museum features quite a bit of large, dark, and heavy machinery, and really looks closely at the technology behind the industrial revolution. The placards inside are tinged with a nicely archaic boosterism: "Precision makes mass production possible," reads one. "Machine tools: the foundation of man's development," reads another. The museum is located in the 1846 Robbins, Lawrence and Kendall armory, itself an historic site.

Ashael Hubbard put Windsor on the map in the early 19th century, when he moved here from Connecticut and invented the hydraulic pump. Other inventions followed, not only from Hubbard, but from his relatives and other inspired Windsor residents. These include the coffee percolator, the underhammer rifle, the lubricating bullet, and an early variant of the sewing machine. The museum covers this unique history with varied displays. It's open Memorial Day through October daily 10am to 5pm. Admission is $5 for adults, and $3 for seniors, $2 students. Children under 6 are free.

North of Winsdor on Route 5 is the Windsor Industrial Park, which is more interesting than it sounds. The focus here is on local crafts, and it's the home of some of the Simon Pearce manufacturing (pottery and glass), and the **Catamount Brewing Company** (☎ **802/674-6700**). The brewers here have attracted a broad regional audience for its amber ales, gold ales, porters, and specialties beers like bock, Octoberfest, and Christmas ale. A brewery tour provides a quick education in the making of a fine beer, and (more important) samples are offered at the conclusion. Tours are held daily July through October at 11am, 1pm, and 3pm (no 11am tour on Sundays). From November through June, tours are Saturdays only at 11am, 1pm, and 3pm. Tours are free and include a sampling.

Note also that Windsor is just a short hop across the Connecticut River from the lovely Saint-Gaudens Historical Site (see chapter 6).

## Fun for Kids

✪ **Montshire Museum of Science.** Montshire Rd., Norwich. ☎ **802/649-2200.** $5.50 adults, $4.50 children 3–17, under 3 free. MC, V. Daily 10am–5pm. Use Exit 13 off I-91 and head east; look for museum signs almost immediately.

This is not your average New England science museum of dusty stuffed animals in a creaky building in need of attention. Located on the border between New Hampshire and Vermont (hence the name), the Montshire is a modern, architecturally engaging, hands-on museum that draws kids back time and again. The Montshire took root in 1976, when area residents gathered up the leavings of Dartmouth's defunct natural history museum and put them on display in a former bowling alley in Hanover. The museum grew and prospered, largely owing to the dedication of hundreds of volunteers. In 1989, the museum moved to this beautiful 100-acre property sandwiched between I-91 and the Connecticut River.

Exhibits are housed in an open, soaring structure inspired by the region's barns. The museum contains some live animals (don't miss the leaf-cutter ant exhibit on the second floor), but it's mostly fun, interactive exhibits that involve kids deeply, teaching them the principles of math and science on the sly. Even preschoolers are entertained here at "Andy's Place," a play area with aquariums, bubble-making exhibits, and other magical things. Outside, there's a science park masquerading as a playground, and four nature trails that wend through this riverside property of tall trees and chirpy birds.

## WHERE TO STAY

Thanks to its location at the crossroads of two interstates, White River Junction has several chain hotels near the highways. The **Best Western at the Junction,** Rte. 5, Exit 11 off I-91 (☎ **802/295-3015**) features 112 rooms, an indoor and outdoor pool, and an exercise room. The **Comfort Inn,** 8 Sykes Ave., (☎ **802/295-3051**) offers 71 rooms, free continental breakfast, an outdoor pool, and a guest laundry room.

**Hotel Coolidge.** 17 N. Main St., White River Junction, VT 05001. ☎ **800/622-1124** or 802/295-3118. www.hotelcoolidge.com. E-mail: hotel.coolidge@valley.net. 53 units. A/C TV TEL. Weekdays $39–$59 double; weekends $49–$69 double. Rates $10 higher during foliage season. AE, DISC, MC, V.

This railroad-era downtown hotel (named after John Coolidge, the father of Calvin) is a stout, three-story brick structure that once bustled with jobbers, salesmen, and wholesalers during the heyday of rail travel. That era has passed, more or less leaving the hotel behind with it. The handsome lobby promises a low-key hospitality, with Doric columns, a brick fireplace, and reasonably modern furniture. The service is cheerful and helpful. Like the town itself, however, the guest rooms tend toward the threadbare and worn. The furnishings might have been au courant in the early 1970s, but are now a bit tired with age. If you're looking for fairly basic shelter, this is a great find for adventurous travelers on a budget. There's also a youth hostel section with rates of $18 per person per night.

**Dining:** The adjacent River City Cafe (accessible through the lobby) is under separate ownership and offers basic fare like burgers and sandwiches.

**Juniper Hill Inn.** Juniper Hill Rd. (RR#1, Box 79), Windsor, VT 05089. ☎ **800/359-2541** or 802/674-5273. www.juniperhillinn.com. E-mail: innkeeper@juniperhillinn.com. 16 units. $95–$175 double, including full breakfast. 2-night minimum during foliage, on holiday weekends, and in fireplace rooms on all weekends. DISC, MC, V. Closed first 3 weeks of April and first 2 weeks of Nov. Children 12 and older welcome.

The Juniper Hill Inn is about 12 miles south of White River Junction in Windsor, and it's one of the more inviting retreats in the state. Set high atop a hill overlooking the Connecticut River Valley, this monumental 1902 manor home is a true period piece—

guests half expect to run into Bertie Wooster lounging by the pool or playing croquet on the grounds. (The three resident Welsh corgis add to the English-country house atmosphere.) It's more mannered and elegant than many Vermont inns, taking its architectural inspiration from various Colonial Revivals. Palladian windows, a slate roof, and six chimneys grace the exterior; the richly appointed lobby features coffered paneling. The common rooms are spacious and lovely—especially the library with its leather wingback chairs—and are reason enough to stay here. The 16 guest rooms are each different, but all feature amenities like fresh flowers, hair dryers, and a decanter of sherry. Room 1 is a bright corner room with a four-poster bed and attractive bathroom; the smallest is Room 8, which is still cozy and appealing with its wood-burning fireplace. (Eleven rooms have either wood-burning or propane fireplaces.)

**Dining:** Four-course candlelit dinners are served at 7pm to guests by reservation ($32.50); 1-day advance notice is requested. The lovely dining room is quietly romantic with classical styling and magenta walls; the fare is regional, with dishes like rack of lamb and pork tenderloin.

**Norwich Inn.** Main St., Norwich, VT 05055. ☎ **802/649-1143.** www.norwichinn.com. 28 units (includes 2 2-bdrm apartments). A/C TV TEL. June–Oct $69–$149 double, off-season $55–$129. Rates include continental breakfast. AE, CB, DC, DISC, MC, V. Dogs allowed in motel only.

Innkeepers Sally and Tim Wilson bought the once-dowdy Norwich Inn about 10 years ago, and have steadily improved the place, most recently recreating the original tower (with suite) on the front of the building. Many guest rooms at this historic inn, parts of which date back to 1797, feature brass and canopy beds; history buffs should opt for the 16 comfortable rooms in the main inn rather than those in the motel-style annex out back, where the rooms are less expensive. The main building is alleged to host one uninvited guest: the ghost of Mary Walker, who local lore has it as atoning for the sin of selling bootleg liquor at the inn during Prohibition.

**Dining:** The dining room has a good reputation, with guests seated in either a handsome formal room or on the porch in summer. Keeping in the tradition of Mary Walker, in 1993 the inn opened Jasper Murdock's Alehouse, which is certainly among America's smallest breweries. Tim, the brewer, loves to talk beer. Pub fare is available, along with a selection of hand-crafted ales, porters, and stouts, in the tiny pub.

## WHERE TO DINE

**Karibu Tulé.** 1 S. Main St., White River Junction. ☎ **802/295-4250.** Main courses $10.25–$15.95. MC, V. Wed–Sun 5–9pm. AFRICAN.

This spacious, colorfully decorated storefront at a prime corner across from the Amtrak station is the handiwork of Damaris and Mel Hall. (Damaris is from Kenya.) Here you'll find bright colors and tangy spices you might not normally associate with quaint Vermont—to wit, chicken with a mint and yogurt sauce, Kenyan curried goat, and peanut chicken stew. Wednesday night features Ethiopian specialties.

✪ **La Poule à Dents.** Carpenter St. (off Main St. across from the Citgo station), Norwich. ☎ **802/649-2922.** www.lapoule.com. Reservations recommended. Main courses $18–$27. AE, CB, DC, DISC, MC, V. Daily 6–8:30pm. FRENCH.

La Poule à Dents, in the sleepy town of Norwich, wakes up visitors with some of Vermont's most elegant and exquisite dining. Housed in an historic 1820 home with a canopied terrace off one side, this fine restaurant has the feel of an elegant French auberge—quiet, dark, and intimate. It's a perfect spot for a romantic meal, or to celebrate a major occasion. The meals might best be described as sumptuous. Begin by selecting from the inviting array of appetizers, which range from a light lobster and saffron broth with a grilled sea scallop to a meaty charcuterie, with three homemade sausages served with fig bread. Pastas and risottos may be ordered either as appetizers of entrees (one tempting offering: lobster and goat cheese ravioli with a grilled arti-choke sauce). Entrees include potato-encrusted trout with ratatouille, peppered venison served with an herb spaetzle, and leg of lamb with a pistachio rosmary sausage.

**Polka Dot.** N. Main St. and Joe Reed Dr., White River Junction. ☎ **802/295-9722.** Breakfast and lunch $1.25–$4.25; dinner $4.75–$7.50. Daily Mon 5am–2pm, Tues–Sun 5am–7pm. Closed Thanksgiving and Christmas. DINER.

Classic diner fare is served up daily in this local institution, a relic of the days when a slew of White River Junction diners catered to railwaymen working the frequent freight and passenger trains. (Amtrak still makes a stop across the way.) The interior is painted a robin's egg blue, and the walls are hung with railroad photos and train models. You can sidle up to the counter and order a fried egg sandwich ($1.50), or grab one of the booths for a filling, decently prepared meal (think: liver and onions) that's not likely to cost much more than $5 or $6. If you're here for breakfast, be sure to try the delicious homemade doughnuts. Architecturally, it's not a classic brushed-steel diner, but the place has all the atmosphere of one.

## 5  Killington & Rutland

Killington is 12 miles east of Rutland, 160 miles northwest of Boston, and 93 miles southeast of Burlington.

In 1937, a travel writer described the town near Killington Peak as "a small village of a church and a few undistinguished houses built on a highway three corners." The area was rugged and remote, isolated from the commercial center of Rutland to the west by imposing mountains and accessible only through daunting Sherburne Pass.

That was before Vermont's second highest mountain was developed as the Northeast's largest ski area; and before a wide, 5-mile-long access road was slashed through the forest to the mountain's base; and before Route 4 was widened and improved, easing access to Rutland. In fact, that early travel writer would be hard-pressed to recognize the region today.

Killington is plainly not the Vermont pictured on calendars and placemats, but Killington boasts Vermont's most lively winter scene, with loads of distractions both on and off the mountain. The area has a frenetic, where-it's-happening feel in winter. (That's not the case in summer, when empty parking lots can trigger mild melancholia.) Those most content here are skiers who like their skiing BIG, singles in search of aggressive mingling, and travelers who want a wide selection of amenities and are willing to sacrifice the quintessential New England charm in exchange for a broader choice of diversions.

About a dozen miles to the west, the rough-hewn city of Rutland lacks the immediate charm of many other Vermont towns, but has a rich history and an array of convenient services for travelers. If you like the action of Killington but are looking for a lower-budget alternative, bivouacking in Rutland and traveling by day to the ski area is a popular option. There's even a ski bus from Rutland to the slopes.

### KILLINGTON

Killington lacks a town center, a single place that makes you feel that you've arrived. Killington is wherever you park. Since the mountain was first developed for skiing in 1957, dozens of restaurants, hotels, and convenience stores have sprouted along Killington Road to accommodate the legions of skiers who descend upon the area during the long skiing season, which typically runs October to May, and sometimes into June.

Killington's current owner—the American Skiing Co.—has heard the complaints about the lack of the village feel, and is setting out to make some changes. The resort hired the same group of architects who conceived the village at British Columbia's Whistler-Blackcomb to come up with a design that would be pedestrian-friendly, and give the resort more of a focal point. Among the plans: an amphitheater and a mix of lodges and restaurants to appeal to folks of various means. The construction is targeted to begin in spring 2001, and it's anticipated that the new village center will be built in phases over the next 2 decades. It's located on the hill between Killington Base Lodge and Ram's Head.

Until the new village comes to life, Killington *is* the access road. It's brightly lit and highly developed, and there's not much to remind visitors of classic Vermont between Route 4 and the base lodge. Suburban-style theme restaurants dot the route (The Grist Mill has a waterwheel; Casey's Caboose has a red caboose), along with dozens of hotels and condos ranging from high-end fancy to low-end dowdy. If you're in search of classic New England, consider staying in quaint Woodstock (see above) and commuting the 20 miles to the slopes.

## ESSENTIALS

**GETTING THERE**   Killington Road extends southward from Routes 4 and 100 (marked on some maps as Sherburne). It's about 12 miles east of Rutland on Route 4. Many of the inns offer shuttles to the Rutland airport. **Amtrak** (☎ **800/USA-RAIL**) offers service from New York to Rutland, with connecting shuttles to the mountain and various resorts.

The **Marble Valley Regional Transit District** (☎ **802/773-3244**) operates the **Skibus,** offering service between Rutland and Killington ($1), as well as up and down the access road (free during the day, $1 evenings).

**VISITOR INFORMATION**   The **Killington & Pico Areas Association,** P.O. Box 114, Killington, VT 05751 (☎ **802/773-4181**), supplies lodging and travel-package information. The association also staffs an information booth on Route 4 at the base of the access road; it's open Monday to Friday 9am to 5pm, and weekends 10am to 2pm. For information about accommodations in the area and travel to Killington, contact the **Killington Lodging and Travel Service** (☎ **800/621-6867**).

## DOWNHILL SKIING

**Killington.** Killington, VT 05751. ☎ **800/621-6867** for lodging or 802/422-3261. Vertical drop: 3,150 ft. Lifts: 2 gondolas, 30 chairlifts (6 high-speed), 2 surface lifts. Skiable acreage: 1,200. Lift tickets: $56.

Killington is by far New England's largest and most bustling ski area, and offers more vertical drop than any other New England mountain. It's the skier's equivalent of the Mall of America: huge and run with a certain efficiency but not offering much of a personal touch. That said, Killington has a broad selection of slopes, with trails ranging from long, old-fashioned narrow runs with almost no discernible downhill angle, to killer bumps high on its flanks. Thanks to this diversity, it has long been the destination of choice for serious skiers.

In 1996, Killington's owner—the American Skiing Company—acquired struggling Pico, a middling but respected ski area just over the ridge. Plans call for connecting the two areas with ski trails and lifts, making Killington even more gargantuan. (Environmental permitting has made the timetable for this hard to predict.)

It's already a huge mountain and easy to get lost on, double-sided maps notwithstanding. My advice: Ask about the free tours of the mountain, led by the ski ambassadors based at Snowshed. Alternatively, at the outset focus on one lift and follow the *lift* signs—don't even try to figure out the trail signs. After a couple of runs, the layout of that part of the mountain will start to make sense. Then move on to another lift.

## CROSS-COUNTRY SKIING

Nearest to the downhill ski area (just east of the Killington Road on Route 100/Route 4) is **Mountain Meadows Cross Country Ski Resort** (☎ **800/221-0598** or 802/775-7077), with 34 miles of trails groomed for both skating and classic skiing. The trails are largely divided into three pods, with beginning skiing trails closest to the lodge, an intermediate area a bit farther along, and an advanced 6-mile loop farthest away. Rentals and lessons are available at the lodge. A full-day pass is $13, or $10 for half-day.

The intricate network of trails at the **Mountain Top Inn** (☎ **800/445-2100** or 802/483-2311) has had a loyal local following for years, but it's now attracting considerable attention from far-flung skiers as well. The 66-mile trail network runs through mixed terrain with pastoral views and is groomed for both traditional and skate-skiing. The area is often deep with snow owing to its high ridge-top location in the hills east of Rutland, and snowmaking along key portions of the trail ensure that you won't have to walk across bare spots during snow droughts. The resort maintains three warming huts along the way, and lessons and ski rentals are available. The trails have a combined elevation gain of 670 feet. Trail passes are $15 for adults, $12 for children.

## OTHER OUTDOOR PURSUITS

**MOUNTAIN BIKING**    Mountain bikers challenge themselves on Killington's mountains as they explore 50 miles of trails. One gondola is equipped to haul bikes and riders to the summit, delivering spectacular views. Riders then give their forearms a workout applying brakes with some vigor and frequency while bumping down the slopes. Explore on your own, or sign up for a full- or half-day tour.

The **Mountain Bike Shop** (☎ **802/422-6232**) is located at the Killington Base Lodge and is open from June to mid-October from 9am to 6pm daily. Two-hour instructional tours (reservations required) are $25 adult, $20 junior, which doesn't include a trail pass or lift ride. A trail pass is $8; trail pass with a two-time gondola ride is $20; and unlimited gondola rides are $30 per day. Bike rentals are also available, starting at $20 for 2 hours, or $32 for a day. Helmets are required ($3 per day).

**HIKING**    Area hikers often set their sights on **Deer Leap Mountain** and its popular 3-hour loop to the summit and back. The trail departs from the Inn at Long Trail off Route 4 at Sherburne Pass. Park across from the inn, then head north through the inn's parking lot onto the Long Trail/Appalachian Trail and into the forest. Follow the white blazes (you'll return on the blue-blazed trail you'll see entering on the left). In a ¹/₂ mile you'll arrive at a crossroads. The Appalachian Trail veers right to New Hampshire's White Mountains and Mt. Katahdin in Maine; Vermont's Long Trail runs to the left. Follow the Long Trail, and after some hiking through forest and rock slab over the next ¹/₂ mile or so, turn left at the signs for Deer Leap Height. Great views of Pico and the Killington area await you in ²/₅ miles. After a snack break here, continue down the steep, blue-blazed descent back to Route 4 and your car. The entire loop is about 2¹/₂ miles.

## AN HISTORIC SITE

**President Calvin Coolidge State Historic Site.** Rte. 100A, Plymouth. ☎ **802/ 672-3773.** Admission $6 adults, free for children 14 and under. Daily 9:30am–5pm. Closed mid-Oct–late May.

When told that Calvin Coolidge had died, literary wit Dorothy Parker is said to have responded, "How can they tell?" Even in his death, the nation's most taciturn president had to fight for respect. A trip to the Coolidge Historic District should at least raise Silent Cal's reputation among visitors, who'll get a strong sense of the president reared in this mountain village, a man shaped by harsh weather, unrelieved isolation, and a strong sense of community and family.

Situated in a high upland valley, the historic district consists of a group of about a dozen unspoiled buildings open to the public and a number of other private residences that may be observed from the outside only. It was at the Coolidge Homestead (open for tours) that in August 1923, Vice President Coolidge, on a vacation from Washington, was awakened in the middle of the night and informed that President Warren Harding had died. His father, a notary public, administered the presidential oath of office.

Be sure to stop by the **Plymouth Cheese Factory** (☎ 802/672-3650), in a trim white shop just uphill from the Coolidge Homestead. Founded in the late 1800s as a farmer's cooperative by President Coolidge's father, the business was until the late 1990s owned by the president's son. Excellent cheeses are available here, including a spicy pepper cheddar. "It's got some authority," the clerk warned me, and she was right. The cheese factory is open daily from 9:30am to 5pm; in winter, it's best to call ahead to make sure it's open.

## WHERE TO STAY

Skiers headed to Killington for a week or so of skiing should consider the condo option. A number of condo developments spill down the hillside and along the low ridges flanking the access road. These vary in elegance, convenience, and size. **Highridge** features units with saunas and two-person Jacuzzis, along with access to a compact health club. **Sunrise Village** has a more remote setting, along with a health club and easy access to the Bear Mountain lifts. **The Woods at Killington** are farthest from the slopes (free shuttle) but offer access to the finest health club and the road's best restaurant. Rates fluctuate widely, depending on time of year, number of bedrooms, and number of days you plan to stay. Prices typically range from $100 to $130 per person per day, which includes lift tickets.

You can line up a vacation—or request more information—with a phone call to the **Killington Lodging and Travel Bureau** (☎ 800/621-6867), which also arranges stays at area inns and motels.

✪ **Blueberry Hill Inn.** Goshen-Ripton Rd., Goshen, VT 05733. ☎ **800/448-0707** or 802/247-6735. Fax 802/247-3983. www.blueberryhillinn.com. E-mail: info@blueberryhillinn.com. 12 units. $200–$260 double. Rates include breakfast and dinner. MC, V.

The wonderfully homey Blueberry Hill Inn is in the heart of the Moosalamoo recreation area, on a quiet road about 45 minutes northwest of Killington. (It's slightly closer to Middlebury.) With superb hiking, biking, canoeing, swimming, and cross-country skiing, it's a delightful destination for those inclined toward spending time outdoors and away from the bother of everyday life. (From the inn's brochure: ". . . we offer you no radios, no televisions, no bedside phones to disturb your vacation.") The inn dates to 1813 and has been gracefully added to over the years, including a greenhouse walkway (appropriately called "The Jungle") that leads to the guest rooms, which are comfortable and cozy. The best of the lot is Norse Sky (the rooms are all named after types of blueberries), with skylights, a hardwood floor, and a handsome oak bed. Four rooms have sleeping lofts, which are perfect for families.

**Dining:** Meals are served family-style in a rustic dining room, with a great stone fireplace and homegrown herbs drying from the wooden beams. The menu changes with the season but might feature an herb-crusted salmon or juniper and black-pepper-crusted venison steak. The dining room is open to outside guests; the four-course meal (including hors d'oeuvres) is $35 per person (BYOB), plus tax and tip.

**Amenities:** The inn is situated on 180 acres and is surrounded by national forest laced with hiking and cross-country-skiing trails. Lake swimming is just down the road, and there's a ten-person sauna for guests. Also: bike rentals, free coffee, and baby-sitting services are available.

**Cortina Inn & Resort.** Rte. 4 (1¹/₂ miles west of Pico), Killington, VT 05751. ☎ **800/ 451-6108** or 802/773-3333. Fax 802/775-6948. www.cortinainn.com. E-mail: cortina1@ aol.com. 96 units. A/C TV TEL. Winter and foliage season $169–$199 double; summer and off-season $109–$189. Rates include full breakfast. 5-night minimum stay Christmas week, 3-night minimum Columbus and Presidents' Day weekends. AE, CB, DC, DISC, MC, V. Pets allowed; $5 per pet per night.

The innkeepers here do a fine job making this inn, with nearly 100 rooms, feel like a smaller and more intimate place. Especially appealing is the attention paid to service and detail—the hotel staff even brushes guests' car windows in the morning after a snow. The lodge, set back slightly from busy Route 4 between Pico and Rutland, was built in 1966, with additions in 1975 and 1987. The interior has somewhat retro ski chalet character dating from the original construction—there's even a sunken conversation pit with a two-sided fireplace and a spiral staircase twisting up to a second level. (What, no "Twister?") Guest rooms vary slightly in their modern country style, but all are nicely furnished.

**Dining:** Evening meals are available on premises at Zola's Grill, which specializes in regional fare ($10.95 to $21.95). There's also a tavern for smaller appetites, and afternoon tea is served near the fireplaces in the lobby in winter.

**Amenities:** Indoor pool, fitness room, mountain-biking center, eight tennis courts, two game rooms (one for adults only), small canoeing pond, Jacuzzi, sauna, children's center, conference rooms, sundeck, free shuttle to Killington during ski season, concierge, limited room service, dry cleaning, laundry service, newspaper delivery, baby-sitting, currency exchange, express check-out, and safe-deposit box.

**Inn at Long Trail.** Rte. 4, Killington, VT 05751. ☎ **800/325-2540** or 802/775-7181. www.innatlongtrail.com. E-mail: ilt@vermontel.com. 19 units. Midweek $84–$104 double. Rates include full breakfast. 2-night minimum stay on weekends and during foliage season at $320–$408 double, including 2 nights, 2 dinners, and 2 breakfasts. AE, MC, V. Closed late Apr–late June. Pets allowed by advance arrangement (with damage deposit).

The Inn at Long Trail is situated in an architecturally undistinguished building at the intersection of Route 4 and the Long and Appalachian trails (about a 10-minute drive from Killington's ski slopes). The interior of this rustic inn is far more charming than the exterior. Tree trunks support the beams in the lobby, which sports log furniture and banisters of yellow birch along the stairway. The older rooms in this three-floor hotel (built in 1938 as an annex to a long-gone lodge), are furnished simply in ski-lodge style. Comfortable, more modern suites with fireplaces, telephones, and TVs are offered in a motel-like addition.

**Dining/Diversions:** The dining room maintains the Keebler-elf theme, with a stone ledge that juts through the wall from the mountain behind. The menu features a selection of hearty meals, including the inn's famed Guinness stew, corned beef and cabbage, and chicken pot pie (entrees $11.95 to $16.95). There's live Irish music in the pub on weekends during the busy seasons.

**Inn of the Six Mountains.** 2617 Killington Rd. (P.O. Box 2900), Killington, VT 05751. ☎ **800/228-4676** or 802/422-4302. Fax 802/422-4321. www.sixmountains.com. 103 units. TV TEL. Winter holidays $249–$299 double; weekend $179–$249 double; midweek $159–$199 double. Summer and off-season discounts available. Rates include continental breakfast. AE, CB, DC, DISC, MC, V.

With its profusion of gables and dormers, the Inn of the Six Mountains stands among the more architecturally intriguing of the numerous hotels along Killington Road. The lobby is welcoming in a modern, Scandinavian sort of way, with lots of blonde wood and stone, and the location is convenient to Killington's base lodge, just a mile up the road; but for a luxury hotel that offers only deluxe rooms and suites and charges accordingly, the attention to detail at times comes up short. While the guest rooms are tastefully decorated in a Shaker-inspired sort of way, several I inspected had scuffed walls, weary carpeting, and bruised furniture.

**Dining:** The inn features dining on the premises at the Six Mountains Grille. The fare is hearty country, with dinner entrees like grilled filet mignon, roasted half-chicken, and breast of duck with lingonberries ($10.95 to $18.95).

**Amenities:** Game rooms, indoor lap pool, outdoor pool (seasonal), Jacuzzi, conference rooms, health club, sauna, sundeck, tennis court, limited room service, and guest safe.

**Killington Grand.** 228 E. Mountain Rd. (near Snowshed base area), Killington, VT 05751. ☎ **802/422-5001.** Fax 802/422-6881. www.killington.com. E-mail: killingtongrand@ killington.com. 200 units. A/C TV TEL. Spring–fall $175–$195 double; ski season $250 midweek, $300 weekend, $350 holiday. 5-night minimum during Christmas and school holidays; 2-night minimum on weekends. AE, DISC, MC, V.

This is the newest addition to the vast strip of hotels along the access road (it opened in 1998), and it's a good if pricey choice for travelers seeking contemporary accommodations on the mountain. More than half (133 units) feature kitchen facilities, and most are quite spacious if decorated in a blandly generic country-condo style. Some units can sleep up to six people (priced higher), and the resort has placed an emphasis on attracting families. You pay a premium for convenience compared to other spots near the mountain, but that convenience is hard to top during ski season. The common area is nicely designed in a understated Mission style, and the helpful service is a step above that typically experienced at large ski hotels.

**Dining:** The hotel has two restaurants: Ovations is open daily for breakfast and dinner, with dinner entrees divided between a bistro menu (pasta and pizza, mostly, price $12.95 to $17.95) and a fine dining menu, with entrees like veal and lobster tail in a sundried tomato cream ($13.95 to $27.50). The Alpine Cafe is open daily for lunch and offers sandwiches, salads, and create-your-own pizzas ($5.75 to $7.95).

**Amenities:** Fitness center, heated outdoor pool (year-round), 2 tennis courts, hot tub, sauna, on-site day care and summer day camp, business center and conference rooms, limited room serivce, valet parking, massage, concierge, washer-dryer, same-day dry cleaning, and safe-deposit boxes.

**Mountain Top Inn.** 195 Mountain Top Rd., Chittenden, VT 05737. ☎ **800/445-2100** or 802/ 483-2311. Fax 802/483-6373. www.mountaintopinn.com. E-mail: info@mountaintopinn. com. 55 units (20 have 1–4 bedrooms). A/C TEL. Summer and fall $176–$268 double; winter $176–$268 double midweek; $196–$268 double weekends and holidays; off-season $168–$268 double. AE, MC, V.

The Mountain Top Inn was carved out of a former turnip farm in the 1940s but has left its root-vegetable heritage long behind. Situated on 1,300 ridge-top acres with expansive views of the rolling Vermont countryside, the inn is a modern inn with country charm, and has the feel of a classic, small Pocono resort hotel, where the hosts make sure you've got something to do every waking minute. Guest rooms are unremarkable but comfortable, and have understated country accents, like quilts and pine furnishings. Rooms are classed as either superior or deluxe—the latter are a bit larger and have views of the lake. Overall, the Mountain Top doesn't offer much value to travelers simply looking for room and board, but those who like to be active outdoors and who prefer to stay put during their vacation can keep busy for their money. The inn is located about a 25-minute drive from Killington's slopes.

**Dining:** The pleasant dining room, with heavy beams and rustic, rawhide-laced chairs, features regional American cuisine with a continental twist. Entrees, which range from $17.95 to $23.95, might include pork tenderloin served with roasted garlic cream sauce, or salmon en papillote. Breakfast and dinner are available to guests for $42 per person per day.

**Amenities:** Outdoor pool, horseback riding, beach swimming, five-hole golf course, driving range, shooting clays, and 66 miles of cross-country-skiing trails,

**The Summit.** Killington Rd. (P.O. Box 119), Killington, VT 05751. ☎ **800/635-6343** or 802/422-3535 (800/897627 in the U.K.). Fax 802/422-3536. 45 units. TV TEL. Summer $88 double (no meals); winter $90–$144 double, including breakfast. AE, DC, MC, V.

Think plaid carpeting and Saint Bernards. Those two motifs seem to set the tone at this inviting spot on a knoll just off the access road. The inn has the big dogs, photos, and illustrations of Saint Bernards throughout. Although built only in the 1960s, it has a suprisingly historic character, with much of the common space constructed of salvaged barn timbers. The guest rooms are less distinguished, with clunky pine furniture and little ambience, although all have balconies or terraces. You may not spend all that much time in your rooms, however, since the numerous common spaces are so inviting. Read some of the *Reader's Digest* condensed books filling the bookshelves, or play a game of Twister! The Summit has more character than most self-styled resorts along the access road and offers good value for the price.

**Dining:** Maxwell's Restaurant is spacious and rustic, with wide boards and terracotta floors. Expect standard resort fare, with entrees like grilled pork chop, chicken parmigiana, and prime rib. Entrees range from $15.95 to $20.

**Amenities:** A circular tiled hot tub in the basement seats about a dozen. The tiny heated outdoor pool can accommodate about the same number in winter; the summer pool is larger. There's also virtual indoor golf on the property, five clay tennis courts, limited room service, coin laundry, massage, and a game room.

## WHERE TO DINE

The mere mention of the restaurants along Killington's access road no doubt provokes a deep horror at poultry farms across the nation. It's my impression that *every* Killington restaurant serves up chicken wings—and plenty of them. If you love wings, especially free wings, you'll be in heaven. Alas, if you're looking for something more adventurous, the access road is home to an astonishing level of culinary mediocrity—bland pasta, tired pizza, and soggy nachos—capped off with indifferent, harried service. Most restaurants are OK spots to carbo-load for a day on the slopes or hiking the mountains, and if you're with a group of friends, you may not mind the middling quality; but for the most part, you shouldn't expect much of a dining adventure.

A handful of happy exceptions exist:

**Charity's.** Killington Rd. ☎ **802/422-3800.** Reservations not accepted. Lunch items $5.95–$7.95; main dinner courses $12.95–$17.95. AE, MC, V. Daily 11:30am–10pm. PUB FARE.

Rustic, crowded, bustling, and boisterous, Charity's is the place if you like your food big and your company young. The centerpiece of this barn-like restaurant adorned with stained-glass lamps and Victorian prints is a handsome old bar crafted in Italy, then shipped to West Virginia, where it completed a run of nearly a century before being dismantled and coming to Vermont in 1971. The menu offers a good selection of burgers, plus a half-dozen vegetarian entrees, like veggie stir-fry and red pepper ravioli.

**Choices.** Killington Rd. (at Glazebook Center). ☎ **802/422-4030.** Main courses $12.50–$21.75. AE, MC, V. Sun–Thurs 5–10pm; Fri–Sat 5–11pm; Sun brunch 11am–2:30pm. BISTRO.

One of the locally favored spots for consistently good, unpretentious fare is Choices, located on the access road across from the Outback and Ppeppers. Full dinners come complete with salad or soup and bread, and will amply restore calories lost on the slopes or the trail. Fresh pastas are a specialty (try the Cajun green peppercorn fettuc-cine); other inviting entrees include meats from the rotisserie. The atmosphere is nothing to write home about and the prices are higher than at nearby burger joints, but the high quality of the food and care taken in preparation make up for that.

✪ **Hemingway's.** Rte. 4 (between Rte. 100 N. and Rte. 100 S.). ☎ **802/422-3886.** Reservations strongly recommended. Fixed-price menu $50–$55; vegetarian menu $45; wine-tasting menu $75. AE, MC, V. Open Wed–Sun (open selected Mon and Tues during ski and foliage season; call first); Fri–Sat 6–10pm; Sun–Thurs 6–9pm. Closed mid-Apr–mid-May and early Nov. NEW AMERICAN.

Hemingway's is an uncommonly elegant spot and ranks among the half-dozen best restaurants in New England (that's including Boston). Located in the 1860 Asa Briggs House, a former stagecoach stop now fronting a busy stretch of highway between Killington and Woodstock, Hemingway's seats guests in three formal areas. The wine cellar has an old-world intimacy and is suited for groups out for a celebration; the two upstairs rooms are elegant with damask linen, silver flatware, crystal goblets, fresh flowers, and contemporary art on the walls. Fellow diners tend to be dressed casually but neatly (no shorts or T-shirts). The food is expertly prepared, and the three- or four-course dinner (including extras like bread, canapes, and coffee) is offered at a price that turns out to be rather reasonable given the quality of the kitchen and the unassailable service.

The menu changes often to reflect available stock. A typical meal might start with a cured salmon on a crispy potato waffle or wild mushroom raviolis. Then it's on to the splendid main course: perhaps duck steaks with autumn slaw and crisp yams in fall, or cod prepared with lobster, corn and vanilla in summer. For sheer architectural bravado, little tops the caged deserts, like the pumpkin crème brûlée with apple-cider sauce.

**Mother Shapiro's.** Killington Rd. ☎ **802/422-9933.** Reservations not accepted. Breakfast and lunch $3–$8.95; dinner entrees $10.95–$18.95. AE, DISC, MC, V. Daily breakfast 7–11am; lunch and munchies 11am–3pm; dinner 4:30–10pm. PUB FARE.

Mother's is the place for breakfast or brunch. You'll find omelets, lox, corned beef hash, and pancakes (served with real maple syrup—"first pitcher on us"). At Sunday brunch, there's a unique Bloody Mary bar—you get a glass with vodka and formulate your own spicy concoction from a line-up of ingredients. It's a fun place that kids adore—it's done up in a comic-book Victorian vaudeville/brothel look, and the menu nags. ("No whining," "Don't make a mess," and "No substitutions concerning this menu unless it's not too busy, then we'll talk.") Although it's open for lunch and late for bar food, the quality of the food seems to slip and service gets less attentive as the day progresses.

**Panache.** Killington Access Rd., Killington. ☎ **802/422-8622.** Reservations recommended. Main courses $20–$32. AE, CB, DC, DISC, MC, V. Sun–Thurs 6–9pm; Fri–Sat 6–10pm. EXOTIC GAME.

Panache's isn't for everyone. For starters, the restaurant—located at The Woods condo complex—offers giraffe, camel, cobra, and other fare that's not likely to show up any time soon on the McDonald's menu. The exotic offerings attract adventurous gourmands in search of new flavors, but there's also a good selection of more traditional fare, like bison, elk, filet mignon, and veal; and once you get beyond the eye-popping menu, you'll discover a superior restaurant with a deft touch and a creative flair. The service is good, the decor is colorful and modern, and the food presentation is excellent. As an added bonus, parents who make reservations can drop off their kids (no infants or toddlers) at a wonderful adjacent game room with air hockey and video games; the staff will keep an eye on them and feed them free pizza.

**Ppeppers.** Killington Rd. ☎ **802/422-3177.** Reservations not accepted. Lunch items $4–$7.95; main dinner courses $7.95–$12.95. AE, DC, MC, V. Daily 7am–midnight. PASTA/ECLECTIC.

This 1950s-style retro restaurant is a festive, upbeat place—and almost always crowded with visitors and locals who've just enjoyed a long day on the slopes or the trails. Situated in a strip-mallish complex near the top of Killington Road, Ppeppers sets the mood with a black-and-white tile floors, red lightshades, and red chili-pepper accent lighting. Take a seat at a genuine naugahyde booth, or grab a stool at the wooden counter. Despite the name, the food isn't all spicy here—the menu is diner fare, expanded for a more sophisticated clientele, but the hamburgers are great, the pasta above average, and the service far more friendly than you'll find in many ski mountain establishments.

## NIGHTLIFE

Killington has more going on after dark than any other Vermont ski resort, with a variety of dance clubs and live music venues along the access road. A few of the more popular are listed below.

**Happy hour** is a religion at Killington in the winter. Many of the restaurants and bars along the access road go to considerable lengths to lure folks in between 3 and 6pm, with free munchies, happy hour entertainers, and drink specials. Just look for the signs along the road, or check the ads in the local paper to find the most tempting offers.

**Mother Shapiro's.** Killington Rd. ☎ **802/422-9933.**

This lively, popular restaurant often features live blues on the small stage later in the evening. It's also a good choice for late-night snacking.

**Pickle Barrel.** Killington Rd. ☎ **802/422-3035.** www.picklebarrelnightclub.com.

The Pickle Barrel is Killington's largest and loudest nightclub, and lures in B-list national acts like Eddie Money, Little Feat, and the Mighty Mighty Bosstones. Cover charge ranges from a couple of bucks to nearly $20.

**Outback/Nightspot.** Killington Rd. ☎ **802/422-9885.**

The music tends to be mellower than the other hot spots in town, with acoustic musicians often heading the lineup. It's the place if you want to chat with friends while enjoying music and wood-fired pizza. Note the resourceful beer-mug cooling system.

**Pickle Barrel.** Killington Rd. ☎ **802/422-3035.** www.picklebarrelnightclub.com.

The Pickle Barrel is Killington's largest and loudest nightclub, and lures in B-list national acts like Eddie Money, Little Feat, and the Mighty Mighty Bosstones. Cover charge ranges from a couple of bucks to nearly $20.

**Wobbly Barn.** Killington Rd. ☎ **802/422-3392.** www.wobblybarn.com.

The Wobbly is best known for its popular happy hour, but also packs in the crowds for dancing and mingling until late in the evening. Expect bands that play good, hard-driving rock. This pioneer establishment, located in an old barn, is owned by American Skiing Co., who also owns the ski resort.

# RUTLAND

Rutland is a no-nonsense, blue-collar town that's never had much of a reputation for charm. Today, it's undergoing a low-grade renaissance, attracting new residents who like the small-city atmosphere and easy access to the mountains, especially Killington in winter.

Located in the wide valley flanking Otter Creek, Rutland was built on the marble trade, which was mined out of bustling quarries in nearby Proctor and West Rutland. By 1880, Rutland boasted more residents than Burlington, and had the distinguished honorific of "Marble City." Many fine homes from this era still line the streets, and the intricate commercial architecture, which naturally incorporates a fair amount of marble, hints at a former prosperity.

Rutland remains the regional hub for central Vermont, with much of the economic energy along bustling Route 7 north and south of downtown. The downtown itself shares its turf with an oddly incongruous strip mall, which appeared during one of those ill-considered spasms of 1950s urban renewal. That said, Rutland has the feel of a real place with real people, a good antidote for those who've felt they've spent a bit too much time in tourist-oriented ski resorts.

## ESSENTIALS

**GETTING THERE**    Rutland is at the intersection of Route 7 and Route 4. Burlington is 67 miles to the north; Bennington is 56 miles south. **Amtrak** (☎ **800/872-7245**) offers daily train service from New York via the Hudson River Valley. Rutland is also served by scheduled air service by **US Airways Express** (☎ **800/247-8786**).

**VISITOR INFORMATION**    The **Rutland Chamber of Commerce,** 256 N. Main St., Rutland, VT 05701 (☎ **802/773-2747**) staffs an information booth at the corner of Route 7 and Route 4 West from Memorial Day through Columbus Day. It's open daily from 10am to 6pm. The chamber's main office is open year-round Monday to Friday 8am to 5pm.

**FESTIVALS**    The **Vermont State Fair** (☎ **802/775-5200**) has attracted fairgoers from throughout Vermont for more than a century and a half. It's held the first week of September at the fairgrounds on Route 7 south of city. Gates open at 8am daily.

## EXPLORING THE TOWN

A stroll through Rutland's historic downtown will delight architecture buffs. Look for the detailed marblework on many of the buildings, such as the Opera House, the Gryphan's Building, and along Merchant's Row. Note especially the fine marble exterior of the Chittenden Savings Bank at the corner of Merchant's Row and Center Street. Nearby South Main Street (Route 7) also has a good selection of handsome homes built in elaborate Queen Anne style.

Shoppers can also look for small finds at a variety of unique downtown shops tucked under awnings here and there. Among those worth seeking out is **Michael's Toys,** 13 Center St. (☎ **802/773-1488**), which will make young kids wide-eyed. It's located at the head of a creaky Dashiel Hammett–esque stairway in a second-floor workshop filled with rocking cows, wooden trucks, and hand-carved wooden signs. You half expect to find a gnome hard at work. The shop is generally open Monday through Saturday from 9am to 5pm.

A stop worth making, especially as a rainy-day diversion, is the **Chaffee Center for the Visual Arts,** 16 S. Main St. (☎ **802/775-0356**). Housed in a Richardsonian structure dating from 1896, with a characteristically prominent turret and a mosaic floor in the archway vestibule, the Chaffee showcases the abundant artistic talent from Rutland and beyond. While it owns no permanent collections, it does feature changing exhibits of local artists, and much of the work is for sale. The building is on the National Register of Historic Places, and the glorious parquet floors have been restored to their original luster. The Chaffee is open daily except Tuesdays from 10am to 5pm (noon to 4pm on Sundays), and admission is by donation.

## OUTSIDE OF TOWN

A worthy detour from Rutland is to the amiable town of **Proctor,** about 6 miles north-west of Rutland center. (Take Route 4 west, then follow Route 3 north to the town.) This quiet town is nestled in the folds of low hills, with some homes and bridges made of marble, and was once a noted center for its exceptionally fine-grained marble, which found its way to the U.S. Supreme Court, Lincoln Memorial and other notable structures. The quarry closed and the factory shut down in 1991, but the heritage lives on at the expansive **Vermont Marble Exhibit** (☎ **802/459-3311**), one of the most popular attractions in New England. You start off by viewing an 11-minute video about marble, then walk through the "Earth Alive" displays about geology, see a sculptor working in marble, and explore the Hall of Presidents, with life-sized bas-relief sculptures of all past presidents. The vast size of this former factory is impressive in itself. There's also a gift shop with a great selection of reasonably priced marble products.

It's open Memorial Day to late October daily from 9am to 5:30pm (closed the rest of the year). Admission is $5 adult, $3.50 seniors, and children under 12 free. Look for signs to the exhibit from Route 3 in Proctor.

## WHERE TO STAY

Rutland has a selection of basic roadside motels and chain hotels, mostly clustered on or along Route 7 south of town. Room rates at the **Comfort Inn at Trolley Square,** 19 Allen St. (☎ **800/228-5150** or 802/775-2200), include a free continental breakfast. The **Holiday Inn,** 476 US Rte. 7 South, (☎ **800/462-4810** or 802/775-1911) has an indoor pool, hot tub, and sauna. Likewise, the **Howard Johnson Rutland,** 401 US Rte. 7 South (☎ **802/775-4303**), features an indoor pool and sauna, with the familiar orange-roofed restaurant next door. The **Best Western Hogge Penny Inn** (☎ **800/828-3334** or 802/773-3200), which is on Route 4 East, offers individual rooms and suites, along with a swimming pool and tennis court.

## WHERE TO DINE

**The Coffee Exchange** (☎ **802/775-3337**) is a casually hip cafe housed in a former downtown bank at 101–103 Merchant's Row. You've got your choice here: grab a seat at a sidewalk table, or move inside and pick a room. (The bank vault is tiny and painted enchantingly, and you can have a lively conversation with your own echo.) A good selection of coffees is available, along with delectable baked goods like banana-nut tarts, croissants, and cheese Danishes.

**Little Harry's.** 121 West St. ☎ **802/747-4848.** Reservations recommended. Main courses $9.95–$16.95. AE, MC, V. Wed–Sun 5–10pm. GLOBAL.

This is an offshoot of the popular Harry's outside of Ludlow. It's located in downtown Rutland on the first floor and basement of a strikingly unattractive building; but Little Harry's has a wonderfully eclectic menu, with main selections ranging from grilled steak sandwich to duck in a "searing" red Thai curry. (Thursday is Thai night.) Appetizers are equally eclectic, with choices along the lines of marinated green olives, gazpacho, pad thai, and hummus. As you might guess, the dishes here span the globe and will appeal to anyone with an adventurous palate.

**Royal's Hearthside.** 37 N. Main St. ☎ **802/775-0856.** Reservations recommended on weekends. Lunch items $6.75–$10.95; main dinner courses $15.95–$21.95. AE, MC, V. Mon–Sat 11am–3pm and 5–10pm, Sun noon–9pm. AMERICAN.

Royal's Hearthside, a local institution since 1962, falls under the category of "old reliable." Situated at the busy intersection of Route 4 and Route 7, Royal's is calming and quiet on the inside, done up in a sort of Ye Olde Colonial American style. Expect spindle-backed chairs, faux pewter sugar bowls, and Brandenburg concertos playing in the background. Meals don't tax the staff in the creativity department, but entrees are solidly prepared. All the sauces are homemade, as are the popovers, breads, and pastries. They even butcher their own meat. Selections run along the lines of baked stuffed shrimp, grilled rack of lamb, broiled salmon, an assortment of grilled meats, and an array of specials. Luncheons include sandwiches, burgers, and omelets. The restaurant is also noted for its traditional puddings, like grapenut, Indian and bread pudding. If you're looking for a dinner bargain, arrive early (before 6:30pm) for one of the early bird specials. "We take care of people who come early," the waitresses say.

# Northern Vermont    5

Northern Vermont is well-represented on either end of the development spectrum. On the western side, along the shores of Lake Champlain, you'll find Burlington, the state's largest and most lively city, which is ringed by fast-growing suburban communities; but drive east a couple of hours, and you'll be deep into the Northeast Kingdom, which is the state's least developed and most remote region. For travelers, there's a tremendous variety of activities within and between these two extremes—exploring Lake Champlain's rural islands, dining in Burlington's creative restaurants, hiking the Long Trail across the state's most imposing peaks, mountain biking on abandoned lanes, and exploring the quirky museums of St. Johnsbury.

In winter, there's excellent skiing at Stowe and Jay Peak. The north is also far enough from the Boston–New York megalopolis that weekend crowds tend to be lighter, and the sense of space here more expansive.

## 1 Middlebury

Middlebury is a gracious college town set amid rolling hills and pastoral countryside. The town center is idyllic in a New-England-as-envisioned-by-Hollywood sort of way. All that's lacking is Jimmy Stewart wandering around, muttering confusedly to himself.

The town centers on an irregular sloping green; above the green is the commanding Middlebury Inn. Shops line the downhill slopes. In the midst of the green is a handsome chapel, and the whole scene is lorded over by a fine, white-steepled Congregational church, built between 1806 and 1809. Otter Creek tumbles dramatically through the middle of town and is flanked by a historic district where you can see the intriguing vestiges of former industry. In fact, Middlebury has 300 buildings listed on the National Register of Historic Places. About the only disruption to the historical perfection is the growl of trucks downshifting as they drive along the main routes through town.

Middlebury College, which is within walking distance of downtown, doesn't so much dominate the village as coexist nicely alongside it. The college has a sterling reputation for its liberal-arts education but may be best known for its intensive summer language programs. Don't be surprised if you hear folks gobbling in exotic tongues while walking through town in summer. Students commit to total immersion, taking the "Language Pledge," which means no lapsing by speaking in English while they're enrolled in the program.

## ESSENTIALS

**GETTING THERE**   Middlebury is located on Route 7 about midway between Rutland and Burlington. It's served by bus through Vermont Transit (☎ **800/451-3292** or 802-388-4373).

**VISITOR INFORMATION**   The **Addison County Chamber of Commerce,** 2 Court St., Middlebury, VT 05753 (☎ **800/733-8376** or 802/388-7951; www.midvermont.com), is located in a handsome, historic white building just off the green, facing the Middlebury Inn. Brochures and assistance are available weekdays during business hours and often on weekends from early June to mid-October. Ask also for the map and guide to downtown Middlebury, published by the Downtown Middlebury Business Bureau, which lists shops and restaurants around town.

## EXPLORING THE TOWN

The best place to begin a tour of Middlebury is the Addison County Chamber of Commerce (see above), where you can request the chamber's self-guided walking-tour brochure.

The **Vermont Folklife Center,** 3 Court St., ☎ **802/388-4964,** is located in the 1823 Masonic Hall, a short walk from the Middlebury Inn. You'll find a gallery of changing displays featuring various folk arts from Vermont and beyond, including music and visual arts. The small gift shop has intriguing items, including heritage foods and traditional crafts. It's open between May and December Tuesday to Saturday 11am to 4pm, and in winter on Saturdays only 11am to 4pm. Admission is by donation. On the Web, visit www.vermontfolklifecenter.com.

The historic **Otter Creek** district, set along a steep hillside by the rocky creek, is well worth exploring. While here, you can peruse top-flight Vermont crafts at the **Vermont State Crafts Center at Frog Hollow,** 1 Mill St. (☎ **802/388-3177**). The center, situated overlooking tumbling Otter Creek, is open daily (closed Sundays in winter) and features the work of some 300 Vermont craftspeople, with exhibits ranging from extraordinary carved-wood desks and metalwork to glass and pottery. The Middlebury center also features a pottery studio and a resident potter who's often busy at work. The Crafts Center also maintains shops in Manchester Village and at the Church Street Marketplace in Burlington. Visit the center's Web site for a listing of monthly exhibits: www.froghollow.org.

From Frog Hollow, wander across the pedestrian footbridge over the river, and find your way up to **The Marbleworks,** an assortment of wood and rough-marble industrial buildings on the far bank that have been converted to a handful of shops and restaurants. (Scenes from the Jim Carey gross-out film "Me, Myself, and Irene" were filmed here in 1999.)

Brewhounds should schedule a stop at the **Otter Creek Brewing Co.,** 793 Exchange St. (☎ **800/473-0727**), for a tour (at 1, 3, and 5pm daily) and free samples of their well-regarded beverages, including the flagship Copper Ale and a robust Stovepipe Porter. The brewery opened in 1989; within a few years, it had outgrown its old space and moved into the new 40-barrel brewhouse on 10 acres. The gift shop is open daily from 10am to 6pm.

Located atop a low ridge with beautiful views of both the Green Mountains to the east and farmlands rolling toward Lake Champlain in the west, prestigious **Middlebury College** has a handsome, well-spaced campus of gray-limestone and white-marble buildings that's best explored by foot. The architecture of the college, founded in 1800, is primarily Colonial Revival, which lends it a rather stern Calvinist demeanor. Especially appealing is the prospect from the marble Mead Memorial Chapel, built in 1917 and overlooking the campus green.

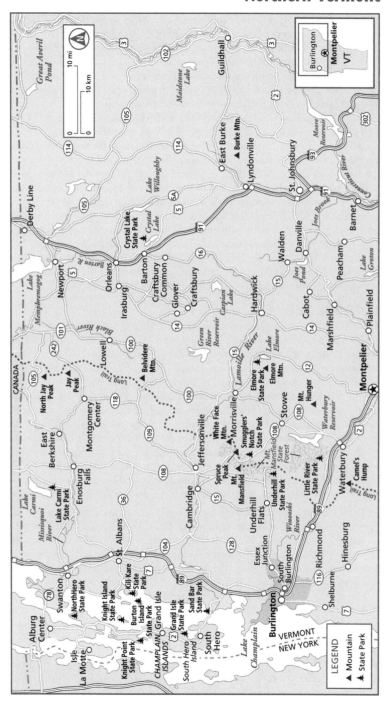

At the edge of campus is the **Middlebury College Center for the Arts.** This architecturally engaging center houses the **Middlebury College Museum of Art** (☎ 802/443-5007), a small museum with a selective sampling of European and American art, both ancient and new. Classicists will savor the displays of Greek painted urns and vases; modern art aficionados can sample from the museum's permanent and changing exhibits. The museum is located on Route 30 and is open Tuesday to Friday from 10am to 5pm, weekends from noon to 5pm. Admission is free.

A couple of miles outside of Middlebury is the **Morgan Horse Farm** (☎ 802/388-2011), which is owned and administered by the University of Vermont. The farm dates back to the late 1800s and was for a time owned by the federal government, which in turn gave the farm to the university in 1951. Col. Joseph Battell, owner of the farm from the 1870s to 1906, is credited with preserving the Morgan breed, a horse of considerable beauty and stamina that has served admirably in war and exploration. The breed is now prized as show horses and family pleasure horses alike. The farm, with its 60 to 80 registered stallions, mares, and foals, is open for guided tours May through October from 9am to 4pm daily. There's also a picnic area and gift shop with loads of equine-themed items. Admission is $4 for adults, $3 for teens, $1 for children 5 to 12, and free for kids 4 and under. To reach the farm, take Route 125 to Weybridge Street (Route 23 north), and head north for a ³/₄ mile, then turn right at the sign for the farm and continue on approximately 2 miles.

## OUTDOOR PURSUITS

**HIKING**   The Green Mountains roll down to Middlebury's eastern edge, making for easy access to the mountains. Stop by the **U.S. Forest Service's Middlebury Ranger District office,** south of town on Route 7 (☎ 802/388-4362), for guidance and information on area trails and destinations. Ask for the brochure *Day Hikes on the Middlebury & Rochester Ranger Districts,* which lists 14 hikes.

One recommended stroll for people of all abilities—and especially those of poetic sensibilities—is the **Robert Frost Interpretive Trail,** dedicated to the memory of New England's poet laureate. Frost lived in a cabin on a farm across the road for 23 summers. (The cabin is now a National Historic Landmark.) Located on Route 125 about 6 miles east of Middlebury, this relaxing loop trail is just a mile long, and excerpts of Frost's poems are placed on signs along the trail. Also posted is information about the trail's natural history. The trail, which is managed by the Green Mountain National Forest, offers pleasant access to the gentle woods of these lovely intermountain lowlands.

**SKIING**   Downhill skiers looking for a low-key, low-pressure mountain invariably head to **Middlebury College Snow Bowl** (☎ 802/388-4356), near Middlebury Gap on Route 125 east of town. This historic ski area, founded in 1939, has a vertical drop of just over 1,000 feet served by three chairlifts. The college ski team uses the ski area for practice, but it's also open to the public at rates of about half what you'd pay at Killington. Adult tickets are $30 for weekends, $25 midweek.

There's also cross-country skiing nearby at the **Rikert Ski Touring Center** (☎ 802/388-2759) at Middlebury's Bread Loaf Campus on Route 125. The center offers 25 miles of machine-groomed trails through a lovely winter landscape. Adult ski passes are $10, students and children are $5. Half-day passes also available ($6 and $3).

## WHERE TO STAY

Middlebury offers a handful of motels in addition to several inns. Two well-kept, reasonably priced motels are located south of town on Route 7: The **Blue Spruce Motel,** 2428 Rte. 7 S. (☎ 800/640-7671 or 802/388-4091), and the **Greystone Motel,** 1395 Rte. 7 S. (☎ 802/388-4935).

**۞ Inn on the Green.** 19 S. Pleasant St., Middlebury, VT 05753. ☎ **888/244-7512** or 802/388-7512. Fax 802/388-4075. 11 units (includes 2 suites). A/C TV TEL. $125–$175 weekends and summer, $155–$195 foliage season, $90 midweek winter. 2-night minimum on weekends. AE, DC, DISC, MC, V.

This village inn occupies a house that dates back to 1803 (it was Victorianized with a mansard tower later in the century), and opened as an inn in 1997. Both historic and comfortable, it's the best choice for those wishing to be in downtown Middlebury. The rooms are furnished with a mix of antiques and reproductions; lustrous wood floors and boldly colored walls (harvest yellow, peach, and burgundy) lighten the architectural heaviness of the house. The suites are naturally the most spacious, but most rooms offer plenty of elbow room. Those in the front of the house are flooded with afternoon light.

**Middlebury Inn and Motel.** 14 Courthouse Sq., Middlebury, VT 05753. ☎ **800/ 842-4666** or 802/388-4961. www.middleburyinn.com. E-mail: midinnvt@sover.net. 80 units. A/C TV TEL. Midweek $86–$195 double; weekends $96–$215 double; $156–$355 suites. Rates include continental breakfast. AE, DC, DISC, MC, V. Pets accepted (limited; $6 additional per day).

The historic Middlebury Inn traces its roots back to 1827, when Nathan Wood built a brick public house he called the Vermont Hotel. It's come a long way since then and now contains 80 modern guest rooms equipped with most conveniences. The rooms are on the large side, and most come furnished with a sofa or upholstered chairs in addition to the bed; rooms are decorated in dark hues and Colonial-reproduction furniture; many of the fixtures in the bathrooms are vintage. Rooms 116 and 246 are among the more desirable—they're spacious corner rooms entered via a dark foyer/ sitting room. Room 129, while smaller, has a four-poster bed, view of the village green, and a Jacuzzi. The ten guest rooms in the Porterhouse Mansion next door also have a pleasant, historic aspect. An adjacent motel with 20 units is decorated in an early American motif, but it feels like veneer—underneath it's just a motel. Stick with the main inn if you're seeking a taste of history.

**Dining:** The inn's dining rooms offer breakfast, lunch, and dinner. The Morgan Tavern features informal fare like salads, crabcakes, and Reubens (priced $6 to $11). The more formal Founder's Room has a regional menu with steak, seafood, and pasta offerings, priced at $14.95 to $19.95. During busy times meals are served buffet style ($18.95).

**Swift House Inn.** 25 Stewart Lane, Middlebury, VT 05753. ☎ **802/388-9925.** Fax 802/ 388-9927. www.swifthouseinn.com. E-mail: shi@together.net. 21 units, 1 with detached bathroom. A/C TV TEL. $100–$225 double. Rates include continental breakfast. 2-night minimum stay some weekends. AE, CB, DC, DISC, MC, V.

The Swift House Inn is a compound of three graceful old homes set in a residential area just a few minutes' walk from the town green. The main Federal-style inn dates back to 1814; inside, it's decorated in a simple, historical style that still has a modern crispness. Guests rooms are well-appointed with antique and reproduction furnishings. Especially appealing is the Swift Room, with its oversize bathroom, whirlpool, and private terrace. About half of the 21 rooms have fireplaces or whirlpools or both; all but two have TVs; most also have coffeemakers and hair dryers. Light sleepers may prefer the main inn or the Carriage House rather than the Gatehouse down the hill; the latter is on Route 7, and the truck noise can be a minor irritant at night.

**Dining:** The dining room is divided among three rooms. The menu is eclectic with global influences and features dishes like Moroccan lamb stew, risotto stuffed acorn squash, and mussels in a spicy black-bean sauce. Main courses are priced $9 to $24.

Open daily in summer from 6 to 9:30pm; winter from Thursday to Saturday 5 to 9pm.
   **Amenities:** Limited room service, steam room, sauna, and safe.

**Waybury Inn.** Rte. 125, East Middlebury, VT 05753. ☎ **800/348-1810** or 802/388-4015.
Fax 802/388-1245. www.wayburyinn.com. E-mail: thefolks@wayburyinn.com. 14 units. (1
with private hall bath.) $95–$135 double, including breakfast. Off-season rates available.
DISC, MC, V. Pets allowed with restrictions; call first.

Photos of Bob Newhart and "Daryll and his other brother, Daryll" grace the wall
behind the reception desk at this classic 1810 inn. There's a simple reason: This was
the inn featured in Newhart's show (at least the exterior; the interior was created on a
sound stage). The architecturally handsome Waybury has loads of integrity in that
simple farmhouse kind of way, but inside it's a bit disappointing with worn carpeting,
chipped paint, and furniture past its prime. A new innkeeper acquired the place in late
1999, and plans call for long-overdue renovations in 2000, so it may be worth checking
out. Even in its former incarnation, some of the guest rooms (all carpeted) were inviting, like Number 9, the largest of the bunch with canopy bed, sofa, and coffee table.
Number 1 is also more sizeable than most, with a nicely turned four-poster. The inn
is close to the road, and the front rooms can be a bit noisy at night; the two attic rooms
are dark and garret-like.
   **Dining:** The Colonial-style dining room serves creative favorites like Cornish game
hen, bourbon steak, and seafood ravioli in a sherry cream sauce. Entrees are $13.50 to
$21.95.

## WHERE TO DINE

**Storm Café.** 3 Mill St. ☎ **802/388-1063.** Reservations highly recommended. Main courses,
lunch $7–$8.50, dinner $12.95–$17.95. MC, V. Tues–Sat 11am–3pm and 5–9pm. NEW
AMERICAN.

This tiny, casual spot tucked down in Frog Hollow is a chef-owned restaurant that's
popular with locals and travelers alike. Given the dearth of tables and the popularity
of the food, reservations are all but essential on weekends. The menu is quite simple,
but tremendous care has been taken in the preparation of the dishes. Lunches include
smoked salmon, jerk chicken, and hummus; at dinnertime, look for sirloin with porta-
bellos and oyster mushrooms, penne carbonara, and grilled shrimp.

**Woody's.** 5 Bakery Lane (on Otter Creek just upstream from the bridge in the middle of
town). ☎ **802/388-4182.** Reservations recommended on weekends and during college
events. Lunch items $4.50–$8.50; main dinner courses $12.95–$17.95. AE, MC, V. Mon–Sat
11:30am–9:30pm; Sun 10:30am–9:30pm. Light menu only 3–5pm. Closed Tues in winter.
PUB FARE/PASTA.

Woody's is not Ye Olde New Englande. It's a bright and colorful multilevel restaurant
overlooking the creek, made all the more appealing by its surprising location down a
small, dark alley. It's the kind of fun, low-key, and hip place destined to put you in a good
mood the moment you walk in. Angle for a table perched over the creek. Lunches
include burgers, sandwiches, and salads, along with burritos and beer-steamed mussels.
Dinner is heavy on the pasta selections (the bourbon shrimp with linguine is popular)
but also features appetizing selections from the grill, like the mixed seafood grill with
fettuccine, and medaillons of pork with a ginger, allspice, and sage rub.

## 2  Mad River Valley

Warren is 3 miles south of Waitsfield, 205 miles northwest of Boston, and 43 miles southeast
of Burlington.

The Mad River Valley is one of Vermont's better kept secrets. This scenic valley surrounding the towns of Warren and Waitsfield has something of a Shangri-la quality to it. In places, it has changed little since first settled in 1789 by Gen. Benjamin Wait and a handful of Revolutionary War veterans, including half a dozen said to have served as Minutemen at the battles of Concord Bridge and Lexington.

Since 1948, ski-related development has competed with the early farms that were the backbone of the region for 2 centuries, but the newcomers haven't been too pushy or overly obnoxious, at least so far. Save for a couple of telltale signs, you could drive Route 100 past the sleepy villages of Warren and Waitsfield and not realize that you've passed close to some of the choicest skiing in the state. The region hasn't fallen prey to unbridled condo or strip-mall developers, and the valley seems to have learned the lessons of haphazard development that afflicted Mount Snow and Killington to the south. Other towns could still learn a lot from Waitsfield: note the Mad River Green, a tidy strip mall disguised as an old barn on Route 100 just north of Route 17. It's scarcely noticable from the main road. Longtime Vermont skiers say the valley today is like Stowe used to be 25 years ago.

The region's character becomes less pastoral along the Sugarbush Access Road, but even then, development isn't heavily concentrated, not even at the base of Sugarbush, the valley's preeminent ski area. The better lodges and restaurants tend to be tucked back in the forest or set along streams, and it behooves travelers to make sure they have good directions before setting out in search of accommodations or food. Hidden up a winding valley road, Mad River Glen, the area's older and grumpier ski area, has a pleasantly dated quality that eschews glamour in favor of the rustic.

As yet, the whole valley maintains a friendly and informal attitude, even during the peak of ski season; and valley residents hope to keep it that way, even in the face of certain growth.

## ESSENTIALS

**GETTING THERE**   Warren and Waitsfield straddle Route 100 between Killington and Waterbury. The nearest interstate access is from Exit 10 (Waterbury) on I-89; drive south on Route 100 for 14 miles to Waitsfield.

**VISITOR INFORMATION**   The **Sugarbush Chamber of Commerce,** P.O. Box 173, Waitsfield, VT 05673 (☎ **800/828-4748** or 802/469-3409), is at 4601 Main St. (Route 100) in the General Wait House, next to the elementary school. It's open daily from 9am to 5pm Monday to Friday during slow times expect limited hours and days. On the Web, go to www.madrivervalley.com.

## EXPLORING THE VALLEY

An unusual way to explore the region is atop an Icelandic pony. **The Vermont Icelandic Horse Farm** (☎ **802/496-7141**) specializes in tours on these small, sturdy, strong horses. Day and half-day rides are available, but to really appreciate both the countryside and the horses, you should sign up for one of the multiday treks. These range from 1 to 5 nights and include lodging at area inns, all your meals (lunches are either picnics or enjoyed at a local restaurant), your mount, and a guide to lead you through the lush hills around Waitsfield and Warren. In winter, there's also **skijoring,** that can best be described as waterskiing behind a horse. Call for pricing information and reservations.

The classic **Warren General Store** (☎ **802/496-3864**) anchors the former bustling timber town of Warren. Set along a tumbling stream, the store has uneven wooden floorboards, a potbellied stove, and shelf stock fully updated for the 1990s with a good selection of gourmet foods and wines. Get coffee or a sandwich at the back deli counter, and enjoy it on the deck overlooking the water. Afterwards, browse upstairs, where you'll find an assortment of leather goods, clothing, and jewelry. The store is located in Warren Village just off Route 100 south of the Sugarbush Access Road.

Visitors can explore local rivers or lakes with the help of **Clearwater Sports** (☎ 802/496-2708) on Route 100 in Waitsfield, just north of the covered bridge. These outgoing guides rent canoes and kayaks, and offer shuttle services for intrepid paddlers looking for adventures ranging from whitewater (best in the spring) to a placid summer afternoon paddle on the Waterbury Reservoir. Rates are $37 per day for canoe rental; guided tours run from 9am to 3pm and cost $48 per person, including transportation, equipment and instruction (bring your own picnic lunch). They also rent sea kayaks, bikes, tents, and sleeping bags. In winter, Clearwater offers snowshoe, ice-skate, and telemark-ski rentals, and hosts 2- and 4-hour snowshoe tours.

South of Warren, Route 100 pinches through **Granville Gulf,** a wild and scenic area of tumultuous streams and sheer hillsides. The highway twists and winds through 6 miles of this troll-like defile, which stands in contrast to the more open vistas along most of Route 100. Look for the roadside pull-off at **Moss Glen Falls,** one of the state's loveliest cascades.

## SKIING

**Sugarbush.** Warren, VT 05674. ☎ **800/537-8427** for lodging or 802/583-2381. www. sugarbush.com. Vertical drop: 2,650 ft. Lifts: 14 chairlifts (4 high-speed), 4 surface lifts. Skiable acreage: 432. Lift tickets: $53 every day.

Sugarbush is part of the American Skiing Company empire, and that company has invested in giving the ski area some flash and zip to broaden its classic New England ski resort appeal. The two main ski mountains—Lincoln Peak and Mount Ellen— are linked with a 2-mile, 10-minute high-speed chairlift that crosses three ridges (no more irksome shuttle buses) and additional high-speed, detachable quad chairlifts have been added at both mountains. Snowmaking has been significantly upgraded, and the improved slopes started generating some buzz. Happily, Sugarbush is still a low-key area with great intermediate cruising runs on the north slopes and some challenging, old-fashioned expert slopes on Castlerock. Sugarbush is a good choice if you find the sprawl of Killington overwhelming but don't want to sacrifice great skiing in the search for a quieter and more intimate resort area.

**Mad River Glen.** Waitsfield, VT 05763. ☎ **802/496-3551.** www.madriverglen.com. E-mail: ski@madriverglen.com. Vertical drop: 2,000 ft. Lifts: 4 chairlifts. Skiable acreage: 115. Lift tickets: $29 midweek, $36 weekends, $38 holidays.

Mad River Glen is the curmudgeon of the Vermont ski world. Its motto is "Ski it if you can." High-speed detachable quads? Forget it. The main lift is a 1948 *single*-chair lift that creaks its way 1 mile to the summit. (It may receive National Historic Landmark status.) Snowmaking? Don't count on it. Only 15 percent of the terrain benefits from the fake stuff; the rest is dependent on Mother Nature. Snowboarding? Nope. It's forbidden at Mad River.

Mad River's slopes are twisting and narrow, and hide some of the steepest drops you'll find in New England (nearly half of the slopes are classified as expert). Mad River Glen long ago attained the status of a cult mountain among serious skiers, and its fans seem bound and determined to keep it that way. Longtime owner Betsy Pratt sold the ski area to a cooperative of about 1,000 Mad River skiers in 1995, making it the only cooperative-owned ski area in the country. The new owners seem especially proud of the mountain's funky traditions (how *about* that single chair?) and say they're determined to maintain the spirit.

## HIKING & BIKING

A rewarding 14-mile bike trip along paved roads begins at the village of Waitsfield. Park your car near the covered bridge, and follow East Warren Road past the Inn at Round Barn Farm and up into the hilly, farm-filled countryside. (Don't be discouraged by the unrelenting hill at the outset.) Near the village of Warren, turn right at Brook Road to connect back to Route 100. Return north on bustling but generally safe and often scenic Route 100 to Waitsfield.

Hikers in search of good exercise and a spectacular view should strike out for **Mount Abraham,** west of Warren. Drive west up Lincoln Gap Road (it leaves Route 100 just south of Warren Village), and continue until the crest, where you'll cross the intersection with the Long Trail. Park here and head north on the trail; about 2 miles along you'll hit the Battell Shelter. Push on another ⁴/₅ mile up a steep ascent to reach the panoramic views atop 4,006-foot Mount Abraham. Enjoy. Retrace your steps back to your car. Allow 4 or 5 hours for the round-trip hike.

For a less demanding adventure that still yields great views, head *south* from Lincoln Gap Road on the Long Trail. In about ³/₅ mile, look for a short spur trail to **Sunset Rock** with sweeping westward vistas of the farms of the Champlain Valley, along with Lake Champlain and the knobby Adirondacks beyond. A round-trip hike requires a little more than an hour.

## WHERE TO STAY

Sugarbush isn't overrun with condos and lodges, although it has its share. Some 200 of the condos nearest the mountain are managed by the **Sugarbush Resort** (☎ 800/ 537-8427 or 802/583-3333), with accommodations ranging from one to four bedrooms. Guests have access to a slew of amenities, including a modern health club and five pools. The resort also manages the attractive Sugarbush Inn, right on the access road, with 46 hotel rooms and two restaurants. Shuttle buses deliver guests around the mountain, keeping driving to a minimum. During major winter holidays, there's a minimum stay of 5 days. Rates vary widely, and most rooms are sold as packages that include lift tickets in winter; call for more information.

✪ **Inn at Round Barn Farm.** 661 E. Warren Rd., Waitsfield, VT 05673. ☎ 802/ **496-2276.** Fax 802/496-8832. www.innattheroundbarn.com. E-mail: roundbarn@madriver. com. 12 units. $135–$250 double. Rates include full breakfast. $20 surcharge on holidays and during foliage season; 3-night minimum stay foliage and holiday weekends. AE, MC, V. Closed Apr 15–30. No children under 15.

This ranks among my favorite B&Bs in northern New England. Those seeking the romance of Vermont will find a surplus of it. You arrive after passing through a covered bridge just off Route 100; a couple of miles later, you come upon a regal barn and farmhouse, set along a sloping hill with views of fields all around. The centerpiece of the inn is the eponymous Round Barn, a strikingly beautiful 1910 structure that's used variously for weddings, arts exhibits, and Sunday church services. Each guest room is furnished with an impeccable country elegance. The less expensive rooms are in the older part of the house and are comfortable if small. The larger luxury rooms in the old attached horse barn feature stunning soaring ceilings under old log beams and include extras like steam showers and gas fireplaces. They're worth a splurge.

**Amenities:** Indoor lap pool, 18-mile cross-country ski center, game rooms, guest safe, and turndown service.

✪ **Inn at the Mad River Barn.** Rte. 17 (R.R. #1; P.O. Box 88), Waitsfield, VT 05673. ☎ **800/631-0466** or 802/496-3310. Fax 802/496-6696. www.madriverbarn.com. E-mail: madriverbarn@madriver.com. 15 units. Summer $74–$95 double; winter $110 double. Discounts midweek. Rates include breakfast. 2-night minimum stay holiday and winter week-ends. AE, DISC, MC, V.

The Inn at the Mad River Barn, run by former Mad River Glen ski-area owner Betsy Pratt, is a classic, 1960s-style ski lodge that attracts a clientele nearly fanatical in its devotion to the place. It's best not to come here expecting anything fancy—carpets and furniture are both more than a little threadbare. Do come expecting to have some fun once you're settled in. It's all knotty pine, with spartanly furnished guest rooms and rustic common rooms where visitors feel at home putting their feet up. Guests stay either in the two-story barn behind the white-clapboard main house, or in one of the eight rooms in the annex building up the lawn, which is better kept but has less character. In winter, guests can elect to get their dinners on the premises ($15), served in boisterous family style. In summer, the mood is slightly more sedate (only breakfast is offered) but enhanced by a beautiful pool a short walk away in a grove of birches. Most rooms have televisions; there's also a great game room in the main lodge with full-service bar.

✪ **The Pitcher Inn.** 275 Main St., Warren, VT 05674. ☎ **888-867-8424** or 802/496-6350. Fax 802/496-6354. www.pitcherinn.com. E-mail: pitcher@madriver.com. 10 units (including 2 2-bdrm suites). A/C TV TEL. $300–$550 double, $600 suites. Rates include full breakfast. Minimum stay applies on weekends (2 nights), holiday weekends (3 nights), and Christmas (5 nights). Children under 12 in suites only. AE, MC, V.

Set in the timeless village of Warren, the remarkable Pitcher Inn was newly built from the ground up following a fire that leveled a previous home; only the barn (housing the two suites) is original. This architect-created inn seamlessly blends modern conveniences and subtle whimsy with historic New England proportions and styling. The common areas are appointed in a sort of American fusion style, with a little Colonial Revival, a little Mission, and a little Adirondack sporting camp to cap it off. It melds perfectly. Be sure to stop by the basement lounge, called Tracks, to admire the wondrous door closing mechanism on the game room, inside which you'll find pool, tabletop shuffleboard, and darts.

The architect-and-artist-designed guest rooms are extraordinary. They're themed rooms, mostly related to Vermont, but done with such cleverness and wit that they're more like elegant puzzles. (My favorite feature: the carved goose in flight on the ceiling of the Mallard Room is attached to a weathervane on the roof, and it's head indicates wind direction.) There's not a bad room in the house. Colonial is the smallest and most traditional. The cozy School Room has a quirky schoolhouse feel (the TV is hidden behind the Gilbert Stuart portrait of Washington); the Chester Arthur Room has presidential memorabilia set amid regal 19th-century furnishings, including a wood fireplace and a richly hued landscape over the massive bed. The three most requested rooms (and justly so, in my opinion) are Trout, with a detached sitting room and octagonal pavillion; Lodge, with a fraternal order theme, lots of obelisks, and a TV hidden in an old podium; and Mountain, with a rock wall, firetower-like sleeping area, slate countertops, and a luxurious steam shower. All rooms have CD players, hidden TVs, and Jacuzzis; nine have fireplaces (seven are wood-burning, two gas); five have steam showers. One room (Ski) has a kitchenette.

**Dining:** The dining room is an airy and bright amalgam of brick, granite, maple, carpets, Mission-style lamps, and country Windsor chairs, with a dash of modern art. (Like the rest of the inn, the styles blend together harmoniously.) The menu is ambitious, and the New American regional meals almost always hit the mark. Look for

# You Paid What?

47,000 hotels, 700 airlines, 50 rental car companies. And a few million ways to save money.

**Travelocity.com**
A Sabre Company

**Go Virtually Anywhere.**

Will you have enough stories to tell your grandchildre

Yahoo! Travel

entrees like grilled sea bass with Thai green curry and coconut rice, and roast duck breast with a dried cherry and green peppercorn sauce. Entree prices range from $24 to $30. For a special meal celebrating a major milestone, ask about the private five-course dinners in the romantic wine cellar, which can accommodate parties up to six. (At last count, about a dozen engagments had been proffered here.)

**West Hill House.** 1496 W. Hill Rd., Warren, VT 05674. ☎ **800/898-1427** or 802/496-7162. Fax 802/496-6443. www.westhillhouse.com. E-mail: westhill@madriver.com. 7 units. Summer, foliage, and ski seasons $105–$160 double; spring $95–$140 double. Rates include full breakfast. 3-night minimum stay foliage and holiday weekends; 2-night minimum on other weekends. AE, DISC, MC, V. Children 12 and older are welcome.

Nestled on a forested hillside along a lightly traveled country road, the West Hill Inn offers the quintessential New England experience within a few minutes' commute to the slopes at Sugarbush. Built in the 1850s, this farmhouse boasts three common rooms, including a modern and bright addition with a handsome fireplace for warmth in winter and an outdoor patio for summer lounging. The guest rooms are well-appointed in an updated country style, and all have gas fireplaces or gas "woodstoves." For sheer character it's hard to beat the two small Hobbit-like rooms tucked under the eaves above a narrow staircase in the old part of the home. Three rooms have air-conditioning, and TVs are available on request. The newer guest rooms over the living room include steam showers and Jacuzzis. Country breakfasts are served around a large dining-room table, and the day's first meal tends to be an event as much as it is nourishment.

## WHERE TO DINE
✪ **Bass Restaurant.** 527 Sugarbush Access Rd., Warren. ☎ **802/583-3100.** www.bassrestaurant.com. Main courses $11–$21. AE, MC, V. Sun–Thurs 4–10pm, Fri and Sat 4–11pm. NEW AMERICAN.

If your choice of valley restaurants were limited to one, this would be the place. Bass Restaurant is located in a multilevel, modern ski-lodge building with a circular stone fireplace and a handsome blonde-wood bar. Light jazz plays in the background, and modern sculpture discretely enlivens the space. Appetizers are displayed on a tray tableside and change often ($5 to $7.50). The main courses range from crab cakes and garlic-marinated shrimp to prime rib and braised lamb shank with black-eyed peas. It's a quiet and romantic spot (tables are well-spaced and lit with individual spotlights) and offers excellent value—most entrees are around $15 and includes a house salad. Bass Restaurant delivers more than you might expect for that price.

**The Common Man.** German Flats Rd., Warren. ☎ **802/583-2800.** Reservations recommended in season. Main courses $12–$22. AE, DISC, MC, V. Daily 6–9pm. Open at 5:30pm on Sat and till 10pm on busier nights. Closed Mon from mid-Apr–mid-Dec. CONTINENTAL.

The Common Man is located in a century-old barn, and the interior is soaring and dramatic. Chandeliers, floral carpeting on the walls (weird, but it works), and candles on the tables meld successfully and coax all but cold-hearted guests into a relaxed frame of mind. You'll be halfway through the meal before you notice there are no windows. The menu strives to be as ambitious and appealing as the decor. It doesn't hit the mark as consistently as it once did, and guests often find themselves poking at a bland offering or two. Entrees range from roast duck served with raspberry vinegar and honey, to rainbow trout with sage leaves and pinenuts. The extravagant *Schnee-ballen* (vanilla ice cream with coconut and hot fudge) makes for a good conclusion.

**The Den.** Junction of Rtes. 100 and 17, Waitsfield. ☎ **802/496-8880.** Lunch items $4.95–$6.95; main dinner courses $8.95–$13.95. AE, MC, V. Daily 11:30am–11pm. AMERICAN.

Good food, decent service, no frills. That's The Den in a nutshell. Since 1970 a local favorite for its well-worn, neighborly feel, it's the kind of spot where you can plop yourself down in a pine booth, help yourself to the salad bar while awaiting your main course, then cheer on the Red Sox (or Patriots or Celtics) on the tube over the bar. The menu offers the usual pub fare, with all manner of burgers, plus Reubens, roast-beef sandwiches, meal-size salads, fried chicken, bowls of chili, homemade soups, and pork chops with apple sauce and french fries.

**John Eagan's Big World Pub.** Rte. 100, Warren. ☎ **802/496-3033.** Main courses $11–$16.50; burgers and sandwiches $6.25. AE, MC, V. Tues–Sun 5:30–9:30pm. GRILL/INTERNATIONAL.

Extreme skier John Eagan starred in ten Warren Miller skiing films over the years but *really* took a risk when he opened his own restaurant 5 years ago. Located in a 1970s-style motel dining room decorated with skiing mementos (including a bar made of ski sections signed by skiing luminaries like Tommy Moe), the Big World Pub compensates with a small but above-average pub menu that the chef often pulls off with unexpected flair. Wood-grilled items are crowd pleasers, including the wood-grilled chicken breast glazed with Vermont cider, ginger, and lime. Also tasty (especially in the winter) is the Hungarian goulash, made with pork and sauerkraut.

**The Spotted Cow.** Bridgestreet Marketplace (at corner of Rte. 100 and East Warren Rd.), Waitsfield. ☎ **802/496-5151.** Reservations suggested. Main courses, lunch $7.95–$10.50, dinner $16.95–$23.95. MC, V. Daily 11:30am–3pm, 5:30–9pm. ECLECTIC.

Set on the ground floor of a small and rustic retail complex in Waitsfield, the Spotted Cow is a low-ceilinged, modern, natural-wood spot with cherry banquettes and windows facing out on to a walkway. The place has the comfortably cozy feel of a bistro only locals know about and is cultivated rather than funky. The inventive lunch menu features brie sandwiches, shiitake soup, and vegetarian paté. At dinner, the kitchen shines with options like pork tenderloin with a maple, mustard, and thyme glaze; game hen and shrimp fricaseee with morels and leeks; and grilled duck breast with foi gras and a maple-cranberry sauce. There's always a vegetarian special available.

**Warrren House Inn.** Sugarbush Access Rd., Warren. ☎ **802/583-2421.** Reservations recommended. Main courses, $13.95–$18.95. AE, MC, V. Ski season daily 5:30–9:30pm (till 10pm Fri–Sat). NEW AMERICAN.

The Warren House has a cozy location in a 1958 sugarhouse decorated with the work of local artists, and it's a popular and casual spot not far from the slopes. The menu is creative but doesn't stray too far from the familiar—call it eclectic comfort food. For starters, there are crab cakes made with ginger and cilantro, and a wide array of salads, including goat cheese wrapped in walnuts and served on baby greens. For main courses, look for maple-marinated pork chops with a roasted garlic barbecue sauce, or bouillabaisse with prawns, scallops, clams and mussels. The kitchen can be inconsistent, but on a good night this is a fun destination.

# 3 Montpelier, Barre & Waterbury

Montpelier is 13 miles southeast of Waterbury, 9 miles northwest of Barre, 178 miles northwest of Boston, and 39 miles southeast of Burlington.

Montpelier is easily the most downhome, low-key state capital in the United States. There's a hint of that in every photo of the glistening gold dome of the state capitol. Rising up behind it isn't a bank of mirror-sided skyscrapers, but a thickly forested hill. Montpelier, it turns out, isn't a self-important center of politics, but a small town that happens to be home to state government.

The state capitol is worth a visit, as is the local art museum and historical society; but more than that, it's worth visiting just to experience a small, clean, New England town that's more than a little friendly. Montpelier centers on two main boulevards: State Street, which is lined with state government buildings, and Main Street, where many of the town's shops are located. It's all very compact, manageable, and cordial.

The downtown has two hardware stores next door to one another. (one had this sign posted on its front door when I visited: "We just oiled our floor and it may be slippery when wet until it gets wore in.") The **Savoy,** 26 Main St. (☎ **802/ 229-0509**), is one of the best art movie houses in northern New England. At the Savoy, a large cup of cider and a popcorn slathered with real, unclarified butter cost me less than a small popcorn with flavored oil at a mall cinema.

Nearby Barre (pronounced "Barry") is more commercial but shares an equally vibrant past. Barre has a more commercial, blue-collar demeanor than Montpelier. The historic connection to the thriving granite industry is seen here and there, from the granite curbstones lining its long Main Street, to the signs for commercial establishments carved out of locally hewn rock. Barre attracted talented stoneworkers from Scotland and Italy (there's even a statue of Robert Burns), that once gave the town a lively, cosmopolitan flavor.

About 10 miles west of Montpelier, **Waterbury** lies at the juncture of Route 100 and I-89, making it a commercial center by default, if not by design. Waterbury is set along the Winooski River but tends to sprawl more than other Vermont towns, perhaps in part because of the flood of 1927, which came close to leveling the town. It's also because the town has attracted an inexplicable number of food companies (including Ben & Jerry's Ice Cream and Green Mountain Coffee) that have built factories and outlets in outlying former pastures. With its location between Montpelier and Burlington and with easy access to Stowe and Sugarbush, Waterbury has started to attract more emigrees looking for the good life.

The downtown, with its brick commercial architecture and sampling of handsome early homes, is worth a brief tour, but most travelers are either passing through or looking for "that ice cream place." Despite its drive-thru quality, Waterbury makes a decent home base for further explorations in the Green Mountains, in Burlington 25 miles to the west and in Montpelier to the east.

## ESSENTIALS

**GETTING THERE**    Montpelier is accessible via Exit 7 off I-89. For Barre, take Exit 8. Waterbury is located at Exit 10 off I-89. For bus service to Montpelier, contact **Vermont Transit** (☎ **800/451-3292** or 802/223-7112). Waterbury is served by Vermont Transit (☎ **802/244-6943**) and Amtrak's *Vermonter,* with daily departures from New York (☎ **800/USA-RAIL**).

**VISITOR INFORMATION**    The **Central Vermont Chamber of Commerce,** P.O. Box 336, Barre, VT 05641 (☎ **802/229-5711**), is located on Stewart Road off Exit 7 of I-89. Turn left at the first light; it's a $^1$/$_2$ mile on the left. The chamber is open weekdays 9am to 5pm. Information is also available on the Web at **www.central-vt.com**.

The Waterbury Tourism Council, P.O. Box 149, Waterbury, VT 05676 (☎ **802/ 244-7822**), operates a small, unstaffed booth stocked with helpful brochures on Route 100 just north of I-89. It's open daily from 7am to 10pm.

## EXPLORING MONTPELIER & BARRE

Start your exploration of Montpelier with a visit to the gold-domed **State House** (☎ **802/828-2228**). A statue of Ethan Allen guards the doors. Three capitol buildings rose on this site since 1809; the present building retained the impressive portico designed during the height of Greek Revival style in 1836. It was modeled after the temple of Theseus in Athens and is made of Vermont granite. Inside, note the handsome black-and-white marble floor; look for fossils in the black marble. Self-guided tours of the capitol are offered when the building is open, Monday to Friday (except holidays) 7:45am to 4:15pm; in summer, it's also open Saturdays 11am to 3pm. Free guided tours are offered twice daily, once in the morning and once in the afternnoon; ask in the main lobby about times.

A short stroll from the State House, at 109 State St., is the **Vermont Historical Society** (☎ 802/828-2291). This is a great spot to admire some of the rich tapestry of Vermont's history. The museum is housed in a replica of the elegant old Pavilion Building, a prominent Victorian hotel, and contains a number of artifacts, including the gun once owned by Ethan Allen. The society's museum is open Tuesday to Friday 9am to 4:30pm, Saturday 9am to 4pm, and Sunday noon to 4pm. Admission is $3 adult, $2 student and senior.

## FOR ROCK FANS

**Rock of Ages Quarry.** Graniteville. ☎ 802/476-3119. www.rockofages.com. Tours $4 adults, $3.50 seniors 62 and over, $1.50 children 6–12, free for children under 6. Narrated tours: Jun–mid-Oct 9:15am–3pm, visitor center May–Oct Mon–Sat 8:30am–5pm, Sun noon–5pm. Closed July 4. From Barre, drive south on Rte. 14, turn left at lights by McDonald's; watch for signs to quarry.

When in or around Barre, listen for the deep, throaty hum of industry. That's the Rock of Ages Quarry, set on a rocky hillside high above town near the aptly named hamlet of Graniteville. A free visitor center presents informative exhibits, a video about quarrying, a glimpse at an old granite quarry (no longer active), and a selection of granite gifts. The self-guided tour is free.

For a closer look at the active quarry, sign up for a guided half-hour tour of the world's largest quarry (note the tour season, hours, and prices above). An old bus groans up to a viewer's platform high above the 500-foot, man-made canyon, where workers cleave huge slabs of fine-grained granite and hoist them out using 150-foot derricks anchored with a spider's web of 15 miles of steel cable. It's a spectacle to behold. Afterwards, visitors are invited to stop by the nearby manufacturing plant to see the granite carved into memorials, architectural adornments, and other pieces.

For a more poignant display of the local stonecutters' craft, head to **Hope Cemetery,** located on a hillside in a wooded valley north of Barre on Route 14. The cemetery is filled with columns, urns, and human figures carved of the fine-grained gray granite. It's more than a memorial park—it's also a remarkable display of the talent of area stonecutters.

## HIKING CAMEL'S HUMP

A short drive from Waterbury is ✪ **Camel's Hump,** the state's fourth highest peak at 4,083 feet. (It's also the highest Vermont mountain without a ski area.) Once the site of a popular Victorian-era summit resort, the mountain still attracts hundreds of hikers who ascend the demanding, highly popular trail to the barren, windswept peak. It's not the place to get away from crowds on sunny summer weekends, but it's well worth the effort for the spectacular vistas and to observe the unique alpine terrain along the high ridge.

One popular round-trip loop-hike is about 7¹/₂ miles (plan on 6 hours or more of hiking time), and departs from the Couching Lion Farm 8 miles southwest of Waterbury on Camel's Hump Road. (You're best off asking locally for exact directions.) At

# The Story of Ben & Jerry

The doleful cows standing amid a bright green meadow on Ben & Jerry's ice cream pints have become almost a symbol for Vermont, but Ben & Jerry's cows—actually, they're Vermont artist Woody Jackson's cows—have also become a symbol for friendly capitalism ("hippie capitalism," as some prefer).

The founding of the company has become a legend in business circles. Two friends from Long Island, New York, Ben Cohen and Jerry Greenfield, started up their company in Burlington in 1978 with $12,000 and a few mail-order lessons in ice-cream making. The pair experimented with the flavor samples they obtained free from salesmen and sold their products out of an old downtown gas station. Embracing the outlook that work should be fun, they gave away free ice cream at community events, staged free outdoor films in summer, and plowed profits back into the community. Their free-spirited approach, along with the exceptional quality of their product, built a successful corporation with sales rising to the hundreds of millions of dollars.

While competition from other gourmet ice-cream makers and a widespread consumer desire to cut back fat consumption has made it tougher to have fun and turn a profit at the same time, Ben and Jerry are still at it, expanding their manufacturing plants outside New England and concocting new products. As of early 2000, Ben & Jerry were weighing offers from outside buyers, but it seems likely that the company's heart will remain in Vermont and New England, no matter who the actual owner is. The firm has too much invested in the region to simply walk away. At least, that's what everybody says and hopes.

The main factory in Waterbury, about 10 miles south of Stowe, is among the most popular tourist attractions in Vermont. The plant is located about a mile north of I-89 on Route 100, and the grounds have a festival marketplace feel to them, despite the fact that there's no festival and no marketplace. During peak summer season crowds mill about waiting for the 30-minute factory tours. Tours are first-come, first-served, and start at 10am; afternoon tours fill up quickly, so get there early if you want to avoid a long wait. Once you've got your ticket, browse the small ice-cream museum (learn the long, strange history of Cherry Garcia), buy a cone of your favorite flavor at the scoop shop, or lounge along the promenade, which is scattered with Adirondack chairs and picnic tables. Tours are $2 for adults, $1.75 senior, free for children under 12.

For kids, there's the "Stairway to Heaven," which leads to a playground, and a "Cow-Viewing Area," which is pretty much self-explanatory. The tours are informative and fun, and conclude with a sample of the day's featured product. For more information on the tours, call ☎ 802/244-8687.

the summit, seasonal rangers are on hand to answer questions and to admonish hikers to stay on the rocks to avoid trampling the rare and delicate alpine grasses, found in Vermont only here and on Mt. Mansfield to the north.

## WHERE TO STAY
### IN MONTPELIER

**Capitol Plaza Hotel.** 100 State St., Montpelier, VT 05602. ☎ **800/274-5252** or 802/223-5252. Fax 802/229-5427. www.capitolplaza.com. E-mail: capitolplaza@ibm.net. 57 units. A/C TV TEL. $89 double; foliage season $105 double. AE, DISC, MC, V.

The Capitol Plaza is the favored hotel of folks coming into town on business with the government, but is well-located (across from the state capitol) to serve visitors exploring the town. The carpeted lobby is small and has a colonial cast to it; the rooms on the three upper floors also adopt a light, faux-colonial tone and feature the usual hotel amenities, including in-room coffeemakers. The hotel is nothing fancy, but it is clean, comfortable, and convenient.

**Dining:** The hotel operates a locally popular steakhouse called J. Morgan's on the first floor, with steaks and other meats priced at $12.95 to $23.95. Less expensive dishes include pizza, pasta, and sandwiches. Open for all three meals daily.

**Inn at Montpelier.** 147 Main St., Montpelier, VT 05602. ☎ **802/223-2727.** Fax 802/223-0722. www.innatmontpelier.com. E-mail: innkeeper@innatmontpelier.com. 19 units. A/C TV TEL. $99–$169 double (premium charged during foliage season). Rates include continental breakfast. AE, DC, DISC, MC, V.

Two historic in-town homes house guests at the Inn at Montpelier, and both offer welcoming accommodations and most amenities. The main, cream-colored Federal-style inn, built in 1827, features a mix of historical and up-to-date furnishings, along with a sunny sitting room and deck off the rear of the second floor. The larger front rooms are nicely appointed, but so too are the much smaller rooms in the former servants' wing. Room 27 is especially pleasant and features a large private deck. The inn is a shade more antiseptic and spartanly furnished than other historic inns I've visited, but it's certainly more intriguing and comfortable than any chain hotel.

## IN WATERBURY

**The Old Stagecoach Inn.** 18 N. Main St., Waterbury, VT 05676. ☎ **800/262-2206** or 802/244-5056. 11 units (3 rooms share 1 bathroom). TEL. Foliage season, Christmas week, and President's Day weekend $55–$130 double; other times $45–$100 double. Rates include full breakfast. 2-night minimum during peak periods. AE, DISC, MC, V. Pets allowed; $10 per pet.

This handsome, gabled home, within walking distance of downtown, is full of wonderful details like painted wood floors, a pair of upstairs porches to observe the town's comings and goings, an old library with a stamped tin ceiling, and a chessboard awaiting a game. Originally built in 1826, the house was gutted and revamped in 1890 in ostentatious period style by an Ohio millionaire. In 1987, after some years of quiet disuse, it was converted to an inn by owners who took good care to preserve the historical detailing. The inn has a living room with a resident parrot. Guest rooms are furnished in a understated Victorian style, mostly with oak and pine furniture and a selection of antiques. It's not a polished inn (expect some worn carpeting), but it's quite comfortable. The two third-floor rooms have the original exposed beams and skylights, and are pleasant and open. The three back rooms share a bath and offer guests the feel of boarding at a friendly farmhouse; these are a good choice for budget travelers. Room 1 is among the best, with Victorian detailing, large dressing area, and marble sink.

**Dining:** The informal dining room offers a casual menu inspired by the meals of historic taveners (back ribs, strip steak, pasta, crab cakes) that's served mostly to inn guests. There's a children's menu, and a full bar. Entrees are priced from $8.95 to $15.95, and meals are served Wednesday through Saturday 5:30 to 8pm.

**Thatcher Brook Inn.** Rte. 100, Waterbury, VT 05676. ☎ **800/292-5911** or 802/244-5911. Fax 802/244-1294. www.thatcherbrook.com. E-mail: info@thatcherbrook.com. 22 units. TEL. Peak season (including holidays, Christmas week, Presidents' Day weekend, and foliage season) $99–$205 double; other times $80–$175 double. Rates include full breakfast. 2-night minimum during foliage season; 3-night minimum during Christmas. AE, CB, DC, DISC, MC, V.

Thatcher Brook Inn is located on busy Route 100 near the Ben & Jerry's factory, but the innkeepers have pulled off the illusion that guests are considerably further away from this major artery. The circa-1899 white-clapboard building has a nice historical character, even though it's undergone significant renovations and expansions in recent years. The new additions have kept its Queen Anne–style architectural integrity intact. The common areas downstairs are worn to a nice patina, whether it's the sitting area in front of the fireplace, or the newer bar and grill with its Windsor chairs. The guest rooms are all carpeted and individually decorated with furniture varying from Ethan Allen new to flea-market oak, but the overall character takes its cue from a somewhat fussy country look. Four rooms have fireplaces (two wood, two propane), and six have Jacuzzis. Rooms 14 through 17 are a bit larger and more spacious; Rooms 8 through 11 have balconies off the back that face a quiet wooded hillside. Some rooms have air-conditioning; ask first if it's important.

**Dining:** The inn's dining room serves country-traditional fare like filet mignon wrapped with bacon, seafood stew, and portobellos stuffed with goat cheese and roasted red peppers. Main courses are $13.95 to $20.95. Guests choosing from four dining areas, including one room for couples only. There's also a Bailley's Fireside Tavern, a bar and grill with American fare.

## WHERE TO DINE

A creation of the New England Culinary Institute, **La Brioche Bakery & Cafe** (☎ **802/229-0443**) occupies the corner of Montpelier's State and Main streets. It's a little bit of Europe in one of New England's more continental cities (Montpelier could slip into the Black Forest or the Vienna Woods without causing much of a stir). A deli counter offers baked goods like croissants and baguettes. Get them to go, or settle into a table in the afternoon sun outdoors.

### IN MONTPELIER

**Horn of the Moon.** 8 Langdon St., Montpelier. ☎ **802/223-2895.** Reservations not accepted. Breakfast $2.50–$6; lunch $5–$7; dinner $6–$10. No credit cards (out-of-state checks OK). Tues–Sat 7am–9pm; Sun 9am–7pm (open Sun until 9pm summer and early fall). VEGETARIAN.

This relaxed, informal, and inexpensive restaurant overlooking a tributary of the Winooski was the first vegetarian restaurant in Vermont, and it remains one of the best. In fact, it's appealing enough to attract plenty of carnivores, drawn by the robust pastas, tasty sandwiches made on whole-wheat flat bread, and the Mexican-style dishes like burritos and tostadas. If you're looking for a full three-course meal with dinner rolls and linens, you're better off around the corner at the Main Street Grill; but if you want wholesome, inexpensive food, get here early and often.

**Main Street Grill & Bar.** 118 Main St., Montpelier. ☎ **802/223-3188.** Reservations accepted. Lunch items $3.75–$7.95; dinner entrees $5.95–$12.75. AE, DISC, MC, V. Mon–Fri 7–10am and 11:30am–2pm; Sat 8:30–10:30am and 11:30am–2pm; Sun 10am–2pm; daily 5:30–9pm. AMERICAN/ECLECTIC.

This airy, modern grill serves both as a classroom and an ongoing exam for students of the New England Culinary Institute, which is located just down the block. It's not unusual to see knots of students, toques at a rakish angle, walking between the restaurant and class. Diners can eat in the first-level dining room, watching street life through the broad windows (in summer, there's seating on a narrow porch outside the windows), or burrow in the homey bar downstairs. Dishes change with the semester, but might include sautéed rainbow trout with rock shrimp, wood-grilled flank steak, or autumn squash ravioli. The breakfasts here are a superb way to begin a day, with items like breakfast burritos stuffed with scrambled eggs.

Also of note is the second-floor **Chef's Table,** which is open weekdays for lunch and dinner, and Saturdays for dinner only. This intimate and well-appointed dining room with Cherokee red walls offers more refined fare, including a three-course tasting menu with two glasses of wine for $40 per person. (A la carte prices are $14.50 to $18.75.) Entrees range from a smoked pork chop with apple-fennel salad, to grilled yellowfin tuna with an olive-caper sauce.

## IN WATERBURY

**Marsala Salsa.** 13–15 Stowe St. ☎ **802/244-1150.** Reservations recommended on weekends. Main courses $6.95–$12.95. MC, V. Mon–Sat 5–9:30pm. INDIAN/MEXICAN.

Here's the story: The owner is from Trinidad and was raised on the cuisine of India, but spent time working at a Mexican restaurant in Nevada. The result? Marsala Salsa, a hybrid that offers two international cuisines, both well-prepared at reasonable prices. The restaurant, located in a funky storefront in Waterbury's historic downtown, is decorated with a light and culturally ambiguous touch. Service is friendly and informal. Mexican entrees include carne asada and bistec picado—strips of sirloin charbroiled with a homemade avocado-lime butter. If you're more tempted by the Asian subcontinent, try the curries or tandoori chicken, or a wonderful shrimp shaag—a light curry with sautéed shrimp, spinach, and carrots. Desserts include flan, deep-fried bananas, and coconut-cream caramel. Marsala Salsa is an unexpected oasis deep behind local culinary battle lines manned primarily by cheddar cheese and maple syrup.

# 4 Stowe

Stowe is 22 miles north of Waitsfield, 198 miles northwest of Boston, and 36 miles east of Burlington.

Stowe is a wonderful destination, summer, fall, and winter. It was one of Vermont's first winter destination areas, but it has managed the decades-long juggernaut of growth reasonably well and with good humor. There are condo developments and strip-mall-style restaurants, to be sure. Stowe has a more depth and breadth of lodging and restaurants than comparably sized ski towns—this small town with a year-round population of just 3,400 boasts some 62 lodging establishments and more than 50 restaurants. By and large, the village has managed to preserve its essential character rather well, including trademark views of the surrounding mountains and vistas across the fertile farmlands of the valley floor. Thanks to its history and charm, Stowe tends to attract a more affluent clientele than, say, Killington or Okemo.

Stowe is quaint, compact, and home to what may be Vermont's most gracefully tapered church spire, located atop the Stowe Community Church. It's one of the most appealing of the ski areas in summer. Because the mountain is a few miles from the village, the town doesn't take on that woebegone emptiness that many ski areas do. You can actually park your car and enjoyably explore by foot or bike, which isn't the case at ski resorts that grew up around large parking lots and condo clusters.

Most of the development of recent decades has taken place along Mountain Road (Route 108), which runs northwest of the village to the base of Mount Mansfield and the Stowe ski area. Here you'll find an array of motels, restaurants, shops, bars, and even a three-screen cinema, with many establishments nicely designed or tastefully tucked out of view. The road has all the convenience of a strip-mall area but with little of the aesthetic blight.

The one complaint about Mountain Road: it invariably backs up at the end of the ski day in winter and on foliage weekends, and can make a trip into the village an interesting experiment in blood-pressure management. Fortunately, a free trolley-bus

# Maple Syrup & How It Gets That Way

Maple syrup is at once simple and extravagant: simple because it's made from the purest ingredients available, extravagant because it's an expensive luxury.

Two elemental ingredients combine to create maple syrup: sugar-maple sap and fire. Sugaring season slips in between northern New England's long winter and short spring; it usually lasts around 4 or 5 weeks, typically beginning in early to mid-March. When warm and sunny days alternate with freezing nights, the sap in the maple trees begins to run from roots to the branches overhead. Sugarers drill shallow holes into the trees and insert small taps. Buckets (or plastic tubing) are hung from the taps to collect the sap that drips out bit by bit.

The collected sap is then boiled off. The equipment for this ranges from a simple backyard fire pit cobbled together of concrete blocks, to elaborate sugarhouses with oil or propane burners. It requires between 32 and 40 gallons of sap to make 1 gallon of syrup, and that means a fair amount of boiling. The real cost of syrup isn't the sap; it's in the fuel to boil it down.

Vermont is the nation's capital of maple syrup production, producing some 550,000 gallons a year, with a value of about $12 million. The fancier inns and restaurants all serve native maple syrup with breakfast. Other breakfast places will charge $1 or so for real syrup rather than the flavored corn syrup that's so prevalent elsewhere. (Sometimes you have to ask if the real stuff is available.)

You can pick up the real thing in almost any grocery store in the state, but I'm convinced it tastes better if you buy it right from the farm. Look for handmade signs touting syrup posted at the end of driveways around the region throughout the year. Drive on up and knock on the door.

A number of sugarers invite visitors to inspect the process and sample some of the fresh syrup in the early spring. Ask for the brochure "Maple Sugarhouses Open to Visitors," available at information centers, or by writing or calling the **Vermont Department of Agriculture** (116 State St., Montpelier, VT 05620; ☎ **802/828-2416**). The list is also posted on the Web at: www.state.vt.us/agric/sugarhouses.htm.

connects the village with the mountain during ski season, so you can let your car get snowed in, and prevent outbreaks of village traffic from getting under your skin.

## ESSENTIALS

**GETTING THERE**    Stowe is located on Route 100 north of Waterbury and south of Morrisville. In summer, Stowe may also be reached via Smugglers Notch on Route 108. This pass, which squeezes narrowly between the rocks and is not recommended for RVs or trailers, is closed in winter.

There is no direct train or bus service to Stowe. Travel to Waterbury, 10 miles south of Stowe, via **Vermont Transit** ☎ **800/451-3292** or 802-244-6943 or **Amtrak** ☎ **800/872-7245,** then connect to Stowe via rental car (**Thrifty,** ☎ **802/244-8800**), limo (**Richard's Limosine Service,** ☎ **800/698-3176** or 802/253-5600), or taxi (**Peg's Pick Up,** ☎ **800/370-9490** or 802/253-9490).

**VISITOR INFORMATION**    The **Stowe Area Association,** P.O. Box 1320, Stowe, VT 05672 (☎ **800/247-8693** or 802/253-7321), maintains a handy office on Main Street in the village center, which is open from 9am to 8pm Monday to Friday, and 10am to 5pm weekends (limited hours during slower times). Also see **www.stoweinfo.com.**

The **Green Mountain Club** (☎ 802/244-7037), a venerable statewide association devoted to building and maintaining backcountry trails, has a visitor center on Route 100 between Waterbury and Stowe.

**FESTIVALS**    The weeklong **Stowe Winter Carnival** (☎ 802/253-7321) takes places annually at the end of January, as it has since 1921. The fest features a number of wacky events involving skis, snowshoes, and skates, as well as nighttime entertainment in area venues. Don't miss the snow sculpture contest, or "turkey bowling," which involves sliding frozen birds across the ice.

## DOWNHILL SKIING

**Stowe Mountain Resort.** Stowe, VT 05672. ☎ **800/253-4754** for lodging or 802/253-3000. www.stowe.com. E-mail: stosales@sover.net. Vertical drop: 2,360 ft. Lifts: 1 gondola, 8 chairlifts (1 high-speed), 2 surface lifts. Skiable acreage: 480. Lift tickets: $56 holiday, $54 non-holiday.

Stowe was once *the* place to ski in New England—one of the first, one of the classiest, and one of the best ski resorts anywhere in the world. Killington, Sunday River, and Sugarloaf—among others—have all captured other superlatives, and never mind the Rocky Mountain resorts much more accessible to easterners now than they were 50 years ago. But this historic resort, first developed in the 1930s, still has loads of charm and plenty of great runs. It's one of the best places for the full New England ski experience and one of the most beautiful ski mountains, and it still offers tremendous challenges to advanced skiers with its winding, old-style trails. Especially notable are its legendary "Front Four" trails (National, Starr, Lift Line, and Goat), that have humbled more than a handful of skiers attempting to claw their way from advanced-intermediate to expert. The mountain has four good, long lifts, that go to the top—not the usual patchwork of shorter lifts you find at other ski areas. Beginning skiers don't have to be intimidated on the main mountain—they can start out across the road at Spruce Peak, which features gentle, wide, and sunny trails.

## CROSS-COUNTRY SKIING

Stowe is an outstanding destination for cross-country skiers, offering no fewer than four groomed ski areas with a combined total of more than 100 miles of trails traversing everything from gentle valley floors to challenging mountain peaks. Note that a single trail pass purchased at any of the four areas listed below is good at all the others, but your car needs to be parked where you buy your ticket.

The **Trapp Family Lodge Cross-Country Ski Center,** on Luce Hill Rd., 2 miles from Mountain Rd. (☎ **800/826-7000** or 802/253-8511; www.trappfamily.com), was the nation's first cross-country ski center. It remains one of the most gloriously situated in the Northeast, set atop a ridge with views across the broad valley and into the folds of the mountains flanking Mount Mansfield. The center features 36 miles of groomed trails on its 2,200 acres of rolling forestland. Rates are $14 for a trail pass, $16 for equipment rental, and $14 for a group lesson. A package of all three is $35.

The **Edson Hill Manor Ski Touring Center** (☎ **800/621-0284** or 802/253-8954) has 33 miles of wooded trails just off Mountain Road ($10 for a day pass). Also offering appealing ski touring are the **Stowe Mountain Resort Cross-Country Touring Center** (☎ **800/253-4754** or 802/253-7311), with 48 miles at the base of Mount Mansfield ($11), and **Topnotch Resort** (☎ **800/451-8686** or 802/253-8585), with 24 miles of groomed trails in the forest flanking Mountain Road ($12).

# OTHER OUTDOOR PURSUITS

Stowe's history is linked to winter recreation, but it's also an outstanding fair-weather destination, surrounded by lush, rolling green hills and open farmlands and towered over by craggy **Mount Mansfield,** Vermont's highest peak at 4,393 feet.

Deciding how to get atop Mount Mansfield is half the challenge. The **toll road** (☎ **802/253-7311**) traces its lineage back to the 19th century, when it served horse-drawn vehicles bringing passengers to the old hotel sited near the mountain's crown. (The hotel was demolished in the 1960s.) Drivers now twist their way up this road and park below the summit of Mansfield; a 2-hour hike along well-marked trails will bring you to the top with its unforgettable views. The toll road is open from late May to mid-October. The fare is $12 per car with up to six passengers, $2 per additional person. Ascending by foot or bicycle is free.

Another option is the Stowe **gondola** (☎ **802/253-7311**), which whisks visitors to within 1¹/₂ miles of the summit at the Cliff House Restaurant. Hikers can explore the rugged, open ridgeline, then descend before twilight. The gondola runs from mid-June to mid-October and costs $10 round-trip for adults, $6 for children 6 to 12.

The budget route up Mount Mansfield (and to my mind, the most rewarding) is on foot, and you have at least nine choices for an ascent. The easiest but least pleasing route is up the toll road. Other options require local guidance and a good map. Ask for information from knowledgeable locals (your inn might be of help), or stop by the Green Mountain Club headquarters, open weekdays, on Route 100 about 4 miles south of Stowe. GMC can also assist with advice on other area trails.

One of the most understated, most beloved local attractions is the **Stowe Recreation Path,** which winds 5.3 miles from behind the Stowe Community Church up the valley toward the mountain, ending behind the Topnotch Tennis Center. This exceptionally appealing pathway is heavily used by locals for transportation and exercise in summer; in winter, it serves as a cross-country ski trail. Connect to the pathway at either end or at points where it crosses side roads that lead to Mountain Road. No motorized vehicles or skateboards are allowed.

All manner of recreational paraphernalia is available for rent at **The Mountain Sports & Bike Shop** (☎ **802/253-7919**), which is right on the Rec Path. This includes full-suspension demo bikes, baby joggers, and bike trailers. Basic bike rentals are $16 for 4 hours, which is plenty long enough to explore the path. The shop is on Mountain Road (across from the Golden Eagle Resort) and is open from 9am to 6pm daily in summer. (This is also a good spot for cross-country ski and snowshoe rentals in winter.)

Guided mountain bike tours are offered by **Steer Off Road Tours,** (☎ **802/253-2999;** www.steeroffroad.com) which will take between one and six riders out to explore Stowe's extensive off-road trail network. Tours are tailored to your experience (adults only), and range in price from $25 for an hour to $69 for a full day. Bikes are not included, but rentals are available in town (see above).

Fans of paddle sports should seek out **Umiak Outdoor Outfitters,** located at 849 S. Main St. in Stowe, (☎ **802/253-2317**). The folks here feature a whole slew of guided river trips (flatwater or light rapids) and instruction (learn how to roll that kayak!), which range from 3 hours to 3 days ($35 to $225). They also offer canoe, kayak, and raft rentals ($25 to $35 per day).

Anglers should allow ample time to peruse **The Fly Rod Shop** (☎ **802/253-7346**), located on Route 100 2 miles south of the village. This well-stocked shop offers fly and spin tackle, along with camping gear, antique fly rods, and rentals of canoes and fishing videos. Also in town is **Bob Shannon's Fly Fish Vermont,**

954 S. Main St. (☎ 802/253-3964), with full retail shop and outfitting operation that can arrange for guides or guided instructional tours.

## WHERE TO STAY

Stowe has a number of motels to serve travelers who don't require the amenities offered by some of the more elaborate properties. The **Sun and Ski Motor Inn,** 1613 Mountain Rd. (☎ **800/448-5223** or 802/253-7159), has 26 servicable but utilitarian units, all of which have air-conditioning, telephones, TVs, and small refrigerators. There's a year-round pool heated to 102 degrees, perfect for thawing after a cold day skiing. Rates are $67 to $160 for two.

The **Stowe Motel,** 2043 Mountain Rd. (☎ **800/829-7629** or 802/253-7629), offers 60 rooms spread among three buildings. It's a basic motel, but with rooms slightly larger than average and a bit more stylish and comfortable, with pine furniture, couches, and coffee tables. All rooms have TVs, telephones, small refrigerators and air-conditioning, and there's a Jacuzzi, heated pool (summer only), game room, and free use of snowshoes. Rates are $62 to $96 double ($98 to $148 during holidays). Add $10 to $20 for an efficiency unit. Winter ski packages are available.

**Edson Hill Manor.** 1500 Edson Hill Rd., Stowe, VT 05672. ☎ **800/621-0284** or 802/253-7371. www.stowevt.com. 25 units. TEL. High season $199–$259 double, including breakfast and dinner; regular season $119–$179 double, including full breakfast; off-season (Apr, May, and Nov) $75 double midweek, $95 weekend. AE, DISC, MC, V. Pets and young children welcome in carriage house only.

The Edson Hill Manor is set up a long, quiet drive 2 miles from Mountain Road and has a wonderfully quirky charm. There's a main lodge, which dates to the 1940s, and four carriage houses just up the hill, which are of newer vintage. The whole compound is set amid a rolling landscape of lawns, hemlocks, and maples. The comfortable common room in the main house is like a movie set for a country retreat—tapestries, pastels, and oils adorn the walls. It could be outside London or maybe in Connecticut horse country. Nine guest rooms are in the main lodge, and most have pine walls and floors, wood-burning fireplaces, Colonial maple furnishings, wingback chairs, and four-poster beds. Most are modestly sized; Room #2 is bigger and brighter with white-washed pine walls. The Honeymoon Suite (#3) has a skylight over the bed, picture window, and a small living room. The 16 carriage-house rooms are somewhat larger but lack the cozy charm of the main inn, and feel more like motel units (albeit *nice* motel units). Manor rooms are air-conditioned; some rooms have televisions.

**Dining:** The dining room is open daily 6 to 9pm (weekends only in the slower seasons) and has heavy beams, slate floors, ladderback chairs, and pink tablecloths. Starters include crab and corn fritters and white bean and tomato soup; main courses range from grilled salmon with oyster mushrooms, rack of lamb, and grilled strip steak with fennel and a greeen peppercorn sauce. Entrees are $15.50 to $24.50. There's a great bar downstairs for a pre- (or post-) dinner libation.

**Amenities:** Edson Hill has riding stables with guided trail rides and hayrides in summer, sleighrides in winter, and private lessons by appointment. Also: fishing pond and access to nearby pool (not on inn grounds).

**The Gables Inn.** 1457 Mountain Rd., Stowe, VT 05672. ☎ **802/253-7730.** Fax 802/253-8989. www.gablesinn.com. E-mail: inngables@aol.com. 19 units. A/C. Foliage season $110–$250 double; winter $90–$175 double; off-season $75–$175 double. Holidays higher. All rates include breakfast. 2-night minimum stay applies weekends, holidays, and foliage season. AE, DC, DISC, MC, V.

This cozy inn, housed in a gray farmhouse facing Mountain Road, is a relaxed kind of place—the hot tub next to the front door makes that point clear. The main farmhouse has 13 comfortable rooms of varying size and shape simply furnished with country antiques; a newer "carriage house" in the back offers four rooms, mostly with cathedral ceilings, canopy beds, fireplaces, Jacuzzis, and air-conditioning. Two other "Riverview Suites" in an adjacent building are more opulently appointed, and include telephones, TVs, fireplaces, and VCRs.

**Dining:** Hearty breakfasts are served in a pleasant sunroom with grand views across the road to distant Mount Mansfield. The inn also offers tasty, basic dinners (steak, veal chicken, scallops, and pasta) with entrees priced at $8.95 to $16.95. Beer and wine are served.

**Green Mountain Inn.** 18 Main St. (P.O. Box 60), Stowe, VT 05672. ☎ **800/253-7302** or 802/253-7301. Fax 802/253-5096. www.greenmountaininn.com. E-mail: info@gminn.com. 76 units. A/C TV TEL. $119–$209 double, $139–$235 foliage and Christmas. Discount in spring and late fall. Ask about packages. 2-night minimum summer/winter weekends and foliage season. AE, DISC, MC, V. Pets allowed in some rooms; ask first.

This tasteful, historic structure sits right in the village. It's a sprawling place with 76 guest rooms spread through several buildings, but it feels far more intimate, with quirky narrow hallways and guest rooms tastefully decorated in an early–19thcentury motif that befits the 1833 vintage of the main inn. About a dozen rooms feature Jacuzzis and/or gas fireplaces, and the newer Mill House has nice-size rooms with small CD players, sofas, and Jacuzzis that open into the bedroom from behind folding wooden doors. Rooms also have those essential tools for weekend relaxing: wine glasses and a corkscrew. Note that some older rooms are heated with balky radiators, and a few of the guest rooms overlook noisy kitchen ventilators; ask when you book.

**Dining:** The Whip Bar and Grill is in the lower level of the main inn and is a cozy, classy grill with loads of pubby charm and a menu featuring everything from burgers ($6.50) and filet mignon ($18.95) to sesame ginger chicken stir fry ($11.95). There's also a vegetarian menu (garden burgers, tempeh, and tofu curry).

**Amenities:** Heated outdoor pool (summer), fitness club, Jacuzzi, sauna, library, lawn games, game room (air hockey, video games, Ping Pong, billiards), limited room service, in-room massage, afternoon tea and cookies, and safe-deposit boxes.

**Inn at The Mountain.** 5781 Mountain Rd., Stowe, VT 05672. ☎ **800/253-4754** or 802/253-3000. www.stowe.com. E-mail: stowresv@sover.net. 34 units (inn rooms; condos also available). TV TEL. Peak season $145–$160, mid-season $90–$135; off-season $70–$85. 5-day minimum stay Christmas week. AE, DC, DISC, MC, V.

This is the "official" hotel of Stowe Mountain Resort—located near the base of the mountain (but not ski-in-ski-out) and owned and operated by the ski mountain. It's a low-key casual spot, more like an upscale motel than a fancy lodge. The rooms are clean and attractive, more spacious than average motel rooms, with veneer furniture, small refrigerators, and tiny balconies that face toward the pools and the woods. Ask also about the 39 nearby condos, which are suitable for families (to $325 in peak season). Some rooms have air-conditioning and fireplaces.

**Dining:** Fireside Restaurant is open daily for breakfast and dinner. The fare is resort-continental, with dishes like beef medaillons with burgundy wine sauce, and braised lamb shank. Entrees are $15.50 to $22.50.

**Amenities:** Heated outdoor swimming pool (summers only), hot tub, sauna, fitness room, six tennis courts, conference center, afternoon refreshments, safe-deposit boxes, and limited room service.

**Inn at Turner Mill.** 56 Turner Mill Lane, Stowe, VT 05672. ☎ **800/992-0016** or 802/253-2062. E-mail: itmstwvt@sover.net. 8 units. TV TEL. Winter $90–$110 double, suites $110–$210; spring–fall $70–$150 doubles and suites (prices increase during foliage). Summer/ fall rates include breakfast. AE, MC, V.

Set in a narrow wooded valley along a bubbling stream, this homey 1936 building was originally built as a residence and inn. In the winter, some of the rooms are combined into suites to accommodate groups, including one with a kitchen, two baths, and a brick fireplace. The inn is eclectic in style, with everything from alarmingly orange wall-to-wall carpeting in some areas, to attractive and rustic log furniture made by the innkeeper in others. Most memorable may be the monolithic stone walkway outside and the steep staircase to the upper floors. In the summer, the rooms rent separately (all have private bath), and rates include breakfast. The inn is a short trip from the mountain and just across the road from the recreation path, making it a good destination for bike-trippers. Afterwards, plan to splash around in the outdoor pool and river swimming hole. The innkeepers can also provide a guide service (extra charge) for those serious about getting outdoors.

**Stonehilll Inn.** 89 Houston Farm Rd. (just off Mountain Rd. midway between village and ski area), Stowe, VT 05672. ☎ **802/253-6282.** www.stonehillinn.com. E-mail: stay@ stonehillinn.com. 9 rooms. A/C TV. Ski season $385 double, Christmas and foliage $425, summer and late fall $295, spring $250. Rates include full breakfast. 2-night minimum on weekends and foliage season; 3-night minimum holiday weekends; 4-night minimum Christmas week. Not suitable for children. AE, DC, MC, V.

The Stonehill Inn brings a measure of contemporary elegance to Stowe. With just nine rooms, the inn offers personal service and a handy location, along with room amenities that include king-size beds, in-room safes, VCRs, Egyptian cotton towels, and double-sided gas fireplaces that also front double Jacuzzis in the sizeable bathrooms. (Note that there are no phones in the rooms, but a private phone booth allows guests to stay in touch.) The rooms are large enough for a small sitting area, have different color schemes and detailing, but are by and large identical. The high-ceilinged common rooms have fireplaces and billiard tables, and there's a well-stocked guest pantry with complimentary beverages and mixers. An outdoor hot tub provides guests with a relaxing soak. Breakfasts are in a bright morning room where every table is window-side; tasty hors d'ouevres are set out each evening. Stonehill lacks a patina of age and may strike some visitors as somewhat sterile, but it will please those willing to forego timeworn character in exchange for quiet and luxury.

**Stoweflake.** 1746 Mountain Rd. (P.O. Box 369), Stowe, VT 05672. ☎ **800/253-2232** or 802/253-7355. Fax 802/253-6858. www.stoweflake.com. E-mail: stoweflk@sover.net. 95 units (includes 10 suites, plus 12 townhouses). A/C TV TEL. $150–$236 double, suites to $295; peak season $160–$256, suites to $340. Call for townhouse or package info. 4-night minimum stay during holidays; 2-night minimum on most weekends. AE, DC, DISC, MC, V.

Stoweflake is located on Mountain Road 1.7 miles from the village and has been playing catchup with the more up-market Topnotch resort and spa. The newer guest rooms are nicer than those at Topnotch—they're regally decorated and have amenities like two phones and wet bars. The resort has five categories of guest rooms in two wings; the "superior" rooms in the old wing are a bit cozy. They're OK for an overnight, but you're better off requesting "deluxe" or better if you're planning to stay a few days. The spa and fitness facilities are perfectly adequate, but lack the over-the-top sybaritic elegance of Topnotch (what, no waterfalls?). The fitness facilities include a decent-size fitness room with Cybex equipment, a squash/racquetball court, coed Jacuzzi, and a small indoor pool. The spa also offers a variety of massages and treatments.

**Dining:** Charlie B's offers pub fare, including meat loaf, blackened chicken sandwiches, and pastas (pub fare $7.50 to $13.50, dinners to $18.75). Next door is Winfield's in a understated, classical setting serving upscale resort fare along the lines of venison medaillons, smoked apple chicken, or pan-seared sturgeon ($16.50 to $22).

One welcome feature: both restaurants share the wine list, with nearly 50 wines available by the glass.

**Amenities:** In addition to the spa and fitness center, there's a large outdoor pool set amid gardens, two tennis courts, a jogging trail, children's program, conference rooms, in-room massage, beauty salon, limited room service, laundry and dry-cleaning services, baby-sitting, safe-deposit boxes, and afternoon cookies and refreshments. For golfers, there's a practice facility and the adjacent Stowe Country Club.

**Stowehof.** 434 Edson Hill Rd. (P.O. Box 1139), Stowe, VT 05672. ☎ **800/932-7136** or 802/253-9722. Fax 802/253-7513. E-mail: stowehof1@aol.com. 50 units, 2 guest houses. A/C TV TEL. Ski season $138–$250, summer $69–$125 double, off-season $35–$70. Rates higher during holidays; rates include full breakfast. 4-night minimum stay during holidays; 2-night minimum on some weekends. AE, DC, MC, V. Pets allowed.

Stowehof is situated high on a hillside and feels far removed from the hubbub of the valley floor. The exterior architecture features that aggressive neo-Tyrolean ski-chalet styling, but inside, the place comes close to magical—it's pleasantly woodsy, folksy, and rustic, with heavy beams and pine floors, ticking clocks, and massive maple tree trunks carved into architectural elements. Guests may feel a bit like characters in the Hobbit. The guest rooms are furnished without a lot of fanfare, and each is decorated individually: Some are bold and festive with sunflower patterns, others subdued and quiet. Four have wood-burning fireplaces, and all have good views. Among the best: Rooms 43 and 44, both with high ceilings, balconies with expansive views, and sofas.

**Dining:** Diners are served in a cozy, multilevel dining room, with entrees like ginger-roasted leg of venison, crab and shrimp cakes, and the house specialty, Wiener schnitzel. Entrees range from $17.95 to $24.95.

**Amenities:** Outdoor heated pool, outdoor hot tub, four all-weather tennis courts, horseback riding (extra fee), game room, nearby jogging track, nature trails, business center, nearby health club, sauna, sundeck, dry cleaning, laundry service, in-room massage, valet parking, and safe. In winter, there are sleigh rides (extra fee). The lodge is next to Wiessner Woods, with 80 acres laced with hiking and cross-country ski trails.

✪ **Topnotch.** 4000 Mountain Rd. (P.O. Box 1458), Stowe, VT 05672. ☎ **800/451-8686** or 802/253-8585. Fax 802/253-9263. www.topnotch-resort.com. E-mail: topnotch@sover.net. 92 units. A/C TV TEL. Ski season and midsummer $220–$310 double, $355–$710 suite; off-season $160–$230 double, $280–$550 suite. Higher prices and 6-night minimum Christmas week. Town-home accommodations $185–$715 depending on season and size. AE, DC, DISC, MC, V. Pets allowed.

A boxy, uninteresting exterior hides a creatively designed interior at this upscale resort and spa located on a knoll just off Mountain Road. The main lobby is ski-lodge modern, with lots of stone and wood and a huge moose head hanging on the wall. The guest rooms, linked by long, motel-like hallways, are attractively appointed, most in country pine; renovations completed in 1999 made the rooms brighter and more cheerful. The "moderate" rooms are the least expansive and are cozy and suitable for those who plan to spend most of their time outdoors or in the spa; the other classes of rooms are all more spacious. (The third floor rooms have cathedral ceilings and seem even larger; a premium is charged). Ten rooms have wood-burning fireplaces; 18 have Jacuzzis. All rooms have robes, slippers, coffeemakers, irons, hair dryers, mini-fridges, and safes.

**Dining:** The resort is home to Maxwell's for fine dining, featuring attentive service and continental dishes, with entrees priced from $19 to $28. Low-fat spa entrees are always available. Those staying for several days or more may wish to select a plan that doesn't tie them to the restaurant every night; restaurants in the valley offer more variety. The resort also features Buttertub Bistro for more casual fare, and a cozy lounge for drinks and light fare.

**Amenities:** Guests spend much of their time around the 60-foot indoor pool with bubbling fountain and 12-foot whirlpool. There's an outdoor pool for summer use as well. Next to the pool is the spa (ask if your package includes access and treatments, otherwise there's an additional charge). The two-level spa has an aerobics room, cardiovascular room, and a weight room with Cybex equipment. The locker rooms feature fireplaces and casual lounges. Plans for 2000–01 call for expanding the spa by 15,000 square feet, including larger locker rooms. Other activities arranged by the resort include horseback riding, sleigh rides, snowshoeing, and cross-country skiing. Other amenities include four indoor tennis courts (plus outdoor courts), hot tub, nature trails, children's center, beauty salon, room service (7am to 10pm), and a business center.

**Trapp Family Lodge.** 700 Trapp Hill Rd., Stowe, VT 05672. ☎ **800/826-7000** or 802/253-8511. Fax 802/253-5740. www.trappfamily.com. E-mail: info@trappfamily.com. 116 units. TV TEL. Winter $140–$235 double ($344–$384 during school vacation, includes meals); summer $98–$235 double. 5-night minimum stay Christmas week; 3-night minimum Presidents' Day weekend and foliage season. AE, DC, DISC, MC, V. Depart Stowe village westward on Rte. 108; in 2 miles, bear left at fork near white church; continue up hill following signs for lodge.

The Trapp Family of *Sound of Music* fame bought this sprawling farm high up in Stowe in 1942, just 4 years after fleeing the Nazi takeover of Austria. The descendants of Maria and Baron von Trapp continue to run this Tyrolean-flavored lodge on 2,200 mountainside acres. The original lodge burned in 1980, and some longtime guests still grouse that its replacement lacks the time-worn character of the old place, but it's a comfortable resort hotel, if designed more for efficiency than elegance. The guest rooms are a shade or two better than your standard hotel room, and most come with fine valley views and private balconies. In summer 2000, another 23 modern rooms and suites have been added, all with Austrian accents. Common areas with blonde wood and comfortably upholstered chairs abound and make for comfortable idling.

**Dining:** The restaurant offers well-prepared continental fare (Wiener schnitzel and lamb tenderloin). Dinner is fixed-price at $36; dinner and breakfast is $47 per person per day in addition to room rates (meal prices plus gratuity and tax). The informal Austrian Tea Room across the road from the main inn is open for lunch and offers three kinds of wurst and more.

**Amenities:** Fitness center, heated indoor pool, two outdoor pools (one for adults only), sauna, extensive cross-country-ski and hiking trail network, game rooms, children's program, room service (7:30am to 10am only), four clay tennis counts, in-room massage, baby-sitting ($10/hour), currency exchange (Canadian), self-service laundry, dry cleaning, courtesy shuttle to mountain for skiing, and guest safe.

## WHERE TO DINE

The **Harvest Market,** 1031 Mountain Rd. (☎ **802/253-3800**), is the place for gourmet-to-go. Browse the Vermont products and exotic imports, then pick up some of the fresh-baked goods, like the pleasantly tart raspberry squares, to bring back to the ski lodge or take for a picnic along the bike path. The high prices may cause one's eyebrows to arch involuntarily, but if you're not traveling on a tight budget, it's a good place to splurge.

✪ **Blue Moon Café.** 35 School St. ☎ **802/253-7006.** Reservations recommended. Main courses $15.75–$22. AE, CB, DC, DISC, MC, V. Daily 6–9:30pm. Open weekends only in shoulder seasons. Closed late fall and early spring. NEW AMERICAN.

The delectable crusty bread on the table, Frank Sinatra crooning in the background, and vibrant local art on the walls offer clues that this isn't your typical ski-area pub-fare restaurant. Located a short stroll off Stowe's main street in a contemporary setting within an older village home, the Blue Moon serves up the village's finest dining. The menu changes every Friday, but count on at least one lamb, beef, and veggie dish, plus a couple of seafood offerings. Chef Jack Pickett has superb instincts for spicing and creates inventive dishes like sirloin strip steak with carmelized onions and blue cheese, roast pheasant with gooseberries, and grilled sea scallops with gumbo sauce. Desserts are simple yet pure delights: profiteroles with espresso ice cream, Belgian chocolate pot, and three sorbets with cookies.

**Mes Amis.** 311 Mountain Rd. ☎ **802/253-8669.** Reservations accepted for 8 or more. Dinner entrees $14.95–$17.95. DC, MC, V. Tues–Sun 5:30–10pm (open for appetizers at 4:30pm). BISTRO.

The friendly Mes Amis is located in a cozy structure above Mountain Road not far from the village. It was once a British-style pub, but the new owners have done a nice job taking the half-timber Tudor decor and making it more broadly European. It's a quiet and friendly spot, and lacks even the smallest iota of pretention. The menu is rather limited (only five entrees), but the specials round out the offerings. The restaurant has three cozy dining rooms and a bar. Appetizers include smoked salmon on toast points and baked stuffed clams; entrees feature steaks and fish. The house specialty is a half-duck roasted with a hot and sweet sauce.

**Miguel's Stowe-Away.** Mountain Rd. ☎ **800/254-1240** or 802/253-7574. Reservations recommended weekends and peak ski season. Main courses $7.95–$17.95 (mostly under $14). AE, CB, DC, DISC, MC, V. Daily 5–10pm. MEXICAN/SOUTHWEST.

Located in an old farmhouse midway between the village and the mountain, Miguel's packs in folks looking for the tangiest Mexican and Tex-Mex food in the valley. Start off with a margarita or Vermont beer, then try out appetizers like the empanadas or mussels Mexicana (served with salsa ranchera). Follow up with sizzling fajitas or one of the filling combo plates. Desserts range from the complicated (apple-mango compote with cinnamon tortilla and ice cream) to simple (chocolate chip cookies). Like the national chains, Miguel's has grown popular enough to offer its own brand of chips, salsa, and other products, which turn up in specialty food shops and grocery stores throughout the Northeast. Expect the place to be loud and boisterous on busy nights.

**Mr. Pickwick's.** 433 Mountain Rd. ☎ **802/253-7558.** Reservations accepted for parties of 6 or more. Main courses, lunch $6.95–$12.95, dinner $11.95–$22.95. AE, MC, V. Daily 11am–1am. BRITISH PUB FARE.

As a matter of policy I usually refuse to consider any establishment with "Ye Olde" in its name, but I'm happy to make an exception for Mr. Pickwick's, a pub and restaurant that's part of Ye Old English Inne. It could justly be accused of being a theme-park restaurant, with the theme being, well, ye olde Englande, but it's been run since 1983 with such creative gusto by British ex-pats Chris and Lyn Francis that it's hard not to enjoy yourself here. You can start by admiring the Union Jack tchotches and Anglo geegaws while relaxing at handsome wood tables at the booths (dubbed "pews" here). Then sample from the 150 beers (many British) before ordering off the menu, which includes house specialties like bangers and mash (sausages and mashed potatoes), fish and chips, and beef Wellington. For patriotic colonials who have yet to forgive the oppressive Brits, there's also burgers, salmon in potato crust, and an intriguing game menu that includes boar, rabbit, and kangaroo.

**The Shed.** 1859 Mountain Rd. ☎ **802/253-4364.** Reservations recommended weekends and holidays. Lunch items $5–$8.95; main dinner courses $10.95–$16.95. AE, DC, DISC, MC, V. Daily 11:30–midnight (light fare only 10pm–midnight); Sun brunch 10am–2pm. PUB FARE.

Stowe has plenty of options for pub fare, but The Shed is the most consistently reliable. Since it first opened 3 decades ago, this friendly, informal place has won fans by the sleighload with its filling fare and feisty camaraderie. There's a bar area with free popcorn and a good selection of beverages, ranging from the craft beers brewed on premises to frozen rum drinks to homemade root beer. The dining room has more of a chain-restaurant feel to it than the pub, but the bright solarium in the rear is the perfect spot to perch during a sunny Sunday brunch. Meals are pub-fare eclectic: nachos (a little soggy), burgers (including a veggie burger), chicken alfredo, grilled tuna, prime rib, Asian stir-fry noodles, and taco salads.

# 5  Burlington

Burlington is 215 miles northwest of Boston, 98 miles south of Montreal, and 154 miles northeast of Albany, NY.

Burlington is a vibrant college town that's continually, valiantly resisting the onset of middle age. It's the birthplace of hippies-turned-mega-corporation Ben & Jerry's. (Look for the sidewalk plaque at the corner of St. Paul and College streets commemorating the first store, in 1978.) It elected a socialist mayor in 1981, Bernie Sanders, who's now Vermont's lone representative to the U.S. Congress. Burlington is also home to the eclectic rock band Phish, which has been anointed by many as the heir to the Grateful Dead hippie-rock tradition; and just look at the signs for offices as you wander downtown—an uncommonly high number seem to have the word "polarity" in them.

It's no wonder that Burlington has become a magnet for those seeking alternatives to big-city life with its big-city problems. The city has a superb location overlooking Lake Champlain and the Adirondacks of northern New York. To the east, visible on your way out of town, the Green Mountains rise dramatically, with two of the highest points (Mount Mansfield and Camel's Hump) rising above the undulating ridge.

In the mid-20th century, Burlington turned its back for a time on its spectacular waterfront. Urban redevelopment focused on parking garages and highrises; the waterfront lay fallow, open to development by light industry. In recent years, the city has sought to regain a toehold along the lake, acquiring and redeveloping parts for commercial and recreational use. It's been successful in some sections, less so in others.

In contrast, the downtown is thriving. The pedestrian mall (Church Street) that has failed in so many other towns works here. As a result, the scale is skewed towards pedestrians in the heart of downtown. It's best to get out of your car as soon as feasible.

## ESSENTIALS
**GETTING THERE**    Burlington is at the junction of I-89, Route 7, and Route 2.

**Burlington International Airport,** about 3 miles east of downtown, is served by **Continental Express** (☎ 800/732-6887), **United Airlines** (☎ 800/241-6522), **US Airways** (☎ 800/428-4322), and **Delta Connection** (☎ 800/345-3400).

Amtrak's *Vermonter* offers daily departures for Burlington from Washington, Baltimore, Philadelphia, New York, New Haven, and Springfield, Massachusetts. Call ☎ **800/872-7245** for more information.

# Burlington

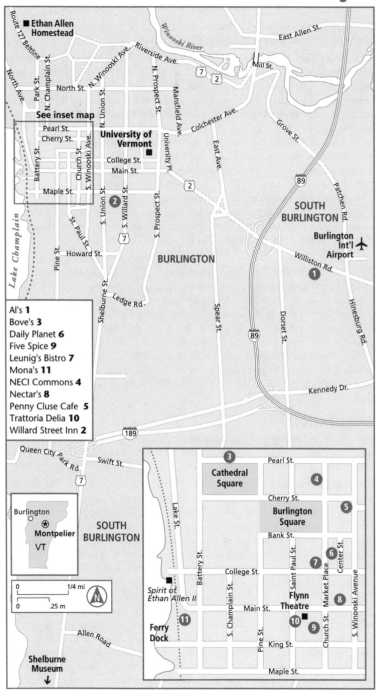

Al's **1**
Bove's **3**
Daily Planet **6**
Five Spice **9**
Leunig's Bistro **7**
Mona's **11**
NECI Commons **4**
Nectar's **8**
Penny Cluse Cafe **5**
Trattoria Delia **10**
Willard Street Inn **2**

**Vermont Transit Lines** (☎ 802/864-6811), with a depot at 345 Pine St., offers bus connections from Albany, Boston, Hartford, New York's JFK Airport, and other points in Vermont, Massachusetts, and New Hampshire.

**VISITOR INFORMATION**    The **Lake Champlain Regional Chamber of Commerce,** 60 Main St., Burlington, VT 05401 (☎ 802/863-3489), maintains an information center in a stout 1929 brick building on Main Street just up from the waterfront and a short walk from Church Street Market. The center is open weekdays from 8:30am to 5pm. On weekends, helpful maps and brochures are left in the entryway for visitors.

A seasonal information booth is also staffed summers on the Church Street Marketplace at the corner of Church and Bank streets. There's no phone. Information can also be requested via e-mail (**vermont@vermont.org**) or the Web (**www.vermont. org**).

Burlington's free weeklies keep residents and visitors up to date on local events and happenings. (To confuse matters somewhat, the *Free Press*—the local daily—is the one paper that costs money.) *Seven Days* carries topical and lifestyle articles along with listings. The *Vermont Times* emphasizes local politics. Look for them at downtown stores and restaurants.

**SPECIAL EVENTS    First Night Burlington** (☎ 802/863-6005; www.1stnight. together.com) turns the whole of downtown into a stage on New Year's Eve. Some 500 performers—from alternative rockers to vaudevillians—play at 34 venues (mostly indoors) for 10 hours beginning at 2pm. The evening finishes with a bang at the midnight fireworks. Admission is $12 (or $9 if you purchase before Christmas) and covers all performances.

The **Vermont Mozart Festival** (☎ 800/639-9097 or 802/862-7352; www. vtmozart.together.com) takes place in various locales in and around Burlington (and even further afield) from mid-July to August. Tickets range from $19 to $32. Call for a schedule and information.

## ORIENTATION

Burlington is comprised of three distinct areas: the UVM campus atop the hill, the downtown area flanking the popular Church Street Marketplace, and the waterfront along Lake Champlain.

**University of Vermont**    The University of Vermont was founded in 1791, funded by a state donation of 29,000 acres of forestland spread across 120 townships. In the 2 centuries since, the university has grown to accommodate 7,700 undergraduates and 1,200 graduate students, plus 300 medical students. The school is set on 400 acres atop a hill overlooking downtown and Lake Champlain to the west, and offers a glorious prospect of the Green Mountains to the east. The campus has more than 400 buildings, many of which were designed by the most noted architects of the day, including H. H. Richardson and McKim, Mead and White. (By the way, UVM stands for "Universitas Virdis Montis," which translates as University of the Green Mountains.)

UVM doesn't have a college neighborhood with bars and bookstores immediately adjacent to the campus, as is common at many universities. Downtown serves that function. The downtown and the campus are 5 blocks from one another, connected via aptly named College Street. A shuttle, which looks like an old-fashioned trolley, runs daily on College Street between the Community Boathouse on the waterfront and the campus. It's in operation year-round between 11am and 9pm, and it's free.

**Church Street Marketplace**    The downtown centers around the Church Street Marketplace, a pedestrian mall that's alive with activity throughout the year. (See

"Shopping," below.) This is the place to wander without purpose and watch the crowds; you can always find a cafe or ice cream shop to rest your feet. While the shopping and grazing is good here, don't overlook the superb historic commercial architecture that graces much of downtown. Radiating out from Church Street are a number of side streets, which contain an appealing amalgam of restaurants, shops, and offices.

**The Waterfront**    The waterfront has benefited from a $6 million renovation centered around Union Station at the foot of Main Street. This includes some newly constructed buildings like The Wing Building, an appealingly quirky structure of brushed steel and other nontraditional materials, which blends in nicely with the more rustic parts of the waterfront. Next door is the Cornerstone Building, with a restaurant and offices, which offers better views of the lake from its higher vantage. Nearby is the city's Community Boathouse, which is an exceptionally inviting destination on a summer's day (see below). Bear in mind that Burlingtonians accept a fairly liberal definition of the adjective "lakeside." In some cases, this might mean the shop or restaurant is 100 yards or so from the lake.

## EXPLORING BURLINGTON

✪ **Shelburne Museum.** Rte. 7 (P.O. Box 10), Shelburne, VT 05482. ☎ **802/985-3346.** www.shelburnemuseum.org. Summer admission (good for 2 consecutive days) $17.50 adults, $10.50 students with ID, $7 children 6–14; winter tours $8.75 adults, $3.50 children. MC, V. Late May–mid-Oct daily 10am–5pm. Selected buildings only open April–late May, and mid-Oct–Dec 31; call for information.

Established in 1947 by Americana collector Electra Havemeyer Webb, the museum contains one of the nation's most outstanding collections of American decorative, folk, and fine art. The museum is spread over 45 rolling acres 7 miles south of Burlington; the collections occupy some 37 buildings. The more mundane exhibits include quilts, early tools, decoys, and weather vanes; b the museum also collects and displays *whole* buildings from around New England and New York State. These include an 1890 railroad station, a lighthouse, a stagecoach inn, an Adirondack lodge, and a round barn from Vermont. There's even a 220-foot steamship, eerily landlocked on the museum's grounds. Spend a few hours here, and you're bound to come away with a richer understanding of regional culture. If you're planning to visit only one museum during your New England trip, this is the one. The grounds also contain a museum shop, cafeteria, and picnic area.

**Ethan Allen Homestead.** Rte. 127. ☎ **802/865-4556.** Admission $4 adults, $3.50 seniors, $2 children 6–16. Mid-May–mid-June daily 1–5pm; mid-June–mid-Oct Mon–Sat 10am–5pm, Sun 1–5pm. Take Rte. 127 northward from downtown; look for signs.

A quiet retreat on one of the most idyllic, least developed stretches of the Winooski River, the Ethan Allen Homestead is a shrine to Vermont's favorite son. While Allen wasn't born in Burlington, he settled here later in life on property confiscated from a British sympathizer during the Revolution. The reconstructed farmhouse is an enduring tribute to this Vermont hero; an orientation center offers an intriguing multimedia account of Allen's life and other points of regional history. The house is open for tours mid-October to mid-May by appointment only (one day's notice is required). The grounds are open daily year-round from dawn to dusk. Admission to the park is free.

**Lake Champlain Ferries.** King St. Dock, Burlington. ☎ **802/864-9804.** www.ferries.com. $12.75 one-way fare for car and driver from Burlington to Port Kent; $6.50 round-trip for adult passengers; $2.50 children 6–12; free for children under 6. Burlington ferry operates mid-May–mid-Oct. Frequent departures in summer between 7:45am and 7:30pm. Schedule varies in spring, fall, and foliage season; call for current departure times. AE, MC, V.

# Ethan Allen, Patriot and Libertine

In 1749, the governor of New Hampshire began giving away land to settlers willing to brave the howling wilderness of what is now Vermont. Two decades later, the New York State courts decreed those grants void, which opened the door for New York speculators to flood into the region vowing to push the original settlers out of the valleys and up into the Green Mountains.

Not too surprisingly, this didn't sit very well with those already there. They established a network of military units called the Green Mountain Boys, who promised to drive out the New Yorkers. A hale fellow named Ethan Allen headed up the new militia, which launched a series of effective harrying raids against the impudent New Yorkers. Green Mountain Boys destroyed their homes, drove away their livestock, and chased the New York sheriffs back across the border.

The American Revolution soon intervened, and Ethan Allen and the Green Mountain Boys took up the revolutionary cause with vigor. They helped sack Fort Ticonderoga in New York in 1775, rallied to the cause at the famed Battle of Bennington, and generally continued to make nuisances of themselves to the British effort throughout the war.

Allen's fame grew as word spread about him and his Green Mountain Boys. A hard-drinking, fierce-fighting, large-living sort of guy, Allen became a legend in his own time. He could bite the head off a nail one story claimed; another said that he was once bit by a rattlesnake, which promptly belched and died.

While Allen's apocryphal exploits lived on following his death in 1789, he also left a more significant legacy. Vermont's statehood in 1791 was due in large part to the independence and patriotism the region showed under Allen; and today you can't drive very far in Vermont without a reminder of Allen's historic presence—parks are named after him, inns boast that he once slept there, and you'll still hear the occasional story about his bawdy doings.

Car ferries chug across the often placid, sometimes turbulent waters of Lake Champlain from Burlington to New York State between late spring and foliage season. It's a good way to cut out miles of driving if you're heading west toward the Adirondacks. It's also a good way to see the lake and the mountains on a pleasant, inexpensive cruise. Between June and mid-October, you can also take a 90-minute narrated lake cruise; the cost is $7.25 adult, $3.75 children, under 6 free.

Ferries also cross Lake Champlain between Grande Isle, Vermont, and Plattsburgh, New York (year-round), and Charlotte, Vermont, and Essex, New York (April to early January). Call the above number for more information.

**The Spirit of Ethan Allen II.** Burlington Boathouse, Burlington. ☎ **802/862-8300.** www.soea.com. Narrated cruises ($1^1/_2$ hr.) $8.75 adults, $3.95 children 3–11. Sunset cruises ($2^1/_2$ hours) $9.50 adults, $4.95 children. Specialty cruises (dinner, brunch, and mystery theater) priced higher, call for information. Daily late May–mid-Oct.

This is Burlington's premier tour boat. Accommodating 500 passengers on three decks, the sleek ship offers a good way of viewing Lake Champlain and the distant Adirondacks. The views haven't changed much since the area was explored by Samuel de Champlain, who first came here in 1609. Food is available on all cruises, including all-you-can-eat buffets at dinner and Sunday brunch. The scenic cruise departs daily every other hour beginning at 10am through 4pm. The sunset cruise departs at 6:30pm. Parking is $2 additional.

**Robert Hull Fleming Museum.** 61 Colchester Ave. (UVM campus). ☎ **802/656-0750.** Admission $3 adult, $5 family, $2 seniors and students. Year-round Sat–Sun 1–5pm; Labor Day–Apr Tues–Fri 9am–4pm; May–Labor Day Tues–Fri noon–4pm.

This University of Vermont facility houses a fine collection of art and anthropological displays, mostly European and American. A selection of paintings by 20th-century Vermont artists are on permanent display, and changing exhibitions roam widely though world cultures (in fall 2000, look for an exhibit of Chinese paintings). Near-by metered parking is available weekends only. Call for a schedule of lectures and other special events.

## OUTDOOR PURSUITS

Burlington is blessed with numerous attractive city parks. The most popular is **Leddy Park** (☎ 802/864-0123) on North Avenue, with an 1,800-foot beach, tennis courts, ballfields, walking trails, and a handsome indoor skating rink. **North Beach** (☎ 802/862-0942) also features a long sandy beach, and a campground for those looking to pitch a tent or park an RV.

On the downtown waterfront, look for the **Burlington Community Boathouse** (☎ 802/865-3377), a modern structure built with Victorian flair. A lot of summer action takes place at this city-owned structure and along the 900-foot boardwalk. You can rent a sailboat or rowboat, sign up for kayak or sculling lessons, or just wander around and enjoy the sunset.

Burlington's commitment to taking back its lake is best seen in the 9-mile ✪ **Burlington Bike Path,** that runs picturesquely along the shores of Lake Champlain to the mouth of the Winooski River. A superb way to spend a sunny afternoon, the paved bike route over a former railbed passes through shady parklands and Burlington's backyards. Along the banks of the Winooski, you can admire the remains of an old bridge and scout around for marble chips.

Bike rentals are available downtown at the **Skirack,** 85 Main St. (☎ 802/658-3313), for $14 to $16 for 4 hours (enough time to do the whole trail), and up to $22 for a whole day. Skirack also rents inline skates ($10 for 4 hours), which are also commonly used on the bike path. **North Star Cyclery,** 100 Main St. (☎ 802/863-3832), also rents bicycles at comparable rates.

When at the bike shops or the chamber of commerce, ask for the free map, *Cycling the City,* which will help you plot a course around town.

## WHERE TO STAY

Burlington's motels are located along the two major access roads to the south and east. On Route 7 south of town, try the **Super 8 Motel** (1016 Shelburne Rd., ☎ 800/800-8000 or 802/862-6421), the **Bel-Aire Motel** (111 Shelburne Rd., ☎ 802/863-3116), or the **Town & Country Motel** (490 Shelburne Rd., ☎ 802/862-5786).

Clustered on and around Route 2 near I-89 and the airport are several chain hotels, including the **Holiday Inn** (1068 Williston Rd, ☎ 802/863-6363) and **Best Western Windjammer Inn** (1076 Williston Rd., ☎ 800/371-1125 or 802/863-1125), and the **Hawthorne Suites Hotel** (410 Dorset St., ☎ 800/527-1133 or 802/860-1212). For those with fewer needs for amenities, nearby is the clean, budget-priced **Swiss Host Motel and Village** (1272 Williston Rd., ☎ 802/862-5734).

✪ **Basin Harbor Club.** Basin Harbor Rd., Vergennes, VT 05491. ☎ **800/622-4000** or 802/475-2311. Fax 802/475-6545. www.basinharbor.com. E-mail: info@basinharbor.com. 105 units (38 inn rooms, 77 cottages). TEL. Summer $210–$345 (to $425 suite), including breakfast, lunch, and dinner; early summer and fall $185–$285 (to $315 suite) including breakfast and dinner. Closed mid-Oct–mid-May. 2-day minimum on summer weekends. MC, V. Pets allowed in cottages ($6.50 per day).

Situated on 700 rolling lakeside acres 30 miles south of Burlington, the Basin Harbor Club offers a detour to a slower-paced time. The club was established in 1886, and the current owners are descendants of the founders. It's the kind of resort you can spend a week at and not get bored—at least if you're a self-starter and don't need a perky recreational director to plan things for you. There's a marina, an 18-hole golf course, tennis courts, a fitness room, and great birdwatching. There's the historic gardens on the property, including the largest collection of annuals in Vermont (15,000) and an active herb garden used by the kitchen. Best of all are the trademark Adirondack chairs, which are scattered all over the property and invite the most exquisite indolence (bring books!). Thirty-eight rooms are located in the main lodge. Most guests prefer the rustic cottages, which are tucked along the shore and in shady groves of trees; all but one were built prior to 1940, and about half have wood-burning fireplaces. Nothing's too fancy, yet nothing's too shabby; it's all pretty comfortable in a New England old-money kind of way. (The occasional cobweb and Venetian blind that looks like it went through the spin cycle seems to add to the charm.) Most rooms have air-conditioning; none have televisions.

**Dining:** The main dining room is formal (jackets on men) with a great view of the harbor. The cuisine is traditional New England resort fare, and it's usually adequate or a notch above—it's not likely to knock your socks off. Most meals are included in the room rates; for outside guests, dinner is $29.95. More informal fare is available at the Red Mill Restaurant near the airfield and golf course, which serves up sandwiches, quesadillas, and meat loaf platter; prices are $5.95 to $23.95.

**Amenities:** Heated outdoor pool, lake beach, marina with boat rentals (windsurfers, kayaks, canoes, day sailers, and outboards) and lake cruises, fitness room, bike rentals, aerobic classes, fishing, art workshops, lecture series, walking trails, airfield, golf course, five tennis courts, children's program in summer, safe-deposit boxes, baby-sitting, dry cleaning, laundry service, concierge, and limited room service.

✪ **The Inn at Shelburne Farms.** 1611 Harbor Rd., Shelburne, VT 05482. ☎ **802/985-8498.** 24 units (7 units share 4 bathrooms). TEL. Fall $105–$350 double; spring and summer $95–$310 double. 2-night minimum stay on weekends. Closed mid-Oct–mid-May. AE, CB, DC, DISC, MC, V.

The numbers behind this exceptional mansion on the shores of Lake Champlain tell the story: 60 rooms, 10 chimneys, 1,400 acres of land. Built in 1899 by William Seward and Lila Vanderbilt Webb, this sprawling Edwardian "farmhouse" is the place to fantasize about the lifestyles of the *truly* rich and famous. From the first glimpse of the mansion as you come up the winding drive, you'll know you've left the grim world behind. That's by design—noted landscape architect Frederick Law Olmsted had a hand in the shaping the grounds, and noted forester Gifford Pinchot helped with the planting. The 24 guest rooms are splendidly appointed. The inn is owned and operated as part of a non-profit environmental education center, with the emphasis on the sensitive stewardship of our agricultural resources.

**Dining:** Meals aren't included in the rates, but the Marble Restaurant on the property offers outstanding breakfasts and dinners, with a focus on contemporary regional cuisine. Chef David Hugo aims to showcase locally grown ingredients, with entrees such as par-roasted chicken with a ragout of artichoke and lemon, and roasted rack of lamb with asparagus and Shelburne Farms cheddar. Entree prices range from $18 to $28.

**Amenities:** Tours of the farm, tennis court, lake for swimming, children's farmyard, nature trails, baby-sitting, and afternoon tea.

**Radisson Hotel Burlington.** 60 Battery St., Burlington, VT 05401. ☎ **802/658-6500.**
Fax 802/658-4659. 256 units. A/C TV TEL. Summer $139–$199 double; winter $99–$149
double. AE, CB, DC, DISC, ER, MC, V.

The nine-story Radisson offers the best views, as well as the best downtown location.
As might be expected, it also offers the amenities of an upscale national hotel chain,
including an indoor pool, covered parking, and two dining areas. Though built in
1976, renovations have kept the weariness at bay. Ask for a room with a lake view,
which is far more dramatic than the downtown view. Families with kids might request
one of the five cabana rooms that open up to the pool area.

**Dining/Diversions:** Seasons on the Lake offers great views and American and continental fare (rack of lamb and beef tournedos with béarnaise), with entrees priced
from $17.95 to $22.95. Dinner is served Tuesday through Saturday. For a quick bite
or a drink, there's also the Oak Street Cafe off the lobby.

**Amenities:** Indoor pool, tiny fitness room, Jacuzzi, gift shop, concierge, dry cleaning,
laundry service, baby-sitting, newspaper delivery, limited room service, express check-
out, courtesy car to airport, in-room safes, and free business center.

**Sheraton Burlington Hotel & Conference Center.** 870 Williston Rd., Burlington, VT
05403. ☎ **800/325-3535** or 802/865-6600. Fax 802/865-6670. E-mail: sheratonvt@
aol.com. 309 units. A/C TV TEL. $139–$215 double. AE, CB, DC, DISC, MC, V.

The largest conference facility in Vermont, the Sheraton also does a decent job catering
to individual travelers and families. This sprawling and modern complex (with 15
conference rooms) just off the interstate, a 5-minute drive east of downtown, features
a sizable indoor garden area. The guest rooms all have two phones and in-room
Nintendos (families take note); rooms in the addition are a bit nicer, furnished in a
simpler, lighter country style. Ask for a room facing east (no extra charge) to enjoy the
views of Mount Mansfield and the Green Mountains.

**Dining:** G's, the complex's main restaurant, is located in and around an indoor
garden, complete with gazebo, and serves three meals daily. The Sunday brunch is the
most elaborate in town. Also serving meals is Tuckaway's, which features an English
pub motif.

**Amenities:** Indoor pool with retractable skylights for summer, two Jacuzzis, a fitness
room, outdoor sundeck, limited room service, concierge, secretarial services, courtesy
cars, video rentals (extra charge), and laundry service.

**Willard Street Inn.** 349 S. Willard St. (2 blocks south of Main St.), Burlington, VT 05401.
☎ **800/577-8712** or 802/651-8710. Fax 802/651-8714. www.willardstreetinn.com. E-mail:
wstinn@vermontel.com. 14 units (1 with private hall bathroom). A/C TEL. $115–$225 double.
Rates include full breakfast. 2-night minimum on weekends. AE, DISC, MC, V.

This impressive inn is located in a splendid Queen Anne–style brick mansion near the
university. The inn has soaring first-floor ceilings, cherry woodwork, and a beautiful
window-lined breakfast room with a bold black-and-white tile floor. The home was
originally built in 1881 by a bank president and served as a retirement home for a time
before its conversion to an inn. Rooms in the former servants wing are more cozy than
those in the core of the house, and the second-floor rooms have higher ceilings. The
third-floor rooms are slightly less elegant and priced accordingly. Among the best
rooms are No. 12, which boasts a small sitting area and the best views of the lake, and
No. 4, which is spacious, has a sizable private bathroom, and also features lake views.
Newly built in late 1999 was the Woodhouse Suite, created by combining two rooms
that formerly shared a bathroom.

## WHERE TO DINE

**Al's.** 1251 Williston Rd. (Rte. 2, just east of I-89), South Burlington. ☎ **802/862-9203.** Sandwiches 75¢–$3.55. No credit cards. Mon–Wed 10:30am–11pm; Thurs–Sat 10:30am–midnight; Sun 11am–10pm. BURGER JOINT.

Two words: french fries.

✪ **Bove's.** 68 Pearl St. ☎ **802/864-6651.** www.boves.com. Sandwiches $1.40–$4.15; dinner items $4.25–$7.70. No credit cards. Tues–Sat 10am–8:45pm. ITALIAN.

A Burlington landmark since 1941, Bove's is a classic red-sauce-on-spaghetti joint just a couple of blocks from the Church Street Marketplace. ("What was here in 1941 is here today," says Richard Bove.) The facade is stark black and white, its octagonal windows closed to prying eyes by Venetian blinds. Step through the doors and into a lost era; grab a seat at one of the vinyl-upholstered booths and browse the menu, which offers spaghetti with meat sauce, spaghetti with meatballs, spaghetti with sausage, and . . . well, you get the idea. The red sauce is rich and tangy; the garlic sauce packs enough garlic to knock you clear out of your booth. Cocktails are only $2.30 and include favorites like stingers, pink ladies, and sloe gin fizzes.

**Daily Planet.** 15 Center St. ☎ **802/862-9647.** Reservations recommended for parties of 5 or more. Lunch items $5.75–$7.25; main dinner courses $11.25–$19.95. CB, DC, DISC, MC, V. Mon–Fri 11:30am–3pm; Sun–Thurs 5–9:30pm; Fri–Sat 5–10pm. Sept–May Sat–Sun brunch 11am–3pm. ECLECTIC.

This popular spot is usually brimming with college students and downtown workers evenings and weekends. The mild mayhem usually adds to the charm, enhancing the eclectic and interesting menu. The meals are better prepared than the one might expect from a place that takes its cues from a pub. There's a bar menu that features fajitas, grilled eggplant sandwiches, and chicken wings. In the dining room, look for lunch dishes like lamb stew, seafood Newburg, and original salads. For dinner, there's strip steak with a gorgonzola-green peppercorn sauce, rainbow trout with peach-red-onion relish, and a vegetable stir fry with tempeh.

**Five Spice.** 175 Church St. ☎ **802/864-4045.** Reservations recommended on weekends and in summer. Lunch items $5.75–$8.95; main dinner courses $10.75–$17.95. AE, CB, DC, DISC, MC, V. Mon–Sat 11:30am–10:30pm; Sun 11am–9:30pm. PAN-ASIAN.

Located upstairs and down in an intimate setting with rough wood floors and aquamarine wainscoting, Five Spice is a popular draw among college students and professors. But customers pour in for the exquisite food, not for the scene. The cuisine is multi-Asian, drawing on the best of Thailand, Vietnam, China, and beyond. Try the excellent hot-and-sour soup. Then gear up for Thai red snapper or the superior kung-pao chicken. The dish with the best name on the menu—Evil Jungle Prince with Chicken—is made with a light sauce featuring a combination of coconut milk, garlic, and lemongrass.

**Inn at Essex.** 70 Essex Way, Essex Junction. ☎ **800/727-4295** or 802/878-1100. www.innatessex.com. Reservations recommended at Butler's; usually not needed at The Tavern. Tavern: lunch items $4.50–$6.95, main dinner courses $4.50–$9.95; Butler's: lunch $6.95–$12.95, dinner $16–$23. AE, CB, DC, DISC, MC, V. Tavern daily 11:30am–11pm; Butler's: daily 11:30am–10pm. REGIONAL/CONTINENTAL.

The Inn at Essex Junction, about a 15-minute drive from Burlington, is the auxiliary campus of the Montpelier-based New England Culinary Institute. It offers both formal and informal dining rooms with meals prepared and served by New England's rising culinary stars. Both restaurants are housed in a large faux-farmhouse complex located along the fringe of Burlington's suburban sprawl. Inside, the setting is quiet and comfortable. In the light and airy tavern, you might be tempted by the Caribbean grilled chicken with a black-bean salsa, or the honey-glazed pork chop. Amid the more intimate, country-inn elegance of Butler's, the dinner fare is a bit more ambitious, with entrees like Dijon peppered rack of lamb, grilled salmon and shrimp with a horseradish cream, and oven-roasted veggies with goat cheese burritos.

**Leunig's Bistro.** 115 Church St., Burlington. ☎ **802/863-3759.** Reservations suggested weekends and holidays. Dinner $8.95–$22.95. AE, DC, DISC, MC, V. Open Mon–Thurs 7am–10pm; Fri 7am–midnight, Sat 9am–midnight, Sun 9am–10pm. REGIONAL/CONTINENTAL.

This boisterous, fun place has a retro-old-world flair, with washed walls, a marble bar, crystal chandeliers, and a Victorian back bar painted white and topped with cherubim. In summer, the inside spills onto the outside, with diners becoming part of the street scene at tables in the marketplace. The inventive and large menu features regional foods prepared with a continental touch. Breakfasts are great (consider the poached eggs and crabcakes), and lunches feature filling sandwiches like turkey cranberry melt, and a cheeseburger of locally raised natural beef and locally made cheese. Dinner offerings change seasonally; in summer, there's poached asparagus with smoked salmon, or soft-shelled crabs with a lemongrass-coconut broth; in fall look for more hearty fare like pork chops with green-peppercorn apple cider sauce or duck breast with a dried cherry and ginger chutney.

**Mona's.** 3 Main St. (in the Cornerstone Building). ☎ **802/658-6662.** Reservations recommended. Lunch items $5.95–$8.95; main dinner courses $13.95–$19.95. AE, CB, DC, MC, V. Mon–Thurs 11:30am–9pm; Fri–Sat 11:30am–11pm; Sun 10am–9pm. NEW AMERICAN.

This urbane but relaxed restaurant overlooking the waterfront is sleeker and more modern than the average Burlington bistro. Located next to the old train station at the foot of Main Street, Mona's is an up-tempo place rich with copper tones throughout. The ceiling in the first-floor jazz bar is made of copper and seems to emit a lurid, unearthly glow at sunset. For the best views of Lake Champlain and the Adirondacks, head to the upstairs dining room. In good weather, angle for a table on the 65-seat deck. The Mediterranean shrimp features shrimp, veggies and garlic served over pasta; meat lovers will enjoy the rib eye with portobello and oatmeal-stout sauce. Sundays (until 2pm) there's a lavish buffet brunch ($12.95), with selections ranging from the usual suspects (waffles and bagels) to vegetable tarts and marinated flank steak.

✪ **NECI Commons.** 25 Church St. ☎ **802/862-6324.** Call before arrival for priority seating. Brunch $5.75–$6.95; lunch $5.95–$8.50; dinner $9.95–$19.95. AE, DC, DISC, MC, V. Daily 11:30am–2pm and 5–9:30pm; Sun brunch 11am–3pm. BISTRO.

NECI Commons opened in 1997 and quickly attracted foodies from around the region. Yet another in the New England Culinary Institute empire (the Inn at Essex and Montpelier's Main Street Grill & Bar are others), this lively, spacious, and busy spot is also a training ground for aspiring chefs and restaurateurs. You can eat upstairs in the main dining room, which has soaring windows overlooking the Church Street Marketplace, or downstairs where you can watch the chef-trainees prepare meals in the open kitchen. The fare is at once simple and creative, and often riding the crest of popular trends. At Sunday brunch, there's a wood-fired breakfast pizza, featuring eggs, bacon, tomato, and cheddar. Lunchtime, there are delectable sandwiches (crabcake with chipotle sauce on a toasted roll) and more filling dishes like crispy calamari salad and a mixed grill with lamb medaillons and sausage, and chicken satay. For dinner, look for sirloin served with the restaurant's famous Vermont cheddar potatoes or blackened sea bass with wilted spinach. The prices are reasonable; the service excellent.

**Nectar's Restaurant and Lounge.** 188 Main St. ☎ **802/658-4771.** Breakfast items $1.75–$6; lunch/dinner items $2.20–$6.75. No credit cards. Daily 5:45am–2am (1am on Sat). Breakfast served until 11am. CAFETERIA.

Burlington in microcosm parades through Nectar's over the course of a long day. Early in the morning you'll find blue-collar workers and elderly gentlemen in ties enjoying heaping plates of eggs and hash browns. Midday finds downtown office workers in for lunch; and late in the evening, it adopts a sort of retro chic as clubbers from nearby clubs and Nectar's own lounge next door file through the cafeteria line for hamburgers, a plate of meat loaf, or just to get a local microbrew and hang with friends.

**Penny Cluse Café.** 169 Cherry St. ☎ **802/651-8834.** Breakfast dishes $3.50–$6.50, sandwiches and lunch dishes 6.25–$8. MC, V. Mon–Fri 6:45am–3pm, Sat–Sun 8am–3pm. CAFE/LATINO.

This gets my vote as the city's best choice for a casual lunch or breakfast. Located a block off the Church St. Marketplace, Penny Cluse is a casual, bright, and popular spot decorated in a vaguely Southwest/Latino motif with worn wood floors and plain pine tables laden with hot sauces. Both the breakfast and lunch menu are available all day. Among the better breakfasts: the Zydeco breakfast with eggs, black beans, andouille sausage, and corn muffins. Lunch ranges from salads to sandwiches (the veggie Reuben with mushrooms, spinach, and red onions is excellent) to slightly more elaborate fare like grilled flank steak with black beans and adobo pork chops with a plantain cake.

**Trattoria Delia.** 152 St. Paul St. ☎ **802/864-5253.** Reservations recommended. Main courses, $13.50–$19.50. DC, MC, V. Daily 5–10pm. ITALIAN.

Locally foraged mushrooms served over polenta with fontina. If that causes you to sit up and take notice, then this is your place. Serving the best Italian food in Burlington, Trattoria Delia is in a low-traffic location, almost hidden through a speakeasy-like door beneath a large building. Inside, you'll find culinary magic, with dishes like wild boar, filet mignon with white truffle butter, and classic pasta dishes, like tagliattelle alla Bolognese. Afterwards, choose from Italian dessert wines and traditional desserts lke tiramisu and panna cotta.

## SHOPPING

The **Church Street Marketplace** is one of the more notable success stories of downtown development. Situated along 4 blocks that extend southward from the austerely elegant 1816 Congregational church, the marketplace buzzes with the sort of downtown energy that makes urban planners everywhere envious. While the marketplace has been discovered by the national chains (Banana Republic, Borders, Pier 1, Eddie Bauer, and Urban Outfitters), it still makes room for used bookstores and homegrown shops. In summer, leave time to be entertained by drummers, pan-flutists, buskers, sidewalk vendors, and knots of young folks just hanging out.

Most of the shops listed below are either in the marketplace or within walking distance downtown.

**Architectural Salvage Warehouse.** 212 Battery St. ☎ **802/658-5011.**

Anyone who owns (or aspires toward) an old home will enjoy browsing this store, located at the corner of Maple and Battery streets southwest of the Church St. Marketplace. There's clawfoot tubs, plenty of old doors, and mantels, but also souvenirs for those who'd rather travel light: crystal doorknobs, brass hardware, and other portable items you can toss in the trunk.

**Bennington Potters North.** 127 College St. ☎ **802/863-2221.**

A good selection of creative and elegant stuff for your dining room table and kitchen can be found on three floors in this handsome, century-old building just off Church Street.

**Frog Hollow.** 85 Church St. ☎ **802/863-6458.**

One of the stores of the Vermont State Craft Center (others are in Middlebury and Manchester), Frog Hollow has a broad selection of work of some of the best Vermont craftspeople, with selections ranging from pottery to woodwork to glassware.

**Kiss the Cook.** 72 Church St. ☎ **802/863-4226.**

This is a good spot to stock up on Vermont gourmet products and craft foods, along with cookware both traditional (bean pots, apple peelers) and modern (Calphalon pans and Oxo gadgets).

**Mesa International Factory Store.** 131 Battery St. ☎ **802/652-0800.**

Save up to 70 percent off imported handicrafts, including a good selection of items for the kitchen and dining room—like hand-painted dinnerware and colorful glassware—at this bright and spacious shop. Look also for wrought iron geegaws and attractive accessories for the garden.

**North County Books.** 2 Church St. ☎ **802/862-6413.**

Located downstairs at the head of the marketplace, this used bookstore has the endearing habit of interspersing rare and valuable volumes amid the paperback reading copies. The selection is better honed than many used bookstores, and the prices reflect that.

**Pompanoosuc Mills.** 50 Church St. ☎ **802/862-8208.**

This upscale New England chain specializes in austerely simple hardwood furniture (cherry, birch, maple, and oak) but also carries carpets, lamps, frames, and a selection of other decorative arts.

# BURLINGTON AFTER DARK
## PERFORMING ARTS

**Flynn Theatre for the Performing Arts.** 153 Main St. ☎ **802/652-4500.** www.flynntheatre.org. Tickets $8–$75.

The Flynn is the anchor for the downtown fine-arts scene. Run as a non-profit and housed in a wonderful art-deco theater dating to 1930, the Flynn stages events ranging from touring productions of Broadway shows (Penn and Teller) to concerts (Diana Krall) to dance (Paul Taylor) to performers and writers (Lily Tomlin and David Sedaris). Call or visit their Web site for the current schedule.

**Royall Tyler Theatre.** University of Vermont campus. ☎ **802/656-2094.** Tickets $8–$20.

Plays are performed by the University of Vermont theater department and local theater groups at this handsomely designed performance hall. Shows ranging from Shakespeare to student-directed one-act plays are staged throughout the year; call for current schedule.

**UVM Lane Series.** Various venues. ☎ **802/656-4455.** www.uvm.edu/~dceweb/lane. Tickets $15–$36.

This university series brings renowned performers from around the country and the globe to Burlington for performances at the Flynn Theatre, Ira Allen Chapel, and the acoustically superb UVM Recital Hall. The series runs from September through April.

Performers have included the San Francisco Opera performing *The Marriage of Figaro,* flutist Eugenia Zuckerman, and the Modern Mandolin Quartet.

**Vermont Symphony Orchestra.** 2 Church St. ☎ **800/876-9293** or 802/864-5741. www.vso.org. Tickets $9–$35.

Outdoor pops performances punctuated by fireworks take place at various locations throughout Burlington and Vermont during the summer. In winter, the classical series moves indoors, including regular performances at the Flynn Theatre. Call for the current schedule.

## NIGHTCLUBS

There's always something going on in the evening, although it might take a little snooping to find it. Burlington has a thriving local music scene. Check the local week-lies for information on festivals and concerts during your visit, and to find out who's playing at the clubs. Online information about local music and arts events may be found at **www.bigheavyworld.com.**

**Nectar's,** 188 Main St. (☎ 802/658-4771), is an odd amalgam—part funky cafeteria-style restaurant, part no-frills lounge. No wonder this is the place Phish got its start and where the band occasionally shows up. Live bands play 7 days a week, and there's never a cover charge. On weekends it's packed with UVM students and abuzz with a fairly high level of hormonal energy. Look for the revolving neon sign (the last of its kind in Vermont).

**Club Metronome,** 188 Main St. (☎ 802/865-4563), is a loud and loose nightspot that features a wide array of acts with a heavy dose of world beat. It's right above Nectar's. You can dance or shoot a game of pool (or do both at once, as seems popu-lar). This is a good spot to sample some of the local talent pool, which runs quite deep. Cover is $3 to $15.

For gay nightlife, head to **135 Pearl** (☎ 802/863-2343), located naturally enough at 135 Pearl St. It's Burlington's only gay bar. You can get a bite to eat, dance to the DJ, or give karaoke a go (Wednesdays only). Open Monday to Thursday 7:30pm to 1am, Friday and Saturday from 5pm to 1am.

# 6 The Champlain Islands

Few travelers studying a map of Vermont can stare at the archipelago of islands in northern Lake Champlain, hard against the Canadian border, and not wonder what's up there.

Well, here's what: not much, and therein lies the appeal.

These islands, connected by bridges, causeways, and roads, are linked primarily by a rich history. There are few amenities for tourists—just a handful of accommodations and only slightly more restaurants—but there's a stark, mercurial beauty in these low, largely open islands against the lake, which is sometimes placid and improbably blue, sometimes a hostile, dull gray flecked with frothy white.

The 30-mile main road is relatively straight and fast; the posted speed is typically 50 m.p.h. If you're going too slowly, locals in pickup trucks will let you know by blowing by or hugging your tail. When the opportunity arises, veer off on one of the side roads and take it slow, or just pull over at one of the many parks to enjoy the scenery. If you've got a boat or kayak, you can explore several small island parks between the island and the mainland. Camping is available at two parks (Grand Isle and South Hero state parks) along the route described below.

While the area is mostly open and appealing farm country now, especially along the northern stretches, the handwriting is on the wall. Today, you'll pass many signs on former farms offering 1-acre home lots for sale. Travel now to see this special area before it starts resembling former farmlands everywhere.

Further information is available from the **Lake Champlain Islands Chamber of Commerce,** P.O. Box 213, North Hero, VT 05474 (☎ **802/372-5683**).

## Touring the Lake Champlain Islands

**Start:** Exit 17 on I-89. Head northwest on Route 2, which you'll stay on much of this tour.

**Finish:** Burlington.

**Time:** The entire loop from Exit 17 on I-89 is approximately 71 miles and may be done in 3 to 5 hours, depending on the number of stops you make. Within a few minutes you'll arrive at:

**1. Sand Bar State Park.** This nicely maintained park (on the mainland side) has sweeping views to the north, a handful of picnic tables, and relatively protected swimming. There's a small fee in summer.

Cross the water on the causeway (you can guess where the sandbar name comes from) to:

**2. Grande Isle.** This island, the largest of the bunch, is split into two villages, South Hero and Grand Isle. The area around South Hero doesn't quite qualify as rural. It's got a mix of architectural styles, from early stone farmhouse to modular home, and it's also blessed with a good number of convenience stores and small retail plazas. The landscape becomes less developed and more farmlike the farther north you travel.

At **Keeler Bay,** take a detour on Route 314 to the:

**3. Lake Champlain Ferry to Plattsburgh, New York.** The ferry runs year-round (the only one of the three lake ferries to do so) and operates daily between 5am and 1am. This short detour is about 5 miles and offers wonderful views across the lake to the Adirondacks. Stop and watch the ferry operation for a bit; across the road is one of Vermont's several fish hatcheries, where you can learn about the state's stocking programs.

Continue on Route 314 back to Route 2, and head north again through the village of Grand Isle. Just north of the village, look for a rustic log cabin on the right side, next to a historical marker reading:

**4. Pioneer Log Cabin.** This is thought to be the oldest existing log cabin in the U.S., dating back to 1783. Built by Jedediah Hyde, it's furnished with many of the Hyde family possessions. The cabin, which is managed by the Grand Isle Historical Society, is open in summer Thursday to Monday 11am to 5pm; there's a small admission fee.

Continue northward on Route 2 until you cross a bridge to North Hero Island. At this tip is:

**5. Knight Point State Park.** Situated on an old farm, this scenic property offers nice views, picnicking, and sheltered swimming that makes this park especially appealing for parents with young children. A small fee is charged in season.

Shortly beyond this park, you'll come across the summer home of the:

**6. Royal Lipizzan Stallions** (☎ **802/372-5683**). These stunning white horses, famed for their precise steps and leaping ability, take a holiday from their home in Florida by coming to a North Hero farm every summer for about 6 or 7 weeks, usually from early or mid-July to late August. The breed dates back to 1580, and the name derives from Lipizza, which was once part of the Austro-Hungarian Empire. While relatively small, Lipizzans are very powerful and have remarkably expressive eyes. These stallions are trained by the Hermann family, which has been training Lipizzans for 3 centuries. Performances are offered Thursday and Friday evenings, and Saturday and Sunday afternoons. Visitors are welcome to stop by anytime between mid-July and August. Performance tickets are $15 adult, $12 senior, and $8 children 6 to 12.

Northward again, head through the picturesque village of North Hero, with its beautiful natural harbor, lapping waves, and westward views toward the Green Mountains. Continue on until you see signs for Route 129 and a small bridge to:

**7. Isle La Motte.** This is the most pastoral and remote of the Champlain Islands, although the western shore is thick with summer homes. The island was connected to Grand Isle in 1882, and for years there was a toll to cross the bridge (20¢ one-way, 25¢ round-trip). Today, the island's interior is mostly farmland, although economics and the ever-assertive forest are making inroads against the open fields.

Shortly after crossing to the island, turn right, following signs to:

**8. St Anne's Shrine.** This outdoor shrine with stations of the cross, grottoes, and a handsome outdoor chapel is run by the Edmundite Fathers and Brothers. It also happens to mark the first European settlement in Vermont—in 1666, Captain Sieur de La Motte built Fort St. Anne on this very spot. It's the site of the first mass in Vermont. Daily masses are performed in summer; there's also a beach and a cafeteria. Nearby is a heroic statue of Samuel de Champlain originally sculpted for Expo '67 in Montreal.

Continue past the shrine for a slow circumnavigation of the island. The whole loop is about 12 miles, and it's especially appealing by bike. The terrain is flat, the traffic light, and the views are best seen from a bike saddle; a lot is lost through car windows.

Upon leaving Isle La Motte, make a left just after the bridge. This road will take you through quiet farmland and past some dour stone houses to the cheerless town of Alburg. If you're heading to New York State, turn left at the stop sign and continue through Alburg to cross at Rouse Point. If you're returning to the Burlington area, turn right on Route 2, then left on Route 78. After crossing the bridge, you'll pass through:

**9. Missisquoi National Wildlife Refuge** (☎ **802/868-4781**), a 6,338-acre federal property that encompasses the Missisquoi River delta. With its copious wetlands, it's a significant stop for migratory birds, especially ducks and other waterfowl. There are some 200 nesting boxes and cylinders on the refuge, and water levels are managed to provide habitat and food for wildlife; there's a $1^1/_2$-mile interpretive trail that will introduce visitors to the terrain. The grounds are open daily from dawn to dark.

From here, it's a short hop to return to I-89 and southward to Burlington.

## WHERE TO STAY

**Shore Acres.** 237 Shore Acres Dr., North Hero Island, VT 05474. ☎ **802/372-8722.** www.shoreacres.com. E-mail: info@shoreacres.com. 23 units. TV. Peak season (July, Aug, and foliage) $87.50–$129.50, early summer and early fall $82.50–$124.50, spring and late fall $72.50–114.50. Off-season rates include continental breakfast. MC, V. Closed late Oct–mid-May. Pets allowed ($10 first night, $5 additional nights).

Shore Acres is an upscale motel set well off the road on beautifully maintained grounds overlooking the lake. It consists of clean, standard-size motel rooms arrayed along a covered walkway; the rooms are furnished comfortably rather than elegantly with modern oak furniture. Porch chairs are located just outside the doors for relaxing and enjoying the views; all lakeside rooms (19 of them) have screen doors; the four rooms in the annex (in a compound of nearby farmhouses) have air-conditioning. Opt for the lake rooms, if available; among these, Rooms 15 to 18 are somewhat larger than the others. The real draw here is the property—you're surrounded by open space, lush lawns, and farm country, and the owners take obvious pride in their place. Adirondack chairs are scattered about for idle afternoons. This spot is impeccably well-cared for and provides good value.

**Dining:** The modern dining room with fresh flowers and lake views offers a small but intriguing menu well-represented by grilled dishes, including filet mignon, pork loin, and adobo chicken. There's always a fresh fish and vegetarian entree, which changes daily. Entrees are $12.95 to $23.95, with most under $20.

**Amenities:** There's swimming in the lake from dock and float, but no beach. Two clay tennis courts, five-hole practice golf course, croquet, horseshoes, and shuffleboard.

**Thomas Mott Homestead.** 63 Blue Rock Rd., Alburg, VT 05440. ☎ **800/348-0843.** www.thomas-mott-bb.com. E-mail: tmott@together.net. 5 units. $79–$108 double, including full breakfast. Blue Rock Rd. is about 1¹/₂ miles east of Rte. 2 on Rte. 78; look for signs to inn. AE, CB, DC, DISC, MC, V. Children over age 6 welcome.

Built in 1838, this small home has been accommodating travelers since 1987 and is the islands' best destination for those seeking homey comfort and cordial hospitality. Ideally situated on a point overlooking the lake (although lately surrounded by a phalanx of contemporary homes), the Thomas Mott has five guest rooms, most of which are somewhat small, and most decorated in a cozy country style. The best view of the lake is from Ransom's Rest, which also has a balcony and gas fireplace. Few come here for the decor or rooms, but many return thanks to the exceptional attention to small things paid by innkeeper Patrick Schallert, a soft-spoken retired wine dealer from California. Patrick is very knowledgeable about the region and happy to help guests plan day trips or find restaurants. Raspberries, blackberries, and blueberries from his yard are served with morning pancakes. Guests can select other options from the extensive breakfast menu, although why they would is unclear. Schallert also keeps a freezer stocked full of Ben & Jerry's ice cream for guests to help themselves free of charge when the mood strikes.

# 7 The Northeast Kingdom

Vermont's Northeast Kingdom has an edgy, wild, and remote character. Consisting of Orleans, Essex, and Caledonia counties, the region was given its memorable name in 1949 by Sen. George Aiken, who understood the area's allure at a time when few others paid it much heed. What gives this region its character is its stubborn, old-fashioned insularity.

In contrast to the dusky narrow valleys of southern Vermont, the Kingdom's landscape is open and spacious, with rolling meadows ending abruptly at the hard edge of dense boreal forests. The leafy woodlands of the south give way to spiky forests of spruce and fir. Accommodations and services for tourists aren't as plentiful or easy to find here as in the southern reaches of the state, but some superb inns are tucked among the hills and in the forests.

Visitor information is available from the **Northeast Kingdom Chamber of Commerce,** 357 Western Ave. Suite 2, in St. Johnsbury (☎ **800/639-6379** or 802/

748-3678). On the Internet, head to www.vermontnekchamber.org. Another online guide focusing on Vermont's northern reaches is located at www.vtnorthcountry.com.

## Touring the Northeast Kingdom

This is a loose, somewhat convoluted driving tour of the Northeast Kingdom. If your time is limited, make sure you at least stop in St. Johnsbury, which has two of my favorite attractions in the state—the Fairbanks Museum and St. Johnsbury Athenaeum. The total tour, from Hardwick to St. Johnsbury by way of Newport, Derby Line, and Lake Willoughby, is approximately 90 miles. Allow a full day or more if you plan to take advantage of hiking and biking in the region.

**Start:** Hardwick.
**Finish:** St. Johnsbury.
**Time:** One full day.

1. **Hardwick,** a small town with rough edges set along the Lamoille River (at the intersection of Rt. 14 and Rt. 15, about 23 miles northwest of St. Johnsbury and 26 miles northeast of Montpelier). It has a compact commercial main street, some quirky shops, and a couple of casual, family-style restaurants.

   From here, head north on Route 14 a little over 7 miles to the turnoff toward Craftsbury and:

2. **Craftsbury Common.** An uncommonly graceful village, Craftsbury Common is home to a small academy and a large number of historic homes and buildings spread along a sizable green and the village's broad main street. The town occupies a wide upland ridge and offers sweeping views to the east and west. Be sure to stop by the old cemetery on the south end of town, where you can wander among historic tombstones of the pioneers, which date back to the 1700s. Craftsbury is an excellent destination for mountain biking and cross-country skiing and is home to the region's finest inn (see below).

   From Craftsbury, continue north to reconnect to Route 14. You'll wind through the towns of Albany and Irasburg as you head north. At the village of Coventry, veer north on Route 5 to the lakeside town of:

3. **Newport.** This commercial outpost (population 4,400) is set on the southern shores of Lake Memphremagog, a stunning 27-mile-long lake that's just 2 miles wide at its broadest point and the bulk of which is located in Canada. Newport, improbably enough, has a small outlet zone on Main Street. Look for discounted gear from **Bogner** (150 Main St., ☎ **802/334-0135**), **Louis Garneau** (at Vermont Bike & Ski, 194 Main St., ☎ **802/334-7346**), and **Great Outdoors** (177 Main St., ☎ **802/334-2831**).

   From Newport, continue north on Route 5, crossing under I-91, for about 7 miles to the town of **Derby Line** (population 2,000). This border outpost has a handful of restaurants and antique shops; you can park and walk across the bridge to poke around the Canadian town of Rock Island without much hassle. Back in Derby Line, look for the:

4. **Haskell Free Library and Opera House,** at the corner of Caswell Avenue and Church Street (☎ **802/873-3022**). This handsome neoclassical building contains a public library on the first floor and an elegant opera house on the second that's modeled after the old Boston Opera House. The theater opened in 1904 with advertisements promoting a minstrel show featuring "new songs, new jokes, and beautiful electric effects." It's a beautiful theater, with a scene of Venice painted on the drop curtain and carved cherubim adorning the balcony.

What's most curious about the structure, however, is that it lies half in Canada and half in the United States. (The Haskell family donated the building jointly to the towns of Derby Line and Rock Island.) A thick black line runs beneath the seats of the opera house, indicating who's in the United States and who's in Canada. Because the stage is set entirely in Canada, apocryphal stories abound from the early days of frustrated U.S. officers watching fugitives perform on stage. More recently, the theater has been used for the occasional extradition hearing.

From Derby Line, retrace your path south on Route 5 to Derby Center and the juncture of Route 5A. Continue south on Route 5A to the town of Westmore on the shores of:

**5. Lake Willoughby.** This glacier-carved lake is best viewed from the north, with the shimmering sheet of water pinched between the base of two low mountains at the southern end. There's a distinctive Alpine feel to the whole scene, and this underappreciated lake is certainly one of the most beautiful in the Northeast. Route 5A along the eastern shore is lightly traveled and well-suited to biking or walking. To ascend the two mountains by foot, see the "Outdoor Pursuits in the Northeast Kingdom" section, below.

Head southwest on Route 16, which departs from Route 5A just north of the lake. Follow Route 16 through the peaceful villages of Barton and Glover. A little over a mile south of Glover, turn left on Route 122. Very soon on your left, look for the farmstead that serves as home to the:

**6. Bread and Puppet Theater.** For the last 3 decades, Polish artist and performer Peter Schumann's Bread and Puppet Theater staged an elaborate annual summer pageant at this farm, attracting thousands. Attendees participated, watched, and lounged about the hillsides as huge, lugubrious, brightly painted puppets crafted of fabric and papier-mâché marched around the farm, acting out a drama that typically featured rebellion against tyranny of one form or another. It was like Woodstock without the music.

Alas, the summer event became so popular that it eventually overwhelmed the farm; for a brief spell, the event was held on secret dates that only diehard fans figured out. Starting in 1999, the theater opted to stage several shows throughout the season, hoping to spread out the mayhem. The schedule is still in an experimental phase; it's best to call for details (☎ **802/525-3031**).

Regardless of the pageant schedule, anytime between June and October you can visit a venerable, slightly tottering barn on the property that's home to the ✪ **Bread and Puppet Museum,** housing many of the puppets used in past events. This is a remarkable display and shouldn't be missed if you're anywhere near the area. Downstairs in the former cow-milking stalls are smaller displays, such as King Lear addressing his daughters, and a group of mournful washerwomen doing their laundry. Upstairs, the vast hayloft is filled to the eaves with soaring, haunting puppets, some up to 20 feet tall. The style is witty and eclectic; the barn seems a joint endeavor of David Lynch, Red Grooms, and Hieronymus Bosch. Admission is free, although donations are encouraged.

From Glover, continue south through serene farmlands to Lyndonville, where you pick up Route 5 south to:

**7. St. Johnsbury.** This town of 7,600 inhabitants is the largest in the Northeast Kingdom and is the major center of commerce. First settled in 1786, the town enjoyed a buoyant prosperity in the 19th century, largely stemming from the success of platform scales, invented here in 1830 by Thaddeus Fairbanks, and which are still manufactured here. The town, which has not suffered from the depredations of tourist boutiques and brew pubs, has an abundance of fine commercial architecture in two distinct areas, which are joined by steep Eastern Avenue. The more commercial part of town lies along Railroad Street (Route 5) at the base of the hill. The more ethereal part of town, with the library, St. Johnsbury Academy, and a grand museum, is along Main Street at the top of the hill. The north end of Main Street is also notable for its grand residential architecture.

At the corner Main and Prospect streets in St. Johnsbury, look for:

**8.** ✪ **The Fairbanks Museum** (☎ **802/748-2372**). This imposing Romanesque red-sandstone structure was constructed in 1889 to hold the collections of obsessive amateur collector Franklin Fairbanks, the grandson of the inventor of the platform scale. Fairbanks was once described as "the kind of little boy who came home with his pockets full of worms." In adulthood, his propensity to accumulate indiscriminately continued unabated. His artifacts include four stuffed bears, a huge moose with full antlers, art from Asia, and 4,500 stuffed native and exotic birds, and that's just the tip of it.

The soaring, barrel-vaulted main hall, reminiscent of an old-fashioned railway depot, embodies Victorian grandeur. Among the assorted clutter, look for the unique mosaics by John Hampson. Hampson crafted scenes of American history—such as Washington bidding his troops farewell—entirely of mounted insects. In the Washington scene, for instance, iridescent green beetles form the epaulets, and the regal great coat is comprised of hundreds of purple moth wings. Words fail me here; you must see these works, which alone are worth the price of admission.

The museum, at 1302 Main St., is open Monday to Saturday from 10am to 4pm (until 6pm in July and August), and Sunday from 1 to 5pm. Admission is $5 for adults, $4 for seniors, $3 for children 5 to 17, free for children under 5, and $12 per family (maximum of three adults, unlimited children).

Also in town, just south of the museum on Main Street:

**9.** ✪ **The St. Johnsbury Athenaeum** (☎ **802/748-8291**) is in an Edward Hopperesque brick building with a truncated mansard tower and prominent keystones over the windows. This is the town's public library, but it also houses an extraordinary art gallery dating to 1873. It claims to be the oldest unadulterated art gallery in the nation, and I see no reason to question that claim.

Your first view of the gallery is spectacular: After winding through the cozy library with its ticking regulator clock, you round a corner and find yourself gazing across Yosemite National Park. This luminous 10-by-15-foot oil was created by noted Hudson River School painter Albert Bierstadt, and the gallery was built specifically to accommodate this work. (Not everyone was happy about the work moving here. "Now *The Domes* is doomed to the seclusion of a Vermont town, where it will astonish the natives," groused the *Boston Globe* at the time.) The natural light flooding in from the skylight above nicely enhances the painting.

Some 100 other works fill the walls. Most are copies of other paintings (a common teaching tool in the 19th century), but look for originals by other Hudson River School painters including Asher B. Durand, Thomas Moran, and Jasper Cropsey.

The Athenaeum is open Monday and Wednesday from 10am to 8pm; Tuesday, Thursday, and Friday from 10am to 5:30pm; and Saturday from 9:30am to 4pm. Admission is free, but donations are encouraged.

## OUTDOOR PURSUITS IN THE NORTHEAST KINGDOM

**HIKING**   At the southern tip of Lake Willoughby, two rounded peaks rise above the lake's waters. These are the biblically named Mount Hor and Mount Pisgah, both of which lie within Willoughby State Forest. Both summits are accessible via footpaths that are somewhat strenuous but yield excellent views.

For **Mount Pisgah** (elevation 2,751 ft.), look for parking on the west side of Route 5A about 5.7 miles south of the junction with Route 16. The trail departs from across the road and runs 1.7 miles to the summit. To hike **Mount Hor** (elevation 2,648 ft.), drive 1.8 miles down the gravel road on the right side of the above-mentioned parking lot, veering right at the fork. Park at the small parking lot, and continue on foot past the parking lot a short distance until you spot the start of the trail. Follow the trail signs to the summit, a round-trip of about 3¹/₂ miles.

**MOUNTAIN BIKING**    The Craftsbury ridge features several excellent variations for bikers in search of easy terrain. Most of the biking is on hard-packed dirt roads through sparsely populated countryside. The views are sensational, and the sense of being well out in the country very strong. The **Craftsbury Outdoor Center at Craftsbury Common** (☎ 800/729-7751 or 802/586-7767) rents mountain bikes and is an excellent source for maps and local information about area roads. Bike rentals are $25 to $35 per day. A small fee is charged for using bikes on the cross-country ski trail network.

**CROSS-COUNTRY SKIING**    The same folks who offer mountain biking at the Craftsbury Center also maintain 61 miles of groomed cross-country trails through the gentle hills surrounding Craftsbury. The trails, maintained by **Craftsbury Nordic** (☎ 800/729-7751 or 802/586-7767), are forgiving, old-fashioned trails that emphasize pleasing landscapes rather than fast action. Trail passes are $10 for adults, $5 for juniors 6 to 12, and $7 for seniors (discounts available midweek). **Highland Lodge** (☎ 802/533-2647) on Caspian Lake offers 36 miles of trails (about 10 miles groomed) through rolling woodlands and fields.

## DOWNHILL SKIING

**Jay Peak.** Rte. 242, Jay, VT 05859. ☎ **800/451-4449** for lodging or 802/988-2611. E-mail: jaypeak@together.net. Vertical drop: 2,153 ft. Lifts: 1 tram, 4 chairlifts, 2 surface lifts. Skiable acreage: 300-plus. Lift tickets: $49.

Located just south of the Canadian border, Jay is Vermont's best ski mountain for those who get away just to ski and who prefer to avoid all the modern-day glitz and clutter that seem to plague ski resorts elsewhere. (The lower lift prices also save you a few dollars a day.) While some new condo development has been taking place at the base of the mountain, the mountain still has the feeling of a remote, isolated destination, accessible by a winding road through unbroken woodlands.

More than half of Jay's 62 trails are for intermediate skiers, but experts haven't been left behind. Jay has developed extensive glade skiing, taking excellent advantage of its sizable natural snowfall, which averages more than 300 inches annually (more than any other New England ski area). Jay Peak's ski school emphasizes glade skiing, making it a fitting place to learn how to navigate these exciting, challenging trails that have cropped up at other New England ski areas in recent years.

## WHERE TO STAY

**Highland Lodge.** Caspian Lake, Greensboro, VT 05841. ☎ **802/533-2647.** Fax 802/533-7494. www.thehighlandlodge.com. E-mail: hlodge@connriver.net. 11 units, 11 cottages. $190–$245 double. Rates include breakfast and dinner. DISC, MC, V. Closed mid-Mar–May and mid-Oct–Christmas. From Hardwick, drive on Rte. 15 east 2 miles to Rte. 16; drive north 2 more miles to East Hardwick. Head west and follow signs to the inn.

The Highland Lodge was built in the mid-19th century and has been accommodating guests since 1926. Located just across the road from lovely Caspian Lake, this lodge has 11 rooms furnished in a comfortable country style. Nearby are 11 cottages, fully equipped with kitchenettes. A stay here is supremely relaxing—the main activities include swimming and boating in the lake in summer, along with tennis on a clay court; in winter, the lodge maintains its own cross-country ski area with 30 miles of groomed trail. Behind the lodge is an attractive nature preserve, which makes for quiet exploration.

**Dining:** The inn's welcoming dining room serves New England favorites, like Cornish game hen and crab gratin (open to outside guests, entrees $14.50 to $16.75).

✪ **Inn on the Common.** Craftsbury Common, VT 05827. ☎ **800/521-2233** or 802/586-9619. Fax 802/586-2249. www.innonthecommon.com. E-mail: info@innonthecommon.com. 16 units. $240–$260 double; foliage season $270–$290 double. Rates include breakfast and dinner ($40 less for breakfast only). 2-night minimum stay during foliage and Christmas week. AE, MC, V. Pets accepted by prior arrangement ($15 per visit).

This exceedingly handsome complex of three Federal-style buildings anchors the charming ridge-top village of Craftsbury Common, one of the most quintessential of New England villages. Innkeepers Penny and Michael Schmitt have run this place with panache since 1973 and have crafted a stunning, comfortable inn that offers just the right measures of both history and luxury. Guests can unwind in the nicely appointed common rooms or stroll the 15 acres of landscaped grounds. Choose from standard or deluxe rooms; five have wood-burning fireplaces. Ask about special winter and summer packages.

**Dining:** Dinner starts with cocktails at 6pm, then guests are seated family-style amid elegant Federal-era surroundings at 7:30pm. The menu changes nightly but includes well-prepared contemporary American fare like baked cherry planked salmon with shallot, caper and mushroom cream sauce or sautéed breast of duck with berry compote and fresh rosemary.

**Amenities:** Outdoor heated pool (summer only), clay tennis court, croquet, 250-video library. in-room massage, baby-sitting ($4 per hour), nature trails, and conference rooms. In winter, there's cross-country skiing and snowshoeing.

# Southern & Central New Hampshire 6

There are two ways to get New Hampshire old-timers riled up and spitting vinegar. First, tell them you love Vermont. Then tell them you think it's a little weird that New Hampshire doesn't have either a state income tax or sales tax.

At its most basic, New Hampshire defines itself by what it isn't, and that, more often than not, is Vermont—a state regarded by many locals as one of the few communist republics still remaining. No, New Hampshire is not Vermont, and they'll thank you not to confuse the two, despite some outward similarities.

Keep in mind that New Hampshire's state symbol is the Old Man of the Mountains, which is an actual site you can visit in the White Mountains. You'll see this icon just about everywhere you look—on state highway signs, on brochures, on state police cars; and it's an apt symbol for a state that relishes its cranky-old-man demeanor. New Hampshire has long been a magnet for folks who speak of government—especially "big government"—in tones normally reserved for bowel ailments. That "Live-Free-or-Die" license plate? It's for real. New Hampshire stands behind its words. This is a state that still regards zoning as a nefarious conspiracy to undermine property rights. Note that New Hampshire does not have a bottle-deposit law or a law banning billboards. (Heathen Vermont has both, as does its other godless neighbor, Maine.)

New Hampshire savors its reputation as an embattled outpost of plucky and heroic independents fighting the good fight against intrusive laws and irksome bureaucrats. Without a state sales tax or state income tax, it's had to be creative in financing its limited government. Many government services are funded through the "tourist tax" (an 8% levy on meals and rooms at restaurants and hotels) along with a hefty local property tax (the mere mention of which is another way to get locals riled up). In fact, candidates for virtually every office with the possible exception of dogcatcher must take "The Pledge," which means they'll vow to fight any effort to impose sales or income tax. To shirk The Pledge is tantamount to political suicide.

Get beyond New Hampshire's affable crankiness, though, and you'll find pure New England. Indeed, New Hampshire may represent the New England ethic distilled to its essence. At its core is a mistrust of outsiders, a premium placed on independence, a belief that government should be frugal above all else, and a laconic acceptance that, no matter what, you just can't change the weather. Travelers exploring the state with open eyes will find these attitudes in spades.

Travelers will also find wonderfully diverse terrain—from ocean beaches to the broad lakes to the region's impressive mountains. Without ever leaving the state's borders, you can toss a Frisbee on a sandy beach, ride bikes along quiet country lanes dotted with covered bridges, hike rugged granite hills blasted by some of the most severe weather in the world, and canoe on a placid lake in the company of moose and loons. You'll also find good food and country inns you won't want to ever leave; but most of all, you'll find vestiges of that feisty independence that has defined New England since the first settlers ran up their flag 3$^1$/$_2$ centuries ago.

## 1 Enjoying the Great Outdoors

See chapter 7 for details on outdoor pursuits in the White Mountains.

More gentle outdoor recreation is found throughout much of the rest of New Hampshire, from canoeing on the meandering **Connecticut River** (which forms the border with Vermont), to sailing on vast **Lake Winnipesaukee.** If you're so inclined, come prepared for outdoor recreation, because it doesn't take much to find it.

**BACKPACKING**    See chapter 7.

**BIKING**    There's superb road biking throughout the state. Southwest New Hampshire near Mount Monadnock offers a multitude of shady backroads for exploring, especially around Hancock and Greenfield.

A wonderful way to take in sea breezes is to pedal along New Hampshire's diminutive coast, following Route 1A from the beach town of Hampton up to the mini-metropolis of Portsmouth. The road can be a bit crowded with RVs at times, but that's made up for by a bike path that veers along the surf from time to time.

**CAMPING**    Fifteen of New Hampshire's state parks allow camping (two of these for RVs only). About half of these parks are located in and around the White Mountains. For advance **reservations,** call the New Hampshire state park system, at ☎ **603/ 271-3628** between January and May; during the summer season, call the campground directly. Some campgrounds are first-come, first-served. A list of parks and phone numbers is published in the New Hampshire Visitor's Guide, distributed widely through information centers, or by contacting the **Office of Travel and Tourism Development,** P.O. Box 1856, Concord, NH 03302 (☎ **800/386-4664** or 603/ 271-2343).

New Hampshire also has more than 150 private campgrounds. For a free directory, contact the **New Hampshire Campground Owners Association,** P.O. Box 320, Twin Mountain, NH 03595 (☎ **800/822-6764** or 603/846-5511; www.ucampnh.com).

**CANOEING**    New Hampshire has a profusion of river and lakes suitable for paddling, and canoe rentals are available widely around the state. Good flatwater paddling may be found along the **Merrimack and Connecticut rivers** in the southern parts of the state. Virtually any lake is good for dabbling about with canoe and paddle, although beware of stiff northerly winds when crossing large lakes like **Winnipesaukee.**

**FISHING**    A vigorous stocking program keeps New Hampshire's lakes and rivers lively with fish. Brook trout (about half of trout stocked), lake trout, and rainbow trout are in the waters. Other sportfish include small- and largemouth bass, landlocked salmon, and walleye.

Fishing licenses are required for freshwater fishing, but not for saltwater fishing. For detailed information on regulations, request the free *Freshwater Fishing Digest* from the **New Hampshire Fish and Game Department,** 2 Hazen Dr., Concord, NH 03301 (☎ **603/271-3211**). Fishing licenses for non-residents range from $19.50 for 3 days

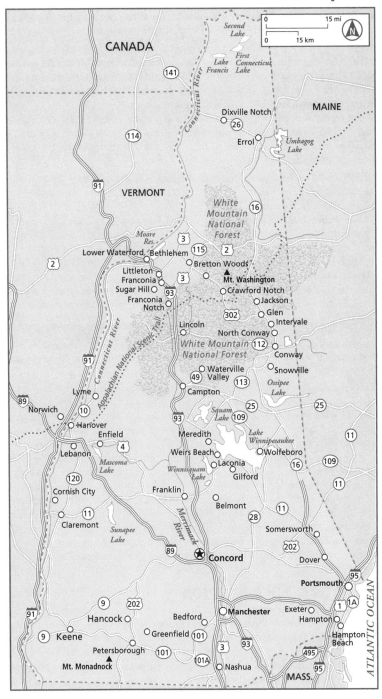

# New Hampshire

CANADA

*Second Lake*

*Lake Francis*

*First Connecticut Lake*

141

*Connecticut River*

114

MAINE

Dixville Notch
26

Errol

*Umbagog Lake*

91

VERMONT

*White Mountain National Forest*

16

*Moore Res.*

3

115

2

Lower Waterford  Bethlehem

Bretton Woods

▲ Mt. Washington

Littleton
Franconia  3
Sugar Hill  93
Franconia Notch

Crawford Notch
Jackson

302  Glen

Intervale

Lincoln

North Conway

*White Mountain National Forest*

112

Conway

2

*Connecticut River*

91

*Appalachian National Scenic Trail*

Waterville Valley
49

Snowville

113

*Ossipee Lake*

Campton

25

25

Lyme

*Squam Lake*

93  109

11

Norwich

89

Hanover

Enfield

Meredith

*Lake Winnipesaukee*

4

Weirs Beach

Wolfeboro

109

Lebanon

*Mascoma Lake*

Laconia

16

11

*Winnisquam Lake*

Gilford

120

Franklin

Cornish City

Belmont

11

Claremont

*Sunapee Lake*

28

Somersworth

202

*Merrimack River*

89  ★ Concord

Dover

95

Portsmouth

9  202

Hancock

Bedford

Manchester

Exeter

1A
1

91

9  Keene

Greenfield
101

Hampton

Petersborough

101

101A

Nashua

3  93

495

95

▲ Mt. Monadnock

MASS.

*ATLANTIC OCEAN*

0        15 mi
0        15 km

**161**

to $28.50 for 15 days. Another helpful booklet, available free from the fish and game department, is *Fishing Waters of New Hampshire.* For online information, point your browser to www.wildlife.state.nh.us.

**HIKING**    In southwest New Hampshire, the premier hike is **Mount Monadnock,** said to be, somewhat implausibly, one of the world's two most popular hikes (second only to Mt. Fuji in Japan). This lone massif, rising regally above the surrounding hills, is a straightforward day hike accessible via several trails.

For other hiking opportunities outside the Whites, *50 Hikes in the White Mountains* and *50 More Hikes in New Hampshire,* both written by Daniel Doan and Ruth Doan MacDougall ($14.95). These are in print and available through your bookstore, or from online retailers like Amazon.com.

**SKIING**    New Hampshire offers a good selection of slopes at some 20 downhill ski areas, although in my opinion the state comes up a bit short in comparison with the winter resorts of Vermont or Maine.

New Hampshire's forte is the small ski area that caters to families. These include Gunstock, Black, Temple Mountain, Mount Sunapee, King Pine, and Pats Peak, all with vertical drops of 1,500 feet or less.

**Ski NH** (☎ **800/887-5464,** or 603/745-9396 in New Hampshire) distributes a ski map and other information helpful in ski-trip planning. The same phone numbers provide recorded ski condition reports. On the Web, point your browser to www.skinh.com for general information and up-to-date ski condition reports.

## 2  The Seacoast

Portsmouth is 11 miles north of Hampton, 10 miles northeast of Exeter, 55 miles north of Boston, and 54 miles south of Portland

Every student of geography at some point registers a small shock when they learn that New Hampshire isn't landlocked—it actually has a coast. Granted, it isn't much of one (just 18 miles of sand, rock, and surf), but travelers quickly learn that it manages to pack a lot of variety into a little space. The coast has honky-tonk beach towns, sprawling mansions, vest-pocket state parks with swaths of warm sand, and a historic seaport city with a vibrant maritime history and culture. Ecologically, it's got low dunes, lush hardwood forests, and a complex system of salt marshes that has blocked development from overtaking the region entirely.

A short drive inland are more historic towns and a slower way of life that has, so far, resisted the inexorable creep of the Boston suburbs. While strip malls are belatedly establishing themselves throughout the region (particularly along Route 1), the quiet downtowns are holding their own and several have established themselves as a fertile breeding grounds for small-scale entrepreneurs who've shunned the hectic life of bigger cities.

### HAMPTON BEACH & HAMPTON

The chamber of commerce's phone number in Hampton Beach is ☎ **800/ GET-A-TAN,** and that about says it all. During the peak of the summer season, as many as 200,000 people, many of them rather young, crowd the beaches on a sunny day, then spill over into the town and cruise the main drag by car, bike, and inline skate. The place bristles with a hormone-fueled energy during the balmy months, then lapses into a deep, shuttered slumber the rest of the year.

The traveler's first impression of this beach town isn't one of sand and surf, however, but rather of asphalt—acres and acres of it—and strikingly undistinguished

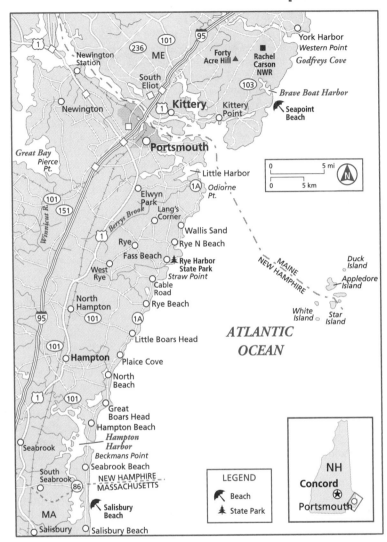

# The New Hampshire Coast

commercial architecture. The town is separated from its sandy strand by a busy four-lane road and a series of parking strips. Along the northern part of the beach, which tends to be less commercial and more residential than the south, the view of the sea from the road is partially blocked by a stout white seawall, which also serves as a handy sunning perch, but stick around for a bit if you're initially less than enchanted; it takes more than a moment for the salty character of the town to reveal itself.

A short drive inland, the more relaxed town of Hampton draws its inspiration less from the sea and more from the classic New England village, although it has a besieged, somewhat bedraggled feel to it in summer. It remains a good destination for shopping, restaurants, and accommodations. Try here if seacoast lodging is booked up.

## Essentials

**GETTING THERE** Hampton Beach is reached from I-95 via Exit 2. Be forewarned that traffic to the beach can be taxing in the summer, particularly on weekends. Route 1A winds north through Rye Beach, ending eventually in Portsmouth. Hampton is on Route 1, a more commercial route that runs parallel to the coast. Traffic can also slow to a crawl here in midsummer.

**VISITOR INFORMATION** The **Hampton Beach Chamber of Commerce,** P.O. Box 790, Hampton Beach, NH 03843 (☎ **800/438-2826** or 603/926-8718), maintains an information center on Ocean Boulevard in the middle of Hampton Beach (across from the casino). It's open weekends only from mid-March until June, then daily to Columbus Day. Hours are 9:30am to 9:30pm. The Web site is www. hamptonbeaches.com.

## Hitting the Beach

What to do here? Head to the beach, of course. Never mind that the ocean water is frigid (60 degrees is *warm* here), or that you'll be comfortable splashing around only if the mercury soars sky-high; and even then, the sweltering heat on shore looks pretty good after a few minutes underwater. The sandy beach is a fine place to roll out a towel, to walk, or just to while away a day.

If you're staying at a Hampton Beach hotel, you're within walking distance of the surf. If not, metered parking is available in and around Hampton Beach, although spots are scarce during prime beachgoing hours. If town parking lots are full, head inland a block or so and search out commercial lots.

Six state parks and beaches, none of them very large, dot the seacoast between Hampton Beach and Portsmouth. All charge a nominal parking or entrance fee during the summer. **Hampton Beach State Park** (☎ **603/926-3784**) is smack in town of Hampton Beach and is the place to be if you like boisterous crowds with your foamy surf. Parking is $5 per car; $8 on weekends. Further up the coast, **Wallis Sands State Beach** (☎ 603/436-9404) offers an inviting, broad sweep of sand and ample parking. It's not quite as crowded or loud as the more southerly beaches. Parking is $5 per car; $8 on weekends. A mile and a half north of Wallis Sands is **Odiorne Point State Park** (☎ 603/436-7406), a 300-acre oceanside park popular among those looking for a more wooded seaside experience. The park marks the site of the first European settlement of New Hampshire (a Scotsman settled here in 1623), and boasts seven types of habitat, picnic areas, and a visitor's center. There's a $2.50 day-use fee (children under 12 free).

## Off the Beach

Splendid flowers and notable garden landscaping are the draw at **Fuller Gardens** (☎ 603/964-5414), located at 10 Willow Avenue in North Hampton just north of the intersection of routes 1-A and 101-D. The 2-acre gardens adorn the grounds of the home of a former Massachusetts governor (the house is long gone), and feature extensive rose collections (more than 2,000 varieties) and hostas, as well as a peaceful Japanese garden within the sound of the surf. The gardens were designed during the mania for all things colonial in the 1920s by landscape architect Arthur Shurtleff,; the grounds were later expanded upon by the noted Olmsted Brothers firm. After visiting the gardens, head to the shore and hike along the footpath. The gardens are open early May through mid-October from 10am to 6pm daily. Admission is $5 adult, $4.50 senior, $2 student, $1 child under 12.

A driving or biking tour north on **Route 1-A** is well worth your while. This twisting oceanside road is dramatic in an understated sort of way (Big Sur it's not), with residential architecture becoming more elegant and imposing as you make your way north to Millionaire's Row. Be forewarned that this won't be an activity you'll enjoy in isolation, particularly during the height of summer. The road is often congested and frustrating to navigate by car, with frequent, unexpected stops and limited visibility behind slow-moving motor homes.

A better option is to view the coast by bicycle, which affords a far saner pace and opens up countless lounging options along the way. Route 1-A has a bike lane that periodically breaks away into a separate bike path with excellent views of the rocky coast.

## WHERE TO STAY

Hampton Beach and Hampton between them have about 70 motels; near the beach itself they tend to clutter in greater density along the southern end near the center of town. Motels along Ocean Boulevard include the **Beachview Inn** (☎ 603/926-2520), **Oceancrest Inn & Motel** (☎ 603/926-6606), and **Jonathan's Motel** (☎ 800/634-8243 or 603/926-6631).

**Ashworth by the Sea.** 295 Ocean Blvd., Hampton Beach, NH 03842. ☎ **800/345-6736** or 603/926-6762. Fax 603/926-2002. 105 units. A/C TV TEL. Peak season $115–$275 double; shoulder seasons $95–$225 double; off-season $74–$205 double. 2- or 3-night minimum stay applies summer weekends. AE, DC, DISC, MC, V.

There are a few subtle architectural clues, but it's still hard to tell that this shorefront hotel was first built in 1912. After a number of renovations, it's all modern and polished to the hilt. The Ashworth is actually two buildings joined at the hip, with the 1912 south building linked to the less distinguished but comfortable north building, constructed in 1979. All but six rooms have private balconies. This friendly hotel does a lively business in conventions and meetings, but not such that it makes individuals or families feel as though they've wandered somewhere they shouldn't.

**Dining:** The hotel has three dining areas. The main dining room has been renovated to recapture its Edwardian flavor (note the stamped-tin ceilings), and serves traditional American fare including lobster Newburg, roast turkey, and filet mignon ($10.95 to $19.95). Sandwiches and other, lighter fare are available at Breakers Cafe Lounge.

**Amenities:** Indoor/outdoor pool and deck on the second level overlooking the road and toward the beach, dry-cleaning ($10 minimum), valet parking (summer only; tip service), and nearby health club ($15 per day).

**Seaside Village Resort.** 1 Ocean Blvd., about 1,000 ft. south of North Hampton Beach (Route 1A), North Hampton, NH 03862. ☎ **603/964-8204.** Fax 603/964-8961. E-mail: ddupuis@nh.ultranet.com. 19 units. A/C TV. $69–$99 daily (when available, usually off-season); $475–$595 weekly for motel units, $650–$1,195 with kitchenettes. Closed Oct 15–May 15. AE, DISC, MC, V. Pets allowed in off-season.

Seaside Village is a classic, gray-shingled beach motel more reminiscent of sandy Cape Cod than of granite-and-spruce New Hampshire. If you're a beach fan, this is your place—it's the only motel in New Hampshire directly on the sand. During the day, you can walk across low dunes to get to mile-long North Hampton Beach. In the evening, guests grill their dinner on the shared hibachis and gas grills, and prepare meals in the handy outdoor galley. All rooms have refrigerators and ceiling fans.

The trick here is to actually get a room. Most book up for the season the previous summer, although if you're in town, it's worth calling to inquire if anything is available for the night. The older units (the Seaside has been operating for more than 60 years) are plain but neatly furnished, and the end units have nice views toward the sea. Expect some ambient noise (like your neighbor's plumbing) in these older rooms.

Eight modern post-and-beam housekeeping cottages were built in the early 1990s and are a better, if more expensive, choice. The newer units are more solidly wrought, and have air-conditioning in the bedrooms. Rooms don't have phones, but you can use the lobby phone jack to check e-mail at certain times of the day.

## WHERE TO DINE

**Ron's Landing.** 379 Ocean Blvd., Hampton Beach. ☎ **603/929-2122.** Reservations recommended in summer. Main courses $14.95–$23.95. AE, CB, DC, DISC, MC, V. Mon–Sat 4–10pm, Sunday noon–10pm. SEAFOOD/AMERICAN.

No surprise: Seafood is the specialty at Ron's Landing, a local institution owned by Ron Boucher, a graduate of the Culinary Institute of America. Ron's has served as an anchor for the often-transient Hampton Beach dining scene and attracts steady traffic in loyal repeat customers. Many return time and again for the fresh seafood, which can be prepared baked, blackened, charbroiled, or steamed and served with an Asian-style sauce. Fish specialties include a mixed seafood grill and (not for the faint of heart) veal-and-lobster pistachio—veal coated with pistachio and served with a lobster stuffing and hazelnut cream sauce. Entrees-not-from-the-sea include chicken, veal, and pasta dishes, but you're best off sticking with fish. Early birds (before 6pm) are rewarded with their own menu with prices at a good discount over the regular menu.

**Widow Fletcher Tavern.** 401 Lafayette Rd., Hampton. ☎ **603/926-8800.** Reservations accepted for parties of 6 or more. Lunch items $4.95–$7.95; main dinner courses $8.95–$16.95. AE, DISC, MC, V. Daily 11am–11pm (closes earlier in winter). BRITISH/AMERICAN.

Situated in what passes for downtown Hampton, a few miles from the sea, the Widow Fletcher has a distinctly British public house feel to it. The tavern sits on hectic Route 1, but when you cross the threshold, you leave the crowds and congestion at the door. This early village home has a comfortable, well-worn patina, with heavy wooden beams and 14-inch pine-plank floors. Dining is both upstairs and down in small rooms decorated with an eclectic selection of antiques, or at the sturdy bar. Guests can continue the British Isles theme with an order of shepherd's pie, or bangers and mash (sausages and mashed potatoes); or branch out and sample something more exotic, like the house specialty, a sirloin steak marinated in soy, ginger, and spicy Chinese hoisin sauce, or the lobster ravioli. The portions are large and will satisfy those who've stoked up sizable appetites after a day on the beach.

## HAMPTON BEACH AFTER DARK

In the evening, the action's in Hampton Beach, which takes on a carnival atmosphere. Much of the town's organized nightlife is centered around **Hampton Beach Casino** (☎ **603/926-4541;** www.casinoballroom.com), situated smack in the middle of town and fronting the ocean at 169 Ocean Boulevard. The casino has shops, video arcades, water slides, and parking for 700 cars (there's no gambling, despite the name). There's also a 2,000-seat performance hall where you can see yesterday's top performers.

## EXETER

The inland town of Exeter is a piece of classic New England. It's got a bandshell around which the local traffic circles, varied commercial architecture in its small but vibrant downtown, and wonderful residential architecture along shady side streets. Bisected by the historic Squamscott River, which once provided power to flanking mills, Exeter now boasts a fine, browsable selection of boutiques and shops; as well as one of the nation's most prestigious prep schools, architecturally, if not culturally, integrated into the town itself. In short, Exeter is a good stop if you want a quick view of what makes New England New England.

## ESSENTIALS

**GETTING THERE**    Exeter is located on Route 108 south of Route 101. Take the Hampton exit on I-95 and head west to Route 108.

**VISITOR INFORMATION**    The **Exeter Chamber of Commerce,** 120 Water St., Exeter, NH 03833 (☎ **603/772-2411**), distributes travel information from its offices weekdays from 8:30am to 4:30pm.

## EXPLORING THE TOWN

Exeter is best viewed on foot. Downtown boasts an eclectic mix of architecture, from clapboarded Georgian homes to intricate brick Victorians. The center of downtown is marked by the **Swasey Pavilion,** a trim 1916 bandstand with an intricate floral mosaic on the ceiling. Brass band concerts are still held here in the summer. Just up the hill from the pavilion is the imposing **Congregational Church,** built in 1798, with its unusually handsome white spire. On Thursdays in summer and early fall, there's a **farmer's market** held from 2:30 to 5:30pm along Swasey Parkway near the river.

I'd strongly recommend picking up the booklet *Walking Tour of Exeter,* published in 1994 by the Exeter Historical Society. It's available for $2 at the American Independence Museum, the Exeter Chamber of Commerce, or the historical society (47 Front St.). This guide and map offers a concise, well-written history of the town, along with historical and architectural facts about notable local buildings, such as 11 Pleasant St., where Abraham Lincoln's son lived while attending Exeter Academy.

With or without the guide, the grounds of the **Phillips Exeter Academy** (just southwest of the town center) are worth a stroll. The predominant style is Georgian-inspired brick buildings—it's hard to imagine misbehaving at a campus this stern (not that this has deterred generations of irksome prep-school kids); but look for the anomalies, like the 1971 prize-winning library by noted American architect Louis I. Kahn on Front Street near Abbot Place.

**American Independence Museum.** 1 Governor's Lane (1 block west of bandshell off Water St.). ☎ **603/772-2622.** Admission $4 adults, $2 children 6–12. May–Oct Wed–Sun noon–5pm. Nov–Apr by appt. only.

This small but ambitious museum offers an insightful glimpse of colonial life during 1-hour tours. Displays in the 1721 Ladd-Gilman House include Revolutionary War and Colonial Revival artifacts and furniture, although you won't see the museum's most prized possession: one of the 25 Declarations of Independence known to exist. It turned up when someone finally got around to cleaning out the attic in the 1980s. Owing to its great delicacy, this revered document is brought out only for special occasions, although copies are always on display.

You'll learn all about the intriguing homestead, built by John Taylor Gilman, who served as governor of New Hampshire for 14 years. Among the functions it served, the home was the state treasury during the American Revolution—look for displays of early currency in the treasury room. Descendants of Gilman occupied this home for decades, and in 1902 it was acquired by the state chapter of the Society of the Cincinnati, the oldest veterans group in the nation. In 1991, the group opened the house to the public (society members still meet here twice a year), and this engaging museum was born. Each year on the third weekend in July, the musuem hosts the free Revolutionary War Festival, which attracts some 10,000 history buffs.

## WHERE TO STAY

**The Inn by the Bandstand.** 4 Front St., Exeter, NH 03833. ☎ **603/772-6352.** www.innbythebandstand.com. 9 units (including 3 suites). A/C TV TEL. $110–$195 double;

suites $195–$299. Rates include breakfast. 2-night minimum holidays and school event week-ends. AE, DISC, MC, V.

You can't help but noticing this regal Federal-style house looming over the bandstand when wandering through downtown Exeter. Hosting guests since 1992, the Inn by the Bandstand is handsomely decorated inside with a supple Victorian richness. The rooms are attractively furnished with a mix of antiques and reproductions; six rooms have propane fireplaces. The first-floor suite is styled with deep maroons and forest greens, and furnished with leather wingback chairs. On the third floor are two rooms with the original hand-hewn beams (the home was built in 1809), and modern amenities include microwaves and refrigerators. Room rates include a continental breakfast, which typically features homemade muffins, coffee cake, fruit, and granola. While the downtown location is certainly handy, it can be a bit noisy as trucks gear down the hill next to the bandstand.

**Inn of Exeter.** 90 Front St., Exeter, NH 03833. ☎ **800/782-8444** or 603/772-5901. www.exeterinn.com. 46 units. A/C TV TEL. $124 double; $199–$245 suite. AE, DC, DISC, MC, V.

Located at the edge of the Exeter Academy campus and within easy walking distance of downtown, the Inn of Exeter has the dark, cool feel of a proper British drinking club. It's all dark wood and maroon carpets, with oil paintings on the walls, statuary in the alcoves, and a basket of apples on the front desk. The inn, which caters in large part to parents and staff associated with the academy next door, was built in 1932. The solid brick building with its prominent chimneys could easily pass for a campus building. The rooms on three floors are tastefully furnished with reproduction American antiques, including some canopy beds. Room sizes vary, but all are welcoming and homey. While the inn isn't budget-priced, it offers good value for the money.

**Dining:** The downstairs lounge and bar is clubby and dim, nicely capturing an era that elsewhere passed by long ago. The nice-but-not-stuffy Terrace Restaurant serves three meals a day. Dinner entrees ($18 to $25) feature upscale resort fare, ranging from veal tenderloin to filet mignon to lime-marinated chicken.

## WHERE TO DINE

**Loaf and Ladle.** 9 Water St. ☎ **603/778-8955.** Main courses $5–$8. AE, CB, DC, DISC, MC, V. Sun–Thurs 8:30am–9pm, Fri–Sat 9am–9pm (closed at 8pm weekdays in winter). CAFE/BAKERY.

A handsome view of the river and colorful piscine art are the only distractions from the superb baked goods and other delicious fare served up with good charm and cheer at the Loaf and Ladle. It's sometimes hard to get a grasp on the ever-evolving menu, which is constantly updated on chalkboards as the day goes on. As one soup is drained by appreciative diners, another offering follows on its heels. Among the savory baked goods, the cinnamon buns are especially fine. The breads are uniformly excellent, as are the pies. Everything is made from scratch, and a number of vegetarian entrees are available. The restaurant has been a mainstay for 26 years, making it clear that the place has been doing something very right.

# PORTSMOUTH

Portsmouth is a civilized seaside city of bridges, brick, and seagulls. Filled with elegant architecture that's more intimate than intimidating, this bonsai-size city projects a strong and proud sense of its heritage without being overly precious about it.

Part of the city's appeal is its variety. Upscale coffee shops and fancy art galleries exist alongside old-fashioned barber shops and tattoo parlors. There's been a steady gentri-fication in recent years, which has brought a wave of shops, but the town still has a

# Portsmouth

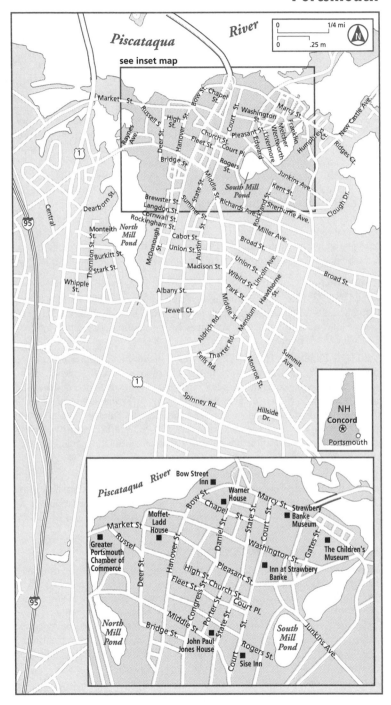

fundamental earthiness that serves as a tangy vinegar for the overly saccharine spots. Portsmouth's humble waterfront must actually be sought out, and when found, it's rather understated.

Portsmouth's history runs deep, a fact that is instantly evident when walking through town. For the past 3 centuries, the city has served as a hub for the region's maritime trade. In the 1600s, Strawbery Banke (it wasn't renamed Portsmouth until 1653) was a center for the export of wood and dried fish to Europe. In the 19th century, it prospered as a center of regional trade. Across the river in Maine, the Portsmouth Naval Shipyard was founded in 1800 and evolved into a prominent base for the building, outfitting, and repair of U.S. Navy submarines. Today, Portsmouth's maritime tradition continues with a lively trade in bulk goods (look for scrap metal and minerals stockpiled along the shores of the Piscataqua River on Market Street). The city's de facto symbol is the tugboat, one or two of which are almost always tied up near the waterfront's picturesque "tugboat alley."

Visitors to Portsmouth will find there's a whole lot to see in a little space. There's good shopping in the boutiques that now occupy much of the historic district, good eating at the many small restaurants, and plenty of history to explore among the historic homes and museums that crop up on almost every block.

## ESSENTIALS

**GETTING THERE**   Portsmouth is served by Exits 3 through 7 on I-95. The most direct access to downtown is via Market Street (Exit 7), which is the last New Hampshire exit before crossing the river to Maine. By bus, Portsmouth is served by Concord Trailways and Vermont Transit.

**VISITOR INFORMATION**   The **Greater Portsmouth Chamber of Commerce,** 500 Market St., Portsmouth, NH 03802 (☎ **603/436-1118**), operates a tourist information center year-round between Exit 7 and downtown. Between Memorial Day and Columbus Day the center is open Monday to Wednesday 8:30am to 5pm, Thursday and Friday 8:30am to 7pm, and Saturday and Sunday 10am to 5pm. The rest of the year, the center is open weekdays only 8:30am to 5pm. In summer, the chamber staffs a second information booth at Market Square in the middle of the historic district.

**PARKING**   Most of Portsmouth can be easily reconnoitered on foot, so you need park only once. Parking can be tight in and around the historic district in summer. The municipal parking garage costs 50¢ per hour; it's located on Hanover Street between Market and Fleet streets. Strawbery Banke (see below) also offers limited parking for visitors.

## EXPLORING PORTSMOUTH'S HISTORY

Portsmouth's 18th-century prosperity can be plainly seen in the regal Georgian-style homes that dot the city. Strawbery Banke occupies the core of the historic area and is well worth visiting. If you don't have the budget, time, or inclination to visit Strawbery Banke, a walking tour will bring you past many other significant homes, some of which are maintained by various historical or colonial societies and are open to the public. A helpful map and brochure describing the key historic homes, entitled *The Portsmouth Trail: An Historic Walking Tour,* is available free at the city's information centers.

✪ **Strawbery Banke Museum.** Hancock St., Portsmouth, NH 03802. ☎ **603/433-1106.** www.strawberybanke.org. Admission $12 adults, $11 seniors, $8 children 7–17, free for children under 7, $28 families. Apr–Oct daily 10am–5pm. Special events held 1st 2 weekends of Dec; otherwise closed Nov–Apr. Look for directional signs posted around town.

If you consider Portsmouth an alfresco festival of historic homes and buildings, Strawbery Banke is the main stage. In 1958, the city planned to raze this venerable neighborhood, first settled in 1653, to make way for urban renewal. A group of local citizens resisted and won, establishing an outdoor history museum that's grown to be one of the largest in New England.

The museum today consists of 10 downtown acres and 46 historic buildings. Ten of these have been restored with period furnishings; eight others feature exhibits. (One admission fee buys access to all homes and exhibits.) While Strawbery Banke employs staffers to assume the character of historic residents (including Thomas Bailey Aldrich, a frequent early contributor to the *Atlantic Monthly*), the emphasis is more on the buildings, architecture, and historic accoutrement, and less on living history as practiced at Sturbridge Village or Plimoth Plantation in Massachusetts.

The neighborhood surrounds an open lawn (formerly a tidal creek) and has a settled, picturesque quality to it. You'll find three working crafts shops on the grounds, where you can watch coopers, boatbuilders, and potters at work. The Shapiro House illustrates the life of a Russian-Jewish immigrant family from around 1919. The most intriguing home may be the split-personality Drisco House, half of which depicts life in the 1790s, and half of which shows life in the 1950s, nicely demonstrating how houses grow and adapt to each era.

**John Paul Jones House.** 43 Middle St. ☎ **603/436-8420.** Admission $5 adults, $2.50 children 6–14, free for children under 6. Mon–Sat 10am–4pm; Sun noon–4pm. Closed late Oct–May.

Revolutionary War hero John Paul Jones ("I have not yet begun to fight") was a boarder in this handsome 1758 home during the Revolutionary War. He was here to oversee the construction of his sloop, *Ranger,* believed to be the first ship to sail under the United States flag (there's a model of it on display). The home has been immaculately restored and maintained by the Portsmouth Historical Society; costumed tour guides offer tours of 45 minutes to an hour.

**Moffatt-Ladd House.** 154 Market St. ☎ **603/436-8221.** $5 adults, $2.50 children under 12. June 15–Oct 15 Mon–Sat 11am–5pm; Sun 1–5pm. Closed mid-Oct to mid-June.

The Moffatt-Ladd House, built for a family of prosperous merchants and traders, is as notable for its elegant garden as for the 1763 home, with its great hall and elaborate carvings throughout. The home stayed within one family between 1763 and 1913, when it became a museum. Many of the furnishings have never left the house. The home will especially appeal to aficionados of early American furniture and painting; it's adorned with portraits of some 15 family members. The home is owned by the National Society of the Colonial Dames of America in the State of New Hampshire.

**Warner House.** 150 Daniel St. ☎ **603/436-5909.** Admission $5 adults, $2.50 children 7–12, free for children 6 and under. Tues–Sat 10am–4pm; Sun 1–4pm. Closed Nov–June 1.

The Warner House, built in 1716, was the governor's mansion in the mid-18th century when Portsmouth served as the state capital. It was lived in privately until the 1930s, and since then, it's been open to the public. This stately brick home with graceful Georgian architectural elements (note the alternating arched and triangular pediments above the dormer windows) is a favorite among architectural historians for its circa-1716 wall murals (said to be the oldest murals still in place in the U.S.), the early wall marbleizing, and the original white-pine paneling.

**Wentworth-Gardner House.** 50 Mechanic St. ☎ **603/436-4406.** Admission $5 adults, $2.50 children 6–14, free for children 5 and under. Tues–Sun 1–4pm. Closed mid-Oct to mid-June.

The Wentworth-Gardner is arguably the most handsome mansion in the entire Seacoast region and is widely considered to be one of the best examples of Georgian architecture in the nation. Built in 1760, the home features many of the classic period elements, including very pronounced quoins (the blocks on the building's corners), pedimented window caps, plank sheathing (meant to make the home appear as if made of masonry), and an elaborate doorway featuring Corinthian pilasters, a broken scroll, and a paneled door topped with a pineapple, the symbol of hospitality. The inside is no less impressive, with hand-painted Chinese wallpaper and a vast fireplace in the kitchen featuring a windmill spit.

## BOAT TOURS

Portsmouth is especially attractive seen from the water. A small fleet of tour boats ties up at Portsmouth, offering scenic tours of the Piscataqua River and the historic Isle of Shoals throughout the summer and fall.

**The Isle of Shoals Steamship Co.** (☎ **800/441-4620** or 603/431-5500) sails from Barker Wharf on Market Street and is the most established of the tour companies. The firm offers a variety of tours on the 90-foot, three-deck *Thomas Laighton* (it's a modern replica of a late-19th-century steamship) and the 70-foot *Oceanic,* which was especially designed for whale watching. Among the most popular excursions are to the Isle of Shoals, allowing passengers to disembark and wander about Star Island, a dramatic, rocky island that's part of an island cluster far out in the offshore swells. Star Island has a rich history and today serves as the base for a summer religious institute. Reservations are strongly encouraged for this trip. Other popular trips include 6-hour whale-watching voyages and a sunset lighthouse cruise. Fares range from $10 to $25 for adults, $6 to $16 for children.

**Portsmouth Harbor Cruises** (☎ **800/776-0915** or 603/436-8084) specializes in tours of the historic Piscataqua River aboard the ***Heritage,*** a 49-passenger cruise ship with plenty of open deck space. Cruise by five old forts, or enjoy the picturesque tidal estuary of inland Great Bay, a scenic trip upriver from Portsmouth. Trips run daily, and reservations are suggested. Fares are $8.50 to $15 for adults, $6 to $9 for children.

## KID STUFF

**The Children's Museum of Portsmouth.** 280 Marcy St. (2 blocks south of Strawbery Banke). ☎ **603/436-3853.** www.childrens-museum.org. $4 adults and children, free for children 2 and under. Open Tues–Sat 10am–5pm; Sun 1–5pm (Also open Mon during summer and school vacations).

The Children's Museum is a bright, lively arts-and-science museum that offers a morning's worth of hands-on exhibits of interest to younger artisans and scientists. Among the more popular displays are exhibits on earthquakes and lobstering, along with the miniature submarine and space shuttle cockpit, both of which invite clambering.

## WHERE TO STAY

Portsmouth has a good selection of places to stay within walking distance of the downtown historic area. Less expensive, less stylish options include chain hotels at the edge of town near I-95. Among them are the **Anchorage Inn,** 417 Woodbury Ave. (☎ 603/431-8111); **Susse Chalet,** 650 Borthwick Ave. (☎ 603/436-6363); and the **Holiday Inn of Portsmouth** 300 Woodbury Ave (☎ 603/431-8000).

**Bow Street Inn.** 121 Bow St., Portsmouth, NH 03801. ☎ **603/431-7760.** Fax 603/433-1680. www.bowstreetinn.com. E-mail: bowstrinn@aol.com. 9 units. A/C TV TEL. High season (summer and holidays) $124–$159 double; low season $94–$140. Rates include continental breakfast. 2-night minimum stay on some holidays. AE, DISC, MC, V.

This is a perfectly adequate destination for travelers willing to give up some charm in order to gain convenience. This former downtown brewery was made over in the 1980s in a bit of inspired adaptive reuse—condos occupy the top floor, and the respected **Seacoast Repertory Theatre** (☎ **603/433-4472**) occupies the first. The second floor is the Bow Street Inn, a modern, nine-room hotel that offers great access to historic Portsmouth. The guest rooms, set off a somewhat sterile hallway, are clean, comfortable, small, and, for the most part, unexceptional in a contemporary motel sort of way. Only rooms 6 and 7 both feature good views of the harbor, and a premium is charged for these. Parking is on the street or at a nearby paid garage; a parking pass is included with harborview rooms.

**Inn at Strawbery Banke.** 314 Court St., Portsmouth, NH 03801. ☎ **603/436-7242.** 7 units. A/C. Summer and early fall $120–$125 double; off-season $90–$95 double. Rates include full breakfast. 2-night minimum stay Aug and Oct weekends. AE, DISC, MC, V. Children 10 and older are welcome.

The Inn at Strawbery Banke, located in a home built in the early 1800s on historic Court Street, is ideally located for exploring Portsmouth. Strawbery Banke is but a block away, and Market Square is just 2 blocks away. The inn has done a nice job taking a cozy antique home and making it comfortable for guests. Rooms are small but bright, and feature stenciling, wooden interior shutters, and beautiful pine floors; one has a bathroom down the hall. There are two sitting rooms with TVs, and a dining room where a full breakfast is served.

**Sise Inn.** 40 Court St., Portsmouth, NH 03801. ☎ **603/433-1200.** Fax 603/433-1200. E-mail: siseinn@cybertours.com. 34 units. A/C TV TEL. June–Oct $145–$225 double; Nov–May $110–$175 double. Rates include continental breakfast. AE, DC, MC, V.

The Sise Inn is a modern, elegant, small hotel in the guise of a country inn. This solid gray Queen Anne–style home with jade and cream trim overlooks the bustling intersection of Court and Middle streets, but inside it's a peaceful world removed from the buzz of town. The original home was built for a prominent merchant in 1881; the hotel addition was constructed in the 1980s. The effect is surprisingly harmonious, with the antique stained glass and copious oak trim meshing well with the more-contemporary elements. An elevator serves the three floors, there's modern carpeting throughout, and many of the rooms and suites feature antique armoires and an updated Victorian styling.

All rooms feature VCRs. Among the most sought-after rooms are Room 406, a suite with soaking tub and private sitting room, and Room 216 with its own sauna and lovely natural light. An elaborate continental breakfast is served in the huge old kitchen and adjoining sunroom, and there's usually something to snack on in the afternoon. This is a popular hotel for business travelers, but if you're here on a holiday, you won't feel out of place.

✪ **Three Chimneys Inn.** 17 Newmarket Rd., Durham, NH 03824. ☎ **888/399-9777** (out of state) or 603/868-7800. Fax 603/868-2964. www.threechimneysinn.com. E-mail: chimney3@threechimneysinn.com. 24 units. A/C TV TEL. Mid-May to mid-Nov $168–$189 double; off-season $149–$169. Rates include full breakfast. 2-night minimum on weekends. AE, DISC, MC, V. Children 6 and older welcome.

Located about 20 minutes northwest of Portsmouth at the edge of the pleasant university town of Durham, the Three Chimney Inn is a wonderful retreat. The main part of the inn dates back to 1649, but later additions and a full-scale renovation in recent years have given it more of a regal Georgian feel. The main house has 7 rooms, but the remaining 17 are located in a restored barn adjacent to the home. All rooms are above average in size, lushly decorated, and all have four-poster or canopied beds, custom-made mahogany armoires, radios, and Belgian carpets. Seventeen rooms have either gas or Duraflame-log fireplaces. My favorites are the William Randolph Hearst Room (#17), with photos of starlets on the walls and a massive bed that's a replica of one at San Simeon; and the Teddy Roosevelt Room (#15), which is richly appointed, much of it Roosevelt-themed. For families, Room #25 is the largest, with king and queen beds plus a pull-out. Note that five rooms are on the ground floor level beneath the barn (all have outside entrances, Jacuzzis, and gas fireplaces), and tend to be a bit more cave-like than the others. The inn is a popular spot for weddings on summer weekends.

**Dining:** Upstairs at the Maples Dining Room expect elegant fare amid an historic setting. Entrees include pan-seared rack of lamb, veal, and shrimp with pepper fettucine, and grilled Atlantic salmon ($17.95 to $23.95). Downstairs in the more informal but equally historic ffrost Sawyer Tavern, you'll find dishes like lamb stew, shrimp ,and scallops in a sherry cream sauce served over linguine, and seafood pie with lobster ($8.95 to $13.95).

## WHERE TO DINE

Portsmouth is blessed with two commendable places to satisfy a sweet tooth. **Ceres Bakery,** 51 Penhallow St. (☎ 603/436-6518), is Portsmouth's original funky bakery, set off on a quiet side street. It's a tiny space with just a handful of tables, so you might be better off getting a cookie or slice of cake to go and then walk the few blocks to the waterfront rose gardens.

**Cafe Brioche,** 14 Market Sq., (☎ 603/430-9225) is more of a high-profile hangout, situated right on Market Square. It's often crowded with folks attracted not only by the central location, but the delectable baked goods and buzz-inducing coffees.

✪ **Blue Mermaid World Grill.** The Hill (between Hanover and Deer sts. facing the municipal parking garage). ☎ 603/427-2583. Reservations recommended for parties of 6 or more. Lunch items $5.75–$11.95; main dinner courses $10.95–$19.95 (most around $15). AE, DC, DISC, MC, V. Mon–Thurs 11:30am–9pm; Fri 11:30am–10pm; Sat noon–10pm; Sun 1–9pm. GLOBAL/ECLECTIC.

The Blue Mermaid ranks among my favorites in Portsmouth for its good food, good value, and refusal to take itself too seriously. It's a short stroll from Market Square, in a historic area called The Hill, whose main feature today is a large parking lot edged by old homes converted to offices. It's not a pretentious place—Tom Waits drones on in the background, and there's outdoor dining in the summer—and the service is casual but professional. More locals than tourists congregate here. The menu is consistently adventurous in a low-key global kind of way—you might try lobster and shrimp pad thai, or a Caribbean pan-seared cod, served with a coconut cream sauce, rice, and beans. There's also seafood, burgers, pasta, and pizza from the wood grill, along with an entertaining drink menu (think: margaritas and mango martinis).

**Dolphin Striker.** 15 Bow St. ☎ 603/431-5222. Reservations recommended. Main courses, lunch $5.95–$11.95, dinner $15.95–$21.95. AE, DC, MC, V. Daily 11:30am–2pm, 5pm–9:30pm; Fri–Sat until 10:30pm. SEAFOOD/NEW ENGLAND.

The Dolphin Striker is located in an historic brick warehouse in the middle of Portsmouth's most charming area and offers a reliable if not terribly exciting selection of traditional New England seafood dishes. There's grilled swordfish with sun-dried tomato butter, lobster and scallops with cheese tortellini, and a broiled scallop casserole. Seafood loathers can find refuge in one of several grilled meat dishes, including beef tenderloin, chicken, and duck breast. The main dining room features a rustic, public house atmosphere with wide pine-board floors and wooden furniture; you can also order meals downstairs in a comfortable pub decorated with a nautical theme.

**Karen's.** 105 Daniel St. ☎ **603/431-1948.** Reservations strongly recommended for dinner. Main courses breakfast $4.95–$7.50, lunch $5.95–$7.95, dinner $12.95–$19.95. AE, DISC, MC, V. Mon–Fri 7am–11:30am, noon–2:30pm; Thurs 5–9:30pm; Sat–Sun 8am–2:30pm, 5:30–9:30pm. (Closed for dinner Sun–Wed.) ECLECTIC.

Karen's is easily overlooked, but it's worth seeking out. It's open for three meals (Thursday to Saturday only for dinner), and you'll find fresh ingredients creatively prepared. For breakfast you can indulge in homemade corned beef hash with poached eggs, or stick with the more basic fare: buttermilk pancakes or fresh fruit with granola and spiced yogurt. Lunches get more intriguing: expect offerings like a tangy red smoked-seafood chowder or blackened salmon fajita. Dinners include a fresh ravioli that changes with the seasons, and hearty meals like pork tenderloin with red cabbage, turnip, sweet potato, and carmelized pineapple. Karen's is the best bet for a visiting vegetarian, offering several dishes nightly for the non-carnivore.

**Lindbergh's Crossing.** 29 Ceres St. ☎ **603/431-0887.** Reservations recommended. Main courses $12–$24. AE, DC, MC, V. Sun–Thurs 5:30–9:30pm; Fri–Sat 5:30–10pm. (Bar opens at 4pm daily; full menu available.) BISTRO.

If you're in the mood for seafood but have a more adventurous palate, head to this restaurant. Located in an old waterfront warehouse (the ooze on the walls is century-old linseed oil), this cozy, two-story restaurant has a bistro menu that's subtly creative without calling too much attention to itself. The braised lamb shank is served over curried sweet potatoes. The salmon is enlivened with sautéed leeks, sun-dried tomato, and a peppercorn crust. There's also beef tenderloin, sautéed seafood and asparagus over couscous, and a roasted pumpkin and mushroom linguini. The preparation is the best in town, although it still comes up a bit short compared to Portland's better restaurants (about an hour north).

**Portsmouth Brewery.** 56 Market St. ☎ **603/431-1115.** Reservations accepted only for parties of 10 or more. Lunch items $5.25–$8.95; main dinner courses $10.95–$13.95. AE, DC, DISC, MC, V. Mon–Sat 11:30am–12:30am; Sun 10am–12:30am (Sun brunch served until 2pm). PUB FARE.

Located in the heart of the historic district (look for the tipping tankard suspended over the sidewalk), New Hampshire's first brew pub opened in 1991 and has since drawn a clientele loyal to the superb beers. The tin-ceilinged, brick-walled dining room is open, airy, echoey, and redolent of hops. The brews are made in 200-gallon batches and include specialties like Old Brown Ale and the delightfully creamy Black Cat Stout. The eclectic menu complements the robust beverages, with selections including burgers, veggie jambalaya, hickory-smoked steak, grilled pizza, and bratwurst. The food's just OK; the beer is excellent.

**The Press Room.** 77 Daniel St. ☎ **603/431-5186.** Reservations not accepted. Sandwiches $3.25–$6.50; main courses $7.50–$12.95. AE, DISC, MC, V. Mon 5–11pm; Sun and Tues–Thurs 4–11pm; Fri–Sat 11:30am–11pm. TAVERN FARE.

Diners flock here more for the convivial atmosphere and the easy-on-the-budget prices than for creative cuisine. Opened in 1976, the Press Room likes to boast that it was the first in the area to serve Guinness Stout, and so it's appropriate that the atmosphere has a Gaelic charm. It's the sort of place where locals like to gather to debate the issues of the day ("BMWs suck") and feel at home. As for character, it's got plenty. During winter and cool coastal days, a fire burns in the woodstove and quaffers flex their elbows at darts amid brick walls, pine floors, and heavy wooden beams overhead. Choose your meal from a basic bar menu, with inexpensive selections, including a variety of burgers, nachos, fish-and-chips, stir fries, and salads.

## SHOPPING

Portsmouth's compact historic district is home to dozens of boutiques offering unique items and antiques. A fine contemporary gallery featuring the work of area crafts-people, the elegant **N. W. Barrett Gallery,** 53 Market St. (☎ **603/431-4262**), offers up a classy selection of creative, exuberant crafts, including ceramic sculptures, glass-ware, lustrous woodworking, and a wide array of handmade jewelry.

Antiques stores are scattered around town. Among my favorites is **Victory Antiques,** 96 State St., (☎ **603/431-3046**), which has a limited yet eclectic selection, often including interesting furniture. About 20 dealers maintain cases here offering a good selection of china and glass.

The **Robert Lincoln Levy Gallery** operated by the New Hampshire Art Association, 136 State St., (☎ **603/431-4230**), has frequently changing exhibits and shows; it's a good destination to view fine art produced by New Hampshire artists.

**City & Country,** 50 Daniel St. (☎ **603/433-5353**), is a contemporary housewares store—a sort of Pottery Barn Lite—with a small but intriguing selection of glasses, table settings, flatware, and cooking implements, along with a mix of furniture and wrought-iron accessories.

**Paradiza,** 63 Penhallow St. (☎ **603/431-0180**), offers up an array of very clever greeting cards (diehards travel here from Boston to stock up), along with exotica like soaps and bath products from Israel and Africa.

Somewhat further down the knicknack foodchain, **Macro Polo,** 89 Market St. (☎ **603/436-8338**) specializes in retro chic gifts, toys, and gadgets. This pleasantly cluttered shop stocks pink flamingos, refrigerator magnets, movie kitsch, candies, coffee mugs, and T-shirts, most of which are embellished with off-beat humor.

## PORTSMOUTH AFTER DARK
### Performing Arts
**The Music Hall.** 28 Chestnut St. ☎ **603/436-2400.** Tickets $12–$51 (average price about $25).

This historic theater dates back to 1878 and was thankfully brought back to its former glory by a local non-profit arts group. A variety of shows are staged here, from magic festivals to comedy revues to concerts by the visiting symphonies and pop artists. Call for the current line-up.

### Bars & Clubs
**Dolphin Striker.** 15 Bow St. ☎ **603/431-5222.**

Live jazz, classical guitar, and low-key folk rock is offered most Tuesday through Sunday evenings.

**Muddy River Smokehouse.** 21 Congress St. ☎ **603/430-9582.**

Blues are the thing at Muddy River's downstairs lounge on the weekends, which is open evenings Wednesday through Saturday. Weekends offers blues with well-known performers from Boston, Maine, and beyond; the rest of the week, it's usually comedy or alternative rock.

**The Press Room.** 77 Daniel St. ☎ **603/431-5186.** No cover Mon–Thurs; around $5 Fri–Sun.

A popular local bar and restaurant (see "Where to Dine," above), the Press Room offers casual entertainment virtually every night, either upstairs or down. Tuesday nights are the popular Hoot nights, with an open mike hosted by local musicians. Fri-day nights are set aside for contemporary folk, starring name performers from around the region; but the Press Room might be best known for its live jazz on Sunday, when the club brings in quality performers from Boston and beyond.

# 3 Manchester & Concord

Manchester is 51 miles west of Portsmouth, 53 miles northwest of Boston, and 19 miles south of Concord

These two Merrimack Valley cities tend to be overlooked by tourists making tracks for the lakes district or the White Mountains to the north. Quite frankly, neither town deserves billing as a top-of-the-ticket tourist destination, but to their credit, both have made considerable strides to exert their magnetism on cars speeding by on the interstate. Manchester is making the most of its industrial heritage with conversions of its grandly monolithic riverside mills; and, in the last decade, Concord has opened a modern and engaging history museum and a fine new planetarium.

The two cities are vastly different. Manchester is a small city, Concord a big town. The humming industry of Manchester once centered on the profusion of mills along the river—and it's an impressive sight to see these brick mastodons, since converted to more contemporary use, grazing at the river's edge. Smaller Concord is lorded over by the prominent dome of the State House and has a more proper and genteel demeanor.

## MANCHESTER

The history of Manchester is the history of its mills. Stoic brick buildings today line both shores of the Merrimack River, reflecting a time when New England was one of the vast and rumbling centers of manufacturing for the nation. French-Canadian workers pored into the city from Quebec to work the mills, and many of their descendants still live and work in the city, giving Manchester a multicultural flavor. The industrial era has passed, but visitors to Manchester can still be impressed by the old mills, some of which have been converted to restaurants and offices, others of which serve as university classrooms, and one of which has leapt eras by housing a technology center, complete with heliport on the roof. Some even remain active as working mills.

With 100,000 residents, Manchester is northern New England's largest city, and it has a grittier, more urban feel than anywhere else in the three states. It's a good place for gathering supplies, visiting the fine art museum, and—most of all—for getting a glimpse of the region's proud industrial heritage.

### ESSENTIALS

**GETTING THERE**   Manchester is accessible from both I-93 and I-293. From the south, the easiest access is to get off at Exit 2 on I-293, then follow Elm Street into the town center.

The **Manchester Airport, ☎ 603/624-6539,** has grown dramatically in the past few years since budget air carrier **Southwest Airlines, ☎ 800/435-9792,** started flights here. It's quickly become one of the preferred gateways to northern New England. Other airlines serving Manchester include Delta (☎ **800/221-1212**), Comair (☎ **800/354-9822**), Continental (☎ **800/525-0280**), Northwest (☎ **800/ 225-2525**), United (☎ **800/241-6522**), and US Airways (☎ **800/428-4322**).

Bus service is provided by **Vermont Transit** (☎ **802/864-6811**) and **Concord Trailways** (☎ **800/639-3317** or 603/228-3300), both of which make stops at the Manchester Transportation Center, 119 Canal St., at the intersection of Granite Street (☎ **603/668-6133**).

**VISITOR INFORMATION**   The **Manchester Chamber of Commerce,** 889 Elm St., Manchester, NH 03101 (☎ **603/666-6600**), provides brochures, maps, and a handy city guide from its third-floor office.

## EXPLORING MANCHESTER

The best way to view the **mill district** is to head off into these canyons of brick. Don't sweat it; you'll eventually find your way out. Note also that you won't miss much if you're touring by car: these buildings are so massive you don't lose much detail driving by slowly.

A new orientation center is slated for 2000 or 2001. It is run by the Manchester Historic Association in the mill district, located in a brick behemoth (Mill #3) at the corner of Commercial and Pleasant streets. The new center will feature exhibits and displays about life and work in the mills. At press time it wasn't clear when the center would be completed, and hours and ticket prices were as yet undetermined., but the ambitious plans make it worth stopping by to see if it's open.

The two main thoroughfares through the mill area are Commercial and Canal streets, which parallel the river. To explore by foot, you can leave your car at the small waterfront park beneath the bridge at Bridge Street. For more adventurous exploring, walk around the hillside above the mill area, where you'll see a range of housing where millworkers lived in tenements and managers occupied more stately homes, all within walking distance of the mills that served as the hub of their lives.

**Amoskeag Fishways.** Fletcher St. ☎ **603/626-3474.** Free admission. Year-round Mon–Sat 9:30am–5pm; fish migration season May–June. Cross from downtown Manchester on the Amoskeag Bridge; turn left immediately after.

If you're here during the brief, 6-week fish run in early summer, be sure to stop by this small but intriguing center with its underwater window that allows visitors to view herring, shad, and other species of fish as they make their way up the Merrimack. (A modern exhibit hall is open year-round, but a visit is most compelling when the fish are running.) The center is designed mostly for young children with some simple interactive exhibits, but older kids and adults will also find it intriguing. Some 54 concrete pools, each slightly higher than the next, skirt the hydroelectric dam, allowing the fish to leap from one to the other. You'll learn why Amoskeag (the Native American name for the falls and later for the mills) means "Great Fishing Place." On your way out, be sure to stop by the 1924 hydroelectric plant just above the center, which has three massive turbines in action, and is imbued with a sort of classic, art-deco/industrial-age heroism. Kids love it.

**Currier Gallery of Art.** 201 Myrtle Way. ☎ **603/669-6144.** $5 adults, $4 students and seniors, free for children under 18. Free Sat 10am–1pm. Sun–Mon and Wed–Thurs 11am–5pm, Fri 11am–8pm, Sat 10am–5pm. From I-93 take Exit 8, bear right onto Bridge St.; continue 1$^1$/2 miles then turn right on Ash St.; Myrtle Way is the third st. on the left.

The Currier is one of northern New England's premier art museums—made all the more magical by its location in a weary industrial city. Housed in an elegant, very classical 1932 beaux-arts building in a residential neighborhood a few blocks from downtown's main drag, the Currier benefited from a major renovation when it reopened several years ago after a year's closure. The permanent collections include some 12,000 works of European and American art, with surprisingly fine pieces by Degas, Picasso, Monet, and John Singer Sargeant. Look for an especially haunting painting by Edward Hopper entitled *The Bootleggers*. In addition to the extensive painting and sculpture on display, the museum has fine exhibits of silver, glass, furniture, and pewter.

**Manchester Historic Assocation.** 129 Amherst St. ☎ **603/622-7531.** www.mv.com/org/mha. Free admission. Tues–Fri 9am–4pm, Sat 10am–4pm.

A quick and lively overview of Manchester's history can be had at this handsome 1931 neoclassical building overlooking Victory Park. The building contains three galleries, two of which feature changing exhibitions. Downstairs is the Manchester Stories gallery, where you can learn about Manchester natives from Revolutionary War hero Gen. John Stark to *Peyton Place* author Grace Metalious.

**Robert Frost Farm.** Rte. 28, Derry. ☎ **603/432-3091.** $2.50 adults, children under 18 free. Spring and fall Sat–Sun 10am–6pm; summer Thurs–Mon 10am–6pm. Closed late Oct–Memorial Day.

One of several New England spots to claim Robert Frost's affections, this graceful white-clapboard farmhouse in Derry, about 8 miles southeast of Manchester, was Frost's home between 1901 and 1909. Learn about the poet and his era while touring the house, and about the abundant wildlife on the property while exploring a network of trails through forest and field. The house and property are owned and managed by the New Hampshire Dept. of Parks and Recreation.

✪ **Zimmerman House.** c/o Currier Gallery of Art, 201 Myrtle Way. ☎ **603/626-4158.** Standard tours $7 adults, $5 seniors and students; longer tours $12 and $9. Price includes admission to Currier Gallery. Tours Fri and Mon 2pm, Sat 1pm, Sun 1 and 2:30pm. Reservations required; children must be 7 or older. Tours depart from the Currier Gallery.

From the 1930s through the 1950s, iconoclastic architect Frank Lloyd Wright designed a number of "Usonian" homes—small-scaled, useful, elegant, and inexpensive to build. The Zimmerman House, built in a Manchester residential neighborhood in 1950, was one such home, although the owners didn't cut corners on costs here. (In truth, few Usonian owners did and most houses came in well over budget.) The furniture and even the gardens were designed by Wright, and the home features luxe touches like Georgia cypress trim and red-glazed brick.

Only five Wright homes were built in the Northeast, and the Zimmerman home is the sole Wright home open to the public. Visitors are shuttled to the house from the Currier Gallery via van. (As a bonus, you'll pass two other privately owned Wright homes in a nearby suburb.) Choose from two tour lengths, 1 hour and 15 minutes, or 2 hours and 15 minutes. Note that advance reservations are required; make them well in advance if you have your heart set on touring the home.

## WHERE TO STAY

Manchester offers few interesting accommdation options for travelers. The most centrally located downtown hotel is the business-friendly **Holiday Inn,** 700 Elm St., ☎ **603/625-1000.**

## WHERE TO DINE

**Café Pavone.** 75 Arms Park Dr. ☎ **603/622-5488.** Reservations recommended. Lunch items $4.50–$8.95; main dinner courses $8.95–$19.95. AE, DC, DISC, MC, V. Mon–Thurs 11:30am–9:30pm, Fri 11:30am–10pm, Sat 4–10pm, Sun 4–9pm. CONTEMPORARY/ITALIAN.

Since 1989, Cafe Pavone has been run by the husband and wife team of Claudia Rippee and Edward Aloise. This lively upbeat trattoria is housed in a small brick building amid a complex of huge old mills. It's a place of simple wood tables, a checkerboard ceramic tile floor, and massive granite slabs along the rear wall; there's outdoor dining in the arbor-enclosed terrace in summer. The menu is built around

### A Gay Bar

**The Frontrunner** at 22 Fir St. (☎ **603/623-6477**) is open to members only, but that just means that you need to sign in when you get there. Cover charges apply on some evenings. Visit their Web site at www.frontrunner.org.

homemade pastas and the wood-fired grill. Look for well-prepared dishes like scallop puttanesca (black pepper fettucine with kalamata olives, capers, and anchovies), duck ragout with wild mushrooms served over fusilli, and wood-grilled filet mignon with wild mushroom demiglace. On Friday evenings, there's live jazz.

**Chez Vachon.** 136 Kelley St. ☎ **603/625-9660.** Main courses, breakfast $1.60–$4.70, dinner $4.50–$7.50, sandwiches $1.95–$4.95. DISC, MC, V. Mon–Thurs 6am–2pm, Wed–Sat 6am–8pm, Sun 7am–8pm. Directions: Head west on Bridge St. across river (turns to Armory St.,) bear right at second light, take left at top of hill on to Kelley St. DINER.

Manchester's French-Canadian heritage lives on at this popular neighborhood diner, located a short drive across the river from downtown Manchester. It's a non-descript place with a plastic Coca-Cola sign out front in an area of triple-decker homes in the traditionally Francophone part of town. The menu is basic diner fare, although if you look a bit harder you'll find traditional favorites like *poutine*—a heart-stopping mass of french fries, melted cheese, and gravy. It's a good destination for aficionados of neighborhood joints (my last waitress had been tending tables here for 16 years), and for hungry travelers on a budget—the all-you-can-eat dinner is just $7.50.

# CONCORD

New Hampshire's capital is a graceful, compact city of 36,000 anchored by the distinguished gold dome of the State House. Visitors can wander a few blocks' radius from the dome and see a wide range of architectural styles; from the commercial brick architecture with elaborate cornices, to grand Richardsonian state office buildings, to buildings that draw heavily on classical tradition. This is one state capital where everything is on a smaller scale, more comforting than overwhelming.

The one regret is that the city has turned its back on its Merrimack River, which flows picturesquely through the valley. Downtown is more or less blocked off from the riverside by I-93, parking lots, and uninspired commercial plazas. Adventurers must strike north or south to get access to the shores. One good spot for a riverside stroll is the 17-acre preserve and conservation center that's also headquarters of the **Society for the Protection of New Hampshire Forests** (☎ **603/224-9945**). The grounds are open daily from dawn to dusk at 54 Portsmouth St. in East Concord just across the river.

## ESSENTIALS

**GETTING THERE**    Concord is located near the junction of I-93 and I-89, and on the east-west State Route 9. The city is also served by **Concord Trailways** (☎ **800/639-3317** or 603/228-3300) and **Vermont Transit** (☎ **802/864-6811**). The Concord Bus Terminal is located on Depot Street (☎ **603/228-3300**).

**VISITOR INFORMATION**    In mid- to late 2000, the **Chamber of Commerce of Greater Concord** will open a new visitor center at the new Concord conference center, 40 Commercial St. For an update on the new hours and location, contact the chamber at ☎ **603/224-2508** during regular business hours Monday to Friday, or visit the Web at **www.concordnhchamber.com**.

## EXPLORING CONCORD

**Christa McAuliffe Planetarium.** 3 Institute Dr. ☎ **603/271-7831.** $7 adults, $4 seniors and children 3–17. Exhibit area open 10am–5pm Tues–Sun; planetarium schedule changes with the seasons, but shows typically slated afternoons Tuesday through Sunday; call for current schedule and reservations. Located at New Hampshire Technical Institute; take Exit 15E on I-93 and follow signs.

Housed beneath a glass pyramid on the technical institute campus a 5-minute drive from downtown Concord, the McAuliffe Planetarium is the state's memorial to

Christa McAuliffe, the Concord schoolteacher who died in the 1986 Challenger explosion. The 92-seat theater presents four different hour-long astronomy shows throughout the week, showcasing its high-tech Digistar computerized projection system. Shows are tailored to different interests and age levels (some feature Sesame Street characters); be sure to ask before you enter. Visitors can peruse a handful of intriguing exhibits in the waiting area before the show, or buy astronomy-related trinkets at the gift shop.

**Museum of New Hampshire History.** Eagle Sq. (across from the State House, $^1/_2$ block off Main St.). ☎ **603/226-3189.** Admission $5 adults, $4 seniors, $2.50 children 6–18. Free Thurs and Fri evenings. Mon–Wed and Sat 9:30am–5pm, Thurs and Fri 9:30am–8:30pm, Sun noon–5pm. Closed Mon mid-Oct–Nov and Jan–June. Free parking in museum lot off Storrs St.

The New Hampshire Historical Society opened this handsome, modern and lively museum after years of displaying its collection in its more staid and formal head-quarters up the block. The museum is housed in a sturdy, stone-faced warehouse built in 1870; the exhibits focus primarily on New Hampshire's 19th-century heritage, and include several interactive displays to keep kids amused. Permanent displays, including a handsome Concord Coach stagecoach, occupy the first floor; upstairs you'll find exhibits that change throughout the year. Children especially enjoy the "fire tower," which pokes through the roof and allows glimpses of the Merrimack River and the state-house dome.

Plan also to stop by the original museum site at the historical society's headquarters at 30 Park St. A handful of paintings and furniture is still on display, but it's most impressive for the classical architecture wrought from New Hampshire granite. The rotunda inside is impressive; be sure also to note the portal sculpture above the front door by Daniel Chester French, who's best known for his sculpture of Lincoln in Washington's Lincoln Memorial.

**State House.** 107 N. Main St. ☎ **603/271-2154.** Free admission. Self-guided tours Mon–Fri 8am–4:30pm. Guided tours by reservation.

New Hampshire's state legislature consists of 412 representatives and senators, making it the third-largest legislative body in the English-speaking world (only the U.S. Congress and the British Parliament are bigger). Despite its formidable size, the legislature still occupies the original chambers, built starting in 1816. Indeed, New Hampshire boasts the oldest state capitol in which the legislature still meets in its original chambers. New Hampshire's numerous citizen legislators are paid just $100 per year—an amount that hasn't changed since 1889.

Both chambers were restored in the mid-1970s, and visitors can catch a glimpse of both hallowed halls during a self-guided tour of the building. Stop by the visitors center in Room 119 and pick up a map and brochure, then wander the halls lined with portraits of dour legislators. Especially impressive are the portrait of Benning Wentworth, New Hampshire's first governor, and the statue of revered native son Daniel Webster, who stands guard on the lawn in front.

## WHERE TO STAY

In addition to the inn mentioned below, Concord has several basic chain hotels that cater primarily to businesspeople in the capital. Well-located within easy walking distance of downtown attractions is the **Holiday Inn,** 172 North Main St. (☎ **603/ 224-9593**), with an indoor pool and locally popular restaurant. Among the newest additions to Concord accommodations is the **Fairfield Inn Concord,** 4 Gulf St. (☎ **603/224-4011**), which has an indoor pool and guest laundry.

# A Road Trip to Canterbury Shaker Village

A 20-minute drive north of Concord in Canterbury (take I-93 to Exit 18 and follow the signs) is one of the best-preserved ✪ Shaker communities of the 18 that once dotted the inland east from Kentucky to Maine. This village was founded in 1792; at its heyday in the late 19th century, some 300 Shakers communally owned 4,000 acres and more than 100 buildings, supporting themselves by selling herbs, making furniture, and growing most of the food they needed.

Today, this graceful outdoor museum features about two dozen buildings on 694 acres. Tours are offered on the hour and last about 90 minutes. You'll see the active herb gardens, the apiary, an impressive laundry facility, and an intriguing schoolhouse. Along the way, you'll learn a lot about this fascinating group of people who not only believed in equality of the sexes, but practiced it as well. They also practiced celibacy and pacifism, although they may be best remembered for the beguiling grace with which they crafted their signature furniture and storage boxes, and the distinguished style in which they built and maintained their buildings. After the tour, wander the trails that lace the property and enjoy the simple pleasures of the country air, or browse the extensive gift shop for Shaker reproduction furniture, books, and New Hampshire handicrafts.

Call ☎ 603/783-9511 or visit the Web at www.shakers.org for additional information. Admission is $10 adults, $4 children 6–15, $25 for a family. It's open daily May through October from 10am to 5pm; in April, November, and December open weekends 10am to 4pm.

A special treat is the candlelight dinner served Friday and Saturday nights at the Creamery. There's a single seating at 6:45pm, with all guests gathered at long tables. The four-course meal is prepared from Shaker recipes; afterwards (in season) you'll be guided on a candlelight tour of the village. The price is $34.50 per person, which includes tax and tip, as well as the village tour. Reservations are essential. The Creamery is also open for lunch and Sunday brunch.

Plans also call for a new Marriot Courtyard Hotel to open adjoining Concord's new conference center, slated to open mid- to late 2000. Contact the **Chamber of Commerce of Greater Concord,** (☎ 603/224-2508), for more information.

**Centennial Inn.** 96 Pleasant St., Concord, NH 03301. ☎ **603/227-9000.** Fax 603/225-5301. 32 units. A/C TV TEL. $125–$164 double, suites $165–$210 double. Rates include continental breakfast. 2-night minimum some weekends. AE, DC, DISC, MC, V.

This 1892 brick mansion with twin turrets sits a little over a ¹/₂ mile from downtown and is popular with Men Having Meetings. It's been thoroughly modernized—most guests enter through the large glass doors facing the parking lot in back, not the pedimented main entrance facing the street. Inside it has a dusky, strong, and masculine feel appropriate to a house of its era, and the owners have furnished it with Mission-influenced accents. Room sizes vary as they will in a rambling old house; suites include sitting areas or reading nooks in the turrets. Ask about rooms that open to private decks.

**Dining:** The stately and very oaky first-floor dining room features a regional menu with a few international dishes (dinner entrees $15 to $24). Appetizers include wild-rice-pecan spring roll, New England clam chowder, and crab cakes; entrees are along the likes of rack of lamb, duck breast, and grilled sirloin.

### WHERE TO DINE

Concord has a wonderful, old-fashioned candy shop in **Granite State Candies,** 13 Warren St., south of the State House (☎ **603/225-2591**). Hand-dipped milk and dark chocolates are the specialty in this palace of high-calorie delights, but you'll also find a wide selection of plain and fancy truffles, hard candies, marzipan, and just about anything else to tame a belligerent sweet tooth.

**The Moxy Grill.** 6 Pleasant St. Extension. ☎ **603/229-0072.** Reservations recommended weekends. Main courses lunch $5.95–$8, dinner $7.95–$12.95. MC, V. Sun–Fri 11:30am–2:30pm, daily 5–9pm (until 10pm Fri–Sat).

Tucked off Main Street in a street-level basement is this appealing small restaurant that's creatively decorated with local art (for sale) and centered around a low, customer-friendly bar (beer and wine only). It's a simple and austere setting for a creative and fun menu—far more fun than you might expect for Concord, which has a notably drowsy culinary scene. Moxy Grill has developed a following for its creative salads (nicoise salad with peppered tuna steak, Caribbean chicken salad with diced fruit), but both lunch and dinner menus are wide-ranging and inviting, with entrees spanning the globe from a sushi plate to herbed chicken breast with stuffing and homemade gravy. Lunches include sandwiches like Cajun spiced blackened meatloaf, and a Southwestern tofu wrap with a black bean cake. Desserts are homemade and include truffle brownie sundae, Key lime pie, and a traditional New England apple crisp.

## 4 The Monadnock Region & the Connecticut River Valley

Peterborough is 71 miles northwest of Boston and 38 miles southwest of Manchester, NH.

New Hampshire's southwestern corner is a pastoral region of rolling hills, small villages, rustic farmsteads, and winding backroads. What the area lacks in major attractions, it makes up for in peaceableness and bucolic charm. The inns tend to be more basic and less elegant than those you'll find across the river in southern Vermont, but lodging prices will also appeal more to budget travelers looking to get a taste of history with their room and board. This is a popular area for Bostonians seeking a weekend respite from city life.

For most visitors, chief activities include woodland walks, porch sitting, and idle drives to nowhere in particular. In fact, the best strategy for exploring the area may be to put away the map and turn randomly on a side road to see where you'll end up. Wherever it is, the odds are you'll find a gentle Currier & Ives quality.

### PETERBOROUGH & ENVIRONS

Peterborough (pop. 5,000) was first settled in 1749, but it's no quaint colonial town gathered primly around a village green. It has more the feel of a once-prosperous commercial center, where the hum of industry provided harmony for a thriving economy. While the hum is a bit quieter these days, Peterborough is still a beautiful town with diverse architecture, and is set picturesquely in a valley at the confluence of the Contoocook and Nubanusit rivers. Improbably enough, Peterborough has carved out a niche in the high-tech world as a publishing center for national computer magazines.

In the literary universe, Peterborough remains famous for inspiring Thornton Wilder to write *Our Town.* It's also home to the noted McDowell Colony, founded in 1907 to provide a retreat for artists, musicians, and writers to tap their creative talents without the distractions of cooking or attending to errands. It's hard to find a writer of note who didn't spend some time at McDowell. (The colony isn't open to the public.)

## ESSENTIALS

**GETTING THERE**    Peterborough is between Keene and Nashua on Route 101. A decent map is essential for exploring the outlying villages and towns on winding state and county roads. Unless, of course, you choose to get lost.

**VISITOR INFORMATION**    The **Greater Peterborough Chamber of Commerce,** P.O. Box 401, Peterborough, NH 03458 (☎ **603/924-7234**), provides helpful advice either over the phone or at their year-round information center located at the intersection of routes 101 and 202.

## EXPLORING THE REGION

The archipelago of three dozen or so villages that surrounds Peterborough and Keene has a strongly traditional New England demeanor; you half expect to hear town criers wandering through loudly offering the day's news. *Yankee* magazine and the *Old Farmer's Almanac,* which have done perhaps more than any other publications to shape the popular image of New England, are based in the unassuming town of Dublin to the west of Peterborough.

Exploring the hidden villages by car (or, for the more ambitious, by bike), could easily eat up a day or two. **Peterborough** itself offers great browsing, with art galleries, bookstores, antique shops, and boutiques, with most of the wares outside the orbit of the usual mass-market trinketry. Notable is the Sharon Arts Center, Depot Square (☎ **603/924-27987**), with a great selection of eclectic local crafts (pottery, glasswork, paintings, and ironwork) in a capacious and attractive gallery.

A sampling of the other villages: **Fitzwilliam** is about 16 miles southwest of Peterborough at the intersection of Route 12 and Route 119, and is presided over by the proudly columned Fitzwilliam Inn (see "Where to Stay," below), and is home to several antique stores. There's a triangular green with a Civil War obelisk ("soldiers who died for their country in the rebellion of 1861"), a cast-iron Victorian fountain; facing the green are some wonderful Greek Revival homes, and an impressively columned 1817 church, which has been the town hall since 1858.

**Hancock** is picture-postcard-perfect New England, with a quiet street of early homes. It was first settled in 1764, and renamed after the first signer of the Declaration of Independence in 1779. A former center for cotton farming, Hancock is home to one of the oldest operating inns in the region (see "Where to Stay," below).

**Francestown,** incorporated in 1752, is rife with remarkable Federal homes, and has a general store, an inviting library, and an 1801 meeting house. Up until 1891, when the quarry closed, Francestown was famous for producing some of the finest soapstone in the world. **Jaffrey Center** (west of Jaffrey itself) is an aristocratic roadside village all but hidden in the abundant maples, and filled with notable early homes and small, tidy barns. **Troy** is the antidote for the tidy priminess of many of the area villages; tucked in a river valley, where you can get a sense of the heady days of the industrial revolution; local industry still hums in a remaining mill building along the river.

Between Rindge and Jaffrey on Cathedral Road (look for signs along Route 124) is the unique **Cathedral of the Pines,** (☎ **603/899-3300**). This outdoor "cathedral" is located on an open knoll amid a stately grove of swaying pines with views toward Mt. Monadnock. It's a quietly spectacular spot, with rustic wooden benches and fieldstone altars and pulpits. The cathedral was built by the parents of Lt. Sanderson Sloane, a bomber crewman who died in World War II. Multidenominational services are held Saturdays and Sundays in summer. It's open daily 9am to 5pm May through October; donations are encouraged.

## OUTDOOR PURSUITS

Mt. Monadnock stands impressively amid the gentler hills of southern New Hampshire. Although it's only 3,165 feet high (about half the height of Mt. Washington far to the north), its solitary grandeur has attracted hikers for more than 2 centuries. The knobby peak has been ascended by New England luminaries including Ralph Waldo Emerson and Henry David Thoreau. Today, more than 100,000 hikers strike for the summit each year to enjoy the views and follow in the footsteps of countless other pilgrims.

Some 40 miles of trails lace the patchwork of public and private lands on the slopes of the mountain. The most popular (and best marked) trails leave from near the **Mt. Monadnock State Park** (☎ **603/532-8862**) entrance about 4 miles northwest of Jaffrey Center. (Head west on Route 124; after 2 miles, follow the park signs to the north.) A round-trip on the most direct routes will take someone in decent shape about 3 to 4 hours. Admission to the park is $2.50 for adults and children 12 and older; 11 and under is free. No pets are allowed in the park.

An 18-mile drive north of Monadnock, not far from the towns of Hancock and Peterborough, is one of my favorite small parks in the region: **Greenfield State Park** (☎ **603/547-3497**). This 400-acre park is a gem for car campers and geology buffs. The park was profoundly shaped by glaciers during the last Ice Age, and eskers, bogs, kames, and other intriguing geological formations may be spotted by knowing eyes (or ask a ranger). For more sedentary pleasures, the park boasts a small beach along scenic Otter Lake. There's also a 900-foot beach set aside for campers who avail themselves of the 252 wooded, well-spaced campsites. On weekends, the campground bustles with activity, but midweek it's a peaceable oasis.

The entire region offers fine terrain for leisurely bike rides, although many of the hills will require some huffing and puffing. Rentals are avaialble in Peterborough at **The Eclectic Bike,** 76 Grove St., (☎ **603/924-9797**). Rates are $15 per day for a road/mountain bike hybrid.

## WHERE TO STAY

**Benjamin Prescott Inn.** 433 Turnpike Rd. (Rte. 124), Jaffrey, NH 03452. ☎ **603/532-6637.** 10 units (including 3 suites). $75–$100 double; suites $95–$150. Rates include full breakfast. 2-night minimum some holidays and peak-season weekends. AE, MC, V. Children age 10 and older are welcome.

Col. Benjamin Prescott fought at the Battle of Bunker Hill, then came to Jaffrey in 1775. This three-story home built by his sons dates to 1853 and is a handsome yellow Greek Revival farmhouse along the (often busy) road in a pastoral area 2 miles east of town. Throughout this pleasant inn, you'll find a strong sense of history and a close connection to the past.

The interior appropriately matches the exterior, decorated in classical country-farmhouse style with stenciling on the walls and traditional pine farmhouse furniture. It's not overly austere—the innkeepers display folk art, ceramics, and other collectibles. The guest rooms are named after Prescott family members and are comfortably furnished; all have ceiling fans and phone jacks (phones provided on request), and two suites have air-conditioning. My choice for the best room in the house? The Col. Prescott, which is bright and airy and features two comfortable armchairs and a writing desk. Guests can wander the farmlands beyond the inn, or set off to hike Mt. Monadnock, a short drive down the road.

✪ **Birchwood Inn.** Rte. 45 (1¹/₂ miles south of Rte. 101), Temple, NH 03084. ☎ **603/878-3285.** E-mail: wolfe@birchwood.mv.com. 7 units, 1 with hall bathroom. TV. Foliage season $79 double; other times $60–$70 double. Rates include full breakfast. 2-night minimum stay during foliage season. No credit cards. Children over 10 are welcome.

This is a quiet village retreat, offering good rooms at a good price. Thoreau visited this inn on his travels, and neither the town nor the inn feel as if they've changed all that much since. This handsome brick farmhouse with white-clapboard ell is in the middle of the country crossroads town of Temple, near the Grange and a park with three war memorials (including one to the heroes of 1776). It's also an easy stroll to a historic cemetery with headstones dating back to the 18th century. The inn is decorated throughout in a pleasantly informal country style. The seven rooms are each decorated in different themes (musical instruments, train memorabilia, historic newspapers, and country store), which borders on kitschy but doesn't quite step over the line. Rooms have small, non-cable TVs. My favorite is the Seashore Room, which is spacious, bright, and summery.

**Dining:** The common rooms are imbued with a rich sense of history. The dining room, where traditional New England meals ($17.95–$19.95 complete) are served, has wide pine floors and historic wall murals painted by the early 19th-century itinerant painter Rufus Porter. The blackboard menu changes nightly; there's usually duck on Saturday night. The BYOB tavern is also comfortable. Judy and Bill Wolfe, who've been running this inn with considerable graciousness since 1980, make guests feel comfortable and at home.

**Fitzwilliam Inn.** Rte. 119, Fitzwilliam, NH 03447. ☎ **603/585-9000.** Fax 603/585-3495. E-mail: fitz9000@aol.com. 25 units (plus 3 in annex), about half have private bathrooms; the remainder share hall bathrooms. TEL. $50–$70 double with private bathroom; $50 double for shared bathroom. DISC, MC, V. Located at the intersection of Rte. 12 and Rte. 119. The village center is just east of Rte. 12.

This handsome, three-story Greek Revival building towers over this quiet crossroads and its triangular green. An inn since 1796, the Fitzwilliam Inn has a lot of history and a locally popular dining room, but elegance isn't its strong suit. Nor is upkeep. Some of the rooms have an old boarding-house feel to them, with beds crammed in every which way, and about half sharing hallway bathrooms, but if you have a mind to associate "worn" with "charming," you'll do fine here, finding a piece of New England heritage at a reasonable price. Rooms 3 and 4 are the best in the house; both are corner rooms (#3 is brighter) with simple maple furnishings and small bathrooms. Avoid the tiny rooms in the back hallway over the dining room. The yellow-clapboard annex across the street has three rooms; S-3 is the largest and cheeriest. Downstairs the sitting rooms have an eclectic mix of Victorian-era and contemporary country furniture, set on time-burnished pine floors.

**Dining:** A quaint country dining room with baskets hung on heavy beams is in the back of the inn. The dining room serves three meals a day, mostly New England classics like lobster Newburg, stuffed chicken breast, or broiled steak. Complete dinners range from $12.95 to $21.95.

**Hancock Inn.** 33 Main St., Hancock, NH 03443. ☎ **800/525-1789** or 603/525-3318. Fax 603/525-9301. www.hancockinn.com. E-mail: innkeeper@hancockinn.mv.com. 15 units. A/C TV TEL. $130–$210 double, including full breakfast. AE, DC, DISC, MC, V. Children 12 and older welcome.

The austere and simple Hancock Inn was built in 1789, and today sits along the Main Street of a small town that doesn't appear to have changed all that much since then. You'll find classic Americana inside, from the creaky floors and braided oval rugs, to the guest rooms appointed in understated Colonial decor. One room—The Rufus Porter Room—features an evocative wall mural from the inn's early days. Three rooms have gas fireplaces; three have soaking tubs. The inn has four suites, including the new Ballroom and Bell Tower Room, the former with a domed ceiling, the latter with a cannonball king bed and gas fireplace; both have soaking tubs. This inn has the historic charm of the other inns mentioned above, but with a more upscale sensibility.

**Dining:** The colonial American theme of the inn extends to the dining room, which features early classics (the house specialty is the Shaker cranberry pot roast) as well as more updated fare, like rib eye served on a ragout of bacon, mushrooms, sweet potato, and pecans. Entrees are $16 to $26.

**The Inn at Jaffrey Center.** 379 Main St., Jaffrey Center, NH 03452. ☎ **603/532-7800.** Fax 603/532-7000. 14 units, 6 share 2 bathrooms. $65–$85 double, including continental breakfast. DISC, MC, V. Pets allowed with advance permission.

This historic gambrel-roofed inn was built in 1830 in the middle of one of New Hampshire's most gracious villages. It's had a dodgy reputation under recent ownership and under a different name (and thus lapsed from this guide), but in 1999, it was reacquired by Sally Roberts, the former innkeeper who was largely responsible for its earlier good reputation. The rooms are nothing fancy and many have small bathrooms, but it's clean, basic, and affordably priced. Room 110 is bright and has a large four-poster surrounded by windows; Room 206 is a two-bedroom suite that looks into a maple tree and has a clawfoot tub. Frommer's wasn't able to give this a full review since renovations and improvements were underway when we visited, but it promises to be much improved.

**Dining:** The inn's Colonial-style dining room is historic without being too formal, with spindle chairs and a pleasant dining porch. The menu features "Yankee comfort food," with dishes like lamb shanks, pot roast, sautéed scallops, and bean and sausage soup. It's open weekdays for lunch and daily for dinners. Dinner entrees run $12 to $21.

## WHERE TO DINE

**Acqua Bistro.** 9 School St., Peterborough. ☎ **603/924-9905.** Reservations accepted for 5 or more. Entrees $11.95–$17.95. MC, V. Tues–Sun 4–11pm. NEW AMERICAN/BISTRO.

Hidden away off Peterborough's main thoroughfares (near Twelve Pine and the Sharon Arts Center), Acqua is a modern and agreeable restuaurant offering a contemporary twist on regional fare. This is Peterborough's best choice for a well-crafted meal. Entrees include linguine with lobster and wilted spinach, steak au poive with portobellos, and rainbow trout prepared in a skillet with bacon, scallions, and tomato.

**Peterborough Diner.** 10 Depot St., Peterborough. ☎ **603/924-6202.** Breakfast items $2.95–$6.60; lunch and dinner items $1.95–$11.95. AE, DISC, MC, V. Daily 6am–9pm. DINER.

This is a classic 1940s throwback on a Peterborough side street. Behind the faded yellow and green exterior is a beautiful interior of wood, aluminum, tile, and ceiling fans, along with one of the best easy-listening jukeboxes in New England. The meals are just what you'd expect: filling, cheap, and basic. Look for the great hot oven grinders (served with cheese and chips), Reubens, burgers, and grilled cheese and bacon at lunchtime. (Although blasphemous to diner aficionados, croissant sandwiches are also on the menu.) Dinner selections are what you'd expect: Yankee pot roast; meatloaf; chicken kiev; pasta; and fried fish.

**Twelve Pine.** Depot Sq., Peterborough. ☎ **603/924-6140.** Sandwiches $4.50; other items priced by pound, generally $6–$7. MC, V. Mon–Fri 8am–7pm, Sat–Sun 9am–4pm. DELI.

This gourmet deli located in an airy former railroad building tucked away behind Peterborough's trim main street is a great place to nosh and linger. You select your pre-made meal (like chicken burritos or one of four homemade soups) from a deli counter, and it gets popped in a microwave if need be. You bring it to a table. You enjoy it. Simple . . . like lunch should be. Sandwiches are on homemade bread and contain a heaping of fillings; excellent cheeses are available by the pound, and fresh juices round out a meal. This is relaxed place where you'll find decent value for your dollar.

## CORNISH REGION

Artists flocked to this untroubled region in the late 19th century, and the subtle beauty of the area, still prevalent today, makes it abundantly clear why. The first artistic immigrants to arrive were painters and sculptors, who showed up in the late 1880s and early 1890s, building modest homes in the hills. They were followed by politicians and the affluent, who eventually established a thriving summer colony. Among those who populated the rolling hills that looked across the river toward Mt. Ascutney were sculptor Daniel Chester French, painter Maxfield Parrish, and New Republic editor Herbert Crowley. Prominent visitors included Ethel Barrymore and presidents Woodrow Wilson and Theodore Roosevelt. A 1907 article in the *New York Daily Tribune* noted that artists made their homes in Cornish not "with the idea of converting it into a 'fashionable' summer resort, but rather to form there an aristocracy of brains and keep out that element which displays its lack of grey matter by an expenditure of money in undesirable ways."

The social allure eventually peaked, and the area has lapsed since into a peaceful slumber. Those who come here now do so for the beauty and seclusion, not for the gatherings and parties. Indeed, the country's most famous recluse—J. D. Salinger—lives in Cornish today.

The region lacks obvious tourist allure—there are no fancy hotels, no four-star restaurants—but it's well worth visiting and exploring. At twilight, you can see where Maxfield Parrish found his inspiration for the rich, pellucid, azure skies for which his prints and paintings are so noted.

### ESSENTIALS

**GETTING THERE**    Don't bother looking for Cornish proper; you won't find it. Cornish is really a few scattered villages with names like Cornish Flats and, somewhat grandiloquently, Cornish City. The best route for exploring the area is Route 12A along the Connecticut River north of Claremont.

**VISITOR INFORMATION**    Your best bet for local guidance is the **Greater Claremont Chamber of Commerce,** Tremont Sq., Claremont, NH 03743 (☎ 603/543-1296), which dispenses travel information from the Moody Building in town.

### EXPLORING THE CORNISH AREA

The region's premier monument to the former arts colony is the ✪ **Saint-Gaudens National Historic Site** (☎ 603/675-2175), located off Route 12A. Noted sculptor Augustus Saint-Gaudens first arrived in this valley in 1885, shortly after receiving an important commission to create a statue of Abraham Lincoln. His friend Charles Beaman, a lawyer who owned several houses and much land in the Cornish area, assured him he would find a surfeit of "Lincoln-shaped men" in the area. Saint-Gaudens came and pretty much stayed the rest of his life.

His home and studio, which he called "Aspet" after the village in Ireland where he was raised, is a superb place to learn more about this extraordinary artist. A brief tour of the house, which is kept pretty much as it was when Saint-Gaudens lived here, provides a brief introduction to the man. Visitors learn about Saint-Gaudens the artist at several outbuildings and on the grounds, where many replicas of his most famous statues are on display.

The 150-acre grounds also feature short nature trails, where visitors can explore the hilly woodlands, passing along streams and a millpond. The historic site is open daily from 9am to 4:30pm from late May through October. Admission is $4 for adults; free for children under 17.

Covered-bridge aficionados will want to seek out the **Cornish-Windsor Covered Bridge,** which happens to be the nation's longest covered bridge. Spanning the Connecticut River between Vermont and New Hampshire, this bridge has an ancient and interesting lineage. A toll bridge was first built here in 1796 to replace a ferry; the current bridge was built in 1866, and extensively restored in 1989. When the late afternoon light hits it just right, this also vies for the title of the most handsome covered bridge in New England.

For a fisheye view of the bridge and the scenic, forested shores of the Connecticut River, rent a canoe a few miles downstream from the bridge at **Northstar Canoe Livery** (☎ 603/542-5802). For $20 per person, Northstar will shuttle you 12 miles upstream, allowing a leisurely paddle back to your car over the next few hours; or rent for just a half day ($12.50 per person) and dabble in the currents.

## WHERE TO STAY

**Chase House.** Rte. 12A, Cornish, NH 03745. ☎ **800/401-9455** or 603/675-5391. Fax 603/675-5010. www.chasehouse.com. E-mail: chasehouse1@fcgnetworks.net. 8 units. A/C. $105–$150 double. Rates include full breakfast. Closed Nov and Dec 25. MC, V.

Every guest room in the Chase House has a biography of noted 19th-century politician Salmon P. Chase, who was born here in 1808. To refresh your memory: Chase was a founder of the Republican party, Lincoln's Treasury Secretary, Chief Justice of the Supreme Court, and namesake of Chase Manhattan Bank; his portrait appears on the $10,000 bill. His regal house, parts of which were built as early as 1766, is decorated appropriately in an early American style, with antiques and nice period touches. Serious history fans may think the house overly remodeled in a glossy, Yield-House sort of way, but others will find it comfortable and welcoming. Especially appealing is the new and spacious second floor common room, made from the timbers of an 1810 house moved from East Topsham, Vermont. The best guest rooms are the queen suites in the new part of the house, which innkeeper Barbara Lewis has decorated with a light country touch. The Chase House is especially popular with wedding parties, which rent the entire house and avail themselves of the 160-acre property. There's a small fitness room on the premises.

## HANOVER

If your idea of New England involves a sweeping green edged with stately brick buildings, be sure to visit Hanover, a thriving university town agreeably situated in the Connecticut River Valley. First settled in 1765, the town was home to early pioneers who were granted a charter by King George III to establish a college. The school was named after the second Earl of Dartmouth, the school's first trustee. Since its founding, Dartmouth College, the most northerly of the Ivy League schools, has had a large hand in shaping the community. One alumnus has aptly said of the school, "Dartmouth is the sort of place you're nostalgic for even if you've never been there."

Dartmouth has produced more than its share of illustrious alumni, including poet Robert Frost, Vice-President Nelson Rockefeller, author Louise Erdrich, former Treasury Secretary and gadfly Robert Reich, former Surgeon General and anti-tobacco crusader C. Everett Koop, and the late children's book author Dr. Seuss. Perhaps the most noted son of Dartmouth was the renowned 19th-century politician and orator, Daniel Webster. In arguing for the survival of Dartmouth College in a landmark case before the U.S. Supreme Court in 1816 (when two factions vied for control of the school), Webster offered his famous closing line: "It is a small college, gentlemen, but there are those who love it." This has served as an informal motto for school alumni ever since.

Today, a handsome, oversize village green marks the permeable border between college and town. In the summer, the green is an ideal destination for strolling and lounging. The best way to explore Hanover is by foot, so your first endeavor is to park your car, which can be trying during peak seasons. Try the municipal lots west of Main Street.

The town boasts a compact and prosperous commercial area, offering some good browsing and shopping. While the area clearly caters to the affluent with shops like Simon Pearce, The Gap, and several excellent bookshops, there's a good selection of small stores that are light on frills and fluff.

Just south of Hanover is the working-class town of **Lebanon,** a commercial center that has a well-grounded feel to it. The town has a village green to be proud of, a variety of shops, a handful of appealing restaurants, and a quirky mall carved out of an old brick powerhouse. If you're looking for the *New York Times,* head to Hanover; if you need a wrench, head for Lebanon.

## ESSENTIALS

**GETTING THERE**    Hanover is north of Lebanon, New Hampshire, and I-89 via Route 10 or Route 120. Amtrak serves White River Junction, Vermont, across the river.

**VISITOR INFORMATION**    Dartmouth College alumni and chamber volunteers maintain an **information center** (☎ 603/643-3512) on the green in the summer. It's open 7 days a week from June through September (9:30am to 5pm in July and August; 10am to 5pm in June and September.) In the off-season, head to the **Hanover Chamber of Commerce,** P.O. Box 5105, Hanover, NH 03755 (☎ 603/643-3115), located on Main Street across from the post office. It's open Monday through Friday 9am to 4:30pm.

**SPECIAL EVENT**    In mid-February, look for the massive, intricate ice sculptures from the Dartmouth Winter Carnival, held annually; contact **Dartmouth College** (☎ 603/646-1110) for more information on this traditionally beer-soaked event.

## EXPLORING HANOVER

Hanover is a superb town to explore by foot, bike, and even canoe. Start by picking up a map of the campus, available at the Dartmouth information center on the green or at the Hanover Inn. (Free guided tours are also offered in the summer.) The expansive, leafy campus is a delight to walk through; be sure to stop by the Baker Memorial Library to view the murals by Latin American painter José Orozco. He painted *The Epic of American Civilization* while teaching here between 1932 and 1934. The huge murals wrap around a basement study room and are as colorful as they are densely metaphorical. There's a helpful printed interpretation in a free brochure available at the front desk in the room.

South of the green next to the Hanover Inn is the modern **Hopkins Center for the Arts** (☎ 603/646-2422; www.dartmouth.edu/~hop/). The center attracts national acts to its 900-seat concert hall and stages top-notch performances at the Moore Theater. Call for information on current shows. If the building looks vaguely familiar, there may be a reason for that. It was designed by Wallace Harrison, the architect who later went on to design New York's Lincoln Center.

Adjacent to the Hopkins Center is the **Hood Museum of Art** (☎ **603/646-2808;** www.dartmouth.edu/~hood/). Although it houses one of the oldest college museums in the nation, it's a decidedly contemporary, open building, constructed in 1986. The austere, three-story structure displays selections from the permanent collection, including a superb selection of 19th-century American landscapes and a fine grouping of Assyrian reliefs dating from 883 B.C. to 859 B.C. The museum is open Tuesday and Thursday to Saturday from 10am until 5pm, Wednesday from 10am to 9pm, and Sunday from noon to 5pm. Admission is free.

A fine way to spend a lazy afternoon is drifting along the Connecticut River in a canoe. Dartmouth's historic **Ledyard Canoe Club** (☎ **603/643-6709**) is located just down the hill from the campus off West Wheelock Street (turn upstream at the bottom of the hill before crossing the river, then follow the signs to the clubhouse). While much of the club's focus is on competitive racing (the club has won 20 national titles since 1967), it's a good place to get a boat and explore the tree-lined river. It's open whenever the river temperature tops 50 degrees. Canoes and whitewater kayaks can be rented for $5 per hour, or $15 per day ($25 on weekends), with boats available first-come, first-served. Summer hours are 9am to 8pm weekends and 10am to 8pm weekdays. In spring and fall, the club is open 10am to 6pm weekends, noon to 6pm weekdays.

A minute or two across the river is the **Montshire Museum of Science,** an excellent children's museum; see Vermont chapter 4 for more information.

## A ROAD TRIP TO MT. KEARSARGE

Mt. Monadnock to the south is the most heavily visited peak in the area, but 2,931-foot Mt. Kearsarge ranks among the most accessible. Located in the Sunapee Lake region southeast of Lebanon, Kearsarge can be ascended most of the way by car along a paved carriage road. The entrance is just outside the town of Warner (Exit 9 on I-89). State park rangers collect a toll at the base ($2.50 per person over age 12), then drivers snake their way $3^1/2$ miles past dramatic vistas to a gravel parking lot high on the mountain's shoulder. From here, it's a simple $^1/2$-mile hike to the summit along a well-marked, rocky trail with remarkable views to the south and southwest along the way.

The rocky, knobby summit offers superb panoramas of south-central New Hampshire's lakes and hills, although the views are cluttered slightly by an old fire tower and several small buildings bristling with antennae and other visual pollution of the information age. Another caveat: On crisp fall weekends, the summit of Mt. Kearsarge has all the seclusion of Christmas Eve at the mall. You're better off avoiding it then and looking for your own peaks away from the crowds.

## SHAKER LIFE

Southeast of Hanover in the town of Enfield is the Enfield Shaker Museum, a cluster of historic buildings on peaceful Lake Mascoma. "The Chosen Vale," as it was called by its first inhabitants, was founded in 1793; by the mid-1800s, it had 350 members and 3,000 acres. From that peak, the community dwindled, and by 1927, the Shakers abandoned the Chosen Vale and sold the village lock, stock, and barrel.

Today, much of the property is either owned by the state of New Hampshire or the museum, which was founded in 1986. The village is picturesque and contains some extraordinary specimens of architecture; it's well worth stopping by for a self-guided walking tour and to view the small museum, which emphasizes Shaker industry rather than Shaker aesthetics.

After a few moments in the museum, ramble through the village and read about the buildings in the walking-tour guide (free with admission). Be sure to note the gardens and the communal grave. Across the road is a lovely hillside, where you can ascend to a former Shaker ceremonial area. The overall historic feel of the village is a tad compromised by a new condominium development along the lakeshores, although as these developments go the scale and design is quite sympathetic to the original village.

Dominating the village is the imposing **Great Stone Dwelling,** an austere but gracious building of granite erected between 1837 and 1841. When constructed, it was the tallest building north of Boston, and it remains the largest dwelling house in any of the Shaker communes. The Enfield Shakers lived and dined here, with as many as 150 Shakers at a time eating at long trestle tables. In 1997, the museum acquired the stone building, and in 1998, a new restaurant and inn opened to the public (see below).

The **Enfield Shaker Museum** (☎ **603/632-4346;** www.valley.net/~esm) is on Route 4A, and between Memorial Day and Halloween, it's open Monday to Saturday from 10am to 5pm, and Sunday from noon to 5pm. (The rest of the year it's open Saturday from 10am to 4pm and Sunday from noon to 4pm.) Admission is $7 for adults, $6 for seniors, $5 students, and $3 for children 10 to 18.

## WHERE TO STAY

Several hotels and motels are located off the interstate in Lebanon and West Lebanon, about 5 miles south of Hanover. Try the **Airport Economy Inn** (☎ 800/433-3466 or 603/298-8888) at 45 Airport Rd. (Exit 20 off I-89); **Holiday Inn Express** (☎ 603/ 448-5070) 135 Rte. 120, (Exit 18 off I-89); the **Radisson Inn North Country** (☎ 603/298-5906) 25 Airport Rd. (Exit 20 off I-89); or **Sunset Motor Inn** (☎ 603/298-8721), 305 N. Main St. (Rte. 10, 4 miles off Exit 19 off I-89).

**Alden Country Inn.** On the Common, Lyme, NH 03768. ☎ **800/794-2296** or 603/ 795-2222. Fax 603/795-9436. www.aldencountryinn.com. E-mail: info@aldencountryinn. com. 15 units. A/C TV TEL. Summer and fall $125–$160 double; off-season $95–$145. Rates include breakfast or Sunday brunch. 2-night minimum on weekends Apr to mid-Oct. AE, DC, DISC, MC, V.

Ten miles north of Hanover is the quiet crossroads village of Lyme with its tidy common and handsome church. Overlooking the common is the 1809 Alden Country Inn, a regal four-story building with a high triangular gable. Over the years it has served as a stagecoach stop and Grange Hall. The guest rooms are varied, and decorated with light historic styling; some are simply furnished with white walls and stenciling, others are more floral in character. Most feature painted floors that show off the wide boards. My favorite is room #9 with its mustard-yellow floors and somewhat larger bathroom. (Common to many old inns, the bathrooms are typically on the small side, often tucked into closets.) Beware that stairs get narrower and steeper the higher your room is in the building.

**Dining:** The Alden Tavern and Grille on the first floor (open to the public) has a nice burnished glow, with maple and pine floors, a fireplace, and a collection of colonial era tools on the walls. Meals tend to be classical New England fare, with entrees like Shaker cranberry pot roast and Atlantic salmon with apple chutney. Entrees are $14.95 to $19.95.

✿ **Hanover Inn.** Wheelock St. (P.O. Box 151), Hanover, NH 03755. ☎ **800/443-7024** or 603/643-4300. Fax 603/646-3744. www.hanoverinn.com. E-mail: hanover.inn@dartmouth.edu. 92 units. A/C TV TEL. $237–$297 double. AE, DC, DISC, MC, V. Valet parking $5 per day. Pets accepted; $15 per night.

The Hanover Inn was founded in 1780 and is New Hampshire's oldest continuing business, but founder Gen. Ebenezer Brewster would be hard pressed to recognize it today. Most of the current five-story inn was built in 1924, 1939, and 1968, and this large, modern hotel is thoroughly up-to-date, with brisk and professional service, tidy rooms, dataports for laptops, and subterranean walkways to the art museum and performing arts theater. Yet the inn maintains an appealing old-world graciousness. It's informed by that mildly starchy neo-Georgian demeanor trendy in the 1940s, and you'll find accents in forest green everywhere you turn. (It's owned and operated by Dartmouth College, and alumni are almost cultish in their wearing of the green, the school color.)

Overlooking the Dartmouth Green, the Hanover Inn is perfectly situated for exploring campus and town. Rooms are priced according to size and view, and each is nicely furnished in a contemporary Colonial style. Most have canopy or four-poster beds and down comforters along with amenities like hair dryers, multiple phones, and bathrobes. Room prices are quite stiff; you pay a premium for the prime location, excellent service, and the honor of being part of the Dartmouth family.

**Dining:** The inn has two dining rooms; see "Where to Dine," below.

**Amenities:** Valet parking, room service (7am to 11pm), laundry/dry cleaning, safe-deposit boxes, turndown service, newspaper delivery, and access to Dartmouth's fitness and athletic facilities.

**Mary Keane House.** Rte. 4 (Shaker Village), Enfield, NH 03748. ☎ **888/239-2153** or 603/632-4241. www.marykeanehouse.com. E-mail: mary.keane.house@valley.net. 5 units. A/C TV. $85–$145 double, including full breakfast. AE, DISC, MC, V. Pets accepted.

Situated at Lower Shaker Village about 20 minutes from Dartmouth, this is an ideal spot for the gentle recuperation of a harried soul. Built in 1929 (2 years after the Shakers had abandoned the village), this two-story grayish-lavender Georgian Revival doesn't share much with the Shaker village in architecture or spirit—in fact, it's filled with lovely Victorian antiques, including a rosewood concert grand piano, which seem to be anathema to the Shaker sensibility; but it's kept immaculately clean (something the Shakers would appreciate), and it's right in the Shaker village, so guests can explore the buildings and museum by day (the grounds are especially peaceful at twilight), paddle the inn's canoes on Lake Mascoma, or swim at the small private beach.

**Shaker Inn at the Great Stone Dwelling.** Rte. 4, Enfield, NH 03748. ☎ **888/707-4257** or 603/632-7810. www.theshakerinn.com. E-mail: info@theshakerinn.com. 24 units. $105–$155 double. Rates include breakfast. AE, CB, DC, DISC, MC, V.

Part of the Enfield Shaker Museum, the Shaker Inn offers a unique destination for those curious about the Shakers and early American history. The rooms are spread among the upper floors of the hulking stone dwelling built by the Enfield Shaker community. It's an astounding edifice that was all the more impressive when constructed in the late 1830s, when it was the tallest building north of Boston. Some of the rooms have original built-in Shaker cabinets (you can stow your socks in something that would bring five figures at a New York auction house). All rooms are furnished with simple and attractive Shaker reproductions; the bigger and more expensive rooms are on the lower floors. The inn is run by the same folks who operate the Red Hill Inn in Center Harbor.

**Dining:** The ground-floor restaurant (formerly the Shaker dining hall) seats 150 and features upscale regional fare that draws on Shaker flavors and traditions, including lamb with rosemary, duckling with a raspberry maple gaze, and sirloin with smothered onions and a whiskey sauce. Entrees are priced from $12.95 to $24.95.

## WHERE TO DINE

Another good option for dining is the excellent La Poule à Dents, located in Norwich, Vermont, just across the river. See the Vermont chapter four for more information.

**Daniel Webster Room.** In the Hanover Inn, Wheelock St. ☎ **603/643-4300.** Reservations recommended. Breakfast items $4.25–$9.50; lunch items $6.95–$13.50; main dinner courses $17–$26. AE, CB, DC, DISC, MC, V. Mon 7–10:30am, 11:30am–1:30pm; Tues–Fri 7–10:30am, 11:30am–1:30pm, 6–9pm; Sat 7am–10:30am, 6–9pm; Sun 11:30am–1:30pm. CONTEMPORARY AMERICAN.

The neoclassical Daniel Webster Room of the Hanover Inn will appeal to those looking for fine dining amid a formal (not to say staid) New England atmosphere. The inn's proper dining room is reminiscent of a 19th-century resort hotel, with fluted columns, floral carpeting, and regal upholstered chairs. The dinner menu isn't extensive, but that doesn't make it any less appealing. When in season, produce from the college's organic farm is used. Entrees are eclectic and creative, and usually please meat eaters. Entrees change with the season but might include braised rabbit leg served with tuffled pappardelle, or a sirloin steak with a roasted garlic and smoked onion tomato jam. Diners can choose from an excellent selection of wines.

Off the inn's lobby is the more informal Zins, a wine bistro that serves some 30 wines by the glass. It's open daily from 11:30am to 10pm, and has lunches for under $10 and dinners like crispy half duck with glazed acorn squash and cider, and lobster and crab ravioli. Most dinner entrees are $13 to $15.

✪ **Lou's.** 30 S. Main St. ☎ **603/643-3321.** Breakfast items $3–$7; lunch items $4–$7. AE, MC, V. Mon–Fri 6am–3pm; Sat 7am–5pm; Sun 7am–3pm. Bakery open for snacks until 5pm. BAKERY/COMFORT FOOD.

Lou's has been a Hanover institution since 1947, attracting hungry crowds for breakfast on weekends and a steady clientele for lunch throughout the week. The mood is no-frills New Hampshire, with a black-and-white linoleum checkerboard floor, maple-and-vinyl booths, and a harried but efficient crew of waiters. Breakfast is served all day here (real maple syrup on your pancakes is $1 extra), and the sandwiches are huge and delicious, served on fresh-baked bread. This is definitely the place for breakfast or lunch in Hanover. Every fourth year, expect to rub elbows with presidential contenders, who eventually show up here while campaigning in the state's first-in-the-nation presidential primary.

**Monsoon.** 18 Centerra Pkwy. (Rte. 120), Lebanon. ☎ **603/643-9227.** Main courses lunch $5–$14, dinner $8–$15. Mon–Fri 11:30am–2pm, 5–9pm (9:30pm on Fri), Sat 5–9:30pm, Sun 5–9pm. Follow Rte. 120 south from Hanover to the Centerra Marketplace in Lebanon. PAN-ASIAN.

Monsoon is run by the same folks who run Sweet Tomatoes (in Lebanon and Burlington, Vermont), and it bills itself—accurately—as an "Asian bistro and satay bar." It's anything but traditional New England. Housed in a sleek, airy, and modern restaurant at the edge of upscale strip mall, it's boldly furnished with laminated wood and brushed steel. The menu is built around creative interpretations of Asian dishes, including appetizers of chicken, beef, and scallop satays with dipping sauces, and excellent lemongrass mussels. Wood-grilled entrees are a specialty and include selections such as kaffir lime-citrus salmon, and the improbable but tasty Thai cowboy steak. There's also a broad selection of filling Asian noodle dishes. Monsoon offers good value for budget-conscious diners.

## 5  The Lake Winnipesaukee Region

Lake Winnipesaukee is the state's largest lake and sprawls immoderately across New Hampshire's central region just east of I-93. Oddly enough, when you're out on the lake, it rarely seems all that huge. That's because the 180-mile shoreline is convoluted and twisting, warped around dozens of inlets, coves, and bays, and further fragmented with some 274 islands. As a result, intermittent lake views from the shore give the illusion you're viewing a chain of smaller lakes and ponds rather than one massive body of water that measures 12 miles by 20 miles at its broadest points. (Incidentally, there's no agreement on the meaning of the lake's Indian name. Although "beautiful water in a high place" and "smile of the great spirit" are the most poetic interpretations, the more commonly accepted translation is "good outlet.")

How to best enjoy the lake? If you're traveling with kids, settle in at Weirs Beach for a day or two, and take in the gaudy attractions. If you're looking for isolation, consider renting a lakeside cabin for a week or so on the eastern shore, track down a canoe or sailboat, then explore much the same way travelers did a century ago. If your time is limited, a driving tour around the lake with a few well-chosen stops will give you a nice taste of the region's woodsy flavor.

## WESTERN SHORE

Lake Winnipesaukee's western shore has a more frenetic atmosphere than its sibling shore across the lake. That's partly for historic reasons—the main stage and rail routes passed along the western shore—and partly for modern reasons: I-93 runs west of the lake, serving as a sluice for harried visitors streaming in from the Boston megalopolis to the south. Laconia is the region's largest town. It has some attractive historic architecture and nice vistas, but also is home to an outsized measure of tacky sprawl and isn't really much of a tourist destination. Travelers are better off exploring farther north along the lakeshore, where you'll find plenty of diversions, especially for those with short attention spans.

### ESSENTIALS

**GETTING THERE**    Interstate access to the western shore is from I-93 at Exit 20 or Exit 23. From Exit 20, follow Route 3 north through Laconia to Weirs Beach. (It's less confusing and more scenic to stay on Business Route 3.) From Exit 23, drive 9 miles east on Route 104 to Meredith, then head either south on Route 3 to Route 11, or strike northeast on Route 25.

**VISITOR INFORMATION**    The **Greater Laconia/Weirs Beach Chamber of Commerce,** 11 Veterans Sq., Laconia, NH 03246 (☎ **603/524-5531**), maintains a seasonal information booth on Business Route 3 about halfway between Laconia and Weirs Beach. It's open daily in summer from 10am to 6pm. Information is also available year-round at the chamber's office at the **old railway station** in Laconia. It's open Monday to Friday from 9am to 5pm. On the Web, point your browser to www.laconia-weirs.org.

The **Lakes Region Association,** P.O. Box 430, New Hampton NH 03256 (☎ **800/605-2537**) doesn't maintain an information booth but is happy to send out a handy vacation kit with maps and extensive information about local attractions. Web information is available at www.lakesregion.org.

### ENJOYING WEIRS BEACH

Weirs Beach is a compact resort town that reflects its Victorian heritage. Unlike beach towns that sprawl for miles, Weirs Beach clusters in that classic pre-automobile fashion, spread along a boardwalk that happens to be near a sandy beach. At the heart of the town is a working railroad that still connects to the steamship line—a nice throwback to an era when summer vacationers weren't dependent on cars. The town attracts a broad mix of visitors, from history and transportation buffs to beach nuts and young video-game warriors.

Most of all, it attracts families. Lots of families. In fact, Weirs Beach is an ideal destination for parents with kids possessed by an insatiable drive for new games and flashing lights. Families might start the morning at **Endicott Beach** (named after the Royal Governor of Massachusetts Bay Colony, who sent surveyors here in 1652), swimming in the clear waters of Winnipesaukee. Arrive early if you want to find public parking, which costs 50¢ an hour with a 5-hour maximum.

Afterwards, stroll along the boardwalk into town, which offers a modest selection of penny arcades, bumper cars, jewelry outlets, leather shops, and tasty if unnutritious fare like crispy caramel corn.

Along the access roads to Weirs Beach are a number of activities that delight young kids and parents desperate to take some of the energy out of them. The **Surfcoaster** (☎ 603/366-4991) has a huge assortment of wave pools, water slides, and other moist diversions for most ages. It's on Route 11B just outside of Weirs Beach and costs $20 adult, $15 for those under 4 feet tall.

Also on Route 11B is **Daytona Fun Park** (☎ 603/366-5461), which has go-carts, miniature golf, and batting cages; and the **Funspot** (☎ 603/366-4377) will keep kids (and uninhibited adults) occupied with upwards of 500 games, including video games, candlepin bowling, and a driving range. There's no charge to enter. Games are priced individually (for example, bowling is $2.75 per game per person), or you can get a better deal by purchasing tokens in bulk: $20 gets you 125 tokens.

## EXPLORING BY LAND & BY LAKE

Scenic train rides leave from town on the **Winnipesaukee Scenic Railroad** (☎ 603/279-5253 or 603/745-2135), which offers 1- and 2-hour excursions from Weirs Beach during the summer. It's an unusual way to enjoy views of lake and forest; kids are provided a hobo lunch packed in a bundle on a stick ($6.95). The 2-hour ride is $8.50 for adults and $6.50 for children ages 4 to 11. The 1-hour trip is $7.50 adult and $5.50 children.

The stately *M/S Mount Washington* is an exceptionally handsome 230-foot-long vessel with three decks and a capacity of 1,250 passengers (☎ 603/366-2628; www.msmountwashington.com). This ship, by far the largest of the lake tour boats, is the best way to get to know Winnipesaukee, with excellent views of the winding shoreline and the knobby peaks of the White Mountains rising over the lake's north end. As many as four cruises a day are offered in summer, ranging from a 2¹/₂-hour excursion ($16 adults, $8 children 4 to 12) to a 3-hour dinner cruise ($31 to $41) that includes dinner and live entertainment on two decks. The dinner cruises offer different themes, but don't look for alternative rock; most are along the lines of classic rock, oldies nights, and country and western. (A comprehensive listing of upcoming dinner cruises and bands may be found on the Web page listed above.) The ship operates from the end of May to mid-October, departing from the train station in Weirs Beach. (You can't miss it when it's at the dock.)

## SKIING

**Gunstock.** Rte. 11A between West Alton and Gilford. ☎ 800/486-7862. Vertical drop: 1,420 ft. Lifts: 5 chairlifts, 2 surface lifts. Tickets: $39 weekends, $28 Wed–Fri, $19 Mon–Tues (non-holidays).

Gunstock is a good destination for families and intermediate skiers who like good views as part of their ski experience. This venerable ski area, with a vertical drop of 1,420 feet, has the comfortably burnished patina of a rustic resort dating from a much earlier era—no garish condos, no ski-theme lounges, no forced frivolity. The mountain managers pride themselves on maintaining excellent ski conditions throughout

# Hog Heaven!

Laconia and Weirs Beach get very loud in mid-June, when some 150,000 motorcyclists descend on the towns to fraternize, party, and race during what's become the legendary Motorcycle Week.

This bawdy event dates back to 1939, when motorcycle races were first staged at the newly built Belknap Gunstock Recreation Area. The annual gathering gained some unwelcome notoriety in 1965, when riots broke out involving bikers and locals. The mayor of Laconia attributed the problems to the Hell's Angels, claiming he had evidence that they had trained in Mexico before coming here to foment chaos. This singular episode was documented in Hunter S. Thompson's classic 1966 book, *The Hell's Angels.*

Laconia and Weirs Beach eventually recovered from that unwanted publicity, and today, bike races take place at the Loudon Speedway just north of Concord and at the Gunstock Recreation Area, which hosts the Hill Climb; but the whole of the Weirs Beach area takes on a leather-and-beer carnival atmosphere throughout the week, with bikers cruising the main drag and enjoying one another's company until late at night. Many travelers would pay good money to avoid Weirs Beach at this time, but they'd be missing out on one of New England's more enduring annual phenomena.

Details may be found on the Web site: www.laconiamcweek.com.

---

the day on the 45 trails, and the views of iced-over Winnipesaukee and the White Mountains to the north are superb. Gunstock also offers night skiing on 15 trails.

## OTHER OUTDOOR PURSUITS

Few finer sights exist than watching the *M/S Mount Washington* steam cross the broad waters of the lake from atop **Mt. Major,** a popular and accessible peak near the lake's southern tip. The mountain isn't major by White Mountain standards (it's just 1,780 feet), but yields a great view of the waters and the more legitimate mountains to the north. The well-used ascent is 1 1/2 miles long; plan on somewhat more than an hour to get to the summit. The trailhead is located 4 miles north of Alton Bay on Route 11.

Also near the lake is the **Gunstock Recreation Area** (☎ 603/293-4341), a four-season area on Route 11A that's been attracting outdoorspeople since it was founded more than a half-century ago. This heavily forested, 2,000-acre park in the upland hills southeast of the lake features camping at 420 sites, fishing, swimming, and plethora of hiking trails that wind through the scenic Belknap Mountains. (There's also skiing in winter.)

A lower-elevation destination popular with swimmers is **Ellacoya State Beach** (☎ 603/293-7821), on Route 11 between Alton Bay and Weirs Beach. The 600-foot sandy beach has superb views across the waters to the rolling hills on the opposite shore and offers basic amenities like changing areas and a snack bar. The beach also has RV camping with 38 sites featuring full hookups.

In Laconia, the **Winni Sailboarders School and Outlet,** 687 Union Ave. (☎ 603/528-4110), will put you on the water in either a kayak or on a sailboard on Opechee Bay, a long, finger-like lake inlet. Lessons are also available. Along the lake's northern shore, **Wild Meadow Canoes,** on Route 25 between Meredith and Center Harbor (☎ 800/427-7536 or 603/253-7536), rents canoes, kayaks, and small boats for exploring the big lake and some of the smaller waters nearby. A canoe rents for $25 per day.

## WHERE TO STAY

The **Half Moon Motel and Cottages** (☎ 603/366-4494) is situated on a hillside overlooking the town and the lake beyond. It's a good choice if you're looking for the full 1940s experience. The cinderblock-walled rooms all have views, although they tend toward, well, the monastic in their decor, with weary industrial carpeting and less-than-spanking-new beds. There's also a somewhat murky pool for splashing around. Summer rates are $69 to $79 double (premium charged Saturday and Motorcycle Week); rates start at $49 in the spring and fall.

**Manor on Golden Pond.** Rte. 3, Holderness, NH 03245. ☎ **800/545-2141** or 603/968-3348. Fax 603/968-2116. www.manorongoldenpond.com. 27 units. A/C TV TEL. Summer $210–$375 double; winter $150–$375. Rates include breakfast. 2-night minimum stay on holidays and foliage season. AE, MC, V. No children under 12.

This regal stucco-and-shingle mansion, located a short drive north of Winnipesaukee in Holderness, was built between 1903 and 1907, and was owned by *Life* magazine editor Harold Fowler in the 1940s. Set on a low hill overlooking Squam Lake, the Manor is nicely situated on 14 landscaped acres studded with white pines that whisper in the breeze. Inside, it has the feel of an English manor house, with rich oak paneling, leaded windows, and mounted pheasants on the mantel. The guest rooms vary in size and decor—the larger, more expensive rooms are more creatively furnished and are far more inviting than the smaller, less expensive rooms in the first-floor wing. Innkeepers David and Bambi Arnold recently added four new cottages with views to the lake, all of which are open year-round.

**Dining:** Meals are served in three dark-hued dining rooms, including the former billiards hall with a beautiful green-tile fireplace. Meals are upscale New American, with main dishes changing nightly. Entrees might include a filet mignon with boursin and chanterelles, or trout with a crab filling served in a sage-brown butter sauce. Wine selections are extensive. A five-course dinner is $50 per person ($38 for three courses).

**Amenities:** Boathouse with canoes and private lakefront beach on 3 acres (nearby), pool, one clay tennis court (lights available for night play), croquet, horseshoes, volleyball, and shuffleboard.

**Red Hill Inn.** Rte. 25B, Box 99M, Center Harbor, NH 03226. ☎ **800/573-3445** or 603/279-7001. Fax 603/279-7003. www.redhillinn.com. E-mail: info@redhillinn.com. 25 units. A/C TEL. $105–$195 double; $195 cottage. Rates include full breakfast. 2-night minimum stay on weekends. Ask about packages. AE, CB, DC, DISC, MC, V. From Center Harbor, drive northwest 2.9 miles on Rte. 25B. Children over 5 are welcome.

The Red Hill Inn is tucked in the rolling hills between Winnipesaukee and Squam Lake, but borrows more of its flavor from the mountains than the lakeshore. Housed in an architecturally austere three-story brick home dating from the turn of the last century, the inn looks down a long meadow toward a small complex of elegant green-and-red shingled farm buildings at the foot of a hill. Two of these have been converted into well-appointed guest quarters. Room prices are based on views and size (21 have wood-burning fireplaces), but my favorite room, the Kearsarge, is one of the less expensive, with a private brick and chocolatey-brown paneled sitting room, off which lies a small bathroom with clawfoot tub. The downside? It's on the third floor of a no-elevator building.

**Dining:** The inn's dining room serves lunch, Sunday brunch, and dinner, with evening entrees such as rack of lamb with feta cheese and Dijon mustard, and roast duckling served with either an orange or cranberry glaze. Dinner entrees range from $10.95 to $22.95.

**Amenities:** Outdoor heated pool and outdoor hot tub (year-round).

## WHERE TO DINE

**Kellerhaus** (☎ 603/366-4466) is the classic house of sweets. Located in a storybook-like stone-and-half-timber structure on Route 3, a 0.3 mile north of Endicott Beach, this old-fashioned place overlooking the lake features a diet-busting ice-cream buffet where fanatics can select from a battery of toppings, including macaroon crunch, butterscotch, chocolate, and whipped cream. The smorgasbord is $3 to $6.25, depending on the number of scoops you begin with. There's also a sizable gift shop with homemade candies providing snacks for the road. The shop is open year-round; from Father's Day to Columbus Day it's open 8am to 11pm daily, with limited hours in the off-season (call first).

**Hart's Turkey Farm Restaurant.** At the junction of Rte. 3 and Rte. 104, Meredith. ☎ 603/279-6212. www.hartsturkeyfarm.com. Main courses $9.25–$17.95. AE, CB, DC, DISC, MC, V. Summer daily 11:15am–9pm; fall through spring daily 11:15am–8pm. TURKEY/AMERICAN.

Hart's Turkey Farm Restaurant is bad news if you're a turkey. On a typically busy day, this popular spot dishes up more than a ton of America's favorite bird, along with 4,000 dinner rolls and 1,000 pounds of potatoes. (Let's not even mention the Thanksgiving carnage.) Judging by name alone, Hart's Farm sounds more rural than it is. In fact, it's in a nondescript roadside building on a busy, non-descript part of Route 3. Inside, it's comfortable in a faux–Olde New Englande sort of way, and the service has that sort of rushed efficiency found in places where waitresses have been hoisting heavy trays for years, (Servers don't even blink when bus tours show up unannounced.) but diners don't return time and again to Harts for the charm. They come for turkey that's cooked moist and perfect every time. There's a good children's menu for kids 10 and under.

**Hickory Stick Farm.** 66 Bean Hill Rd., Belmont. ☎ 603/524-3333. www.hickorystickfarm. com. Reservations highly recommended. Main courses $12.95–$21.95. AE, DISC, MC, V. Memorial Day–Columbus Day Tues–Sat 5pm–9pm, Sun 10am–2pm, 4–8pm; Columbus Day–Memorial Day Fri–Sat 5–9pm, Sun 10am–2pm. AMERICAN.

The Hickory Stick Farm is a local institution well off the beaten path in the countryside outside of Laconia. Despite its hidden location, it's managed to attract and keep diners happy since it first opened its doors in 1950. Ask for a seat on the screened-in gazebo room during the balmy weather. When it turns chilly, angle for a table near the fireplace in the brick-floored dining room. The restaurant is famous for its distinctive duck dishes, served with an orange-sherry sauce. The duck is slow-roasted for hours, with the fatty layer removed from beneath the skin. This method yields delicate and crispy skin, but wonderfully moist meat. The duck attracts diners from Boston and beyond, but tasty country fare like Yankee braised beef and baked chicken breast with apple pecan stuffing keeps local folks happy. Lest you fear this spot might be too fancy for a casual summer night out, note that dinner includes a "molded zippy pineapple salad."

**Las Piñatas.** 9 Veteran's Sq., Laconia. ☎ 603/528-1405. Reservations recommended for parties of 5 or more. Lunch items $4–$8; main dinner courses $11–$16. AE, DISC, MC, V. Mon–Thurs 11am–2pm and 5–9pm; Fri–Sat 11am–2pm and 5–9:30pm; Sun 5–8pm. Closed Tues in winter. MEXICAN.

Armando Lezama first came to Laconia from Mexico City in 1979 as a high-school exchange student. He liked it, so he moved here with his family, opening one of the more authentic Mexican restaurants in New Hampshire. Housed in the handsome stone railroad station on the edge of Laconia's downtown, Las Piñatas has a good menu of Mexican dishes and frozen margaritas that always seem especially tasty after a long day at the lake. The menu includes Mexican regulars like empanadas, tacos al carbón, and fajitas. Among the specialties are the delectable enchiladas de mole, made with the Lezamas' homemade mole sauce.

## EASTERN SHORE

Winnipesaukee's east shore recalls Gertrude Stein's comment about Oakland: "There's no there there." Other than the low-key town of Wolfeboro, the east shore is mostly islands and coves, mixed forests and rolling hills, rocky farms and the occasional apple orchard. While it's a large lake, its waters are also largely inaccessible from this side. Old summer homes and new gated condominium communities occupy some of the best coves and points; but narrow roads do touch on the lake here and there, and most roads are nicely engineered for leisurely cruising. The secret to getting the most out of the east shore is to take it slow and enjoy the small villages and quiet forests as if they were delicately crafted miniatures, not vast panoramas.

### ESSENTIALS

**GETTING THERE**    Lake Winnipesaukee's east shore is best explored on Route 28 (from Alton Bay to Wolfeboro) and Route 109 (from Wolfeboro to Moultonborough). From the south, Alton Bay can be reached via Route 11 from Rochester, or from Route 28, which intersects routes 4 and 202 about 12 miles east of Concord.

**VISITOR INFORMATION**    The **Wolfeboro Chamber of Commerce,** P.O. Box 547, Wolfeboro, NH 03894 (☎ **800/516-5324** or 603/569-2200), offers regional travel information and advice from its offices in a converted railroad station at 32 Central Ave, 1 block off Main Street in Wolfeboro. It's open daily in summer 10am to 5pm, in the off-season 10am to 3pm Monday through Friday. The chamber maintains a high-quality Web site: www.wolfeboroonline.com.

### EXPLORING WOLFEBORO

The town of Wolfeboro claims to be the first summer resort in the United States, and the documentation makes a pretty good case for it. In 1763, John Wentworth, the nephew of a former governor, built a summer estate on what's now called Lake Wentworth, along with a road to it from Portsmouth. Wentworth didn't get to enjoy his holdings for long—his Tory sympathies forced him to flee when the political situation heated up in 1775. The house burned in 1820, but the site now attracts archeologists.

Visitors are lured to **Wentworth State Beach** (☎ **603/569-3699**) not so much because of history but because of the attractive beach, refreshing lake waters, and shady picnic area. The park is located 5 miles east of Wolfeboro on Route 109.

The town of Wolfeboro (population 2,800) has a vibrant, homey downtown that's easily explored on foot. Park near Depot Square and the gingerbread Victorian train station, and stock up on brochures and maps at the Chamber of Commerce office inside. Behind the train station, running along the former tracks of the rail line, is the Russell C. Chase Bridge-Falls Path, a rail-trail that runs pleasantly along Back Bay to a set of small waterfalls.

Near the falls, look for the **Wright Museum of American Enterprise,** 77 Center St. (Route 77; ☎ **603/569-1212**), open 10am to 4pm daily in summer. This is an unusual museum, easily identified by the tank "crashing" out through the crumbling front wall. Founded in 1984, the Wright Museum celebrates life on "the home front" between 1939 and 1945, when America's boys were abroad fighting the good fight. If the good old days for you means Frank Sinatra in saddle shoes and strawberry parfaits at a marble-topped fountain, you'll find a lot to bring back memories here. Admission is $5 adults, $4 seniors, and $3 students.

For a superb view of the eastern shore, head 7 miles north of Wolfeboro on Route 109 to the Abenaki Tower. Look for a parking lot and wooden sign on the right side of the road at the crest of a hill. From the lot, it's an easy 5-minute hike to the sturdy log tower, which rises about 60 feet high and is ascended by a steep staircase. (This is not a good destination for acrophobes.) Those who soldier on to the top are rewarded with excellent views of nearby coves, inlets, and the Belknap Mountains southwest of the lake.

## A Quirky Castle

**Castle in the Clouds.** Rte. 171 (4 miles south of Rte. 25), Moultonborough. ☎ **800/729-2468** or 603/476-2352. Admission $11 adults, $10 seniors, $8 student, children under 6 free. Mid-May to mid-June Sat–Sun 9am–5pm; mid-June to Labor Day daily 9am–5pm; Labor Day–3rd week of Oct daily 9am–4pm. Closed Nov–Apr.

Cranky millionaire Thomas Gustav Plant built this eccentric stone edifice high atop a mountain overlooking Lake Winnipesaukee in 1913, at a cost of $7 million. The home is a sort of rustic San Simeon East, with orange roof tiles, cliff-hugging rooms, stained-glass windows, and unrivaled views of the surrounding hills and lakes. Visitors drive as far as the carriage house (nicely converted to a snack bar and restaurant), where they park and are taken in groups through the house by knowledgeable guides.

Even if the castle holds no interest, the 5,200-acre grounds are worth the admission price. The long access road is harrowingly narrow and winding (kids, don't try this in your mobile home!), with wonderful vistas and turnouts for stopping and exploring along the way. I'd advise taking your time on the way up; the separate exit road is fast, straight, and uninteresting. The grounds are also home to a bottled water plant and a microbrewery, both of which are open for tours.

## Where to Stay & Dine

**Wolfeboro Inn.** 90 N. Main St., Wolfeboro, NH 03894. ☎ **800/451-2389** or 603/569-3016. Fax 603/569-5375. www.wolfeboroinn.com. 44 units. A/C TV TEL. Mid-May to Oct 139–$235 double; Nov to mid-May $79–$175 double. Rates include continental breakfast. 2-night minimum in peak season. AE, MC, V.

This small, elegant hotel strives to mix modern and traditional, and succeeds admirably in doing so. Located a short stroll from downtown Wolfeboro, the inn dates back to 1812 but was extensively expanded and updated in the mid-1980s. The modern lobby features a small atrium with wood beams, slate floor, and a brick fireplace, and has managed to retain an old-world elegance and grace. Comfortable guest rooms vary in size, and most are furnished with early American reproductions. The inn also has some nice extras, including its own 75-passenger excursion boat (a free trip is included in room rates in summer). On the downside, for an inn of this elegance it has only a disappointing sliver of lakeshore and a miniature beach for guests.

**Dining/Diversions:** The upscale 1812 Room serves both regional and Italian fare. Dinner entrees range from $14 to $25. The atmospheric Wolfe's Tavern has pewter tankards hanging from the low beams, 60 brands of beer, a sizeable salad bar and a selection of basic pub fare. Prices run from $7 to $16.

**Amenities:** Beach swimming, conference rooms, nearby health club, concierge, limited room service, dry cleaning, laundry service, and baby-sitting.

# 7

# The White Mountains & North Country

**V**isitors coming from the West scoff at the low elevations of New England's peaks. ("Four thousand feet? *Four thousand feet?* We'd need a steamshovel to reach that elevation where we come from!")

Savvy eastern hikers indulge their guests with good humor. Then they take them to the White Mountains' brutally rugged, steep trails to force them to beg for mercy—never mind the plentiful oxygen at these low elevations. After that, boastful visitors tend to stay quiet.

The White Mountains' famed network of hiking trails will test anyone's mettle. The hard granite hills of the ancient mountains of New England resist the sort of gently graded trail through the crumbly earth found so often in the American West. The White Mountains' early trailblazers were evidently a humorless lot, who found their amusement in building trails straight up sheer pitches and through tortuous boulderfields.

Despite (or perhaps because of) these trails, the White Mountains are the destination in New England for serious outdoorspeople. There's superb hiking in the summer, and fine skiing (both cross-country and downhill) in the winter. It's also a good place to test your meteorological acumen—the weather can change almost instantly on the high ridges, so backcountry explorers have to keep a sharp eye out. A pleasant afternoon picnic can turn into a harrowing and frigid experience for the unwary. Atop Mt. Washington, the region's highest peak, it's not unusual to see snow anytime of the year—midsummer flurries aren't all that uncommon.

The **Kancamagus Highway,** links Conway with Lincoln and provides some of the most spectacular White Mountain vistas in the region. Along the way, frequent roadside pull-offs and interpretive exhibits allow casual explorers to admire cascades, picnic along rivers, and enjoy sweeping mountain views. Several less-demanding nature hikes are also easily accessible from various roadside turnouts.

Keep in mind that the White Mountains are *a national forest*, not *a national park*, a distinction that's sometimes lost on urban visitors and foreign travelers. There's a big difference. National forests are managed for multiple uses, which includes timber harvesting, wildlife management, recreational development, and the like. This may disappoint those offended by clear-cutting and logging roads. Fortunately, the level of cutting is not as extensive as at many Western national forests, and the regrowth here also tends to be more rapid than in the arid

West. Also bear in mind that about 15 percent of the White Mountains is formally designated as wilderness, from which mechanical devices (including mountain bikes) are prohibited. Strike for these areas if you're looking to step deep into the wilds.

As for accommodations, it should be easy to find an area to suit your mood and inclinations. North Conway is the motel capital of the region, with hundreds of rooms, many quite charmless but often available at reasonable rates. The Loon Mountain and Waterville Valley areas have a sort of planned condo village graciousness that delights some travelers and gives others the creeps. Jackson, Franconia Notch, Crawford Notch, and the Bethlehem-Littleton area are the best destinations for old-fashioned hotels and inns.

## 1 Enjoying the Great Outdoors

The White Mountains are northern New England's undisputed outdoor-recreation capital. This cluster of ancient mountains is a sprawling, rugged playground that attracts kayakers, mountaineers, rock climbers, skiers, mountain bikers, bird-watchers, and hikers.

Especially hikers. The **White Mountain National Forest** encompasses some 773,000 acres of rocky, forested terrain, more than 100 waterfalls, dozens of remote backcountry lakes, and miles of clear brooks and cascading streams. An elaborate network of 1,200 miles of hiking trails dates back to the 19th century, when the urban gentry took to the mountains in droves to build character, build trails, and experience the raw sublimity of nature. Trails ranging from easy to extraordinarily demanding lace the hillside forests, run along remote valley rivers, and traverse barren, windswept ridgelines where the weather can change dramatically in less time than it takes to eat your lunch.

The center of the White Mountains—in spirit if not in geography—is its highest point: 6,288-foot **Mount Washington,** an ominous, brooding peak that's often cloud-capped, and often mantled with snow early and late in the season. This blustery peak is accessible by cog railroad, car, and foot, making it one of the more popular destinations in the region. You won't find wilderness here, but you will find abudant natural drama.

Flanking this colossal peak are the brawny **Presidential Mountains,** a series of wind-blasted granite peaks named after U.S. presidents and offering spectacular views. Surrounding these are numerous other rocky ridges that lure hikers looking for challenges and a place to experience nature at its most elemental.

As for **camping,** you can do it in some style by staying in shared cabins that hold several dozen overnight guests in bunk beds (sometimes stacked three high). They are situated in some of the most dramatic locations in the high mountains and are managed by the Appalachian Mountain Club. Meals are included at the huts, but the whole package is surprisingly pricey, especially for a family or group. (See below for more information.) Three-sided log lean-tos are also scattered throughout the White Mountains, providing overnight shelter for backcountry campers. Shelters are sometimes free, sometimes a backcountry manager will collect a small fee. Backcountry tent camping is free throughout the White Mountains, and no permit is needed, although you'll need to purchase a parking permit to leave your car at the trailhead. Check with one of the ranger stations for current restrictions on camping in the backcountry.

Travelers whose idea of fun doesn't involve steep cliffs or icy dips in mountain streams still have plenty of opportunity for milder adventures. A handful of major arteries provide easy access to mountain scenery. Route 302 carries travelers through

# The White Mountains & Lake Winnipesaukee

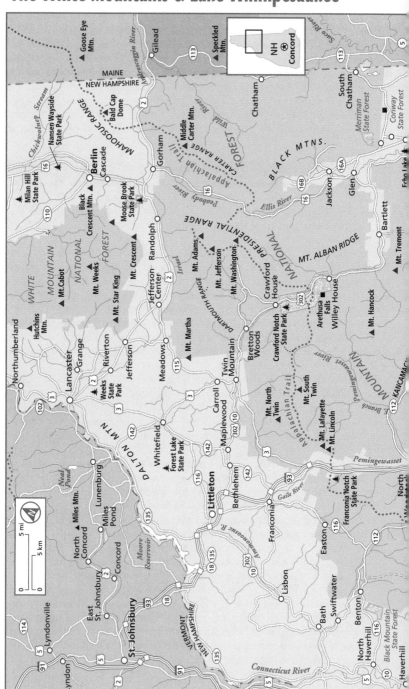

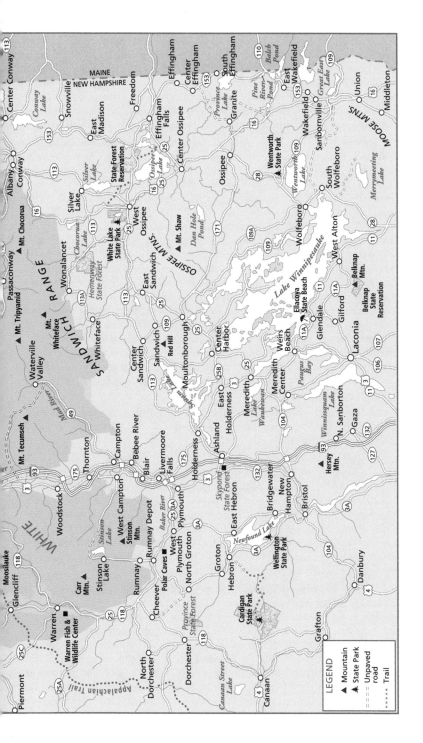

LEGEND

▲ Mountain
🔺 State Park
= = = Unpaved road
······ Trail

**205**

North Conway and Crawford Notch to the pleasant towns of Bethlehem and Littleton. Route 16 travels from southern New Hampshire through congested North Conway before twisting up dramatic Pinkham Notch at the base of Mt. Washington. Wide and fast, Route 2 skirts the northern edge of the mountains, offering wonderful views en route to the town of Jefferson. I-93 gets my vote for the most scenic interstate in northern New England, passing through spectacular Franconia Notch as it narrows to a two-lane road in deference to its natural surroundings (and local political will).

**BACKPACKING**   The White Mountains of northern New Hampshire offer some of the most challenging and scenic backpacking in the Northeast. The best trails are located within 773,000-acre White Mountain National Forest, which encompasses several 5,000-plus-foot peaks and more than 100,000 acres of designated wilderness. Trails range from easy lowland walks along bubbling streams to demanding ridgeline paths buffeted by fierce winds. The **Appalachian Mountain Club** (☎ 603/ 466-2727) is an excellent source of general information about the New Hampshire outdoors, and their huts offer shelter in eight dramatically situated cabins that offer basic shelter and a certain spartan comfort. Reservations are essential.

In addition, a number of three-sided Adirondack-style shelters are located throughout the backcountry on a first-come, first-served basis. Some are free; others have a small fee. Pitching a tent in the backcountry is free, subject to certain restrictions, and no permits are required. It's best to check with the **White Mountain National Forest** headquarters (☎ 603/528-8721) or a district ranger station (see number in White Mountains section below) for rules and regulations. The **Appalachian Trail** passes through New Hampshire, entering the state at Hanover, running along the highest peaks of the White Mountains, and exiting into Maine along the Mahoosuc Range northeast of Gorham. The trail is well-maintained, although it tends to attract teeming crowds along the highest elevations in summer.

**Rental Equipment**   Everything, including sleeping bags and pads, tents, and backpacks, is available at **Eastern Mountain Sports** (☎ 603/356-5433), in North Conway, at reasonable rates.

**BIKING**   There's some challenging road biking near Sugar Hill northeast of the White Mountains; you'll be rewarded with great vistas and charming villages.

The White Mountains have plenty of opportunities for mountain bikers; trails are open to bikers unless otherwise noted. (Bikes are not allowed in wilderness areas.) The upland roads outside of Jackson offer some superb country biking, as does the steep terrain around Franconia and Sugar Hill. **Great Glen Trails** (☎ 603/466-2333), near Mt. Washington, and **Waterville Valley Base Camp** (☎ 800/468-2553), at the southwest edge of the park, both offer bike rentals and maintained mountain-bike trails for a fee. Waterville Valley also has lift-serviced mountain biking.

**CAMPING**   Car campers shouldn't have any problem finding a place to pitch a tent or park an RV, especially in the northern half of the state. The White Mountain National Forest maintains 20 campgrounds with a total of 819 sites (no hookups), some very small and personal, others quite large and noisy. Sites tend to be fairly easy to come by midweek, but on summer or foilage weekends, you're taking a chance if you arrive without reservations. For National Forest Campground reservations, call the **National Recreation Reservation Service** (☎ 877/444-6777). Reservations may also be made via the Web at **www.reserveusa.com**, a useful and sophisticated site that allows you to read up on individual campsites (including how many feet to the nearest water faucet, and its suitability for RVs or the disabled) and reserve the exact campsite you want online.

For advance **reservations** at one of the state parks located in and around the White Mountains, call ☎ **603/271-3628** between January and May; during the summer season, call the campground directly. Some campgrounds are first-come, first-served. A list of parks and phone numbers is published in the New Hampshire Visitor's Guide, distributed widely through information centers, or by contacting the **Office of Travel and Tourism Development,** P.O. Box 1856, Concord, NH 03302 (☎ **800/ 386-4664** or 603/271-2343).

**CANOEING**    In the far north, 8,000-acre **Lake Umbagog** is home to bald eagles and loons, and is especially appealing to explore by canoe. In general, the further north you venture, the wilder and more remote the terrain.

In the north, the **Androscoggin River** offers superb Class I-II whitewater and swift flatwater upstream of Berlin; below, the river can be faintly noxious with paper-mill pollution, although it's rarely noticeable. Serious whitewater enthusiasts head to the upper reaches of the **Saco River** during spring run-off, where the Class III-IV rapids are intense if relatively short-lived along a 6¹/₂-mile stretch paralleling Route 302.

**FISHING**    See "Enjoying the Great Outdoors" in chapter 6 for details on obtaining a fishing license.

**HIKING**    The White Mountains offer 1,200 miles of trails; serious hikers will want to bypass much of the state and beeline for the Whites. The essential guide to hiking trails is the Appalachian Mountain Club's *White Mountain Guide,* which contains up-to-date and detailed descriptions of every trail in the area. The guide is available at most book- and outdoor shops in the state. See the section on the White Mountains later in this chapter for further suggestions on hikes.

**ROCK CLIMBING**    The White Mountains are renowned for their impressive, towering granite cliffs, especially Cathedral and White Horse ledges, which attract legions of rock climbers from throughout the United States and Europe. Ascents range from rather easy to extraordinarily difficult. The North Conway area hosts three climbing schools, and experienced and aspiring climbers alike have plenty of options for improving their skills. Classes range from 1 day to a week.

Contact Eastern Mountain Sports Climbing School (☎ 603/356-5433), the International Mountain Climbing School (☎ 603/356-7064), or the Mountain Guides Alliance (☎ 603/356-5310) for more information.

**SKIING**    The best ski areas in the White Mountains are Cannon Mountain, Loon Mountain, Waterville Valley, Wildcat, and Attitash Bear Peak, with vertical drops of 2,000 feet or so and featuring services one would expect of a professional ski resort.

The most impressive ski run in New Hampshire isn't served by a lift. **Tuckerman Ravine** drops 3,400 feet from a lip on the shoulder of Mt. Washington down to the valley floor. Skiers arrive from throughout the nation to venture here in the early spring (it's dangerously avalanche-prone during the depths of winter), first hiking to the top then speeding to the bottom of this dramatic glacial cirque. The slope is sheer and unforgiving; only very advanced skiers should attempt it. Careless or cocky skiers are hauled out every year on stretchers, and few years seem to go by without at least one skier's death. Contact the AMC's **Pinkham Notch Camp** (☎ **603/466-2727**) for information on current conditions.

The state boasts some 26 cross-country ski centers, which groom a combined total of more than 500 miles of trails. The state's premier cross-country destination is the **Jackson** (☎ **603/383-9355**), with 55 miles of groomed trail in and around an exceptionally scenic village in a valley near the base of Mt. Washington. Other favorites include **Bretton Woods** (☎ **800/232-2972** or 603/278-5181) at the western entrance to Crawford Notch, also with more than 50 miles of groomed trails, and the spectacularly remote **Balsams/Wilderness** cross-country ski center (☎ **800/255-0600** or 603/255-3951) in the northerly reaches of the state.

**SNOWMOBILING**    Snowmobilers will find nearly 6,000 miles of groomed, scenic snowmobile trails lacing the state, interconnected via a trail network maintained by local snowmobile clubs. All snowmobiles must be registered with the state; this costs $47 for non-residents ($37 for residents) and can be done through any of the 248 off-highway recreational-vehicle agents in the state. More information may be obtained from the **New Hampshire Snowmobile Association,** 722 Rte. 3A, Bow, NH 03304 (☎ **603/224-8906**). For current trail conditions, call 603/743-5050. On the Web, head to www.nhsa.com.

The state's most remote and spectacular destination for snowmobilers is that nubby finger that thrusts up into Canada. It also happens to be the snowiest part of the state. The **Connecticut Lakes Tourist Association** (☎ **603/538-7405**) can provide information on services and lodging in the area.

**WINTER CAMPING/MOUNTAINEERING**    The White Mountains attract experienced recreationists who test their mettle against the blustery mountain peaks. The experience is unparalleled, if you're properly equipped—the Whites are never more untrammeled or peaceful than after a heavy winter's snowfall, and there are few other times you can enjoy the crystalline views from atop the region's highest peaks without sharing the experience with dozens of others.

Guided day hikes to the top of Mt. Washington are offered throughout the winter and are suitable for people in reasonable shape with some hiking experience—no winter mountaineering experience is needed. **Eastern Mountain Sports Climbing School** (☎ **603/356-5433**) will outfit you with crampons and ice axe, and teach you their use on the lower slopes of the mountain. Many of the excursions fail to make the summit because of deteriorating weather conditions, but the experience of even being on the shoulders of wind-driven Mt. Washington is memorable nonetheless. Think of it as a low-rent trip to the Arctic.

Two of the AMC huts (Zealand Falls and Carter Notch) are kept open during the winter. Meals aren't served, but hikers need only bring food; the use of gas stoves and kitchenware is included in the rates. Heat is provided by a woodstove at night in the common room (although not in the bunkrooms, so bring a heavy-duty sleeping bag); during the day, you're free to explore these magnificent, snowy regions. Both huts require long ski or snowshoe hikes to reach them, although Zealand Falls is the less demanding of the two. There's a modest overnight fee. Contact the AMC for more information at ☎ **603/466-2727.**

## FEES & INFORMATION
### BACKCOUNTRY FEES
The White Mountain National Forest requires anyone using the backcountry—whether for hiking, mountain biking, picnicking, skiing, or any other activity—to pay a recreation fee. Anyone parking at a trailhead must display a backcountry permit on the dashboard of their car. The fees go to develop and maintain recreational facilities at the forest. Those lacking a permit face a fine. Permits are available at ranger stations and many stores in the region. Two permits are sold: an annual permit for $20 and a 7-day pass for $5. For information about the permit program, contact the **Forest Service's White Mountains office** at ☎ **603/528-8721.**

## RANGER STATIONS & INFORMATION

The Forest Service's **central White Mountains office** is at 719 Main Street in Laconia (☎ **603/528-8721**), which actually is near Lake Winnipesaukee. Your best general source of information is the **Saco Ranger Station** (☎ **603/447-5448**) in Conway; the office is at 33 Kancamagus Highway just 100 yards west of Route 16. Other district offices are: **Androscoggin Ranger Station** (☎ **603/466-2713**), 300 Glen Rd. in Gorham; **Ammonoosuc Ranger Station** (☎ **603/466-2713**) 660 Trudeau Rd. in Bethlehem; and **Pemigewasset Ranger Station** (☎ **603/536-1315**) on Route 175 in Holderness, near the Plymouth town line. The **Evans Notch Ranger Station** (☎ **207/824-2134**), which covers the Maine portion of the White Mountains (about 50,000 acres), is in Bethel at 18 Mayville Rd., off Route 2 just north of town.

Additional information and advice about recreation in the White Mountains is also available at the **AMC's Pinkham Notch Camp** (☎ **603/466-2727**) on Route 16 between Jackson and Gorham. The center is open daily from 6am to 10pm.

## SPECIALIZED GUIDEBOOKS

For serious exploration of the White Mountains, you'll need supplemental guides and maps to keep you on track. Here's a short list of recommended guides, most of which are available at area bookstores:

- *AMC White Mountain Guide* (Appalachian Mountain Club, 1998, $21.95). This comprehensive 576-page book is chock-full of detailed information on all the hiking trails in the White Mountains. It comes with a handy set of maps. This is the definitive hiker's bible for the region.
- *50 Hikes in the White Mountains* (Backcountry Publications, 1997, $14.95). The fifth edition of this popular guide, written by Daniel Doan and Ruth Doan MacDougall, offers a good selection of mountain rambles in the high peaks region around Mt. Washington. You'll find everything from easy strolls to overnight backpack trips.
- *Ponds & Lakes of the White Mountains* (Backcountry Publications, 1998, $16). The White Mountain high country is studded with dramatic tarns (many left by retreating glaciers). This 350-page guide by Steven D. Smith offers 68 trips to help get you there.
- *Waterfalls of the White Mountains* (Backcountry Publications, 1999, $18). Waterfall lovers will get their money's worth from Bruce and Doreen Bolnick's guide to 100 mountain waterfalls, including roadside cascades and backcountry cataracts.

# Suggested Itineraries

### If You Have 1 Day

Head to Franconia Notch State Park on the west side of the White Mountains. Visit the Flume, take a tram ride to the tip of Cannon Mountain, enjoy roadside views of the Old Man of the Mountain, and enjoy a walk or bike ride along Echo Lake. You'll get a good introduction to the drama of the White Mountains without a lot of scurrying from place to place.

### If You Have 2 Days

**Day 1** Start at the town of Lincoln at Exit 32 of I-93, and drive to North Conway via the scenic Kancamagus Highway. Allow a few brief shopping forays in town, and savor the views of the Mt. Washington Valley. Head to the village of Jackson for lunch and secure accommodations for the night. Spend the rest of the afternoon relaxing at Jackson Falls, hiking area trails, or exploring by car or bike up Carter Notch Road and the other scenic backroads in the hills above the village.

**Day 2**    Retrace your path down Route 16 back to Route 302, turn right and drive through Crawford Notch. If weather and time allows, hike to one of the scenic water-falls. (See Crawford Notch section, below.) Go to the Mt. Washington Cog Railway on the far side of the Notch. Take the train ride to the summit of Mt. Washington (dress warmly). Upon your return, stop by the grand Mt. Washington Hotel for a celebratory snack. Continue west on Route 302 until reaching Route 3. Turn left (south) to I-93. Continue southward through scenic Franconia Notch, and tour the attractions as time allows.

### If You Have 3 Days

**Day 1**    See Day 1 of the 2-day itinerary above.

**Day 2**    Spend the day exploring by foot around Pinkham Notch. Stop at Glen Ellis Falls en route to the base of Mt. Washington. Park at Pinkham Notch and hike to dramatic Tuckerman's Ravine for a picnic lunch. Return to your car and continue north to Wildcat Ski Area. Take the chairlift to the summit for spectacular views of Mt. Washington, the Presidentials, and the Carter Range. Return to Jackson for the night.

**Day 3**    See Day 2 of the 2-day itinerary above.

## 2  North Conway & Environs

North Conway is 150 miles north of Boston and 62 miles northwest of Portland

North Conway is the commercial heart of the White Mountains. Shoppers adore it because of the profusion of outlets, boutiques, and restaurants along routes 302 and 16. (The two state highways overlap through town.) Outdoor purists abhor it, considering it a garish interloper to be avoided at all costs, except when seeking pizza and beer.

No doubt, North Conway itself won't strike anyone as nature's wonderland. The shopping strip south of the village is basically one long turning lane flanked with outlet malls, motels, and chain restaurants of every architectural stripe. On rainy weekends and during the foliage season, the road can resemble a linear parking lot.

The sprawl notwithstanding, North Conway is beautifully situated along the eastern edge of the broad and fertile Saco River Valley (often called the Mt. Washington Valley by local tourism boosters). Gentle, forest-covered mountains, some with sheer cliffs that suggest the distant, stunted cousins of Yosemite's rocky faces, border the bottomlands. Northward up the valley, the hills rise in a triumphant crescendo to the blustery, tempestuous heights of Mt. Washington.

The village itself is trim and attractive (if often congested), with an open green, quaint shops, Victorian frontier-town commercial architecture, and a distinctive train station. It's a good place to park, stretch your legs, and find a cup of coffee or a snack. (*Hint:* There's a Ben & Jerry's off the green near the train station.)

Visitors who'd prefer a more scenic, less commercial route bypassing North Conway's strip malls should detour to **West Side Road.** Arriving from the south on Route 16, turn north at the light in Conway Village on to Washington Street. One-half mile further, bear left on West Side Road. The road passes near two covered bridges in the first $^1/_2$ mile, then dips and winds through the broad farmlands of the Saco River Valley. You'll pass working farms and farm stands, and some architecturally distinctive early homes.

You'll also come upon dramatic views of the granite cliffs that form the western wall of the valley. Stop for a swim at **Echo Lake State Park** (it's well-marked, on your left).

At the first stop sign, turn right for North Conway village, or turn left to connect to Route 302 in Bartlett, passing more handsome ledges and cliffs.

## ESSENTIALS

**GETTING THERE**   North Conway and the Mt. Washington Valley are on Route 16 and Route 302. Route 16 connects to the Spaulding Turnpike, which intersects with I-95 outside of Portsmouth, New Hampshire. Route 302 begins in Portland, Maine.

Do not underestimate how vexing the traffic can be in the Mt. Washington Valley during peak visiting times, including holiday weekends in summer and foliage weekends in fall. I've seen traffic backups of several miles, which do little to help one appreciate the surroundings. Try valiantly to plan around these busy times in order to preserve your own sanity.

**VISITOR INFORMATION**   The **Mount Washington Valley Chamber of Commerce,** P.O. Box 2300, North Conway, NH 03860 (☎ **800/367-3364** or 603/ 356-3171), operates a seasonal information booth opposite the village green with brochures about attractions and inns. The staff can arrange for local accommodations. It's open daily in summer 9am to 6pm. In winter, it's open weekends only. Information is also available on the Web at www.4seasonresort.com.

The state of New Hampshire also operates an information booth with rest rooms and telephones at a vista with fine views of Mt. Washington on Routes 16 and 302 north of North Conway.

## RIDING THE RAILS

The **Conway Scenic Railroad** (☎ **800/232-5251** or 603/356-5251; www. conwayscenic.com) offers regularly scheduled trips in comfortable cars pulled by either steam or sleek early diesel engines. Trips depart from a distinctive 1874 train station just off the village green, recalling an era when tourists arrived from Boston and New York to enjoy the country air for a month or two each summer. The 1-hour excursion heads south to Conway; the more scenic 1³/₄-hour trip heads north to the village of Bartlett. For a real show, sign up for the 5¹/₂-hour excursion through dramatic Crawford Notch, with stupendous views of the mountains from high along this beautiful glacial valley. You even get a great view of the remarkable Mt. Washington Hotel. Ask also about the railway's dining excursions ($20.95 to $42.95 including lunch or dinner).

The train runs mid-April to mid-December, with more frequent trips scheduled daily in midsummer. Coach and first-class fares are available; first-class passengers sit in "Gertrude Emma," an 1898 parlor car with wicker and rataan chairs, mahogany woodwork, and an observation platform. Tickets are $8.50 to $17.50 for adults ($31 to $42 for the Crawford Notch trip), $6 to $12.50 for children 4 to 12 ($16 to $27 for Crawford Notch). Kids under 4 ride free on the two shorter trips; there's a charge on the Crawford Notch trip. Reservations are accepted for the dining car and the Crawford Notch train.

## ROCK CLIMBING

The impressive granite faces on the valley's west side are for more than admiring from afar—they're also for climbing. **Cathedral Ledge** and **Whitehorse Ledge** attract rock climbers from all over the Eastern seaboard who consider these cliffs (along with the Shawangunks in New York State and Seneca Rocks in West Virginia) as sort of an eastern troika where they can put their grace and technical acumen to the test.

Experienced climbers will have their own sources of information on the best access and routes. Inexperienced climbers should sign up for a class taught by one of the local outfitters, whose workshops run from 1 day to 1 week. Try the **Eastern Mountain Sports Climbing School** (☎ 603/356-5433), the **International Mountain Climbing School** (☎ 603/356-7064), or the **Mountain Guides Alliance** (☎ 603/356-5310).

To tone up or keep in shape on rainy days, the **Cranmore Sports Center** (☎ 603/356-6301) near the Mt. Cranmore base lodge has an indoor climbing wall open weekdays 5 to 9pm and weekends 2 to 8pm. The fee is $14 Monday to Friday, and $16 on weekends. Newcomers must pass a belay test (free) before climbing; if their skills aren't up to snuff, they'll be asked to take a lesson. Private, semiprivate, and group lessons are available.

## SKIING

**Cranmore Mountain Resort.** North Conway Village, NH 03860. ☎ **603/356-5544.** www.cranmore.com. E-mail: info@cranmore.com. Vertical drop: 1,200 ft. Lifts: 7 chairlifts (1 high-speed quad), 2 surface lifts. Skiable acreage: 192. Lift tickets: $29 all week.

Mt. Cranmore is sort of within walking distance of the village of North Conway, although it's far enough that you wouldn't want to try it in ski boots. The oldest operating ski area in New England, Mt. Cranmore is unrepentantly old-fashioned and doesn't display an iota of pretense. It's not likely to challenge advanced skiers, but it will delight beginners and intermediates, as well as those who like the old-style New England cut of the trails. It's very popular with families, thanks to both the relaxed attitude and budget ticket prices (kids 6 to 12 are $15 anytime).

## WHERE TO STAY

Route 16 through North Conway is packed with basic motels, reasonably priced in the off-season (around $40 to $60), but more expensive in peak travel times such as summer and ski-season weekends and fall foliage season. Fronting the commercial strip, these motels don't offer much in the way of a pastoral environment, but most are comfortable and conveniently located. Try the budget **School House Motel** (☎ 603/356-6829), with a heated outdoor pool; **The Yankee Clipper Motor Lodge** (☎ 800/343-5900 or 603/356-5736), with a pool and miniature golf (the cheaper rooms lack phones); or the slightly pricier **Green Granite Inn** (☎ 800/468-3666 or 603/356-6901), with 88 rooms, whirlpool suites, and a free continental breakfast.

**Albert B. Lester Memorial Hostel.** 36 Washington St., Conway, NH 03818. ☎ **800/909-4776** ext. 51 or 603/447-1001. Fax 603/447-3346. www.angel.net/~hostel. E-mail: hiconway@nxi.com. 45 beds. $16 per person, $45 for family rooms. Rates include continental breakfast. JCB, MC, V. Closed Nov 1–30. Turn north on Washington St. at the light in Conway; it's the 2nd house on the left.

Conveniently situated near the center of Conway Village, the Lester Hostel is the best choice for those traveling on a shoestring but not enamored of camping. Rooms in this gracious black and white farmhouse are set up hostel-style and accommodate 45 people (some private family rooms are available). Not only will you save money here, but the congenial atmosphere offers a great way to swap tips on area trails and bike rides with newfound friends. You can borrow a bike or repair your own in the bike repair room. Music and impromptu performances are staged periodically at the new amphitheater, made of straw bales and packed earth. The hostel is open for check-in or check-out daily from 7:30 to 9:30am and 5 to 10pm.

**Cranmore Inn.** 80 Kearsarge St., North Conway, NH 03860. ☎ **800/526-5502** or 603/356-5502. www.cranmoreinn.com. E-mail: cranmore@cranmoreinn.com. 18 units, 3 with private hall bathrooms. TEL. Foliage season and ski weekends $86–$128 double; summer $64–$88 double; off-season $59–$88 double. Rates include full breakfast. 2-night minimum weekends, holidays, and foliage season. AE, MC, V.

The Cranmore Inn has the feel of a 19th-century boarding house—which is appropriate, since that's what it is. Open since 1863, this three-story Victorian home is hidden on a side street a short walk from North Conway's village center. Its distinguished heritage—it's the oldest continuously operating hotel in North Conway—adds considerable charm and quirkiness, but comes with some minor drawbacks, like uneven water pressure in the showers and some sinks with cracked or stained enamel. That said, I'd return here in a second because of its charm, its good value, and the gracious hospitality of the innkeepers. There's also a heated outdoor pool in summer to cool off after a day of hiking.

**The Forest Country Inn.** Rte. 16A (P.O. Box 37), Intervale, NH 03845. ☎ **800/448-3534** or 603/356-9772. Fax 603/356-5652. www.forest-inn.com. E-mail: forest@ncia.net. 11 units, 1 with detached bathroom. A/C TEL. July–Oct and mid-Dec to Mar $95–$140 double ($20 surcharge in foliage season); off-season $80–$120. Rates include full breakfast. AE, DISC, MC, V. Children 6 and older welcome. Closed Apr.

Ten minute's drive north of North Conway is a spur road that leads through the village of Intervale, which has several lodges and a feeling quite removed from the clutter of the outlet shops. The Forest was built in 1850, with a mansard-roofed third floor added in 1890 when it became an inn. Typical for the era, the rooms are more cozy than spacious, and today are decorated mostly with reproductions and a smattering of country Victorian antiques. (Room #4 is a bit larger than most of the standard rooms.) The best rooms are the two in the nearby stone cottage, which early in the 1900s housed the offices of one of the first female lawyers to practice hereabouts. Ask for the Cottle Room, with its wood-burning fireplace, wing chairs, and small porch with Adirondack chairs. The common areas include a glass-front porch with both wicker and plastic furniture, and another room with a small TV and two chairs. There's a small pool and 25 acres to explore out back.

**Four Points Hotel.** Rte. 16 at Settler's Green (P.O. Box 3189), North Conway, NH 03860. ☎ **800/648-4397** or 603/356-9300. 200 units. A/C TV TEL. Summer $89–$179 double; off-season $69–$149. AE, CB, DC, DISC, MC, V.

If you're looking for convenience, modern amenities, and easy access to outlet shopping, this Sheraton-run hotel is your best bet. Built on the site of North Conway's old airfield, the Four Points is a four-story, gabled hotel adjacent (and architecturally similar) to Outlet Village Plus, one of the two or three million outlet centers based in North Conway. The Four Points offers clean, comfortable, basic hotel rooms with amenities including HBO, coffeemakers, hair dryers, irons and ironing boards, and data ports.

**Amenities:** Guests have access to an attractive brick-terraced indoor pool and Jacuzzi. Other extras include tennis courts, an outdoor pool, a fitness room, game room, Laundromat, safe-deposit boxes, and a basic restaurant and tavern.

**Stonehurst Manor.** Rte. 16 (1.2 miles north of N. Conway Village; P.O. Box 1937), North Conway, NH 03860. ☎ **800/525-9100.** Fax 603/356-3217. www.stonehurstmanor.com. E-mail: smanor@aol.com. 24 units, 2 with shared bathroom. A/C TV. $80–$140 double ($20–$30 surcharge during foliage season); $106–$166 double with breakfast and dinner included. 2-night minimum on weekends. AE, MC, V. Pets accepted; $25 extra.

This imposing, architecturally eclectic Victorian stone-and-shingle mansion, originally built for the family that owned Bigelow carpet, is set amid white pines on a rocky knoll above Route 16 one mile north of North Conway village. Oddly, it wouldn't seem at all out of place in either the south of France or the moors of Scotland. One's immediate assumption is that it caters to the stuffy and affluent, but the main focus here is on outdoor-adventure vacations, and it attracts a youngish crowd. My advice is to request one of the 14 rooms in the regal 1876 mansion itself (another 10 are in a comfortable but less elegant wing built in 1952). These mansion rooms are all individually furnished appropriately to the building's era.

**Dining:** See "Where to Dine," below.

**Amenities:** Outdoor pool, Jacuzzi, tennis court, and nature trails.

**White Mountain Hotel and Resort.** West Side Rd. (5.4 miles west of N. Conway; P.O. Box 1828), North Conway, NH 03860. ☎ **800/533-6301** or 603/356-7100. Fax 603/356-7100. www.whitemountainhotel.com. E-mail: infor@whitemountainhotel.com. 80 units. A/C TV TEL. Summer $129–$219 double; foliage season $149–$219 double; winter $79–$159 double; other times $59–$119 double. 2-night minimum on weekends. AE, DISC, MC, V.

This modern resort has the best location of any lodge in North Conway. Sited at the base of dramatic White Horse Ledge near Echo Lake State Park and amid a contemporary golf-course community, the White Mountain Hotel was built in 1990 but borrows from the rich legacy of classic White Mountain resorts. Its designers have managed to take some of the more successful elements of a friendly country inn—a nice deck with a view, comfortable seating in the lobby, a clubby tavern area—and incorporate them into a thoroughly contemporary resort. Guest rooms are comfortably appointed with dark wood and an earthy maroon carpeting, and are a solid notch or two above standard hotel furnishings. All have hair dryers, coffeemakers, and irons and ironing boards.

**Dining:** The pleasant Ledges Dining Room offers mountain panoramas through tall windows. Entrees include veal Oscar, shrimp stuffed with crabmeat, and charbroiled steaks, priced from $14.95 to $19.95.

**Amenities:** Nine-hole golf course, two tennis courts, game room, year-round outdoor heated pool, Jacuzzi, sauna, fitness center, nature trails, conference rooms, self-service Laundromat, limited room service, dry cleaning, laundry service, and baby-sitting.

## WHERE TO DINE

**Bellini's.** 33 Seavey St., North Conway. ☎ **603/356-7000.** www.bellinis.com. Reservations not accepted. Main courses $11–$20. AE, CB, DC, DISC, MC, V. Sun–Mon and Wed–Thurs 5–10pm; Fri–Sat 5–11pm. COUNTRY ITALIAN.

Bellini's has a fun, quirky interior that's more informal than its Victorian exterior might suggest. Inside it features Cinzano umbrellas and striped awnings, vintage Italian posters, black-and-white-checkerboard floors, and huge potted plants—it's the kind of place to put you in a good mood right off. It's run by the third generation of the Marcello family, who opened their first place in Rhode Island in 1927. (They call it Bellini's because North Conway alread had a Marcello's restaurant, run by an entirely unrelated family.) The food runs the Italian gamut from fettuccine chicken pesto to braciola, and most everything is homemade—soups, breads, pastas, and desserts. Particularly good are the toasted raviolis. There's a fine selection of beverages—you can order fresh-squeezed juices, concoctions from the espresso or martini bar, or wine from a limited but inviting list. One drink gives pause: the trademarked "espresso martini," served in a chocolate dipped martini glass.

**Shalimar of India.** 27 Seavey St., North Conway. ☎ **603/356-0123.** Reservations recommended in peak summer and winter seasons. Main courses lunch $5.25–$6.25, dinner $7.95–$15.95. DISC, MC, V. Sun noon–3pm and 5–10pm, Mon 5–10pm, Tues–Thurs 11am–2:30pm and 5–10pm, Fri 11am–2:30pm and 5–10:30pm, Sat noon–3pm and 5–10:30pm. NORTHERN INDIAN.

Shalimar is a pleasant surprise in a town where adventurous ethnic cuisine once meant "nachos fully loaded." Run by the same family who runs a restaurant of the same name in Portland, Maine, Shalimar offers a wide variety of tasty, tangy dishes of northern India. The meals are wonderfully prepared, and the chef is very accommodating to ensure just the right level of spice for your palate. The restaurant, located a short walk from the village green, offers several tandoori dishes, and a wonderfully tangy lamb vindaloo.

**Stonehurst Manor.** Rte. 16 (1.2 miles north of the village), North Conway. ☎ **800/ 525-9100** or 603/356-3113. Reservations recommended. Main courses $14.75–$21.75; pizza $9.95–$12.95. MC, V. Daily 6–10pm. AMERICAN/PIZZA.

The restaurant added wood-fired pizza to the menu when the owners noticed that inn guests arriving late on Friday nights from Boston didn't feel up to a full meal. So they started making pizza in a number of surprising variations (chicken sausage and wild mushrooms; grilled vegetables), and the word spread. Stonehurst's pizza has become a local institution, complementing the other dishes served here. Diners have a choice of four dining areas on the first floor of this 1876 mansion, and each area is decorated informally and comfortably. (The deep, overly low rattan chairs may have outlived their charm, however.) In addition to pizza, the chef serves up a raft of other hearty dishes, including wood-oven baked lobster stuffed with scallops and shrimp, and grilled buffalo steak topped with goose liver.

## SHOPPING

North Conway is one of northern New England's major outlet centers, with 200-plus shops located along its strip, which extends about 3 miles northward from the junction of Route 302 and Route 16 in Conway into to the village of North Conway itself. It's a town planner's nightmare, but a shopper's paradise.

Among the more notable outlet clusters are **Outlet Village Plus** at Settler's Green, with more than than 30 name-brand shops, including GAP, Van Heusen, Haggar, and Foreside; the **Tanger Factory Outlet,** which hosts the popular L.L. Bean factory outlet and several others; and **Willow Place,** with 11 shops like Dress Barn, Bed & Bath, and the Lingerie Factory. Other outlets scattered along the strip include Anne Klein, American Tourister, Izod, Dansk, Donna Karan, Levi's, Polo/Ralph Lauren, Reebock/Rockport, J. Crew, and Eddie Bauer. **Chuck Roast Mountainwear** (☎ **603/356-5589**), a North Conway–based manufacturer of outerwear, backpacks, and soft luggage, has a shop at the Mount Washington Outlet Center, the plaza next door to the L.L. Bean outlet.

For those setting out on a White Mountain expedition, outdoor equipment suppliers in town include **International Mountain Equipment** (☎ **603/356-7013**) and **Eastern Mountain Sports** (☎ **603/356-5433**), both on Main Street just north of the green. There's also **Ragged Mountain Equipment** (☎ **603/356-3042**), 3 miles north of town in Intervale on Routes 16 and 302.

## 3 Jackson & Environs

Jackson is 8 miles north of North Conway

Jackson is like an eddy swirling gently on its own out of the flow of the tourist mainstream. Situated in a picturesque valley just off Route 16 about a 15-minute drive north of North Conway, Jackson still attracts plenty of travelers, but the rich history is strong enough here to absorb much of the tourist impact.

You enter Jackson, somewhat tentatively, on a single-lane covered bridge. The village center is tiny, but touches of old-world elegance remain here and there—vestiges of a time when Jackson was a favored destination for the East Coast upper middle class, who fled the summer heat in the cities to board at rambling wooden hotels or relax at shingled country homes.

With the Great Depression and the subsequent rise of the motel trade in the 1940s and 1950s, Jackson and its old-fashioned hostelries slipped into a long slumber. Then along came the 1980s, which brought developers in private helicopters, condo projects sprouting in fields where cows once roamed, vacation homes flanking the hills, and the resuscitation of the two vintage wooden hotels that didn't burn or collapse during the dark ages.

Thanks to a rebuilt golf course and one of the most elaborate and well-maintained cross-country ski networks in the country, Jackson is today again a thriving resort, both summer and winter. While no longer undiscoverd, it still feels out of the mainstream and is a peaceful spot, especially when compared to commercial North Conway. Settle into one of the old summer homes converted to an inn, park yourself on a rocker on a porch, and you'll suspect that not all that much has changed in the intervening century.

## ESSENTIALS

**GETTING THERE**    Jackson is just off Route 16 about 11 miles north of North Conway. Look for the covered bridge on the right when heading north.

**VISITOR INFORMATION**    The **Jackson Chamber of Commerce,** P.O. Box 304, Jackson, NH 03846 (☎ **800/866-3334** or 603/383-9356), can answer your questions about area attractions or make lodging reservations for you. On the Web, point your browser to www.jacksonnh.com.

## EXPLORING MOUNT WASHINGTON

Mount Washington, located just north of Jackson in the national forest, is home to numerous superlatives. At 6,288 feet, it's the highest mountain in the Northeast. (Mt. Mitchell in North Carolina is slightly higher, robbing Mt. Washington of the "highest in the East" title.) It's said to have the worst weather in the world outside of the polar regions. It holds the world's record for the highest surface windspeed ever recorded—231 m.p.h. in 1934. Winds over 150 m.p.h. are routinely recorded every month except June, July, and August, due in part to the mountain's location at the confluence of three major storm tracks.

Mt. Washington may also be the mountain with the most options for getting to the summit. Visitors can ascend by cog railroad (see the "Crawford Notch" section, below), by car, by guide-driven van, or by foot. There's an annual bike race and foot race to the summit, and each year, winter mountaineers test their mettle by inching their way to the top outfitted with crampons and ice axes.

Despite the raw power of the weather, the summit of Mt. Washington is not the best destination for those seeking wild and untamed wilderness. There's a train platform, a parking lot, a snack bar, a gift shop, a museum, and a handful of outbuildings, some of which house the weather observatory, which is staffed year-round, and there are the crowds, which can be thick on a clear day. Then again, on a clear day the views can't be beat, with vistas extending into four states and to the Atlantic Ocean.

The best place to learn about Mt. Washington and its approaches is the rustic **Pinkham Notch Camp** (☎ **603/466-2721**), operated by the Boston-based Appalachian Mountain Club. Located at the crest of Route 16 between Jackson and Gorham, Pinkham Notch offers overnight accommodations and meals (see below), maps, a limited selection of outdoor supplies, and plenty of advice from the helpful staff. A number of hiking trails depart from Pinkham Notch, allowing for several loops and side trips.

About a dozen trails lead to the mountain's summit, ranging in length from 3.8 to 15 miles. (Detailed information is available at Pinkham Notch Camp.) The most direct and, in many ways, most dramatic trail is the Tuckerman Ravine Trail, which departs from Pinkham Notch. It's a full day's endeavor: Healthy hikers should allow 4 to 5 hours for the ascent, an hour or two less for the return trip. Be sure to allow enough time to enjoy the dramatic glacial cirque of Tuckerman Ravine, which attracts extreme skiers to its snowy chutes and sheer drops as late as June, and often holds patches of snow well into summer.

The **Mount Washington Auto Road** (☎ 603/466-3988) opened in 1861 as a carriage road, and has since remained one of the most popular White Mountain attractions. The steep, winding 8-mile road (it has an average grade of 12%) is partially paved and incredibly dramatic; your breath will be taken away at one curve after another. The ascent will test your iron will; the descent will test your car's brakes.

If you'd prefer to leave the driving to someone else, custom vans ascend throughout the day, allowing you to relax, enjoy the views, learn about the mountain from informed guides, and leave the fretting about overheating brakes to someone else.

The Auto Road, which is on Route 16 north of Pinkham Notch, is open mid-May to late October from 7:30am to 6pm (more limited hours early and late in the season). The cost for cars is $16 for vehicle and driver, and $6 for each additional adult ($4 for children 5 to 12). The fee includes an audiocassette featuring narration pointing out sights along the way (available in English, French, and German). The management has imposed some curious restrictions on automobiles; for instance, Acuras and Jaguars with automatic transmissions must show a "1" on the shifter to be allowed on the road, Saturns with automatic transmissions are limited to 300 lbs. capacity (passengers and luggage), and no Lincoln Continentals from before 1969 are permitted.

Van tours are $20 for adults, $10 for children 5 to 12, including a half-hour stay on the summit. More information is available on the Web at www.mt-washington.com.

One additional note: The average temperature atop the mountain is 30°F. (The record low was –43°F, and the warmest temperature ever recorded atop the mountain, in August, was 72°.) Even in summer, visitors should come prepared for blustery, cold conditions.

If you'd prefer to observe Mt. Washington from a safe and respectful distance, head up **Wildcat Mountain** (☎ 800/255-6439 or 603/466-3326) on the enclosed gondola for a superb view of Tuckerman Ravine and Mt. Washington's summit. The lift operates weekends from Memorial Day to mid-June, then daily through October. The base lodge is located just north of Pinkham Notch on Route 16.

## CROSS-COUNTRY SKIING

Jackson regularly makes rankings in the top five cross-country ski resorts in the nation. The reason for that: the non-profit **Jackson Ski Touring Foundation** (☎ 603/383-9355), which created and now maintains the extensive trail network. The terrain around Jackson is wonderfully varied, with 93 miles of trails maintained by the foundation (56 miles are regularly groomed).

Start at the foundation headquarters in the center of Jackson, located near the Wentworth Resort. There's parking right there, and you can ski from here through the village and into the hills. Gentle trails traverse the valley floor, with more advanced trails winding up the flanking mountains. One-way ski trips with shuttles back to Jackson are also available; ask if you're interested. Given how extensive and well-maintained the trails are, passes are a good value at $12 Saturdays and holidays, $10 all other days. Ski rentals are available in the ski center ($16 per day). Ask about packages. More information is available on the Web at www.jacksonxc.com.

## DOWNHILL SKIING

**Black Mountain.** Jackson, NH 03846. ☎ **800/698-4490** or 603/383-4490. www.blackmt. com. Vertical drop: 1,100 ft. Lifts: 2 chairlifts, 2 surface lifts. Skiable acreage: 132. Lift tickets: $32 weekends, $20 weekdays.

Dating back to the 1930s, Black Mountain is one of the White Mountains' pioneer ski areas. It remains the quintessential family mountain—modest in size, thoroughly non-threatening, and ideal for beginners. (The newest trail is Sweet Dreams, which offers novices a peacefully rolling descent though a lovely forest.) The mountain offers some great views of Mt. Washington from the top to boot. It feels a bit like you're skiing in a farmer's unused hayfield, which just adds to the charm. The mountain claims to have the first overhead lift in the country—the original lift featured shovel handles passing by on a cable, which skiers grabbed hold of. The ski area offers two compact terrain parks for snowboarders.

**Wildcat.** Rte. 16, Pinkham Notch, NH 03846. ☎ **800/255-6439** or 603/466-3326. www.skiwildcat.com. Vertical drop: 2,100 ft. Lifts: 1 gondola, 1 detachable high-speed quad, 4 chairlifts. Skiable acreage: 225. Lift tickets: $49 weekends and holidays, $39 weekdays.

Wildcat Mountain has a rich heritage as a venerable New England ski mountain. It also happens to offer the best mountain views of any ski area in the Whites. Situated on national forest land just across the valley from Mount Washington and Tuckerman Ravine, Wildcat has strong intermediate trails and some challenging expert slopes. This is skiing as it used to be—there's no base-area clutter, just a simple ski lodge. While that also means there's no on-slope accommodations, you've got an abundance of choices within a 15-minute drive. Also ask about the occasional midweek specials (such as two-for-one tickets) that can bring down the cost of the lift tickets.

## OTHER OUTDOOR PURSUITS

The Jackson area offers an abundance of outdoor activities. In addition to exploring around Mt. Washington, hiking opportunities abound in the Carter Range to the north and on the various peaks surrounding Mt. Washington. Space here doesn't permit even a brief inventory of trails. Consult the AMC White Mountain Guide, or ask for advice from your innkeeper or at Pinkham Notch Camp.

One suggested 4-hour (round-trip) hike offering a wonderful view is to the top of **Doublehead.** The hike departs from a trailhead located 2.9 miles east of Jackson on Dundee Road (look for the sign). It's unrelentingly uphill and quite demanding on legs and lungs. Views of the Presidential Range may be had from scattered ledges off the summits of both North and South Doublehead; it's a prime place to weigh more ambitious hiking options.

North of the village is **Great Glen Trails** (☎ 603/466-2333), near the Mt. Washington Auto Road entrance. Hiking and mountain biking is offered on their scenic, carriage path-like trails near the base of Mt. Washington. Walking is free (donations are encouraged); a full-day bike pass is $7. Mountain-bike rentals are $20 for a half day, $30 full day, and include a helmet and bike pass.

Golfers can tee up at the scenic **Wentworth Golf Resort** (☎ 603/383-9126), whose fairways and greens wind their way in and around the village of Jackson. The 17th hole even includes a covered bridge. Golf is also available in the pastoral upland valley spread out before the **Eagle Mountain House** (☎ 603/363-9111), a short drive from Jackson up beautiful Carter Notch Road.

Those less afflicted with ambition will enjoy an agreeable day at **Jackson Falls,** along Carter Notch Road just up the hill from the Wentworth Resort. A series of cataracts tumble down the rocky hillside, forming pools here and there that are custom-made for chilling out on warm afternoons. Bring a book and a picnic, and while away a few peaceful hours.

## KID STUFF

Parents with young children who find majestic mountains about as interesting as watching C-Span can buy peace of mind at two area attractions. **StoryLand,** at the northern junction of Routes 16 and 302 (☎ **603/383-4293**), is filled with 30 acres of improbably leaning buildings, magical rides, fairy-tale creatures, and other enchanted beings. Kids can take a ride in a Pumpkin Coach, float in a swan boat, ride the watery Bamboo Chute, wander through a Dutch village, or spin on an antique carousel. A "sprayground" features a 40-foot water-spurting octopus—if they're so inclined, kids can get a good summer soaking. From Memorial Day to mid-June, StoryLand is open weekends only 10am to 5pm; mid-June to Labor Day open daily from 9am to 6pm; and Labor Day to Columbus Day weekends only from 10am to 5pm. Admission, which includes all rides and entertainment, is $18 for all visitors over 4 years old.

Next door is **Heritage New Hampshire** (☎ **603/383-9776**), which endeavors to make state history easily digestible for both adults and kids. It's an indoor theme park in a Georgian-style building with a theme of old-time New Hampshire. Visitors learn about the famous Concord Coach and hear prominent politician Daniel Webster discourse about his life and times. The attraction is open daily mid-May to mid-October from 9am until 5pm. Admission is $10 for adults, $4.50 for children 6 to 12, and free for children under 6.

## WHERE TO STAY & DINE

**Eagle Mountain House.** Carter Notch Rd., Jackson, NH 03846. ☎ **800/966-5779** or 603/383-9111. Fax 603/383-0854. www.eaglemt.com. E-mail: reservations@eaglemt.com. 93 units. TV TEL. Summer $99–$149 double, $139–$179 suite. Winter $69–$129 double, $109–$159 suite. Ask about package plans. AE, CB, DC, DISC, MC, V.

The Eagle Mountain House is a fine and handsome relic that happily survived the ravages of time, fire, and the capricious tastes of tourists. Built in 1916 and fully renovated in the 1980s, this five-story gleaming, white wooden classic is set in an idyllic valley above the village of Jackson. The lobby is rich with earth tones, polished brass, and oak accenting. The guest rooms, set off wonderfully wide and creaky hallways, are furnished with a country pine look and feature stenciled blanket chests, pine armoires, and feather comforters. There's a premium for rooms with mountain views, but it's not really worth the extra cash. Just plan to spend your free time lounging on the wide porch with the views across the golf course toward the mountains beyond.

**Dining:** There's a handsome oak tavern off the lodge for light snacks. The spacious, formal Highfields dining room seats about 150 guests and provokes a distinct "well-here-we-are!" sense of glee when one first settles in for dinner under the high ceilings. The menu features updated New England classics, with offerings like rainbow trout in cornbread crumbs, topped with crabmeat. Entrees are $13.95 to $20.95.

**Amenities:** Nine-hole golf course, two tennis courts (one lit for night play), outdoor pool (summer), small health club, game room, conference rooms, dry cleaning, and safe-deposit boxes.

✪ **Inn at Thorn Hill.** Thorn Hill Rd. (P.O. Box A), Jackson, NH 03846. ☎ **603/383-4242.** www.innatthornhill.com. E-mail: thornhll@ncia.net. 19 units including 3 cottages. A/C TEL. $190–$300 double off-season; foliage season and Christmas $225–$345 double; cottages $275–$300. Rates include breakfast and dinner. 2-night minimum on weekends, 3 nights some holidays. AE, DISC, MC, V. Children 10 and older are welcome.

This is a truly elegant inn. The classic shingle-style home was designed by scandal-plagued architect Stanford White in 1895 (alas, it is now swathed in yellow siding). The Inn at Thorn Hill is just outside of the village center, surrounded by wooded hills that seem to greet it in a warm embrace. Inside, there's a comfortable Victorian feel, although mercifully sparing on the frilly stuff. The two sitting parlors are well-designed for lounging; cookies and tea are served here in the afternoon. There's also a TV room with jigsaw puzzles and a decent selection of books on the shelves. The hospitality is warm and top-notch. Three of the guest rooms have gas fireplaces.

**Dining:** The dining room, which is open to the non-guests, is decorated in what might be called Victorian great-aunt style, with rich green carpeting, press-backed oak chairs, and pink tablecloths. It's one of the best in New Hampshire and serves "New England fusion." The menu changes to reflect the availability of choice fresh ingredients, but you're likely to find entrees ($19.95 to $25.95) like pan-roasted chicken garnished with braised lobster and a black truffle sauce, or cornmeal-crusted salmon with a crab-meat cream sauce.

**Amenities:** Outdoor pool, hot tub, sundeck, nature trails, conference rooms, baby-sitting, laundry service, turndown service, free videos, afternoon tea, and room service (mornings and evenings only).

**Joe Dodge Lodge at Pinkham Notch.** Rte. 16, Pinkham Notch, N.H. (Mailing address: AMC, P.O. Box 298, Gorham, NH 03581). ☎ 603/466-2727. www.outdoors.org. 108 beds in bunk rooms of 2, 3, and 4 beds. All with shared bathroom. Peak season $49 per adult, $33 per child (discount for AMC members); off-peak $46 and $30. Rates include breakfast and dinner. MC, V. Children should be at least 3 years old.

Guests come to the Pinkham Notch Camp more for the camaraderie than the accommodations. Situated spectacularly at the base of Mount Washington and with easy access to numerous hiking and skiing trails, the lodge is operated like a tightly run Scandinavian youth hostel, with guests sharing bunk rooms and enjoying boisterous, filling meals (turkey, beef stew, and baked chicken) at long family-style tables in the main lodge. Some family and private rooms are available at an additional cost. The accommodations are spartan, basic and compact (you'll sleep just feet from snoring strangers if you end up sharing a room), but that's often overcome by the festive atmosphere. It's a place to meet others and swap information about what to do in the area.

**Wentworth Resort Hotel.** Jackson, NH 03846. ☎ 800/637-0013 or 603/383-9700. Fax 603/383-4265. www.thewentworth.com. 76 units (includes 20 condominum suites). A/C TV TEL. Weekends $155–$295, weekdays $145–$285 double. Rates include full breakfast and five-course dinner. Higher rates during foliage season and Christmas week; discounts available Mar to mid-June. 2-night minimum some weekends and holidays. AE, CB, DC, DISC, ER, MC, V.

The venerable Wentworth sits in the middle of Jackson Village, all turrets, eaves, and awnings. Built in 1869, this Victorian shingled inn once had 39 buildings (including a dairy and electric plant) but edged to the brink of deterioration in the mid-1980s. The seven remaining buildings were acquired, refurbished, and added to with a number of condominium clusters around the newly expanded and upgraded golf course. The inn upgraded again in recent years, with an owner and chef both formerly with Four Seasons. The large guest rooms are decorated with a Victorian-inspired grace and elegance. Some rooms feature propane fireplaces, whirlpools, or clawfoot tubs. Those of stouter constitution can stroll up the road and plunge into the cold waters of Jackson Falls.

**Dining:** The regal first-floor dining room serves updated regional favorites like beef tenderloin with wild mushrooms, almond-crusted rainbow trout, and rack of lamb. Entree prices are $17 to $24.

**Amenities:** Outdoor heated pool, 18-hole PGA golf course, clay tennis court, billiards, and cross-country skiing.

**Wildcat Inn & Tavern.** Rte. 16A, Jackson, NH 03846. ☎ **800/228-4245** or 603/
383-4245. 14 units, 2 share bathroom. A/C TV TEL. $109–$149 double, including breakfast.
Surcharge during foliage season. AE, DC, MC, V.

The Wildcat Inn occupies a three-story farmhouse-style building in the middle of
Jackson, directly across from the cross-country ski center. It's a comfortable, informal
kind of place, better known for its restaurant and tavern than for its accommodations.
Most guest rooms are cozy, two-room suites, carpeted and furnished with a mish-mash
of furniture. Sitting rooms typically contain contemporary sofas, chairs, and pine furniture, and offer cozy sanctuary after a day of hiking or skiing.

**Dining:** The downstairs dining room resembles a traditional country farmhouse,
with old wood floors and pine furniture. Country-style meals are prepared with flair
and include a beef tenderloin topped with lobster, asparagus, and Hollandaise sauce
(main courses are $13.95 to $25.95). In the winter, stake out a toasty spot in front of
the tavern fireplace—one of the most popular gathering spots in the valley—to sip
soothing libations and order from the bar menu, which has lighter fare like chicken
quesadillas and spanakopita ($6.95 to $8.95).

## 4 Crawford Notch

Crawford Notch is a wild, rugged mountain valley that angles through the heart of the
White Mountains. Within the notch itself lies plenty of legend and history. For years
after its discovery by European settlers (Timothy Nash stumbled upon it in 1771), it
was an impenetrable wilderness, creating a barrier to commerce by blocking trade
between the upper Connecticut River valley and commercial harbors in Portland and
Portsmouth. This was eventually surmounted by a plucky crew who hauled the first
freight through.

Nathaniel Hawthorne immortalized the notch with a short story about a real-life
tragedy that struck in 1826. One dark and stormy night (naturally), the Willey family
fled its home when they heard an avalanche roaring toward the valley floor. As fate
would have it, the avalanche divided above their home and spared the structure; the
seven who fled were killed in tumbling debris. You can still visit the site today; watch
for signs when driving through the notch.

The notch is accessible via Route 302, which is wide and speedy on the lower sections, becoming steeper as it approaches the narrow defile of the notch itself. Modern
engineering has taken most of the kinks out of the road. The views up the cliffs from
the road can be spectacular on a clear day; on an overcast or drizzly day, the effect is
foreboding.

### ESSENTIALS
**GETTING THERE**   Route 302 runs through Crawford Notch for approximately
25 miles between the towns of Bartlett and Twin Mountain.

**VISITOR INFORMATION   Twin Mountain Chamber of Commerce,** P.O. Box
194, Twin Mountain, NH 03595 (☎ **800/245-8946** or 603/846-5407), offers general information and lodging referrals at their information booth near the intersection
of Routes 302 and 3. Open year-round; hours vary.

### SKIING
**Attitash Bear Peak.** Rte. 302, Bartlett, NH 03812. ☎ **800/223-7669** or 603/374-2368.
www.attitash.com. E-mail: info@attitash.com. Vertical drop: 1,750 ft. Lifts: 12 chairlifts
(including 2 high-speed quads), 3 surface lifts. Skiable acreage: 280. Lift tickets: $48 week-
ends, $50 holidays, $42 weekdays.

Attitash Bear Peak is a good mountain for intermediate-to-advanced skiers, with a selection of great cruising runs and a handful of more challenging drops. The ski terrain covers two peaks: the 1,750-foot Attitash and the adjacent 1,450-foot Bear Peak. In 2000, the resort added an additional 25 acres of glades for advanced skiers. It's also one of the region's most scenic ski areas—it's dotted with rugged rock outcroppings, and you'll get stunning views of Mt. Washington and some of the Presidentials from its peaks; there's an observation tower you can scramble up on the main summit. The base area tends to be pretty quiet in the evenings, so those looking for nightlife typically head 15 minutes away to North Conway.

**Bretton Woods.** Rte. 302, Bretton Woods, NH 03575. ☎ **800/232-2972** or 603/278-3307. www.brettonwoods.com. E-mail: skibw@brettonwoods.com. Vertical drop: 1,500 ft. Lifts: 8 chairlifts (including 1 high-speed quad), 4 surface lifts. Skiable acreage: 330. Lift tickets: $49 weekends and holidays, $39 weekdays.

In 1999, Bretton Woods expanded to include the formerly undeveloped West Mountain, doubling the number of chairlifts and skiable acreage (it now has the most skiing terrain in New Hampshire). The new trails and lifts bring a welcome vitality to the mountain, which has long been popular with beginners and families. The new trails include glades and wide cruising runs, along with more challenging trails for advanced skiers. (Note that it still doesn't rival the more demanding slopes of Vermont or Maine, however.)

The resort continues to do a great job with kids (the Family Learning Center is a wonderful spot for tykes to attempt their first descents) and offers a pleasantly low-key attitude that families lap up. Accommodations are available on the mountain and nearby, notably at the Mount Washington Hotel, but evening entertainment tends to revolve around hot tubs, TVs, and going to bed early. For those so inclined, there's an excellent cross-country ski center nearby. The mountain hasn't finished expanding: Plans call for a new detachable quad chair in 2001 and new trails and lifts on adjacent Mt. Stickney for the 2002–03 ski season.

## WATERFALLS & SWIMMING HOLES

Much of the mountainous land flanking Route 302 falls under the jurisdiction of **Crawford Notch State Park,** which was established in 1911 to preserve land that elsewhere had been decimated by overly aggressive logging. The headwaters of the Saco River form in the notch, and what's generally regarded as the first permanent trail up Mt. Washington also departs from here. Several turnouts and trailheads invite a more leisurely exploration of the area. The trail network on both sides of Crawford Notch is extensive; consult the *AMC White Mountain Guide* for detailed information.

Engorged by snowmelt in the spring, the Saco River courses through the notch's granite ravines and winds past sizable boulders that have been left by retreating glaciers and crashed down from the mountainsides above. It's a popular destination among serious whitewater boaters and makes for a good spectator sport if you're here early in the season. During the lazy days of summer, the Saco offers several good swimming holes just off the highway. They're unmarked, but watch for local cars parked off the side of the road for no apparent reason, and you should be able to find your way to a good spot for soaking and splashing.

Up the mountain slopes that form the valley, hikers will spot a number of lovely waterfalls, some more easily accessible than others. A few to start with:

**Arethusa Falls** has the highest single drop of any waterfall in the state, and the trail to the falls passes several attractive smaller cascades. These are especially beautiful in the spring or after a heavy rain, when the falls are at their fullest. The trip can be done as a $2^3/5$-mile round-trip to the falls and back on Arethusa Falls Trail, or as a $4^1/2$-mile loop hike that includes views from stunning Frankenstein Cliffs. (These are named not after the creator of the famous monster, but after a noted landscape painter.)

If you're arriving from the south, look for signs to the trail parking area shortly after passing the Crawford Notch State Park entrance sign. From the north, the trailhead is a $^1/2$ mile south of the Dry River Campground. At the parking lot, look for the sign and map to get your bearings, then cross the railroad tracks to start up the falls trail.

Another hike begins a short drive north on Route 302. Reaching tumultuous **Ripley Falls** requires an easy hike of a little more than 1 mile, round-trip. Look for the sign to the falls on Route 302 just north of the trailhead for Webster Cliff Trail. (If you pass the Willey House site, you've gone too far.) Drive in and park at the site of the Willey Station. Follow trail signs for the Ripley Falls Trail, and allow about a half hour to reach the cascades. The most appealing swimming holes are at the top of the falls.

Two attractive falls may be seen from the roadway at the head of the notch, just east of the crest. **Flume Cascades** and **Silver Cascades** tumble down the hills in white braids that are especially appealing during a misty summer rain. These falls were among the most popular sites in the region when tourists alighted at the train station about 1 mile away. They aren't as spectacular as the two mentioned above, but they're accessible if you're in a hurry. Travelers can park in the lots along the road's edge for a slower paced view.

## AN HISTORIC RAILWAY

✪ **Mount Washington Cog Railway.** Rte. 302, Bretton Woods. ☎ **800/922-8825** or 603/846-5404. Fare $44 adults, $30 children 6–12, free for children under 6. MC, V. Runs daily Memorial Day–late Oct, plus weekends in May. Frequent departures; call for schedule. Reservations recommended.

The cog railway was a marvel of engineering when it opened in 1869, and it remains so today. Part moving museum, part slow-motion roller-coaster ride, the cog railway steams to the summit with a determined "I think I can" pace of about 4 m.p.h. but there's still a *frisson* of excitement on the way up and back, especially when the train crosses Jacob's Ladder, a rickety-seeming trestle 25 feet high that angles upward at a grade of more than 37%. Passengers enjoy the expanding view on this 3-hour round-trip (there are stops to add water to the steam engine, to check the track switches, and to allow other trains to ascend or descend). There's also a 20-minute stop at the summit to browse around. Be aware that the ride is noisy and sulfurous, and you should dress expecting to acquire a patina of cinder and soot; but it's hard to imagine anyone (other than those fearful of heights) not enjoying this trip—from kids marveling at the ratchety-ratchety noises and the thick plume of black smoke, to curious adults trying to figure out how the cog system works, to naturalists who get superb views of the bony, brawny uplands leading to Mt. Washington's summit.

## WHERE TO STAY & DINE

**The Bernerhof.** Rte. 302, Glen, NH 03838. ☎ **603/383-9132.** Fax 603/383-0809. www.bernerhofinn.com. E-mail: stay@bernerhofinn.com. 9 units. A/C TV TEL. Midweek $75–$130 double; weekends $95–$150. Rates include full breakfast. 2-night minimum peak season and weekends. AE, DISC, MC, V.

Situated overlooking busy Route 302 en route to Crawford Notch, The Bernerhof occupies a century-old home that's all gables and squared-off turrets on the outside. Inside, the guest rooms are eclectic and fun, crafted with odd angles and corners. All are tastefully furnished in a simple country style that's sparing with the frou-frou.

Spacious Room 7 (a suite) is tucked under the eaves on the third floor and has a two person Jacuzzi and in-room sauna. Room 8 (not a suite) is also romantic and appealing, with a Jacuzzi under a skylight, wood floors, a brass bed, and a handsome cherry armoire.

**Dining:** The rustic Black Bear Pub is oakey and mellow—there's a bear skin on the wall and over 70 varieties of bottled beers. The meals in the adjacent Prince Place dining room can be memorable on a good night. Middle European fare, including several traditional veal dishes, is the specialty, but other entrees are always available (for example, smoked salmon and shrimp linguini, and hazelnut chicken saute). Dining is open to the public nightly in season, with entrees ranging from $16.95 to $21.95.

○ **Mount Washington Hotel.** Rte. 302, Bretton Woods, NH 03575. ☎ **800/258-0330** or 603/278-1000. www.mtwashington.com. E-mail: info@mtwashington.com. 200 units. TV TEL. Weekends and holidays $249–$499 double; midweek $209–$459 double; suites up to $1,199. Rates include breakfast and dinner. Minimum stays required during holidays. AE, DISC, MC, V.

This five-story wooden resort, with its gleaming white clapboards and cherry-red roof, seems something out of a fable. Built in 1902 by railroad and coal magnate Joseph Stickney, the resort attracted luminaries like Babe Ruth, Thomas Edison, Woodrow Wilson, and silent-movie star Mary Pickford. In 1944, it hosted the famed Bretton Woods International Monetary Conference, which secured the dollar's role as the world's currency.

After large resorts fell out of fashion, the Mount Washington went through a succession of owners and fell on lean times. Threatened with demolition and put on the auction block in 1991, it was purchased by a group of local business folks, who have gradually made long-overdue improvements to both grand public areas and the guest rooms. The biggest change? Starting in the winter of 1999–2000, the resort opened year-round, a feat that required the replacement of some 800 old windows with double panes. (The old windows are now used as picture frames in the hallways.) Guest rooms vary in size and decor; most are furnished simply and comfortably, and many have grand views of the surrounding mountains and countryside. A broad 900-foot wrap-around veranda makes for relaxing afternoons. The decor isn't lavish, and while the innkeepers are gradually making improvements, the hotel can still feel a bit unfinished in parts—such as in the wide upstairs hallways that lack either furniture or artwork. That said, this remains still one of my favorite spots, partly for the sheer improbability of it all, and partly because of its direct and tangible link with a lost era.

**Dining:** Meals are enjoyed in the impressive octagonal dining room, designed such that no guest would be slighted by being seated in a corner. (Jackets are requested for men at dinner.) A house orchestra provides entertainment during the dinner, and guests often dance between courses. The meals are delightful, with a continental bent but global influences. The fixed-price meal is $50 per person for outside visitors. The resort also has several other spots for a bite to eat, including lunches poolside and at the Cave, said to be a former speakeasy, in the basement.

**Amenities:** A 27-hole golf course, 12 red-clay tennis courts, indoor and outdoor pools, horseback riding, carriage and sleigh rides, cross-country and downhill skiing, bike rentals, sauna, children's program, Jacuzzi, coin-op laundry, game room, shopping concourse, concierge, baby-sitting, valet parking, and safe-deposit boxes.

○ **Notchland Inn.** Rte. 302, Hart's Location, NH 03812. ☎ **800/866-6131** or 603/ 374-6131. Fax 603/374-6168. www.notchland.com. E-mail: notchland@aol.com. 13 units (includes 6 suites). Foliage season and holidays $275–$325; off-season $225–$285 double. Rates include breakfast and dinner. (B&B rates from $165.) 2-night minimum on weekends; 3-night minimum foliage and some holidays. AE, DISC, MC, V. Children over 12 are welcome.

The inn is located off Route 302 in a wild, remote section of the Crawford Notch, looking every bit like a redoubt in a Sir Walter Scott novel. Built of hand-cut granite for a prosperous dentist between 1840 and 1862, Notchland is classy yet informal, and perfectly situated for exploring the wilds of the White Mountains. All 13 guest rooms are tastefully appointed with antiques and traditional furniture, and all feature wood-burning fireplaces, high ceilings, and individual thermostats. Five two-room suites are available; three suites have Jacuzzis and two have soaking tubs. Two rooms are located in the adjacent schoolhouse; the upstairs room has a wonderful soaking tub. Kinsman is the largest room in the main inn and decorated with Asian artwork; Hancock has a Jacuzzi with skylight, and a fireplace in the bedroom. The inn is also home to two affable Bernese mountain dogs.

**Dining:** Dinners in the bright, often noisy dining room are eclectic and nicely presented. Five-course dinners are served at 7pm, with a choice of three creative entrees or so each evening. These might include a Thai curry, five-pepper-crusted roast beef, or scallops with walnuts and a lime-ginger sauce. Dinners are available to the public (very few outside spaces are available; reservations essential) at a fixed price of $35, not including tax, tip, or beverage.

**Amenities:** River swimming (just across the road), outdoor hot tub, nature trails, game room, and baby-sitting by advance appointment.

## 5  Waterville Valley & Loon Mountain

In the southwestern corner of the White Mountains are two ski resorts occupying attractive mountain valleys. **Waterville Valley,** which lies at the end of a 12-mile dead-end road, was the first to be developed. Incorporated as a town in 1829, Waterville Valley became a popular destination for summer travelers during the heyday of mountain travel late in the 19th century. Skiers first started descending the slopes in the 1930s after a few ski trails were hacked out of the forest by the Civilian Conservation Corps and local ski clubs, but it wasn't until 1965, when a skier named Tom Corcoran bought 425 acres in the valley, that Waterville began to assume its current modern air.

While the village has a decidedly manufactured character—it's also at a lower elevation than the ski area, requiring a drive or shuttle bus to the slopes—Corcoran's initial vision has kept the growth within bounds. The village is reasonably compact, with modern lodges, condos, and restaurants located within a loop road. In the center is the "Town Square," itself a sort of minor mall complex with a restaurant and a few shops. If there's any complaint, it's that Waterville Valley has the unnatural, somewhat antiseptic quality of planned communities everywhere.

One of the nicer features of Waterville Valley is the Athletic Club, an attractive and modern complex with cardiovascular equipment, tennis courts, racquetball, an Olympic-size pool, a restaurant, and more. Admission to the complex is ostensibly "free" to valley hotel guests, who pay an involuntary 15% resort tax (13% in winter) on their hotel bills. (Combined with the sales tax, that adds up to a hefty 21% to 23% tax on room rates—rather steep for a state that likes to boast of being tax-free.)

Some 25 miles to the north is **Loon Mountain,** which is located just outside the former paper-mill town of Lincoln. In summer, a shorter route crosses Thornton Gap on Tripoli Road. The resort was first conceived in the early 1960s by Sherman Adams, a former New Hampshire governor and Eisenhower administration official. The mountain opened in 1966 and was quickly criticized for its mediocre skiing, but some upgrading and expanding since then has brought the mountain greater respect.

Loon has evolved from a friendly intermediate mountain served by a few motels to a friendly intermediate mountain served by dozens of condos and vast, modern hotels.

At times it seems that Lincoln underwent not so much a development boom in the 1980s as a development spasm. Clusters of chicken-coop style homes and condos now blanket the lower hillsides of this narrow valley, and fast-food restaurants and strip-mall-style shops line Route 112 from I-93 to the mountain.

The Loon area includes the towns of Lincoln and North Woodstock, which flank I-93. North Woodstock has more of the feel of a town that's lived in year-round. Lincoln and the Loon Mountain base village are lively with skiers in the winter, but in the summer, the area can have a post-nuclear-fallout feel to it, with lots of homes but few people in evidence. The ambience is also compromised by that peculiar style of resort architecture that's simultaneously aggressive and bland.

## ESSENTIALS

**GETTING THERE**   Waterville Valley is located 12 miles northwest of Exit 29 on I-93 via Route 49. Lincoln is accessible off I-93 on Exits 32 and 33.

**VISITOR INFORMATION**   The **Waterville Valley Chamber of Commerce,** RFD #1, Box 1067, Campton, NH 03223 (☎ **800/237-2307** or 603/726-3804), staffs a year-round information booth on Route 49 in Campton, just off Exit 28 of I-93. On the Web: www.watervillevalleyregion.com. The **Lincoln-Woodstock Chamber of Commerce,** P.O. Box 358, Lincoln, NH 03251 (☎ **800/227-4191** or 603/745-6621), has an information office open daily at Depot Plaza on Route 112 in Lincoln. Go to www.linwoodcc.org.

The most comprehensive place for information about the region is the **White Mountains Visitor Center,** P.O. Box 10, North Woodstock, NH 03262 (☎ **800/ 346-3687** or 603/745-8720), located just east of Exit 32 on I-93. They'll send a visitor kit, and they offer brochures and answer questions from their center, which is open year-round from 8:30am to 5pm daily.

## SKIING

**Loon Mountain.** Lincoln, NH 03251. ☎ **800/227-4191** for lodging or 603/745-8111. www.loonmtn.com. Vertical drop: 2,100 ft. Lifts: 8 chairlifts (1 high-speed), 1 high-speed gondola, 1 surface lift. Skiable acreage: 275. Lift tickets: $47 weekends, $40 weekdays.

Located on U.S. Forest Service land, Loon has been stymied in past expansion efforts by environmental concerns regarding land use and water withdrawals from the river. Loon eventually got the go-ahead for expansion and has expanded and reshaped the ski mountain, adding uphill capacity, 15 acres of glade skiing (in 2000), and improved snowmaking. The expansion has reduced some of the congestion of this popular area, but it's still crowded on weekends. Most of the trails are solid intermediate runs and cluster toward the bottom. Experts head to the north peak, which has a challenging selection of advanced trails served by a triple chairlift. For kids, there's a new snow-tubing park off the Little Sister chairlift.

**Waterville Valley.** Waterville Valley, NH 03215. ☎ **800/468-2553** or 603/236-8311. www.waterville.com. E-mail: info@waterville.com. Vertical drop: 2,020 ft. Lifts: 8 chairlifts (2 high speed), 4 surface lifts. Skiable acreage: 255. Lift tickets: $47 weekends, $40 weekdays.

Waterville Valley is a classic intermediate skier's mountain. The trails are uniformly wide and well-groomed, and the ski area is compact enough that no one will get confused and end up staring down a double-diamond trail. Over the past 3 years, the mountain's new owners invested $4 million in improvements (including a second high-speed chair and more extensive snowmaking), making it a fine place to learn to ski or brush up on your skills. Advanced skiers have a selection of black-diamond trails, but the selection and steepness doesn't begin to rival larger ski mountains. A new terrain park served by a poma lift above the base lodge is popular with both advanced and beginning boarders.

## HIKING & MOUNTAIN BIKING

Impressive mountain peaks tower over both Lincoln and Waterville Valley, making both areas great for hiking and mountain biking. As always, your single best source of information is the Appalachian Mountain Club's *White Mountain Guide,* which offers a comprehensive directory of area trails. Also check with Forest Service staff at the White Mountains Visitor Center for information on local outdoor destinations.

From Waterville Valley, a popular 4-hour hike runs to the summit of **Mt. Tecumseh.** The hiking trail starts about 100 yards north of the ski lodge and offers wonderful views as you climb. From the 4,003-foot summit, you can return via the **Sosman Trail,** which winds its way down beneath the ski lifts and along ski runs closed for summer.

Outdoor novices who prefer their adventures neatly packaged will enjoy the **Adventure Center at Waterville Valley** (☎ **800/468-2553**). The center offers mountain-bike rentals, in-line skates, guided tours, lift access for bikers and hikers, and information on area trails. Rates start at $18 for 2-hour mountain-bike rental, to $50 for a private 4-hour guided hike. (The center also offers cross-country skiing and snowshoeing in winter.)

In the Lincoln area, a level trail that's excellent for hikers in any physical shape is the **Wilderness Trail** along the East Branch of the Pemigewasset River. Head eastward on Route 112 (the Kancamagus Highway) from I-93 for 5 miles then watch for the parking lot on the left just past the bridge. Both sides of the river may be navigated; the Wilderness Trail on the west side runs just over 3 miles to beautiful, remote Black Pond; on the east side, an abandoned railroad bed makes for smooth mountain biking. The two trails may be linked by fording the river where the railbed is crossed by a gate.

Additionally, hikers will find easy access to various trailheads along the Kancamagus Highway (see below).

## THE KANCAMAGUS HIGHWAY

The Kancamagus Highway—locally called "the Kanc"—is among the White Mountains' most spectacular drives. Officially designated a National Scenic Byway by the U.S. Forest Service, the 34-mile roadway joins Lincoln with Conway through 2,860-foot Kancamagus Pass. When the highway was built from 1960 to 1961, it opened up 100 square miles of wilderness—a move that irked preservationists but has proven very popular with folks who prefer their sightseeing by car.

The route begins and ends along wide, tumbling rivers on relatively flat plateaus. The two-lane road rises steadily to the pass. Several rest areas with sweeping vistas allow visitors to pause and enjoy the mountain views. The highway also makes a good destination for hikers; any number of day and overnight trips may be launched from the roadside. One simple, short hike along a gravel pathway (it's less than a 0.3 mile each way) leads to **Sabbaday Falls,** a cascade that's especially impressive after a downpour. Six national forest campgrounds are also located along the highway.

To get the most out of the road, take your time and make frequent stops. Think of it as a scavenger hunt as you look for a covered bridge, cascades with good swimming holes, a historic home with a quirky story behind it, and spectacular mountain panoramas. All of these things and more are along the route.

# WHERE TO STAY
## IN WATERVILLE VALLEY

Guests at hotels in Waterville Valley pay a mandatory 15% resort tax (13% in winter) on their bills, which gains them admission to the Valley Athletic Club. If you don't plan to use the complex (at some hotels, that can mean an additional $30 a day), you might think about staying in Lincoln or North Woodstock.

**Golden Eagle Lodge.** 6 Snowsbrook Rd., Waterville Valley, NH 03215. ☎ **800/910-4499** or 603/236-4600. Fax 603/236-4947. www.goldeneaglelodge.com. 118 units. TV TEL. Summer $98–$188; winter $89–$218 per unit; spring $78–$148. Premium charged on holidays. Resort fee of 13%–15% is additional. Minimum stay requirements on certain holidays. AE, DC, DISC, MC, V.

This dominating, contemporary condominium project is centrally located in the village, and from the outside, the five-story shingle-and-stone edifice looks like one of the grand White Mountain resorts of the 19th century. Inside it's also regal in a cartoon-Tudor kind of way, with lots of stained wood, columns, and tall windows to let in the views. The hotel accommodates two to six people in each one- or two-bedroom unit, which have kitchens and basic cookware (very handy given the dearth of available eateries during crowded times). While outwardly grand, some of the furnishings and construction feel low budget, which compromises the experience somewhat.

**Amenities:** Indoor and outdoor pools, whirlpool, bike rental, nearby nine-hole golf course, game rooms, nearby indoor jogging track, nature trails, conference rooms, access to valley Athletic Club across the street, self-service Laundromat, sauna, and outdoor and indoor tennis courts nearby.

**Snowy Owl Inn.** 4 Village Rd., Waterville Valley, NH 03215. ☎ **800/766-9969** or 603/236-8383. Fax 603/236-4890. ww.snowyowlinn.com. 80 units. TV TEL. Winter weekends $128–$158 double, $228 suite; winter non-holiday midweek $98–$128 double, $188 suite; summer $78–$108 double, $158 suite. Rates include continental breakfast. Resort fee of 13%–15% is additional. AE, DISC, MC, V.

The Snowy Owl will appeal to those who like the amiable character of a country inn but prefer modern conveniences like in-room hair dryers. A modern, four-story resort project near Town Square, the inn offers a number of dramatic touches like a towering fieldstone fireplace in the lobby (adorned with a moose head), a handsome octagonal indoor pool, and a curious rooftop observatory reached via spiral staircase. The rooms are a notch above basic motel-style rooms. A number of small but long-overdue improvements in recent years have reversed the slide into dowdiness, making it quite a pleasant lodge.

**Amenities:** Indoor and outdoor pools, Jacuzzis, game room, VCR room, and free access to the Athletic Club.

**Valley Inn.** 1 Tecumseh Rd. (P.O. Box 1), Waterville Valley, NH 03215. ☎ **800/343-0969** or 603/236-8336. Fax 603/236-4294. www.valleyinn.com. E-mail: info@valleyinn.com. 52 units. A/C TV TEL. Winter weekends $78–$148 double, $248 suite; midweek $68–$128 double, $228 suite; discounts in summer and off-season, premium charged during winter holidays. Resort fee of 13%–15% additional. Minimum-stay policy during certain holidays. AE, CB, DISC, MC, V.

The Valley Inn is one of the smaller complexes in the valley, and a bit more intimate than its neighbors. The rooms are larger than those in a standard motel, and most feature a sitting area and petite dining table in a bay window. Most rooms have a wet bar; suites have kitchenettes. The inn is conveniently located near the village center and within walking distance of the Athletic Club and Town Square.

**Dining:** You have your choice of two dining areas. The main Red Fox dining room serves nicely prepared resort fare like lemon-pepper chicken and beef tournedos ($11.95 to 19.95). The cozy tavern, located downstairs, has burgers and the like starting at $4.95, and live entertainment during the busier season.

**Amenities:** Indoor/outdoor year-round heated pool, sauna, Jacuzzi, game room, free access to valley Athletic Club, room service (5 to 9pm), and self-service Laundromat.

## IN LINCOLN & NORTH WOODSTOCK

In addition to the places listed below, Lincoln offers a range of motels that will appeal to budget travelers. Among them: the **Kancamagus Motor Lodge** (☎ 800/346-4205 or 603/745-3365), the **Mountaineer Motel** (☎ 800/356-0046 or 603/745-2235), and **Woodward's Motor Inn** (☎ 800/635-8968 or 603/745-8141).

**Mountain Club at Loon.** Rte. 112 (R.R. #1; Box 40), Lincoln, NH 03251. ☎ 800/229-7829 or 603/745-2244. Fax 603/745-2317. www.mtnclubonloon.com. 234 units. A/C TV TEL. Winter weekend $209–$429 double; winter midweek $169–$399 double; summer and off-season $114–$259 double. AE, DC, DISC, MC, V.

Set at the foot of Loon Mountain's slopes, the Mountain Club is a large and contemporary resort of prominent gables and plate glass built during the real-estate boom of the 1980s. It was managed for several years as a Marriott, and the inoffensive but unexciting decor tends to reflect its chain-hotel heritage. Guest rooms are designed to be rented either individually or as two-room suites; each pair features one traditional hotel-style bedroom with king-size bed, along with a studio with a kitchen, sitting area, and a fold-down queen-size bed. The high room rates reflect the proximity to the slopes and the excellent health-club facilities connected to the hotel via covered walkway.

**Dining:** The resort features a lounge with pub-style noshing, and more upscale offerings at Rachel's Restaurant. Look for dishes like grilled salmon with tomatilla salsa, or seared duck breast with corn cakes. Entrees are priced from $11.95 to $18.95.

**Amenities:** Ski-out access, indoor and outdoor pools, year-round outdoor whirlpool, limited room service, concierge, list of local baby-sitters, health club and fitness facility (including basketball, walleyball, and aerobics rooms), sauna, game room, Laundromat, and two outdoor tennis courts.

**Wilderness Inn.** Rte. 3, North Woodstock, NH 03262. ☎ 800/200-9453 or 603/745-3890. E-mail: wildernessinn@juno.com. 7 units, 1 cottage. $55–$135 double. Rates include full breakfast. AE, MC, V. Located just south of Rte. 112.

The Wilderness Inn is located at the southern edge of North Woodstock village—it's not the wilderness that the name or the brochure might suggest, but it's a friendly, handsome bed-and-breakfast, with six guest rooms in a large bungalow-style home that dates to 1912. The interior features heavy timbers in classic Craftsman style, creaky maple floors, a somewhat spare mix of antiques and reproductions, and games to occupy an evening. Five rooms have TVs, the second floor rooms are air-conditioned, and there's a VCR and TV in the living room for all guests to enjoy. The nearby cottage is a good spot to relax, with a gas fireplace and a Jacuzzi tub. If you're arriving by bus in Lincoln, the innkeepers will pick you up (no charge).

**Woodstock Inn.** Main St. (P.O. Box 118), North Woodstock, NH 03262. ☎ 800/321-3985 or 603/745-3951. Fax 603/745-3701. www.woodstockinnnh.com. E-mail: relax@woodstockinnnh.com. 21 units, 8 with shared 13 with private bathroom. A/C TV TEL. Foliage season $75–$150 double; off-season $55–$135 double. Rates include breakfast. AE, DISC, MC, V.

The Woodstock Inn has a Jekyll-and-Hyde thing going on. In the front, it's a white Victorian with black shutters amid Woodstock's commercial downtown area—one of the few older inns in the land of condos and modern resorts. In the back, it's a modern, boisterous brew pub that serves up hearty fare along with robust ales (see Woodstock Station under "Where to Dine," below). The inn features 19 guest rooms spread among three houses. If you're on a tight budget, go for the shared-bathroom units in the main house and the nearby Deachman house; the slightly less personable Riverside building across the street offers rooms with private bathrooms, but at a premium. Rooms are individually decorated in a country Victorian style, furnished with both reproductions and antiques. Three have Jacuzzis.

## WHERE TO DINE

Waterville Valley offers a limited selection of restaurants, which too often seem to be either closed for the night or too crowded. No one place is outstanding. The Athletic Club has its own restaurant on the second floor, **Wild Coyote Grill** (☎ 603/236-4919), which offers regional favorites like potato-crusted salmon and grilled sirloin with mashed potatoes ($10.95 to $16.95). Decent pub fare (including commendable french fries) can be had in the **Red Fox Tavern** (☎ 603/236-8336) located in the basement of the Valley Inn.

**Woodstock Station.** Main St. ☎ 603/745-3951. Reservations accepted for Clement Room only. Breakfast items $3.95–$9.50; lunch and dinner items $5.50–$16 (dinner in Clement Room $9.95–$22.95). AE, DISC, MC, V. Clement Room daily 7–11:30am and 5:30–9:30pm; Woodstock Station daily 11:30am–10pm. PUB FARE/AMERICAN.

You've got a choice here: Dine amid the casually upscale Clement Room Grille on the enclosed porch of the Woodstock Inn, or head to the brew pub in the back, housed in an old train station. In the Clement Room, there's an open grill and fare that aspires toward some refinement (for instance, ostrich quesadilla, cedar-plank salmon, stuffed sole, and roast duck). The pub has high ceilings, knotty pine, and a decor that draws on vintage winter recreational gear. The pub menu rounds up the usual suspects, like nachos, chicken wings, burgers, and pasta, none of which is prepared with much creative flair. Better are the porters, stouts, and brown and red ales, which are brewed on premises.

## 6  Franconia Notch

Franconia Notch is rugged New Hampshire writ large. As travelers head north on I-93, the Kinsman Range to the west and the Franconia Range to the east begin to converge, and the road swells upward. Soon, the flanking mountain ranges press in on either side, forming tight and dramatic Franconia Notch, which offers little in the way of civilization but a whole lot in the way of natural drama. Most of the notch is included in a well-managed state park that to most travelers will be indistinguishable from the national forest. Travelers seeking the sublime should plan on a leisurely trip through the notch, allowing enough time to get out of the car and explore forests and craggy peaks.

## ESSENTIALS

**GETTING THERE**   I-93 runs through Franconia Notch, gearing down from four lanes to two (where it becomes the Franconia Notch Parkway) in the most scenic and sensitive areas of the park. Several roadside pull-outs and scenic attractions dot the route.

**VISITOR INFORMATION**   Information on the park and surrounding area is available at the **Flume Information Center** (☎ 603/823-5563) at Exit 1 off the parkway. The center is open daily in summer from 9am to 4:30pm. North of the notch, head to the **Franconia Notch Chamber of Commerce,** P.O. Box 780, Franconia, NH 03580 (☎ **603/823-5661**), on Main Street next to the town hall. It's open spring through fall, Tuesday through Sunday from 10am to 5pm (days and hours often vary depending on staff availability). For information via the Web, head to www.franconianotch.org.

## EXPLORING FRANCONIA NOTCH STATE PARK

Franconia Notch State Park's 8,000 acres, nestled within the surrounding White Mountain National Forest, hosts an array of scenic attractions easily accessible from I-93 and the Franconia Notch Parkway. For information on any of the follow attractions, contact the park offices (☎ **603/823-8800**).

Without a doubt, the most famous park landmark is the **Old Man of the Mountains,** located near Cannon Mountain. From the right spot on the valley floor, this 48-foot-high rock formation bears an uncanny resemblance to the profile of a craggy old man—early settlers said it was Thomas Jefferson. If it looks familiar, it's because this is the logo you see on all the New Hampshire state highway signs. The profile, which often surprises visitors by just how tiny it is when viewed from far below (bring binoculars), is best seen from the well-marked roadside viewing area at Profile Lake. In years past, harried tourists craning their necks to glimpse the Old Man while speeding onward resulted in some spectacular head-on collisions. Take your time and pull over. It's free.

**The Flume** is a rugged, 800-foot gorge through which the Flume Brook tumbles. The gorge, a hugely popular attraction in the mid-19th century, is 800 feet long, 90 feet deep, and as narrow as 20 feet at the bottom; visitors explore by means of a network of boardwalks and bridges. Early photos of the chasm show a boulder wedged in overhead; this was swept away in an 1883 avalanche. If you're looking for simple and quick access to natural grandeur, it's worth the money. Otherwise, set off into the mountains and seek your own drama with fewer crowds. Admission is $7 for adults, $4 for children 6 to 12.

**Echo Lake** is a picturesquely situated recreation area, with a 28-acre lake, a handsome swimming beach, and picnic tables scattered about all within view of Cannon Mountain on one side and Mount Lafayette on the other. A bike path runs alongside the lake and continues onward in both directions. Admission to the park is $2.50 for visitors over 12 years old.

For a high-altitude view of the region, set off for the alpine ridges on the **Cannon Mountain Tramway.** The old-fashioned cable car serves skiers in winter; in summer, it whisks up to 80 travelers at a time to the summit of the 4,180-foot mountain. Once at the top, you can strike out by foot along the Rim Trail for superb views. Be prepared for cool, gusty winds. The tramway costs $9 round-trip for adults, $7 for children 6 to 12. It's located at Exit 2 of the parkway.

Also near the base of Cannon Mountain is the **New England Ski Museum** (☎ **603/823-7177**), with its compact but interesting collection of ski memorabilia like early clothing, posters, and historic equipment. The old ski films shown in the theater are especially entertaining. It's open daily from the end of May to mid-October, and daily except Wednesdays during ski season. Admission is free.

## HIKING

Hiking opportunities abound in the Franconia Notch area, ranging from demanding multiday hikes high on exposed ridgelines to gentle valley walks. Consult AMC's *White Mountain Guide* for a comprehensive directory of area hiking trails.

A pleasant woodland detour of 2 hours or so can be found at the **Basin-Cascades Trail** (look for well-marked signs for the Basin off I-93 about 1$^1$/2 miles north of the Flume). A popular roadside waterfall and natural pothole, the Basin attracts teeming crowds, but relatively few visitors continue on the trail to a series of cascades beyond. Look for signs for the trail, then head off into the woods. After about a $^1$/2 mile of easy hiking you'll reach **Kinsman Falls,** a beautiful 20-foot cascade. Continue on another $^1$/2 mile beyond that to Rocky Glen, where the stream plummets through a craggy gorge. Retrace your steps back to your car.

For a more demanding hike, set off for rugged **Mt. Lafayette,** with its spectacular views of the western White Mountains. Hikers should be well-experienced, well-equipped, and in good physical condition. Allow 6 to 7 hours to complete the hike. A popular and fairly straightforward ascent begins up the **Old Bridle Trail,** which departs from the Lafayette Place parking area off the parkway. This trail climbs steadily with expanding views to the AMC's **Greenleaf Hut** (2.9 miles). From here, continue to the summit of Lafayette on the **Greeleaf Trail.** It's only 1.1 miles farther, but it covers rocky terrain and can be demanding and difficult, especially if the weather turns on you. If in doubt about conditions, ask advice of other hikers or the AMC staff at Greenleaf Hut.

## SKIING

**Cannon Mountain.** Franconia Notch Pkwy., Franconia. ☎ **603/823-8800.** Vertical drop: 2,146 ft. Lifts: 70-person tram, 5 chairlifts, 1 surface lift. Skiable acreage: about 175. Lift tickets: $42 weekend, $30 weekday.

During skiing's formative years, this state-run ski area was *the* place to ski in the East. One of New England's first ski mountains, Cannon remains famed for its challenging runs and exposed faces, and the mountain still attracts skiers serious about getting down the hill in style. Many of the old-fashioned New England–style trails are narrow and fun (if often icy, scoured by the notch's winds), and the enclosed tramway is an elegant way to get to the summit. There's no base scene to speak of; skiers tend to retire to inns around Franconia or retreat southward to the condo villages around Lincoln.

## FROST, YOU SAY?

**The Frost Place.** Ridge Rd., Franconia. ☎ **603/823-5510.** Admission $3 adults, $1.50 children 6–15, free for children under 6. Late May–June Sat–Sun 1–5pm; July to mid-Oct Wed–Mon 1–5pm. Head south on Rte. 116 from Franconia 1 mile to Ridge Rd. (gravel); follow signs a short way to the Frost House; park in lot below the house.

Robert Frost lived in New Hampshire between the ages of 10 and 45. "Nearly half my poems must actually have been written in New Hampshire," Frost said. "Every single person in my 'North of Boston' was a friend or acquaintance of mine in New Hampshire." The Frost Place is a humble farmhouse, where Frost lived simply with his family. Wandering the grounds, it's not hard to see how his granite-edged poetry evolved at the fringes of the White Mountains. First editions of Frost's works are on display; a slide show offers a glimpse into the poet's life, and a nature trail in the woods near the house is posted with excerpts from his poems.

## WHERE TO STAY & DINE

**Franconia Inn.** 1300 Easton Rd., Franconia, NH 03580. ☎ **800/473-5299** or 603/823-5542. Fax 603/823-8078. www.franconiainn.com. E-mail: info@franconiainn.com. 32 units. Weekends $96–$156 double; midweek $86–$126 double. Rates include breakfast. Meal plan rates also available. 3-night minimum on holiday weekends. Closed Apr to mid-May. AE, MC, V.

This is a pleasant inn that offers good value. Owned by brothers Alec and Richard Morris, it's set along a quiet road in a bucolic valley 2 miles from the village of

Franconia. The inn itself, built in 1934 after a fire destroyed the original 1886 inn, has a welcoming and informal feel to it, with wing-back chairs around the fireplace in one common room, and jigsaw puzzles half completed in the paneled library. Guest rooms are nicely appointed in a relaxed country fashion; three feature gas fireplaces and four have Jacuzzis. The inn is a haven for cross-country skiers—38 miles of groomed trails start right outside the front door.

**Dining:** The handsome first-floor dining room serves a delicious breakfast each morning and is open daily for dinner. The New American menu (entrees $16.95 to $20.95) includes dishes like rack of lamb dijonaise, portobello mushroom en papillote, and pepper-broiled salmon with dill.

**Amenities:** Heated pool, outdoor hot tub, four clay tennis courts, mountain bikes (free), game rooms, sauna, golf course nearby, tour desk, bridle trails and horse rentals, and cross-country ski trails.

## 7  Bethlehem & Littleton

More than a century ago, **Bethlehem** was the same size as North Conway to the south, and home to numerous sprawling resort hotels, summer homes, and even its own semiprofessional baseball team. (Joseph Kennedy, patriarch of the Kennedy clan, once played for the team.) Bethlehem subsequently lost the race for the riches (or won, depending on your view of outlet shopping), and today is again a sleepy town high on a hillside.

Once famed for its lack of ragweed and pollen, Bethlehem teemed with vacationers seeking respite from the ravages of hay fever late in the 19th century and early 20th century. When antihistamines and air-conditioning appeared on the scene, the sufferers stayed home. The now-empty resorts burned down one by one. Around the 1920s, Bethlehem was discovered by Hasidim from New York City, who soon arrived in number to spend the summers in the remaining boarding houses. In fact, that tradition has endured, and it's not uncommon today to see resplendently bearded men in black walking the village streets or rocking on the porches of Victorian-era homes.

Nearby **Littleton,** set in a broad valley along the Ammonoosuc River, is the area's commercial hub, but it still has a plenty of busy small-town charm. The town's long main street has an eclectic selection of shops—you can buy a wrench, a foreign magazine or literary novel, locally brewed beer, pizza, whole foods, or camping supplies. It's an active working downtown, which has avoided the migration of businesses to the mall by not having a mall.

The Littleton Area Chamber of Commerce (see below) has a free brochure outlining a walking tour of downtown Littleton. It includes 12 historic buildings, mostly representing traditional commercial styles from the mid- to the late 19th century. Littleton's cultural and industrial past is the also subject of the local history displays at the **Littleton Area Historical Society Museum,** 1 Cottage St. (☎ **603/444-6586**), housed in the town's former fire station. It's open in summer Wednesday and Saturday 1:30 to 4:30pm; admission is free.

Several pleasant natural trails are located on the outskirts of Littleton, with the most extensive at Pine Hill. (Drive uphill at Jackson Street—a couple of blocks east of the post office—and park at the end). You'll find a network of old roads and trails, and a number of glacial erratics left behind by the retreating ice sheet. Ask for the *Guide to Littleton* by the Littleton Conservation Commission at the chamber's office.

Neither town offers much in the way of must-see attractions, but both have good lodging, decent restaurants, and pleasing environs. Either town makes a peaceful alternative for travelers hoping to avoid the tourist bustle to the south. Note that some visitors find Bethlehem melancholy and full of unpolished charm; others find it a bit eerie and prefer to push on.

## ESSENTIALS

**GETTING THERE**   Littleton is best reached via I-93; get off at either Exit 41 or 42. Bethlehem is about 3 miles east of Littleton on Route 302. Get off I-93 at Exit 40 and head east. From the east, follow Route 302 past Twin Mountain to Bethlehem.

**VISITOR INFORMATION**   The **Bethlehem Chamber of Commerce,** P.O. Box 748, Bethlehem, NH 03574 (☎ **603/869-2151**), maintains an information booth in summer on Bethlehem's Main Street across from the town hall. The **Littleton Area Chamber of Commerce,** P.O. Box 105, Littleton, NH 03561 (☎ **603/444-6561**), offers information from its office at 120 Main St. and on the Web at www. littletonareachamber.com.

## EXPLORING BETHLEHEM

Bethlehem once was home to 38 resort hotels, but little evidence of them remains today. For a better understanding of the town's rich history, track down a copy of *An Illustrated Tour of Bethlehem, Past and Present,* available at many shops around town. This unusually informative guide offers a glimpse into the town's past, bringing to life many of the most graceful homes and buildings. Bethlehem consists of Main Street and a handful of side streets. Several antiques stores clustered in what passes for downtown are worth browsing.

Harking back to its more genteel era, Bethlehem still offers two well-maintained 18-hole golf courses amid beautiful North Country scenery. Call for hours and green fees. Both the municipal **Bethlehem Golf Course** (☎ **603/869-5754**) and private **Maplewood Casino and Country Club** (☎ **603/869-3335**) are on Route 302 (Main Street) in Bethlehem.

Just west of Bethlehem on Route 302 is **The Rocks** (☎ **603/444-6228;** www. therocks.org), a classic, Victorian gentleman's farm that today is the northern headquarters for the Society for the Protection of New Hampshire Forests. Set on 1,200 acres, this gracious estate was built in 1883 by John J. Glessner, an executive with the International Harvester Company. A well-preserved shingled house and an uncommonly handsome barn grace the grounds. Several hiking trails meander through meadows and woodlands on a gentle hillside, where visitors can enjoy open vistas of the wooded mountains across the rolling terrain. The Society operates a Christmastree farm here, as well as regular nature programs. Admission is free; open daily dawn to dusk.

## WHERE TO STAY

✪ **Adair.** 80 Guider Lane (just off Exit 40 on Rte. 93), Bethlehem, NH 03574. ☎ **888/ 444-2600** or 603/444-2600. Fax 603/444-4823. www.adairinn.com. E-mail: adair@connriver .net. 10 units (includes 2-bedroom cottage). A/C. $145–$245 double; cottage $295 double. Rates include breakfast. 2-night minimum on cottage, and during weekends and foliage season. AE, MC, V. Children 12 and over welcome.

Adair opened in 1992, but is still one of New England's better kept secrets. Guests enter via a winding drive flanked by birches and stone walls to arrive at a peaceful Georgian Revival home dating from 1927 that seems far more regal than its years. The inn is set on 200 acres, including beautifully landscaped grounds around the home. Inside, the common rooms are open, elegant, and spacious. Downstairs is the memorable Granite Tap Room, a huge, wonderfully informal, granite-lined, stone-floored rumpus room with a VCR, antique pool table, and fireplace. The guest rooms are impeccably well-furnished with a mix of antiques and reproductions in a light country fashion. Six feature fireplaces. The best of the lot is the Kinsman suite with a Jacuzzi the size of a small swimming pool, a small library, gas woodstove, and a petite balcony looking out toward the Dalton Range. A two-bedroom, one-bath cottage on the grounds is available for a 2-night minimum stay. The innkeepers are Judy and Bill Whitman, who are making a special effort to restore the gardens, which were originally laid out by the Olmsted Brothers.

**Dining:** See Tim-Bir Alley under "Where to Dine," below.

**Amenities:** All-weather tennis court, nature trails, and game room with billiards.

**Hearthside Village Cottage Motel.** Rte. 302 (midway between Bethlehem Village and I-93), Bethlehem, NH 03574. ☎ **603/444-1000.** www.hearthsidevillage.com. E-mail: cottages@hearthsidevillage.com. 16 cottages. TV. $54.95–$64.95 ($10 less in off-season). 2- or 3-night minimum during foliage season. MC, V. Closed mid-Oct to mid-May.

Hearthside Village is quirky motel court that feels a bit like an installation by Red Grooms. A little bit weird and a little bit charming at the same time, Hearthside claims to be the first motel court built in New Hampshire. A colony of steeply gabled miniature homes, the village was built by a father and son in two construction bursts, the first in the 1930s, the second in the late 1940s. The six 1940s-era cottages are of somewhat better quality, with warm knotty-pine interiors. Many of the cottages have fireplaces, some have kitchenettes, and several are suitable for small families. There's a small pool, an indoor playroom filled with toys for tots, and another recreation room with video games and Ping-Pong for older kids. Hasidic families from New York often stay here in summer, which lends the place a curiously multicultural air.

**Rabbit Hill Inn.** Rte. 18, Lower Waterford, VT 05848. ☎ **800/762-8669** or 802/748-5168. Fax 802/748-8342. www.rabbithillinn.com. E-mail: info@rabbithillinn.com. 20 units. $235–$370 double. Rates include breakfast, dinner, afternoon tea, and gratuities. 2-night minimum on weekends. AE, MC, V. Closed early Apr and early Nov. From I-93, take Rte. 18 northwest from Exit 44 for approximately 2 miles. Children over 12 are welcome.

A short hop across the Connecticut River from Littleton is the lost-in-time Vermont village of Lower Waterford with its perfect 1859 church and small library. Amid this cluster of buildings is the stately Rabbit Hill Inn, constructed to last in 1795. With its prominent gabled roof and imposing columns, the inn easily ranks among the most refined structures in the Connecticut River Valley. More than half of the rooms have gas fireplaces, all but two have air-conditioning, and several feature Jacuzzis. The innkeepers go the extra mile to make this an appealing destination for couples in search of quiet romance.

**Dining:** Dinner is included in the rates, and the menu changes every 2 months. The menu is uncommonly creative, offering entrees like braised pheasant wrapped in bacon and served with a blackberry-honey syrup and beef tenderloin with a black-pepper-raisin sauce. Proper attire is expected in the dining room ("Though jacket and tie are appropriate, they are not required."). The public is welcome with reservations; a five-course meal is $37 per person.

**✪ Thayers Inn.** 111 Main St., Littleton, NH 03561. ☎ **800/634-8179** or 603/444-6469. www.thayersinn.com. 42 units, 3 with shared bathroom. A/C TV. $39 double shared bathroom; $49–$100 double private bathroom. Rates include continental breakfast. AE, DC, DISC, MC, V. Dogs allowed if not left in room.

Thayers offers some the best value of any White Mountain inn. It's a clean, well-run hostelry in an impressive Greek Revival downtown building that dates to 1850. You'll find a mix of rooms furnished comfortably if eclectically with high quality flea-market antiques (lots of old maple) on four floors; in some rooms it feels a bit like a trip back into the 1940s. The $49 rooms aren't spacious but are perfectly adequate and comfortable. Room 11 is a family suite, with two bedrooms, two TVs, a queen plus two twins. The top floor is a bit of a hike—Room 47 ($39) is a bargain for a solo travelers on a budget, with maple furniture, air-conditioning, sink and mirror in the room, and a shared bath. The inn has a video library of 140 movies; you can borrow a VCR and films for free. Don't leave before climbing to the cupola for a great panoramic view of the town. Local trivia: President Ulysses S. Grant once addressed a crowd from a balcony under the grand eaves out front.

## WHERE TO DINE

**✪ Tim-Bir Alley.** 80 Guider Rd., Bethlehem. ☎ **603/444-6142.** Reservations required. Main courses $14.95–$18.95. No credit cards. Summer Wed–Sun 5:30–9pm; winter Wed–Sat 5:30–9pm. Closed Apr and Nov. REGIONAL/CONTEMPORARY.

The best dining in the White Mountains is at Tim-Bir Alley, housed in the area's most gracious country inn. Owners Tim and Biruta Carr have created an elegant and romantic setting, and prepare meals from ingredients that are wholesome and basic; even simple side dishes flirt with the remarkable. Diners might start with Moroccan sweet potato soup with spiced almonds, or corriander- and cumin-spiced lamb sausage with a banana-honey barbecue sauce, then tuck into a main course of beef tournedos with smoked bacon and grilled leeks, or sea scallops with sundried tomatoes and capers on pastry. Save room for the superb deserts, which range from peach-blueberry tart to a chocolate-hazelnut pâté. Attentive service isn't the strong suite here, so come expecting to enjoy a leisurely meal; beer and wine is available.

## 8 The North Country

I've been traveling to New Hampshire's North Country for more than 25 years, and it's come to serve as a touchstone for me. **Errol** is a town that regards change with high suspicion, something that held true even during the go-go times of the 1980s. The clean if basic Errol Motel is always there. The Errol Restaurant still serves the best homemade donuts north of Boston; and the land surrounding the town remains an outpost of rugged, raw grandeur that hasn't been at all compromised, as have many of the former wildlands to the south.

Of course, there's a problem with these lost-in-time areas. It's the nothing-to-see-nothing-to-do syndrome that especially seems to afflict young families with children. You can drive for miles and not see much other than spruce and pine, an infrequent bog, a glimpse of a shimmering lake, and—if you're real lucky—a roadside moose chomping on sedges, but there *is* plenty to do: Whitewater kayaking on the Androscoggin River; Canoeing on Lake Umbagog; Bicycling along the wide valley floors; and visiting one of the Northeast's grandest, most improbable historic resorts, which continues to thrive despite considerable odds.

Some recent developments are encouraging for those who'd like to see the area remain unchanged. The piney shoreline around spectacular Lake Umbagog was protected as a National Wildlife Refuge in the 1990s. Part was acquired outright by the federal and state governments (Umbagog straddles the Maine–New Hampshire border), and part was protected through the purchase of development rights from timber companies. The upshot? Umbagog should remain in its more-or-less pristine state for all time.

As for Errol, some shops have closed, some have opened, but the Androscoggin River still flows through, and the police still set up a radar at the bend near the river to catch Canadian speeders heading south toward Old Orchard Beach on Friday, then turn around to catch them heading north on Sundays.

# ESSENTIALS

**GETTING THERE**    Errol is at the junction of Route 26 (accessible from Bethel, Maine) and Route 16 (accessible from Gorham, New Hampshire).

**VISITOR INFORMATION**    The **Northern White Mountains Chamber of Commerce,** 164 Main St., Berlin, NH 03570 (☎ **800/992-7480** or 603/752-6060), offers travel information from its offices weekdays between 8:30am and 4:30pm and on the Web at www.northernwhitemountains.com.

# OUTDOOR PURSUITS

**Dixville Notch State Park** (☎ **603/788-2155**) offers limited hiking, including a delightful 2-mile round-trip hike to Table Rock. Look for the small parking area just east of the Balsams resort on the edge of Lake Gloriette. The loop hike (it connects with a ¹/₂-mile return along Route 26) ascends a scrabbly trail to an open rock with fine views of the resort and the flanking wild hills.

A great place to learn the fundamentals of whitewater is at **Saco Bound's Northern Waters** whitewater school (☎ **603/447-2177**), located where the Errol bridge crosses the Androscoggin River. The school offers 2- to 5-day workshops in the art of getting downstream safely, if not dryly. Classes involve videos, dry-land training, and frequent forays onto the river—both at the Class I to III rapids at the bridge, and more forgiving trips downstream. The base camp is also a good place for last-minute boat supplies and advice for paddlers exploring the river on their own. Classes are $170 for 2 days, with the price including equipment and a riverside campsite.

Excellent lake canoeing may be found at Lake Umbagog, which sits between Maine and New Hampshire. The lake, which is home to the **Lake Umbagog Wildlife Refuge** (☎ **603/482-3415**), has some 40 miles of shoreline, most of which is wild and remote. Look for osprey, eagles, otters, and mink. More than 20 primitive campsites are scattered around the shoreline and on the lake's islands. (Canoes are available for rent at Saco Bound's Errol outpost for $27 per day; see above). These backcountry campsites are managed by New Hampshire parks department; call ☎ **603/271-3628** for more information.

The area around Errol offers excellent roads for **bicycling**—virtually all routes out of town make for good exploring (although it's mighty hilly heading east). An especially nice trip is south on Route 16 from Errol. The occasional logging truck can be unnerving, but mostly it's an easy and peaceful riverside trip. Consider pedaling as far as what's locally called the Brown Co. Bridge—a simple, wooden logging road bridge that crosses the Androscoggin River. It's a good spot to leap in the river and float through a series of gentle rips before swimming to shore. Some small ledges on the far side of the bridge provide a good location for sunning and relaxing.

Biking information and rentals ($15 per day) are available in Gorham at **Moriah Sports,** 101 Main St. (☎ **603/466-5050**).

# WHERE TO STAY & DINE

✪ **Balsams Grand Resort Hotel.** Dixville Notch, NH 03576. ☎ **800/255-0600,** 800/255-0800 in N.H., or 603/255-3400. Fax 603/255-4221. www.thebalsams.com. E-mail: thebalsams@aol.com. 204 units. TEL. Summer $275–$480 double, including all meals and entertainment; winter $200–$350 double, including breakfast, dinner, and lift tickets; year-round $550–$700 suite. 4-night minimum on weekends July–Aug. AE, DISC, MC, V. Closed early Apr–late May and mid-Oct to mid-Dec.

Located on 15,000 private acres (yes, 15,000) in a notch surrounded by 800-foot cliffs, the Balsams is a rare gem hidden deep in the northern forest. The inn is but one of a handful of the great New England resorts dating back to the 19th century still in operation, and its survival is all the more extraordinary given its exceedingly remote location. What makes this Victorian grande dame even more exceptional has been its refusal to compromise or bend to the trend of the moment. Bathing suits and jeans are prohibited from the public areas, you'll be ejected from the tennis courts or golf course if you're not neatly attired, and men are required (not requested) to wear jackets at dinner. The resort has also maintained strict adherence to the spirit of the "American plan"—everything but booze is included in the room rate, from greens fees, tennis, and boats on Lake Gloriette to evening entertainment in the three lounges. Even the lift tickets at the resort's downhill ski area are covered.

**Dining/Diversions:** Meals are superb. Especially famous is the sumptuous luncheon buffet, served in summer and featuring delightful salads, filling entrees like linguine with clam sauce and fried shrimp, and time-warp deserts (when did you last gorge on chocolate eclairs?). There are also three lounges.

**Amenities:** The resort is noted for its two golf courses (one 18-hole, one nine-hole). Also: concierge, limited room service, dry cleaning, laundry service, newspaper delivery, turndown service, baby-sitting, currency exchange, valet parking, six tennis courts (both clay and all-weather), heated outdoor pool, 45 miles of groomed cross-country ski trails, bicycle rentals, game rooms, nature trails, children's programs, business center, conference rooms, sundeck, water-sports equipment, beauty salon, boutiques, and shopping arcade.

✪ **Philbrook Farm Inn.** 881 North Rd. (off Rte. 2 between Gorham, N.H., and Bethel, Maine), Shelburne, NH 03581. ☎ **603/466-3831.** 18 units, 6 summer cottages (6 units have shared bathrooms). $120–$150 double, including full breakfast and dinner; cottages $700 weekly. No credit cards. Closed Apr and Nov–Dec 25. Pets allowed in cottages only.

The Philbrook Farm Inn is a New England classic, a period piece that can easily trace its lineage to the 19th century, when farmers opened their doors to summer travelers to earn some extra cash. Set on 1,000 acres between the Mahoosuc Range and the Androscoggin River, this country inn has been owned and operated by the Philbrook family continuously since 1853. The inn has expanded haphazardly, with additions in 1861, 1904, and 1934. As a result, the cozy guest rooms on three floors are eclectic— some have a country farmhouse feel, others a more Victorian flavor. Guests spend their days at leisure, swimming in the outdoor pool, playing croquet, exploring trails in the nearby hills. or just reading in the sun on the porch. Philbrook Farm is a wonderful retreat, well out of the tourist mainstream, and worthy of protection as a local cultural landmark.

**Dining:** The dining room has a farmhouse-formal feel to it; guests are assigned one table for their stay and are served by waitresses in crisp white uniforms. Meals tend toward basic New England fare, with specialties like cod cakes and baked beans with brown bread.

# Coastal Maine 8

Professional funny guy Dave Barry once suggested that Maine's state motto should be "Cold, but damp."

Cute, but true. There's spring, which tends to last a few blustery, rain-soaked days; there's November, in which Arctic winds alternate with gray sheets of rain; and then winter brings a character-building mix of blizzards and ice storms to the fabled coast and rolling mountains.

Ah, but then there's summer. Summer in Maine brings osprey diving for fish off wooded points; gleaming cumulus clouds building over the steely-blue rounded peaks of the western mountains; and the haunting whoop of loons echoing off the dense forest walls bordering the lakes. It brings languorous days when the sun rises well before most visitors, and by 8am, it seems like noontime. Maine summers bring a measure of gracious tranquillity, and a placid stay in the right spot can rejuvenate even the most jangled nerves.

The trick comes in finding that right spot. Those who arrive here without a clear plan may find themselves rueing their travel decision. Maine's Route 1 along the coast has its moments, but for the most part, it's rather charmless—an amalgam of convenience stores, tourist boutiques, and restaurants catering to bus tours. Acadia National Park can be congested, Mt. Katahdin's summit overcrowded, and some of the more popular lakes have become defacto racetracks for jet skis; but Maine's size works to the traveler's advantage.

Maine is roughly as large as the other five New England states combined. It has 3,500 miles of coastline, some 3,000 coastal islands, and millions of acres of undeveloped woodland. In fact, more than half of the state exists as "unorganized territories," where no town government exists, and the few inhabitants look to the state for basic services. With all this space and a little planning, you'll be able to find your piece of Maine.

Wherever your travels take you, be sure to look for the varied layers of history, both natural and human. You'll find the mark of the great glaciers on the scoured mountaintops. You'll find the hand of man in 2-century-old mansions on remote coves that bespeak a former affluence when Maine ruled the waves (or at least much of the early trade on those waves). You'll find the 18th and 19th centuries overlapping in coastal villages, where handsome Georgian and Victorian homes sit side by side. Picking these layers apart is much of the fun in exploring Maine.

## 1　Enjoying the Great Outdoors

No other northern New England state offers as much diversity in its outdoor recreation as Maine. Bring your mountain bike, hiking boots, sea kayak, canoe, fishing rod, and snowmobile—there'll be plenty for you to do here. See chapter 9 for more on enjoying the outdoors in the Western Lakes & Mountains and the North Woods.

If your outdoor skills are rusty or non-existent, consider brushing up at the **L.L. Bean Outdoor Discovery Schools** (☎ **888/552-3261**). The "schools" are actually a series of lectures and workshops that run anywhere from 2 hours to 3 days. Classes are offered at various locations around the state covering a whole range of subjects, including map and compass, fly tying, bike maintenance, canoeing, kayaking, and cross-country and telemark skiing. L.L. Bean also hosts popular canoeing, sea-kayaking, and cross-country skiing festivals that bring together instructors, lecturers, and equipment vendors for 2 or 3 days of learning and outdoor diversion. Call for a brochure.

**BEACHGOING**　Swimming at Maine's ocean beaches is for the hearty. The Gulf Stream, which prods warm waters toward the Cape Cod shores to the south, veers toward Iceland south of Maine and leaves the state's 3,500-mile coastline washed by the brisk Nova Scotia current, an offshoot of the arctic Labrador Current. During the summer months, water temperatures along the south coast may top 60°F during an especially warm spell where the water is shallow, but it's usually cooler than that. The average ocean temperature at Bar Harbor in summer is 54°F.

Maine's beaches are found mostly between Portland and the New Hampshire border. Northeast of Portland a handful of fine beaches await—including popular **Reid State Park** and **Popham Beach State Park**—but rocky coast defines this territory for the most part. The southern beaches are beautiful but rarely isolated. Summer homes occupy the low dunes in most areas; mid-rise condos give Old Orchard Beach a "mini-Miami" air. For my money, the best beaches are at **Ogunquit,** which boasts a 3-mile-long sandy strand, some of which has a mildly remote character, and **Long Sands Beach** at York, which has a festive, carnival atmosphere right along Route 1A.

The sandy beaches at Maine's wonderful lakes bear close scrutiny if want to spend some some any significant time in the water during your trip. The water is tepid by comparison to the frigid Atlantic. The state is rife with swimming holes and swimmable lakes and rivers. Most are a matter of local knowledge; look for cars inexplicably pulled over along the road near a river or lake, and there's probably a good place to swim a short walk away. See chapter 9 for details on the Western Lakes.

**BIKING**　**Mount Desert Island** and **Acadia National Park** are arguably the premier destination for visiting bikers, especially mountain bikers who prefer easy-riding terrain. The 57 miles of well-maintained carriage roads in the national park offer superb cruising through thick forests and to the tops of rocky knolls with ocean views. No cars are permitted on these grass and gravel lanes, so bikers and walkers have them to themselves. Mountain bikes may be rented in Bar Harbor, which has at least three bike shops. The Park Loop Road, while often crowded with slow-moving cars, offers one of the more memorable road-biking experiences in the state. The rest of Mount Desert Island is also good for road biking, especially on the quieter western half of the island.

Also, don't overlook the islands for relaxed biking. In Casco Bay, **Chebeague Island** offers a pleasant wooded excursion. **Vinalhaven** and **North Haven** in Penobscot Bay, and **Swan's Island** in Blue Hill Bay are also popular destinations for bikers.

There's plenty of serious mountain biking for those who like to get technical on two wheels. Your best bet is to consult with area bike shops for the best trails, which are usually a matter of local knowledge.

# Maine

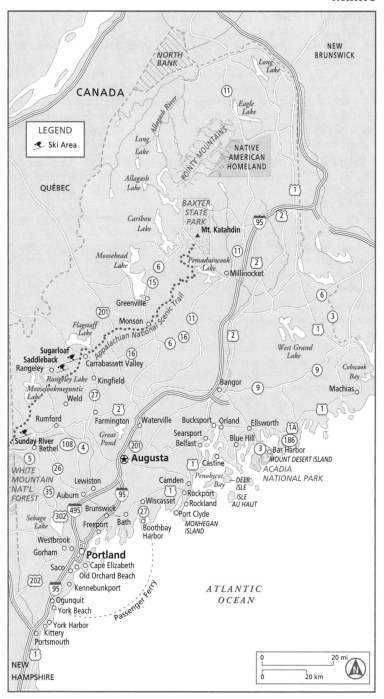

**LEGEND**
🎿 Ski Area

CANADA

QUÉBEC

NEW BRUNSWICK

NORTH BANK

*Allagash River*

*Long Lake*

⑪

*Eagle Lake*

*Long Lake*

POINTY MOUNTAINS

NATIVE AMERICAN HOMELAND

*Allagash Lake*

*Caribou Lake*

BAXTER STATE PARK

▲ Mt. Katahdin

① ②

95

*Moosehead Lake*

⑥

⑮

⑪

*Pemadumcook Lake*

○ Millinocket

② ⑥

Greenville

⑥

③

201

Monson

⑪ ⑥ ⑯

②

⑥

① ③

*Flagstaff Lake*

**Appalachian National Scenic Trail**

**Sugarloaf**
**Saddleback**
Rangeley

⑯ Carrabassett Valley

② ⑨ *West Grand Lake*

⑨

*Cobscook Bay*

*Rangeley Lake*

Kingfield

*Mooselookmeguntic Lake*

27 Weld

Bangor

⑨

Machias ○

② Farmington

Waterville

Bucksport  Orland

Ellsworth

① 1A

**Sunday River**
108 ④ Bethel

*Great Pond*

Searsport

Blue Hill

186

⑤

26

201

Augusta

① Castine

③ Bar Harbor

*MOUNT DESERT ISLAND*

*ACADIA NATIONAL PARK*

Rumford

WHITE MOUNTAIN NAT'L FOREST

Lewiston

35 Auburn

Belfast ○

*Penobscot Bay*

*DEER ISLE*

Camden

① Rockport

○ Rockland

*ISLE AU HAUT*

495

Brunswick

Wiscasset

Port Clyde

*MONHEGAN ISLAND*

*Sebago Lake*

302 Freeport  Bath

27 Boothbay Harbor

Westbrook

Gorham

**Portland**

Saco ○ Cape Elizabeth

Old Orchard Beach

202

95 Kennebunkport

**Passenger Ferry**

*ATLANTIC OCEAN*

Ogunquit ○

York Beach

York Harbor ○

Kittery

Portsmouth

①

NEW HAMPSHIRE

| 0 | 20 mi |
| 0 | 20 km |

N

**BIRDING**   Birders from southern and inland states should be able to lengthen their life lists along the **Maine Coast,** which attracts migrating birds cruising the Atlantic flyway and boasts populations of numerous native shorebirds, such as plovers (including the threatened piping plover), whimbrels, sandpipers, and dunlins. You'll see a surfeit of herring and great black-backed gulls along with the common tern; less frequently seen are Bonaparte's gull, laughing gull, jaegers, and the arctic tern. Far up the coast near Lubec, look for members of the alcid family, including razorbills and guillemots. Puffins (another alcid) nest on several offshore islands; tour boats to view puffins depart from Boothbay Harbor, Bar Harbor, and Jonesport.

For a recording of recent sightings of rare birds, call ☎ **207/781-2332.**

**CANOEING**   For many outdoor enthusiasts in the northeast, Maine means canoeing. From the thousands of acres of lakes and ponds to the tumbling whitewater of mountain rivers, Maine is very alluring to serious paddlers. See "Canoeing the Saco River" in chapter 9.

There's also the upper West Branch of the **Penobscot River,** which winds through moose country and connects to one of Maine's more pristine lakes.

In fact, you can't travel very far in Maine without stumbling upon a great canoe trip. Two excellent sources of information are the *AMC River Guide: Maine* and *Quiet Water Canoe Guide: Maine,* both published by the Appalachian Mountain Club, 5 Joy St., Boston, MA 02108.

**FISHING**   Maine draws anglers from throughout the Northeast who indulge their grand obsession on Maine's 6,000 lakes and ponds and its countless miles of rivers and streams.

For options on rustic fishing camps statewide, request one of the attractive brochures that describes more than 50 sporting camps between the Rangeley Lakes and Eagle Lake near Fort Kent from **Maine Sporting Camp Association,** P.O. Box 89, Jay, ME 04239.

Non-resident licenses are $50 for the season, or $21 for 3 days. Seven- and 15-day licenses are also available. You can purchase licenses at many outdoor shops or general stores. For a booklet of fishing regulations, contact the Fisheries Division at **Inland Fisheries and Wildlife,** 284 State St., Station # 41, Augusta, ME 04333 (☎ **207/287-5261**).

Ice fishing is also enormously popular throughout the winter, and you'll see the huts of anglers clustered on lakes throughout the state from the time the ice freezes until the season winds down at the end of March. If anyone tells you that Maine's waters are fished out, consider this: A Maine man landed a 23$\frac{1}{2}$-pound brown trout while ice fishing in March 1996 at a pond in southwestern Maine.

**HIKING**   Maine is home to hundreds of miles of maintained trails and ten peaks over 4,000 feet. Acadia National Park offers superb hiking, although the trails can be crowded during the peak of the summer season. In western Maine, 50,000 acres of the White Mountains spill over the border from New Hampshire and boast an excellent network of trails. There are a number of pathways in and around Evans Notch that offer opportunities for hikers of all levels. Finally, there's the dramatic Bigelow Range near the Sugarloaf/USA ski resort, which offers challenging trails and stunning vistas from high, blustery ridges. The Appalachian Trail traverses the range; a good source of trail information is the AT guide.

Two guides to the state's trails are highly recommended. *50 Hikes in Southern and Coastal Maine,* by John Gibson, is a reliable directory to trails at Evans Notch, Acadia, and the Camden Hills area. *50 Hikes in the Maine Mountains,* by Chloe Chunn, is the best guide for the Bigelow Range and Baxter State Park. Both are published by Backcountry Publications, and are available through local bookstores.

**SEA KAYAKING**  Paddlers nationwide migrate to Maine in the summer for world-class sea kayaking. The 3,500 miles of rocky coastline and the thousands of offshore islands have created a wondrous kayaker's playground. It's a sport that can be extremely dangerous (when the weather shifts, the seas can turn on you in a matter of minutes) but can yield plenty of returns for those with the proper equipment and skills.

The nation's first long-distance water trail was created here in 1987 when the **Maine Island Trail** was established. This 325-mile waterway winds along the coast from Portland to Machias, and incorporates some 70 state and privately owned islands along the route. Members of the Maine Island Trail Association, a private non-profit, help maintain and monitor the islands, and in turn are granted permission to visit and camp on them as long as they follow certain restrictions (for example, don't visit designated islands during seabird nesting season). Membership is $40 per year; contact the **Maine Island Trail Association,** P.O. Box C, Rockland, ME 04841 (☎ **207/596-6456** or 207/761-8225).

For novices, Maine has a number of kayak outfitters offering guided excursions ranging from an afternoon to a week. Outfitters include **Maine Island Kayak Co.,** 70 Luther St., Peaks Island, ME 04108 (☎ **207/766-2373**), and **Maine Sports Outfitters,** P.O. Box 956, Rockport, ME 04856 (☎ **800/244-8799** or 207/236-8797). Write or call to request information on upcoming trips.

**SKIING**  Maine has two major destination downhill ski resorts, as well as ten smaller areas. The two big resorts, Sugarloaf and Sunday River, are under the same ownership, but both have distinct characters. **Sugarloaf** is compactly arrayed on a single large peak and offers the highest vertical drop in New England after Vermont's Killington. The resort's base area is self-contained like an established campus and is a big hit with families.

**Sunday River** seems to keep growing lengthwise along an undulating ridge—the local nickname for it is "Someday Bigger." It's a less established resort ,and its base area is still a bit rough around the edges—think of it as more of a brash community college; but it offers diverse skiing terrain and state-of-the-art snowmaking and grooming.

The medium and small mountains cater primarily to the local market but offer good alternatives for travelers who'd just as soon avoid the flash and crowds of the two larger areas. Of the midsize areas, **Shawnee Peak** and **Saddleback** have small resort complexes at or near their bases, and offer better bargains and fewer crowds; Shawnee Peak is open for night skiing until 10pm 6 nights each week. **Mount Abram,** which is near Sunday River, has developed a solid reputation among telemark skiers. **Squaw Mountain** overlooking Moosehead Lake is the best choice for an old-fashioned bargain and features twisty, narrow trails and great views from the summit.

For a pamphlet with basic information about Maine's ski areas, contact **Ski Maine Association** (P.O. Box 7566, Portland, ME 04112), or visit www.skimaine.com on the Web. The Web site also offers up to date reports on ski conditions during the winter.

Cross-country skiers have a glorious mix of terrain to choose from, although groomed cross-country ski areas aren't as extensive in Maine as in neighboring New Hampshire or Vermont. Sunday River, Saddleback, and Sugarloaf all have cross-country ski areas at or near their downhill complexes. A more remote destination is **The Birches** (☎ **800/825-9453**) on Moosehead Lake with 24 miles of groomed trails. Among the best places to combine remote backcountry lodging and skiing is **Little Lyford Pond Camps** (☎ **207/280-0016** via cell phone) outside of Greenville—it's accessible in winter only by skiplane or snowmobile. For further information about cross-country ski areas in Maine, contact the **Maine Nordic Council** (☎ **800/754-9263**).

**WHITE-WATER RAFTING**    Maine's three northern rivers are dam-controlled, which means that good rafting is available throughout the season. The **Dead River** has a limited release schedule; it's opened only a half-dozen times for rafting in early summer and fall; smaller releases allow paddling in inflatable kayaks during the summer. The **Kennebec River** offers monstrous waves just below the dam, then tapers off into a gentle afternoon paddle as you float out of a scenic gorge. The west branch of the **Penobscot River** has a challenging, technical section called the Cribworks at the outset, several serious drops and falls after that, and dramatic views of Mt. Katahdin along the route.

**Raft Maine** (☎ **800/723-8633** or 207/824-3694) is a trade association of whitewater outfitters in Maine. Call their toll-free line, and they'll connect you to one of their member outfitters. You can also learn more about rafting at their Web site, www.raftmaine.com.

## 2 The South Coast

Maine's southern coast runs roughly from the state line at Kittery to Portland and is the destination of the majority of travelers into the state (including many day-trippers from the Boston area). While it will take some doing to find privacy and remoteness here, you'll turn up at least two excellent reasons for a detour: the long, sandy beaches that are the region's hallmark, and the almost tactile sense of history in the coastal villages.

Thanks to quirks of geography, nearly all of Maine's sandy beaches are located in this 60-mile stretch of coastline. It's not hard to find a relaxing sandy spot, whether you prefer dunes and the lulling sound of the surf or the carny atmosphere of a festive beach town. The waves are dependent on the weather—during a good Northeast blow (especially prevalent in spring and fall), they pound the shores and threaten beach houses built decades ago. During the balmy days of midsummer the ocean can be as gentle as a farm pond, with barely audible waves lapping timidly at the shore.

One thing all beaches share in common: They're washed by the chilled waters of the Gulf of Maine. Except in the very young, who seem immune to blood-chilling temperatures, swimming sessions here tend to be very brief and often accompanied by shrieks, whoops, and agitated hand-waving. The beach season itself is also brief and intense, running from July 4th to Labor Day. The season is stretching out into fall at an increasing number of beach towns (Columbus Day is accompanied by the sound of the remaining businesses shuttering up), but after Labor Day, shorefront communities tend to take a adopt a slower, more somnolent pace.

On foggy or rainy days, plan to search out the South Coast's rich history. More than 3 centuries ago, the early European newcomers first settled here, only to be driven out by Native Americans, who had been pushed to the brink by treaty-breaking British settlers and prodded by the mischievous French. Settlers later re-established themselves, and by the early 19th century, the southern Maine Coast was one of the most prosperous regions in the nation. Shipbuilders constructed brigantines and sloops, and ship captains plied the Eastern seaboard, the Caribbean, and far beyond. Merchants and traders constructed vast warehouses along the rivers to store their goods. Many handsome and historic homes near the coast today attest to the region's former prosperity.

# The Southern Maine Coast

Bethel
Bryant Pond
Livermore
5
17
219
26
Winthrop
North Waterford
117
Turner
5
South Paris
4
Norway
202
11
118
Waterford
117
Mechanic Falls
495
201
Lovell
Auburn
**Lewiston**
Richmond
302
Bridgton
*Long Lake*
196
Lisbon Falls
95
Casco
26
136
Bath
Naples
Brunswick
Freeport
123
5
117
11
*Saco R.*
Hiram
N. Windham
Yarmouth
*Harpswell Peninsula*
209
Cornish
*Sebago Lake*
302
*Orrs Island*
5
35
202
*Bailey Island*
*Casco Bay*
25
Westbrook
295
Limerick
4
**Portland**
Hollis Center
South Portland
Shapleigh
5
Cape Elizabeth
95
Old Orchard Beach
11
Alfred
111
Saco
*Saco Bay*
109
Biddeford
TNPK.
Sanford
1
202
4
109
Kennebunk
**Rochester**
North Berwick
Kennebunkport
MAINE
*ATLANTIC OCEAN*
Berwick
95
Somersworth
Wells
Ogunquit
**Dover** MAINE
York
Durham
Kittery
108
**Portsmouth**
NEW HAMPSHIRE
1A

## LEGEND

Ferry routes - - - - -

0 ____ 20 mi
0 ____ 20 km

ME
Augusta
⊛
Portland

A second wave of settlers came in the mid– to late 19th century, when wealthy city dwellers from Boston and New York sought respite from the summer heat and congestion by fleeing to Maine's coast. They built shingled estates (which they coyly called "cottages") with views of the Atlantic. At the beginning of the 20th century, aided by trolleys and buses, wealthy rusticators were followed by the emerging middle class, who built bungalows near the shore and congregated at oceanside boarding houses to splash in the waves.

# KITTERY & THE YORKS

Driving into Maine from the south, as most visitors do, the first town you'll come to is **Kittery.** Kittery was once famous nationally for its naval yard (it's still operating), but regionally at least, Kittery is now better known for the dozens of factory outlets that cluster here. (Why they chose to blossom here and not a couple of miles away in sales-tax-free New Hampshire remains an enduring mystery.) Maine has the second highest number of outlet malls in the nation (only California has more), and Kittery is home to a good many of them.

"The Yorks," just to the north, are comprised of three towns that share a name but little else. In fact, it's rare to find three such well-defined and diverse New England archetypes in such a compact area. **York Village** is redolent with early American history and architecture. **York Harbor** reached its zenith during America's late Victorian era, when wealthy urbanites constructed rambling cottages at the ocean's edge. **York Beach** has an Edwardian beach town feel, with loud amusements, taffy shops, a modest zoo, and small gabled summer homes set in crowded enclaves near the beach.

## ESSENTIALS

**GETTING THERE**    Kittery is accessible from I-95 or Route 1, with exits well-marked. The Yorks are reached most easily from Exit 1 of the Maine Turnpike. From the exit, look for Route 1A just south of the turnpike exit. This route connects all three York towns.

**VISITOR INFORMATION**    Travelers entering the state on I-95 can stock up on travel information for the region and beyond at the **Kittery Information Center** (☎ 207/439-1319), located at a well-marked rest area. It's open 9am to 5:30pm year-round (hours usually extended in summer). It's amply stocked with brochures, and the helpful staff can answer most questions.

The **York Chamber of Commerce,** P.O. Box 417, York, ME 03909 (☎ 207/363-4422), operates an attractive, helpful information center at 571 Route 1 near the turnpike exit. It's open 9am to 4pm daily (until 5pm Fridays). A trackless trolly (a bus retrofitted to look like an old-fashioned trolley) regularly links all three York towns and provides a convenient way to explore without having to scare up parking spots at every stop. Hop on the trolley at one of the well-marked stops for a 1-hour narrated tour ($3) or disembark along the way and explore by foot ($1.50 for a partial trip).

## EXPLORING KITTERY

The historic Portsmouth Naval Shipyard is located on the waterfront, just across the harbor from Portsmouth, New Hampshire. It's an active shipyard and isn't open to the public, but you can visit the base's **Naval Shipyard Museum** (☎ 207/439-3080), which is open summers Monday to Saturday 10am to 4pm, or the rest of the year by appointment. You'll find engaging displays, especially those related to the history of submarines, which is the shipyard's specialty. Admission is $3 adult, $1.50 children, $6 family.

From Kittery, an attractive route north to York follows winding Route 103. (Perfect for a drive, it's a bit busy and narrow for a bike ride.) The road passes through the historic village of Kittery Point, where homes seem to be located just inches from the roadway, and past two historic forts (both in parks open to the public). Look for the **Lady Pepperell House** on your right at the first left elbow in the road. The handsome cream-colored Georgian home was built in 1760 and is considered one of the most elegant of its kind in the nation(not open to the public).

Just before coming into the village of York, keep an eye on your left near the marshes and tidal inlets for the Wiggly Bridge (see "Two Wonderful Walks," below).

Kittery's consumer mecca is 4 miles south of York on Route 1. Some 120 factory outlets flank the highway, scattered among more than a dozen strip malls. Name-brand retailers include Dansk, Eddie Bauer, Corning Revere, Ann Klein, Coldwater Creek, Le Creuset, Calvin Klein, Crate & Barrel, Donna Karan, Converse, Olga/Warner, Bose, Nautica, and Noritake. The area can be aggravating to navigate during the summer owing to the four lanes of often heavy traffic and capricious restrictions on turns. Information on current outlets is available from ☎ 888/548-8379 or on the Web at www.thekitteryoutlets.com

My advice: If you're headed north, wait until Freeport (60 miles away) to indulge the shopping bug. In Freeport (as in Manchester, Vermont), you can park once and reconnoiter much of the outlet village on foot.

## DISCOVERING LOCAL HISTORY

**Old York Historical Society.** Route 1A (York St.), York. ☎ **207/363-4974.** $7 adults, $3 children 6–16, includes admission to all buildings. Tues–Sat 10am–5pm; Sun 1–5pm. (Last tour leaves at 4pm.) Closed Oct–May.

John Hancock is nationally famous for his oversize signature on the Declaration of Independence, his tenure as governor of Massachusetts, and the insurance company named after him. What's not so well known is his earlier checkered past as a businessman. Hancock was the proprietor of Hancock Wharf, a failed enterprise that's but one of the intriguing historic sites in York Village.

First settled in 1624, York Village has several early homes open to the public. Tickets are available at any of the properties, but a good place to start is **Jefferds Tavern,** across from the handsome old burying ground. Changing exhibits here document various facets of early life. Next door is the **School House,** furnished as it might have been in the mid–19th century. A 10-minute walk along lightly traveled Lindsay Road will bring you to **Hancock Wharf,** which is next door to the George Marshall Store. Also nearby is the **Elizabeth Perkins House** with its well-preserved Colonial Revival interiors.

If you're in a hurry, the two don't-miss buildings in the society's collection are the intriguing **Old Gaol,** built in 1719 with its now-musty dungeons for criminals and debtors. The jail is the oldest surviving public building in the United States. Just down the knoll from the jail is the **Emerson-Wilcox House,** built in the mid-1700s. Added to periodically over the years, it's a virtual catalog of architectural styles and early decorative arts.

## TWO WONDERFUL WALKS

Two local strolls will allow visitors to stretch their legs and get the cobwebs out of their heads.

York Harbor and York Village are connected by a quiet pathway that follows a river and passes through gently rustling woodlands. **Fisherman's Walk** departs from below Edward's Harborside Inn, near the Stage Neck Inn. (There's limited parking at tiny

York Harbor Beach.) Follow the pathway along the river, past lobster shacks and along lawns leading up to grand shingled homes. Cross Route 103 and walk over the Wiggly Bridge (said to be, not implausibly, the smallest suspension bridge in the world), then head into the woods. You'll soon connect with a dirt lane; follow this and you'll emerge at Lindsay Road near Hancock Wharf. The entire walk will require a half hour to 45 minutes.

Also departing from near York Harbor Beach is the **Cliff Walk,** a trail that follows rugged terrain along rocky bluffs and offers wonderful views of the open ocean and glimpses of life in some of the town's more grand cottages. The far end of this trail was destroyed by forceful ocean waves some years back; you'll have to retrace your steps back to the beach. There have also been local squabbles over public access, so watch for any newly posted "no trespassing" signs.

## BEACHES

York Beach actually consists of two beaches—**Long Sands Beach** and **Short Sands Beach**—separated by a rocky headland and a small island capped by scenic **Nubble Light.** Both offer plenty of room for sunning and frisbees when the tide is out. When the tide is in, they're both a bit cramped. Short Sands fronts the town of York Beach with its candlepin bowling and video arcades. It's the better bet for families traveling with kids who have short attention spans. Long Sands runs along Route 1A, across from a profusion of motels, summer homes, and convenience stores. Parking at both beaches is metered (50¢ per hour).

## WHERE TO STAY

For basic accommodations, try York Beach, which has a proliferation of motels and guest cottages facing Long Sands Beach. Even with this abundance, it's advisable to reserve ahead during prime season.; and don't expect any real bargains midsummer, even among the most basic of motels. Among those offering basic accommodation on or very near the beach are: **The Anchorage Motor Inn** (☎ 207/363-5112), **Long Beach Motor Inn** (☎ 207/363-5481), and the **Nevada Motel** (☎ 207/363-4504).

### In Kittery

**Inn at Portsmouth Harbor.** 6 Water St., Kittery, ME 03904. ☎ **207/439-4040.** Fax 207/438-9286. www.innatportsmouth.com. E-mail: innph@cybertours.com. 6 units. A/C TV TEL. Apr–Oct $135–$155 double; Nov–Mar $85–$125. Rates include full breakfast. 2-night minimum in summer, holidays. AE, MC, V. Children over 16 welcome.

This 1899 home is located just across the river from Portsmouth, New Hampshire, about a ¹/₂-mile walk across a bridge. Guests here get a taste of small coastal town life, but with access to the restaurants and shopping of Portsmouth. Most of the rooms are on the cozy side, but all are boldly furnished and fun—"Valdra" has ruby red walls, attractive antiques, and an above-average size bathroom with historic accents; "Royal Gorge" is on the third floor and has limited skylight views of the harbor and cast-iron tub with handheld shower. The whimsically decorated sitting room downstairs has two couches, plus some of the more intriguing and readable books I've seen at any inn. Breakfasts are flat-out great: large and tasty with fresh-squeezed juice and selections like corn pancakes with smoked salmon.

### In York

**Dockside Guest Quarters.** Harris Island (P.O. Box 205), York, ME 03909. ☎ **207/ 363-2868.** Fax 207/363-1977. www.docksidegq.com. E-mail: info@docksidegq.com. 25 units (2 with shared bathroom). TV. Mid-June–early Sept $119–$179 double; early summer/late fall $100–$140; winter–spring (open weekends only) $90–$140. 2-night minimum July–Sept. DISC, MC, V. Drive south on Route 103 from Route 1A in York Harbor; after bridge over York River, turn left and follow signs.

David and Harriet Lusty established this quiet retreat in 1954, and recent additions (mostly new cottages) haven't changed the friendly, maritime flavor of the place. Situated on an island connected to the mainland by a small bridge, the inn occupies nicely landscaped grounds shady with maples and white pines. Five of the rooms are in the main house, built in 1885, but the bulk of the accommodations are in small, modern townhouse-style cottages constructed between 1968 and 1998. These are simply furnished, bright, and airy, and all have private decks that overlook the entrance to York Harbor. (Several rooms also feature wood stoves.) The inn operates a locally popular restaurant on the property, serving traditional New England meals like broiled halibut, baked stuffed lobster, and braised lamb. Entrees are $13 to $17. Breakfast is available for $3. Amenities include rowboats, badminton, croquet, ocean swimming, laundry service, bicycle rental, and a sundeck.

**Stage Neck Inn.** Stage Neck (P.O. Box 70), York Harbor, ME 03911. ☎ **800/222-3238** or 207/363-3850. www.stageneck.com. E-mail: reserve@stageneck.com. 60 units. A/C TV TEL. June–Labor Day $165–$230 double; early fall $135–$200 double; winter $110–$145 double; spring $135–$165 double. AE, DISC, MC, V. Head north on 1A from Rte. 1; make second right after York Harbor post office.

A hotel in one form or another has been housing guests on this windswept bluff located between the harbor and the open ocean since about 1870. The current incarnation was constructed in 1972 and offers understated elegance to guests. The hotel, while indisputably up-to-date, successfully creates a sense of old-fashioned intimacy and avoids the overbearing grandeur to which many modern resorts aspire (often with poor results). Almost every room has a view of the water, and guests enjoy low-key recreational pursuits. York Harbor Beach is but a few steps away.

**Dining:** The inn has two dining rooms—Sandpiper Bar and Grille, and Harbor Porches. Both offer three meals daily. Dinner entrees at the more elegant Harbor Porches range from blackened Maine crab cakes to grilled pork medaillons with apple-Dijon-garlic glaze ($17 to $24). More informal fare is served up at Sandpiper's.

**Amenities:** Indoor and outdoor pools, ocean swimming, Jacuzzi, tennis courts, fitness room, and sauna.

## WHERE TO DINE
### In Kittery
**Bob's Clam Hut.** Rte. 1, Kittery. ☎ **207/439-4233.** Reservations not accepted. Sandwiches $1.50–$3.95; dinners $3.95–$18.45. AE, MC, V. Daily Memorial Day–Labor Day 11am–9pm (Sat–Sun until 9:30pm). Open year-round but closing times varies in off-season; call ahead. Located just north of the Kittery Trading Post. FRIED FISH.

Operating since 1956 (although take-out only until 1989), Bob's manages to retain an old-fashioned flavor—despite now being surrounded by slick new factory outlet malls—while serving up heaps of fried clams and other diet-busting enticements with great efficiency. (From Bob's brochure: "Our suppliers marvel at the amount of fry-olator oil we order.") Order at the front window, get a soda from a vending machine, then stake out a table inside or on the deck with a Route 1 view while waiting for your number to be called. The food is surprisingly light, cooked in cholesterol-free vegetable oil; the onion rings are especially good. To ensure your that your diet plans have been irrevocably violated, Bob's also offers Ben & Jerry's ice cream.

**Chauncey Creek Lobster Pier.** Chauncey Creek Rd., Kittery Point. ☎ **207/439-1030.** No reservations. Lobsters priced to market; other items $1.50–$8.95. MC, V. Daily 11am–8pm (until 7pm during shoulder seaons); closed Mon after Labor Day. Closed Columbus Day–Mother's Day. Located between Kittery Point and York on Route 103; watch for signs.

It's not on the wild, open ocean, but Chaucey's remains one of the most scenic lobster pounds in the state, not the least because the Spinney Family, which has been selling lobsters here since the 1950s, takes such obvious pride in their place. You reach the pound by walking down a wooden ramp to the water's edge, where a broad deck and some 42 festively painted picnic tables await. Lobster, served hot and fresh, is the specialty, of course, but they also offer up steamed mussels (in wine and garlic) and clams. This is an à la carte place—buy a crock of baked beans or sodas and a bag of ice while waiting for your lobsters to cook. It's BYOB, and you can bring in any other food you want provided they don't sell it here. Afterwards, wash up at the outdoor sink (labelled "finger bowl") on the deck.

### In The Yorks

✪ **Cape Neddick Inn Restaurant.** 1233 Rte. 1, Cape Neddick. ☎ **207/363-2899.** Reservations recommended. Main courses $16–$28. DISC, MC, V. Late June–Labor Day daily 5:30–9:30pm (open year-round Wed–Sat; call ahead for other days in off-season). CONTEMPORARY AMERICAN.

This fine inn has offered some of the consistently best dining in southern Maine since 1979, and continues to do so under its current ownership. Located in an elegant structure on a relatively quiet stretch of Route 1, the Cape Neddick Inn has an open, handsome dining area that mixes traditional and modern. The old comes in the cozy golden glow of the room. The modern is the artwork, which changes frequently and showcases some of the region's better painters and sculptors. The creative menu changes seasonally to make the most of local products. There's an extensive selection of appetizers, including goat cheese with a roasted beet terrine, and applewood-smoked seafood (smoked on premises) served tossed in an apple-cider vinaigrette on Rhode Island johnnycakes. Depending on the season, main courses could include chargrilled steak with Vidalia onions and cob-smoked bacon, or salmon glazed with a Sichuan barbecue sauce. Diners can select from more than 100 wines, a selection recognzied by *Wine Spectator* awards in 1998 and 1999.

**Goldenrod Restaurant.** Railroad Rd. and Ocean Ave., York Beach. ☎ **207/363-2621.** www.thegoldenrod.com. Breakfast $2.50–$5.25; lunch and dinner entrees $2.75–$7.50. MC, V. Memorial Day–Labor Day daily 8am–10pm (until 9pm in June); Labor Day–Columbus Day Wed–Sun 8am–3pm. Closed Columbus Day–Memorial Day. FAMILY STYLE.

This beach town classic is the place for local color—it's been a summer institution in York Beach since it first opened in 1896. It's easy to find: look for visitors gawking through plate-glass windows at the ancient taffy machines hypnotically churning out taffy in volumes enough (63 tons a year) to make busloads of dentists very wealthy. The restaurant is behind the taffy and fudge operation, and is low on frills and long on atmosphere. Diners sit on stout oak furniture around a stone fireplace, or at the marble soda fountain. There are dark beams overhead and the sort of linoleum floor you don't see much anymore. Breakfast offerings are the standards: omelets, waffles, griddle cakes and bakery items. Lunch is equally predictable American fare (soups, club sandwiches, hamburgers, and hot dogs), but well-presented. As for dinner, you'd probably be better served heading to some place more creative.

## OGUNQUIT

Ogunquit is a bustling beachside town that's attracted vacationers and artists for more than a century. While notable for its abundant and elegant summer-resort architecture, Ogunquit is most famous for its $3^1/2$-mile white-sand beach, backed by grassy dunes. The beach serves as the town's front porch, and most everyone drifts over there at least once a day when the sun is shining.

Ogunquit's fame as an art colony dates to around 1890, when Charles H. Woodbury arrived and declared the place an "artist's paradise." He was followed by artists Walt Kuhn, Elihu Vedder, Yasuo Kuniyoshi, and Rudolph Dirks, who was best known for creating the "Katzenjammer Kids" comic strip.

In the latter decades of the 19th century, the town found quiet fame as a destination for gay travelers, at a time when one's sexual orientation was not publicly acknowledged. (Well, at least if you weren't hetero.) Ogunquit has retained its appeal for gays through the years, and many local enterprises are run by gay entrepreneurs. The scene is very low-key compared to Provincetown, Massachusetts. It's more like an understated family resort, where a good many family members just happen to be gay.

Despite the architectural gentility and the overall civility of the place, the town can feel overrun with tourists during the peak summer season, especially on weekends. The teeming crowds are part of the allure for some Ogunquit regulars. If you're not a crowd person, you would probably do well to visit here in the off-season.

## ESSENTIALS

**GETTING THERE**   Ogunquit is located on Route 1 between York and Wells. It's accessible from either Exit 1 or Exit 2 of the Maine Turnpike.

**VISITOR INFORMATION**   The **Ogunquit Welcome Center,** P.O. Box 2289, Ogunquit, ME 03907 (☎ **207/646-5533** or 207/646-2939), is located on Route 1 south of the village center. It's open daily 9am to 5pm April to Columbus Day (until 8pm during the peak summer season) and 10am to 2pm daily during the off-season. On the Web, head to www.ogunquit.org.

**GETTING AROUND**   The village of Ogunquit is centered around an intersection that seems fiendishly designed to cause massive traffic foul-ups in summer. Parking in and around the village is also tight and relatively expensive (expect to pay $6 per day or more). As a result, Ogunquit is best reconnoitered on foot or by bike.

A number of trackless trollies (with names like Dolly and Ollie—you get the idea) run all day long from mid-May to Columbus Day between Perkins Cove and the Wells town line to the north, with detours to the sea down Beach and Ocean streets. The cost is $1 per adult, 50¢ per child per boarding; the driver can't make change. It's well worth the small expense to avoid the hassles of driving and parking.

## EXPLORING OGUNQUIT

The village center is good for an hour or two of browsing among the boutiques, or sipping a cappucino at one of the several coffee emporia.

From the village you can walk to scenic Perkins Cove along **Marginal Way,** a mile-long oceanside pathway once used for herding cattle to pasture. Earlier in the last century, the land was bought by a local developer who deeded the right-of-way to the town. The pathway, which is wide and well-maintained, departs across from the Seacastles Resort on Shore Road. It passes tide pools, pocket beaches, and rocky, fissured bluffs, all of which are worth exploring. The seascape can be spectacular (especially after a storm), but Marginal Way can also be spectacularly crowded during fair-weather weekends. To elude the crowds, head out in the very early morning.

**Perkins Cove,** accessible either from Marginal Way or by driving south on Shore Road and veering left at the "Y" intersection, is a small, well-protected harbor that seems custom-designed for a photo opportunity. As such, it attracts visitors by the busload, carload, and boatload, and is often heavily congested. A handful of galleries, restaurants, and T-shirt shops catering to the tourist trade occupy a cluster of quaint buildings between the harbor and the sea. An intriguing pedestrian drawbridge is operated by whomever happens to be handy, allowing sailboats to come and go.

Perkins Cove is also home to a handful of deep-sea fishing and tour boat operators, who offer trips of various durations. Try the *Deborah Ann* (☎ 207/-361-9501) for whale watching (two tours daily) or the *Ugly Anne* (☎ 207-646-7202) for deep-sea fishing. One last bit of advice: If teeming crowds and tourist enterprises are not the reason you came to Maine, steer clear of Perkins Cove.

Not far from the cove is the **Ogunquit Museum of American Art,** 183 Shore Rd. (☎ 207/646-4909), one of the best small art museums in the nation. Set back from the road in a grassy glen overlooking rocky shore, the museum's spectacular view initially overwhelms the artwork as visitors walk through the door.; but stick around a few minutes—the changing exhibits in this architecturally engaging modern building of cement block, slate, and glass will get your attention soon enough, since the curators have a track record of staging superb shows and attracting national attention. (Be sure to note the bold, underappreciated work of Henry Strater, the Ogunquit artist who founded the museum in 1953.) A 1,400-square-foot wing opened recently adding welcome new exhibition space. The museum is open July 1 to September 30 from 10:30am to 5pm Monday to Saturday, and 2 to 5pm on Sunday. Admission is $4 for adults, $3 for seniors and students, and children under 12 are free.

For evening entertainment, head to the **Ogunquit Playhouse,** Rte. 1 (☎ 207/646-5511), a 750-seat summer-stock theater that has garnered a solid reputation for its careful, serious attention to stagecraft. The theater has entertained Ogunquit since 1933, attracting noted actors such as Bette Davis, Tallulah Bankhead, and Gary Merrill. Stars of recent seasons have included Gavin McLeod and Kitty Carlisle Hart.

## BEACHES

Ogunquit's **main beach** is more than 3 miles long, and three paid parking lots ($2 per hour) are located along its length. The most popular access point is at the foot of Beach Street, which runs into Ogunquit Village. The beach ends at a sandy spit, where the Ogunquit River flows into the sea; here you'll find changing rooms and a handful of informal restaurants. It's also the most crowded part of the beach. Less congested options are at **Footbridge Beach** (turn on Ocean Avenue off Route 1 north of the village center) and **Moody Beach** (turn on Eldridge Avenue in Wells).

## A ROAD TRIP TO LAUDHOLM FARM

A short drive north of Ogunquit, just above the beach town of Wells, is the **Laudholm Farm** (☎ 207/646-1555), an historic saltwater farm owned by the non-profit Laudholm Trust since 1986. The 1,600-acre property was originally the summer home of 19th-century railroad baron George Lord, but has been used for estaurine research since taken over by the trust. The farm has 7 miles of trails through diverse ecosystems, which range from salt marsh to forest to dunes. A visitor center in the regal Victorian farmhouse will get you oriented. Tours are available, or you can explore the grounds on your own. Parking costs $5 in summer; it's free the rest of the year. There's no admission charge to the grounds or visitor center. The farm is open daily 8am to 5pm; the visitor center is open 10am to 4pm Monday to Saturday, and noon to 4pm on Sunday.

The farm is reached by turning east on Laudholm Farm Road at the blinking light just north of Harding's Books (which, incidentally, is located in Lord's former private railroad station). Bear left at the fork, then turn right into the farm's entrance.

## WHERE TO STAY

Just a few steps from Ogunquit's main downtown intersection is the meticulously maintained **Studio East Motel,** 43 Main St. (☎ 207/646-7297). It's open April to mid-November, with peak-season rates running $94 to $119. Rooms are basic, but all have refrigerators; microwaves are available free to those staying 3 nights or more. A restaurant serving traditional New England fare is on the premises.

**Beachmere Inn.** 12 Beachmere Rd., Ogunquit, ME 03907. ☎ **800/336-3983** or 207/646-2021. Fax 207/646-2231. www.beachmereinn.com. 53 units. A/C TV TEL. Peak season $110–$195 double, mid-season $75–$145, off-season $65–110. Rates include continental breakfast. 3-night minimum in summer. Closed mid-Dec–April. AE, CB, DC, DISC, MC, V.

Run by the same family since 1937, the Beachmere Inn sprawls across a grassy hillside (the inn occupies about 4 acres) and nearly every room has a view northward up Ogunquit's famous beach. Guests choose from two buildings. The Beachmere Victorian dates to the 1890s and is all turrets and porches. Next door is the dated but fun Beachmere South, a two-story motel-like structure done up in 1960s modern style, featuring concrete slathered with a stucco finish. The rooms at Beachmere South are spacious (some are mini-suites), interestingly angled, and all have private balconies or patios and great views. The motel is on Marginal Way, which is great for walks, and offers foot access to the beach. When rooms in the two main buildings are filled, guests are offered rooms in the Bullfrog Cottage nearby. The five units are darker, lack views, and are less impressively furnished, but they are spacious and popular with families.

**Grand Hotel.** 102 Shore Rd. (P.O. Box 1526), Ogunquit, ME 03907. ☎ **207/646-1231.** www.thegrandhotel.com. E-mail: info@thegrandhotel.com. 28 suites. A/C TV TEL. Peak season $150–$200 double, mid-season $95–$200, off-season $75–$140. Ask about spring and fall packages. Rates include continental breakfast. 2- or 3-night minimum on weekends and peak season. AE, DISC, MC, V. Closed early Nov–early Apr.

The modern Grand Hotel seems a bit ill at ease in Victorian Ogunquit. Constructed in a vaguely Frank Lloyd Wright–inspired style, the hotel centers around a three-story atrium and consists of 30 two-room suites. All rooms have refrigerators and VCRs (tapes may be rented downstairs). The modern, tidy guest rooms have an unfortuante generic, chain-hotel character, but all have private decks on which to enjoy the woodsy Maine air. The five top-floor penthouses are airier and brighter, with cathedral ceilings and Duraflame-log fireplaces. The hotel is located on busy Shore Road and is about 10 minute's walk to the beach. Other nice touches: Parking is underground and connected to the rooms by elevator, and there's a small indoor pool.

**Nellie Littlefield House.** 9 Shore Rd., Ogunquit, ME 03907. ☎ **207/646-1692.** 8 units. A/C TV TEL. Peak season $150–$210, mid-season $95–$150, off-season $80–$125. Rates include full breakast. 2-night minimum weekends, 3 nights on holidays. DISC, MC, V. Closed late Oct–Apr. Children over 12 welcome.

This 1889 home stands impressively at the edge of Ogunquit's compact commercial district, and the prime location and the handsome Queen Anne architecture are the main draws here. All rooms are carpeted and feature a mix of modern and antique reproduction furnishings; several have refrigerators. Four rooms to the rear have private decks, but views are limited, mostly of the unlovely motel next door. The most spacious room is the third-floor J. H. Littlefield suite, with two TVs and a Jacuzzi. The most unique? The circular Grace Littlefield room, located in the upper turrent and overlooking the street. The basement features a compact fitness room with modern equipment.

## WHERE TO DINE

✪ **Arrows.** Berwick Rd. ☎ **207/361-1100.** Reservations strongly recommended. Main courses $35–$40. MC, V. Mid-April–Memorial Day weekend Fri–Sun 6–9:30pm; June–Columbus Day Tues–Sun 6–9:30pm; Columbus Day–mid-Dec Fri–Sun 6–9:30pm. Open Thanksgiving Day. Closed mid-Dec–mid-Apr. Turn uphill at the Key Bank in the village; the restaurant is 1.9 miles on your right. NEW AMERICAN.

When owner/chefs Mark Gaier and Clark Frasier opened Arrows in 1988, they quickly put Ogunquit on the national culinary map. They've done so by not only creating an elegant and intimate atmosphere, but by serving up some of the freshest, most innovative cooking in New England. The emphasis is on local products—often very local. The salad greens are grown in gardens on the grounds, and much of the rest is grown or raised locally. The food transcends traditional New England and is deftly prepared with exotic twists and turns. Frasier lived and traveled for a time in Asia, and his Far Eastern experiences tend to influence the menu, which changes nightly. Among the more popular recurrent dishes is the homemade prosciutto (hams are strung up around the restaurant to cure in the off-season) served with pears, toasted pumpkin seeds, and olive oil. The "bento box" includes marinated lamb brochettes, orange cabbage, and "strange flavored eggplant"; the grilled beef tenderloin is spiced with a Szechuan peppercorn marinade. The wine list is top-rate. The chief complaint? The entree prices are way beyond what you'll pay elsewhere in northern New England, and may make even New Yorkers wince.

✪ **Hurricane.** 52 Oarweed Rd., Perkins Cove. ☎ **800/649-6348** (ME and NH only) or 207/646-6348. www.perkinscove.com. Reservations recommended for either lunch or dinner. Lunch items $7–$15; main dinner courses $16–$28; lobster dishes priced daily (to $39). AE, DC, DISC, MC, V. Daily 11:30am–3:30pm, 5:30–10:30pm May–Oct, 5:30–9:30pm Nov–Apr. Closed briefly in January (call ahead). NEW AMERICAN.

Tucked away amid the T-shirt kitsch of Perkins Cove is one of southern Maine's classiest and most enjoyable dining experiences. The plain shingled exterior of the building, set along a curving, narrow lane, doesn't hint at what you'll find inside. The narrow dining room is divided into two smallish halves, but soaring windows overlooking the Gulf of Maine create the sense that the place is larger than it actually is. Hurricane's menu changes daily, and owner Brooks MacDonald is known for his consistently creative concoctions, like the appetizer of deviled Maine lobster cakes served with a tangy fresh salsa (so popular it's always available). At lunch, look for salmon burgers or seared jerked scallops. At dinner, there's delectable lobster cioppino (the signature dish), a pistachio-coated veal chop, or swordfish served with a pecan-plum sauce. Among the more intriguing desserts: a vanilla ginger crème brûlée, and white chocolate with coconut mousse. Added bonus: Hurricane makes the best martinis in town.

## THE KENNEBUNKS

"The Kennebunks" consist of the villages of **Kennebunk** and **Kennebunkport,** both situated along the shores of small rivers, and both laying claim to a portion of rocky coast. The region was first settled in the mid-1600s and flourished after the American Revolution, when ship captains, shipbuilders, and prosperous merchants constructed the imposing, solid homes. The Kennebunks are famed for their striking historic architecture and expansive beaches.

While summer is the busy season along the coast, winter has its charm: the grand architecture is best seen through leafless trees. When the snow flies, guests find solace curling up in front of a fire at one of the inviting inns.

### ESSENTIALS

**GETTING THERE**    Kennebunk is located off Exit 3 of the Maine Turnpike. Kennebunkport is 3¹/₂ miles southeast of Kennebunk on Port Road (Route 35).

**VISITOR INFORMATION    The Kennebunk-Kennebunkport Chamber of Commerce,** P.O. Box 740, Kennebunk, ME 04043 (☎ **800/982-4421** or 207/967-0857), can answer your questions year-round by phone or at their offices on

Route 9 next to Meserve's Market. The **Kennebunkport Information Center** (☎ 207/967-8600) is off Dock Square (next to Ben & Jerry's) and is open daily throughout the summer and fall.

The local trolley (bus) (☎ 207/967-3686), makes several stops in and around Kennebunkport and also serves the beaches. The fare is $7 per person per day, which includes unlimited trips.

## EXPLORING KENNEBUNK

Kennebunk has its downtown inland just off the turnpike and is a dignified, small commercial center of white clapboard and brick. The **Brick Store Museum,** 117 Main St. (☎ 207/985-4802), hosts shows of historical art and artifacts throughout the summer, switching to contemporary art in the off-season. The museum is housed in a historic former brick store (that is, a store that once sold bricks), as well as the three adjacent buildings, which have been made over and inside have the polished gloss of a well-cared-for gallery. Admission is $5 adult, $2 student, under 17 free. Open Tuesdays through Saturdays 10am to 4:30pm between June and December. Call for winter hours.

**Tom's of Maine,** (☎ 207/985-3874), a natural toothpaste maker, is also headquartered here. Tom and Kate Chappell sell their all-natural toothpaste and other personal care products worldwide, but are almost as well known for their green, socially conscious business philosophy. (Tom wrote a book on the subject.) Tom's factory outlet sells firsts and seconds of its own products (some at a tremendous markdown), as well as a selection of other natural products. The shop is at Lafayette Center, an historic industrial building converted to shops and offices at the corner of Main and Water streets. It's open Monday to Saturday 10am to 5pm.

When en route to or from the coast, be sure to note the extraordinary homes that line Port Road (Route 35). This includes the famous "Wedding Cake House," which you should be able to identify on your own. Local lore claims that the house was built by a guilt-ridden ship captain, who left for sea before his bride could enjoy a proper wedding cake. It's made of brick, with a surfeit of ornamental trim. The house is privately owned but can be enjoyed from the outside.

## EXPLORING KENNEBUNKPORT

Kennebunkport is the summer home of former Pres. George Bush, whose family has summered here for decades. Given that, it has the tweedy, upper-crust feel that one might expect of the place. This historic village, whose streets were laid out during days of travel by foot and horse, is subject to monumental traffic jams around the town center. If the municipal lot off the square is full, head north on North Street a few minutes to the free long-term lot and catch the trolley back into town.; or walk—it's a pleasant 10- to 15-minute from the lot to Dock Square.

**Dock Square** has a pleasantly wharf-like feel to it, with low buildings of mixed vintages and styles (you'll find mansard, gabled, and hip roofs side by side), but the flavor is mostly clapboard and shingles. The boutiques in the area are attractive, and many feature creative artworks and crafts, but Kennebunkport's real attraction is found in the surrounding blocks, where the side streets are lined with one of the nation's richest assortments of early American homes. The neighborhoods are especially ripe with examples of Federal-style homes; many have been converted to bed-and-breakfasts (see "Where to Stay," below).

A bit farther afield, in the affluent neighborhood near the Colony Hotel (about 1 mile east on Ocean Avenue), is a superb collection of homes of the uniquely American shingle style. It's worth a detour on foot or bike to ogle these icons of the 19th and early 20th century leisure class.

Aimless wandering is a good tactic for exploring Kennebunkport, but at least, make an effort to stop by the **Richard A. Nott House** (8 Maine St., ☎ 207/967-2751) in your travels. Situated on Maine Street at the head of Spring Street, this imposing Greek Revival house was built 1853 and is a Victorian-era aficionado's dream. It remained untouched by the Nott family through the years and was donated to the local historical society with the stipulation that it remain forever unchanged. It still boasts the original wallpaper, carpeting, and furnishings. Tours run about 40 minutes; it's open 1 to 4pm Tuesday to Friday from mid-June to mid-October. Admission is $5 adult, $2 children under 18.

Ocean Drive from Dock Square to Walkers Point and beyond is lined with opulent summer homes overlooking surf and rocky shore. You'll likely recognize the former president's home at Walkers Point when you arrive. If it's not familiar from the several years it spent in the national spotlight, look for the crowds with telephoto lenses. If they're not out, look for the shingle-style secret service booth at the head of a drive. That's it.

✪ **The Seashore Trolley Museum.** 195 Log Cabin Rd., Kennebunkport. ☎ **207/ 967-2800.** www.trolleymuseum.org. $7 adults, $4.50 children 6–16, $5 seniors, $23 family. Open daily May 29–Oct 21 10am–5pm; weekends only May 6–May 27 and Oct 22–Nov 5. Closed early Nov–early May. Head north from Kennebunkport on North St. for 1.7 miles; look for signs.

A short drive north of Kennebunkport on Log Cabin Road is a local marvel: a scrapyard-masquerading-as-a-museum ("world's oldest and largest museum of its type"). This quirky and engaging museum was founded in 1939 to preserve a disappearing way of life, and today the collection contains more than 200 trolleys from around the world, including specimens from Glasgow, Moscow, San Francisco, and Rome. (Rest assured, there's also a streetcar named "Desire" from New Orleans.)

About 40 of the cars still operate, and the admission charge includes rides on a 2-mile track. The other cars, some of which still contain early–20th century advertising, are on display outdoors and in vast storage sheds. A good museum inspires awe and educates its visitors on the sly. This one does so deftly, and not until visitors are driving away are they likely to realize how much they learned about how America got around before there was a car in every garage.

## BEACHES

The coastal area around Kennebunkport is home to several of the state's finest beaches. Southward across the river (technically this is Kennebunk although it's closer to Dock Square than to downtown Kennebunk) are **Gooch's Beach** and **Kennebunk Beach.** Head eastward on Beach Street (from the intersection of Routes 9 and 35) and you'll soon wind into a handsome colony of eclectic, shingled summer homes (some improbably grand, some modest). The narrow road twists past sandy beaches and rocky headlands. The area can be frightfully congested when traveling by car in the summer; avoid the local version of gridlock by opting to travel via foot or bike.

**Goose Rocks Beach** is north of Kennebunkport off Route 9 (watch for signs), and is the better destination for those who prefer to avoid crowds, and are more drawn to beaches than the beach scene. You'll find an enclave of beach homes set amid rustling oaks off a fine sand beach. Just offshore is a narrow barrier reef that has historically attracted flocks of geese—which in turn lent their name to the beach.

## BIKING THE KENNEBUNKS

The Kennebunks are well-suited to exploring by bicycle. Bikes may be rented at **Cape Able Bike Shop** north of Kennebunkport (☎ **800/220-0907** or 207/967-4382). Some inns also will rent bikes to guests; ask when you reserve a room.

## WHERE TO STAY

A unique choice for budget accomodations is the **Franciscan Guest House,** Beach Street, (☎ **207/967-2011**) a former dormitory on the 200-acre grounds of the St. Anthony's Monastery. The 60 rooms are institutional, basic, and clean, and have private baths; guests can stroll the attractive riverside grounds or walk over to Dock Square, about 10 minutes away. Rooms are $43 to $49. No credit cards; open mid-June to mid-September.

**Beach House Inn.** 211 Beach Ave., Kennebunk Beach, ME 04043. ☎ **207/967-3850.** Fax 207/967-4719. www.beachhseinn.com. E-mail: innkeeper@beachhseinn.com. 34 units. Peak season $190–$325 double; off-season $95–$190. Rates include continental breakfast. 2-night minimum on weekends. AE, MC, V.

This is a good choice if you'd like to be amid the action of Kennebunk Beach. The inn was built in 1891 but has been extensively modernized and expanded—it's now owned by the same folks who own the legendary White Barn Inn, and has been upgraded with down comforters and pillows. The rooms aren't necessarily historic but are carpeted, and most have Victorian furnishings and accenting. The main draw is the lovely porch, where you can stare out at the pebble beach across the road and idly watch bikers and in-line skaters pass by. The inn has touring bikes and canoes for guests to use, and provides beach chairs and towels.

**Captain Jefferds Inn.** 5 Pearl St. (P.O. Box 691), Kennebunkport, ME 04046. ☎ **800/839-6844** or 207/967-2311. www.captainjefferdsinn.com. E-mail: capjeff@captainjefferdsinn.com. 16 units. $135–$285 double. Rates include full breakfast. 2-night minimum weekends July–Oct and holidays. AE, MC, V. Dogs $20 additional by advance reservation.

This 1804 Federal home surrounded by other historic homes was fully done over recently, and the innkeepers have done a superb job in coaxing out the historic feel of the place while giving each room its own personality. Fine antiques abound throughout, and guests will need some persuading to come out of their wonderful rooms once they've settled in. Among the best are Manhanttan, with a four-poster bed, fireplace, and beautiful afternoon light; and Assissi, with a restful indoor fountain and rock garden (sounds weird, but it works). The wide price range reflects the varying room sizes, but even the smallest rooms—like Katahdin—are comfortable and far beyond merely adequate. Bright common rooms on the first floor offer alluring lounging space; an elaborate breakfast is served before a fire on cool days, and on the terrace when summer weather permits.

✪ **Captain Lord.** Pleasant St. and Green St. (P.O. Box 800), Kennebunkport, ME 04046. ☎ **207/967-3141.** Fax 207/967-3172. www.captainlord.com. E-mail: captain@biddeford.com. 16 units. A/C TEL. Summer and fall $199–$399 double; winter and spring from $99 midweek, from $175 weekends. Rates include full breakfast. 2-night minimum weekends and holidays year-round (some holidays 3-night minimum). DISC, MC, V. Children 12 and older welcome.

Captain Lord is one of the most architecturally distinguished inns anywhere, housed in a pale-yellow Federal-style home that peers down a shady lawn toward the river. The adjective "stately" is laughably inadequate. When you enter the downstairs reception area, you'll know immediately that this is the genuine article, with grandfather clocks and Chippendale highboys—and that's just the front hallway. Off the hall is a comfortable common area with piped-in classical music and a broad brick fireplace. Downstairs is a conference room with sofa and TV for those who need their fix (no TVs in rooms).

Head up the elliptical staircase to the guest rooms, which are furnished with splendid antiques; all feature gas fireplaces. The Captain Lord does not have a single unappealing room (although some may find "Union" a little dark). Among my favorites: "Excelsior," a large corner room with a massive four-poster bed, a love seat in front of the gas fireplace, and a two-person Jacuzzi in the bathroom with a heated tile floor; "Hesper," which is the nicest of the less expensive rooms, featuring a burnished historic gloss and a bathroom with a large stained-glass window; and "Merchant," a spacious first-floor suite that pampers you with two large rooms, a marble-floored bathroom with a large Jacuzzi, and a mini-spa with NordicRider bike and foot massager. Four rooms are at Phebe's, an historic gray-clapboard home behind the main inn, where guests are served breakfast at a long table in a Colonial-style kitchen. The rooms here are less opulent but still very well-appointed.

○ **The Colony Hotel.** 140 Ocean Ave. (P.O. Box 511), Kennebunkport, ME 04046. ☎ **800/552-2363** or 207/967-3331. Fax 207/967-8738. www.thecolony hotel.com/maine. E-mail: reservations@thecolonyhotel.com. 123 units. TEL. $175–$425 double in July and August; off-season rates available. Rates include breakfast. 3-night minimum on summer weekends and holidays in main hotel. AE, MC, V. Closed mid-Oct–mid-May. Pets allowed.

The Colony is one of the handful of oceanside resorts that has preserved intact the classic New England vacation experience. This mammoth white Georgian Revival (built in 1914) lords over the ocean and the mouth of the Kennebunk River. The three-story main inn has 91 rooms, all of of which have been renovated over the last 3 years. The rooms are bright and cheery, simply furnished with summer cottage antiques. Rooms in two of the three outbuildings carry over the rustic elegance of the main hotel; the exception is the East House, a 1950s-era motor hotel at the back edge of the property with 20 uninteresting motel-style rooms.

Guest rooms lack TVs in the main inn, and that's by design. The Boughton family, which has owned the hotel since 1948, encourages guests to socialize in the evening downstairs in the lobby, on the porch, or at the shuffleboard court, which is lighted for nighttime play. A staff naturalist leads guided coastal ecology tours Saturday mornings in July and August.

**Dining:** The massive, pine-panelled dining room seats up to 400, and guests are assigned one table throughout their stay. Dinners begin with a relish tray but quickly progress to creative regional entrees. Entrees are priced $15 to $28. On Fridays, there's a lobster buffet, and Sunday, a jazz brunch during summer months. Lunch is served daily (poolside in July and August), and a pub menu is available for those seeking lighter fare. Live music is offered in the Marine Room lounge on weekends.

**Amenities:** Bike rental, putting green, library, heated saltwater pool, small beach, conference rooms, poolside sundeck, cocktail lounge, gift shop, weekday afternoon tea in lobby, room service, social director, free newspaper, safe-deposit boxes, and health club 3 miles away.

**Old Fort Inn.** 8 Old Fort Rd. (P.O. Box M), Kennebunkport, ME 04046. ☎ **207/967-5353.** Fax 207/967-4547. www.oldfortinn.com. E-mail: oldfort@cybertours.com. 16 units (includes 2 suites). A/C MINIBAR TV TEL. $150–$195 double; from $325 suite. Rates include full breakfast. AE, DISC, MC, V.

The sophisticated Old Fort Inn is located in a quiet and picturesque neighorbhood of magnificent late-19th-century summer homes about 2 blocks from the ocean and not far from The Colony Hotel. Guests check in at the tidiest antique shop I've ever seen, and most park around back at the large carriage house, an interesting amalgam of stone, brick, shingle, and stucco. The 14 rooms here are modern (once inside you could be in a building constructed last year), but are solidly wrought and delightfully decorated with antiques and reproductions. About half of the rooms have in-floor heated tiles in the bathrooms; all have welcome amenities like robes, refrigerators, irons, coffeemakers, hair dryers, Neutrogena products, and a reasonably priced self-serve snack bar.

Two 500-square-foot suites are located in the main house; #216 faces east and the pool, and is flooded with morning light. A full buffet breakfast is served in the main house; in nice weather guests often take waffles, pancakes, croissants, or fresh fuit on wicker trays outside to enjoy the morning sun.

**Amenities:** The inn is located on 15 acres that include a heated outdoor pool and tennis court (1 hour free daily). A beach is within walking distance; two golf courses are within 5 minutes. Also Laundromat or laundry service, and dry cleaning

**The Tides Inn.** Goose Rocks Beach, Kennebunkport, ME 04046. ☎ **207/967-3757.** www.tidesinnbythesea.com. 22 units (4 share 2 bathrooms). Peak season $185–$245 double with private bath (from $125 off season), $105 with shared bath (from $95 off season). 3-night minimum in peak season (mid-June–Labor Day and all weekends). AE, MC, V. Closed mid-Oct–mid-May.

This is the best bet in the region for a quiet getaway. Located just across the street from Goose Rocks Beach, the Tides Inn is a yellow-clapboard and shingle affair dating from 1899 that retains a seaside boarding-house feel while providing up-to-date comfort. (Past guests have included Teddy Roosevelt and Arthur Conan Doyle.) The rooms tend toward the small side, as they often do in historic hostelries, but are comfortable, and you can hear the lapping of the surf from all of them. Among the brightest and most popular are rooms 11, 15, 24, and 29, some of which have bay windows and all of which have ocean views. The parlor has old wicker, TV, and chess for those rainy days. The pub is cozy and features a wood stove and dartboard.

**Dining:** The Belvedere Room offers upscale traditional dining in a Victorian setting with options such as rack of lamb, shellfish ragout, filet mignon, and boiled lobster. Entrees are $16.95 to $27.95. Less elaborate meals are served in the pub, including salads, burritos, and burgers ($5.95 to $10.25). Breakfast is also offered, but note that it's not included in room rates.

✪ **White Barn Inn.** 37 Beach Ave. (¹/₄ mile east of junction of rtes. 9 and 35; P.O. Box 560), Kennebunkport, ME 04046. ☎ **207/967-2321.** Fax 207/967-1100. www.whitebarninn. com. E-mail: innkeeper@whitebarninn.com. 25 units. A/C TEL. $220–$250 double; suite $365–$550. Rates include continental breakfast and afternoon tea. 2-night minimum weekends; 3 nights holiday weekends. AE, MC, V.

The White Barn Inn pampers its guests like no other in Maine. Upon checking in, guests are shown to one of the inn's parlors and offered port or brandy while valets in crisp uniforms gather luggage and park the cars. A tour of the inn follows, then guests are left to their own devices. They can avail themselves of the inn's free bikes (including a small fleet of tandems) to head to the beach, or walk cross the street and wander the quiet, shady pathways of St. Anthony's Franciscan Monastery. The rooms are individually decorated in a refined country style that's elegant without being obtrusive. The inn has an atmosphere that's distinctly European, and the emphasis is on service. I'm not aware of any other inn of this size that offers as many unexpected niceties, like robes, fresh flowers in the rooms, bottled water, and turndown service at night. Nearly half the rooms have wood-burning fireplaces.

**Dining:** See "Where to Dine," below.

**Amenities:** Concierge, room service (breakfast only), free newspaper, in-room massage, twice-daily maid service, valet parking, guest safe, afternoon tea, outdoor heated pool, bicycles, nearby ocean beach, conference rooms, and sundeck.

## WHERE TO DINE

**Federal Jack's Restaurant and Brew Pub.** 8 Lower Village (south bank of Kennebunk River), Kennebunkport. ☎ **207/967-4322.** www.federaljacks.com. Lunch items $5.25–$12.95; main dinner courses $6.25–$21.95. AE, DISC, MC, V. Daily 11:30am–10 pm. PUB FARE.

This light, airy, and modern restaurant is in a retail complex of recent vintage that sits a bit uneasily amid the scrappy boatyards lining the south bank of the Kennebunk River. From the second-floor perch (look for a seat on the spacious 3-season deck in warmer weather) you can gaze across the river toward the shops of Dock Square. The upscale pub menu features regional fare with an international influence, and also offers standard fare like hamburgers, steamed mussels, and pizza. Most everything is well-prepared. Watch for specials like the grilled crab and Havarti sandwich. Don't leave without sampling the Shipyard ales, lagers, and porters brewed downstairs, which are among the best in New England. Consider the ale sampler, which provides tastes of various brews. Non-tipplers can enjoy a zesty homemade root beer, or imbibe fresh-roasted coffees at the coffee bar.

**Grissini.** 27 Western Ave., Kennebunkport. ☎ **207/967-2211.** Reservations encouraged. Main courses $7.95–$18.95. AE, MC, V. Sun–Fri 5:30–9:30pm; Sat 5–9pm (closed Wed Jan–Mar). TUSCAN.

Opened by the same folks who run the White Barn Inn, Grissini is a handsome trattoria that offers good value. The mood is rustic Italian writ large: oversize Italian advertising posters line the walls of the soaring, barn-like space, and burning logs in the handsome stone fireplace take the chill out of a cool evening. In fact, everything seems larger than life, including the plates, flatware, and water goblets. The meals are also luxuriously sized and nicely presented, and include a wide range of pastas and pizza, served with considerable flair. (The linguini tossed with seafood is simple, filling, and tasty.) The desserts are competent, not stellar, and include old friends like creme caramel and tiramasu.

✪ **White Barn Inn.** 37 Beach Ave., Kennebunkport. ☎ **207/967-2321.** Reservations recommended. Fixed-price dinner $72. AE, MC, V. Daily 6–9pm. Closed 2 weeks in Jan. REGIONAL/NEW AMERICAN.

The setting is magical. The restaurant (attached to an equally magical inn, see "Where to Stay," above) is housed in an ancient, rustic barn with a soaring interior. There's a copper-topped bar off to one side, rich leather seating in the waiting area, a pianist setting the mood, and an eclectic collection of country antiques displayed in the hay loft above. On the tables are floor-length tablecloths, and the chairs feature imported Italian upholstery. The service is impeccable, although those accustomed to more informal settings might find it overly attentive.

The excellent menu changes frequently, but depending on the season, you might start with a lobster spring roll with daikon, carrots, snow peas and cilantro, then graduate to a crab-glazed poached fillet of halibut on sweet-pea puree, or pan-seared veal and venison on bacon-roasted butternut squash. Among the more popular dishes is the Maine lobster on homemade fettucini with cognac corral butter sauce. Anticipate a meal to remember. The White Barn won't let you down.

# 3 Portland

Portland is 106 miles north of Boston

Portland is Maine's largest city, and it's easily one of the more attractive and livable small cities on the East Coast. Strike up a conversation with a resident, and you're likely to get an earful about how easy it is to live here. You can buy superb coffee, see movies with subtitles, and get delicious pad thai to go. Yet it's still small enough to walk from one end of town to the other, and postal workers and bank clerks know your name soon after you move here. Despite its outward appearance of being an actual metropolis, Portland has a population of just over 65,000, or roughly half that of Peoria, Illinois.

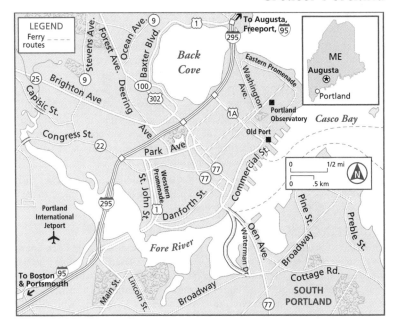

In some ways, Portland is still figuring out just what it wants to be when it grows up. It was a center for maritime trade in the 19th century, when a forest of masts obscured the view of the harbor. It's been a manufacturing hub, with locomotive factories, steel foundries, and fish-packing facilities. It's been a mercantile center with impressive downtown department stores and a slew of wholesale dealers. Today, as the mall area of South Portland siphons off much of the local economic energy, the city is striving to re-invent downtown as a tourist destination and a regional center for the arts. (Plans for a $50-million modern aquarium are underway, and there's talk of a new convention center). But best of all, it's a great place to see a mix of simple rowhomes and extravagant mansions, fishermen and stock brokers, pickup trucks and Saabs, all getting along rather harmoniously.

## ESSENTIALS

**GETTING THERE** Portland is located off the Maine Turnpike (I-95). Coming from the south, downtown is most easily reached by taking Exit 6A off the turnpike, then following I-295 to downtown. Exit at Franklin Street and follow this eastward until you arrive at the waterfront at the Casco Bay Lines terminal. Turn right on Commercial Street, and you'll be at the lower edge of the Old Port. Continue on a few blocks to the visitor's center (see below).

**Concord Trailways** (☎ 800/639-3317 or 207/828-1151) and **Vermont Transit** (☎ 800/537-3330 or 207/772-6587) offer bus service to Portland from Boston and Bangor. The Vermont Transit bus terminal is located at 950 Congress Street. Concord Trailways, which is a few dollars more expensive, usually offers movies and headsets on its trips. The Concord terminal is inconveniently located on Sewall Street (a 35-minute walk from downtown), but offers free parking for outbound travelers and is served by local buses from nearby Congress Street ($1 fare).

The **Portland International Jetport** is served by regularly scheduled flights on several airlines, including **Delta/Business Express** (☎ 800/438-7300), **Continental**

(☎ 800/525-0280), **US Airways** (☎ 800/428-4322), **United** (☎ 800/241-6522), and **Northwest Airlines** (☎ 800/225-2525). The airport is located just across the Fore River from downtown and is compact and easy to navigate, although ongoing construction and tight parking can be frustrating at times. Metro buses ($1) connect the airport to downtown; cab fare runs about $12.

**VISITOR INFORMATION**    The **Convention and Visitor's Bureau of Greater Portland,** 305 Commercial St., Portland, ME 04101 (☎ **207/772-5800** or 207/772-4994), stocks a large supply of brochures and is happy to dispense information about local attractions, lodging, and dining. The center is open in summer weekdays 8am to 6pm and weekends 10am to 5pm; hours are shorter during the off-season. Ask for the *Greater Portland Visitor Guide* with map.

**PARKING**    Parking is notoriously tight in the Old Port area, and the city's parking enforcement is notoriously efficient. Several parking garages are convenient to the Old Port, with parking fees around $1 per hour.

## EXPLORING THE CITY

Any visit to Portland should start with a stroll around the historic **Old Port.** Bounded by Commercial, Congress, Union, and Pearl streets, this several-square-block area near the waterfront contains the city's best commercial architecture, a plethora of fine restaurants, a mess of boutiques, and one of the thickest concentrations of bars on the eastern seaboard. (The Old Port tends to transform as night lengthens, with the crowds growing younger and rowdier.) The narrow streets and intricate brick facades reflect the mid-Victorian era; most of the area was rebuilt following a devastating fire in 1866. Leafy, quaint Exchange Street is the heart of the Old Port, with other attractive streets running off and around it.

Just outside the Old Port, don't miss the **First Parish Church,** at 425 Congress St., an uncommonly beautiful granite meeting house with an impressively austere interior that's changed little since it first opened its doors in 1826. A few doors down the block is Portland's **City Hall,** at the head of Exchange Street. Modeled after New York's City Hall, Portland's seat of government was built of granite in 1909. In a similarly regal vein is the **U.S. Custom House,** at 312 Fore St. During business hours, feel free to wander inside to view the elegant woodwork and marble floors dating back to 1868.

**Portland Public Market.**  25 Preble St. (¹/₂ block west of Monument Sq.).  ☎ **207/ 228-2000.** Open year-round. Mon–Sat 9am–6pm, Sun 10am–5pm.

The Portland Public Market features more than 2 dozen vendors selling fresh foods and flowers, much of which is Maine-grown. The architecturally distinctive building houses fishmongers, butchers, fresh fruit dealers, and a seafood cafe. It's a much-recommended spot for a quick snack, or just to sit and watch Portland pass by.

**Children's Museum of Maine.**  142 Free St. (next to the Portland Museum of Art).  ☎ **207/828-1234.** Admission $5 per child or adult, under 1 free. MC, V. Mon–Sat 10am–5pm, Sun noon–5pm; closed Mon–Tues fall through spring. Discounted parking at Free St. Parking Garage.

The centerpiece exhibit here is the camera obscura, a room-sized "camera" located on the top floor of this stout, columned downtown building next to the art museum. Children gather around a white table in a dark room, where they see magically projected images that include cars driving on city streets and boats plying the harbor. The camera obscura never fails to enthrall, and it provides a memorable lesson in the workings of a lens—whether in a camera or an eye.

**ACCOMMODATIONS**
Holiday Inn **6**
Inn at Park Spring **4**
Portland Regency Hotel **10**

◆ **DINING**
Back Bay Grill **1**
Bella Cucina **3**
Federal Spice **12**
Fore Street **11**
Katahdin **5**
Natasha's **2**
Stone Coast Brewing Co. **7**
Street & Co. **9**
Three Dollar Dewey's **8**

That's just one attraction; there's plenty more to do here, from running a super-market checkout counter to sliding down the firehouse pole to piloting the mock space shuttle from a high cockpit. The new Explore Floor (1999) offers a series of interactive science exhibits focusing on Maine's natural resources. Leave time for lunch at the cafe, where you can order up a peanut butter and jelly sandwich, a tall glass of milk, and an oatmeal cookie. (Living large!) Make a deal with your kids: They behave during a trip to the art museum (just next door), and they'll be rewarded with a couple of hours in their own museum.

✪ **Portland Head Light & Museum.** Fort Williams Park, 1000 Shore Rd., Cape Elizabeth. ☎ **207/799-2661.** www.portlandheadlight.com. Grounds free; museum admission $2 adults, $1 children 6–18. Park grounds open daily year-round sunrise–sunset (until 8:30pm in summer); museum open daily June–Oct 10am–4pm; open weekends only in spring and late fall. From Portland, follow State St. across the Fore River; continue straight on Broadway. At third light, turn right on Cottage Rd., which becomes Shore Rd.; follow until you arrive at the park, on your left.

Just a 10-minute drive from downtown Portland, this 1794 lighthouse is one of the most picturesque in the nation. (You'll probably recognize it from its cameo role in numerous advertisements and posters.) The light marks the entrance to Portland Harbor and was occupied continuously from its construction until 1989, when it was automated and the graceful keeper's house (1891) converted to a small, town-owned museum focusing on the history of navigation. The lighthouse itself is still active and thus closed to the public, but visitors can stop by the museum, browse for lighthouse-themed gifts at the gift shop, wander the park grounds, and watch the sailboats and cargo ships come and go. The park has a pebble beach, grassy lawns with ocean vistas, and picnic areas well-suited for informal barbecues.

**Portland Museum of Art.** 7 Congress Sq. (corner of Congress and High sts.). ☎ **207/ 775-6148.** www.portlandmuseum.org. E-mail: pma@maine.rr.com. $6 adults, $5 students and seniors, $1 children 6–12. (No admission charged Fri 5–9pm.) Tues–Wed and Sat–Sun 10am–5pm (June–mid-Oct also open Mon 10am–5pm), Thurs–Fri 10am–9pm.

This bold, modern museum was designed by I.M. Pei Associates and features selections from its own fine collections along with a parade of touring exhibits. (Summer exhibits are usually targeted at a broad audience.) The museum is particularly strong in American artists who had a connection to Maine, including Winslow Homer, Andrew Wyeth, and Edward Hopper, and has fine displays of early American furniture and crafts. The museum shares the Joan Whitney Payson Collection with Colby College (the college gets it one semester every other year). The collection also features wonderful European works by Renoir, Degas, and Picasso. Guided tours are daily at 2pm, and at 6pm on Thursday. A cafe serves light fare.

**Victoria Mansion.** 109 Danforth St. ☎ **207/772-4841.** $6 adults, $3 children 6–17, under 6 free. May–Oct Tues–Sat 10am–4pm, Sun 1–5pm; tours offered at 15 min. before and after each hour. Closed Nov–Apr, except for holiday tours from late Nov–mid-Dec. From the Old Port, head west on Fore St., veer right on Danforth St. at light near Stonecoast Brewing; proceed 3 blocks to the mansion, at the corner of Park St.

Widely regarded as one of the most elaborate Victorian brownstone homes ever built in the United States, this mansion (also known as the Morse-Libby House) is a remarkable display of high Victorian style. Built between 1859 and 1863 for a Maine businessman who made a fortune in the New Orleans hotel trade, the towering, slightly foreboding home is a prime example of the Italianate style once in vogue. Inside, it appears that not a square inch of wall space was left unmolested by craftsmen or artisans (11 painters were hired to create the murals). The decor is ponderous and somber, but it offers an engaging look at a bygone era. This home is a must for architecture buffs and is often mentioned in books on the history of American architecture. A gift shop sells Victorian-themed gifts and books.

**Wadsworth-Longfellow House & Center for Maine History.** 489 Congress St. ☎ **207/879-0427.** www.mainehistory.com. Gallery and Longfellow house tour $5 adults, $1 children under 12. Gallery-only $2 adults, $1 child. Longfellow House June–Oct daily 10am–4pm, gallery 10am–6pm; Nov–May gallery only Wed–Sat noon–4pm.

Maine Historical Society's "history campus" includes three widely varied buildings on busy Congress Street in downtown Portland. The austere brick Wadsworth-Longfellow House dates to 1785 and was built by Gen. Peleg Wadsworth, father of noted poet Henry Wadsworth Longfellow. It's furnished in an early-19th-century style, with many samples of Longfellow family furniture on display. Adjacent to the home is the Maine History Gallery, located in a garish post-modern building, formerly a bank. Changing exhibits here explore the rich texture of Maine history. Just behind the Longfellow house is the library of the Maine Historical Society, a popular destination among genealogists.

## ON THE WATER

The 3¹/₂-mile **Back Cove Pathway** loops around Portland's Back Cove, offering attractive views of the city skyline across the water, glimpses of Casco Bay, and a bit of exercise. The pathway is the city's most popular recreational facility; after work in summer, Portlanders flock here to walk, bike, jog, and windsurf (there's enough water $2^1/_2$ hours before and after high tide). Part of the pathway shares a noisy bridge with I-295 (and it can be a bit fulsome at a dead low tide), but when tides and weather cooperate, it's a pleasant spot for a walk. The main parking lot is located across from Shop 'n Save Plaza at the water's edge. Take Exit 6 (Forest Avenue north) off I-295; turn right at the first light on Baxter Boulevard; at the next light, turn right again and park in the lot ahead on the left.

Another fine place to take in a water view is the **Eastern Prom Pathway,** which wraps for about a mile along the waterfront between the Casco Bay Lines ferry terminal and the East End Beach. The paved pathway is suitable for walking or biking, and offers wonderful views out toward the islands and the boat traffic on the harbor. The easiest place to park is near the beach and boat ramp. From downtown, head east on Congress Street until you can't go any farther; turn right, then take your first left on the road down the hill to the water's edge.

**Casco Bay Lines.** Corner of Commercial and Franklin sts. ☎ **207/774-7871.** Fares vary depending on the run and season, but summer rates are typically $5.25–$13.75 round-trip. Frequent departures 6am–midnight.

Six of the Casco Bay islands have year-round populations and are served by scheduled ferries from downtown Portland. Except for Long Island, the islands are part of the city of Portland. The ferries offer an inexpensive way to view the bustling harbor and get a taste of island life. Trips range from a 20-minute (one-way) excursion to Peaks Island (the closest thing to an island suburb with 1,200 year-round residents), to the $5^1/_2$-hour cruise to Bailey Island (connected by bridge to the mainland south of Brunswick) and back. All of the islands are well-suited for walking; Peaks Island has a rocky back shore that's easily accessible via the island's paved perimeter road (bring a picnic lunch). Cliff Island is the most remote of the bunch, and has a sedate turn-of-the-century island-retreat character.

**Eagle Island Tours.** Long Wharf (Commercial St.) ☎ **207/774-6498.** $16.50 adults, $13.50 seniors, $9.50 children under 12 (includes state park fee of $1.50 adult, 50¢ child). 1 departure daily at 10am.

Eagle Island was the summer home of famed Arctic explorer and Portland native Robert E. Peary, who claimed in 1909 to be the first person to reach the North Pole. (His accomplishments have been the subject of exhaustive debates among Arctic scholars, some of whom insist he inflated his claims.) In 1904, Peary built a simple home on a remote, 17-acre island at the edge of Casco Bay; in 1912, he added flourishes in the form of two low stone towers. After his death in 1920, his family kept up the home, then later donated it to the state, which has since managed it as a state park. The home is open to the public, maintained much the way it was when Peary lived here. Island footpaths through the scant forest allow exploration to the open, seagull-clotted cliffs at the southern tip. Eagle Tours offers one trip daily from Portland. The 4-hour excursion includes a $1^1/_2$-hour stopover on the island.

**Old Port Mariner Fleet.** Commercial St. (Long Wharf and Custom House Wharf). ☎ **207/775-0727.** www.marinerfleet.com. Excursions $10–$75. Several departures daily.

The *Indian II* offers deep-sea fishing trips far beyond Portland Harbor in search of cod, cusk, hake, pollack, and more. Most are daylong trips (8am to 5pm), but several times each summer they offer marathons (5am to 5pm) for diehards. The *Odyssey* is a cruise boat that offers daylong whale watches (10am to 4pm) and evening music parties, including a 2-hour "floating Irish pub" on Saturday and Sunday evenings (departs at 6:30pm) for $10.

## MINOR LEAGUE BASEBALL

**Portland Sea Dogs.** Hadlock Field, P.O. Box 636, Portland, ME 04104. ☎ **800/936-3647** or 207/879-9500. www.portlandseadogs.com. Tickets $4–$6. Season runs Apr–Labor Day.

The Portland Sea Dogs are the Double-A team affiliated with the Florida Marlins. The team plays throughout the summer at Hadlock Field, a small stadium near downtown that still retains an old-time feel despite aluminum benches and other updating. Activities are geared towards families, with lots of entertainment between innings and a selection of food that's a couple of notches above basic hot dogs and hamburgers. (Try the tasty french fries and grilled sausages.)

## WHERE TO STAY

The **Holiday Inn** by the Bay, 88 Spring St. (☎ **207/775-2311**), offers great views of the harbor from about half the rooms, along with the usual chain-hotel creature comforts, including a ground-floor restaurant. Peak-season rates are approximately $150 double.

Budget travelers may choose to seek accommodations near the Maine Mall in South Portland, about 10 minutes' drive away from the attractions of downtown. Try **Days Inn** (☎ 207/772-3450) or **Coastline Inn** (☎ 207/772-3838).

✪ **Black Point Inn.** 510 Black Point Rd., Prouts Neck, ME 04074. ☎ **800/258-0003** or 207/883-2500. Fax 207/883-9976. www.blackpointinn.com. 80 units (includes 12 2-room suites). A/C TV TEL. July–Labor Day $345–$470 double, cottages $420–$520 double; spring and fall from $290; winter from $210. Rates include breakfast and dinner. AE, CB, DC, DISC, MC, V.

Located about 15 minutes' drive from downtown Portland, the Black Point inn is a Maine classic. Situated on 9 acres on a point with views along the coast both north and south, the Black Point was built as a summer resort in 1873 in an area enshrined in some of the work of noted American painter Winslow Homer. It's the same ownership as the Portland Regency, and the new owners have retained its famous old-world graciousness and charm. Sixty guest rooms are located in the main shingled lodge; the others are spread about four tidy cottages on the property. Even the smaller rooms are generously sized, with enough room for two wing chairs and a writing desk. All are carpeted and have a quaint, summery feel, with Martha Washington bedspreads, original glass door knobs, and reproduction furnishings, along with robes, irons, and hair dryers. The guest rooms in the cottages have more of a rustic L.L. Bean look to them; my pick would be the Sprague Cottage, with its flagstone floors in the common area and five rooms with private balconies, some with ocean views. Note that it's popular for weddings on summer weekends, when you'll encounter the attendent bustle and noise.

**Dining:** The main dining room has heavy beams, Windsor chairs, toile wallpaper, views of garden or ocean, and a menu that favors creative resort fare, like seaood fettucine, cedar-planked salmon, crusted rack of lamb and, of course, boiled lobster with butter and lemon. On-staff is a social director and, in summer, a children's program director.

**Amenities:** Olympic-size outdoor pool, indoor pool, ocean swimming at two adjacent beaches, shuttle to five area golf courses, hot tub, sauna, fitness room, nearby tennis courts, trails through bird sanctuary, massage, children's program (summers), free valet parking, limited room service, laundry and dry cleaning, baby-sitting, safe-deposit boxes, afternoon refreshments, and coffee delivery to room.

**The Danforth.** 163 Danforth St., Portland, ME 04102. ☎ **800/991-6557** or 207/879-8755. Fax 207/879-8754. www.danforthmaine.com. E-mail: danforth@maine.rr.com. 10 units. A/C TV TEL. $95–$285 double. Rates include continental breakfast; discounts available in off-season. AE, MC, V. Pets sometimes allowed ($10 fee); ask first.

Located in an exceptionally handsome brick home constructed in 1821, The Danforth is one of Portland's most desirable small inns. The guest rooms are handsomely decorated, many in rich and vibrant tones. The inn's extra touches are exceptional throughout, from working fireplaces in all guest rooms but one to the richly panelled basement billiards room to the direct-line phones. Especially appealing is Room 1 with a sitting room and private second-floor deck, and Room 2 with high ceilings and superb morning light; rooms 5 and 6 are smaller, housed in the old servant's wing. The inn is located at the edge of the Spring Street Historic District and is within 10 minutes' walk of downtown attractions. It's very popular for weddings and other events, so if you're in search of a quiet weekend retreat, ask first if anything is planned.

**Amenities:** Newspaper delivery, in-room massage, billiards room, bicycle rental, sundeck, and access to in-town health club.

**Inn at Park Spring.** 135 Spring St., Portland, ME 04101. ☎ **800/437-8511** or 207/774-1059. www.innatparkspring.com. E-mail: psinn@javanet.com. 6 units. A/C. May–Oct $135–$145 double; Nov–Apr $105. Rates include full breakfast and off-street parking. 2-night minimum weekends. AE, MC, V.

This small, tasteful B&B is located on a busy downtown street in an historic brick home that dates back to 1835. It's well-located for exploring the city on foot. The Portland Museum of Art is just 2 blocks away, the Old Port about 10 minutes, and great restaurants are all within easy walking distance. Guests can linger or watch TV in the front parlor, or chat at the table in the kitchen. The rooms are all corner rooms, and most are bright and sunny. Especially nice is "Spring," with its great morning light and wonderful views of the historic rowhouses on Park Street, and "Gables," on the third floor, which gets abundant afternoon sun.

**The Percy Inn.** 15 Pine St., Portland, ME 04104. ☎ **207/871-7638.** Fax 207/775-2599. www.percyinn.com. E-mail: innkeeper@percyinn.com. 4 units. A/C TV TEL. June–Oct $89–$179 double; Nov–May $79–$129. Rates include continental breakfast. MC, V. Children over 8 welcome.

The handsome Percy Inn run by innkeeper Dale Northrup at the edge of Portland's west end. (Small world note: Dale wrote *Frommer's Northern New England* in the mid-1990s.) Housed in a brick 1830 townhouse in a up-and-coming but mixed area (there's an adult bookstore just down the block), the inn is close to good restaurants and the Center for Cultural Exchange (see "Performing Arts," below), and is about a 15-minute walk to the Old Port. The four guest rooms are arrived at after an ascent up a narrow and twisting staircase. The third-floor Dorothy Parker Room has a Dickensian view of the brick skyline, along with a decent-size bathroom and dressing area. The second-floor Henry W. Longfellow Room has wonderful random-width floorboards, a small snack room with mini-fridge, and a corner sitting area with a marble cafe table. Nice touches abound: all rooms have weather radios, CD players, VCRs, complimentary soft drinks, and coolers with beach blankets for day trips. There's limited common space; self-serve breakfasts are offered in a second-floor breakfast room.

**✪ Pomegranate Inn.** 49 Neal St., Portland, ME 04102. ☎ **800/356-0408** or 207/772-1006. Fax 207/773-4426. www.pomegranateinn.com. 8 units. A/C TV TEL. Summer and fall $135–$175 double; winter and spring $95–$135. Rates include full breakfast. 2-night minimum summer weekends; 4 nights at Christmas and Thanksgiving. AE, DISC, MC, V. On-street parking. From the Old Port, take Middle St. (which turns into Spring St.) to Neal St. in the West End (about 1 mile); turn right and proceed to inn. Children 16 and older are welcome.

This is Portland's most appealing B&B, and one of the better choices in all of northern New England. Housed in an imposing, dove-gray 1884 Italianate home in the architecturally distinctive Western Prom neighborhood, the interiors are wondrously decorated with whimsy and elegance—a combination that can be fatally cloying if attempted by someone without impeccably good taste. Look for the bold and exuberant wall paintings by a local artist, and the eclectic antique furniture collected and tastefully arranged by owner Isabel Smiles. If you have the chance, peek in some of the unoccupied rooms—they're all different with painted floors and boisterous faux-marble woodwork. Most rooms have gas fireplaces; the best of the lot is in the carriage house, which has its own private terrace, kitchenette, and fireplace. Tea and wine is served upon arrival, and the sit-down breakfasts in the cheery dining room are invariably creative and tasty. The inn is well-situated for exploring the West End, and downtown is about a 20-minute walk away.

**Portland Regency Hotel.** 20 Milk St., Portland, ME 04101. ☎ **800/727-3436** or 207/774-4200. Fax 207/775-2150. www.theregency.com. E-mail: public@theregency.com. 95 units. A/C MINIBAR TV TEL. Summer $199–$249 double; off-season $159–$239. AE, CB, DISC, MC, V.

Centrally located on a cobblestone courtyard in the middle of the trendy Old Port, the Regency boasts the city's premier hotel location; but it's got more than location going for it—it's also one of the more architecturally striking and well-managed hotels in the state. Housed in an 1895 brick armory, the hotel inside is thoroughly modern, and offers attractive guest rooms nicely appointed and furnished with all the expected amenities. The architects have had to work within the quirky layout of the the building; as a result, the top floor rooms lack windows but have skylights, and the windows are at knee-height in some other rooms. The hotel has three different style suites; for a spluge, ask for Room 332 or Room 336, both corner rooms with handsome (non-working) brick fireplaces and sitting areas, where some of the glory of the old armory peeks through. The one complaint I've heard is about the noise: The interior guest room walls are a bit thin so noise travels from room to room, and on weekends, the revelry in the Old Port streets sometimes penetrates even the dense brick walls.

**Dining:** The hotel is home to The Armory Restaurant, which serves breakfast, lunch, and dinner. Dinners include traditional favorites like steak au poive and surf-and-turf, with entree prices ranging from $14.95 to $26.95.

**Amenities:** Limited room service, valet parking, dry cleaning (Monday to Friday), baby-sitting (with prior notice), valet parking ($8 per day), courtesy car to airport, safety-deposit boxes, Jacuzzi, VCR rental, sauna, fitness club, conference rooms, and aerobics classes.

# WHERE TO DINE
## EXPENSIVE

✪ **Back Bay Grill.** 65 Portland St. ☎ **207/772-8833.** Reservations recommended. Main courses $18–$27. AE, DC, DISC, MC, V. Mon–Thurs 5–9pm, Fri and Sat 5–9:30pm. NEW AMERICAN.

Back Bay Grill offers an upscale, contemporary ambience amid a rather downscale neighborhood near the main post office. There's light jazz in the background and bold artwork on the walls that's several notches above mere atmosphere. Chef Larry Matthews has been serving up some of Maine's most innovative meals for more than a decade, and he's developed a loyal following. Diners might launch an evening with a seared jumbo sea scallop served with an Indian curry vinaigrette, or house-cured gravlax with Spoonbill caviar. The menu changes seasonally; main dishes emphasize local produce and meats when available. Look for resourceful dishes like free-range chicken with an apple, walnut, and cornbread stuffing, or halibut with a chorizo-saffron sauce. The fresh pastas are notable and might include fettuccini with smoked tomatoes and oyster mushrooms, or ravioli filled with maple-butternut squash and served with a tangy cranberry, orange, and ginger sauce. The restaurant offers a good selection of moderately priced wines by the glass.

**Fore Street.** 288 Fore St. ☎ **207/775-2717.** Reservations recommended. Main courses, $14.95–$25.95. AE, MC, V. Daily 5:30–10pm. CONTEMPORARY GRILL.

During the long summer evenings, light floods in through the huge windows at this loftlike space with narrow-plank maple floors and copper-topped tables; later at night, it takes on a more intimate glow with soft lighting against the brick walls and buttery wooden floors. The place always feels bustling—the sprawling open kitchen is located in the middle of it all, filled with a team of chefs busy with stoking the wood-fired brick oven and grilling fish and meats. Grilled foods are the specialty here. The menu changes nightly, but you might start with the local quail roasted in the wood oven or mussels served with a garlic almond butter, then move on to the turnspit-roasted Maine rabbit or one of the selection of applewood-grilled dishes, including steak, chicken, duckling, venison, or fresh fish. Meals are consistently well-prepared here, and the service attentive on all but the busiest nights.

**Street & Co.** 33 Wharf St. ☎ **207/775-0887.** Reservations recommended. Main courses $13.95–$23.95. AE, MC, V. Sun–Thurs 5:30–9:30pm, Fri–Sat until 10pm. MEDITERRANEAN/ SEAFOOD.

A pioneer establishment on now-bustling Wharf Street, Street & Co. specializes in seafood cooked just right. There's no smoke and mirrors—you pass the open kitchen as you're seated, and you can watch the talented chefs peform their magic in their tiny space. This intimate spot is a bit like something you might imagine stumbling onto while touring Provence: Low beams, dim lighting, and drying herbs hanging overhead nicely set the mood. Diners are seated at copper-topped tables, designed such that the waiters can deliver steaming skillets right from the stove. Looking for lobster? Try it grilled and served over linguini in a butter-garlic sauce. If you're partial to calamari, this is the place. They know how to cook it so it's perfectly tender, a knack that's been lost elsewhere. Street & Co. fills up early, so reservations are strongly recommended. One-third of the tables are reserved for walk-ins each night, so it can't hurt to ask if you're in the neighborhood. In summer, there's outdoor seating at tables along the cobblestone street.

## MODERATE

**Bella Cucina.** 653 Congress St. ☎ **207/828-4033.** Reservations recommended. Main courses, $9–$17. AE, CB, DISC, MC, V. Open daily 5–10pm. RUSTIC ITALIAN.

Situated in one of Portland's less elegant commercial neighborhoods, Bella Cucina sets an inviting mood with rich colors, stylized fish sculptures, soft lighting, and pinpoint spotlights over the tables that carve out alluring islands of light. The eclectic menu changes frequently but dances deftly between rustic Italian and regional, with options like a robust ciopinno with haddock and lobster, and a melange of veal, pork, and chicken served with a prosciutto and mushroom ragout. Three or four vegan entrees are always offered. About half the seats are kept open for walk-ins, so take a chance and stop by even if you don't have reservations. There's a fitting selection of wines, and free parking evenings behind Joe's Smoke Shop.

**Katahdin.** 106 High St. ☎ **207/774-1740.** Reservations not accepted. Main courses $9.95–$15.95. DISC, MC, V. Tues–Thurs 5–9:30pm, Fri–Sat until 10:30pm. CREATIVE NEW ENGLAND.

Katahdin is a lively, often noisy spot that prides itself on its eclectic cuisine. Artists on slim budgets dine on the nightly blue-plate special, which typically features something basic like meatloaf or pan-fried catfish. Wealthy business folks one table over dine on more delicate fare, like the restaurant's much-remarked-upon (in a good way) crab cakes. Other recommended specialties include an appetizer of pan-seared oysters, and main courses of grilled sea scallops with a spicy lime vinaigrette, or London broil marinated in a ginger, scallion, and garlic mix. Sometimes the kitchen nods, but for the most part, food is good, made more palatable by the reasonable prices. Several dishes can be made to order for vegetarians; there's a small but decent selection of wines. No reservations are accepted, but you can enjoy one of the restaurant's fine martinis while waiting for a table at the bar.

**Natasha's.** 40 Portland St. ☎ **207/774-4004.** Reservations recommended. Main courses, brunch $4.50–$8.50, lunch $5–$9.95, dinner $13–$20. AE, DISC, MC, V. Mon–Fri 8am–2:30pm, Sat–Sun 8am–2:30pm, Thurs–Sat 5–9:30pm. NEW AMERICAN.

Natasha's, located between the main post office and the Portland Public Market, has a setting that borders on industrial chic—battered concrete floors and drop ceilings, combined with tomato-red walls, a handsome black pew-like bench that lines the wall, and white tablecloths topped with butcher's paper. The menu is delightfully creative in its simplicity—a smoked salmon chowder, and Maine crab and goat cheese rangoon for starters. Dinner entrees include lobster and crab ravioli served with leeks and lemon, pork loin grilled and served with a spicy pepper jam, and a crispy peanut tofu with pad thai seasoning. Brunch features great omelets, corned beef hash, and granola. (Try the tortillas with scrambled eggs and other fixin's.) Lunch is equally inviting, with options including novel sandwiches (like a grilled vegetarian Napoleon with artichoke hearts) and salads, along with wraps and noodles. Owner Natasha Carleton believes in giving back to the community: On Mondays, lunch is pay-what-you-can-afford, with the more affluent covering the cost for the less so.

## INEXPENSIVE

✪ **Becky's.** 390 Commercial St. ☎ **207/773-7070.** Breakfast items $3–$6.25, sandwiches $1.75–$4.75. AE, DISC, MC, V. Daily 4am–9pm. BREAKFAST/LUNCH JOINT.

Becky's got a glowing write-up by noted food writers Jane and Michael Stern in *Gourmet* magazine in 1999, but it obviously hasn't gone to the proprietor's head (she's a mother of six and doesn't have time for a swelled head). This waterfront institution is located in a squat maroon building of concrete block on the non-quaint end of the waterfront, and has drop ceilings, fluorescent lights, scruffy counters, booths, and tables. It's populated early (it opens 4am) and often by local fishermen grabbing a cup of joe and a plate o' eggs before setting out; later in the day, it attracts high school kids and businessmen and just about everyone else. The menu is extensive but offers about what you'd expect, including lots of inexpensive sandwiches (fried haddock and cheese, corn dogs, and tuna melt). It's most noted for its breakfasts, including 13 different omelets, eggs any other way you'd like them, fruit bowls (made with fresh fruit in season), pancakes, and French toast. And where else have you seen five different types of homefries?

**Federal Spice.** 225 Federal St. ☎ **207/774-6404.** Main courses $2.50–$6. No credit cards. Mon–Sat 11am–9pm. WRAPS/GLOBAL.

This is Portland's best bet for a quick, cheap, and filling nosh. Located beneath a parking garage (just off Temple Street), Federal Spice is a breezy, informal spot with limited dining inside and a few tables outside. You'll find quesadillas, salads, and soft tacos here, along with great wraps full of inventive, taste-bud-awakening stuffings (the curried coconut chicken is my favorite). The yam fries are excellent and nicely accompany just about everything on the menu.

✪ **Silly's.** 40 Washington Ave. ☎ **207/772-0360.** Lunch and dinner $2.25–$6.50; pizza $7.50–$20. MC, V. Mon–Sat 10am–10pm; closed Sun. ECLECTIC/TAKEOUT.

Silly's is the favored cheap-eats joint among even jaded Portlanders. Situated on an aggressively charmless urban street, the interior is informal, bright and spunky, with an excellent selection of mismatched 1950s-era dinettes and funky-retro accessories. The menu is creative, the selections tasty, and everything made fresh and from scratch. The place is locally noted for its "fast abdullahs," which consist of tasty fillings rolled up in fresh tortillas. (Among the favorites: the shish kebab with feta cheese, and the big and sloppy "Diesel," made with pulled pork barbeque and cole slaw. The pizza is also excellent, and there's beer on tap. Don't overlook the great mound of handcut french fries, or the huge old-fashioned milk shakes and malts.)

## SHOPPING

Aficionados of antique and secondhand furniture stores love Portland. Good browsing may be had on Congress Street. Check out the stretches between State and High streets in the arts district, and from India Street to Washington Avenue on Munjoy Hill. About a dozen shops of varying quality will be found in these two areas.

More serious antique hounds may choose to visit an **auction** or two. Two or three times per week you'll be able to find an auction within an hour's drive of Portland. A good source of information is the *Maine Sunday Telegram.* Look in the classifieds for listings of auctions scheduled for the following week.

For new items, the Old Port, with its dozens of boutiques and storefronts, is well worth browsing. There are few chain stores, and the commercial neighborhood is especially strong in contemporary one-of-a-kind clothing that's a world apart from stuff you'll find at a mall. Artisan and crafts shops are also well-represented.

**Abacus American Crafts.** 44 Exchange St. ☎ **207/772-4880.**

A wide range of bold, inventive crafts of all variety—from furniture to jewelry—is displayed on two floors of this centrally located shop. Even if you're not in a buying frame of mind, this is a great place for browsing.

**Amaryllis Clothing Co.** 41 Exchange St. ☎ **207/772-4439.**

Portland's original creative clothing store, Amaryllis offers unique clothing for women that's as comfortable as it is casually elegant. The colors are rich, the patterns unique, and some items are designed by local artisans. It's open until 9pm daily in summer.

**D. Cole Jewelers.** 10 Exchange St. ☎ **207/772-5119.**

Dean and Denise Cole are longtime Old Port denizens, producing wonderfully hand-crafted gold and silver jewelry. Browse from elegant traditional designs as well as more eccentric work at their brightly lit, low-pressure shop.

**Decorum.** 231 Commercial St. ☎ **207/775-3346.**

Anyone living in an old house will enjoy a stroll through Decorum, which sells both old and new "architectural curiosities." You'll see slate sinks, cast-iron tubs, curious pewter and chrome faucets, and a good selection of unique lighting fixtures. Even if you can't lug home, say, a tub, you might find the cabinet pulls, furniture waxes, or bathroom accessories that will coax your wallet out.

**Fibula.** 50 Exchange St. ☎ **207/761-4432.**

Original, handcrafted jewelry by Maine's top designers is beautifully displayed at this tasteful shop in the heart of the Old Port. There's also a collection of loose gemstones on display.

**Green Design Furniture.** 267 Commercial St. ☎ **207/775-4234.**

This inventive furniture shop sells a line of beautiful, Mission-inspired furniture that disassembles for easy storage and travel. These beautiful works, many creatively crafted of cherry, should be seen to be appreciated.

**Harbor Fish Market.** 9 Custom House Wharf (across from end of Pearl St.). ☎ **800/ 370-1790** or 207/775-0251.

This classic waterfront fish market is worth a trip just to see the mounds of fresh fish piled in the cases. It's a great spot for lobsters to go if you're flying home from Portland (they're packed for travel and will easily last 24 hours), or to buy smoked fish for a local picnic.

**Maine Potters Market.** 376 Fore St. ☎ **207/774-1633.**

Maine's largest pottery collective has been in operation for nearly 2 decades. You can select from a variety of high-end styles; shipping is easily arranged.

**Resourceful Home.** 111 Commercial St. ☎ **207/780-1314.**

Environmentally sound products for the home and garden, including linens and cleaning products, are the specialty here.

**Stonewall Kitchen.** 182 Middle St. ☎ **207/879-2409.**

Stonewall is a frequent winner in food trade shows for its innovative and delicious mustards, jams, and sauces. Among them: ginger peach tea jam, sun-dried tomato and olive relish, and maple chipotle grill sauce. You can browse and sample at their Old Port store (also stores in Camden and in York).

# PORTLAND AFTER DARK
## FILM

Downtown Portland is blessed with three movie houses, allowing travelers in the mood for a flick to avoid the disheartening slog out to the boxy, could-be-anywhere mall octoplexes. The **Keystone Theatre Cafe,** 504 Congress St. (☎ 207/871-5500), offers surprisingly good pub fare and beer while you enjoy second-run films that are usually more arty than you'll find at the mall. **Nickelodeon Cinemas,** 1 Temple St. (☎ 207/772-9751), has six screens showing second-run films at discount prices. **The Movies,** 10 Exchange St. (☎ 207/772-9600), is a compact art-film showcase in the heart of the Old Port, featuring a line-up of foreign and independent films of recent and historic vintage.

## MUSIC

Portland is usually lively in the evenings, especially on summer weekends when the testosterone level in the Old Port seems to rocket into the stratosphere with young men and women prowling the dozens of bars and and spilling out onto the streets.

Among the Old Port bars favored by locals are **Three-Dollar Dewey's** at the corner of Commercial and Union streets (try the great french fries), **Gritty McDuff's Brew Pub** on Fore Street near the foot of Exchange Street, and **Brian Ború,** on Center Street. All three bars are casual and pubby, with guests sharing long tables with new companions.

Beyond the active Old Port bar scene, a number of clubs offer a mix of live and recorded entertainment throughout the year. As is common in other small cities where there's more venues than attendees, the clubs have come and gone, sometimes quite rapidly. Check one of the two free weekly newspapers, *Casco Bay Weekly* or the *Portland Phoenix,* for current venues, performers, and showtimes.

Among the more reliable spots for live music is **Stone Coast Brewing Co.,** 14 York St. (☎ **207/773-2337**), a sizeable brew pub in an old brick cannery at the edge of the Old Port. Downstairs there's a no-smoking bar and restaurant overlooking the brewery. Upstairs is "The Smoking Room," with pool tables, dart lanes, sales of hand-rolled cigars, and live music. Music features local acts, as well as touring bands. Cover charges range from $1 to $20, but are typically $3 to $5 for local and regional acts.

Outside the Old Port near the art museum is the **Free Street Taverna,** 128 Free St. (☎ **207/774-1114**), a popular spot with 20- and 30-somethings for sipping beer, sampling pubby Greek fare, and listening to an eclectic mix of local bands.

## PERFORMING ARTS

Portland has a growing creative corps of performing artists. Theater companies typically take the summer off, but it doesn't hurt to call or check the local papers for special performances.

**Center for Cultural Exchange.** 1 Longfellow Sq. (corner of Congress and State sts.) ☎ **207/761-1545.** www.artsandculture.org. Tickets $8–$27.

The center is devoted to bringing acts from around the globe to Portland. Venues range from area theaters and churches, to the center's small but handsome performance space in a former dry cleaning establishment facing a statue of the pensive poet, Henry Wadsworth Longfellow. Acts range from pan-Caribbean dance music to klezmer bands to Quebecois step-dancing workshops. It's worth stopping by the center (it hosts a tiny cafe for an afternoon caffeine boost) to see what coming up. You just never know.

**Portland Stage Company.** Portland Performing Arts Center, 25A Forest Ave. ☎ **207/774-0465.** www.portlandstage.com. Tickets $19–$29.

The best-polished and most consistent of the Portland theater companies, Portland Stage offers crisply produced shows staring local and imported equity actors in a handsome, second-story theater just off Congress Street. About a half-dozen shows are staged throughout the season, which runs from October into May. Recent (spring 2000) shows included Graham Green's *Travels with My Aunt* and Pearl Cleage's *Blues for an Alabama Sky.*

# SIDE TRIPS

**OLD ORCHARD BEACH**    About 12 miles south of Portland is the unrepentantly honky-tonkish beach town of Old Orchard Beach, a venerable Victorian-era resort famed for its amusement park, pier, and long, sandy beach. Be sure to spend time and money on the stomach-churning rides at the beachside amusement park of **Palace Playland** (☎ **207/934-2001**), then walk on the 7-mile-long beach past the mid-rise condos that sprouted in the 1980s.

The beach is broad and open at low tide; at high tide, space to plunk your towel down is at a premium. In the evenings, teens and young adults dominate the town, spilling out of the video arcades and cruising the main strip. For dinner, do as the locals do and buy hot dogs, pizza, and cotton candy; save your change for the arcades.

Old Orchard is just off Route 1 south of Portland. The quickest route is to leave the turnpike at Exit 5, then follow I-195 and the signs to the beach. Don't expect to be alone here: Parking is tight, and the traffic can be horrendous during the peak summer months.

**SEBAGO LAKE & DOUGLAS HILL**    Maine's second-largest lake is also its most popular. Ringed with summer homes of varying vintages, many dating from the early part of the last century, Sebago Lake attracts thousands of vacationers to its cool, deep waters.

You can take a tour of the outlying lakes and the ancient canal system between Sebago and Long lakes on the *Songo Queen,* a faux-steamship berthed in the town of Naples (☎ 207/693-6861); or just lie in the sun along the sandy beach at bustling **Sebago Lake State Park** (☎ 207/693-6613) on the lake's north shore (the park is off Route 302; look for signs between Raymond and South Casco). The park has shady picnic areas, a campground, a snack bar, and lifeguards on the beach (entrance fee charged). It can be uncomfortably crowded on sunny summer weekends; it's best on weekdays. Bring food for barbecuing. The park's campground has its own beach and is at a distance from the day-use area, so it is less congested during good weather. It books up early in the season, but you might luck into a cancellation if you need a spot to pitch your tent.

To the west of the lake, the rolling wooded uplands hold some surprises. For a low-key excursion, head to the **Jones Museum of Glass and Ceramics** (☎ 207/787-3370), a place that captivates even visitors who have little interest in the history of glass or ceramics. Housed in a beautiful old farm building near a compound of summer homes, the museum has hundreds of pieces of old and contemporary glass displayed in highly professional and engaging exhibits.

The museum is located just off Route 107 south of Sebago (the town, not the lake) on the lake's west side. The museum is conscientious about posting directional signs; watch for them. It's open daily 10am to 5pm mid-May through mid-November (1 to 5pm on Sunday). Admission is $5 for adults, $3 for students.

A short hop up the hill from the museum is **Douglas Mountain,** whose summit is capped with a medieval-looking 16-foot stone tower. The property is owned by The Nature Conservancy and is open to the public; the summit is reached via an easy ¼-mile trail from the parking area. Look for wild berries in late summer.

**❂ SABBATHDAY LAKE SHAKER COMMUNITY**    Route 26 from Portland to Norway is a speedy state highway that passes through new housing developments as it heads toward hilly farmland and pine forests. At one point, the road pinches through a cluster of stately historic buildings that stand proudly beneath towering shade trees. That's the Sabbathday Lake Shaker Community (☎ 207/926-4597), the last active Shaker community in the nation. The half-dozen or so Shakers living here today still embrace the traditional Shaker beliefs and maintain a communal, pastoral way of life. The bulk of the community's income comes from the sale of herbs, which have been grown here since 1799.

Tours are offered daily from Memorial Day to Columbus Day except on Sundays (when visitors are invited to attend Sunday services). Docents provide tours of the grounds and several buildings, including the graceful 1794 meeting house. Exhibits in the buildings showcase the famed furniture handcrafted by the Shakers, and include antiques made by Shakers at other U.S. communes. You'll learn plenty about the Shaker ideology with its emphasis on simplicity, industry, and celibacy. After your tour, browse the gift shop for Shaker herbs and teas. Tours last 1 hour ($6 adult, $2 children 6 to 12). In July and August, the community also offers an optional extended tour, lasting 1 hour and 45 minutes ($7.50 adult, $2.75 children). Open daily except Sunday Memorial Day to Columbus Day from 10am to 4:30pm. The last tour is at 3:30pm.

The Shaker village is about 45 minutes from Portland. Head north on Route 26 (Washington Avenue in Portland). The village is 8 miles from Exit 11 (Gray) of the Maine Turnpike.

## 4  The Mid-Coast

Bath is 33 miles northeast of Portland. Boothbay Harbor is 23 miles east of Bath and 41 miles west of Rockland

Veteran Maine travelers contend this part of the coast is fast losing its native charm—it's too commercial, too developed, too much like the rest of the United States. The grousers do have a point, especially regarding Route 1's roadside, but get off the main roads and you'll find pockets where you can catch glimpses of another Maine. Backroad travelers will stumble upon quiet inland villages, dramatic coastal scenery, and a rich sense of history, especially maritime history.

The best source of information for the region in general is found at the **Maine State Information Center** (☎ 207/846-0833) just off Exit 17 of I-95 in Yarmouth. This state-run center is stocked with hundreds of brochures and a selection of free newspapers, and staffed with a helpful crew that can provide information on the entire state, but is particularly well-informed about the mid-coast region.

Note that just across the road is the ✪ **DeLorme Map Store** (☎ 888/227-1656). Here you'll find a wide selection of maps, including the firm's trademark state atlases and a line of CD-ROM map products. The store's fun to browse even if you're not a map buff, but what makes the place worth a detour off the interstate is Eartha, "the world's largest rotating and revolving globe." The 42-foot-diameter globe, which occupies the whole of the atrium lobby, is constructed on a scale of 1:1,000,000, and is the largest satellite image of the earth ever produced.

## FREEPORT

If Freeport were a mall (and that's not a far-fetched analogy), L.L. Bean would be the anchor store. It's the business that launched Freeport, elevating its status from just another town off the interstate to one of the two outlet capitals of Maine (the other is Kittery). Freeport still has the form of a classic Maine village, but it's a village that's been largely taken over by the national fashion industry. Most of the old homes and stores have been converted to upscale shops, and now sell name-brand clothing and housewares. Banana Republic occupies an exceedingly handsome brick Federal-style home; even the McDonald's is in a tasteful, understated Victorian farmhouse—you really have to look for the golden arches.

While a number of more modern structures have been built to accommodate the outlet boom, strict planning guidelines have managed to preserve much of the local charm, at least in the village section. Huge parking lots off Main Street are hidden from view, making this one of the more aesthetically pleasing places to shop; but even with these large lots, parking can be scarce during the peak season, especially on rainy summer days when every cottage-bound tourist between York and Camden decides that a trip to Freeport is a winning idea. Bring a lot of patience, and expect teeming crowds if you come at a busy time.

### ESSENTIALS

**GETTING THERE**    Freeport is on Route 1 but is most commonly reached via I-95 from either Exit 19 or 20.

**VISITOR INFORMATION**    The Freeport Merchants Association, P.O. Box 452, Freeport, ME 04032 (☎ **800/865-1994** or 207/865-1212) publishes a map and directory of businesses, restaurants, and overnight accommodations. The free map is available widely around town at stores and restaurants, or contact the association to have them send you one. On the Web, head to www.freeportusa.com.

## SHOPPING

Freeport has more than 100 retail shops between Exit 19 of I-95 at the far lower end of Main Street and Mallett Road, which connects to Exit 20. Shops have recently begun to spread south of Exit 19 toward Yarmouth. If you don't want to miss a single shopping opportunity, get off at Exit 17 and head north on Route 1. The bargains can vary from extraordinary to "eh?," so plan on racking up some mileage if you're intent on finding outrageous deals. Among national chains with a presence in Freeport are The Gap, The Body Shop, Levi's, Calvin Klein, Patagonia, North Face, Nike, J. Crew, Nine West, Chaudier Cookware ("the cookware of choice aboard Air Force One"), Timberland, Maidenform, and many others.

To avoid hauling your booty around for the rest of your vacation, stop by the **Freeport Trading & Shipping Co.,** 18 Independence Dr. (☎ 207/865-0421), which can pack and ship everything home.

**Cuddledown of Maine.** 475 U.S. Rte. 1 (Exit 19 off I-95). ☎ **888/235-3696** or 207/865-1713. www.cuddledown.com.

Down pillows are made right in this shop, which carries a variety of European goose-down comforters in all sizes and thicknesses. Look also for linens and home furnishings.

**Freeport Knife Co.** 148 Main St. ☎ **207/865-0779.**

The largest selection of knives for kitchen and camp is found in this shop. Look for the custom knives, and bring your dull camp blade for sharpening.

**J.L. Coombs, Fine Casuals and Footwear.** 15 Bow St. and 278 Rte. 1 (between exits 17 and 19). ☎ **800/683-5739** or 207/865-4333.

A Maine shoemaker since 1830, J.L. Coombs today carries a wide assortment of imported and domestic footwear at its two Freeport shops, including a wide selection of footwear, with manufacturers including Finn Comfort, Dr. Martens, Ecco, and Mephisto. There's also outerwear by Pendleton and Jackaroos.

**L.L. Bean.** Main and Bow sts. ☎ **800/221-4221.** www.llbean.com.

Monster outdoor retailer L.L. Bean traces its roots to the day Leon Leonwood Bean decided that what the world really needed was a good weatherproof hunting shoe. He joined a watertight gum shoe with a laced leather upper. Hunters liked it. The store grew. An empire was born.

Today, L.L. Bean sells millions of dollars worth of clothing and outdoor goods to customers nationwide through its well-respected catalogs, and it continues to draw hundreds of thousands through its door. This modern, multilevel store is the size of a regional mall, but tastefully done with its own indoor trout pond, lots of natural wood, even a separate kid's ship (L.L. Kids), and a space for live summer performances out back. Don't worry about arriving when it's open—L.L. Bean is open 365 days a year, 24 hours a day (note the lack of locks or latches on the front doors), and it's a popular spot even in the dead of night, especially in summer and around holidays. Selections include Bean's own trademark clothing, along with home furnishings, books, shoes, and plenty of outdoor gear for camping, fishing, and hunting.

L.L. Bean also stocks an outlet shop with a relatively small but rapidly changing inventory at discount prices. It's located in a back lot between Main Street and Depot Street—ask at the front desk of the main store for walking directions. L.L. Bean also has outlets in Portland, Ellsworth, and North Conway, New Hampshire.

**Mangy Moose.** 112 Main St. ☎ **207/865-6414.**

A cute souvenir shop with a twist: Virtually everything in the place is moose-related. There are moose hackey sacks, moose wine glasses, moose trivets, moose cookie-cutters, and, of course, moose T-shirts, and much more. The merchandise is a notch above what you'll find in other tourist-oriented shops.

**Thos. Moser Cabinetmakers.** 149 Main St. ☎ **207/865-4519.**

Classic furniture reinterpreted in lustrous wood and leather are the focus at this shop, which thanks to a steady parade of ads in The New Yorker and elsewhere has become almost as much an icon of Maine as L.L. Bean, Shaker, Mission, and Modern styles have been wonderfully re-invented by the shops designers and woodworkers, who produce heirloom-quality signed pieces. Deliveries nationwide are easily arranged.

## EXPLORING FREEPORT & ENVIRONS

While Freeport is nationally known for its frenetic shopping, that's not all it offers. Just outside of town, you'll find a lovely pastoral landscape, picturesque country walks, and scenic drives that make for a handy retreat from shopping.

Head by car east on Bow Street (down the hill from the L.L. Bean's main entrance), and wind around for 1 mile to the sign for **Mast Landing Sanctuary** (☎ **207/ 781-2330**). Turn left, then turn right in 0.1 mile into the sanctuary parking lot. A network of more than 3 miles of trails criss-cross through a landscape of long-ago eroded hills and mixed woodlands; streams trickle down to the marshland estuary. The 140-acre property is owned by the Maine Audubon Society and is open to the public until dusk.

Back at the main road, turn left and continue eastward for 1.4 miles, then turn right on Wolf Neck Road. Continue 1.7 miles, then turn left for $^1/_2$ mile on a dirt farm road. **Wolfe's Neck Farm,** owned and operated by a non-profit trust, has been experimenting with ways to produce beef without any chemicals, and sells its own line of organic meat. All this happens to take place at one of the most scenic coastal farms in Maine (it's especially beautiful near sunset). Stop at the gray farmhouse and pick up some tasty steaks or flavorful hamburger. Ask about the hiking trails, which the farm has been working on the past couple of years. Open Monday through Friday 1 to 5pm and Saturday 10am to 4pm (☎ **207/865-4469**).

## WHERE TO STAY

**Harraseeket Inn.** 162 Main St., Freeport, ME 04032. ☎ **800/342-6423** or 207/865-9377. www.harraseeketinn.com. E-mail: harraseeke@aol.com. 84 units. A/C TV TEL. Summer and fall $175–$260 double; spring and early summer $130–$250; winter $100–$235. All rates include breakfast buffet. AE, DC, DISC, MC, V. Take Exit 20 off I-95 to Main St.

The Harraseeket Inn is a large, thoroughly modern hotel 2 blocks north of L.L. Bean. It's to the inn's credit that, despite its size, a traveler could drive down Main Street and not immediately notice it. A late-19th-century home is the soul of the hotel, but most of the rooms are in later additions. Guests can lounge about in the well-regarded dining room, relax in the common room with the baby-grand player piano, or sip a cocktail in the homey Broad Arrow Tavern with its wood-fired oven and grill. The guest rooms are on the large side and tastefully done, with quarter-canopy beds and a nice mix of contemporary and antique furniture. All have hair dryers and coffeemakers; about a quarter have gas or wood-burning fireplaces, and more than half feature single or double whirlpools.

**Dining:** There are two restaurants on the premises. The Maine Dining Room offers New American dining with an emphasis on local ingredients; entree prices are $13 to $26. The Broad Arrow Tavern has a more informal setting with a less ambitious menu, which includes an array of pizzas and pastas; entrees range from $10 to $21.

**Amenities:** Concierge, room service (7am to 10pm), dry cleaning, laundry service, safe-deposit boxes, indoor heated lap pool, business center, and conference rooms.

**Isaac Randall House.** 5 Independence Dr., Freeport, ME 04032. ☎ **800/865-9295** or 207/865-9295. Fax 207/865-9003. 12 units (1 with private hall bathroom). A/C TEL. $70–$135 double. 2-night minimum on holiday and midsummer weekends. AE, DISC, MC, V. Located ¹/₂ mile south of the L.L. Bean store on Rte. 1. Pets accepted.

Freeport's first bed-and-breakfast, the Isaac Randall House is located in an 1823 farmhouse that's been refurbished with a dozen handsome guest rooms, all with private bathrooms and about half with televisions. The most charming of the bunch is the "Pine" room, built in an adjoining shed with rustic barnboards and decorated in a Southwestern motif. (It also features a unique antique copper tub.) The least charming are the two smaller, modern rooms in an addition in back, and a dark "Loft" room upstairs. Breakfast is served in a homey country kitchen with a Glenwood stove and ticking Regulator clock. The inn is well-situated for exploring Freeport; its main disadvantage is its location sandwiched between busy Route 1 and I-95. The sound of traffic is never far away.

**Kendall Tavern.** 213 Main St., Freeport, ME 04032. ☎ **800/341-9572** or 207/865-1338. 7 units (showers only). Peak season $100–$125 double; off-season $75–$95. Rates include full breakfast. AE, DISC, MC, V.

If you want to be out of the bustle of town but not too far from the shopping, this is a good choice. This handsome B&B is in a cheerful yellow farmhouse on 3¹/₂ acres at a bend in the road, a ¹/₂ mile north of the center of Freeport. The rooms are all plushly carpeted and appointed with comfort in mind. Everything is decorated in a bright and airy style, with framed posters on the walls and a mix of antique and new furniture. The rooms facing Route 1 (Main Street) may be a bit noisier than the others, but the traffic is still not likely to be too disruptive. There's a piano in one of the two downstairs parlors, and a sizable hot tub in a spacious private room in the back (no extra charge). The breakfast, served in the pine-floored dining room, is all-you-can-eat.

**✪ Maine Idyll Motor Court.** 325 Rte. 1, Freeport, ME 04032. ☎ **207/865-4201.** 20 cottages. TV. $44–$70 double (2- and 3-bedroom cottages $68–$90). No credit cards (checks accepted). Closed early Nov–late April. Pets allowed.

The 1932 Maine Idyll Motor Court is a Maine classic—a cluster of 20 cottages scattered about a grove of beech and oak trees. Each has a tiny porch, wood-burning fireplace (birch logs provided), TV, modest kitchen facilities (no ovens), and time-worn furniture. The cabins are not lavishly sized, but are comfortable and spotlessly clean. If you need a phone, you're out of luck—the cabins lack them, and there's no pay phone on the premises (the owners are good about letting guests use the office phone if they're in a pinch). The only interruption to an idyll here is the omnipresent sound of traffic: I-95 is just through the trees on one side, Route 1 on the other side. Get past the drone, and you'll find very good value for your money here.

## WHERE TO DINE

For a quick and simple meal, you might head down Mechanic Street (near the Mangy Moose at 112 Main Street) to the **Corsican Restaurant** (9 Mechanic St.; ☎ **207/ 865-9421**) for a 10-inch pizza, calzone, or king-size sandwich. A popular spot for quick, reasonably priced lunch close to L.L. Bean is the **Falcon Restaurant** (8 Bow St.; ☎ **207/865-4031**).

**Harraseeket Lunch & Lobster.** Main St., South Freeport. ☎ **207/865-4888.** Lobsters market price (typically $8–$12). No credit cards. Open daily 11:30am–8:30pm. Closed mid-Oct–May 1. From I-95, take Exit 17 and head north on Route 1; turn right on S. Freeport Rd. at the huge Indian statue; continue to stop sign in S. Freeport; turn right to waterfront. From Freeport take South St. (off Bow St.) to Main St. in South Freeport; turn left to water. LOBSTER POUND.

Located at a boatyard on the Harraseeket River about 10 minutes' drive from Freeport's main shopping district, this lobster pound is an especially popular destination on sunny days—although with its heated dining room, it's a worthy destination any time. Order a crustacean according to how hungry you are (from 1 lb. on up), then take in the river view from the dock while waiting for your number to be called. Be prepared for big crowds; a good alternative is to come in late afternoon between the crushing lunch and dinner hordes.

**Jameson Tavern.** 115 Main St. ☎ **207/865-4196.** Reservations encouraged. Main courses, tap room $5.95–$16.95; dining room lunch $5.25–$10.95, dinner $11.95–$21.95. AE, DC, DISC, MC, V. Tap room daily 11am–11pm; dining room daily in summer 11am–10pm, winter 11:30am–9pm. AMERICAN.

Located in a handsome, historic farmhouse literally in the shadow of L.L. Bean (it's just north of the store), the Jameson Tavern touts itself as the birthplace of Maine. In 1820, the papers were signed here legally separating Maine from Massachusetts. Today, it's a dual restaurant under the same ownership. As you enter the door, you can head left to the historic Tap Room, a compact, often crowded spot filled with the smell of fresh-popped popcorn. (Ask to sit outside on the brick patio if the weather's good.) Meals here include fare like crabcake burgers, lobster croissants, and a variety of build-your-own burgers. The other part of the house is the Dining Room, which is rather more formal in a country-colonial sort of way. Meals here are more sedate and gussied up, with an emphasis on steak and hearty fare. Entrees include filet mignon Oscar (with asparagus, crabmeat, and hollandaise), seafood fettucini, and pan-blackened haddock. (Look also for heart-healthy selections.) While not overly creative, the meals in both the dining room and tap room will hit the spot if you've worked up one of those fierce hungers peculiar to marathon shopping adventures.

# BRUNSWICK & BATH

Brunswick and Bath are two handsome and historic towns that share a strong commercial past. Many travelers heading up Route 1 pass through both towns eager to reach the areas with higher billing on the marquee. That's a shame, for both are well worth the detour to sample the sort of slower pace that's being lost elsewhere.

**Brunswick** was once home to several mills along the Androscoggin River; these have since been converted to offices and the like, but Brunswick's broad Maine Street still bustles with activity. (Idiosyncratic traffic patterns can lead to snarls of traffic in the late afternoon, when local businesses let out.) Brunswick is also home to Bowdoin College, one of the nation's most respected small colleges. The school was founded in 1794, offered its first classes 8 years later, and has since amassed an illustrious roster of prominent alumni, including writer Nathaniel Hawthorne, poet Henry Wadsworth Longfellow, President Franklin Pierce, and arctic explorer Robert E. Peary. Civil War hero Joshua Chamberlain served as president of the college after the war.

Eight miles to the east, **Bath** is pleasantly situated on the broad Kennebec River and a noted center of shipbuilding. The first U.S.-built ship was constructed downstream at the Popham Bay colony in the early 17th century; in the years since, shipbuilders have constructed more than 5,000 ships hereabouts. Bath shipbuilding reached its heyday in the late 19th century, but the business of shipbuilding continues to this day. Bath Iron Works is one of the nation's preeminent boatyards, constructing and repairing ships for the U.S. Navy. The scaled-down military has left Bath shipbuilders in a somewhat tenuous state, but it's still common to see the steely gray ships in the drydock (the best view is from the bridge over the Kennebec), and the towering red-and-white crane moving supplies and parts around the yard.

Bath is gaining attention from young professional emigres attracted by the fine old housing stock, but it's still at heart a blue collar town, with massive traffic tie-ups each weekday at 3pm when the shipyard changes shifts. Architecture buffs will find a detour here worthwhile. (Look for the free brochure, *Architectural Tours: Walking and Driving in the Bath Area* available at the local information centers listed below.) The Victorian era in particular is well-represented here. Washington Street, lined with maples and impressive homes, has to be one of the better preserved displays in New England of impressive late-19th-century homes. The compact downtown, on a rise overlooking the river, is also home to notable Victorian commercial arhitecture.

## ESSENTIALS

**GETTING THERE**    Brunswick and Bath are both situated on Route 1. Brunswick is accessible via Exit 22 and 23 off I-95. If you're bypassing Brunswick and heading north up Route 1 to Bath or beyond, continue up I-95 and exit at the "coastal connector" exit in Topsham, which avoids some of the slower going through Brunswick.

For bus service from Portland or Boston, contact **Vermont Transit** (☎ **800/451-3292**) or **Concord Trailways** (☎ **800/639-3317**).

**VISITOR INFORMATION**    The **Bath-Brunswick Region Chamber of Commerce,** 59 Pleasant St., Brunswick, ME 04011 (☎ **207/725-8797** or 207/443-9751) offers information and lodging assistance Monday to Friday 8:30am to 5pm from its offices near downtown Brunswick. The chamber also staffs an information center 10am to 7pm daily in summer on Route 1 between Brunswick and Bath.

**A FESTIVAL**    In early August, look for posters for the ever-popular ✪ **Maine Festival** (☎ **207/772-9012**), which takes place at Thomas Point Beach between Brunswick and Bath. What started as a sort of counterculture celebration of Maine people and crafts has evolved and grown to a hugely popular mainstream event. Performers from throughout Maine gather at this pretty coveside park (it's a private campground the rest of the summer), and put on shows from noon past dark throughout the first weekend in August. Displays of crafts, artwork, and the products of small Maine businesses are also on display. An admission fee is charged.

## EXPLORING BRUNSWICK & BATH

**Bowdoin College Museum of Art.** Walker Art Bldg., Bowdoin College, Brunswick. ☎ **207/725-3275.** Free admission. Tues–Sat 10am–5pm, Sun 2–5pm.

This stern, neoclassical building on the Bowdoin campus was designed by the prominent architectural firm of McKim, Mead, and White. While the collection is small, it has a number of exceptionally fine paintings, along with artifacts from classical antiquity and choice examples of early furniture. The artists include Andrew and N. C. Wyeth, Marsden Hartley, Winslow Homer, and John Singer Sargent. The older upstairs galleries have soft, diffused lighting from skylights high above; the basement galleries feature temporary exhibits (almost all are excellently conceived) and are modern and spacious.

**Maine Maritime Museum & Shipyard.** 243 Washington St., Bath. ☎ **207/443-1316.** Admission $8.50 adult, $5.75 child 6–17, $25 family. Open daily 9:30am–5pm.

On the shores of the Kennebec River, this museum (it's just south of the very obivous Bath Iron Works shipyard) features a wide array of displays and exhibits related to the boatbuilder's art. It's sited at the former shipyard of Percy and Small, which built some 42 schooners in the late 19th and early 20th century. The largest wooden ship ever built in America—the 329-foot *Wyoming*—was constructed on this lot in 1909.

The centerpiece of the museum is the handsomely modern Maritime History Building. Here, you'll find changing exhibits of maritime art and artifacts. (There's also a gift shop with a great selection of books about ships.) The 10-acre property houses a fleet of additional displays, including an intriguing exhibit on lobstering and a complete boatbuilding shop. Here, you can watch handsome wooden boats take shape in this active program. Kids enjoy the play area (they can search for pirates from the crow's nest of the play boat). Be sure to wander down to the docks on the river to see what's tied up or to inquire about river cruises (extra charge).

**Peary-MacMillan Arctic Museum.** Hubbard Hall, Bowdoin College, Brunswick. ☎ **207/ 725-3416.** Free admission. Tues–Sat 10am–5pm, Sun 2–5pm.

While Admiral Robert E. Peary (class of 1887) is better known for his accomplishments (he "discovered" the North Pole at age 53 in 1909), Donald MacMillan (class of 1898) also racked up an impressive string of achievements in Arctic research and exploration. You can learn about both men and the wherefores of Arctic exploration in this altogether manageable museum on the Bowdoin campus. The front room features mounted animals from the Arctic, including some impressive polar bears. A second room outlines Peary's historic 1909 expedition, complete with excerpts from Peary's journal. The last room includes varied displays of Inuit arts and crafts, some historic, some modern. This compact museum can be visited in about 20 minutes or so; the art museum (see Bowdoin College Museum of Art, above) is just next door.

## WHERE TO STAY

**The Kennebec Inn.** 1024 Washington St., Bath, ME 04530. ☎ **800/822-9393** or 207/443-5202. 7 units. A/C TV TEL. $100–$165 double, including full breakfast. AE, DISC, MC, V. Children over 12 are welcome. 2-night minimum on weekends.

The historic Kennebec Inn was built in 1860 for a shipbuilder and sea captain. This imposing mansion, located on a street of notable homes, was built with bricks shipped from England and looks more like a small bank than a home. Leaded glass sets a tone of elegance in the entryway; the downstairs common rooms have 14-foot ceilings, while the second-floor guest rooms make do with 12-foot ceilings. All rooms have custom-made armoires and data ports; bathrooms range in size from generous to somewhat cramped. The four larger guest rooms are in the front of the house and were formerly used by the family members. The best of the lot is room #2, with two wing chairs, large windows, pocket shutters, and a great old pedestal sink and Jacuzzi in the bathroom. The smallest is the very adequate room #5, with simple pine floors and four-poster queen bed. The breakfast buffet is set out in the butler's pantry and is enjoyed by candlelight in the formal dining room with mahogany panelling and tapestry wall coverings.

**Moses Galen House.** 1009 Washington St., Bath, ME 04530. ☎ **888/442-8771.** www.galenmoses.com. E-mail: galenmoses@clinic.net. 4 units (1 with detached bathroom). $69–$119 double, including full breakfast. 2-night minimum on summer weekends. MC, V.

The four-guest-room Moses Galen House was built in 1874 and is an extravagant, three-story Italianate home done up in exuberant colors by innkeepers Jim Haught and Larry Keift. The whole of the spacious first floor is open to guests and includes a TV room, lots of loudly ticking clocks, and an appropriately cluttered Victorian double parlor. (Emma, the resident greyhound, makes herself at home here.) Note the old friezes and stained glass original to the house. The guest rooms vary in decor and size, but all are quite welcoming. The Victorian Room occupies a corner and gets lots of afternoon light, although the bathroom is dark; the Suite is ideal for families, with two sleeping rooms and a small kitchen.

# THE HARPSWELL PENINSULA

Extending southwest from Brunswick and Bath is the picturesque Harpswell Peninsula. It's actually three peninsulas, like the tines of a pitchfork, if you include the islands of Orrs and Bailey, which are linked to the mainland by bridges. While close to some of Maine's larger towns (Portland is only 45 minutes away), the Harpswell Peninsula has a remote, historic feel with sudden vistas across meadows to the blue waters of northern Casco Bay. Toward the southern tips of the peninsulas, the character changes as clusters of colorful Victorian-era summer cottages displace the farmhouses found farther inland. Some of these cottages rent by the week, but savvy families book up many of them years in advance. Ask local real-estate agents if you're interested.

There's no set itinerary for exploring the area. Just drive south on Route 123 until you can't go any farther, then backtrack for a bit and strike south again. Among the "attractions" worth looking for are the wonderful ocean and island views from **South Harpswell** at the tip of the westernmost peninsula (park and wander around for a bit), and the clever **Cobwork Bridge** connecting Bailey and Orrs islands. The humpbacked bridge was built in 1928 of granite blocks stacked in such a way that the strong tides could come and go and not drag the bridge out with it. No cement was used in its construction.

This is a good area for a bowl of chowder or a boiled lobster. One of the premier places for chowder off-the-beaten track is at the down-home ✪ **Dolphin Marina** (☎ **207/833-6000**) at Basin Point in South Harpswell. (Drive 12.2 miles south of Brunswick on Route 123, turn right at Ash Point Road near the West Harpswell School, then take your next right on Basin Point Road and continue to the end.) Find the boatyard, then wander inside the adjacent building, where you'll discover a tiny counter seating six and a handful of pine tables and booths with stunning views of Casco Bay. The fish chowder and lobster stew are reasonably priced and absolutely delicious, and the blueberry muffins are warm and have a crispy crown. The servers are easily flummoxed at times, so bring your patience.

## BEACHES

This part of Maine is better known for rocky cliffs and lobster pots than swimming beaches. There are two notable exceptions.

**Popham Beach State Park** (☎ 207/389-1335) is located at the tip of Route 209 (head south from Bath). This handsome park has a long, sandy strand and great views of knobby islands just offshore. This includes Seguin Island, capped with a lonesome lighthouse. There's a state park here that provides parking and basic services, including changing rooms. Admission is $2 adult, 50¢ children 5 to 11.

At the tip of the next peninsula to the east, is **Reid State Park** (☎ 207/371-2303), another uncommonly beautiful spot, and an idyllic place to picnic on a lazy summer day. Arrive early enough and you can stake out a picnic table among the wind-blasted pines. The mile-long beach is great for strolling and splashing around. Services include changing rooms and a small snack bar. Admission is $2.50 adult, 50¢ children 5 to 11. To reach Reid State Park, follow Route 127 south from Bath and Route 1.

## WHERE TO STAY

✪ **Driftwood Inn & Cottages.** Washington Ave., Bailey Island, ME 04003. ☎ **207/833-5461,** off-season 508/947-1066. 24 units plus 6 cottages (most units share hallway bathrooms). $70–$110 double; weekly $375 per person, including breakfast and dinner (July and Aug only); cottages $550–$600 per week. No credit cards. Open late May–mid-Oct; dining room open late June–Labor Day.

The oceanside Driftwood Inn dates back to 1910 and is a coastal New England classic. A rustic summer retreat on three acres at the end of a dead-end road, the inn is a compound of four weathered, shingled buildings and a handful of housekeeping cottages on a rocky, oceanside property. The spartan rooms of time-aged pine have a simple turn-of-the-last-century flavor that hasn't been gentrified in the least. Most rooms share bathrooms down the hall, but some have private sinks and toilets. Your primary company will be the constant sound of surf surging in and ebbing out of the fissured rocks. The inn has an old saltwater pool and porches with wicker furniture to while away the afternoons; bring plenty of books and board games.

**Dining:** The dining room serves basic fare (roasts, fish, and so on) in a wonderfully austere setting overlooking the sea; meals are extra, although a weekly American plan is available. Dining is open to outside guests if you call ahead.

✪ **Grey Havens.** Seguinland Rd., Georgetown Island, ME 04548. ☎ **207/371-2616.** Fax 207/371-2274. www.greyhavens.com. E-mail: greyhavens@clinic.net. 13 units (2 with private hall bathrooms). $100–$210 double, including full breakfast. Closed Nov–May. From Route 1, head south on Route 127, then follow signs for Reid State Park; watch for inn on left. MC, V. No children under 7.

Located on Georgetown Island off the beaten track southeast of Bath, Grey Havens is worth seeking out if you'd like a place to idly watch the ocean while you unwind. This graceful, 1904 shingled home with prominent turrets sits on a high, rocky bluff overlooking the sea. Inside, it's all richly mellowed pine paneling, and a spacious common room where you can relax in cozy chairs in front of the cobblestone fireplace while listening to classical music. The guest rooms are simply but comfortably furnished. In the turret rooms, the managers have even placed binoculars to help guests better monitor the comings and goings on the water. The oceanfront rooms command a premium but are worth it. (If you're looking to save a few dollars, ask for an oceanfront room that has a private bath just across the hall.) Guests have the run of the old kitchen and can use the inn's canoe and bikes to explore the outlying area. One caveat: The inn has been only lightly modernized, which means rather thin walls. If you have loud neighbors, you'll learn more about their lives than you may care to know.

**Sebasco Harbor Resort.** Route 217, Sebasco Estates, ME 04565. ☎ **800/225-3819** or 207/389-1161. Fax 207/389-2004. www.sebasco.com. E-mail: info@sebasco.com. 115 units. TEL. July–Labor Day $169–$249 double; May–June $129–$209; Sept–Oct $149–$229. 15% service charge additional. 2-night minimum on weekends. Closed late Oct–early May. South from Bath 11 miles on Rte. 209; look for Rte. 217 and signs for Sebasco. AE, DISC, MC, V.

Sebasco is a grand old seaside resort under new management that's fighting a generally successful battle against time and irrelevance. It's a self-contained resort of the sort that flourished 50 years ago and today is being rediscovered by families. Some guests have been coming here for 60 years and love the timelessness of it; newcomers are starting to visit now that much of it has benefited from a facelift.

The 664-acre grounds remain the real attraction here—guests enjoy sweeping ocean views, a lovely seaside pool, and great walks around well-cared-for property. The guest rooms, it should be noted, are adequate rather than elegant, and may seem a bit short of the mark given the high prices charged. Most lack a certain style—especially the 40 rooms in the old inn, which are dated, and I don't mean that in a good way. (The small wooden decks on many rooms are a plus, though.) Better are the quirky rooms in the octagonal Lighthouse Building—rooms #12 and #20 have among the best views in the state. Most (not all) rooms have TVs; ask first if it's important to you. If you're coming for more than 2 days, it's probably best to book a cottage, which come in all sorts and sizes.

**Dining:** The Pilot House Dining Room is airy, contemporary, and the best place to enjoy the sunsets. You'll find white linens and a jackets-recommended-on-men policy; the menu is contemporary resort style, with dishes like grilled swordfish with a pesto butter, and prime rib with a Parmesan Yorkshire pudding. Another restaurant, Ledges, is a more informal spot downstairs that serves from a lighter menu.

**Amenities:** Swimming in outdoor saltwater pool and ocean, nine-hole golf course, tennis courts, hot tub, sauna, health club, bay cruises, canoe and kayak rentals, shuffleboard, snack bar, children's center and programs, video games, candlepin bowling, movies, nature trails, sailing lessons, and bike rentals. Popham Beach is 5 miles away.

## WHERE TO DINE

**Five Islands Lobster Co.** Rte. 127, Georgetown. ☎ **207/371-2990.** Typically $6–$9 per lobster. MC, V. Daily 11am–8pm in July and Aug; shorter hours during the off-season. Closed Columbus Day–Mother's Day. LOBSTER POUND.

The drive alone makes this lobster pound a worthy destination. It's located about 12 miles south of Route 1 down winding Route 127, past bogs and spruce forests with glimpses of azure ocean inlets. (Head south from Woolwich, which is just across the bridge from Bath.) Drive until you pass a cluster of clapboard homes, then keep going until you can't go any farther.

Wander out to the wharf with its unbeatable island views, and place your order. This is a down-home affair, owned jointly by local lobstermen and the proprietors of Grey Havens, a local inn (see "Where to Stay," above). While you're awaiting your lobster, you can wander next door to the Love Nest Snack Bar for extras like soda or the killer onion rings. Gather up your grub and settle in at one of the wharf picnic tables, or head over to the grassy spots at the edge of the dirt parking lot, and bring some patience: Despite its edge-of-the-world feel, the lobster pound draws steady traffic and it can be crowded on weekends.

**✪ Robinhood Free Meetinghouse.** Robinhood Rd., Robinhood. ☎ **207/371-2188.** Reservations encouraged. Main courses $18–$25. AE, DISC, MC, V. Open daily in May–Oct 5:30–9pm. Limited days late fall–spring; call first. FUSION.

Chef Michael Gagne is ambitious. His menu features between 30 and 40 entrees, and they're wildly eclectic—from Thai-grilled vegetables to Wiener schnitzel to salmon en papillote. Ordering from the menu almost seems like playing stump the chef: Let's see you make *this!* You know what? Gagne almost always hits his notes and rarely serves a mediocre meal. You just can't go wrong here. Gagne has attracted legions of dedicated local followers, who appreciate the extraordinary attention paid to detail. Carbonated water and slices of citrus are served at every table in the sparely decorated, immaculately restored 1855 Greek Revival meeting house. Even the sorbet served between courses is homemade. Eating here is not an inexpensive proposition, but it offers good value for the price.

## BOOTHBAY HARBOR

Boothbay Harbor, 11 miles south of Route 1, is a small and scenic town that seems to exert an outsized allure on passing tourists. This former fishing port was discovered in the late 19th century by wealthy rusticators who built imposing seaside homes and retreated here in summer to avoid the swelter of the cities along the eastern seaboard.

Having embraced the tourist dollar, the harborfront village never really looked back, and in more recent years, it has emerged one of the premier destinations of travelers in search of classic coastal Maine. This embrace has had an obvious impact. The village has been discovered by bus tours, which has in turn attracted kitschy shops and a slew of mediocre restaurants that all seem to specialize in baked stuffed haddock.

Note that Boothbay Harbor is very much a summer town; by and large, it shutters up shortly after Labor Day. Despite it all, there's still an affable charm that manages to rise above the clutter and cheese, especially on foggy days when the horns bleat mournfully at the harbor's mouth.

## ESSENTIALS

**GETTING THERE**   Boothbay Harbor is south of Route 1 on Route 27. Coming from the west, look for signs shortly after crossing the Sheepscot River at Wiscasset.

**VISITOR INFORMATION**   As befits a region where tourism is a major industry, Boothbay and Boothbay Harbor have three visitor information centers, reflecting the importance of the travel dollars to the region. At the intersection of Route 1 and Route 27 is a **visitor center** that's open May through October and is a good place to stock up on brochures. A mile before you reach the village is the seasonal **Boothbay Information Center** on your right (open June to October). If you pass these, don't fret. The year-round **Boothbay Harbor Region Chamber of Commerce,** P.O. Box 356, Boothbay Harbor, ME 04538 (☎ **207/633-2353**) is at the intersection of Route 27 and Route 96.

## EXPLORING BOOTHBAY HARBOR

Compact Boothbay Harbor, clustered along the water's edge, is ideal for exploring by foot. (The trick is parking, which in midsummer will require either persistence or the forking over of a few dollars.) Pedestrians naturally gravitate to the long, narrow **footbridge** across the harbor, first built in 1901. The bridge is more of a destination than a link—other than some restaurants and motels, there's really not much on the other side. The winding, small streets that weave through the town also offer plenty of boutiques and shops that cater to the tourist trade and offer decent browsing.

A short excursion to **Ocean Point** is well worthwhile. Follow Route 96 southward from east of Boothbay Harbor, and you'll pass through East Boothbay before striking toward the point. The narrow road runs through piney forests before arriving at the rocky finger; it's one of the few Maine points with a road edging its perimeter, allowing wonderful ocean views. Bunches of colorful Victorian-era summer cottages bloom along the roadside like wildflowers.

Ocean Point makes for a good **bike loop,** as does a trip around **Southport Island,** which is connected to Boothbay Harbor via a bridge. Follow Route 238 around the island, stopping from time to time to enjoy the occasional sea views or to poke down gravel public roads. Mountain-bike rentals are available from $12 and up at Tidal Transit Kayak Co. (See "Boat Tours," below.)

If dense fog or rain socks in the harbor, bide your time at the vintage **Romar Bowling Lanes** (☎ 207/633-5721). This log and shingle building near the footbridge has a harbor view and has been distracting travelers with the promise of traditional New England candlepin bowling since 1946. On rainy summer days, the wait for one of the eight lanes can be up to an hour. While you're waiting you can play pool and video games, or order a root beer float from the snack bar. It's not hard to find. You'll hear pins crashing, shrieks of victory, and howls of despair from various points around the town.

**Marine Resources Aquarium.** 194 McKown Point Rd., West Boothbay Harbor. ☎ **207/633-9542.** $2.50 adult, $2 children 5–18. Daily 10am–5pm. Closed after Columbus Day to just before Memorial Day.

Operated by the state's Department of Marine Resources, this compact aquarium offers context for life in the sea around Boothbay and beyond. You can view rare albinos and blue lobsters, and get your hands wet at a 20-foot touch tank—a sort of petting zoo of the slippery and slimy. Parking is tight at aquarium, which is located on a point across the water from Boothbay Harbor. A free shuttle bus (look for the Rock-tide trolly) connects downtown with the aquarium and runs frequently throughout the summer.

## BOAT TOURS

The best way to see the timeless Maine coast around Boothbay is on a boat tour. Nearly two dozen tour boats berth at the harbor or nearby, offering a range of trips ranging from an hour's outing to a full-day excursion to Monhegan Island. You can even observe puffins at their rocky colonies far offshore.

**Balmy Day Cruises** (☎ 800/298-2284 or 207/633-2284) runs several trips from the harbor, incuding an all-day excursion to Monhegan Island on the 65-foot *Balmy Days II* (this allows passengers about 4 hours to explore the island before returning—see "Monhegan Island," below). The Monhegan trip is $30 (children $18). The company also offers one-harbor tours for $9 (children $4.50). If you'd rather be sailing, ask about the 90-minute cruises on the *Bay Lady,* a 15-passenger Friendship sloop ($18).

**Windborne Cruises** (☎ 207/882-1020) sails from Smuggler's Cove Motel on Route 96, about 2 miles south of East Boothbay. Passengers report that Capt. Roger Marin is a great storyteller and captivates his temporary crew with local tales. Marin can accommodate just six passengers on the 40-foot *Tribute,* a handsome Block Island sailboat. Two hour cruises depart at 11am and 3pm, and cost $25 per person. You can also charter the boat for a half day ($200) or full day ($375), with both options including lunch.

The most personal way to see the harbor is via sea kayak. **Tidal Transit Kayak Co.** (☎ 207/633-7140), offers morning, afternoon, and sunset tours of the harbor for $30 (sunset's the best bet). Kayaks may also be rented for $12 an hour, or $50 per day. Tidal Transit is open daily in summer (except when it rains) on the waterfront at 47 Townshend Avenue (walk down the alley).

## WHERE TO STAY

**Five Gables Inn.** Murray Hill Rd. (P.O. Box 335), East Boothbay, ME 04544. ☎ 800/451-5048 or 207/633-4551. www.fivegablesinn.com. E-mail: info@fivegablesinn.com. 16 units. TEL. $110–$175 double. Rates include breakfast buffet. MC, V. Closed Nov–mid-May. Drive through E. Boothbay on Rte. 96; turn right after crest of hill on Murray Hill Rd. Children 12 and older are welcome.

The handsome Five Gables Inn sits proudly amid a small colony of summer homes on a quiet road above a peaceful cove. It's nicely isolated from the confusion and hubbub of Boothbay Harbor; the activity of choice here is to sit on the deck and enjoy the glimpses of the water through the trees. It's a good base for bicycling—you can pedal down to Ocean Point or into town. It's also handy to the Lobsterman's Wharf for good, informal dining. The rooms are pleasantly appointed, and five have fireplaces. The common room is nicely furnished in an upscale country style. The breakfast buffet is an inviting affair, with offerings like tomato-basil fritatta, cornbread with bacon and green onions, and blueberry-stuffed French toast.

**Lawnmeer Inn & Restaurant.** Rte. 27, Southport, ME 04576. ☎ 800/633-7645 or 207/633-2544. www.lawnmeerinn.com. E-mail: cooncat@lawnmeerinn.com. 32 units. TV TEL. Summer rates $95–$195 double; spring and fall from $85. 2-night minimum on holiday weekends. MC, V. Closed mid-Oct–mid-May. Pets accepted on limited basis; $10 extra.

The Lawnmeer, situated a short hop from Boothbay on the northern shore of South-port Island, offers easy access to town and a restful environment. This was originally built as a guest home in the late 19th century, and the main inn has been updated with some loss of charm. More than half of the guest rooms are located in a motel-like annex, which makes up for a lack of character with private balconies offering views of the placid waterway that separates Southport Island from the mainland.

**Dining:** American and global cuisine is served in a comfortable, homey dining room with windows overlooking the waterway. Expect contemporary fare, with entrees like linguini aux fruits de mer, and Thai green curry shrimp over basmati rice. Entrees are priced $13 to $22; reservations are recommended.

**Newagen Seaside Inn.** Rte. 27 (P.O. Box 68), Cape Newagen, ME 04552. ☎ **800/ 654-5242** or 207/633-5242. E-mail: seaside@wiscasset.net. 26 units. $140–$240 double, including full breakfast. Ask about off-season discounts. MC, V. Closed mid-Oct–mid-May. Located on south tip of Southport Island; take Rte. 27 from Boothbay Harbor and continue on until the inn sign.

This 1940s-era resort has seen more glamorous days, but it's still a superb small, low-key resort offering stunning ocean views and walks in a fragrant spruce forest. The inn is housed in a low, wide, white-shingled building that's furnished simply with country pine furniture. There's a classically austere dining room, narrow cruise-ship-like hallways with pine wainscotting, and a lobby with a fireplace. The rooms are plain, and the inn is a bit threadbare in spots, but never mind that. Guests flock here for the 85-acre oceanside grounds filled with decks, gazebos, and walkways that border on the magical. It's hard to convey the magnificence of the ocean views, which may be the best of any inn in Maine.

**Dining:** The handsome, simple dining room with ocean views offers a menu with traditional New England fare and a selection of more creative additions (entrees $11.95 to $28.95). Closed Tuesday for dinner.

**Amenities:** Freshwater and saltwater pools, badminton, horseshoes, tennis, sundeck, and free rowboats.

**Spruce Point Inn.** Atlantic Ave. (P.O. Box 237), Boothbay Harbor, ME 04538. ☎ **800/ 553-0289** or 207/633-4152. www.sprucepointinn.com. E-mail: thepoint@sprucepointinn. com. 93 units. TV TEL. Mid-July–Aug $155–$325 double; fall $110–$250; spring $105–$215; early summer $115–$225. 2-night minimum weekends; 3 nights holidays. AE, DC, DISC, MC, V. Closed mid-Oct–Memorial Day. Turn seaward on Union St. in Boothbay Harbor; proceed 2 miles to the inn. Pets accepted; $50 deposit, $100 cleaning fee.

The Spruce Point Inn was originally built as a hunting and fishing lodge in the 1890s, and evolved into a summer resort in 1912. After years of quiet neglect, it has benefited greatly from a makeover that's been ongoing since the late 1980s. A number of new units have been built on the grounds in the late 1990s; they match the older buildings architecturally, and blend in nicely. Those looking for historic authenticity may be disappointed. Those seeking modern resort facilities (Jacuzzis, carpeting, and updated furniture) along with accenting to provide a bit of historic flavor, will be delighted. Anyway, it's hard to imagine anyone being let down by the 15-acre grounds, situated on an rocky point facing west across the harbor. Guests typically fill their time idling in the Adirondack chairs, or partaking of more strenuous activities that include croquet, shuffleboard, tennis on clay courts, or swimming. Children's programs accommodate the growing number of families destined here.

**Dining:** Diners are seated in an elegant formal dining room (men are requested to wear jackets) and enjoy wonderful sunset views across the mouth of Boothbay Harbor as they peruse the evening menu. The menu features adaptations of traditional New England meals. Appetizers include crabcakes with three sauces; sautéed mussels; and a signature cabbage-and-lobster soup with fresh dandelion. Main courses might include pan-roasted filet mignon, or lobster with a bay stuffing of scallops. Entrees range from $15 to $25.

**Amenities:** Two outdoor pools (one heated), Jacuzzi, two outdoor clay tennis courts, fitness center, lawn games (shuffleboard, tetherball, and so on), sundeck, conference rooms, self-service Laundromat, concierge, dry cleaning, laundry service, in-room massage, baby-sitting, safe, game room, and free shuttle to Boothbay.

**Topside.** 60 McKown Hill, Boothbay Harbor, ME 04538. ☎ **207/633-5404.** www.gwi.net/topside. E-mail: topside@gwi.net. 25 units. TEL. July 1–Labor Day $67–$155 double; Apr–June and Sept–Oct $50–$130 double. Rates include continental breakfast. AE, DISC, MC, V. Closed mid-Oct–late Apr.

The old grey house on the hilltop looming over the dated motel buildings may bring to mind the Bates Motel, especially when a full moon is overhead, but get over that. Because Topside offers spectacular ocean views at a reasonable price from a quiet hilltop compound located right in downtown Boothbay. The inn itself—a former boarding house for shipyard workers—features several comfortable rooms, furnished with a somewhat discomfitting mix of antiques and contemporary furniture. At the edge of the inn's lawn are two outbuildings with basic motel units. These are on the small side, furnished simply with dated paneling and furniture. (You won't find this hotel profiled in *House Beautiful*.) Rooms 9 and 14 have the best views, but most rooms offer a glimpse of the water, and many have decks or patios. All guests have access to the wonderful lawn and the endless views, and the Reed family, which owns and operates the inn, is accommodating and friendly.

## WHERE TO DINE

When wandering through Boothbay Harbor, watch for "King" Brud and his famous **hot-dog cart.** Brud started selling hot dogs in town in 1943, and he's still at it. Dogs are $1. He's usually at the corner of McKown and Commercial streets from 10am till 4pm from June through October.

Those wishing for innovative dining should also consider (in addition to Christopher's Boathouse, below) the **Spruce Point Inn,** listed above.

**Boothbay Region Lobstermen's Co-Op.** 99 Atlantic Ave., Boothbay Harbor. ☎ **207/633-4900.** No reservations. Dinners $6.50–$9.95. MC, V. Open daily May–mid-Oct 11:30am–8:30pm. By foot: Cross footbridge and turn right; follow road for $^1/_3$ mile to co-op. SEAFOOD.

"We are not responsible if the seagulls steal your food" reads the sign at the ordering window of this casual, harborside lobster joint., and that sets the tone pretty well. Situated across the harbor from downtown Boothbay, the Lobstermen's Co-op offers no-frills lobster and seafood. This is the best pick from among the cluster of usually dependable lobster-in-the-rough places that line the waterfront nearby. You order at a pair of windows, then pick up your meal and carry your tray to either the picnic tables on the dock or inside a garage-like two-story prefab building. Lobsters are priced to market (figure $8 to $12), with extras like corn on the cob for 95¢. This is a fine place for a lobster on a sunny day, but it's uninteresting at best in rain or fog.

✪ **Christopher's Boathouse.** 25 Union St., Boothbay Harbor. ☎ **207/633-6565.** Reservations recommended during peak season. Lunch $5–$9; dinner $17–$23. MC, V. June 1–Oct 15 daily 5–9pm; July 4–mid-Oct daily 11:30am–3pm. Closed Sun–Mon in winter. CREATIVE AMERICAN/WOOD GRILL.

Christopher's offers a welcome change from the generally unexciting fare found elsewhere around town. Scenically located at the head of the harbor, the restaurant is open, bright, and modern, and a handful of lucky diners get a tremendous view up the harbor. (There's also outside deck dining when the weather is good.) The chef has a deft touch with spicy flavors and deftly combines the expected with the unexpected (to wit: lobster and mango bisque with spicy lobster wontons). The meals from the wood grill are excellent and include an Asian-spiced tuna with Caribbean salsa, and a barbecue-spiced flank steak. Christopher's is a popular destination in the summer months; make a reservation to avoid disappointment.

**Lobsterman's Wharf.** Rte. 96, East Boothbay. ☎ **207/633-3443.** Reservations for parties of 6 or more only. Lunch from $4.50; dinner $13.25–$22.95 (mostly $14–$16). AE, MC, V. Apr–Oct. SEAFOOD.

Slightly off the beaten path in East Boothbay, the Lobsterman's Wharf has the comfortable, pubby feel of a popular neighborhood bar, complete with pool table; and that's appropriate, since that's what it is, but it's that rarest of pubs—a place that's popular with the locals, but also serves up a decent meal and knows how to make travelers feel at home. If the weather's cooperative, sit at a picnic table on the dock and admire the views of a spruce-topped peninsula across the Damariscotta River; you can also grab a table inside amid the festive nautical decor. Entrees include a mixed-seafood grill, a barbecue shrimp and ribs platter, grilled swordfish with béarnaise, and succulent fresh lobster offered four different ways.

## PEMAQUID PENINSULA

The Pemaquid Peninsula is an irregular, rocky wedge driven deep into the Gulf of Maine. It's far less commercial than the Boothbay Peninsula just across the Damariscotta River, and more inviting for casual exploration. The inland areas are leafy with hardwood trees, and laced with narrow, twisting backroads that are perfect for bicycling. As you near the southern tip where small harbors and coves predominate, the region takes on a more remote, maritime feel. Rugged and rocky Pemaquid Point, at the extreme southern tip of the peninsula, is one of the most dramatic destinations in Maine when the ocean surf pounds the shore.

### ESSENTIALS

**GETTING THERE**   The Pemaquid Peninsula is accessible from the west by turning southward on Route 129/130 in Damariscotta, just off Route 1. From the east, head south on Route 32 just west of Waldoboro.

**VISITOR INFORMATION**   The Damariscotta Region Chamber of Commerce, P.O. Box 13, Main Street, Damariscotta, ME 04543 (☎ **207/563-8340**) is a good source of local information, and maintains a seasonal information booth on Route 1 during the summer months.

### EXPLORING THE PEMAQUID PENINSULA

The Pemaquid Peninsula invites slow driving and frequent stops. Start out by heading south on Route 129 toward Walpole from the sleepy head-of-the-harbor village of Damariscotta. Keep an eye on your left for the austerely handsome Walpole Meeting House, one of three meeting houses built on the peninsula in 1772. (Only two remain.) It's usually not open to the public, but services are held here during the summer and the public is welcome.

Just north of the unassuming fishing town of South Bristol, watch for the **Thompson Ice Harvesting Museum** (☎ 207/644-8551). During winter's deep freeze, volunteers from around town carve out huge blocks of ice and relay them to the well-insulated icehouse (a replica of the original icehouse). Summer visitors can peer into the cool, damp depths and see the glistening blocks (the harvest is sold to fishermen throughout the summer to ice down their catch), and learn about the once-common practice of ice harvesting. It's open in July and August on Wednesday, Friday and Saturday 1pm to 4pm or by appointment; admission is $1 adult, 50¢ child.

Continue on Route 129, and you'll soon arrive at picturesque **Christmas Cove,** so named because Capt. John Smith (of Pocahontas fame) anchored here on Christmas Day in 1614. While wandering about, look for the rustic **Coveside Bar and Restaurant** (☎ 207/644-8282) a popular marina with a pennant-bedecked lounge and a basic dining room. The food is okay, but the views are outstanding and you might catch a glimpse of the celebrity yachtsmen who tend to stop off here.

Backtrack about 5 miles north of South Bristol and turn right on Pemaquid Road, which will take you to Route 130. Along the way look for the **Harrington Meeting House** (the other 1772 structure), which is open to the public on occasional afternoons in July and August. It's an architectural gem inside, almost painfully austere, with a small museum of local artifacts on the second floor. Even if it's not open, stop to wander about the lovely cemetery out back, the final resting place of many sea captains.

Head south on Route 130 to the village of New Harbor, and look for signs to **Colonial Pemaquid** (☎ 207/677-2423). Open daily in summer from 9am to 5pm, this state historic site features exhibits on the original 1625 settlement here; archaeological digs take place in the summer. The $1 admission charge (50¢ for children 6 to 12) includes a visit to stout **Fort William Henry,** a 1907 replica of a supposedly impregnable fortress that stood over the river's entrance. There's a sand beach nearby for a bracing ocean dip.

**Pemaquid Point,** which is owned by the town, is the place to while away an afternoon (☎ 207/677-2494). Bring a picnic and a book, and find a spot on the dark, fractured rocks to settle in. The ocean views are superb, interrupted only by somewhat tenacious seagulls that may take a profound interest in your lunch. While here, be sure to visit the **Fishermen's Museum** (☎ 207/677-2726) in the handsome lighthouse. Informative exhibits depict the whys and wherefores of the local fishing trade. There's a small fee ($1 over 12, 50¢ seniors) to use the park in summer; admission to the museum is by donation.

From New Harbor, you can get a great view of the coast from the outside looking in with **Hardy Boat Cruises** (☎ 800/278-3346 or 207/677-2026). Tours are aboard the 60-foot *Hardy III,* and excursions include a 1-hour sunset and lighthouse cruise ($8 adult, $5 child 12 and under), 90-minute puffin tours out to Eastern Egg Rock ($17 adult, $1 child), and full-day ocean safaris, which includes puffin sightings and a 90-minute visit to Monhegan Island ($30 adult, $18 child). Extra clothing for warmth is strongly recommended.

Route 32 strikes northwest from New Harbor, and it's the most scenic way to leave the peninsula if you plan to continue eastward on Route 1. Along the way look for the sign pointing to the ✪ **Rachel Carson Salt Pond Preserve,** a Nature Conservancy property. The noted naturalist Rachel Carson studied these roadside tide pools extensively while researching her 1956 best-seller *The Edge of the Sea,* and today it's still an inviting spot for budding naturalists and experts alike. Pull off your shoes and socks, and wade through the cold waters at low tide looking for starfish, green crabs, periwinkles, and other creatures.

## WHERE TO STAY

**Bradley Inn.** 3063 Bristol Rd, Rte. 130, New Harbor, ME 04554. ☎ **207/677-2105.** Fax 207/677-3367. www.bradleyinn.com. E-mail: bradley@lincoln.modcoast.com. 16 units. TV TEL. Summer and fall $125–$225 double; winter and spring $105–$165. Rates include full breakfast. AE, MC, V.

The Bradley Inn is located within easy walking or biking distance to the point, but there's plenty of reason to lag behind at the inn. Start by wandering the nicely landscaped grounds, or enjoying a game of croquet in the gardens. If the fog's moved in for a spell, settle in for a game of Scrabble at pub, which is decorated with a lively nautical theme. The rooms are tastefully appointed; only three have televisions. The third-floor rooms are my favorites, despite the hike, thanks to the distant glimpses of John's Bay.

**Dining:** The local seafood served in the Ships, the inn's restaurant, gets high marks.

**Amenities:** Free use of bikes, room service (7am to 10pm), and access to nearby beach

## WHERE TO DINE

**Shaw's Fish and Lobster Wharf.** On the water, New Harbor. ☎ **207/677-2200.** Lobster priced to market (typically $8–$12). MC, V. Mid-June–Labor Day daily 11am–9pm; call for hours during shoulder seasons. Closed mid-Oct–late May. LOBSTER POUND.

Shaw's attracts hordes of tourists, but it's no trick to figure out why: It's one of the best-situated lobster pounds, with postcard-perfect views of the working harbor and the boats coming and going through the inlet that connects to the open sea. Customers stand in line to place their orders, then wait for their name to be called. While waiting, you can stake out a seat on either the open deck or the indoor dining room (go for the deck), or order up some appetizers from the raw bar. This is one of the few lobster joints with a full liquor license.

## MONHEGAN ISLAND

Brawny, wild, and remote, Monhegan Island is Maine's premier island destination. Visited by Europeans as early as 1497 (although some historians insist that earlier Norsemen carved primitive runes on neighboring Manana Island), the island was first settled by fishermen attracted to the sea's bounty in the offshore waters. Starting in the 1870s and continuing to the present day, noted artists discovered the island and came to stay for a spell. Their roster included Rockwell Kent, George Bellows, Edward Hopper, and Robert Henri. The artists gathered in the kitchen of the lighthouse to chat and drink coffee; it's said that the wife of the lighthouse keeper accumulated a tremendously valuable collection of paintings.

It's not hard to figure why artists have been attracted to the place: There's a mystical quality to it, from the thin light to the startling contrasts of the dark cliffs and the foamy white surf. There's also a remarkable sense of tranquility to this place, which can only help focus one's inner vision.

If you have the time, I'd strongly recommend an overnight on the island at one of the several hostelries. Day trips are popular and easily arranged, but the island's true character doesn't start to emerge until the last day boat sails away and the quiet, rustic appeal of the island starts to percolate back to the surface.

## ESSENTIALS

**GETTING THERE**    Access to Monhegan Island is via boat from either New Harbor, Boothbay Harbor, or Port Clyde. The hour-and-10-minute trip from Port Clyde is the favored route among longtime island visitors. The trip from this rugged fishing village is picturesque as it passes the Marshall Point Lighthouse and a series of spruce-clad islands before setting out on the open sea.

Two boats make the run to Monhegan from Port Clyde. The *Laura B.* is a doughty workboat (building supplies and boxes of food are loaded on first; passengers fill in the available niches on the deck and in the small cabin). A newer boat—the faster, passenger-oriented *Elizabeth Ann*—also makes the run, offering a large heated cabin and more seating. You'll need to leave your car behind, so pack light and wear sturdy shoes. The fare is $25 round-trip for adults; $12 for children 2 to 12 years old.

Reservations are advised: **Monhegan Boat Line,** P.O. Box 238, Port Clyde, ME 04855 (☎ **207/ 372-8848;** www.monheganboat.com). Parking is available near the dock for an additional $4 per day.

**VISITOR INFORMATION**   Monhegan Island has no formal visitors center, but it's small and friendly enough that you can make inquiries of just about anyone you meet on the island pathways. The clerks at the ferry dock in Port Clyde are also quite helpful. Be sure to pick up the inexpensive map of the island's hiking trail at the boat ticket office or at the various shops around the island.

Because wildfire could destroy this breezy island in short order, smoking is prohibited outside the village.

## EXPLORING PORT CLYDE

Port Clyde's charm lies in the fact that it's still first and foremost a fishing village. While some small-scale tourist enterprises have made their mark on the village, located at the tip of a long finger about 15 miles south of Route 1, it still caters primarily to working fishermen and the ferrymen who keep Monhegan supplied.

Here's a favorite routine for spending a couple of hours in Port Clyde, either while waiting for the ferry or just snooping around. Head to the **Port Clyde General Store** (☎ 207/372-6543), on the waterfront and soak up the cracker-barrel ambience (there's actually a decent selection of wine here, attesting to encroaching "upscalism"). Order a sandwich to go, then drive to the **Marshall Point Lighthouse Museum** (follow the road along the harbor eastward, and bear right to the point).

This small lighthouse received a few moments of fame as the spot where Forrest Gump turned around and headed back west during his cross-country walks in the movie, but it also happens to be one of the most peaceful and scenic lighthouses in the state. Walk with your lunch around to the far side of the lightkeeper's house and settle on one of the granite benches to watch the fishing boats come and go through the thoroughfare. Afterwards, tour through the small but engaging museum (free; donations encouraged) and learn a bit about the culture of lighthouses on the Maine coast.

## EXPLORING MONHEGAN

Walking is the chief activity on the island, and it's genuinely surprising how much distance you can cover on these 700 acres (about 1$\frac{1}{2}$ miles long and a 1/2 mile wide). The village clusters tightly around the harbor; the rest of the island is mostly wildland, laced with some 17 miles of trails. Much of the island is ringed with high, open bluffs atop fissured cliffs. Pack a picnic lunch and hike the perimeter trail, and plan to spend much of the day just sitting and reading, or enjoying the surf rolling in against the cliffs. During one lazy afternoon on a bluff near the island's southern tip, I spotted a half-dozen whale spouts over the course of a half hour, but never did agree with my friend whether it was one whale or several.

The inland trails are appealing in a far different way. Deep, dark **Cathedral Woods** is mossy and fragrant; sunlight only dimly filters through the evergreens to the forest floor.

**Birding** is a popular activity in the spring and fall. Monhegan Island is on the Atlantic flyway, and a wide variety of birds stop at the island along their migration routes. Swapping stories of the day's sightings is a popular activity at island inns and B&Bs.

The sole attraction on the island is the **Monhegan Museum,** located next to the 1824 lighthouse on a high point above the village. The museum, open from July through September, has a quirky collection of historic artifacts and provides some context for this rugged island's history. Also near the lighthouse is a small and select art museum featuring the works of Rockwell Kent and other island artists.

The spectacular view from the grassy slope in front of the lighthouse is the real prize. The vista sweeps across a marsh, past one of the island's most historic hotels, past melancholy Manana Island and across the sea beyond. Get here early if you want a good seat for the sunset; it seems most visitors to the island congregate here after dinner to watch the sinking of the sun. (Another popular place is the island's southern tip, where the wreckage of the *D. T. Sheridan,* a coal barge, washed up in 1948.)

If you time it right, you can also visit the studios of Monhegan artists, who are still attracted here in great number. Artists often open their workspaces to visitors during limited hours, and are happy to have visitors stop by and look at their work, chat with them a bit, and perhaps buy a canvas or sculpture to bring home. Some of the artwork runs along the lines of predictable seascapes and sunsets, but much of it rises above the banal. Look for the bulletin board along the main pathway in the village for walking directions to the studios and a listing of the days and hours they're open.

## WHERE TO STAY & DINE

**Monhegan House.** Monhegan Island, ME 04852. ☎ **800/599-7983** or 207/594-7983. 33 units (all shared bathroom). $95 double. AE, DISC, MC, V. Closed Columbus Day–Memorial Day.

The handsome Monhegan House has been accommodating guests since 1870, and it has the comfortable, worn patina of a venerable lodging house. The accommodations at this four-floor walk-up are austere but comfortable; there are no closets, and everyone uses clean dormitory-style bathrooms. The downstairs lobby with fireplace is a welcome spot to sit and take the fog-induced chill out of your bones (even in August, it can be cool here). The front deck is a nice place to lounge and keep a close eye on the comings and goings of the village. The restaurant offers three meals a day, with a selection of filling but simple meat and fish dishes, along with vegetarian entrees. Main courses range in price from about $9 to $16.

**Trailing Yew.** Monhegan Island, ME 04852. ☎ **207/596-0440.** 37 units in 4 buildings (all but 1 share bathrooms). $120 double, including breakfast, dinner, taxes, and tips. Closed mid-Oct–mid-May. No credit cards. Pets allowed.

At the end of long summer afternoons, guests congregate near the flagpole in front of the main building of this rustic hillside compound. They sit in Adirondack chairs or chat with new-found friends, but mostly they're waiting for the ringing of the bell, which signals them in for dinner, as if at summer camp. Inside, guests sit around long tables, introduce themselves to their neighbors, then pour an iced tea and wait for the delicious, family-style dinner. (You're given a choice, including vegetarian options, but my advice is to opt for the fresh fish whenever it's available.)

The Trailing Yew, which has been taking in guests since 1929, is a friendly, informal place, popular with hikers and birders (meals are a great time to swap tales of sightings) who tend to make fast friends here amid the welcome adversity of Monhegan Island. Guest rooms are eclectic and simply furnished in a pleasantly dated, summer-home style; only one of the four guest buildings has electricity (most, but not all, bathrooms have electricity); guests in rooms without electricity are provided a kerosene lamp and instruction in its use (a small flashlight is helpful . . . just in case).

# 5  Penobscot Bay

Camden is 230 miles northeast of Boston, 8 miles north of Rockland, and 18 miles south of Belfast

Traveling eastward along the Maine Coast, those who pay attention to such things will notice they're suddenly heading almost due north around Rockland. The culprit behind this geographic quirk is Penobscot Bay, a sizeable bite out of the Maine Coast that forces a lengthy northerly detour to cross the head of the bay where the Penob-scot River flows in at Bucksport.

You'll find some of Maine's most distinctive coastal scenery in this area, dotted with broad offshore islands and high hills rising above the blue bay. Although the mouth of Penobscot Bay is occupied by two large islands, its waters can still churn with vigor when the tides and winds conspire.

Penobscot Bay's western shore gets a heavy stream of tourist traffic, especially along Route 1 through the scenic village of Camden. Nonetheless, this is a good destination to get a taste of the Maine coast. Services for travelers are abundant, although during the peak season, a small miracle will be required to find a weekend guest room with-out a reservation.

## ROCKLAND & ENVIRONS

Located on the southwest edge of Penobscot Bay, Rockland has long been proud of its brick-and-blue-collar waterfront town reputation. Built around the fishing industry, Rockland historically dabbled in tourism on the side, but with the decline of the fish-eries and the rise of the tourist economy in Maine, the balance has shifted—in the last decade, Rockland has been colonized by creative restaurateurs and innkeepers and other small-business folks who are painting it with an unaccustomed gloss.

There's a small park on the waterfront from which the fleet of windjammers comes and goes, but more appealing than Rockland's waterfront is its commercial down-town—it's basically one long street lined with sophisticated historic brick architecture. If it's picturesque harbor towns you're seeking, head to Camden, Rockport, Port Clyde, or Stonington; but Rockland makes a great base for exploring this beautiful coastal region, especially if you have a low tolerance for trinkets and tourist hordes.

### ESSENTIALS

**GETTING THERE**    Route 1 passes directly through Rockland. Rockland's tiny air-port is served by **Colgan Air** (☎ **800/272-5488** or 207/596-7604) with daily flights from Boston and Bar Harbor. **Concord Trailways** (☎ **800/639-3317**) offers bus ser-vice from Rockland to Bangor and Portland.

**VISITOR INFORMATION**    The **Rockland/Thomaston Area Chamber of Com-merce,** P.O. Box 508, Rockland, ME 04841 (☎ **800/562-2529** or 207/596-0376; e-mail: rtacc@midcoast.com) staffs an information desk at Harbor Park. It's open daily 9am to 5pm Memorial Day to Labor Day, and weekdays only the rest of the year.

**EVENTS**    The **Maine Lobster Festival** (☎ **800/562-2529** or 207/596-0376) takes place at Harbor Park the first weekend in August (plus the preceding Thursday and Friday). Entertainers and vendors of all sorts of Maine products—especially the local crustacean—fill the waterfront parking lot and attract thousands of festival-goers who enjoy this pleasant event with a sort of buttery bonhomie. The event includes the Maine Sea Goddess Coronation Pageant.

### TWO FINE MUSEUMS

**Farnsworth Museum.** 356 Main St., Rockland. ☎ **207/596-6457.** E-mail: farnsworth@midcoast.com. $9 adults, $8 seniors, $5 students 18 and older, free for 17 and under (prices discounted $1 in winter). MC, V. Summer 9am–5pm daily; winter Tues–Sat 10am–5pm, Sun 1–5pm.

Rockland, for all its rough edges, has long and historic ties to the arts. Noted sculptor Louise Nevelson grew up in Rockland, and in 1935, philanthropist Lucy Farnsworth bequeathed a fortune large enough to establish the Farnsworth Museum, which has since become one of the most respected art museums in New England. Located in the middle of downtown, the Farnsworth has superb collection of paintings and sculptures by renown American artists with a connection to Maine. This includes not only Nevelson and three generations of Wyeths (N.C., Andrew, and Jamie), but Rockwell Kent, Childe Hassam, and Maurice Prendergast. The exhibit halls are modern, spacious, and well-designed, and the shows professionally prepared. The **Farnsworth Center for the Wyeth Family** is housed in the former Pratt Memorial Methodist Church and contains Andrew and Besty Wyeth's personal collection of Maine-related art. Another major expansion into an adjacent dime store is planned for late 2000.

The Farnsworth also owns two other buildings open to the public. The **Farnsworth Homestead,** located behind the museum, offers a glimpse into the life of prosperous coastal Victorians. And a 25-minute drive away in the village of Cushing is the **Olson House,** perhaps Maine's most famous home, immortalized in Andrew Wyeth's noted painting, *Christina's World.* Ask at the museum for directions and information.

**Owls Head Transportation Museum.** Rte. 73, Owls Head. ☎ **207/594-4418.** www.ohtm.org. $6 adults, $5 seniors, $4 children 5–12, families $16. Apr–Oct daily 10am–5pm; Nov–Mar daily 10am–4pm.

You don't have to be a car or plane nut to enjoy a day at this museum, located 3 miles south of Rockland on Route 73. Founded in 1974, the museum has an extraordinary collection of cars, motorcycles, bicycles, and planes, nicely displayed in a tidy, hangar-like building at the edge of the Knox County Airport. Look for the beautiful early Harley-Davidson and the sleek Rolls-Royce Phantom dating from 1929. The museum is also a popular destination for hobbyists and tinkerers, who drive and fly their classic vehicles here for frequent weekend rallies in the summer. Call ahead to ask about special events.

## ✪ WINDJAMMER TOURS

During the long transition from sail to steam, captains of the fancy new steamships belittled the old-fashioned sailing ships as "windjammers." The term stuck, and through a curious metamorphosis, the name evolved into a term of adventure and romance.

Today, windjammer vacations combine adventure with limited creature comforts—sort of like lodging at a backcountry cabin on the water. Guests typically bunk in small two-person cabins, which usually offer cold running water and a porthole to let in fresh air, but not much else. (You'll conclude this isn't like a stay at a fancy inn upon noting that one ship's brochure boasts "standing headroom in all 15 passenger cabins," and another crows that all cabins "are at least 6 feet by 8 feet.")

Maine is the capital of windjammer cruising in the United States, and the two most active Maine harbors are **Rockland** and **Camden** on Penobscot Bay. Cruises last from 3 days to a week, during which these handsome, creaky vessels poke around the tidal inlets and small coves that ring the beautiful bay. It's a superb way to explore Maine's coast the way it's historically been explored—from the water, looking inland. Rates run around $100 to $125 per day per person, with modest discounts early and late in the season.

Cruises vary from ship to ship and from week to week, depending on the inclinations of the captains and the vagaries of the Maine weather. The "standard" cruise often features a stop at one or more of the myriad spruce-studded Maine islands (perhaps with a lobster bake on shore), hearty breakfasts enjoyed sitting at tables below decks (or perched cross-legged on the sunny deck), and a palpable sense of maritime history as these handsome ships scud through frothy waters. A windjammer vacation

# Penobscot Bay

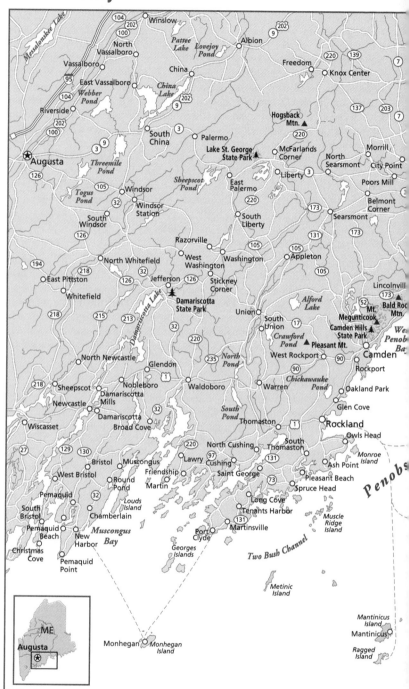

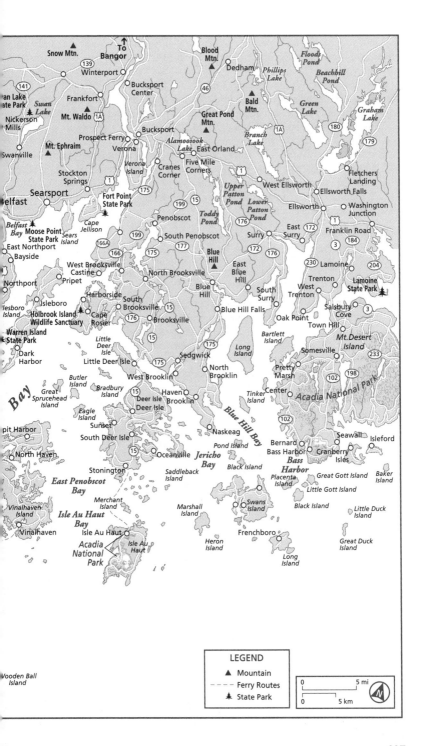

demands you use all your senses, to smell the tang of the salt air, to hear the rhythmic creaking of the masts in the evening, and to feel the frigid ocean waters as you leap in for a bracing dip.

About a dozen windjammers offer cruises in the Penobscot Bay region during the summer season (many migrate south to the Caribbean for the winter). The ships vary widely in size and vintage, and guest accommodations range from cramped and rustic to reasonably spacious and well-appointed. Ideally, you'll have a chance to look at a couple of ships to find one that suits you before signing up.

If that's not practical, call ahead to the **Maine Windjammer Association** (☎ **800/807-9463**) and request a packet of brochures, which allow comparison shopping. The association's Web site is www.midcoast.com/sailmwa/. If you're hoping for a last-minute cruise, stop by the chamber of commerce office at the Rockland waterfront (see above) and inquire if they know of any available berths.

## WHERE TO STAY

**Capt. Lindsey House Inn.** 5 Lindsey St., Rockland, ME 04841. ☎ **800/523-2145** or 207/596-7950. Fax 207/596-2758. www.rocklandmaine.com. E-mail: lindsey@midcoast.com. 9 units. A/C TV TEL. Peak season $100–$170 double; Columbus Day–Memorial Day $65–$110. Rates include continental breakfast. AE, DISC, MC, V.

The three-story, brick Capt. Lindsey House is located just a couple minutes' walk from the Farnsworth Museum. It was originally erected as a hotel in 1835 but went through several subsequent incarnations, including headquarters of the Rockland Water Co. (The inn's front desk is where folks once paid their water bills.) Guests enter through a doorway a few steps off Rockland's Main Street and enter into an opulent first-floor common area done up in rich tones, handsome dark-wood paneling, and a well-selected mix of antique and contemporary furniture. The upstairs rooms are also tastefully decorated in a contemporary country style, generally with bold modern colors and patterns mixed deftly with traditional design. Even the smaller rooms like Room 4 are well-done (this in a sort of steamship-nouveau style); the rooms on the third floor all feature yellow pine floors and antique oriental carpets. All but two rooms have showers only, but all have pleasing extras, like handmade bedspreads, hair dryers, down comforters, and bathrobes. Reliable pub fare is available at the Waterworks next door which is owned by the same people who own the inn.

**East Wind Inn.** P.O. Box 149, Tenants Harbor, ME 04860. ☎ **800/241-8439** or 207/372-6366. Fax 207/372-6320. www.eastwindinn.com. E-mail: info@eastwindinn.com. 26 units (7 with shared bathroom). Summer $90–$138 double, $165–$275 suites and apartments; off-season $72–$125 double. Rates include full breakfast. 2-night minimum on suites and apartments. AE, DISC, MC, V. Closed Dec–Apr. Drive south on Route 131 from Thomaston to Tenants Harbor; turn left at post office. Children 12 and older welcome. $10 extra for pets (by reservation).

The inn itself, formerly a sail loft, is perfectly situated next to the harbor with water views from all rooms and the long porch. It's a classic seaside hostelry with busy wallpaper, simple Colonial reproduction furniture, and tidy rooms. (The 10 guest rooms across the way at a former sea captain's house have most of the private baths.) The atmosphere is relaxed almost to the point of ennui and the service good.

**Dining:** Traditional New England fare is served in an Edwardian-era dining room. The seafood is usually your best bet; the baked haddock is always popular. Entrees are priced $11.95 to $17.95.

**LimeRock Inn.** 96 Limerock St., Rockland, ME 04841. ☎ **800/546-3762** or 207/594-2257. www.limerockinn.com. 8 units. $100–$180 double. Rates include breakfast. MC, V.

This beautiful Queen Anne–style inn is located on a quiet side street just 2 blocks from Rockland's Main Street. Originally built for U.S. Rep. Charles Littlefield in 1890, it served as a doctor's residence from 1950 to 1994, after which it was renovated into a gracious inn. The innkeepers have done a commendable job converting what could be a gloomy manse into one of the region's better choices for overnight accommodation. Excellent attention has been paid to detail throughout, from the choice of country Victorian furniture to the Egyptian cotton bedsheets. All the guest rooms are welcoming, but among the best choices is the Island Cottage Room, a bright and airy chamber wonderfully converted from an old shed and featuring a private deck and Jacuzzi. The Turret Room has French doors into the bathroom, which features a claw-foot tub. If it's big elegance you're looking for, opt for the Grand Manan Room, which has a large four-poster bed, a fireplace, and a double Jacuzzi.

**Samoset Resort.** 220 Rockport, ME 04856. ☎ **800/341-1650** or 207/594-2511. www.samoset.com. E-mail: info@samoset.com. 178 hotel units, plus 72 townhouse units. A/C TV TEL. Early July–Labor Day $259–$289 double ($339 suite); fall $165–$225 ($270); winter $119–$149 ($189); May–mid-June $145–$190 ($230); mid-June–early July $185–$255 ($285). Meals not included; ask about MAP packages. AE, CB, DC, DISC, MC, V.

The Samoset is a wonderful destination for those seeking a self-contained resort that offers contemporary styling, ocean views, and lots of golf. This modern resort is located on 230 acres at the mouth of Rockland Harbor. Both the hotel and townhouses are surrounded by the handsome golf course, which opens up expansive views from almost every window on the property. The lobby is constructed of massive timbers (recovered from an old grain silo in Portland), and the guest rooms all have balconies or terraces. Golfers love the place—it's been called Pebble Beach East—and families will always find plenty of activities for kids (there's a summer camp during high season at $40 additional per day, and baby-sitting the rest of the year). The resort also has the best sunset stroll in the state—you can ramble across the golf course to a break-water that leads out to a picturesque lighthouse. The one downside: for the high prices charged, the staff may be less polished than you would expect.

**Dining:** The Samoset offers four dining areas, including the Clubhouse Grill, Breakwater Cafe, and the Poolhouse. The centerpiece restaurant is Marcel's, where specialty dinners are prepared tableside. These include lobster flambé, rack of lamb for two, and steak Diane. Prices for main courses at Marcel's range from $14 to $29.

**Amenities:** 18-hole golf course, indoor and outdoor pools, modern health club, hot tub, sauna, indoor video golf driving range, four tennis courts (night play), jogging and walking trails, children's program, business center, gift shops, courtesy car, valet parking, massage, free newspaper, concierge, laundry service and dry cleaning, baby-sitting, safe, and safe-deposit boxes.

## WHERE TO DINE

✪ **Cafe Miranda.** 15 Oak St., Rockland. ☎ **207/594-2034.** Reservations strongly encouraged. Main courses $9.50–$16.50. DISC, MC, V. Tues–Sat 5:30–9:30pm (until 8:30 in winter). WORLD CUISINE.

Hidden away on a side street, this tiny, contemporary restaurant features a huge menu with big flavors. The fare draws liberally from cuisines from around the globe ("It's comfort food for whatever planet you're from," says owner-chef Kerry Altiero), and given its wide-ranging culinary inclinations, it comes as something of a surprise just how well-prepared everything is. The char-grilled pork and shrimp cakes served with a ginger-lime-coconut sauce are superb. Other creative entrees include barbecue pork ribs with a smoked jalapeno sauce, and Indian almond chicken. (The menu changes often, so don't set your heart on these dishes in particular.) Cafe Miranda provides the best value for the buck of any restaurant in Maine. Beer and wine is available.

**Cod End Fish House.** Next to the Town Dock, Tenant's Harbor. ☎ **207/372-6782.** Lunch entrees $1.75–$8; dinner $6.95–$12.95. DISC, MC, V. July–Aug daily 7am–9pm; limited hours June, Sept–Oct; closed Nov–May. LOBSTER POUND.

Part of the allure of Cod End is its hidden and scenic location—it seems as though you've stumbled upon a secret. Situated between the Town Landing and the East Wind Inn, Cod End is a classic lobster joint with fine views of tranquil Tenants Harbor. You walk through the fish market (where you can buy fish or lobster to go, along with various lobster-related souvenirs), then place your order at the outdoor shack. While waiting to be called, you can check out the dock or just sit and relax in the sun. (If it's raining, there's limited seating in the market.) Lobsters are the draw here, naturally, but there's plenty else to choose from, including chowders, stews, linguini with seafood, rolls (like the clam or haddock rolls), and simple sandwiches for younger tastes (even peanut butter and jelly). As with most lobster pounds, the less complicated and sophisticated your meal is here, the better the odds you'll be satisfied.

**Market on Main.** 315 Main St. ☎ **207/594-0015.** Main courses $4.95–$7.50. DISC, MC, V. Mon–Sat 10am–7pm, Sun 9:30am–2:30pm. UPMARKET DELI.

Run by the folks from Cafe Miranda, the lively and hip Market on Main is a great choice for a midday break if you're driving up the coast or spending the day at the Farnsworth Art Museum down the block. It's half deli and half restuarant, and determinedly casual with unfinished brick walls, exposed heating ducts, and galvanized steel tabletops. The selections range from sandwiches (including original choices like baked eggplant) to burgers to seafood, and plenty of salads. There's also a children's menu (including that longtime grumpy kid favorite, "Nothing....$0.00").

## CAMDEN

Camden is the quintessential coastal Maine village. Set at the foot of the wooded Camden Hills on a picturesque harbor that no Hollywood movie set could improve, the affluent village of Camden has attracted the gentry of the eastern seaboard for more than a century. The elaboarate mansions of the moneyed set still dominate the shady side streets (many have been converted into bed-and-breakfasts), and Camden is possessed of a grace and sophistication that eludes many other coastal towns; nor have Camden's charms gone unnoticed.

The village and the surrounding communities have become a haven for retired U.S. Foreign Service and CIA personnel, and have attracted its share of summering corporate bigwigs, including former Apple Computer C.E.O. John Sculley. More recently, the town received an economic injection from the rapid growth of MBNA, a national credit card company that has restored historic buildings and contributed significantly to Camden's current prosperity (this explains the high number of clean-cut young men in white shirts and ties you may see in and around town).

The best way to enjoy Camden is to park your car as soon as you can—which may mean driving a block or two off Route 1. The village is of a perfect scale to reconnoiter on foot, which allows a leisurely browse of boutiques and galleries. Don't miss the hidden town park (look behind the library), which was designed by the landscape firm of Frederick Law Olmsted, the nation's most lauded landscape architect.

On the downside: All this attention and Camden's growing appeal to bus tours are having a deleterious impact, say some longtime visitors. The merchandise at the shops seems to be trending downward in appeal to a lower common denominator, and the constant summer congestion distracts somewhat from the village's inherent charm. If you don't come expecting a pristine and undiscovered village, you're likely to enjoy the place all the more.

## ESSENTIALS

**GETTING THERE**    Camden is located on Route 1. Coming from the south, travelers can shave a few minutes off their trip by turning left onto Route 90, 6 miles past Waldoboro, bypassing Rockland. The most traffic-free route from southern Maine is to Augusta via the Maine Turnpike, then via Route 17 to Route 90 to Route 1.

**Concord Trailways** (☎ **800/639-3317**) offers bus service from Camden to Bangor and Portland.

**VISITOR INFORMATION**    The **Rockport-Camden-Lincolnville Chamber of Commerce,** P.O. Box 919, Camden, ME 04843 (☎ **800/223-5459** or 207/236-4404) dispenses helpful information from its center at the Public Landing in Camden. The chamber is open year-round weekdays from 9am to 5pm and Saturdays 10am to 5pm. In summer, it's also open Sundays 10am to 4pm.

## EXPLORING CAMDEN

**Camden Hills State Park** (☎ **207/236-3109**) is located about 1 mile north of the village center on Route 1. This 6,500-acre park features an oceanside picnic area, camping at 112 sites, a winding toll road up 800-foot Mt. Battie with spectacular views from the summit, and a variety of well-marked hiking trails. The day-use fee is $2 adult, 50¢ for children 5 to 11.

One hike I'd recommend is an ascent to the ledges of **Mt. Megunticook,** preferably early in the morning before the crowds have amassed and when the mist still lingers in the valleys. Leave from near the campground and follow the well-maintained trail to these open ledges, which requires only about 30 to 45 minutes' exertion. Spectacular, almost improbable, views of the harbor await, as well as glimpses inland to the gentle vales. Depending on your stamina and desires, you can continue on the park's trail network to Mount Battie, or into the less-trammeled woodlands on the east side of the Camden Hills.

The Camden area also lends itself well to exploring by bike. A pleasant loop of several miles takes you from Camden into the village of Rockport, which has an equally scenic harbor and less tourist traffic. Bike rentals ($15 per day, $9 half day), maps, and local riding advice are available at **Brown Dog Bikes** (☎ **207/236-6664**) at 53 Chestnut Street in Camden.

Try this bike route: Take Bayview Street from the center of town out along the bay, passing by opulent seaside estates. The road soon narrows and becomes quiet and pastoral, overarched with leafy trees. At the stop sign just past the cemetery, turn left and follow this route into Rockport. Along the way, you'll pass the local version of "landscape with cows": in this case, a small herd of belted Galloways. In Rockport, snoop around the historic harbor, then stop by **Maine Coast Artists** (Russell Avenue; ☎ **207/236-2875**), a stately gallery that offers rotating exhibits of local painters, sculptors, and craftsmen. Admission is free.

What to do in the evening? Besides quaffing a lager or ale at the Sea Dog Brewing Co. (see "Where to Dine," below), you might take in a foreign or art film at the **Bayview Street Cinema** (10 Bayview St; ☎ **207/236-8722**), on the second floor a few dozen yards from Camden's central intersection.

## ON THE WATER

Several sailing ships make Camden their home base, and it's a rare treat to come and go from this harbor, which is easily one of the most attractive in the state.

The 57-foot windjammer *Surprise* (☎ 207/236-4687), was launched in 1918, and today takes a maximum of 18 passengers on 2-hour non-smoking cruises from the Camden Public Landing. Fruit juices and cookies are served on-board; children 12 and older only. Four excursions ($25) are offered daily in July and August, three daily in June, September and October; reservations are helpful.

The *Schooner Lazy Jack* (☎ 207/230-0602), has been plying the waters since 1947 and is modeled after the Gloucester fishing schooners of the late 19th century. There's a maximum of 13 passengers; children must be 10 or older. The 2-hour tours are $20 per person; snacks are available on board, and you can BYOB.

For a more intimate view of the harbor, **Maine Sports Outfitters** (☎ **800/722-0826** or 207/236-8797) offers sea-kayaking tours of Camden's scenic harbor. The standard tour lasts 2 hours, costs $30, and takes paddlers out to Curtis Island at the outer edge of the harbor. This beginners tour is offered three or four times daily, and is an easy, delightful way to get a taste of the area's maritime culture. Longer trips and instruction are also available. The Outfitter's main shop, located on Route 1 in Rockport, has a good selection of outdoor gear and is worth a stop for outdoor enthusiasts gearing up for local adventures or heading on to Acadia.

## WHERE TO STAY

Despite the preponderance of B&Bs, the total number of guest rooms (only about 300) is limited relative to the number of visitors, and during peak season, lodging is tight. It's best to reserve well in advance. You might also try **Camden Accommodations and Reservations** (☎ **800/344-4830** or 207/236-6090), which offers assistance with everything from booking rooms at local B&Bs to finding cottages for seasonal rental.

If the inns and B&Bs listed below are unavailable or out of your budget, a handful of area motels and hotels may be able to accommodate you. South of the village center are the **Cedar Crest Motel** (115 Elm St.; ☎ **800/422-4964** or 207/236-4839), a handsome compound with coffee shop and a shuttle-bus connection downtown; and long-time mainstay **Towne Motel** (68 Elm St.; ☎ **207/236-3377**), which is within walking distance of the village. Also right in town, just across the footbridge, is the modern if generic **Best Western Camden Riverhouse Hotel** (11 Tannery Lane; ☎ **800/755-7483** or 207/236-0500), which has an indoor pool and fitness center. Rooms at all three start around $90.

*One warning:* High Street is a-rumble with cars and RVs during the summer months, and you may find the steady hum of traffic diminishes the small-town charm of the establishments that flank this otherwise stately, shady road. Restless sleepers should request rooms at the rear of the property.

**Blue Harbor House.** 67 Elm St., Camden, ME 04843. ☎ **800/248-3196** or 207/236-3196. Fax 207/236-6523. www.blueharborhouse.com. E-mail: balidog@midcoast. com. 10 units. TEL. $95–$150 double including full breakfast. AE, DISC, MC, V.

The Blue Harbor House is located on busy Route 1 just south of town. This pale blue 1810 farmhouse has been an inn since 1978 and is decorated throughout with a sprightly country look. The guest rooms vary in size; some are rather small and noisy with traffic (earplugs and white noise machines are provided in some rooms). Room #3 is especially nice, with wood floors, a handsome quilt, a bright alcove with plants, and a small TV. (Seven rooms have TVs, eight feature air-conditioning, and two have Jacuzzis). The quietest and most spacious quarters are the two suites in the rear of the house, which offer the best value. Guests tend to return to this B&B not so much for the elegance of the accommodations, as for the congeniality of the hosts (they're especially good at helping plan day trips), and the familiar, familial feel of the place.

**Camden Windward House.** 6 High St., Camden, ME 04843. ☎ **207/236-9656.** Fax 207/230-0433. E-mail: bnb@windwardhouse.com. 8 units. A/C TV TEL. Peak season $135–$195 double; off-season $110–$175 (prices $10 less midweek). All rates include full breakfast. AE, MC, V. Children 12 and older are welcome.

One of the common complaints about travelers staying in B&Bs on Camden's High Street is the noise from passing traffic. The Windward's new innkeeper has tackled that issue head-on. He added a sound-muffling facade across the front of this historic 1854 house (you can't tell it's there), and installed double windows to further dampen the drone (all rooms are air-conditioned). As a result, when you walk in this historic house and close the door behind you, it feels as if you're miles away. The welcoming common rooms are decorated with a light Victorian touch, and feature a great collection of cranberry glass; in the library, you'll find a guest refrigerator, icemaker, and afternoon refreshment. The guest rooms are varied in size, but all have televisions and phones with data ports. Three rooms with gas fireplaces also have larger TVs and VCRs. Breakfasts are ordered off the menu in the pleasant dining room, which is furnished with four maple tables.

**Cedarholm Garden Bay.** Rte. 1, Lincolnville Beach, ME 04849. ☎ **207/236-3886.** 6 units (includes 3 2-bedroom cottages). TV. Oceanfront cottages $250–$275 double; oceanview cottages $80–$135 double. Rates include breakfast. 2-night minimum in some cottages. MC, V.

Cedarholm began years ago as a small cottage court with four simple cottages just north of Camden along Route 1. It was operated more or less as a hobby. When Joyce and Barry Jobson took over in 1995, they built a road down to the 460 feet of dramatic cobblestone shoreline and constructed two modern, steeply gabled cedar cottages, each with two bedrooms. These are uniquely wonderful places, with great detailing like pocket doors, cobblestone fireplaces, handsome kitchenettes, and Jacuzzis. They're easily among the region's most quiet and peaceful retreats. Guests staying up the hill in the smaller, older (but recently updated) cottages can still wander down to the shore and lounge on the common deck overlooking the upper reaches of Penobscot Bay. It's noisier up above, where it's closer to Route 1, and the prices reflect that.

**Inn at Sunrise Point.** Route 1 (P.O. Box 1344), Camden, ME 04843. ☎ **800/435-6278** or 207/236-7716. Fax 207/236-0820. www.sunrisepoint.com. E-mail: info@sunrisepoint.com. 7 units (4 in cottages). TV TEL. $175–$225 rooms; $275–$350 cottages. Rates include a full breakfast. AE, MC, V. Closed Nov–late May. No children.

This peaceful, private sanctuary 4 miles north of Camden Harbor seems a world apart from the bustling town. The service is crisp and helpful, and the setting can't be beat. Situated on the edge of Penobscot Bay down a long, tree-lined gravel road, the Inn at Sunrise Point consists of a cluster of contemporary yet classic shingled buildings set amid a nicely landscaped yard. The predominant sounds here are of birds and waves lapping at the cobblestone shore. A granite bench and Adirondack chairs on the front lawn to allow guests to enjoy the bay view; breakfasts are served in a sunny conservatory. Guest rooms are spacious, comfortable, and full of amenities, including VCRs and individual heat controls. The cottages are at the deluxe end of the scale, and all feature double Jacuzzis, fireplaces, wet bars, and private decks.

✪ **Maine Stay.** 22 High St., Camden, ME 04843. ☎ **207/236-9636.** www.mainestay. com. E-mail: innkeeper@mainestay.com. 8 units. $100–$150 double including breakfast; discounts during the off-season. AE, MC, V. Children over age 10 welcome.

The Maine Stay is Camden's premier bed-and-breakfast. Located in a home dating to 1802 but expanded in Greek Revival style in 1840, the Maine Stay is a classic slate-roofed New England homestead set in a shady yard within walking distance of both downtown and Camden Hills State Park. The eight guest rooms on three floors all have ceiling fans and are distinctively furnished with antiques and special decorative touches. My favorite: the downstairs Carriage House Room, which is away from the buzz of traffic on Route 1 and boasts its own stone patio.

The downstairs common rooms are perfect for unwinding, and the country kitchen is open to guests at all times. Hikers can set out on trails right from the yard into the Camden Hills. Perhaps the most memorable part of a stay here, however, will be the hospitality of the three hosts—Peter Smith, his wife Donny, and her twin sister, Diana Robson. The trio is genuinely interested in their guests' well-being, and they offer dozens of day-trip suggestions, which are conveniently printed out from the inn's computer for guests to take with them. Of note is a roomy new suite on the top floor, along with other upgrades and subtle improvements.

✪ **Norumbega.** 61 High St., Camden, ME 04843. ☎ **207/236-4646.** Fax 207/236-0824. www.norumbegainn.com. E-mail: norumbega@acadia.net. 13 units. TV TEL. July–mid-Oct $160–$475 double; mid-May–June and late Oct $125–375; Nov–mid-May $99–$295. All rates include full breakfast and evening refreshments. 2-night minimum weekends and holidays. AE, DISC, MC, V. Children over age 7 welcome.

You'll have no problem finding Norumbega. Just head north of the village and look for travelers pulled over taking photos of this Victorian-era stone castle overlooking the bay. The 1886 structure is both wonderfully eccentric and finely built, full of wondrous curves and angles throughout. There's extravagant carved-oak woodwork in the lobby, and a stunning oak and mahogany inlaid floor. The downstairs billiards room is the place to pretend you're a 19th-century railroad baron (or an information-age baron—the home was owned for a time by Hodding Carter III).

Guest rooms have been meticulously restored and furnished with antiques. Five of the rooms have fireplaces, and the three "garden level rooms" (they're off the downstairs billiards room) have private decks. Two rooms rank among the finest in New England—the Library Suite, housed in the original two-story library with interior balcony, and the sprawling Penthouse with its superlative views. The inn is big enough to ensure privacy but also intimate enough for you to get to know the other guests—mingling often occurs at breakfast, at the evening social hour, and in the afternoon, when the inn puts out its famous fresh-baked cookies.

**Sunrise Motor Court.** Rte. 1 (RR 3, Box 545), Lincolnville Beach, ME 04849. ☎ **207/236-3191.** 13 cottages (all shower only). TV. Peak season $49–$69 double. Rates include continental breakfast. DISC, MC, V. Closed Columbus Day–Memorial Day weekend. Located 4¹/₂ miles north of Camden.

The Sunrise Motor Court, about 10 minutes north of Camden on Route 1, is a vintage 1950s-era establishment with excellent views of Penobscot Bay—though these views are regrettably across Route 1 and through a latticework of utility lines; yet the place boasts a time-worn comfort, like a favorite old sweatshirt. The 13 cozy cottages are arrayed along a grassy hillside at the edge of a wood, and all are simply furnished with a bed and maybe a chair or two. All boast small decks and outdoor chairs, allowing guests to relax and enjoy the serene view. (Note that two cabins behind the manager's house lack a view). This is a good bet for budget-conscious travelers who want to spend some time in the Camden area, yet not spend a small fortune doing so.

**Whitehall Inn.** 52 High St., Camden, ME 04843. ☎ **800/789-6565** or 207/236-3191. Fax 207/236-4427. www.whitehall-inn.com. E-mail: stay@whitehall-inn.com. 50 units (8 units share 4 bathrooms). July–late Oct $165–$185 double with private bath, including breakfast and dinner ($130–$150 with breakfast only); shared bath, $140 breakfast and dinner ($105 breakfast only). Discounts in late May–June. AE, MC, V. Closed late Oct–late May.

The Whitehall is a venerable Camden establishment, the sort of place you half expect to find the young Cary Grant in a blue blazer tickling the ivories on the 1904 Steinway in the lobby. Set at the edge of town on Route 1 in a structure that dates to 1834, this three-story inn has a striking architectural integrity with its columns, gables, and long roofline. This is the place you think of when you think of the classic New England summer inn. Ask for a room away from noisy Route 1.

The antique furnishings—including the handsome Seth Thomas clock, Oriental carpets, and cane-seated rockers on the front porch—are impeccably well-cared-for. Guest rooms are simple but appealing; only some rooms have phones. The Whitehall also occupies a minor footnote in the annals of American literature—a young local poet recited her poems here for guests in 1912, stunning the audience with her eloquence. Her name? Edna St. Vincent-Millay.

**Dining:** The Whitehall's dining room boasts a slightly faded glory and service that occasionally limps along, but remains a good destination for reliable New England fare like scallops with basil and cherry tomatoes, and grilled lamb loin with rosemary and caramelized garlic (entrees $15.75 to $18.) Of course, there's always boiled Maine lobster.

**Amenities:** Tennis court, tour desk, nature trails, conference rooms, baby-sitting, guest safe, and afternoon tea.

## WHERE TO DINE

**Atlantica.** 1 Bayview Landing. ☎ **207/236-6019.** Reservations suggested. Main courses lunch $7.25–$12.50, dinner $6.95–$24.95 (mostly $13–$15). AE, MC, V. Daily in summer 6–9pm. SEAFOOD/ECLECTIC.

Atlantica gets high marks for its innovative seafood menu and its consistently well-prepared fare; alas, the service can be a bit lackluster at times. Located on the waterfront with a small indoor seating area and an equally small deck, Atlantica features global fare like Thai peanut-curry seafood, wok-charred scallops, and seafood pasta provençal. (Lunches are a bit more informal, with dishes like spinach-nut burger, veggie burrito, and fresh fish tacos.) The wine list is solid if unexciting, the microbrew selection is well-chosen, but the Maine native blueberry banana smoothie is the real winner.

**Cappy's Chowder House.** 1 Main St. ☎ **207/236-2254.** Main courses $5.95–$13.95. MC, V. Daily 7:30am–midnight. SEAFOOD/AMERICAN.

"People always remember their meal here," say fans of Cappy's, a local institution smack in the middle of Camden. Travelers, especially families, tend to drift in here more to drink up the atmosphere than to sample rarified cuisine. Prime rib is served every day, there's a hearty seafood stew made with keilbasa, and there's also the famous chowder (it's been noted by *Gourmet* magazine). The Crow's Nest upstairs is a bit quieter and offers glimpses of the harbor. Cappy's is well worth a stop if you're looking for a reasonably priced and filling meal, and you don't expect to be treated like a member of the House of Windsor.

**Peter Ott's.** 16 Bayview St., Camden. ☎ **207/236-4032.** Reservations accepted for large parties. Main courses $13.95–$22.95. MC, V. Daily 5:30–9:30pm during season; usually closed 1 night weekly off-season; call first. AMERICAN.

Peter Ott's has attracted a steady stream of satisfied local customers and repeat-visitor yachtsmen since it opened smack in the middle of Camden in 1974. While it poses as a steakhouse with its simple wooden tables and chairs and its manly meat dishes (like charbroiled Black Angus with mushrooms and onions, and sirloin steak dijonaise), it's grown beyond that to satisfy more diverse tastes. In fact, the restaurant offers some of the better prepared seafood in town, including a pan-blackened seafood sampler and grilled salmon served with a lemon caper sauce. Be sure to leave room for the specialty coffees and its famous desserts, like the lemon-almond crumb tart.

**Sea Dog Brewing Co.** 43 Mechanic St., Camden. ☎ **207/236-6863.** Main courses $6.95–$12.95. AE, DISC, MC, V. Daily 11:30am–9pm (kitchen closed 2–5pm off-season). Located at Knox Mill 1 block west of Elm St. PUB FARE.

This is one of a handful of brew pubs that have found quick acceptance in Maine, and it makes a reasonable destination for quick pub food like nachos or hamburgers. It won't set your taste buds dancing, but it will satisfy basic cravings. On the ground floor of an old woolen mill that's been renovated by MBNA (a national credit-card company), the restaurant has a pleasing, comfortable atmosphere with its booths, handsome bar, and views (through tall windows) of the old millrace. The beers are consistently excellent, although some suffer from regrettable, cute names (for example, Old Gollywobbler Brown Ale).

**The Waterfront.** Bayview St. on Camden Harbor. ☎ **207/236-3747.** Main courses $6.95–$13.95 lunch, $12.95–$22.95 dinner. AE, MC, V. Daily 11:30am–2:30pm and 5–9:30pm. Closes earlier in off-season. SEAFOOD.

The Waterfont disproves the restaurant rule of thumb that "the better the view, the worse the food." Here you can watch multimillion-dollar yachts and handsome wind-jammers come and go (angle for a harborside seat on the deck), yet still be pleased by the food. The house specialty is fresh seafood of all kinds. Lunch and dinner menus are an enterprising mix of old favorites and creative originals. On the old-favorites side are fried clams, crab cakes, boiled lobster, and a fisherman's platter piled with fried seafood. On the more adventurous side is black sesame shrimp salad (served on noodles with a Thai vinaigrette), or seafood linguini with shrimp, mussels, squid, and caramelized balsamic onions. More earthbound fare for non-seafood eaters includes burgers, pitas, and strip steaks. A lighter pub menu is available between 2:30 and 5pm.

## BELFAST TO BUCKSPORT

The northerly stretch of Penobscot Bay is rich in history, especially maritime history. In the mid–19th century, Belfast and Searsport produced more than their share of ships, along with captains to pilot them on trading ventures around the globe. A century ago the now-sleepy village of Searsport had 17 active shipyards, which turned out some 200 ships over the years. In 1856 alone, 24 ships of more than 1,000 tons were launched from Belfast.

When shipbuilding died out at the end of the 19th century, the Belfast area was sustained by a thriving poultry industry. Alas, that too declined as the industry moved south. In recent decades, the area has attracted artisans of various stripes, who sell their wares at local shops. Tourists tend to pass through the region quickly, en route from the tourist enclave of Camden to the tourist enclave of Bar Harbor. It's worth slowing down for.

### ESSENTIALS

**GETTING THERE**    Route 1 connects Belfast, Searsport, and Bucksport.

**VISITOR INFORMATION**    The **Belfast Area Chamber of Commerce,** P.O. Box 58, Belfast, ME 04915 (☎ **207/338-5900**) staffs an information booth at 17 Main St. near the waterfront park that's open May to November daily, 10am to 6pm. Farther north, try the **Bucksport Bay Area Chamber of Commerce,** 263 Main St. (P.O. Box 1880), Bucksport, ME 04416 (☎ **207/469-6818**). Self-serve information is available 24 hours a day; hours with staff depend on volunteer availability.

## EXPLORING THE REGION

When approaching from the south, some splendid historic homes may be viewed by veering off Route 1 and approaching downtown Belfast via High Street (look for the first "Downtown Belfast" sign). The Primrose Hill District along High Street was the most fashionable place for prosperous merchants to settle during the early and mid–19th century, and their stately homes reflect an era when stature was equal to both the size of one's home and the care one took in designing and embellishing it. Downtown Belfast also has some superb examples of historic brick commercial architecture, including the elaborate High Victorian Gothic–style building on Main Street that formerly housed the Belfast National Bank.

At the northern tip of Penobscot Bay, the Penobscot River squeezes through a dramatic gorge near Verona Island, which Route 1 spans on an attractive suspension bridge. This easily defended pinch in the river was perceived to be of strategic importance in the 1840s, when solid and imposing **Fort Knox** was constructed. While it was never attacked, the fort was manned during the Civil and Spanish-American wars, and today is run as a state park (☎ **207/469-7719**). It's an impressive edifice to explore, with graceful granite staircases and subterranean chambers that produce wonderful echoes. Admission is $2 for adults and 50¢ for children under 12.

Across the river from Fort Knox in the paper mill town of Bucksport is **Northeast Historic Film** (☎ **800/639-1636** or 207/469-0924), an organization dedicated to preserving and showing early films related to New England. In 1992, the group bought Bucksport's Alamo Theatre, which was built in 1916 and closed (after a showing of *Godzilla*) in 1956. Films are shown regularly at the recently renovated theater. Call to ask about the ongoing film series. Visitors can also stop by the store at the front of the Alamo to browse through available videos and other items.

✪ **Penobscot Marine Museum.** Church St. at Rte. 1, Searsport. ☎ **207/548-2529.** Adults $6, seniors $5, children 7–15 $2. Memorial Day–mid-Oct Mon–Sat 10am–5pm, Sun noon–5pm. Last ticket sold at 4pm.

The Penobscot Marine Museum is one of the best small museums in New England. Housed in a cluster of eight historic buildings atop a gentle rise in tiny downtown Searsport, the museum does a deft job in educating visitors about the vitality of the local shipbuilding industry, the essential role of international trade to daily life in the 19th century, and the hazards of life at sea. The exhibits are uncommonly well-organized, and wandering from building to building induces a keen sense of wonderment at the vast enterprise that was Maine's maritime trade.

Among the more intriguing exhibits is a wide selection of dramatic marine paintings (including one stunning rendition of whaling in the Arctic), black-and-white photographs of many of the 286 weathered sea captains who once called Searsport home, exceptional photographs of a 1902 voyage to Argentina, and an early home decorated in the style of a sea captain, complete with lacquered furniture and accessories hauled back from trade missions to the Orient. Throughout, the curators do a fine job of both educating and entertaining visitors. It's well worth the price if you're the least bit interested in Maine's rich culture of the sea.

## WHERE TO STAY

**Homeport Inn.** Rte. 1, (P.O. Box 647), Searsport, ME 04974. ☎ **800/742-5814** or 207/548-2259. 10 units (3 share 1 bathroom) $55–$90 double, including full breakfast. AE, ER, DISC, MC, V.

Sitting in the front parlor of the Homeport Inn, guests would be excused for feeling a bit as though they were sitting inside a Persian carpet. The opulently furnished room is filled with tchotchkes from Asia and elaborate decorative touches. In fact, this architecturally striking 1861 sea captain's house is imposing and elegant throughout, furnished appropriately to the period with Victorian furniture and heavy oil portraits. Breakfast is served on an airy enclosed porch along the side (with glimpses of the bay beyond). After your meal, you can wander the grounds down to the water's edge, resting at benches placed for the guest's leisure. The main disadvantage is its location facing a fast-traveled stretch of Route 1 east of Searsport village.

Guest rooms are a tough choice. Choose from either one of the four handsome period rooms in the old section of the house atop a grand staircase, or from six more modern rooms in the adjoining carriage house. The disadvantage of the old rooms is that they share a single bathroom; the disadvantage of the carriage house rooms is that they're somewhat lacking in historic charm. Also available are two-bedroom Victorian cottages, which rent by the week.

## WHERE TO DINE

**Darby's.** 155 High St., Belfast. ☎ **207/338-2339.** Reservations suggested after 7pm. Lunch $3.95–$8.95; dinner $5.75–$13.95. AE, DC, DISC, MC, V. Mon–Sat 11:30am–3:30pm and 5–9pm; Sun 12–3:30pm and 5–8:30pm. AMERICAN/ECLECTIC.

Located in a Civil War–era pub with attractive stamped-tin ceilings and a beautiful back bar with Corinthian columns, Darby's is a popular local hangout that boasts a comfortable, neighborhood-y feel. Order up a Maine microbrew or a single-malt whisky while you peruse the menu, which is more creative than you might expect for the pubby surroundings. Darby's not only serves up basic bar favorites like burgers and Cajun chicken on a bulkie, but also inventive dishes like calamari with ginger soy sauce, mahogany duck, and a steak and crispy onion sandwich. The desserts are all homemade and feature cheesecake, pie, and a decidedly undietetic Scottish toffee pudding cake. If you like the artwork on the wall, ask about it. It's probably painted by a local artist, and it's probably for sale.

**MacLeod's.** Main St., Bucksport. ☎ **207/469-3963.** Reservations recommended on weekends and in summer. Main courses $3.75–$9.95 lunch, $8.95–$14.95 dinner. AE, DC, MC, V. Mon–Fri 11am–9pm, Sat–Sun 5–9pm (closed Sun evenings in off-season); bakery/cafe open daily at 7am. ECLECTIC HOMESTYLE.

MacLeod's is a comfortable, pubby place in downtown Bucksport that teems on weekends with Bucksport residents—from workers at the pulp mill to local businessmen. With its simple wood tables, Windsor chairs, and relentlessly upbeat background music, MacLeod's won't be confused with a place for fancy dining, but it does offer good meals, sizable portions, and consistent quality. For dinner, entrees include grilled lamb shish kabob, raspberry chicken, baked sea scallops, or a unique "lasagne al pescatore," made with shrimp, scallops, and crabmeat with a rich lobster sauce. The chocolate silk pie is much talked about locally.

**Young's Lobster Pound.** Mitchell Ave., East Belfast. ☎ **207/338-1160.** Fax 207/338-3498. No reservations. Main courses $5.95–$16.95. MC, V. Daily 7am–8pm (until 7pm in shoulder seasons). Closed Dec–Mar. From Belfast, take rtes. 1 & 3 eastward across the river; look for signs. LOBSTER POUND.

When you first pull down to the dirt parking lot and come upon the unlovely red corrugated industrial building on the waterfront, you'll think: "There must be some mistake. This doesn't look much like a restaurant at all," but head inside the hangar-sized door, and you'll find a counter where folks will take your order amid the long, green lobster tanks loudly gurgling seawater. After placing your order, scope out what a large lobster operation looks like, then stake out a seat. You can eat upstairs where picnic tables are arrayed in an open, barnlike area, or out on the deck, with views across the river to Belfast. This is a place to get good and messy without embarrassment. While you can order from a variety of dishes, the smart money sticks to the shore dinners and steers away from the stews, which are a bit bland and thin.

## 6 The Blue Hill Peninsula

Blue Hill is 136 miles northeast of Portland, 23 miles north of Stonington, and 14 miles southwest of Ellsworth

The Blue Hill Peninsula is a backroads paradise. If you're of a mind to get lost on country lanes that suddenly dead-end at the sea or inexplicably start to loop back on themselves, this is the place. In contrast to the western shores of Penobscot Bay, the Blue Hill Peninsula has more of a lost-in-time character. The roads are hilly, winding, and narrow, passing through leafy forests, along venerable saltwater farms, and touching on the edge of an azure inlet here or there. By and large, it's overlooked by the majority of Maine's visitors, especially those who like their itineraries well-structured and their destinations clear and simple.

### CASTINE & ENVIRONS

Castine gets my vote for the most settled and gracious village in Maine. It's not so much the stunningly handsome and meticulously maintained mid-19th-century homes that fill the side streets; nor is it the location on a quiet peninsula, 16 miles south of RV-clotted Route 1.

No, what lends Castine its charm are the splendid, towering elm trees, which still overarch many of the village streets. Before Dutch elm disease ravaged the nation's tree-lined streets, much of America once looked like this, and it's easy to slip into a debilitating nostalgia for this most graceful tree, even if you're too young to remember America of the elms. Through perseverance and a measure of luck, Castine has managed to keep several hundred elms alive, and it's worth the drive here for these alone.

For American history buffs, Castine offers much more. This outpost served as a strategic town in various battles between British, Dutch, French, and feisty colonials in the centuries following its settlement in 1613. It was occupied by each of those groups at some point, and historical personages like Miles Standish and Paul Revere passed through during one epoch or another. The town has a dignified, aristocratic bearing, and it somehow seems appropriate that Tory-dominated Castine welcomed the British with open arms during the Revolution.

An excellent brief history of Castine by Elizabeth J. Duff is published in brochure form by the Castine Merchants Association. The brochure, which also includes a walking tour of Castine, is entitled "Welcome to Castine" and is available widely at shops in town and at state information centers.

*One final note:* Castine is likely to appeal most to those who can entertain themselves. It's a peaceful place to sit and read, or take an afternoon walk. If it's outlet shopping you're looking for, you're better off moving on. "This is not Bar Harbor," one local innkeeper noted dryly.

### ESSENTIALS

**GETTING THERE**    Castine is located 16 miles south of Route 1. Turn south on Route 175 in Orland (east of Bucksport) and follow this to Route 166, which winds its way to Castine. Route 166A offers an alternate route along Penobscot Bay.

**VISITOR INFORMATION**    Castine lacks a formal information center, but the clerk at the **Town Office** (☎ 207/326-4502) is often helpful with local questions.

## EXPLORING CASTINE

One of the town's more intriguing attractions is the **Wilson Museum** (☎ 207/326-8753, or ☎ 207/326-8545 between 5 and 9pm) on Perkins Street, an attractive and quirky anthropological museum constructed in 1921. This small museum contains the collections of John Howard Wilson, an archaeologist and collector of prehistoric artifacts from around the globe. His gleanings are neatly arranged in a staid, classical arrangment of the sort that proliferated in the late 19th and early 20th centuries. The museum is open from the end of May to the end of September daily except Monday 2 to 5pm; admission is free.

Next door is the **John Perkins House,** Castine's oldest home. It was occupied by the British during the Revolution and the War of 1812, and a tour features demonstrations of old-fashioned cooking techniques. The Perkins House is open July and August on Wednesday and Sunday only from 2 to 5pm. Admission is $2.

Castine is also home to the **Maine Maritime Academy** (☎ 207/326-8545), which trains sailors for the rigors of life at sea. The campus is on the western edge of the village, and the S.S. *Maine,* the hulking grey training ship, is often docked in Castine, threatening to overwhelm the village with its sheer size. Free, half-hour tours of the ship are offered in summer (assuming the ship is in port) from 10am to noon, and 1 to 4pm.

Also worth exploring is Dyce's Head Light at the extreme western end of Battle Avenue. While the 1828 light itself is not open to the public, it's well worth scrambling down the trail to the rocky shoreline along the Penobscot River just beneath the lighthouse. A small sign indicates the start of the public trail.

## ON THE WATER

This is a lovely, open harbor, with farmland and forest edging the watery expanse. A couple of options exist for cruising on the water.

**New England Outdoor Center** (☎ 800/766-7238; www.neoc.com), offers 6-hour ($90) and 3-hour ($55) sea-kayak tours departing from Dennett's Wharf. Both trips are appropriate for those without experience; a brief intro will get you started with this graceful and often meditative sport. You'll often spot wildlife, like bald eagles, harbor seals, and ospreys. The 6-hour tour includes a bag lunch. Ask also about the 2-hour sunset tours ($35).

Smoke on the water? That's likely to be the 30-foot *Laurie Ellen,* which claims to be "the nation's only wood-powered, steam-driven passenger launch inspected and approved by the U.S. Coast Guard." (Admittedly, I haven't come across any others.) It was launched in 1999 by Capt. Randy Flood, who's the guy behind the **Castine Steamboat Co.** The unique boat has a striped canopy and will hold up to 18 passengers. Tours of the harbor run 1-hour and are offered five times daily from late June to Labor Day, sailing from Dennett's Wharf, next to the town landing. Tickets are $17.50 adult, $10 child. Call ☎ 207/374-2536 (or contact Randy on his cell phone aboard the boat during the summer: ☎ 207/266-2841). Randy's Web site is www.castinesteamboat.com. He plans to expand with a fleet of these small steamboats at different ports up and down the Maine Coast, so keep an eye out.

## WHERE TO STAY

**Castine Harbor Lodge.** Perkins St (P.O. Box 215), Castine, ME 04421. ☎ **207/326-4335.** www.castinemaine.com. E-mail: chl@acadia.net. 9 units (2 share 1 bathroom; 1 with private hall bathroom). $75–$135 double. Rates include continental breakfast. DC, DISC, MC, V. Pets allowed; $10 per night.

This is a great spot for families. Housed in a grand 1893 mansion (the only inn on the water in Castine), it's run with an informal good cheer that allows kids to feel at home amid the regal architecture. The main parlor is dominated by a pool table, and there's Scrabble and Nintendo if you but ask. The front porch has views that extend across the bay to the Camden Hills, and offers one of the best places to unwind in all of Maine. The spacious rooms are eclectically furnished, with some antiques and some modern. Two of the guest rooms share an adjoining bathroom—of note to traveling families. The family dog is welcome; and if you're not traveling with a family? It's still a great spot if you prefer a well-worn comfort to high-end elegance. Last word: The bathrooms have the best views of any in the state.

**Castine Inn.** Main St. (P.O. Box 41), Castine, ME 04421. ☎ **207/326-4365.** Fax 207/326-4570. www.castineinn.com. E-mail: relax@castineinn.com. 19 units. $85–$135 double; $210 suite. Rates include full breakfast. 2-night minimum in July and Aug. MC, V. Closed mid-Dec–May. Children 8 and older are welcome.

The Castine Inn is a Maine Coast rarity—a hotel that was originally built as a hotel (not as a residence), in this case in 1898. This handsome cream-colored village inn, designed in an eclectic Georgian–Federal Revival style, has a fine front porch and attractive gardens. Inside, the lobby takes its cue from the 1940s, with wingback chairs, loveseats, and a fireplace in the parlor. There's also an intimate, dark lounge decked out in rich green hues, reminiscent of an Irish pub. The guest rooms on the two upper floors are attractively if unevenly furnished in early American style—the innkeepers are revamping the rooms one by one to an even gloss, even adding luxe touches. Until they're all renovated, it may be wise to ask to view the available rooms before you sign in.

**Dining:** The elegant dining room serves up Castine's best fare, and some of the best food in the state. Chef/owner Tom Gutow served a stint at Bouley in New York and isn't timid about experimenting with local meats and produce, always to good effect. The menu changes nightly with ingredients varying by the season, but you might expect to find dishes such as lobster with vanilla butter, mango mayonnaise and tropical fruit salsa, or lamb loin with eggplant, green lentils, tomatoes and rosemary jus. Entrees range from $15 to $26.

**Pentagöet Inn.** Main St. (P.O. Box 4), Castine, ME 04421. ☎ **800/845-1701** or 207/326-8616. Fax 207/326-9382. www.pentagoet.com. E-mail: pentagoet@hypernet.com. 16 units (2 with private hall bathrooms). $99–$150 double, including buffet breakfast. 2-night minimum in peak season. MC, V. Closed 3rd week of Oct–early May. Pets by reservation. Suitable for children 12 and older.

Here's the big activity at the Pentagöet: Sit on the wraparound front porch on cane-seated rockers and watch the slow-paced activity on Main Street. That's not likely to be overly appealing to those looking for a fast-paced vacation, but it's the perfect salve for someone seeking respite from urban life. This quirky yellow and green 1894 structure with its prominent turret is tastefully furnished downstairs with hardwood floors, oval braided rugs, and a wood stove. It's comfortable without being overly fussy, professional without being chilly, personal without being overly intimate. A pleasant afternoon tea service is available to guests for an extra charge.

The rooms on the upper two floors of the main house are furnished eclectically, with a mix of antiques and old collectibles. The five guest rooms in the adjacent Perkins Street building—a more austere Federal-era house—are furnished simply and feature painted floors. There's no air-conditioning, but all rooms have ceiling or window fans.

## WHERE TO DINE

The best dinner in town is at the **Castine Inn** (see above).

**Dennett's Wharf.** Sea St. (next to the Town Dock). ☎ **207/326-9045.** Reservations recommended in summer and for parties of 6 or more. Main courses $8.95–$17.95. Daily 11am–midnight. Closed mid-Oct–Apr 30. PUB FARE.

Located in a soaring waterfront sail loft with dollar bills tacked all over the high ceiling, Dennett's Wharf offers upscale bar food amid a lively setting leavened with a good selection of microbrews. If the weather's decent, there's outside dining under a bright yellow awning with superb harbor views. Look for grilled sandwiches, roll-ups, and salads at lunch; dinner includes lobster, stir-fry, and steak teriyaki; and how did all those bills get on the ceiling? Ask your server. It will cost you exactly $1 to find out.

# DEER ISLE

Deer Isle is well off the beaten path but worth the long detour from Route 1 if your tastes run to pastoral countryside with a nautical edge. Loopy, winding roads cross through forest and farmland, and travelers are rewarded with sudden glimpses of the sun-dappled ocean and mint-green coves. An occasional settlement crops up now and again.

Deer Isle doesn't cater exclusively to tourists, as many coastal regions do. It's still occupied by fifth-generation fishermen, farmers, longtime rusticators, and artists who prize their seclusion. The village of **Deer Isle** has a handful of inns and galleries, but its primary focus is to serve locals and summer residents, not transients. The village of **Stonington,** on the southern tip, is a rough-hewn sea town. Despite serious incursions the past 5 years by galleries and enterprises dependent on seasonal tourism, it remains dominated in spirit by fishermen and the occasional quarryworker.

## ESSENTIALS

**GETTING THERE**    Deer Isle is accessible via several winding country roads from Route 1. Coming from the west, head south on Route 175 off Route 1 in Orland, then connect to Route 15 to Deer Isle. From the east, head south on Route 172 to Blue Hill, where you can pick up Route 15. Deer Isle is connected to the mainland via a high, narrow, and graceful suspension bridge, built in 1938, which can be somewhat harrowing to cross in high winds.

**VISITOR INFORMATION**    The **Deer Isle–Stonington Chamber of Commerce** (☎ 207/348-6124) staffs a seasonal information booth just beyond the bridge on Little Deer Isle. The booth is open daily in summer from 10am to 4pm, depending on volunteer availability.

## EXPLORING DEER ISLE

Deer Isle, with its network of narrow roads to nowhere, is ideal for perfunctory rambling. It's a pleasure to explore by car and is also inviting to travel by bike, although hasty and careening fishermen in pickups can make this unnerving at times. Especially tranquil is the narrow road between Deer Isle and Sunshine to the east. Plan to stop and explore the rocky coves and inlets along the way. To get here, head toward Stonington on Route 15, and just south of the village of Deer Isle, turn east toward Stinson Neck and continue along this scenic byway for about 10 miles over bridges and causeways.

Along this road watch for the **Haystack Mountain School of Crafts** (☎ 207/348-2306). The campus of this respected summer crafts school is visually stunning. Designed in the 1960s by Edward Larrabee Barnes, the campus is set on a steep hillside overlooking the cerulean waters of Jericho Bay. Barnes cleverly managed to play up the views while respecting the delicate landscape by building a series of small buildings on pilings that seem to float above the earth. The classrooms and studios are linked by boardwalks, many of which are connected to a wide central staircase, ending at the "Flag Deck," a sort of open-air commons just above the shoreline.

The buildings and classrooms are closed to the public, but summer visitors are welcome to walk to the Flag Deck and stroll the nature trail adjacent to the campus. There's also one public tour weekly on Wednesday at 1pm, during which you can catch glimpses of the studios. Donations are appreciated. Call for further information.

Stonington, at the very southern tip of Deer Isle, consists of one commercial street that wraps along the harbor's edge. While bed-and-breakfasts and boutiques have made inroads here recently, it's still mostly a rough-and-tumble waterfront town with strong links to the sea, and you're likely to observe lots of activity in the harbor as lobstermen come and go. If you hear industrial sounds emanating from just offshore, that's probably the stone quarry on Crotch Island, which has been supplying architectural granite to builders nationwide for more than a century.

You can learn more about the stone industry at the **Deer Isle Granite Museum** on Main Street (☎ **207/367-6331**). The tiny storefront museum features some historical artifacts from the quarry's golden years, but the real draw is a working diorama (8-foot-by-15) of Crotch Island as it would have appeared around 1900. It features a little railroad, little boats, and little cranes moving little stones around. Kids under 10 years old find it endlessly fascinating. The museum is open from late May through August daily 10am to 5pm. (Sunday it opens at 1pm.). Admission is free; donations are requested.

## WHERE TO STAY

Located on the island side of the bridge from the mainlaind is **Eggemoggin Landing,** Route 15, (☎ **207/348-6115**), a recommended lodging option on the island for those looking to spend less than charged at the inns below. It's a standard motel with basic rooms but features a great location on the shores of Eggemoggin Reach with good views of the bridge. It's open from April until Columbus Day, with rates of $69 to $75 in season, $10 less in spring and fall. Pets are allowed spring and fall only (extra charge). There's a restaurant on the premises.

✪ **Goose Cove Lodge.** Goose Cove Rd. (P.O. Box 40), Sunset, ME 04683. ☎ **207/ 348-2508.** Fax 207/348-2624. www.goosecovelodge.com. E-mail: goosecove@ goosecovelodge.com. 23 units. July and August 2-night minimum (1-week minimum in cottages). High season $140–$186 double; off-season $120–$145. Rates include full breakfast. MAP rates also available. MC, V. Open mid-May–mid-Oct.

A rustic compound adjacent to a nature preserve on a remote coastal point, Goose Cove Lodge is a superb destination for families and lovers of the outdoors. The grounds offer an adventure every day. You can hike out at low tide to salty Barred Island, or take a guided nature hike on any of five trails. You can mess around in boats in the cove (the inn has kayaks and canoes), or borrow one of the inn's bikes for an excursion; and after dinner, there's astronomy. When fog or rain puts a damper on things, curl up with a book in front of a fireplace (20 of the rooms offer fireplaces or Franklin stoves). Two recently built, modern cottages sleep six and are available through the winter. My favorites? Elm and Linnea, cozy cabins tucked privately in the woods on a rise overlooking the beach.

**Dining:** Meals here are far above what you would expect to find at the end of a remote dirt road. Each evening begins with a cocktail hour at 5:30 in the lodge, followed by dinner. Guests, seated family style, dine while enjoying views of the cove and distant islands. There's always a vegetarian option at dinner, along with one or two other entrees, like beef tenderloin with a pepper crust and horseradish spaetzle, or salmon with wild mushroom couscous and white truffle essense. The dining room is open to the public (reservations mandatory); come for lunch on the deck, or for dinner as space permits (entrees $18 to $26).

**Inn on the Harbor.** Main St. (P.O. Box 69), Stonington, ME 04681. ☎ **800/942-2420** or 207/367-2420. Fax 207/367-5165. www.innontheharbor.com. E-mail: webmaster@ innontheharbor.com. 14 units. TV TEL. $100–$125 double. Rates include continental breakfast. AE, DISC, MC, V. Closed Jan–mid-Apr. Children 12 and older welcome.

This appealingly quirky waterfront inn has the best location in town—perched over the harbor and right on the main street. In its former incarnation (called the Captain's Quarters), the inn was funky, with small rooms and 1970s-era furnishings. It's now nicely appointed with antiques and sisal carpets, yet the place still retains an unconventional charm.

Guests swap notes about their rooms over complimentary sherry and wine served in the reception room or on the expansive deck in late afternoon. This is a great location for resting up before or after a kayak expedition, or a good base for a day trip out to Isle au Haut. All rooms except the suite, located across town in the innkeeper's home, feature in-room phones. The inn also operates a restaurant a short walk away called the Cafe Atlantic, which features seafood, pasta, and beef (prime rib on weekends) with entrees priced at $11 to $17. Parking is on the street or at nearby lots, and can be inconvenient during busy times.

**Oakland House Seaside Resort/Shore Oaks.** 435 Herrick Rd., Brooksville, ME 04617. ☎ **800/359-7352** or 207/359-8521. www.oaklandhouse.com. E-mail: jim@oaklandhouse. com. 10 inn rooms plus 15 cottages. (3 inn units share 1 bathroom.) Summer $146–$190 double, including breakfast and dinner; off-season $75–$115 including breakfast. Cottages $1,195–$1,573 double per week including breakfast and dinner. 2-night minimum for inn on weekends. MC, V. Closed mid-Oct–early May. No children in inn.

Located on the mainland just north of the bridge to Deer Isle, Oakland House is a classic summer resort that's been in the same family since the American Revolution. For the past half century, the main draw has been the cluster of shoreside cottages, tucked among 50 acres and a $^1/_2$-mile of shorefront with superlative water views. These are mostly set aside for week-long stays (Saturday to Saturday). The cottages are of varying vintages but most have fireplaces with wood delivered daily. For shorter visits, a grand 1907 shorefront home has been converted to a 10-room inn called Shore Oaks; innkeeepers Jim and Sally Littlefield have been making it over in recent years in an arts-and-crafts-inspired style. In peak season, guests take their meals at the old 1889 hotel, with tasty options such as broiled swordfish, roast pork loin, or chicken and lobster verdicchio.

Activities on the grounds include hiking trails (be sure to hike the Blue Dot Trail to Lookout Rock), dubbing around in rowboats, swimming in the frigid saltwater, hiking to a (warmer) lake for swimming (shared with a kid's summer camp), and watching videos in the barn after dinner. Boat charters and a lobster bake are options in the summer.

**Pilgrim's Inn.** Deer Isle, ME 04627. ☎ **207/348-6615.** Fax 207/348-7769. www.pilgrim-sinn.com. 13 units, 2 cottages (3 rooms with shared bathroom). $160–$195 double; cottages $145–$215. Rates include breakfast and dinner. (B&B rates available; call for info.) MC, V. Closed mid-Oct–mid-May (cottages open year-round). Children 10 and older are welcome. Pets allowed in cottages only.

Set just off a town road and between an open bay and a millpond, this is a historic, handsomely renovated inn in a lovely setting. This four-story, gambrel-roofed structure will especially appeal to those intrigued by early American history. The inn was built in 1793 by Ignatius Haskell, a prosperous sawmill owner. His granddaughter opened the home to boarders, and it's been housing summer guests ever since. The interior is tastefully decorated in a style that's informed by early Americana, but not beholden to historic authenticity. The guest rooms are well-appointed with antiques and painted in muted colonial colors; especially intriguing are the rooms on the top floor with impressive diagonal beams. Two nearby cottages are also available. Activities here include strolling around the village, using the inn's bikes to explore farther afield, and taking scenic drives. Ask about bird-watching weekends in May.

**Dining:** Dinners start with cocktails and hors d'ouevres in the common room at 6pm, followed by one seating at 7pm in the adjacent barn dining room. Only one entree is served, but the creative American cuisine is not likely to disappoint. You might feast on tenderloin of beef with lobster risotto, or a bouillabaisse made of locally caught seafood. Dinner is open to the public by reservation at a fixed price of $31.50.

## WHERE TO DINE

For fine dining, check out **Goose Cove Lodge** or the **Pilgrim's Inn** (see above). The following restaurants offer more basic fare.

**Fisherman's Friend.** School St., Stonington. ☎ **207/367-2442.** Reservations recommended peak season and weekends. Sandwiches $2.50–$6.50; dinner entrees $6.95–$15.95. No credit cards. July–Aug daily 11am–9pm; June, Sept, and Oct daily 11am–8pm; April and May Tues–Sun 11am–8pm. Closed Nov–Mar. Located up the hill from the harbor past the Opera House. SEAFOOD.

This lively and boisterous restaurant is usually as crowded as it is unpretentious. Simple tables fill a large room, and long-experienced waitresses hustle about to keep up with demand. The menu features basic homecooked meals, and typically includes a wide range of fresh fish prepared in a variety of styles, including char-broiled. (The locals seem to prefer it fried.) The lobster stew is brimming with meaty lobster chunks and flavored perfectly. It's not a light meal, but travelers often find themselves making excuses to linger in Stonington the next day to indulge in yet another bowl of stew. Desserts selections, including berry pies and shortcake, are extensive and traditional New England; $2 will buy a hearty serving of of grapenut pudding with real whipped cream. Bring your own wine, beer, or cocktails.

## ✪ DAY TRIP TO ISLE AU HAUT

Rocky and remote Isle au Haut offers the most unusual hiking and camping experience in northern New England. This 6-by-3-mile island, located 6 miles south of Stonington, was originally named Ille Haut—or High Island—in 1604 by French explorer Samuel de Champlain. The name and its pronunciation evolved—today, it's generally pronounced "aisle-a-ho"—but the island itself has remained steadfastly unchanged over the centuries.

About half of the island is owned by the National Park Service and maintained as an outpost of Acadia National Park (see "Mount Desert Island & Acadia National Park," below). A 60-passenger "mailboat" makes a stop in the morning and late afternoon at Duck Harbor, allowing for a solid day of hiking while still returning to Stonington by nightfall. At Duck Harbor, the NPS also maintains a cluster of five Adirondack-style lean-tos, which are available for overnight camping. (Advance reservations are essential.) Contact **Acadia National Park,** Bar Harbor, ME 04609, or call ☎ 207-288-3338.

A network of hiking trails radiates from Duck Harbor. Be sure to ascend the island's highest point, 543-foot **Duck Harbor Mountain,** for exceptional views of the Camden Hills to the west and Mount Desert Island to the east. You also should not miss the **Cliff or Western Head trails,** which track along high, rocky bluffs and coastal outcroppings capped with damp, tangled fog forests of spruce. The trails periodically descend to cobblestone coves, which issue forth a deep rumble with every incoming wave. A hand-pump near Duck Harbor provides drinking water, but be sure to bring food and other refreshments in a daypack.

The other half of the island is privately owned, some by fishermen who can trace their island ancestry back 3 centuries, and some by summer rusticators whose forebearers discovered the bucolic splendor of Isle au Haut in the 1880s. The summer population of the island is about 300, with about 50 die-hards remaining year-round. The mailboat also stops at the small harborside village, which has a few old homes, a handsome church, a tiny schoolhouse, post office, and store. Day-trippers will be better served ferrying straight to Duck Harbor.

The **mail boat** (☎ 207/367-6516) to Isle au Haut leaves from the pier at the end of Sea Breeze Avenue in Stonington. In summer (mid-June to mid-September), the *Miss Lizzie* departs for the village of Isle au Haut daily at 7am, 11:30am, and 4:30pm; the *Mink* departs for Duck Harbor daily at 10am and 4:30pm. (Limited trips to Isle au Haut take place the remainder of the year.) The round-trip boat fare is $24 for adults to either the village or Duck Harbor. Children under 12 are $10. The crossing takes about 45 minutes to the village, 1 hour to Duck Harbor. Reservations are not accepted; it's best to arrive at least a half hour before departure.

### SEA KAYAKING & BOATING ALONG "MERCHANT'S ROW"

Peer southward from Stonington, and you'll see dozens of spruce-studded islands between the mainland and the dark, distant ridges of Isle au Haut. These islands, ringed with salmon-pink granite, are collectively called Merchant's Row, and they're invariably ranked by experienced coastal boaters as among the most beautiful in the state. Thanks to these exceptional islands, Stonington is among Maine's most popular destinations for sea kayaking. Many of the islands are open to day visitors and overnight camping, and one of the Nature Conservancy islands even hosts a flock of sheep. Experienced kayakers should contact the **Maine Island Trail Association** (☎ 207/761-8225) for more information about paddling here; several of the islands are open only to association members.

New in the Stonington area is **Old Quarry Charters** (☎ 207/367-8977), which offers guided kayak tours, as well as kayaks for rent (Old Quarry will rent only to those with prior experience, so it's best to call ahead to discuss your needs). Tours range from 2 hours ($27) to a full-day, 7-hour tour that weaves out through the islands and includes a stop for a swim at an abandoned quarry ($100). Overnight camping trips are also offered. Other services: parking and a launch site for those who've brought their own boats (small fee); sailboat tours and lessons; charter tours aboard a 38-foot lobster boat; and primitive cottages and camping on the property (permits for the latter were pending at press time). For more information, visit www.oldquarrycharters.com.

Outfitters based outside the region that offer guided overnight kayak trips around Merchant's Row include **Maine Island Kayak Co.** (☎ 207/766-2373) or **Maine Sports Outfitters** (☎ 207/236-8797).

## BLUE HILL

Blue Hill (pop. 1,900) is fairly easy to find—just look for gently domed, eponymous Blue Hill Mountain, which lords over the northern end of Blue Hill Bay. Set between the mountain and the bay is the quiet and historic town of Blue Hill, which clusters along the bay shore and a burbling stream. There's never much going on in town, and that seems to be exactly what attracts summer visitors back time and again—and may explain why two excellent independent bookstores are located here. Many old-money families still maintain retreats along the water or in the rolling inland hills, but Blue Hill offers several excellent choices for lodging if you're not well-endowed with local relatives. It's a good destination for an escape and will especially appeal to those deft at crafting their own entertainment.

When in the area, be sure to tune into the local community radio station, WERU at 89.9 FM. It was started some years back by Noel Paul Stookey (the Paul in Peter, Paul and Mary) in a chicken coop. The idea was to spread around good music and provocative ideas. It's become slicker and more professional in recent years, but still maintains a pleasantly homespun flavor.

## ESSENTIALS

**GETTING THERE**   Blue Hill is located southeast of Ellsworth on Route 172. Coming from the west, head south on Route 15, 5 miles east of Bucksport (it's well-marked with road signs).

**VISITOR INFORMATION**   Blue Hill does not maintain a visitor information booth. Look for the "Blue Hill, Maine" brochure and map at state information centers, or write the **Blue Hill Chamber of Commerce,** P.O. Box 520, Blue Hill, ME 04614. The staff at area inns and restaurants are usually able to answer any questions you might have.

## EXPLORING BLUE HILL

A good way to start your exploration is to ascend the open summit of **Blue Hill Mountain,** from which you'll have superb views of the azure bay and the rocky balds on nearby Mount Desert Island. To reach the trailhead from the village, drive north on Route 172, then turn west (left) on Mountain Road at the Blue Hill Fairgrounds. Drive 8/10 mile and look for the well-marked trail. An ascent of the "mountain" (elevation 940 feet) is about 1 mile and requires about 45 minutes. Bring a picnic lunch and enjoy the vistas.

Blue Hill has traditionally attracted more than its fair share of artists, especially, it seems, potters. Stop by **Rowantrees Pottery** (☎ 207/374-5535) on Union Street, and **Rackliffe Pottery** on Ellsworth Road (☎ 207/374-2297). Visitors are welcome to watch the potters at work. Both shops are open year-round.

Even if you're not given to swooning over historic homes, you owe yourself a visit to the intriguing **Parson Fisher House** (contact Eric Linnell, ☎ 207/374-2339, for information), located on Routes 176 and 15, one-half mile west of the village. Fisher, Blue Hill's first permanent minister, was a rustic version of a Renaissance man when he settled here in 1796. Educated at Harvard, Fisher not only delivered sermons in six different languages, including Aramaic, but was a writer, painter, and minor inventor whose energy was evidently boundless. On a tour of his home, which he built in 1814, you can see a clock with wooden works he made, and samples of the books he not only wrote, but published and bound himself.

Parson Fisher House is open from July to mid-September daily except Sunday from 2 to 5pm. Admission is $2 adults; children under 12 are free.

If you're an ardent antiques hunter or bibliophile, it's worth your while to detour to the **Big Chicken Barn** (☎ 207/667-7308) on Route 1 between Ellsworth and Bucksport (it's 9 miles west of Ellsworth; 11 miles east of Bucksport). This sprawling antiques mall and bookstore is of nearly shopping-mall proportions—more than 21,000 square feet of stuff in an old poultry barn. The first floor has a mix of very old and recent-old antiques in dozens of stalls maintained by local dealers. Most things for sale are of a size you'll tote away in a bag, although there's some furniture as well. Upstairs are some 90,000 books, which are unusually well-organized by category. There's a huge selection of old magazines in plastic sleeves that are great for browsing through on rainy afternoons

## WHERE TO STAY

The lovely **John Peters Inn** (☎ 207/374-2116; www.johnpetersinn.com), a Blue Hill landmark on 25 waterfront acres, was in the process of being sold as of early 2000. Its fate was unclear at press time. It's worth calling ahead to find out if it's reopened; rates in 1999 were $135 to $220.

**Blue Hill Farm Country Inn.** Rte. 15 (P.O. Box 437), Blue Hill, ME 04614. ☎ **207/ 374-5126.** 14 units (7 with shared bathroom). June–Oct $80–$95 double; off-season $65–$75 double. All rates include continental breakfast. AE, MC, V.

Comfortably situated on 48 acres 2 miles north of the village of Blue Hill, the Blue Hill Country Farm Inn offers some of the most relaxing and comfortable common areas you'll find anywhere. Whether you want to opt for privacy or the company of others, you're sure to find the perfect spot.

It's fortunate that the common areas are so exceptionally well done, because you're not likely to spend much time in the guest rooms, which tend to be small and lightly furnished. The more modern rooms are upstairs in the barn loft and are nicely decorated in a country farmhouse style, but these are a bit motel-like, with rooms set off a central hallway. The older rooms in the farmhouse have more character, but be forewarned that three share a single bathroom with a small tub and handheld shower.

**Blue Hill Inn.** Union St. (P.O. Box 403), Blue Hill, ME 04614. ☎ **207/374-2844.** Fax 207/374-2829. www.bluehillinn.com. E-mail: bluhilin@downeast.net. 12 units. $100–$185 double; suite $160–$230. Rates include breakfast. 2-night minimum in summer. DISC, MC, V. Closed Dec–mid-May. Children 13 and older are welcome.

The Blue Hill Inn has been hosting travelers since 1840. Situated on one of Blue Hill's main thoroughfares and within walking distance of most everything, this Federal-style inn features a convincing Colonial American motif throughout, with the authenticity enhanced by creaky floors and door jambs slightly out of true. Innkeepers Mary and Don Hartley have furnished all the rooms pleasantly with antiques and down comforters; four rooms feature wood-burning fireplaces. A more contemporary luxury suite is located in an adjacent building, which features cathedral ceiling, fireplace, kitchen, and deck. Ask about packages that include kayaking, hiking, or sailing.

**Dining:** The one part of the inn that doesn't feel old is the dining room, which is built in a shed-like addition to the old house, but the superb country cooking makes up for the less interesting atmosphere. The meals are made chiefly with local, organic ingredients. Among the creative dishes are lobster with a vanilla beurre blanc and roast duck with green peppercorn sauce. The wine selection is excellent. The fixed-price dinner ($30) is served Wednesday to Friday and is open to the public; reservations required.

## WHERE TO DINE

**Jean-Paul's Bistro.** Main St., Blue Hill. ☎ **207/374-5852.** Lunch $6.95–$8.95. MC, V. Daily 11am–5pm. Closed mid-Sept–June 30. Located at the intersection of rtes. 172 and 15. UPSCALE SANDWICHES.

You get a lot of mileage for a moderate price at Jean-Paul's, which serves up lunch and tea during its brief summer season (it's open in July, August, and early September only). This is the place to head when the sun's shining overhead and summer blazes in its full glory. Behind this old farmhouse in the village center are stone terraces and a lawn that slopes down to the head of Blue Hill Bay. Choose either a table on the terraces, or plop yourself into one of the wide-armed Adirondack chairs on the lawn overlooking the water. Lunches tend toward quiche, croissant sandwiches, and salads. The walnut tarragon chicken salad is tasty; the delicious desserts make liberal use of local blueberries.

**Jonathan's.** Main St., Blue Hill. ☎ **207/374-5226.** Reservations recommended. Main courses, $14.95–$18.95. MC, V. Daily 5–9:30pm. Closed Mon from Nov–May. ECLECTIC.

Located in the middle of Blue Hill, Jonathan's appeals to almost everyone—from the younger local crowd to the old-money summer denizens. The service is brisk and professional, and the wine list extensive and creative. Guests choose between the barn-like back room with its comfortable knotty-pine feel, or the less elegant front room facing Main Street, and done up in green tablecloths, captain's chairs, and booths of white pine. The menu changes frequently, but among typical dishes are the popular braised lamb shank with maple barbecue sauce; mixed grill of quail, rabbit, and venison sausage; and a simple poached salmon with dill sauce. Appetizers run along the lines of warm smoked mussel and chèvre salad, or pear salad with Maine cheeses.

## 7  Mount Desert Island & Acadia National Park

Mount Desert Island is home to spectacular Acadia National Park, and for many visitors, the two places are one and the same. Yes, visitors to Acadia drive the economy, and their presence defines the spirit of Maine's largest island. The park contains the most dramatic coastal real estate on the eastern seaboard.

Yet the park holdings are only part of the appeal of this immensely popular island, which is connected to the mainland via a short, two-lane causeway. Beyond the parklands are scenic harborside villages and remote backcountry roads, quaint B&Bs and unusually fine restaurants, oversize 19th-century summer "cottages" and the unrepentant tourist trap of Bar Harbor. Those who arrive on the island expecting untamed wilderness invariably leave disappointed. Those who understand that Acadia National Park is but one chapter (albeit a very large one) in the intriguing story of Mount Desert Island will enjoy their visit thoroughly.

Mount Desert (pronounced "de-*sert*") is divided into two lobes separated by Somes Sound, the only legitimate fjord in the continental U.S. (A fjord is a valley carved by a glacier that subsequently filled with rising ocean water.) Those with a poetic imagination see Mount Desert shaped as a lobster, with one large claw and one small. Most of the parkland is on the meatier east claw, although large swaths of park exist on the leaner west claw as well. The eastern side is more developed, with Bar Harbor the center of commerce and entertainment. The western side has a more quiet, settled air, and teems more with wildlife than tourists. The island isn't huge—it's only about 15 miles from the causeway to the southernmost tip at Bass Harbor Head—and visitors can do a lot of adventuring in such a compact space. The best plan is to take it slow, exploring whenever possible by foot, bicycle, canoe, or kayak.

## ACADIA NATIONAL PARK

It's not hard to fathom why Acadia is consistently one of the biggest draws in the U.S. national park system. The park's landscape is a rich tapestry of rugged cliffs, restless ocean, and deep, silent woods. Acadia's landscape, like so much of the rest of northern New England, was carved by glaciers some 18,000 years ago. A mile-high ice-sheet shaped the land by scouring valleys into their distinctive U shapes, rounding many of the once-jagged peaks, and depositing huge boulders about the landscape, such as the famous 10-foot-high "Bubble Rock," which appears to be perched precariously on the side of South Bubble Mountain.

The park's more recent roots can be traced back to the 1840s, when noted Hudson River School painter Thomas Cole packed his sketchbooks and easels for a trip to this remote island, then home to a small number of fishermen and boatbuilders. His stunning renditions of the surging surf pounding against coastal granite were later displayed in New York and triggered an early tourism boom as urbanites flocked to the island to "rusticate." By 1872, national magazines were touting Eden (Bar Harbor's name until 1919) as a desirable summer resort. It attracted the attention of wealthy industrialists and soon became a summer home to Carnegies, Rockefellers, Astors, and Vanderbilts.

Early in the 1900s, the huge popularity and growing development of the island began to concern its most ardent supporters. Boston textile heir and conservationist George Dorr and Harvard president Charles Eliot, aided by the largesse of John D. Rockefeller, Jr., started acquiring large tracts for the public's enjoyment. These parcels were eventually donated to the federal government, and in 1919, the public land was designated Lafayette National Park, the first national park east of the Mississippi. Renamed Acadia in 1929, the park has grown to encompass nearly half the island, with holdings scattered about piecemeal here and there.

## ESSENTIALS

**GETTING THERE**   Acadia National Park is reached from the town of Ellsworth via Route 3. If you're coming from southern Maine, you can avoid the coastal congestion along Route 1 by taking the Maine Turnpike to Bangor, picking up I-395 to Route 1A, then continuing south on Route 1A to Ellsworth. While this looks longer on the map, it's by far the quickest route in summer.

Daily flights from Boston to the airport in Trenton, just across the causeway from Mount Desert Island, are offered year-round by Continental affiliate **Colgan Air** (☎ **800/523-3273** or 207/667-7171).

In summer, **Concord Trailways** (☎ **888/741-8686** or 207/942-8686) offers van service between Bangor (including an airport stop), Ellsworth, and Bar Harbor between late May and mid-September. Reservations are required.

**GETTING AROUND**   The free ✪ **islandwide bus shuttle service** serve six routes that cover nearly the entire island and will stop anywhere you request outside the village centers, including trailheads, ferries, small villages, and campgrounds. All routes begin or end at the Village Green in Bar Harbor, but you're encouraged to pick up the bus wherever you're staying, whether motel or campground, to avoid parking hassles in town. Route #3 goes from Bar Harbor along much of the Park Loop, offering easy access to some of the park's best hiking trails. The buses operate from late June to early September; ask for a schedule at any of the island information centers.

**GUIDED TOURS**   **Acadia National Park Tours** (☎ **207/288-3327**), offers 2¹⁄₂-hour park tours departing twice daily (10am and 2pm) from downtown Bar Harbor. The bus tour includes three stops (Sieur De Monts Springs, Thunder Hole, and Cadillac Mountain) and plenty of park trivia courtesy of the driver. This is an easy way for first-time visitors to get a quick introduction to the park before setting out on their own. Tickets are available at Testa's Restaurant, 53 Main St., Bar Harbor; $15 adult, $5 children under 14.

# Mount Desert Island/Acadia National Park

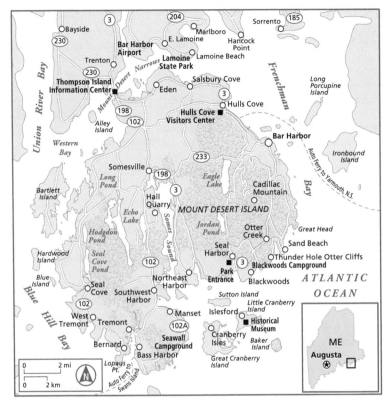

**ENTRY POINTS & FEES**   A 1-week park pass, which includes unlimited trips on Park Loop Road, costs $10 per car; no extra charge per passenger. (No daily pass is available.) The main point of entry to Park Loop Road, the park's most scenic byway, is at the visitor center at **Hulls Cove.** Mount Desert Island consists of an interwoven network of park and town roads, allowing visitors to enter the park at numerous points. A glance at a park map (available at the visitor center) will make these access points self-evident. The entry fee is collected at a toll booth on Park Loop Road, a $1/2$ mile north of Sand Beach.

## Avoiding Crowds in the Park

Early fall is the best time to miss out on the mobs yet still enjoy the weather. If you do come midsummer, try to venture out in the early morning and or early evening to see the most popular spots, like the Thunder Hole or the summit of Cadillac Mountain. Setting off into the woods at every opportunity is also a good strategy. About four out of five visitors restrict their tours to the loop road and a handful of other major attractions, leaving the Acadia backcountry open for more adventurous spirits.

The best guarantee of solitude is to head to the more remote outposts managed by Acadia, especially Isle au Haut and Schoodic Peninsula, located across the bay to the east. Ask for more information at the visitor's centers.

**VISITOR CENTERS**    Acadia staffs two visitor centers. The **Thompson Island Information Center** (☎ 207/288-3411) on Route 3 is the first you'll pass as you enter Mount Desert Island. This center is maintained by the local chambers of commerce, but park personnel are often on hand to answer inquiries. It's open May through mid-October and is a good stop for general lodging and restaurant information.

If you're primarily interested in information about the park itself, continue on Route 3 to the National Park Service's **Hulls Cove Visitor Center** about 7¹/₂ miles beyond Thompson Island. The visitor center includes natural history exhibits, as well as free brochures about hiking trails and the carriage roads. Postcards and more detailed guidebooks are available for sale. The center is open mid-April through October.

Information is also available year-round, by phone or in person, from the park's **headquarters** (☎ 207/288-3338; www.nps.gov/acad) on Route 233 between Bar Harbor and Somesville.

**WHEN TO GO**    Visit Acadia in September if you can. Between Labor Day and the foliage season of early October, the days are often warm and clear, the nights have a crisp northerly tang, and you can avoid the hassles of congestion, crowds, and pesky insects. Not that the park is empty in September; you will still encounter crowds at the most popular sites. Just walk a minute or two off the road to find solitude and an agreeable peacefulness.

Summer, of course, is peak season at Acadia. Weather is perfect for just about any outdoor activity in July and August. Most days are warm (in the '70s or '80s), with afternoons frequently cooler than mornings owing to ocean breezes. While sun seems to be the norm, come prepared for rain and fog, both frequent visitors to the Maine coast. Sometime during the last 2 weeks of August, a cold wind will blow through at night, and you'll smell the approach of autumn, with winter not far behind.

Winter is increasingly popular among travelers who enjoy cross-country skiing on the carriage roads. Be aware, though, that snow is inconsistent and services are very much limited in the off-season.

**RANGER PROGRAMS**    Frequent ranger programs are offered throughout the year. These include talks at campground amphitheaters and tours of various locations around the island. Examples are the Otter Point nature hike, Mr. Rockefeller's bridges walk, Frenchman Bay cruise (rangers provide commentary on commercial trips; make reservations with commercial tour boat owners), and a discussion of changes in Acadia's landscape. Ask for a schedule of events or more information at either of the two visitor centers or campgrounds.

## EXPLORING THE PARK

Try to allow 3 or 4 days at a minimum for visiting the park. One small, motherly tip: When you set out to explore the park, pack a picnic lunch and keep it handy. Having drinks and a bite to eat at hand will prevent breaking up your day with time-wasting backtracking into Bar Harbor or elsewhere in a desperate effort to fend off starvation.

✪ **THE PARK LOOP ROAD**    This 20-mile road is the park's main attraction. It runs along the island's eastern shore, then loops inland along Jordan Pond and Eagle Lake. The road runs high along the shoulders of dramatic coastal mountains, then dips down along the boulder-strewn coastlines. The dark granite is broken by the spires of spruce and fir, and the earthy tones contrast sharply with the frothy white surf and the steely, azure sea. It's easy to make frequent stops to admire the vistas along the way.

Attractions along the coastal loop include: scenic **Sand Beach,** the only sand beach on the island; **Thunder Hole,** a shallow oceanside cavern into which the surf surges, compresses, and bursts out with an explosive force and a concussive sound (young kids seem to be endlessly mesmerized by this); and **Cadillac Mountain,** the highest point on the island at 1,530 feet, and the place in the United States first touched by the sun during much of the year. The mountain top is accessible by car along an old carriage road, but the parking lot at the summit is often crowded and drivers testy. You're better off hiking to the top or scaling a more remote peak.

**LOBSTER POUNDS**   The best lobster restaurants are those right on the water, where there's no pretension or frills. The ingredients for a proper feed at a local lobster pound are a pot of boiling water, a tank of lobsters, some well-worn picnic tables, a good view, and a six-pack of Maine beer. Among the best are **Beal's Lobster Pier** (☎ 207/244-7178) in Southwest Harbor, which is one of the oldest pounds in the area. **Thurston's Lobster Pound** (☎ 207/244-7600) in tiny Bernard (across the water from Bass Harbor) was atmospheric enough to be used as a backdrop for the Stephen King mini-series "Storm of the Century"; it's a fine place to linger toward dusk. **Abel's Lobster Pound** (☎ 207/276-5827) on Route 198, 5 miles north of Northeast Harbor overlooks the deep blue waters of Somes Sound; eat at picnic tables under the pines or indoors at the restaurant. It's quite a bit pricier than other lobster restaurants at first glance, but they don't charge for the extras like many other lobster joints—and some visitors claim that lobsters here are more succulent.

On the mainland just north of the causeway is the wonderful **Oak Point Lobster Pound** (☎ 207/667-6998). This is off the beaten path (although still popular and often crowded), where you can enjoy your lobster with a sensational view of the island's rocky hills. To get here, turn west off Route 3 onto Route 230 before crossing to Mount Desert, then continue 4 miles to the restaurant.

**CARRIAGE RIDES**   Carriage rides are offered by **Wildwood Stables** (☎ 207/276-3622), a national park concessioner located a ¹/₂-mile south of Jordan Pond House. The 1-hour Day Mountain trip departs three times daily, yields wonderful views, and costs $13 for adults, $7 for children 6 to 12, and $4 for children 2 to 5. Longer tours and charters are also available, as is a special carriage designed to accommodate handicapped passengers; reservations are encouraged.

**HIKING**   Acadia National Park has 120 miles of hiking trails in addition to the carriage roads. The **Hulls Cove Visitor Center** offers a one-page chart of area hikes; combined with the park map, this is all you'll need since the trails are well-maintained and well-marked. It's not hard to cobble together loop hikes to make your trips more varied. Coordinate your hiking with the weather; if it's damp or foggy, you'll stay drier and warmer strolling the carriage roads. If it's clear and dry, head for the highest peaks with the best views.

Among my favorite trails is the **Dorr Ladder Trail,** which departs from Route 3 near The Tarn just south of the Sieur de Monts entrance to the Loop Road. This trail begins with a series of massive stone steps ascending along the base of a vast slab of granite, then passes through crevasses (not for the wide of girth) and up ladders affixed to the granite. The views east and south are superb.

An easy lowland hike is around **Jordan Pond,** with the northward leg along the pond's east shore on a hiking trail, and the return via the carriage road. It's mostly level, with the total loop measuring just over 3 miles. At the north end of Jordan Pond, consider heading up the prominent, oddly symmetrical mounds called The Bubbles. These detours shouldn't take much more than 20 minutes each; look for signs off the Jordan Pond Shore Trail.

On the western side of the island, an ascent of **Acadia Mountain** and return takes about an hour and a half, but hikers should schedule in some time for lingering while they enjoy the view of Somes Sound and the smaller islands off Mount Desert's southern shores. This 2½-mile loop hike begins off Route 102 at a trailhead 3 miles south of Somesville. Head eastward through rolling mixed forest, then begin an ascent over ledgy terrain. Be sure to visit both the east and west peaks (the east peak has the better views), and look for hidden balds in the summit forest that open up to unexpected vistas.

**☉ MOUNTAIN BIKING**    Acadia's **carriage roads** offer some of the most scenic, relaxing mountain biking anywhere in the United States. The 57 miles of grassy lanes and gravel roads were built in the early part of the 20th century by John D. Rockefeller, Jr. The roads today are superbly restored and maintained, and are open only to pedestrians, bicyclists, and equestrians. Where the carriage roads cross private land (generally between Seal Harbor and Northeast Harbor), they are closed to mountains bikes. A decent map of the carriage roads is available free at the park's visitor center. More detailed guidebooks are sold at area bookstores.

Mountain bikes may be rented along Cottage Street in Bar Harbor, with rates around $15 to $17 for a full day, $10 to $12 for a half day. Most bike shops include locks and helmets as basic equipment, but ask what's included before you rent. Also ask about closing times, since you'll be able to get a couple extra hours in with a later-closing shop. **Bar Harbor Bicycle Shop** (☎ 207/288-3886) at 141 Cottage St. gets my vote for the most convenient and friendliest; you might also try **Acadia Outfitters** (☎ 207/288-8118) at 106 Cottage St., or **Acadia Bike & Coastal Kayaking** (☎ 207/288-9605) at 48 Cottage St.

**ROCK CLIMBING**    Many of the oceanside rock faces attract experienced rock climbers, as much for the beauty of the climbing areas as the challenge of the climbs. For curious novices, **Acadia Mountain Guides** (☎ 207/288-8186) offers rock-climbing lessons and guide services, ranging from a half-day introduction to rock climbing to intensive workshops on self-rescue and instruction on how to lead climbs. The Bar Harbor shop is located at the corner of Main and Mount Desert Street.

**SEA KAYAKING**    Experienced sea kayakers flock to Acadia to test their paddling skills along the surf at the base of rocky cliffs, to venture out to the offshore islands, and to probe the still, silent waters of Somes Sound. Novice sea kayakers also come to Acadia to try their hand for the first time with guided tours, which are offered by several outfitters. If you're concerned about the waters being too crowded, ask how many paddlers have already signed up. (Insider tip: Rainy days can be magical on the water and surprisngly dry once you're sealed inside a kayak; you're also likely to have a much less crowded experience.) You can turn up a variety of tours by contacting the following guide services: **Acadia Outfitters** (☎ 207/288-8118) at 106 Cottage St., **Coastal Kayaking** (☎ 207/288-9605) at 48 Cottage St., and **National Park Sea Kayak Tours** (☎ 207/288-0342) at 137 Cottage St. Rates typically range from $35 per person for a 2-hour harbor tour, to $65 for a full-day excursion.

## CAMPING

The National Park Service maintains two campgrounds within Acadia National Park. Both are extremely popular; during July and August expect both to fill by early to mid-morning.

The more popular of the two is **Blackwoods** (☎ 207/288-3274), located on the island's eastern side. Access is from Route 3, 5 miles south of Bar Harbor. Bikers and pedestrians have easy access to the loop road from the campground via a short trail. The campground has no public showers, but an enterprising business just outside the campground entrance offers clean showers for a modest fee. Camping fees are $18 per night and reservations are accepted; **reservations** may be made up to 5 months in advance by calling ☎ 800/365-2267. (This is to a national reservation service, whose contract is revisited from time to time by the park service; if it's non-working, call the campground directly to ask for the current toll-free reservation number.) Reservations may also be made on the Web between 10am and 10pm only at http://reservations.nps.gov.

**Seawall** (☎ 207/244-3600) is on the quieter, western half of the island near the fishing village of Bass Harbor. This is a good base for road biking, and several short coastal hikes are within easy striking distance. Many of the sites are walk-ins, which require carrying your gear 100 yards or so to the site. The campground is open late May through September on a first-come, first-served basis. In general, if you get here by 9 or 10am, you'll be pretty much assured of a campsite, especially if you're a tent camper. No showers, but they're available nearby. Camping fees are $12 to $18 per night.

Private campgrounds handle the overflow. The region from Ellsworth south boasts some 14 private campgrounds, which offer varying amenities. The **Thompson Island Information Center** (☎ 207/288-3411) posts up-to-the-minute information on which campgrounds still have vacancies; it's a good first stop for those arriving without camping reservations.

To my mind, two private campgrounds stand above the rest. **Bar Harbor Campground** (Route 3, Salisbury Cove; ☎ 207/288-5185), on the main route between the causeway and Bar Harbor, doesn't take reservations, and you can often find a good selection of sites if you arrive before noon, even during the peak season. Some of its 300 sites are set in piney woods; others are on an open hillside covered with blueberry barrens and offering fine views of northern Frenchman Bay.

At the head of Somes Sound is **Mount Desert Campground** (Route 198; ☎ 207/244-3710), which is especially well-suited for tenters (RVs to a maximum of 20 feet only). This heavily wooded campground has very few undesirable sites, and a great many desirable ones, including some walk-in sites right at the water's edge.

Another option is **Lamoine State Park** (☎ 207/667-4778), which faces Mount Desert from the mainland across the cold waters of northernmost Frenchman Bay. This is an exceptionally pleasant, quiet park with spacious and private sites and a small beach about a half-hour's drive from the action at Bar Harbor. The campground has been discovered by more travelers in recent years, but camping sites are still usually available in summer after the national park sites have all been spoken for.

## BAR HARBOR

Bar Harbor's historical roots are in the grand resort era of the late 19th century. The region was discovered by wealthy rusticators, drawn by landscape paintings exhibited in Boston and New York. Later, sprawling hotels and boarding houses cluttered the shores and hillsides as the newly affluent middle class flocked here in summer by steamboat and rail from eastern seaboard cities. The tourist business continued to grow through the early part of 1900s, then all but collapsed as the Great Depression and the growing popularity of automobile travel doomed the era of the extended vacation.

Bar Harbor was dealt a further blow in 1947 when a fire, fueled by an unusually dry summer and fierce northwest winds, leveled many of the most opulent cottages and much of the rest of the town. The fire destroyed five hotels, 67 grand cottages, and 170 homes. In all, some 17,000 acres of the island were burned. Downtown Bar Harbor was spared, and many of the in-town mansions along the oceanfront were missed by the conflagration.

After a period of quiet slumber (some storefronts were still boarded up as late as the 1970s), Bar Harbor has been rejuvenated and rediscovered in recent years as visitors have poured into this area, followed by entrepreneurs who opened dozens of restaurants, shops, and boutiques. The less charitable regard Bar Harbor as just another tacky tourist mecca, and it does have some of those traits—the downtown hosts a proliferation of T-shirt vendors, ice-cream-cone shops, and souvenir palaces. Crowds spill off the sidewalk and into the street in midsummer, and the traffic and congestion can be truly appalling. Yet Bar Harbor's vibrant history, distinguished architecture, refusal to sprawl, and beautiful location along Frenchman Bay allow it to rise above being only a diversion for tourists.

Most of the island's inns, motels, and B&Bs are located here, as are dozens of restaurants, making it a desirable base of operations. Bar Harbor is also the best destination for the usual supplies and services; there's a decent grocery story and Laundromat, and you can stock up on all the necessities of life.

As for the congestion, it's fortunate that Bar Harbor is compact enough that once you find a parking space or a room for the night, the whole town can be navigated conveniently on foot. Arriving here early in the morning also considerably improves your odds of securing parking within easy striking distance of the town center. *Suggestion:* Explore Bar Harbor before and after breakfast, then set off for the hills, woods, and coast the rest of the day.

## ESSENTIALS

**GETTING THERE**   Bar Harbor is located on Route 3 about 10 miles southeast of the causeway. Seasonal bus service is available in summer; for schedules contact **Concord Trailways** (☎ **800/639-3317**).

**VISITOR INFORMATION**   The **Bar Harbor Chamber of Commerce,** P.O. Box 158, Bar Harbor, ME 04609 (☎ **207/288-5103;** e-mail: bhcc@acadia.net) stockpiles a huge arsenal of information about local attractions at its offices at 93 Cottage St. Write, call, or e-mail in advance for a full guide to area lodging and attractions. The chamber's Web site (www.acadia.net/bhcc) is chock-full of information and helpful links.

## EXPLORING BAR HARBOR

Wandering the compact downtown on foot is a good way to get a taste of the town. Among the best views in town are those from the foot of Main Street at grassy **Agamont Park,** which overlooks the town pier and Frenchman Bay. From here, set off past the Bar Harbor Inn on the **Shore Path,** a winding, wide trail that follows the shoreline for a short distance along a public right of way. The pathway passes in front of many of the elegant summer homes (some converted to inns), offering a superb vantage point to view the area's architecture.

From the path, you'll also have an open view of **The Porcupines,** a cluster of spruce-studded islands just offshore. This is a good spot to witness the powerful force of glacial action. The south-moving glacier ground away at the islands, creating a gentle slope facing north. On the south shore, away from the glacial push (glaciers simply melted when they retreated north), is a more abrupt, cliff-like shore. The resulting islands look like a small group of porcupines migrating southward—or so early visitors imagined.

A short stroll from the Village Green is the **Bar Harbor Historical Society,** 33 Ledgelawn Ave. (☎ **207/288-3807**). The society is housed in a handsome 1918 former convent, and showcases artifacts of life in the old days—dishware and photos from the grand old hotels, and exhibits on noted landscape architect Beatrix Farrand. Leave enough time to spend a few minutes thumbing through the scrapbooks about the devastating 1947 fire. The museum is open June to October, Monday to Saturday from 1 to 4pm; admission is free.

One of the most elaborate of Bar Harbor's magnificent summer cottages—called The Turrets—is now the centerpiece of the **College of the Atlantic** (☎ **207/288-5015**), a

# Bar Harbor

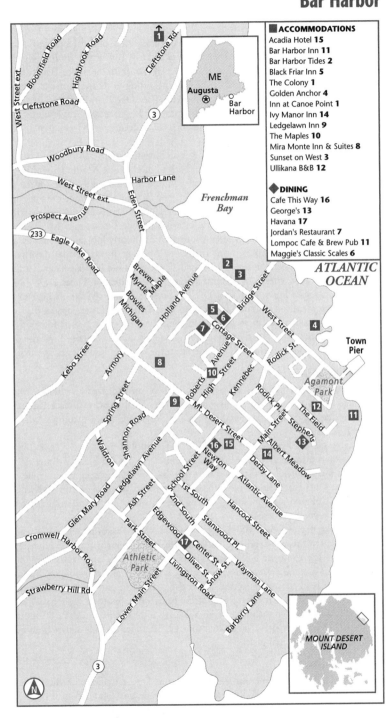

**ACCOMMODATIONS**
Acadia Hotel **15**
Bar Harbor Inn **11**
Bar Harbor Tides **2**
Black Friar Inn **5**
The Colony **1**
Golden Anchor **4**
Inn at Canoe Point **1**
Ivy Manor Inn **14**
Ledgelawn Inn **9**
The Maples **10**
Mira Monte Inn & Suites **8**
Sunset on West **3**
Ullikana B&B **12**

**DINING**
Cafe This Way **16**
George's **13**
Havana **17**
Jordan's Restaurant **7**
Lompoc Cafe & Brew Pub **11**
Maggie's Classic Scales **6**

school founded in 1969 with a strong emphasis on environmental education. The campus is centered around an impressively turreted stone castle built in 1895, featuring a broad porch and drop-dead spectacular views of the bay. Part of the ground floor has been converted to a natural history museum, which is open to the public. The exhibits are well-done and informative, and there's extra in getting to see the former estate and its view. The museum is open daily mid-June to Labor Day 10am to 5pm; the rest of the year, it's open Thursday and Friday 1 to 4pm, Sat 10am to 4pm., and Sunday 1 to 4pm. Admission is $3.50 adults, $2.50 seniors, $1.50 teens, and $1 children 12 and under.

For an eye-opening adventure, consider watching the sunrise from atop Cadillac Mountain followed by a zippy bike descent back to Bar Harbor. **Acadia Downhill** (48 Cottage St.; ☎ 207/288-9605) will haul you and a rental bike to the top of the island's highest peak via van, serve you coffee and a light breakfast while the sun edges over the eastern horizon, then lead you on a delightfully brisk coasting and pedaling trip 6 miles back down the mountain and into Bar Harbor. Beware that this is a *really* early-morning adventure: tours meet at about 4:15am in early July (about 5am by late August), and last about 3 hours. Trips are offered Monday through Friday during the peak season, and reservations are recommended; the price is $34 per person.

One of downtown's less obvious attractions is the **Criterion Theater** (☎ 207/ 288-3441), a movie house built in 1932 in a classic art-deco style and which so far avoided the degradation of multiplexification. The 900-seat theater, located on Cottage Street, shows first-run movies in summer and is worth the price of admission for the fantastic if somewhat faded interiors; the movie is secondary. As once was the case at most movie palaces, it still costs extra to sit in the more exclusive loges upstairs.

## ON THE WATER

Bar Harbor makes a memorable base for several ocean endeavors, including whale watching. Tour operators offer excursions in search of humpbacks, finbacks, minkes, and the infreqently seen endangered right whale. Reservations are encouraged during July and August.

The largest of the fleet is the *Friendship V* (☎ 800/942-5374 or 207/288-2386), which operates from the Holiday Inn wharf 1 mile north of Bar Harbor. Tours are on a fast, twin-hulled three-level excursion boat that can hold 200 passengers in two heated cabins. The tours run 3 hours plus; the cost is $33 per adult. A puffin and whale-watch tour is offered for $38 adult. There's free on-site parking, and a money-back guarantee that you'll see whales.

**Whale Watcher** (☎ 800/508-1499 or 207/288-3322) takes passengers in search of whales aboard the 116-foot, two-deck *Atlantis.* The 3-hour trip is $33 adult, $20 children 6 to 12, $5 under 6. The same folks offer somewhat more rustic bay tours aboard the 42-foot *Katherine,* which is especially popular among younger children. You'll stop to haul lobster traps and inspect the contents, and look at and handle urchins, starfish, and other inhabitants of the briny deep. Spotting harbor seals sunning on the rocks is often the most memorable part of the trip for kids. The 90-minute tour costs $18.75 adult, $14.75 children 6 to 12, $2 under 6. Trips depart from next to Bar Harbor's municipal pier.

## WHERE TO STAY

Bar Harbor is the bedroom community for Mount Desert Island, with hundreds of hotel, motel, and inn rooms. While varied in size, shape, cost, and decor, all share one thing in common: They're invariably filled during the busy days of summer. It's best to book your room as early as possible.

A number of modern hotels and motels cluster along Route 3 just northwest of the village center; these are your best bets if you arrive without reservations. **The Golden Anchor** (55 West St.; ☎ **800/328-5033** or 207/288-5033) is smack on the waterfront, with peak-season rates from $120 to $185. **The Town Motel and Guest House** (12 Atlantic Ave.; ☎ **800/458-8644** or 207/288-5548) has both comfortable motel rooms and inn rooms in a Victorian manor conveniently located near downtown attractions. Peak-season rates are $95 to $140. Great views greet guests at the **Atlantic Eyrie Lodge** (Highbrook Rd.; ☎ **207/288-9786**), perched on a hillside above Route 3. Peak rates are $105 to $151. Some units have kitchenettes and balconies; all share access to the ocean-view pool. Those looking for a bit more tranquility have a good option in the **Edgewater Motel and Cottages** (off Rte. 3, Salisbury Cove; ☎ **888/310-9920** or 207/288-3491; www.acadia.net/edgewater). The 11 cottages are just up from the water's edge—the name doesn't lie. Rates are $82 to $135 during peak season.

## Expensive

**The Bar Harbor Inn.** Newport Dr. (P.O. Box 7), Bar Harbor, ME 04609. ☎ **800/248-3351** or 207/288-3351. www.barharborinn.com. 153 units. A/C TV TEL. Peak season $155–$395 double; spring and late fall $80–$325. Rates include continental breakfast. AE, DISC, MC, V. Closed Dec–late March.

The Bar Harbor Inn, located just off Agamont Park, manages to nicely mix traditional and contemporary. Situated on shady waterfront grounds just a minute's stroll from downtown boutiques (it's also at the start of the Shore Path), the inn offers both convenience and gracious charm. The main shingled inn, which dates back to the turn of the 19th century, has a settled, old-money feel, with its semicircular dining room with ocean views, and the button-down elegance of the lobby. The guest rooms, located in the main inn and two additional structures, are decidedly more contemporary. Guest rooms in the Oceanfront and Main Inn both offer spectacular views of the bay, and many have private balconies; the less expensive Newport building lacks views but is comfortable and up-to-date.

**Dining:** The inn's semi-formal dining room serves up well-regarded resort fare along with one of the best ocean views in town. Entrees include grilled vegetable ravioli, filet mignon, and grilled strip steak. Prices are $16.95 to $23.95. The Terrace Grille, serving simpler fare like chowders, salads, and boiled lobster ($9.95 to $14.95), is downstairs; it also overlooks the bay, features outdoor seating in good weather, and is open daily for lunch and dinner.

**Amenities:** Heated outdoor pool, hot tub, morning newspaper, conference space, limited room service, and afternoon coffee and cookies.

**Bar Harbor Tides.** 119 West St., Bar Harbor, ME 04609. ☎ **207/288-4968.** www.barharbortides.com. E-mail: info@barharbortides.com. 4 units. TV. $175–$325 double, including full breakfast. DISC, MC, V. Closed Nov–mid-June.

The Bar Harbor Tides features just four guest rooms in a wonderful sprawling 1887 cream-colored mansion. It's located at the head of a long, lush lawn that descends to the water's edge, all on 1 1/2 in-town acres in a neighborhood of imposing homes and within easy strolling distance of the village center. When you first enter, it feels as though you're visiting someone's great aunt—someone's very rich great aunt; but soon enough it feels like home, as you unwind in one of the two spacious living rooms (one upstairs and one down) or, more likely, on the veranda, which has an outdoor fireplace. Breakfast is served on the porch in good weather; otherwise, it's enjoyed in the regal dining room with polished wood floors and views out to Bar Island. Plan to return here by sunset to wander down to the foot of the lawn for the end-of-the-day show.

✪ **Inn at Canoe Point.** Rte. 3, Bar Harbor, ME 04609. ☎ **207/288-9511.** Fax 207/288-2870. www.innatcanoepoint.com. E-mail: canoe.point@juno.com. 5 units. A/C. Peak season $160–$265 double; off-season $80–$160 double. Rates include breakfast. DISC, MC, V. Not recommended for children under 16.

The Inn at Canoe Point boasts the best deck on the island—it virtually hangs over the waters of a rocky cove, with great views across the northern bay. There's even a cluster of Adirondack chairs arrayed for sprawling. The inn itself is equally magical, built in 1889 in a style that might best be described as "storybook Tudor." Guests arrive down a short, winding road through an attractive stand of pines. Although the inn is just 75 yards or so off of bustling Route 3, you might as well be on an island far away. The interior is sleekly contemporary and comfortable. The guests' living room has a modern stone fireplace, superb views, and a great selection of reading matter. Rooms vary in size and decor, but all are elegantly appointed. The Garret Suite occupies the whole third floor and is the most spacious; the tiny Garden Room makes up for its relatively diminutive size with wonderful windows on three sides.

**Ivy Manor Inn.** 194 Main St., Bar Harbor, ME 04609. ☎ **888/670-1997** or 207/288-2138. E-mail: ivymanor@acadia.net. 7 units. A/C TV TEL. Peak season $150–$300; off-season $85–$200. Rates include full breakfast. 2-night minimum on holiday weekends. Children over 12 welcome. AE, DISC, MC, V.

Located in a 1940s-era Tudor-style house that was once home and office of a doctor, the Ivy Manor was thoroughly done over in an understated French-Victorian style, mostly in lush, rich colors including burgundy. The rooms are above average in size; most are carpeted and furnished with attractive, tasteful antiques from the innkeeper's collection. Some rooms have antique clawfoot tubs; others have small outdoor sitting decks (none with views to speak of). Among the best rooms are #6—a small suite with a private sitting room and small fireplace—and #1, the honeymoon room with an imposing walnut headboard and matching armoire. All rooms have small TVs. Leave time for a cocktail in the cozy first-floor lounge after you return from your day's outing.

**Dining:** See Michelle's, in "Where to Dine," below.

**Mira Monte Inn.** 69 Mt. Desert St., Bar Harbor, ME 04609. ☎ **207/288-4263** or 800/553-5109. Fax 207/288-3115. www.miramonte.com. E-mail: mburns@miramonte.com. 12 units, 3 suites. A/C TV TEL. $145–$175 double; $215 suite. Rates include breakfast. 2-night minimum in midsummer. AE, DC, DISC, MC, V. Closed mid-Nov–April (suites available by week in winter).

A stay at this impressive greyish-green Italianate mansion, built in 1864, feels a bit like a trip to grandmother's house—a grandmother who inherited most of her furniture from *her* grandmother. The antiques are more flea-markety than elegant, and the common rooms are furnished in a pleasant country Victorian style. The 2-acre grounds, located within a few minutes' walk of Bar Harbor's restaurants and attractions, are attractively landscaped and include a cutting garden to keep the house in flowers. There's a nice brick terrace away from the street, which makes a fine place to enjoy breakfast on warm summer mornings. The guest rooms are blessed with a profusion of balconies and fireplaces—all but two rooms have one or the other; many have both. The room styles vary widely; some are heavy on the Victorian, others have the bright and airy feel of a country farmhouse. If you're a light sleeper, avoid the rooms facing Mt. Desert Street; those facing the gardens in the rear are far more peaceful. Families should inquire about the suites in the adjacent outbuilding.

✪ **Sunset on West.** 115 West St., Bar Harbor, ME 04609. ☎ **207/288-4242.** Fax 207/288-4545. www.sunsetonwest.com. E-mail: sunsetonwest@gwi.com. 4 units. TV. Peak season $175–$275; off-season $95–$155. Rates include full breakfast. MC, V. Closed Dec–Apr. Children 16 and older welcome.

This gracious bed-and-breakfast is one of my favorite small places in Bar Harbor for its great location, bold decor, attention to detail, and over-the-top breakfasts. The newly renovated 1910 shingled cottage is located on elegant West Street, with views of the water but no waterfront property. It has four guest rooms, and guests also have run of much of the downstairs, including a music room with a baby grand piano and wood-burning fireplace, and pantry with a guest refrigerator, stemware, and a selection of Republica teas. All guest rooms feature the plushest towels I've come across, Hammacher Schlemmer robes, down comforters and pillows, and VCRs (you can choose from 150 films in the collection of innkeepers Nancy and Mel Johnson). "Morning Glory" is the smallest of the rooms and doesn't face the water, but is still bright and cheerful and has a clawfoot tub. Two rooms can be rented either as a single room or with an adjoining sitting room as a suite. The "Sunset Suite" has a sitting room with gas fireplace and a large porch with a water view. "Nocturne" is a spacious suite that's perfect for those seeking a getaway; it's got a water view and a large sitting room with television. Breakfasts are elaborate, with choices like ricotta hotcakes with blueberries, and crème fraîche scrambled eggs in dill crepes with smoked salmon.

## Moderate

**Acadia Hotel.** 20 Mt. Desert St., Bar Harbor, ME 04609. ☎ 207/288-5721. www.acadiahotel.com. E-mail: acadiahotel@acadia.net. 10 units. A/C TV. Peak season $75–$150 double; off-season $45–$135. MC, V.

The Acadia Hotel is nicely situated overlooking the Village Green, easily accessible to in-town activities and free shuttles to elsewhere on the island. This handsome, simple home dating from the late 19th century has a wraparound porch and guest rooms decorated in an aggressive floral motif. The rooms vary widely in size and amenities; two have whirlpools, two have phones, one has a kitchenette. Ask for the specifics when you book. The smaller rooms offer good value for those who don't plan to spend much time inside.

**Black Friar Inn.** 10 Summer St., Bar Harbor, ME 04609. ☎ 207/288-5091. Fax 207/288-4197. www.blackfriar.com. E-mail: blackfriar@blackfriar.com. 7 units (3 with private hall bathrooms). A/C. $90–$145 double, including full breakfast. 2-night minimum mid-June–mid-Oct. DISC, MC, V. Closed Dec–May. Children 12 and older welcome.

The Black Friar Inn, tucked on a side street overlooking the municipal building parking lot, is easily overlooked, but this yellow-shingled structure with quirky pediments and a somewhat eccentric air offers good value for Bar Harbor. A former owner "collected" interiors and installed them throughout the house. Among them is a replica of the namesake Black Friar Pub in London, complete with elaborate carved-wood paneling (it's now a common room), stamped-tin walls in the breakfast room, and a doctor's office (now a guest room). The Black Friar's rooms are carpeted and furnished with a mix of antiques, and most are quite small and cozy. The least expensive are the two garret rooms on the third floor, each of which has a private bathroom down the hall.

**The Colony.** Rte. 3, (P.O. Box 56) Hulls Cove, ME 04644. ☎ 800/524-1159 or 207/288-3383. E-mail: thecolony@acadia.net. 55 units. A/C TV TEL. $65–$105 double. AE, DC, DISC, MC, V. Closed mid-Oct–early June.

The Colony is a classic motor court consisting of a handful of motel rooms and a battery of cottages arrayed around a long green. It will be most appreciated by those with a taste for retro chic; others might decide to look for something with more modern amenities. The rooms are furnished in a simple '70s style that won't win any awards for decor, but all are comfortable; many have kitchenettes. It's situated just across Route 3 from a cobblestone beach, and a 10-minute drive from Bar Harbor. The Colony offers one of the better values on the island.

**Ledgelawn Inn.** 66 Mt. Desert St., Bar Harbor, ME 04609. ☎ **800/274-5334** or 207/288-4596. Fax 207/288-9968. E-mail: barhbrinns@aol.com. 33 units. TV TEL. July and August $95–$245 double. Discounts off-season. Rates include full breakfast. AE, DISC, MC, V. Closed late Oct–early May. Pet accepted; $15 per day extra.

If you want a great location with considerably more flair than a motel, this is a good bet. This hulking cream and maroon 1904 "cottage" sits on a village lot amid towering oaks and maples, and has a mid–20th century elegance to it, although updated with modern amenities (some rooms have air-conditioning); on the property, you'll also find a small, no-frills pool. The Ledgelawn first gets your attention with a handsome sun porch lounge with a full bar, and when you first set foot here, you half expect to find Bogart flirting with Bacall in a corner. The guest rooms all vary somewhat as to size and mood, but all are comfortably if not stylishly furnished with antiques and reproductions. Room 221 has a working fireplace, a shared balcony, and a pair of oak double beds; room 122 has an appealing sitting area with a fireplace. Note that some rooms have bathrooms shoehorned into small spaces.

**Maples Inn.** 16 Roberts Ave., Bar Harbor, ME 04609. ☎ **207/288-3443.** E-mail: maplesinn@acadia.net. 6 units (1 with private hall bathroom). Mid-June–mid-Oct $90–$150 double; off-season $60–$95. Rates include full breakfast. 2-night minimum on holiday weekends. DISC, MC, V. No children.

The Maples is a popular destination among those attracted to outdoor activities. You'll often find guests swapping stories of the day's adventure on the handsome front porch, or lingering over breakfast to compare notes about the best hiking trails. The rather modest (by Bar Harbor standards) yellow farmhouse-style home is tucked away on a leafy side street among other B&Bs; it's an easy walk downtown to a movie or dinner. The innkeepers have a good way of making guests comfortable, with board games and paperbacks scattered about, and down comforters in all rooms. The rooms aren't huge, but you're not likely to feel cramped either. (The suite with a fireplace is the largest.) Breakfasts—including dishes like Bananas Holland America—are appropriately filling for a full day outdoors.

**Primrose Inn.** 73 Mt. Desert St., Bar Harbor, ME 04609. ☎ **877/846-3424** or 207/288-4031. www.primroseinn.com. E-mail: primrose@acadia.net. 10 units plus 5 efficiencies. TV TEL. Peak season $90–$175 double, shoulder seasons $75–$125; efficiencies $650–$950 per week. Daily rates include breakfast. AE, DISC, MC, V. Closed late Oct–Apr. Pets allowed (limited; call first).

This handsome pale-green and maroon Victorian stick-style inn, originally built in 1878, is one of the more noticeable properties on mansion row along Mount Desert Street. The inn is comfortable and furnished with "functional antiques" and more modern reproductions; and many rooms have a floral theme and thick carpets. It's not a stuffy place—it has a distinctly informal air that encourages guests to mingle and relax in the common room, decorated in a light country Victorian style, complete with a piano. Two guest rooms feature whirlpools or fireplaces. The suites in the rear are spacious and comfortable, and the efficiencies make sense for families who could benefit from a kitchen (for rent by the week only).

**Ullikana Bed & Breakfast.** 16 The Field, Bar Harbor, ME 04609. ☎ **207/288-9552.** www.ullikana.com. 10 units (2 with detached bathroom), plus 6 across the street in Yellow House. $130–$220 double ($185 in Yellow House). All rates include full breakfast. MC, V. Closed mid-Oct–early May.

This Tudor cottage dates from 1885 and is tucked on a quiet side street near Agamont Park and the Bar Harbor Inn (the owners report that its name has long been shrouded in mystery). The 10-bedroom "cottage" is solidly built, and the downstairs with its oak trim and wainscotting is heavy dark in English gentleman's club kind of way. The guest rooms are varied in size but all are spacious and nicely decorated in a country Victorian mode, some with iron or brass cottage beds. "Audrey's Room" has a pleasant, storybrook feel to it, with pastel colors, high ceilings, and a cozy bathroom with a clawfoot tub. Summery Room #6 has a deck with glimpses of the bay, along with a sofa and clawfoot tub for relaxing. Across the lane is the attractive "Yellow House," which has six additional rooms. The house and rooms are both simpler in style than the main cottage, and it boasts its own large common area on the first floor. Especially appealing here are the porch rockers with views of the whimsical sculpture on the grounds.

### Inexpensive

**YWCA of Mount Desert Island.** 36 Mt. Desert St., Bar Harbor ME 04609. ☎ **207/288-5008.** 26 units (all with shared bathroom). $30 single; $90 per week single, $150 per week double. No credit cards.

If you're a woman, the best deal in Bar Harbor is the $30 bed at the YWCA, which is clean and centrally located. It's available only to women, and rooms can be rented by the night or week. The Y features single and double rooms, as well as a seven-bed dormitory (summer only). If you opt to stay a week or more, you'll be assessed a $10 membership fee and a $25 security deposit (refundable). The Y is open year-round, but during summer, it fills up fast; it's advisable to make reservations early.

## WHERE TO DINE

If you're looking for a low-key sweet after a meal at one of the restaurants reviewed below, head over to **Ben & Bill's Chocolate Emporium** (66 Main St.; ☎ 207/288-3281) for a tasty and generous ice-cream cone. In the evenings, you may have to join in the line spilling out the door. Visitors are often tempted to try the house novelty, lobster ice cream. Visitors often regret giving into that temptation.

**Café This Way.** 14$^1$/$_2$ Mt. Desert St. ☎ **207/288-4483.** Reservations recommended for dinner. Main courses $3.25–$5.95 breakfast, $12–$19 dinner. MC, V. Summer daily 7–11am (8am–1pm Sun), and 6–9pm. Closed for dinner and open for lunch in winter. NEW AMERICAN.

Café This Way has the feel of a casually hip coffeehouse and is much more airy than one might guess upon first looking at this cozy cottage tucked on a side street down from the village green. Bookshelves line one wall, and there's a small bar tucked in a nook. The breakfasts are excellent and mildly sinful, with offerings like eggs Benedict with spinach, artichoke and tomato. The red-skinned potatoes are crispy and delicious; the robust coffee requires two creamers to lighten it. Dinners are equally appetizing, with tasty dishes like butternut squash ravioli, crabcakes with a tequila-lime sauce, and filet mignon grilled with fresh basil.

✪ **George's.** 7 Stephens Lane. ☎ **207/288-4505.** Reservations recommended. Entrees $25; fixed-price $34–$37. AE, DISC, MC, V. Daily 5:30–10pm; shorter hours after Labor Day. Closed Nov–early May. CONTEMPORARY MEDITERRANEAN.

George's takes some sleuthing to find, but it's worth the effort. This is a Bar Harbor classic, offering fine dining in informal surroundings for nearly 2 decades. (It's located in the small clapboard cottage behind Main Street's First National Bank.) George's captures the joyous feel of summer nicely with four smallish dining rooms (and plenty of open windows) and additional seating on the terrace outside, which is the best place to watch the gentle dusk settle over town. The service is upbeat, and the meals wonderfully prepared. All entrees sell for one price ($25), and include salad, vegetable, and potato or rice. You won't go wrong with the basic choices, like steamed lobster or roast chicken, but you're even better off opting for the more adventurous fare like lobster strudel or "George's clay pot," a melange of seafood. The house specialty is lamb in its many incarnations, including charcoal-grilled lamb tenderloin and rolled lamb stuffed with wild mushrooms. The restaurant consistently receives the annual Wine Spector award of excellence.

**✪ Havana.** 318 Main St. ☎ **207/288-2822.** Reservations recomended. Main courses $15–$25. AE, DC, DISC, MC, V. Daily 5:30–10pm. Closed Jan–Mar. LATINO/FUSION.

Havana has established a new creative standard for restaurants in this town of fried-fish and baked-stuffed-haddock. The spare but sparkling decor in the old storefront is as classy as you'll find in Boston or Washington, D.C., and the menu could compete in any urban area as well. Owner Michael Boland says his menu is inspired by Latino fare, which melds nicely with New American ideas. While the offerings change weekly, expect items like appetizers of crab and roasted corn cakes with a cilantro sour cream, or sweet potato ravioli with a crabmeat-chipotle béchamel sauce. Entrees include Catalan tuna (cubed and seasoned with raisins and pinenuts), rack of lamb with a black bean and dijon crust, and a delicious sage and beer-brined pork, served with a side of sautéed cactus. The wine list is small and basic, but won't offend connoisseurs.

**Jordan's Restaurant.** 80 Cottage St. ☎ **207/288-3586.** Breakfast and lunch $1.95–$7.95. MC, V. Daily 5am–2pm. Closed Feb–Mar. DINER.

This unpretentious breakfast and lunch joint has been dishing up filling fare since 1976, and offers a glimpse of old Bar Harbor before the economy was dominated by T-shirt shops. It's a popular haunt of local working folks in town on one errand or another, but the staff is genuinely friendly to tourists. Diners can settle into one of the pine booths or at a laminated table and order off the placemat menu, choosing from basic fare like grilled cheese with tomato or a slight but serviceable hamburger that's just $3. The soups and chowders are all homemade. Breakfast is the specialty here, with a broad selection of three-egg omlets, along with muffins and pancakes made with wild Maine blueberries.

**Lompoc Cafe and Brewpub.** 36 Rodick St. ☎ **207/288-9392.** Reservations not accepted. Sandwiches $4.50–$6.50; dinner $8.95–$15.95. MC, V. May–Nov daily 11:30am–1am. Closed Dec–Apr. AMERICAN/ECLECTIC.

The Lompoc Cafe has a well-worn, neighborhood bar feel to it, and it's little wonder that waiters and other workers from around Bar Harbor congregate here after hours. The on-site brewery produces several unique beers, including a blueberry ale (intriguing concept, but I'd suggest asking for a sample before ordering a full glass), and the smooth Coal Porter, available in sizes up to the 20-oz. "fatty." Whiskey drinkers will be busy here: The Lompoc claims to have the largest selection of single malts north of Boston. The menu has some pleasant surprises, like the Persian plate (hummus and grape leaves), Szechuan eggplant wrap, and crab and shrimp cakes. Vegetarians will find a decent selection. Live music is offered some evenings, when there's a small cover charge.

**Maggie's Classic Scales.** 6 Summer St. ☎ **207/288-9007.** Reservations recommended in July and Aug. Main courses $14.95–$20.95. DISC, MC, V. Daily 5–10pm; closed mid-Oct–mid-June. SEAFOOD.

The slogan for Maggie's is "notably fresh seafood," and the place invariably delivers on that understated promise. (Only locally caught fish is used.) It's a casually elegant spot tucked off Cottage Street, good for a romantic evening with soothing music and attentive service. Appetizers include smoked salmon, lobster tail cocktail, and steamed mussels.

Main courses range from basic boiled lobster and grilled salmon, to more adventurous offerings like Maine seafood provençal and sautéed scallops with fresh corn, bacon, and peppers. Desserts are homemade and well worth leaving room for.

**Michelle's.** 194 Main St. ☎ **207/288-0038.** Reservations recommended during peak season. Main courses $19–$42. Daily 6:30–9:30pm. Closed late Oct–early May. FRENCH.

Michelle's is located in the graceful Ivy Manor Inn (see "Where to Stay," above). The three dining rooms are elegant and set out with fresh roses and candles (there's outside seating when the weather's good). The extensive menu elaborates on traditional French cuisine with subtle New England twists. The appetizers ($8 to $16) include smoked salmon layered with a chervil mousse, and foie gras with black truffle. Main courses are elaborate affairs, with dishes like chateaubriand for two carved at the table, and Michelle's bouillabaisse for two, which includes lobster, mussels, clams, scallops and the fresh catch of the day. Appropriately for Bar Harbor, the seafood selection is extensive.

## SHOPPING

Bar Harbor is chock-full of boutiques and souvenir shops along the two intersecting commercial streets—Main Street and Cottage Street. Many proffer the expected T-shirt and coffee-mug offerings—the stuff that crops up wherever tourists congregate—but look a little harder and you'll find some original items for sale.

**Bar Harbor Hemporium.** 116 Main St. ☎ **207/288-3014.** www.barharborhemp.com.

The Hemporium is dedicated to promoting products made from hemp, an environmentally friendly (and non-psychoactive) fibrous plant that can be used in making paper, clothing, and more.

**Bowl and Board.** 160 Main St. ☎ **207/288-4519.**

Wood products from Maine are the focus here, with items including—in addition to bowls and cutting boards—children's games and puzzles, peg coat racks, and spice racks. Upstairs is the North Woods Center, where you can learn about efforts to create a North Woods National Park in northern Maine.

**Cadillac Mountain Sports.** 26 Cottage St. ☎ **207/288-4532.**

Sleeping bags, backpacks, rugged outdoor clothing, and hiking boots are found at this shop, which caters to the ragged wool and fleece set. There's a good selection of hiking and travel guides to the island.

**Island Artisans.** 99 Main St. ☎ **207/288-4214.**

This is the place to browse for products of local and Maine craftspeople. Products are mostly of the size you can bring home in a knapsack, and include tiles, sweetgrass baskets, pottery, jewelry, and soaps.

**RainWise.** 25 Federal St. ☎ **800/762-5723** or 207/288-5169. www.rainwise.com.

Bar Harbor–based RainWise manufactures high-end weather stations for the serious hobbyist. The factory store, located off Cottage Street, sells the firm's products, along with a variety of third-party thermometers and barometers.

## ELSEWHERE ON THE ISLAND

There's plenty to explore outside of Acadia National Park and Bar Harbor. Quiet fishing villages, deep woodlands, and unexpected ocean views are among the jewels that turn up when one peers beyond the usual places.

## ESSENTIALS

**GETTING AROUND**    The east half of the island is best navigated on Route 3, which forms the better part of a loop from Bar Harbor through Seal Harbor and past Northeast Harbor before returning up the eastern shore of Somes Sound. Routes 102 and 102A provide access to the island's western half. See information on the free islandwide shuttle service in "Getting Around," under "Acadia National Park," above.

**VISITOR INFORMATION**    The best source of information on the island is at the **Thompson Island Information Center** (☎ **207/288-3411**) on Route 3 just south of the causeway connecting Mount Desert Island with the mainland. Another source of local information is **Mount Desert Chamber of Commerce,** P.O. Box 675, Northeast Harbor, ME 04662 (☎ **207/276-5040**).

## EXPLORING THE REST OF THE ISLAND

On the tip of the eastern lobe of Mount Desert Island is the staid, prosperous community of **Northeast Harbor,** long one of the favored retreats among the Eastern Seaboard's upper crust. Those without personal invitations to come as house guests will need be satisfied with glimpses of the shingled palaces set in the fragrant spruce forests and along the rocky shore; but the village itself is worth investigating. Situated on a scenic, narrow harbor, with the once-grand Asticou Inn at its head, Northeast Harbor is possessed of a refined sense of elegance that's best appreciated by finding a vantage point, then sitting and admiring.

One of the best, least publicized places for enjoying views of the harbor is from the understatedly spectacular ✪ **Asticou Terraces** (☎ **207/276-5130**). Finding the parking lot can be tricky: head $1/2$ mile east (toward Seal Harbor) on Route 3 from the junction with Route 198, and look for the small gravel lot on the water side of the road with a sign reading ASTICOU TERRACES. Park here, cross the road on foot, and set off up a magnificent path made of local rock that ascends the sheer hillside with expanding views of the harbor and the town. This pathway, with its precise stonework and the occasional bench and gazebo, is one of the nation's hidden marvels of landscape architecture. Created by Boston landscape architect Joseph Curtis, who summered here for many years prior to his death in 1928, the pathway seems to blend in almost preternaturally with its spruce-and-fir surroundings, as if it were created by an act of God rather than of man. Curtis donated the property to the public for quiet enjoyment.

Continue on the trail at the top of the hillside and you'll soon arrive at Curtis's cabin (open to the public daily in summer), behind which lies the formal **Thuya Gardens,** which are as manicured as the terraces are natural. These wonderfully maintained gardens, designed by noted landscape architect Charles K. Savage, attract flower enthusiasts, students of landscape architecture, and local folks looking for a quiet place to rest. It's well worth the trip. A donation of $2 is requested of visitors to the garden; the terraces are free.

From the harbor visitors can depart on a seaward trip to the beguilingly remote **Cranberry Islands.** You have a couple of options: Either travel with a national park guide to Baker Island, the most distant of this small cluster of low islands, and explore the natural terrain; or hop one of the ferries to either Great or Little Cranberry Island and explore on your own. On Little Cranberry, there's a small historical museum run by the National Park Service that's worth seeing. Both islands feature a sense of being well away from it all, but neither offers much in the way of shelter or tourist amenities, so travelers should head out prepared for the possibility of shifting weather.

When leaving Northeast Harbor, plan to drive out via **Sargent Drive.** This one-way route runs through Acadia National Park along the shore of Somes Sound, affording superb views of this glacially carved inlet.

On the far side of Somes Sound, there's good hiking (see above), and the towns of Southwest Harbor and Bass Harbor. These are both home to fishermen and boat-builders, and are rather more humble than the settlements of the landed gentry at Northeast and Seal harbors across the way.

In Southwest Harbor, look for the intriguing **Wendell Gilley Museum of Bird Carving** (☎ 207/244-7555) on Route 102 just north of town. Housed in a new building constructed specifically to display fine woodcarving, the museum contains the masterwork of Wendell Gilley, a plumber who took up carving birds as a hobby in 1930. His creations, ranging from regal bald eagles to delicate chickadees, are star-tlingly lifelike and beautiful. The museum offers wood-carving classes for those inspired by the displays, and a gift shop sells fine wood carving. It's open daily 10am to 4pm except Monday, June through October; open Friday through Sunday in May, November, and December. The museum is closed January through April. Admission is $3.25 adults, $1 children 5 to 12.

## WHERE TO STAY

**Asticou Inn.** Rte. 3, Northeast Harbor, ME 04662. ☎ **800/258-3373** or 207/276-3344. www.asticou.com. E-mail: asticou@acadia.net. 47 units. TEL. Summer $302–$395 double, including continental breakfast and dinner (from $230 with breakfast only); spring and fall from $130 double, with breakfast. MC, V. Closed Nov–mid-May. Children 6 and older welcome.

The once-grand Asticou Inn, which dates to 1883, occupies a still-prime location at the head of Northeast Harbor. Its weathered gray shingles and layered eaves give it a slightly stern demeanor, but it also has elements of mild eccentricity. The Asticou is more elegant on the exterior and in its location than in the interior, although it has been spruced up a bit. Despite some incipient shabbiness, a wonderful old-world gen-tility seems to seep from the creaking floorboards and through the thin walls, espe-cially at meal time. The rooms are simply furnished in a pleasing summer-home style, as if a more opulent decor was somehow too ostentatious.

**Dining:** Changes have been undertaken the past 2 years to improve the dining room, where longtime guests have noted a decline in quality. It appears to be paying off. The dinner dance and elaborate "grand buffet" on Thursday nights in summer remain hallowed island traditions and worth checking out. (Expect smoked seafood, lobster Newburg, salads and relishes, a dessert tray, and more.) Seatings are on the hour; jackets are requested on men in the evening. The buffet cost approximately $30; the regular fixed-price meal is a couple dollars less.

**Amenities:** Outdoor heated pool, one clay tennis court, concierge, limited room service, laundry, turndown service, baby-sitting, valet parking, safe-deposit boxes, business center, and conference rooms.

✪ **Claremont.** P.O. Box 137, Southwest Harbor, ME 04679. ☎ **800/244-5036** or 207/244-5036. www.theclaremonthotel.com. clmhotel@acadia.net. 30 inn rooms, 12 cot-tages. TEL. July–Labor Day $140–$155 double, including breakfast, $185–$200 including breakfast and dinner; off-season $85–$115 double including breakfast. Cottages: July–Labor Day $158–$198; off-season $100–$140. 3-night minimum on cottages. No credit cards. Closed mid-Oct–early June.

Early prints of the Claremont, built in 1884, show an austere four-story wooden building with a single severe gable overlooking Somes Sound from a low, grassy rise. The place hasn't changed all that much since then. The Claremont offers nothing fancy or elaborate, just simple, classic New England grace. It's wildly appropriate that the state's most high-profile and combative croquet tournament takes place here annu-ally in early August; all those folks in their whites seem right at home. The common areas and dining rooms are pleasantly appointed in an affable country style. There's a library with rockers, a fireplace, and jigsaw puzzles waiting to be assembled. Two other fireplaces in the lobby take the chill out of the morning air.

Most of the guest rooms are bright and airy, furnished with antiques and some old furniture that doesn't quite qualify as "antique." The bathrooms are modern. Guests opting for the full meal plan at the inn are given preference in reserving rooms overlooking the water; it's almost worth it, although dinners are regrettably lackluster. There's also a series of cottages, available for a 3-day minimum. Some are set rustically in the piney woods; others offer pleasing views of the sound.

**Dining:** The dining room is open nightly. Meals are mainly reprises of American classics like salmon, grilled lamb, and steamed lobster; guests report being underwhelmed by the kitchen's flair. The dining room is open to the public; entrees are $17 to $22.

**Amenities:** One clay tennis court, rowboats, bicycles (free to guests), croquet court, and baby-sitting arrangements.

**Inn at Southwest.** 371 Main St. (P.O. Box 593), Southwest Harbor, ME 04679. ☎ **207/ 244-3835.** www.innatsouthwest.com. E-mail: innatsw@acadia.net. 9 units (2 with private hall bathrooms). Summer and early fall $95–$145 double; off-season $65–$105. All rates include full breakfast. DISC, MC, V. Closed Nov–Apr.

Innkeeper Jill Lewis acquired the architecturally quirky Inn at Southwest in 1995, and she's done a fine job making this mansard-roofed Victorian a hospitable place. There's a decidedly late-19th-century air to this elegant home, but it's restrained on the frills. The guest rooms are named after Maine lighthouses and are furnished with both contemporary and antique furniture. All rooms have ceiling fans and down comforters. Among the most pleasant rooms is Blue Hill Bay on the third floor, with its large bath, sturdy oak bed and bureau, and glimpses of the scenic harbor. Breakfasts offer ample reason to rise and shine, featuring specialties like vanilla Belgian waffles with raspberry sauce, and crab potato bake.

✪ **Lindenwood Inn.** 118 Clark Point Rd. (P.O. Box 1328), Southwest Harbor, ME 04679. ☎ **207/244-5335.** 21 units, 2 suites. June–mid-Oct $95–$245 double; mid-Oct–June $75–$195. All rates include full breakfast. AE, MC, V.

The Lindenwood offers a refreshing change from the fusty, overly draperied inns that tend to proliferate along Maine's coast. Housed in a handsome 1902 Queen Anne–style home at the harbor's edge, the inn features rooms that are modern and uncluttered, the colors simple and bold. The adornments are relatively few (those that do exist are mostly from the innkeeper's collection of African and Pacific art and artifacts), but clean lines and bright natural light more than create a relaxing mood—you'll even begin to view the cobblestone doorstops as works of art. Especially appealing is the spacious suite, which features great harbor views. If you're on a tighter budget, ask for a room in the annex, housed in an 1883 home just a minute's walk down the block. The rooms are somewhat less expansive and more simply decorated, but still offer nice touches (like bright halogen reading lamps) and make a superb base from which to explore the area. Eight of the rooms feature fireplaces; most also have telephones, but ask when you book if this is important to you.

**Dining:** The Lindenwood's dining room attracted attention from epicures around the island in 1996–97 but closed in 1998. Plans were underway to reopen the restaurant in 2000.

**Amenities:** Jacuzzi, heated outdoor pool, and boat dock.

## WHERE TO DINE

**The Burning Tree.** Rte. 3, Otter Creek. ☎ **207/288-9331.** Reservations recommended. Main courses $14–$20. Aug daily 5–9pm; mid-June–July, early fall Wed–Mon 5–9pm. Closed Columbus Day–mid-June. REGIONAL/ORGANIC.

Located on busy Route 3 between Bar Harbor and Northeast Harbor, The Burning Tree is an easy restaurant to speed right by, but that's a mistake. This low-key restaurant, with its bright, open and sometimes noisy dining room, serves up the freshest food in the area. Much of the produce and herbs come from its own gardens, with the rest of the ingredients supplied locally wherever possible. Seafood is the specialty here, and it's consistently prepared with imagination and skill. The menu changes often to reflect local availability.

**Jordan Pond House.** Park Loop Rd., Acadia National Park (near Seal Harbor). ☎ **207/ 276-3316.** Advance reservations not accepted; call before arriving to hold table. Lunch $6.25–$12.75; afternoon tea $5.75–$6.75; dinner $9.25–$17.50. AE, DISC, MC, V. Mid-May–late Oct daily 11:30am–8pm (until 9pm July–Aug). AMERICAN.

The secret to the Jordan Pond House? Location, location, location. The restaurant traces its roots back to 1847, when an early farm was established on this picturesque property at the southern tip of a pond looking toward The Bubbles, a pair of towering, glacially sculpted mounds. The spot first caught on during the local mania for tea houses in the late 19th century, but tragedy struck in 1979 when the original structure and its birch-bark dining room was destroyed by fire. A more modern, two-level dining room was built in its place—it has less charm, but it still has the location. If the weather's agreeable, ask for a seat on the lawn with its unrivaled views. Afternoon tea is a hallowed Jordan Pond House tradition. Ladies-Who-Lunch sit next to Mountain-Bikers-Who-Wear-Lyrca, and everyone feasts on the huge, tasty popovers and strawberry jam served with a choice of teas or fresh lemonade. Dinners are reasonably priced, and include classic resort entrees like prime rib, steamed lobster, and baked scallops with a crumb topping.

**✪ Keenan's.** Rte. 102A, Bass Harbor. ☎ **207/244-3403.** Reservations suggested for parties of 5 or more. Sandwiches and main courses $5–$17. No credit cards. Summers 5–9pm daily; weekends only off-season. SEAFOOD.

This classic, informal seafood shack at a fork in the road is one of those local secrets that most travelers zip right by without a second thought, but do yourself a favor: Slow down, pull in, saunter inside, and order up some of the best seafood value for your money. The fried clams are well-prepared, and the spicy gumbo packs a kick. If you're of a mind to gorge on seafood, go with the seafood sampler, which includes lobster, crab, mussels, clams, and corn, all for less than $20.

**Redfield's.** Main St., Northeast Harbor. ☎ **207/276-5283.** Reservations strongly recommended in summer. Main courses $17.95–$25.95. AE, MC, V. June–Oct Mon–Sat 6:30–9pm; Nov–May Fri–Sat only, 6:30–9pm. CONTEMPORARY.

Located in a storefront in Northeast Harbor's tiny downtown, this elegant restaurant is decorated with a subtle and restrained touch. Patrons can enjoy a libation at the wonderful marble bar (it was taken from an old soda fountain), then settle in and peruse the short but tempting menu, which draws its inspiration from cuisines around the world. Choices change with some frequency but might include appetizers of Stilton cheese fondue over artichoke hearts, or smoked lobster with a sauce of corn, tomato, and serrano chili. The entrees are usually prepared with style and care, and include a sesame-dipped salmon fillet with ginger-tamari sauce, and venison with dried cranberry and port compote.

**Restaurant XYZ.** Shore Rd., Manset (across from the town dock). ☎ **207/244-5221.** Reservations recommended. Main courses $15. MC, V. July–Aug daily 5:30–9pm; June, Sept–Oct weekends only 5:30–9pm. Closed Columbus Day–Memorial Day. MEXICAN.

Restaurant XYZ doesn't promise much at first: It's on the ground floor beneath a motel that fronts the harbor, and the interior is adorned with imports from Mexico that might best be described as "stuff," but the food! Drawing on the traditions of central Mexico and the Yucatan, the fare here is spicy, earthy, and tangy. Don't look for thin sauces and melted cheese. Expect a remarkably savory mole (especially good with chicken), and a chipotle salsa that sings. Start with one of the stand-out margaritas (made with fresh lime juice), and peruse the appetizers, which include a seafood coctail made with octopus, scallops, shrimp, and avacado. Among the more inviting entrees are a pork loin baked in a sauce of ancho, guajillo, and chipotle chiles, and chiles stuffed with corn and cheese. Aficianados of authentic Mexican cooking will be delightfully surprised to find such excellent dining deep in the home turf of boiled lobster and fried clams. All entrees are $15 and include salad and tortillas. (Children's entrees are $5.) Beverages include a half-dozen Mexican beers, sangria, and a tiny wine list.

## 8 Downeast Coast

The term "Downeast" comes from the old sailing ship days. Ships heading east had the prevailing winds at their backs, making it an easy "downhill" run to the eastern ports. Heading the other way took more skill and determination.

Today, it's a rare traveler who gets far Downeast to explore the rugged coastline of Washington County. Few tourists venture beyond Acadia National Park, discouraged perhaps by the lack of services for visitors and the low number of high-marquee attractions. They may also be a bit creeped out by the sometimes spooky remoteness of the region, but Downeast Maine has substantial appeal. There's an authenticity that's been lost in much of coastal Maine and is only a distant memory in the rest of New England. Many longtime visitors to the state say that this is how all of Maine used to be back in the 1940s and 1950s, when E. B. White first arrived. Pad thai, the *New York Times,* and designer coffee have not yet crossed the border into Washington County. Those seeking a glimpse of a rugged, hardscrabble way of life where independence is revered above all else aren't likely to go away disappointed.

Many residents still get by as their forebearers did—by scratching a living from the land. Scalloping. lobstering, and fishing remain major sources of income, as do logging and other forest work. Grubbing for bloodworms in spring, picking wild blueberries in the barrens in late summer, and tipping fir trees for wreathmaking in late fall round out the income. In recent years, aquaculture has become an important part of the economy around Passamaquoddy and Cobscook bays; travelers will see vast floating pens, especially around Eastport and Lubec, where salmon are raised for markets worldwide.

### ESSENTIALS

**GETTING THERE**   Downeast Maine is most commonly reached via Route 1 from Ellsworth. Those heading directly to Washington County in summer can take a more direct, less congested route via Route 9 from Brewer (across the river from Bangor), connecting south to Route 1 via Route 193 or Route 192.

**VISITOR INFORMATION**   The **Machias Bay Area Chamber of Commerce,** P.O. Box 606, Machias, ME 04654 (☎ **207/255-4402**) provides tourist information from its offices at 23 East Main St. (Rte. 1). The offices are open 9am to 5pm Tuesday through Saturday (also open Monday in summer).

**EVENTS**   Eastport celebrates **Fourth of July** in extravagant hometown style each year, a tradition that began in 1820 after the British gave up possession of the city

# Downeast Coast

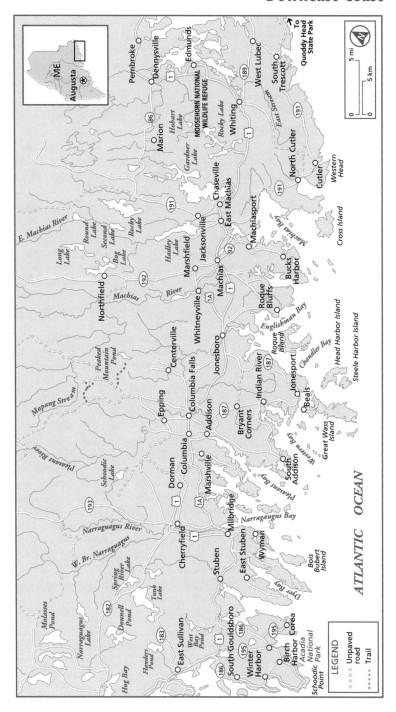

(they captured it during the War of 1812). Some 15,000 people pour into this city of 1,900 for the 4-day event, which includes vendors, games, and contests, culminating with a grand parade on the afternoon of the Fourth.

The **Machias Wild Blueberry Festival** celebrates the local cash crop in mid-August each year. Events include a blueberry pancake breakfast (of course!), a blueberry pie eating contest, performances, and the sales of blueberry-themed gift items. Contact the Chamber of Commerce (☎ **207/255-4402**) for the exact dates.

## EXPLORING DOWNEAST MAINE

Below are some of the highlights of the region, described from west to east. The driving time from Ellsworth to Lubec via Route 1 and Roue 189 is about 2 hours. Allow considerably more time for visiting the sites mentioned below and just plain snooping around.

**Burnham Tavern.** Main St. (Rte. 192), Machias. ☎ **207/255-4432.** $2 adult, 25¢ child. Mid-June–Labor Day Mon–Fri 9am–5pm.

In June 1775, a month after the Battle of Lexington in Massachusetts, a group of patriots hatched a plan at the gambrel-roofed Burnham Tavern that led to the first naval battle of the Revolutionary War. The armed schooner *Margaretta* was in Machias Harbor to obtain wood for British barracks. The patriots didn't think much of this idea, and attacked the ship using much smaller boats they had commandeered, along with muskets, swords, axes, and pitchforks. The patriots prevailed, killing the captain of the *Margaretta* in the process.

Visitors can learn all about this episode during a tour of the tavern, which was built on a rise overlooking the river in 1770. On display are booty taken from the British ship, along with the original tap table and other historic furniture and ephemera. The tour lasts around 1 hour.

✪ **Cutler Coastal Trail.** Rte. 191, Cutler. Contact Maine Bureau of Park and Recreation: ☎ **207/287-3821.** Free admission. Always open. From Cutler, head northeast on Rte. 191; about 4¹/₂ miles out of town, look for parking lot and signs on right.

Marked by a sign at a small parking lot, this dramatic loop trail passes through diverse ecosystems, including bogs, barrens, and dark and tangled spruce forests; but the highlight of this trail, which traverses state-owned land, is the mile-long segment along the rocky headlands high above the restless ocean. Some of the most dramatic coastal views in the state are along this isolated stretch, which overlooks dark-gray-to-black rocks and an often tumultuous sea. Visible on the horizon across the Bay of Fundy are the west-facing cliffs of the Canadian island of Grand Manan. Plan on at least 2 or 3 hours for the whole loop, although more time spent whiling away the afternoon hours on the rocks is well worthwhile. If it's damp or foggy, rain pants are advised to fend off the moisture from the low brush along the trail.

**Eastport Historic District.** Water St., Eastport. From Rte. 1 in Perry, take Rte. 190 south for 7 miles.

In the 1880s, the city of Eastport—3 miles from Lubec by water but 50 minutes by car—had a population of nearly 5,000 and 18 bustling sardine plants. The population is now less than 2,000, and all the sardine plants are gone, but much of the handsome commercial brick architecture remains on downtown's Water Street, a compact thoroughfare that also affords lovely views of Campobello Island and Passamaquoddy Bay. The majority of the buildings between the post office and the library are on the National Register of Historic Places. Here, you'll find the nation's oldest operating ship chandlery (**S. L. Wadsworth & Son,** 42 Water St.; ☎ **207/853-4343**), and the

**Quoddy Maritime Museum,** (Water Street; ☎ 207/853-4297), where you can view a 14-foot-by-16-foot model of the proposed Passamaquoddy Tidal Power Project, an FDR-era attempt to harness the 25-foot tides to produce hydroelectric power.

Just north of Eastport is the Old Sow, said to be the largest whirlpool in the western hemisphere. It's a bit finicky and typically appears only during the highest tides; the best way to see it is to take a seasonal ferry to Deer Island (in New Brunswick, Canada) and back. There'a nominal fee for passengers, and you don't have to go through the cursory Canadian customs check if you don't disembark. The ferry departs from behind the Eastport Fish and Lobster House, 167 Water St.

**Great Wass Preserve.** Black Duck Cove Rd., Great Wass Island, Jonesport. Contact Nature Conservancy: ☎ 207/729-5181. Free admission. Open daylight hours. From Jonesport cross bridge to Beals Island (signs); continue across causeway to Great Wass Island. Bear right at next fork; pavement ends; continue past lobster pound to a small parking lot on the left marked by Nature Conservancy logo (oak leaf).

This exceptional 1,524-acre parcel was acquired by the Nature Conservancy in 1978 and contains an excellent 5-mile loop hike covering a wide cross-section of native terrain, including bogs, heath, rocky coastline, and forests of twisted jack pines. Maps and a birding checklist are found in a stand at the parking lot. Follow one fork of the trail to the shoreline; work your way along the storm-tossed boulders to the other fork, then make your way back to your car. If a heavy fog has settled into the area, as often happens, don't let that deter your hike. The dense mist creates a medieval tableau that makes for magical hiking.

**Roosevelt Campobello International Park.** Rte. 774, Campobello Island, New Brunswick. ☎ 506/752-2922. Free admission. Daily 10am–6pm. Closed mid-Oct–late May.

Take a brief excursion out of the country and across the time zone. The U.S. and Canada maintain a joint national park here, celebrating the life of Franklin D. Roosevelt, who summered here with his family in the early 1900s. Like other affluent Americans, the Roosevelt family made an annual trek to the prosperous colony at Campobello Island. The island lured folks from the sultry cities with a promise of cool air and a salubrious effect on the circulatory system. ("The extensive forests of balsamic firs seem to affect the atmosphere of this region, causing a quiet of the nervous system and inviting sleep," read an 1890 real-estate brochure.) The future U.S. president came to this island every summer between 1883, the year after he was born, and 1921, when he was suddenly stricken with polio. Franklin and his siblings spent those summers exploring the coves and sailing around the bay, and he always recalled his time here fondly. (It was his "beloved island," he said, coining a phrase that gets no rest in local promotional brochures.)

You'll learn much about Roosevelt and his early life both at the visitor center, where you can view a brief film, and during a self-guided tour of the elaborate mansion, which is covered in cranberry-colored shingles. For a "cottage" this huge, it's surprisingly comfortable and intimate. The park is truly an international park—run by a commission with representatives from both the U.S. and Canada, making it like none other in the world.

Leave some time to explore farther afield in the 2,800-acre park, which offers scenic coastline and 8½ miles of walking trails. Maps and walk suggestions are available at the visitor center.

**Ruggles House.** Main St., Columbia Falls. ☎ 207/483-4637. $3.50 adult, $2.50 children. June–mid-Oct Mon–Sat 9:30am–4pm, Sun 11am–4:30pm.

This fine Federal home dates from 1818 and was built for Thomas Ruggles, an early timber merchant and civic leader. The home is very grand and opulent but in an oddly miniature sort of way. There's a flying staircase in the central hallway, pine doors hand-painted to resemble mahogany, and detailed wood carvings in the main parlor, done over the course of 3 years by an English craftsman equipped, legend says, with only a penknife. Locals once said his hand was guided by an angel. Tours last 20 minutes to a half hour.

**Schoodic Point.** Acadia National Park, Winter Harbor. ☎ **207/288-3338.** Free admission charged. Drive east from Ellsworth on Route 1 for 17 miles to W. Gouldsboro, then turn south on Route 186 to Winter Harbor. Outside of Winter Harbor, look for the brown-and-white national park signs.

This remote unit of Acadia National Park is just 7 miles from Mount Desert Island across Frenchman Bay, but it's a long 50-mile drive to get here via Ellsworth. A pleasing loop drive hooks around the tip of Schoodic Point. The one-way road (no park pass required) winds along the water and through forests of spruce and fir. Good views of the mountains of Acadia open up across Frenchman Bay; you'll also see buildings of an historic naval station housed on the point. Park near the tip of this isolated promontory and explore the salmon-colored rocks that plunge into the ocean. It's especially dramatic when the seas are agitated and the surf crashes loudly.

**West Quoddy Head Light & Quoddy Head State Park.** W. Quoddy Head Rd., Lubec. ☎ **207/733-0911.** Lighthouse grounds: free admission. Park: $1 adult, 50¢ children 5–11. Open daylight hours.

This famed red-and-white light (it's been likened to a barbershop pole and a candy cane) marks the easternmost point of the United States and ushers boats into the Lubec Channel between the U.S. and Canada. The light is operated by the Coast Guard and isn't open to the public, but visitors can walk the grounds near the light and along headlands at the adjacent state park. The park overlooks rocky shoals that are ceaselessly battered by high winds, pounding waves, and some of the most powerful tides in the world. Watch for fishing boats straining against the currents, or seals playing in the waves and sunning on the offshore rocks. The park consists of 480 acres of coastline and bog, and several trails wind through the dark conifer forest and crest the tops of rocky cliffs. Some of the most dramatic views are just a short walk down the path at the far end of the parking lot.

## WHERE TO STAY & DINE

**Crocker House Country Inn.** Hancock Point (HC 77, Box 171), ME 04640. ☎ **207/422-6806.** Fax 207/422-3105. www.acadia.net/crocker. E-mail: crocker@acadia. net. 11 units. TEL. Mid-June–mid-Oct $90–$130 double; off-season $70–$90. Rates include breakfast. AE, MC, V. Closed Jan–late Apr. Pets allowed with prior permission.

The handsome, shingled Crocker House inn, built in 1884, is off the beaten track on picturesque Hancock Point, across Frenchmen Bay from Mount Desert Island. It's a cozy retreat, pefect for rest and relaxation and quiet walks (it's about 4 minutes' walk from the water's edge). The rooms are tastefully decorated with comfortable country decor. Two rooms are located in the adjacent carriage house. The common areas are more relaxed than fussy, like the living room of a friend who's always happy to see you. The inn has a few bikes for guests to explore the point; nearby are four clay tennis courts.

**Dining:** Dinners here are a highlight, with tremendous care taken with the meals, and a fun, convivial atmosphere, featuring live piano on weekends. The menu focuses on regional favorites, including French onion soup, artichoke hearts with crabmeat, and oysters Rockefeller for starters. Entrees include a good selection of fresh seafood, including scallops, salmon and shrimp creatively prepared; non-seafood items include filet mignon and rack of lamb. The desserts and breads are homemade. There's a great Sunday brunch during the peak summer months.

✪ **Le Domaine.** Rte. 1 (P.O. Box 496), Hancock, ME 04640. ☎ **800/554-8498** or 207/422-3395. www.ledomaine.com. E-mail: ledomaine@acadia.net. Fax 207/422-2316. 5 units. A/C TEL. $175 double; $260 suites. Rates include full breakfast. AE, DISC, MC, V. Closed mid-Oct–mid-June.

An epicure's delight, Le Domaine long ago established its reputation as one of the most elegant and delightful destinations in Maine. Set on Route 1 about 10 minutes east of Ellsworth, this inn has the continental flair of an impeccable French auberge. While the highway in front can be a bit noisy, the garden and woodland walks out back offer plenty of compensating serenity. The rooms are comfortable and tastefully appointed without being pretentious; in 1999, the innkeeper combined four rooms to create two suites and added air-conditioning and phones to all rooms. The guest rooms are on the second floor in the rear of the property; private terraces face the gardens and the 90 acres of forest owned by the inn. Rooms are loaded with extras, like Bose radios, fresh flowers, lighted makeup mirrors, and wine glasses and corkscrews.

**Dining:** The real draw here is the exquisite dining room, which is famed for its understated elegance. Chef Nicole Purslow carries on the tradition established when her French-immigrant mother opened the inn in 1946, offering superb country cooking in the handsome candlelit dining room with pinewood floors and a sizable fireplace. The ever-changing meals still sing. My favorite appetizer? It's called "My mother's pâté of organic chicken livers that I cannot improve upon." Entrees might include baby grilled lamb chops in a house marinade, or lightly crusted sweetbreads with capers and lemon juice. Plan to check in by 5:30pm; dinner is served Tuesday to Saturday between 6pm and 9pm. Dinner is available to outside guests; entrees are $24.50 to $29.

# 9 Inland Maine

Maine's western mountains comprise a rugged, brawny region that stretches northeast from the White Mountains to the Carrabassett Valley. It isn't as commercialized as the Maine coast, and the villages aren't as quaint as you'll find in Vermont's Green Mountains; but visitors will find azure lakes, ragged forests of spruce, fir, and lichens, and rolling hills and mountains that take on a distinct sapphire hue during the summer hiking season.

Moosehead Lake and Baxter State Park in the North Woods offer numerous outdoor pursuits. About half of Maine is comprised of northern forest lands with no formal local government—called "unorganized townships." While timber companies own and maintain much of the land, visitors will find much to explore on foot or by canoe.

## 1 The Western Lakes & Mountains

Cultural amenities are few here, but natural amenities are legion. Hikers have the famed Appalachian Trail, which crosses into Maine in the Mahoosuc Mountains (near where Route 26 enters into New Hampshire) and follows rivers and ridgelines northeast to Bigelow Mountain and beyond. Canoeists and anglers head to the noted Rangeley Lakes area, a chain of deepwater ponds and lakes that has attracted sportsmen for more than a century; and in the winter, skiers can choose among several downhill ski areas, including the two largest in the state, Sunday River and Sugarloaf.

### FRYEBURG TO GILEAD

Travelers typically scurry through Fryeburg on their way from the Maine Coast to the White Mountains. They might buy a tank of gas or a sandwich here, but they don't give much thought to this town set amid a region of rolling hills and placid lakes. Many don't even realize that 50,000 acres of the White Mountain National Forest spill over from New Hampshire into Maine just north of Fryeburg; and they simply don't know that the White Mountain foothills harbor some of the best hiking and canoeing in the region. Evans Notch has granite peaks and tumbling cascades; and the meandering Saco River is rife with sandbars that invite canoeists to pull over and laze away a sunny afternoon.

This region also contains one of the most pristine and appealing lakes in Maine—scenic Kezar Lake, with its backdrop of the White Mountains. Kezar Lake is made all the more appealing because public access is more difficult than at most lakes, and very few roads touch its shores.

Day-trippers from Portland and Boston have discovered the allure of this region (at about an hour and a half away, it's virtually in Portland's backyard), but it still lacks the crowds and commercialism of the more developed valleys of New Hampshire's White Mountains.

## ESSENTIALS

**GETTING THERE**   Fryeburg is on Route 302 between Portland and North Conway, New Hampshire. It's about 1 1/4 hours northwest of Portland and 15 minutes east of North Conway. Route 113 north to Gilead departs from Fryeburg on the west side of town.

**VISITOR INFORMATION**   The **Fryeburg Information Center** offers general information about lodging and attractions in the area. It's open in summer near the state line on Route 302. For information year-round, try the **Bridgton Lakes Region Chamber of Commerce,** P.O. Box 236, Bridgton, ME 04009 ( ☎ **207/647-3472**). They have a year-round information center (open 9am to 5pm weekdays; extended hours in summer) about 1/4 mile south of the light on Route 302.

Outdoor enthusiasts should head to the **Evans Notch Ranger District,** RR #2, P.O. Box 2270, Bethel, ME 04217 ( ☎ **207/824-2134**). Rangers dispense information from their headquarters at 18 Mayville Rd. just off Route 2 north of Bethel, or write in advance and request their helpful brochure describing a sampling of area hikes.

**SPECIAL EVENTS**   The **Fryeburg Fair** ( ☎ **207/935-3268**) is Maine's largest agricultural fair, held during the 10 days prior to Columbus Day in early October. Staged at the peak of foliage season, this huge fair is even more colorful than its surroundings. It's a classic, old New England extravaganza, with snorting pigs, horse-pulling matches, serene llamas, pumpkins the size of Rhode Island, and contests for the best-looking and best-tasting pies. Tickets are $4 Monday to Thursday, $5 Friday to Sunday; seniors (over 65) and children under 12 get in free.

## A SCENIC DRIVE

The 29-mile drive through Evans Notch from Fryeburg north on Route 113 to the crossroads of Gilead stands as one of the more appealing backroad drives in the state. You'll pass through open farmland hemmed in by rolling hills, and through tiny villages from which most commerce has long since departed. As you enter the national forest, you'll slowly gain elevation as the road narrows. Soon you're twisting up through craggy Evans Notch, before cresting the hill and coasting down through dense forest of birch and fir. The road, which is closed in winter, is narrow enough that the trees arch overhead, forming a shady tunnel in summer that turns a fiery gold in fall.

## HIKING

Superb hiking trails lace the rugged, low hills of Evans Notch on either side of Route 113, offering something for hikers of every stripe and inclination. Far more trails exist than could possibly be covered in the limited space here. Hikers should request the national forest hiking brochure (see "Visitor Information," above), or consult one of the several trail guides covering the area. Among them are the *White Mountain Guide* and the *Maine Mountain Guide* (Appalachian Mountain Club), and *Fifty Hikes in Southern Maine* by John Gibson (Backcountry Publications).

# Maine's Western Lakes & Mountains

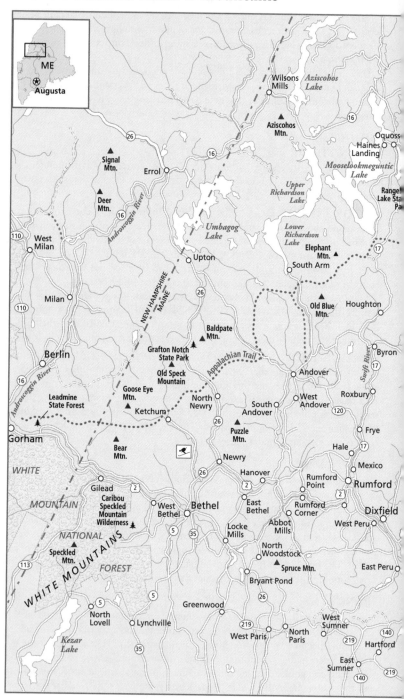

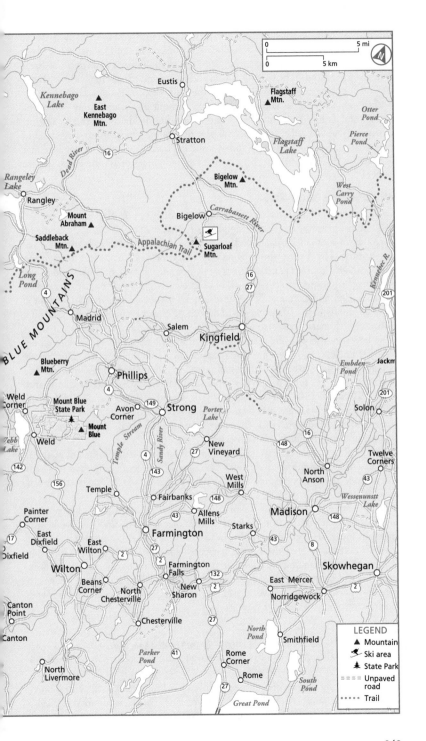

An easy hike for which no trail guide is needed is to the summit of **East Royce Mountain.** The trail leaves from a small parking area on Route 113 just north of the road's high point. This well-marked 3-mile round-trip follows a small stream before it begins a steeper ascent. The summit is bald and rocky, and affords fine views of Kezar Lake and the more imposing mountains to the west. Return via the same path.

Other recommended local hikes include the summit of Caribou Mountain in the heart of the Caribou Wilderness Area, and demanding Baldface Mountain, with its connecting ridgetop trail that follows the edge of a ragged glacial cirque carved out of the mountain eons ago. A loop up and over the Baldfaces is a tough, all-day hike that will reward experienced hikers; check one of the trail guides or ask the Forest Service for details.

## CANOEING THE SACO RIVER

The Saco River is home to some of the most accessible and inviting canoeing in the state. The river rises in the White Mountains near Crawford Notch, then wends its way to the sea south of Portland, passing through the gentle farmlands around Fryeburg en route. The river is slow-moving but steady for much of its run through the region, with gentle rapids to make it interesting but rarely threatening. The land flanking the river is mostly privately owned, but the owners graciously open their land to quiet recreation and camping. (They've also hired a seasonal ranger to make sure it stays clean and fire-free.) Thanks to glacial deposits, the river is notable for its numerous sandbars, which make for superb lounging. Bring your beach towel.

The largest outfitter in the area is **Saco Bound** (☎ 603/447-2177), located on Route 302 in New Hampshire just over the state line. From their busy shop just across the highway from the river, the harried staff provides equipment, advice, shuttle service, and guided trips. For more personal, smaller-scale service, try **Saco River Canoe and Kayak** (☎ 207/935-2369) on Route 5, or **Canal Bridge Canoes** (☎ 207/935-2605) at 125 Main St. in Fryeburg. Rentals typically run about $26 per day for a canoe with all equipment, including river access and parking. (You can often find discounts midweek.) Shuttle service is extra.

A couple of caveats: In early summer, especially following a damp spring, mosquitoes can be unusually irksome along the river. Bring lots of repellent or opt for a trip later in the season. The bug population usually declines after July 4. By August, they're all but gone.

Also, be aware that the Saco's popularity has soared in recent years. The upshot: You're not likely to have a true wilderness experience here, especially on weekends. Lunkheads fueled by beer and traveling in vast armadas descend in great number on summer weekends to lend the river a frat-party atmosphere. In the late 1980s, it became such a problem that the police set up "riverblocks" on busy weekends to check for sobriety and illegal substances. (The courts told the police to cut it out.) It's mostly a weekend phenomenon; midweek, paddlers tend to be more sedate families and couples.

## SKIING

**Shawnee Peak.** Rte. 302, Bridgton, ME 04009. ☎ 207/647-8444. www.shawneepeak.com. Vertical drop: 1,300 ft. Lifts: 4 chairlifts. Skiable acreage: 202. Lift tickets: $38 adult weekend and holiday, $29 midweek; $25 children 7–12 and seniors weekend, $19 midweek.

The friendly family ski area of Shawnee Peak is a solid intermediate hill area located on Pleasant Mountain between Fryeburg and Portland. For skiers of moderate skills, it's a good alternative to the larger, more crowded resorts in the White Mountains and Maine. Shawnee Peak daily tickets are good until 5pm (an hour later than most ski areas), and the mountain also offers the area's best night skiing, with 17 of its 32 trails lit until 10pm every night except Sunday. Since 1997 the mountain has upgraded its chairlifts (one quad, two triples, and one double) and improved snowmaking. The ski lodge scene is low-key and family-oriented. Shawnee Peak is about an hour from Portland and attracts a number of afterwork skiers.

## WHERE TO STAY & DINE

✪ **Quisisana.** Rte. 5, Center Lovell, ME 04016 (Winter address: P.O. Box 142, Larchmont, NY 10538). ☎ **207/925-3500,** or winter 914/833-0293. www.quisisanaresort.com. E-mail: quisisanar@aol.com. 16 rooms, 38 cottages. Lodge $260–$270 double, including all meals; cottages $330–$350 double. 1-week stay required during peak season (Saturday arrival/departure); shorter stays available early in the season. No credit cards. Closed late-Aug to mid-June.

This is not your average lakeside resort. The scenery across Kezar Lake to the White Mountains beyond is spectacular, but what makes this place stand alone is the music. It's everywhere. The 80-person staff consists of students recruited from the better conservatories across the nation, and you're never far from wafting notes, whether it's someone practicing an aria in a rehearsal hall near the lake, or a full-blown production number in a lakeside lodge. The guests (maximum of 150) usually stay for a week, and the musical menu changes day by day—Mondays feature musical theater, Tuesdays piano recitals, Wednesdays one-act operas, and so on. The recitals are performed by exuberant students who rarely slip up—an astonishing feat given that they practice in between sweeping, cooking, laundering, and the other mundane tasks of resort management.

The snug cabins have one, two, or three bedrooms, and are set among white pines along the lakeshore. They have the charm of an old summer camp, but include amenities like private bathrooms (some shared baths within family cabins) and comfortable furniture. Days are spent canoeing, hiking, playing tennis, or simply sunning at the lake's edge. If it's rainy, the staff will often cobble together an extra recital to keep guests entertained.

**Dining:** Dinner is served in a handsome dining hall in the main lodge, and entrees are creative and well-prepared. On Tuesday nights, beer and wine are served on a grassy peninsula along the lake, with chamber-music accompaniment—it's often a magical highlight to an always wondrous stay.

## BETHEL

Until the mid-1980s, Bethel was a sleepy, 19th-century resort town with one of those friendly, family-oriented ski areas that seemed destined for certain extinction. Then a guy named Les Otten came along. This brash young entrepreneur bought Sunday River Ski Area and proceeded to make it into one of New England's most vibrant and successful ski destinations. (Otten subsequently acquired most of the other major ski areas in New England, including Killington, Attitash, Sugarbush, Sugarloaf, Mt. Snow, and Waterville Valley, then set about buying western resorts.)

With the rise of Sunday River, the white-clapboard town of Bethel (located about 7 miles from the ski area) has been dragged into the modern era, although it hasn't yet taken on the artificial, packaged flavor of some other New England ski towns. The village (pop. 2,500) is still defined by the stoic buildings of the respected prep school Gould Academy, the broad village common, and the Bethel Inn, an old-fashioned sprawling resort that's managed to stay ahead of the tide by adding condos, but without losing its pleasant, timeworn character.

## ESSENTIALS

**GETTING THERE**   Bethel is located at the intersection of Routes 26 and 2. It's accessible from the Maine Turnpike by heading west on Route 26 from Exit 11. From New Hampshire, drive east on Route 2 from Gorham.

**VISITOR INFORMATION**   The **Bethel Area Chamber of Commerce,** 30 Cross St., Bethel, ME 04217 (☎ **800/442-5826** for reservations or 207/824-2282), has offices behind the Casablanca movie theater. It's open year-round Monday to Friday from 8am to 8pm, Saturday from 10am to 6pm, and Sunday noon to 5pm.

Across Route 2 from the chamber the **state tourism office** has paired up with the White Mountain National Forest district office to provide information. You can stock up on brochures from across the state and get information on local national forest activities, such as hiking and mountain biking. Open daily in summer 8am to 4:30pm (closed Wednesdays in winter). Call ☎ **207/824-4582.**

## EXPLORING LOCAL HISTORY

Bethel's stately, historic homes ring the **Bethel Common,** a long, rectangular greensward created in 1807 atop a low, gentle ridge. (It was originally laid out as a street broad enough for the training of the local militia.) The town's **historic district** encompasses some 27 homes, which represent a wide range of architectural styles popular in the 19th century.

The oldest home in the district is the **1813 Moses Mason House,** which is now a fine, small museum housing the collections and offices of the **Bethel Historical Society** (☎ 207/824-2908). Mason was a doctor and a local civic leader, and was willing to try anything once, including building his Federal-style house on a stone foundation. His compatriots assured him that the house would topple over in a gale. It didn't, and all local houses were soon built on stone foundations. Mason also commissioned an itinerant painter—possibly the renowned landscape artist Rufus Porter—to paint his foyer and stairwell. The result is an engagingly primitive panorama (still in pristine condition) of boats at anchor at a calm harbor flanked by a still forest of white pine. View this and numerous other artifacts of the early 19th century while exploring the home. The museum, at 14 Broad Street, is open in July and August 1 to 4pm Tuesday to Sunday. Admission is $2 for adults and $1 for children.

Architecture buffs can sustain the Federal-home theme with a side trip to **Waterford,** a wonderfully picturesque village first settled in 1793. About 20 minutes from Bethel along a fast-moving backroad route (head south on Route 5 from the Bethel Common to North Waterford, then continue on Route 35 to Waterford), this village has changed little since the late 19th century. Distinguished white-clapboard homes surround a shady, small green, and the village touches on tranquil Keoka Lake, which has a small municipal beach. Stop for a swim, or head to the trail just off the Green leading summit of Mount Tir'em, a modest hike with a rewarding view.

## GRAFTON NOTCH STATE PARK

Grafton Notch straddles Route 26 as it angles northwest from Newry toward Errol, New Hampshire. The 33-mile drive between the two towns is one of my favorites, both picturesque and dramatic. You initially pass through farmland in a fertile river valley before ascending through bristly forest to a handsome glacial notch hemmed in by rough, gray cliffs on the towering hillsides above. Foreboding Old Speck Mountain towers to the south; views of Lake Umbagog open to the north as you continue into New Hampshire. This route attracts few crowds, although it's popular with Canadians headed to the Maine Coast.

Public access to the park consists of a handful of roadside parking lots near scenic areas. The best of the bunch is **Screw Auger Falls,** where the Bear River drops through several small cascades before tumbling dramatically into a narrow, corkscrewing gorge carved long ago by glacial runoff through granite bedrock. Picnic tables dot the forested banks upriver of the falls, and kids seem inexorably drawn to splash and swim in the smaller pools on warm days. Admission to the park is $1; look for self-pay stations at the parking lot.

## DOWNHILL SKIING

**Sunday River Ski Resort.** P.O. Box 450, Bethel, ME 04217. ☎ **800/543-2754** for lodging or 207/824-3000. www.sundayriver.com. E-mail: snowtalk@sundayriver.com. Vertical drop: 2,340 ft. Lifts: 18 chairlifts (4 high-speed), 3 surface lifts. Skiable acreage: 654. Lift tickets: $49 adults weekends, $47 weekdays; children under 5 ski free.

Sunday River has grown at stunning speed in recent years, and today competes in the same league as longtime New England winter resorts like Stowe and Killington. Unlike ski areas that have developed around a single tall peak, Sunday River has expanded along an undulating ridge about 3 miles wide that encompasses seven peaks. Just traversing the resort, stitching runs together with chairlift rides, can take an hour or more. As a result, you'll rarely get bored making the same run time and again. The descents offer something for virtually everyone, from deviously steep bump runs to challenging glade skiing to wide, wonderful intermediate trails. Sunday River is also blessed with plenty of water for snowmaking, and makes tons of the stuff using a proprietary snowmaking system.

The superb skiing conditions are, alas, offset by an uninspiring base area. The lodges and condos are architecturally dull, and the less-than-delicate landscaping is of the sort created by bulldozers. Efforts are underway to create a new village from scratch at the Jordan Bowl area, where more of a sense of community might develop sometime after 2001.

## OTHER OUTDOOR PURSUITS

**BIKING**   One easy and scenic route perfect for a bike tour follows winding Sunday River Road for several miles into the foothills of the Mahoosuc mountains. Start near the Sunday River ski area, and head west along the river past a tranquil scene with covered bridge and a few miles later past the Outward Bound center. Eventually, you'll head into the forested hills (the road eventually turns to dirt). This dead-end road is lightly traveled, and views from the broad valley floor are rewarding.

More serious mountain bikers should head to the **Sunday River Mountain Bike Park** (☎ 207/824-3000) at the ski area. Mountain-bike trails of every caliber are open to bikers. Experienced trail riders will enjoy taking their bikes by chairlift to the summit, and careening back down on the service roads and bike trails.

**Bethel Outdoor Adventures,** 121 Mayville Rd., Bethel, ☎ 800/533-3607 or 207/836-2708, also rents bikes. The center is located where Route 2 crosses the Androscoggin between Bethel and Sunday River.

**BOATING**   Canoe rentals and shuttles for exploring the Androscoggin River can be arranged by Bethel Outdoor Adventures (see above).

**GOLF**   Duffers should make for the **Bethel Inn** and **Country Club** (☎ 207/ 824-2175), which operates a scenic 18-hole golf course next to the inn. Equipment and golf carts are available for rent, and the club also features a driving range.

**HIKING**   The **Appalachian Trail** crosses the Mahoosuc Mountains northwest of Bethel. Many of those who've hiked the entire 2,000-mile trail say this stretch is the most demanding on knees and psyches. The trail doesn't forgive; it generally foregoes switchbacks in favor of sheer ascents and descents. It's also hard to find water along the trail during dry weather. Still, it's worth the knee-pounding effort for the views and the unrivaled sense of remoteness.

One stretch crosses Old Speck Mountain, Maine's third highest peak. Views from the summit are all but non-existent since the old fire tower closed a while back, but an easy-to-moderate spur trail on the lower end of the trail ascends an 800-foot cliff called "The Eyebrow" and provides a good vantage point for Bear River Valley and the rugged terrain of Grafton Notch. Look for the well-signed parking lot where Route 26 intersects the trail in Grafton Notch State Park. Park your car, then head south on the A.T. toward Old Speck; in 0.1 mile, you'll intersect the Eyebrow Trail, which you can follow to the overlook.

The Appalachian Mountain Club's *Maine Mountain Guide* is highly recommended for detailed information about other area hikes.

## WHERE TO STAY

**Bethel Inn.** On the Common, Bethel, ME 04217. ☎ **800/654-0125** or 207/824-2175. www.bethelinn.com. 56 units. TV TEL. Summer $198–$360 double; winter $158–$280 double. Rates include breakfast and dinner. 2-night minimum on weekends in summer and ski season; 3-night minimum during winter school vacations. Ski packages available. AE, DC, DISC, MC, V. $30 extra for pets; one-time fee.

The Bethel Inn is a classic, old-fashioned resort set on 200 acres in the village. It has a quiet, settled air. This is appropriate, since it was built to house patients of Dr. John Gehring, who put Bethel on the map treating nervous disorders through a regimen of healthy country living, including a lot of wood splitting. (Bethel was once known as "the resting place of Harvard" for all the faculty treated here.) The quaint, homey rooms aren't terribly spacious, but they are welcoming and pleasingly furnished with country antiques. More luxurious are the 16 deluxe rooms and suites added to the inn in 1998. You give up some of the charm of the old inn but gain welcome elbow room.

**Dining:** The dining room remains the resort's Achilles' heel. It's promising at first, offering classic resort specialties like prime rib, shrimp scampi pesto, and cedar-planked salmon (main courses are $14 to $20 for outside guests). Alas, the preparation and service often fail to live up to the promise of these fine surroundings.

**Amenities:** Fitness center with an outdoor heated pool (open year-round), whirlpool, sauna, golf course, tennis, cross-country skiing, shuttle to ski areas, laundry service, baby-sitting, and guest safe. Also lake swimming at the inn's Lake House, picturesquely located amid pines on a small lake a short drive away.

**Black Bear Bed & Breakfast.** Sunday River Rd. (P.O. Box 55), Bethel, ME 04217. ☎ **207/824-0908**. www.bbearbandb.com. E-mail: bbearinn@megalink.net. 6 units. Winter $80–$95 double, including breakfast; summer $70–$80 double. 2-night minimum on ski season weekends. Closed May. AE, MC, V. Pets allowed; ask first.

This 1830s farmhouse is located a short drive beyond the turn-off to Sunday River ski area, and is a great choice for those seeking a casual spot to rest up between ski runs or hiking trips. The rooms vary in size but are each furnished in a simple country style with pine and oak furniture, and with lots of daylight poring through oversized old windows. The common room is a good spot to sit around the wood stove and chat with other guests or innkeepers Faith Spath and Phil Buell, as is the hot tub just off the deck. But the chief amenity is the location: it's on 8 acres in a lovely dead-end valley. You can be on the ski slopes in winter within 5 minutes, yet it feels like you're far off in the country by nightfall. In summer, guests can splash around in the river, or set off on mountain biking and hiking rambles up the valley into the national forest. A new structure in the adjacent field was planned at press time, which will add four deluxe rooms by late 2000, each with fireplace and Jacuzzi ($125 double).

**Holidae House.** 85 Main St., Bethel, ME 04217. ☎ **800/882-3306** or 207/824-3400. 9 units (includes 2 apartments). A/C TV TEL. Winter $89–$150 double; summer $70–$98; apartments $95–$175. Rates include continental breakfast. 2-night minimum on weekends Jan–March; 3-night minimum holiday weekends. AE, MC, V.

The exterior of this century-old village home on Bethel's Main Street is unusually handsome, painted in rich but muted colors. Inside, it's equally exuberant, decorated in a style that nicely straddles high Victorian and low whimsical. Each room is furnished with antiques and Oriental carpets; some have delightful hand-painted ceiling murals and whirlpool tubs. (Room 5 is my favorite, decorated with an abundance of classically inspired elegance.) Among the accommodations are a studio apartment that sleeps four, and a three-bedroom apartment that sleeps eight. The inn is a 5-minute walk from the Bethel Common, and a 10-minute drive to skiing at Sunday River. Avid readers take note: Innkeepers Sandy and Scott Dennis run a fine bookstore in the adjacent carriage house.

**Jordan Grand Resort Hotel.** Sunday River Rd., (P.O. Box 450), Bethel, ME 04217. ☎ **800/543-2754** or 207/824-5000. Fax 207/824-2111. www.sundayriver.com. 195 units. A/C TV TEL. Ski season $155–$225 double; off-season $105–$120. AE, DC, DISC, MC, V.

The Jordan Grand is the anchor for new development slated for the far-flung Jordan Bowl area. Right now, though, the place feels miles away from the rest of the resort, largely because it is—even the staff makes "The Shining" jokes about its remoteness. It's a modern if sprawling hotel that offers little in the way of a personal touch or flair, but boasts a great location for skiers who want to be first on untracked slopes each morning. Owing to the quirky terrain, parking is inconvenient and you often have to walk some distance to your room (opt for the valet parking). The rooms are simply furnished in a durable condo style. Many are quite spacious and most have balconies. It's a popular destination with families, so this isn't the best choice for couples seeking a quiet getaway.

**Dining:** Sunday River has stepped up efforts to improve its food service, and the two restaurants here suggest that it's succeeding. Breakfast and dinner are served daily at the Grand Avenue Cafe, which offers up tasty American cuisine like Jack Daniels duck and sautéed lobster (entrees $16 to $25). Sliders is at the distant other end of the hotel, right on the slopes. Upgraded pub fare (meatloaf, beef stew, and big and sloppy hamburgers) is reasonably priced and large-proportioned. Prices are $5.95 to $8.95.

**Amenities:** Outdoor heated pool (year-round), Jacuzzis, sauna, steam room, fitness room, children's center, conference rooms, business center, valet parking, in-room massage, limited room service, concierge, washer-dryer, dry cleaning, baby-sitting, and safe-deposit boxes.

**The Victoria.** 32 Main St., Bethel, ME 04217. ☎ **888/774-1235** or 207/824-8060. www.victoria-inn.com. E-mail: erickate@megalink.net. 15 units (including 4 family suites). A/C TV TEL. $105–$175 double, $250–$350 loft rooms (from $75 in spring and late fall). Rates include full breakfast. 2-night minimum on weekends and holidays. AE, MC, V.

The Victoria marks the welcome rehabilitation of one of the village's most prominent structures. Built in 1895 and damaged by lightning some years back, the inn has been superbly restored, complete with antique lighting fixtures, period furniture, and the original formidable oak doors guarding the entryway. The guest rooms have a luxurious William Morris feel, with richly patterned wallpaper and handmade duvet covers. Room 1 is the luxurious master suite, with a turret window and a sizeable bathroom; Room 3 is the only room with wood floors (the others are carpeted), but has a tiny bathroom. Most intriguing are the four loft rooms in the attached carriage house, each with gas fireplace, Jacuzzi, and soaring ceilings revealing old beams. These are perfect for families, with spare beds in lofts over the main rooms. Room 7 has spiral stairs leading to bunk beds; Room 9 has a separate sitting room with TV. All guests have access to a bright sitting area with woodstove on the second floor of the carriage house.

**Dining:** The inn's two dining rooms are stately and handsome, as one would expect in this elaborate manse. Dinner is served nightly except Tuesday, with entrees including breast of duck with a raspberry coulis and bordelaise sauce, and grilled salmon with a crabmeat and red pepper garnish. Reservations are requested; entree prices range from $11.95 (spinach manicotti) to $22.95 (veal chop).

## WHERE TO DINE

In addition to the informal establishments listed below, don't overlook **The Victoria** (see above) for the best upscale dining in the village. It's open year-round.

**Great Grizzly/Matterhorn.** 292 Sunday River Rd. ☎ **207/824-6271** or 207/824-6836. Pizza $7.95 and up; other entrees $6.95–$16.95. MC, V. Pizza from 3pm–10pm; steak house menu from 5pm. Open only during ski season. STEAKHOUSE/BRICK-OVEN PIZZA.

These two restaurants share a handsome new timber-frame structure on the Sunday River Road just a couple of minutes from the ski area. It's casual and relaxed, with pool table, pinball, and a handsome metal-top bar. You'll get two menus after you settle in: Great Grizzly offers mostly steaks. Matterhorn specializes in wood-fired pizza, and they're very, very good. The atmosphere is more relaxed and the food significantly better than at the Sunday River Brewing Co. a couple of miles down the road, and the beer-on-tap selection doesn't suffer much for not being a brewpub. Alas, it's closed in summer, though that could change in the future.

**Sunday River Brewing Company.** Rte. 2 (at Sunday River Rd.), Bethel. ☎ **207/824-4253.** Reservations not accepted. Main courses, $5.95–$15.95 (most $7–$9). AE, MC, V. Daily 11:30am–12:30am. PUB FARE.

Sunday River Brewing Co. opened this modern and boisterous brew pub on prime real estate at the corner of Route 2 and the Sunday River access road. This is a good choice if your primary objective is to quaff robust ales and porters. The brews are awfully good; the food (burgers, nachos, and chicken wings) doesn't strive for any culinary heights, and certainly doesn't achieve any. If you want good pub fare, you're better off headed up Sunday River Road a piece to try Great Grizzly/Matterhorn (ski season only). Come early if you're looking for a quiet evening; it gets loud later in the evening when bands take the stage.

## RANGELEY LAKES

Mounted moose heads on the walls, log cabins tucked into spruce forest, and cool August mornings that sometimes require not one sweater but two are the stuff of the Rangeley Lakes region. Although Rangeley Lake and its eponymous town are at the heart of the region, its borders extend much further, consisting of a series of lakes that feed into and flow out of the main lake.

Upstream is Maine's fourth largest lake, Flagstaff, a beautiful, wind-raked body of water created in 1949 when Central Maine Power dammed the Dead River. (Below the dam, it's no longer dead; in fact, it's now noted for its white-water rafting—see "The North Woods," below). From Rangeley Lake, the waters flow into Cupsuptic Pond, which in turn flow to Mooselookmeguntic Lake, through the Upper and Lower Richardson Lakes, down remote Swift River and to Lake Umbagog, which feeds the headwaters of the Androscoggin River.

The town of **Rangeley** (pop. 1,200) is the regional center for outdoor activities. It offers a handful of motels and restaurants, a bevy of fishing guides, a smattering of shops, and little else. Easy-to-visit attractions in the Rangeley area are few, and most regular visitors and residents seem determined to keep it that way. The wise visitor rents a cabin or takes a room at a lodge, then explores the area with the slow pace that seems custom-made for the region. Rangeley is Maine's highest town at 1,546 feet, and usually remains quite cool throughout the summer.

## ESSENTIALS

**GETTING THERE**   Rangeley is 122 miles north of Portland, and 39 miles north-west of Farmington on Route 4. The most scenic approach is on Route 17 from Rumford. En route you'll come upon one of the more stunning overlooks in New England, with a sweeping panorama of Mooselookmeguntic Lake and Bemis Mountain.

If you're coming from New Hampshire, drive 111 miles north on Route 16 from North Conway through Gorham, Berlin, and Errol. Route 16 from Errol to Rangeley is especially remote and scenic.

**VISITOR INFORMATION**   The **Rangeley Lakes Region Chamber of Commerce,** P.O. Box 317, Rangeley, ME 04970 (☎ **800/685-2537** or 207/864-5364), maintains an information booth in town at a small park near the lake that's open year-round Monday to Saturday from 9am to 5pm.

## DOWNHILL SKIING

**Saddleback Ski Area.** P.O. Box 490, Rangeley, ME 04970. ☎ **207/864-5671.** Vertical drop: 1,830 ft. Lifts: 2 double chairs, 3 T-bars. Skiable acreage: 100. Lift tickets: $45 weekends; $29 midweek.

With only two chairlifts, Saddleback qualifies as a small mountain, but Saddleback has an unexpectedly big-mountain feel. It offers a vertical drop of just 1,830 feet, but what makes Saddleback so appealing is its rugged alpine setting (the Appalachian Trail runs across the high, mile-long ridge above the resort) and the old-fashioned trails. Saddleback offered glade skiing and narrow, winding trails well before the bigger ski areas sought to re-create these old-fashioned slopes.

## OTHER OUTDOOR PURSUITS

**CANOEING**   The Rangeley Lakes area is a canoeist's paradise. Azure waters, dense forests, and handsome hills are all part of the allure. Rangeley Lake has a mix of wild forest and classic old cottages lining the lakeshore. The southeast coves of Mooselookmeguntic Lake suffered an unfortunate period of haphazard lakeshore development during the 1980s, but much of the shore, especially along the west shore, is still very remote and appealing.

**HIKING**   The Appalachian Trail crosses Route 4 about 10 miles south of Rangeley. A strenuous but rewarding hike is along the trail northward to the summit of **Saddleback Mountain,** a 10-mile round-trip that ascends through thick forest and past remote ponds to open, arctic-like terrain with fine views of the surrounding mountains and lakes. Saddleback actually consists of two peaks over 4,000 feet (hence the name). Be prepared for sudden shifts in weather, and for the high winds that often rake the open ridgeline.

An easier 1-mile hike may be found at **Bald Mountain** near the village of Oquossuc, on the northeast shore of Mooselookmeguntic Lake. (Look for the trailhead 1 mile south of Haines Landing on Bald Mountain Road). The views have grown over in recent years, but you can still catch glimpses of the clear blue waters from above.

# Odd Science

✪ **Orgonon.** Dodge Pond Rd. (3¹/₂ miles west of Rangeley off Rte. 4). ☎ **207/ 864-3443.** Admission $4 adults, free for children under 12. Open July and August Tuesday to Sunday 1 to 5pm; September Sunday only 1 to 5pm.

Among the few historic sites in Maine relating to the 20th century is Orgonon, former home of controversial Viennese psychiatrist Wilhelm Reich (1897–1957). Reich was an associate of Sigmund Freud during the early days of psychoanalysis. Like Freud, Reich believed that underlying sexual tension governed much of our behavior, but Reich took Freud's work a few steps further, building on the hypothesis that pent-up sexual energy—a sort of psychological blockage—resulted in numerous neuroses.

Reich settled in Rangeley in 1942, where he developed the science of "orgonomy." According to Reich, living matter was animated by a sort of life force called "orgone." This floated freely in the atmosphere and was blue (which Reich believed explained the hue of the sky). To cure orgone imbalances he invented orgone energy boxes, which were said to gather and concentrate ambient orgone. These boxes were just big enough to sit in, and featured 6-inch walls of metal and asbestos.

Reich was sentenced to federal prison for matters related to the interstate transport of his orgone boxes. He died in prison in 1957. While many dismissed Reich's theories as quackery, he still has serious and dedicated adherents, including those who maintain the museum in his memory.

Orgonon, built in 1948 of native fieldstone, has a spectacular view of Dodge Pond and is built in the distinctive American Modern style, which stands apart from the local rustic-lodge motif. Visitors on the 1-hour guided tour of the estate and the architecturally distinctive home can view the orgone boxes along with other intriguing inventions.

## WHERE TO STAY & DINE

The Rangeley area has a scattering of bed-and-breakfasts, but many travelers spend a week or more at a sporting camp or rented waterfront cottage. Among the best known of the sporting camps is **Grant's Kennebago Camps** (☎ **800/633-4815** or 207/864-3608), situated down a long and dusty logging road on Kennebago Lake—the biggest "fly-fishing only" lake east of the Mississippi. Rates are $100 per person per day, including all meals. For weekly rental of a private cabin, advance planning is essential. A good place to start is the local **chamber of commerce's** free *Accommodations and Services* pamphlet (☎ **800/685-2537** or 207/864-5364). The chamber can also book cabins by the week for you.

**Kawahnee Inn.** Rte. 142 (P.O. Box 119), Weld, ME 04285. ☎ **207/585-2000.** www.lakeinn.com. E-mail: maineinn@somtel.com. 9 units (4 with shared bathroom), plus 12 cabins. $65–$105 double ($10 additional for private bath); cabins $125–$165. MC, V. Closed October 15–May 15. Limited accommodations for pets.

The rustic Kawahnee Inn is located about 30 miles southeast of Rangeley, but it's worth the detour if you don't demand luxury and you're looking for that ineffable lakeside Maine experience. Originally built in 1929 to house parents visiting their children at neighboring Camp Kawahnee, the lodge is full of creaks and shadows as befits a spot built by a teacher of industrial arts. There are columns of yellow birch, handsome caned chairs original to the lodge, a cobblestone fireplace with a moose head above, and classic views across the lake to Mt. Blue (a state park that offers tempting hiking). The lodge rooms are spartan but attractive, and noises tend to carry. Five of the rooms have private baths; the other four share one bath. The one-, two-, and three-bedroom cabins are usually booked by the week (rates range from $485 to $700), but some are available on a nightly basis, especially during the shoulder seasons.

**Dining:** The rustic dining room is open nightly mid-June though Labor Day and serves moderately priced fare including lobster, sirloin steak, roast duck, seafood, and a selection of vegetarian dishes including Szechuan vegetable stir fry.

**Amenities:** Lake, beach, and canoe rentals.

**Rangeley Inn.** P.O. Box 160, Rangeley, ME 04907. ☎ **800/666-3687** or 207/864-3341. Fax 207/864-3634. www.rangeleyinn.com. E-mail: rangeinn@rangeley.org. 50 units. TV (in motel units only). $69–$119 double. 2-night minimum winter weekends. AE, DISC, MC, V. Pets allowed (limited); $8 extra per night.

The architecturally eclectic Rangeley Inn dominates Rangeley's miniature downtown. Parts of this old-fashioned, blue-shingled hotel date back to 1877, but the main wing was built in 1907, with additions in the 1920s and the 1940s. A 15-unit motel annex was built more recently behind the inn on Haley Pond, but those looking for creaky floors and a richer sense of local heritage should request a room in the main, three-floor inn. Some rooms in the motel have woodstoves, kitchenettes, or whirlpools; in the inn you'll find a handful of rooms with clawfoot tubs perfect for an evening's soaking.

**Dining:** The gracious, old-worldish dining room serves hearty, filling meals; less formal fare is available in the Rangeley Inn Tavern. During the heavy tour season (especially fall), bus groups tend to dominate.

### TWO LAKESIDE CAMPGROUNDS

While dozens of wilderness campsites may be found throughout the region (check with the chamber of commerce for more information), two of the more accessible campgrounds bear mentioning. **Rangeley Lake State Park** (☎ **207/864-3858**) occupies about a mile of shoreline on the south shore of Rangeley Lake. It has a small swimming area just off a grassy clearing and 50 campsites, some of which offer easy access to the waters of Rangeley Lake. Bring a canoe for exploring. Rates are $16 per night, $12 for Maine residents ($2 additional for reserved sites).

Along a dirt road on the eastern shores of Mooselookmeguntic Lake is the **Stephen Phillips Wildlife Preserve** (☎ **207/864-2003**), a private sanctuary comprised of 400 lakeshore acres, several islands, and 63 campsites. The preserve offers camping on two islands (Toothaker and Students), both of which are easily accessible by canoe. Lakeside campsites are also available in the scrubby spruce forest that lines the lake; most sites are accessible by walking a few hundred feet from scattered parking areas, providing more of a backcountry experience than you'll find at the usual drive-in campgrounds. Canoes are available for rent at the office. The fee is $8 per night for 2 people; additional campers are $4 per night. The preserve is open May through September; reservations are accepted, but credit cards are not.

## CARRABASSETT VALLEY

The Carrabassett Valley can be summed up in six words: big peaks, wild woods, deep lakes. The crowning jewel of the region is Sugarloaf Mountain, Maine's second highest peak at 4,237 feet. Distinct from nearby peaks because of its pyramidal shape, the mountain has been developed for skiing and offers the largest vertical drop in Maine, the best selection of activities daytime and night, and a wide range of accommodations within easy commuting distance.

While Sugarloaf draws the lion's share of visitors, it's not the only game in town. Nearby **Kingfield** is an attractive, historic town with a fine old hotel; it has more of the character of an Old West outpost than of classic New England. Other valley towns offering limited services for travelers include **Eustis, Stratton,** and **Carrabassett Valley.**

Outside the villages and ski resort, it's all rugged hills, tumbling streams, and spectacular natural surroundings. The muscular mountains of the **Bigelow Range** provide terrain for some of the state's best hiking, and Flagstaff Lake is the place for flatwater canoeing amid majestic surroundings.

## ESSENTIALS

**GETTING THERE**    Kingfield and Sugarloaf are on Route 27. Skiers debate over the best route from the turnpike. Some exit at Auburn and take Route 4 north to Route 27; others exit in Augusta and take Route 27 straight through. It's a toss-up time-wise, but exiting at Augusta is marginally more scenic.

**Maine Tour and Travel** (☎ 800/649-5071) offers a private shuttle service from state airports to the mountain.

**VISITOR INFORMATION**    The **Sugarloaf Area Chamber of Commerce** (☎ 207/235-2100) offers information from its offices 9¹/₂ miles north of Kingfield on Route 27. The office is open year-round; their goal is to be open daily 10am to 4pm, but that may vary. The chamber can book lodgings in and around Sugarloaf; call ☎ 800/843-2732. For accommodations on the mountain, contact Sugarloaf/USA directly (see below).

## DOWNHILL SKIING

**Sugarloaf/USA.** RR #1, Box 5000, Carrabassett Valley, ME 04947. ☎ **800/843-5623** or 207/237-2000. www.sugarloaf.com. Vertical drop: 2,820 ft. Lifts: 13 chairlifts, including 2 high-speed quads; 1 surface lift. Skiable acreage: 1,400 (snowmaking on 475 acres). Lift tickets: $49 adults weekends, $47 weekdays.

Sugarloaf is Maine's big mountain, with the highest vertical drop in New England after Vermont's Killington; and thanks to quirks of geography, it actually feels bigger than it is. From the high, open snowfields (which account for much of Sugarloaf's huge skiable acreage) or the upper advanced runs like Bubblecuffer or White Nitro, skiers develop vertigo looking down at the valley floor. Sugarloaf attracts plenty of experts to its hardcore runs, but it's also a fine intermediate mountain with great cruising runs. A gentle bunny slope extends down through the village; the "green" slopes on the mountain itself are a bit more challenging. The main drawback comes in the form of wind. Sugarloaf seems to get buffeted regularly, with the higher lifts often closed due to gusting.

Sugarloaf has more of a destination feel than many New England ski resorts, since it's nearly 3 hours from Portland (5 from Boston) and gets comparatively little day traffic. Most people who ski Sugarloaf stay at the base complex, a well-run, convivial cluster of hotel rooms, condos, and mini-suites offering 7,500 beds. The accommodations, the mountain, the restaurants, and other area attractions are well-connected by chairlifts and shuttle buses, making for a relaxed visit here even during a fierce blizzard.

## CROSS-COUNTRY SKIING

The **Sugarloaf Ski Touring Center** (☎ 207/237-6830) offers 57 miles of groomed trails that weave through the village at the base of the mountain and into the low hills covered with scrappy woodlands along the Carrabassett River. The trails are impeccably groomed for striding and skating, and wonderful views open here and there to Sugarloaf Mountain and the Bigelow Range. The base lodge is simple and attractive, all knotty pine with a cathedral ceiling, and features a cafeteria, towering stone fireplace, and a well-equipped ski shop. Snowshoes are also available for rent. Trail fees are $15 daily for adults; $10 for seniors (60+) and children 12 and under. (Half-day tickets also available.) The center is located on Route 27 about 1 mile south of the Sugarloaf access road. A shuttle bus serves the area in winter.

## HIKING

The 12-mile Bigelow Range has some of the most dramatic high-ridge hiking in the state, a close second to Mt. Katahdin. It consists of a handful of lofty peaks, with Avery Peak (the east peak) offering the best views. On exceptionally clear days, hikers can see Mt. Washington to the southwest and Mt. Katahdin to the northeast.

A strenuous but rewarding hike for fit hikers is the $10^3/_{10}$-mile loop that begins at the **Fire Warden's Trail.** (The trailhead is at the washed-out bridge on Stratton Brook Pond Road, a rugged dirt road that leaves eastward from Route 27 about $2^3/_{10}$ miles north of the Sugarloaf access road.) Follow the Fire Warden's Trail up the steep ridge to the junction with the **Appalachian Trail.** Head south on the AT, which tops the West Peak and South Horn, two open summits with stellar views. One-quarter mile past Horns Pond, turn south on **Horns Pond Trail** and descend back to the Fire Warden's Trail to return to your car. Allow about 8 hours for the loop; a topographical map and hiking guide are strongly recommended.

A less rigorous hike that still yields supremely rewarding views is to **Cranberry Peak,** the Bigelow peak farthest west. Plan on 4 to 5 hours to complete this hike along Bigelow Range Trail, which runs about $6^1/_2$ miles. The trail head is just south of the town of Stratton (from the south, turn right $^2/_{10}$ miles after crossing Stratton Brook, then drive on a dirt road $^1/_2$ mile to a clearing). Follow the trail through woods and over a series of ledges to the 3,213-foot Cranberry Peak. Retrace your steps to your car.

Detailed directions for these hikes and many others in the area may be found in the AMC's *Maine Mountain Guide.*

## OTHER OUTDOOR PURSUITS

Sugarloaf's 18-hole **golf course** (☎ 207/237-2000) is often ranked the number-one golf destination in the state by experienced golfers, who are lured here by the Robert Trent Jones, Jr., course design and dramatic mountain backdrop. Sugarloaf hosts a well-respected golf school during the season.

Other outdoor activities are located in and around the **Sugarloaf Outdoor Center** (☎ 207/237-6830). Through the center, you can arrange for fly-fishing lessons, a mountain-bike excursion at the resort's mountain-bike park (rentals available), or hiking or white-water rafting in the surrounding mountains and valleys.

## A MUSEUM FOR AUTO & PHOTO BUFFS

**Stanley Museum.** School St., Kingfield. ☎ **207/265-2729.** www.stanleymuseum.org. Admission is $2 adults, $1 children. Tues–Sun 1–4pm. Closed weekends Nov–June, except by appointment.

The Stanley Steamer—an automobile powered with steam like a locomotive—is today an anachronistic footnote and prized collectible, but when manufactured between 1897 and 1925, it was state-of-the-art transportation, literally and figuratively smoking the competition. The Stanley Steamer was the first car to reach the summit of Mt. Washington, the first car to break the 2-miles-in-1-minute barrier with a land-speed record of 127 m.p.h. in 1906, and the winner of numerous hill-climb competitions.

The Stanley Museum, housed in a handsome yellow Georgian former schoolhouse in Kingfield, chronicles the rise of the Steamer, and the backgrounds of the two Kingfield inventors, the twins F. O. and F. E. Stanley. Three working Steamers are on display. You'll learn that the Stanleys invented the car as a hobby—they established their first fortune inventing the dry-plate photographic process and building a company that was eventually purchased by George Eastman, the founder of Kodak.

Also on display are extraordinary early photographs taken by their sister, Chansonetta Stanley, who documented life in rural Maine and South Carolina at the turn of the last century—a sort of self-appointed precursor to the WPA photographers. Her work has gained recent respect among serious collectors, and this exhibit will make it abundantly plain why that's so.

## WHERE TO STAY

For convenience, nothing beats staying right on the mountain in winter. Skiers can pop right out the door and on to the lifts. Sugarloaf is nicely designed to allow skiers access to the village; a long, gentle slope extends from the base of the mountain through clusters of condos and hotels, allowing skiers to glide home after a long day. A low chairlift takes you up to the base first thing in the morning.

Many of the condos are booked through the **Sugarloaf/USA Inn** (☎ 800/ 843-5623 or 207/237-2000), which handles the reservations for more than 300 condos and mini-suites. The units are spread throughout the base area, and are of varying vintage and opulence. All guests have access to the Sugarloaf Sports and Fitness Center. Another option at the base village is the **Sugarloaf Mountain Hotel** (☎ 800/ 527-9879), a towering structure right at the lifts with more than 100 guest rooms.

**The Herbert.** Main St. (P.O. Box 67), Kingfield, ME 04947. ☎ **800/843-4372** or 207/ 265-2000. Fax 207/265-4594. www.mainemountaininn.com. E-mail: herbert@somtel.com. 32 units. $59 double midweek; $99 weekend; $110 holiday. Rates include continental breakfast. 3-night minimum during holidays. AE, DC, DISC, MC, V. Pets allowed; some restrictions apply.

The Herbert has the feel of a classic North Woods hostelry—sort of Dodge City by way of Alaska. Built in downtown Kingfield in 1918, the three-story hotel featured all of the finest accoutrements when it was built, including fumed oak paneling and incandescent lights in the lobby (look for the original brass fixtures), a classy dining room, and comfortable rooms. The rooms are furnished in a fairly simple and basic style, featuring flea-market antiques and some newer additions. The Herbert is located about 15 miles from the slopes at Sugarloaf/USA.

**Dining:** See "Where to Dine," below.

**Three Stanley Avenue.** 3 Stanley Ave. (P.O. Box 169), Kingfield, ME 04947. ☎ **207/ 265-5541.** 6 units, 3 share 2 bathrooms. Dec–March $50–$60 double; Apr–Nov $50–$55. All rates include breakfast. 2-night minimum on winter weekends. AE, MC, V.

Three Stanley Avenue is the bed-and-breakfast annex to the well-known restaurant next door, One Stanley Avenue. Set on a shady knoll in a quiet village setting just across the bridge from downtown Kingfield, this B&B has an old-fashioned Victorian boarding house feel to it, complete with an elaborate stained-glass window at the bottom of the stairs. The rooms are comfortably if not luxuriously appointed; three rooms share two baths, the other three have private baths.

**Dining:** The small, well-regarded restaurant is open during ski season only, daily except Monday. The chef says the cuisine is "classical in nature, regional in execution." You might find roast duckling with rhubarb glaze, or sweetbreads with cream sauce flavored with chives and applejack. Northern New England flavors—like berries and fiddleheads—tend to be well-represented. Entrees range from $15 to $29.

## WHERE TO DINE

**The Herbert.** Main St., Kingfield. ☎ **800/843-4372** or 207/265-2000. Reservations recommended. Main courses, $14.95–$22.95. AE, DC, DISC, MC, V. Thurs–Mon 5pm–9pm (until 8pm on Sunday). REGIONAL.

This open but intimate dining room off the lobby of The Herbert hotel recalls the days when hotels served the best meals in town. The place has a nicely worn Edwardian feel to it—right down to the heavy sink in the dining room for guests to wash their hands after disembarking from the stage. The interior has been prettified somewhat, but not enough to lose its charm for tourists and locals who come here for the often tasty, healthy and usually creative meals. The chef offers interpretations of regional classics, like shiitake mushrooms with venison medaillons, and haddock baked with feta cheese and served with a lemon-garlic dressing. The meals are usually good, not excellent, and the service is friendly. Come early to enjoy a glass of wine in the lobby before you dine.

**Hug's.** Rte. 27, Carrabassett Valley. ☎ **207/237-2392.** Reservations recommended, especially on weekends. Main courses $11.95–$17.95. DISC, MC, V. Daily 5–10pm. Closed May–Nov. Located ⁷/₁₀ mile south of the Sugarloaf access rd. NORTHERN ITALIAN.

Hug's takes diners well beyond red sauce, offering a broad selection of pastas far tastier than one should reasonably expect from a restaurant within the orbit of a ski area. This is a small place, set just off the highway in a fairy-tale-like cottage. Inside are two intimate dining rooms; the dominant color is battleship gray, but it's enlivened with lipstick red tablecloths and intriguing early ski pictures on the walls. Dinners are preceded with a tasty basket of pesto bread (very welcome after a day of hiking or skiing). The dinner selections are uncommonly well-prepared. The shiitake ravioli with walnut-pesto Alfredo is superb, as are the veal specials. As for the name: you won't be greeted with a warm embrace. "Hug" was the original owner's nickname.

# 2 The North Woods

There are two versions of the Maine Woods. There's the grand and unbroken forest threaded with tumbling rivers that unspools endlessly in the popular perception, and then there's the reality.

The perception is that this region is the last outpost of big wilderness in the east, with thousands of acres of unbroken forest, miles of free-running streams, and more azure lakes than you can shake a canoe paddle at. A look at a road map seems to confirm this, with only a few roads shown here and there amid terrain pocked with lakes; but undeveloped does not mean untouched.

The reality is that this forest land is a massive plantation, largely owned and managed by a handful of international paper and timber companies. An extensive network of small timber roads (about 25,000 miles at last count) feed off major arteries and open the region to extensive clear-cutting. This is most visible from the air. In the early 1980s, New Yorker writer John McPhee noted that much of northern Maine "looks like an old and badly tanned pelt. The hair is coming out in tufts." That's even more the case today following the acceleration of timber harvesting thanks to technological advances and demands for faster cutting to pay down debts incurred during the buy-and-sell frenzy of the past decade and a half.

While the North Woods are not a vast, howling wilderness, the region still has fabulously remote enclaves where moose and loon predominate, and where the turf hasn't changed all that much since Thoreau paddled through in the mid-19th century and found it all "moosey and mossy." If you don't arrive expecting utter wilderness, you're less likely to be disappointed.

One last note: those who are least impressed by the North Woods are those who try to see it by car. Those who come away most impressed travel by foot and canoe.

# BANGOR, ORONO & OLD TOWN

These three towns along the western banks of Penobscot River serve as gateways to the North Woods. Bangor, Maine's third largest city (after Portland and Lewiston), is the last major urban outpost with a full-fledged mall. It's also a good destination for history buffs curious about the early North Woods economy. Bangor was once a thriving lumber port, shipping out millions of board feet cut from the woods to the north and floated down the Penobscot River. While much of the town burned in 1911 and has since suffered from ill-considered urban renewal schemes, visitors can still discern a robust history just below the surface. Orono and Old Town, two smaller towns to the north, offer an afternoon's diversion on rainy days.

## ESSENTIALS

**GETTING THERE**    Bangor is located just off the Maine Turnpike. Take I-395 east, exit at Main Street (Route 1A), and follow signs for downtown.

It's not as easy to fly in or out of Bangor as it was in recent years. Like many smaller regional airports, the **Bangor International Airport** (☎ 207/947-0384) has had a difficult time persuading airlines to maintain a schedule of full-service flights here; as a result, many flights begin or end via commuter planes to or from Boston. Owing in part to recent airline turnovers, many travelers have reported problems with delays and lost luggage at Bangor. Airlines currently serving Bangor include **Comair/Delta Connection** (☎ 800/221-1212), **Business Express** (☎ 800/345-3400), and **US Airways Express** (☎ 800/428-4322).

**Concord Trailways** (☎ 800/639-3317) and **Vermont Transit** (☎ 800/451-3292 or 800/642-3133) both offer bus service to Bangor from Portland; there's also connecting bus service to Bar Harbor, Houlton, and the Downeast coast, including Machias and Calais.

**VISITOR INFORMATION**    The **Bangor Visitors Information Office** is staffed in summer near the big, scary statue of Paul Bunyan at the convention center on Main Street near I-395. Contact the **Greater Bangor Chamber of Commerce**, P.O. Box 1443, Bangor, ME 04402 (☎ 207/947-0307), open year-round 8am to 5pm Monday through Friday, and extended hours in summer depending on volunteer availability.

## EXPLORING BANGOR, ORONO & OLD TOWN

**IN BANGOR**    The **Bangor Historical Society** (☎ 207/942-5766) offers a glimpse of life in Bangor during the golden days of the late 19th century. The society is housed in a handsome brick home built in 1836 for a prominent businessman and now features displays of furniture and historical artifacts. The society's collections are at 159 Union St. (just off High Street) and are seen during 1-hour guided tours; the price is $5 adult, 12 and under are free. The museum is open April to December Tuesday through Friday from noon to 4pm; from June through September, it's also open Saturdays noon to 4pm.

Vintage-car and early transportation buffs will enjoy a detour to the **Cole Land Transportation Museum** (☎ 207/990-3600), located at 405 Perry Rd. off Exit 45B of I-95 near the intersection with I-395 (go left at the first light, then make next a left onto Perry Road) The museum features old automobiles lined up in a warehouse-size display space, along with quirkier machinery like snow rollers, cement mixers, power shovels, and tractors. The museum is especially well-represented by early trucks, which is appropriate given its connection with Cole Express, a Maine trucking company founded in 1917. The museum is open daily from May through mid-November 9am to 5pm; admission is $3 adult, $2 senior, and free under 18.

Despite the city's rich history and the distinguished architecture of the commercial district, Bangor is probably best known as home to horror novelist and one-man Maine industry Stephen King. King's sprawling Victorian home seems a fitting place for the Maine native author; it's got an Addams Family–like creepiness, which is only enhanced by the wrought-iron fence with bats on it. His home isn't open to the public, but it's worth a drive by. To find the house, take the Union Street exit off I-95, head toward town for 6 blocks, then turn right on West Broadway. I'll leave it to you to figure out which one it is.

**IN ORONO & OLD TOWN**   Orono is home to the University of Maine, which was founded in 1868. The campus is spread out on a plain and features a pleasing mix of historic and contemporary buildings. (The campus was originally designed by noted landscape architect Frederick Law Olmsted, but it's early look has been obscured by later additions.) On campus, the modern and spacious **Hudson Museum** (☎ **207/ 581-1901**) features exhibits on anthropology and native culture. The museum displays crafts and artwork from native cultures around the world, and is especially well-represented with North American displays. Closed Mondays and holidays; admission is free.

A few minutes north on Route 178 is the riverside town of Old Town, famous for its canoes, which have been made here since the turn of the last century. **The Old Town Canoe Company** (☎ **207/827-5513**) is still situated in its original brick factory in the middle of town and sells new and factory-second canoes from its showroom at 58 Middle St. (Open in summer Monday through Saturday 9am to 6pm, Sunday 10am to 3pm.) Old Town no longer offers tours of the creaky old factory, but there's a continuously running video showing techniques used in contemporary canoemaking.

## WHERE TO STAY

Bangor has plenty of guest rooms, many located along charmless strips near the airport and the mall. If you're not choosey or if you're arriving late at night, these are fine. Be aware that even these can fill up during the peak summer season, so reservations are advised. Try the **Comfort Inn,** 750 Hogan Rd. (☎ **800/228-5150** or 207/ 942-7899), **Howard Johnson's Motor Lodge,** 336 Odlin Rd. (☎ **800/654-2000** or 207/942-5251), or the **Fairfield Inn,** 300 Odlin Rd. (☎ **800/228-2800** or 207/990-0001).

Other options: Connected to the Bangor's airport is **Four Points by Sheraton,** 308 Godfrey Blvd. (☎ **800/228-4609** or 207/947-6721); near the Bangor Mall and other chain stores is **Country Inn at the Mall,** 936 Stillwater Ave. (☎ 207/941-0200).; and downtown is the **Holiday Inn,** 500 Main St. (☎ 800/799-8651 or 207/947-8651).

**Phenix Inn.** 20 Broad St., Bangor, ME 04401. ☎ **207/947-0411.** Fax 207/947-0255. 32 units. A/C TV TEL. Summer and foliage season $95–$165 double; spring and winter $80–$140 double. All rates include continental breakfast. AE, CB, DC, DISC, MC, V.

Bangor's only downtown hotel is in a striking brick building dating from 1873 and now on the National Register of Historic Places. The exterior shows a confident Victorian exuberance; trim, attractive guest rooms are comfortably furnished with mahogany reproduction furniture. Some rooms have four-poster beds, but all are

# The Debate Over Maine's North Woods

Much of Maine's outdoor recreation takes place on private lands—especially in the North Woods, 9 million acres of which are owned by fewer than two dozen timber companies. This sprawling, uninhabited land is increasingly at the heart of a simmering debate over land-use policies.

Hunters, fishermen, canoeists, rafters, bird-watchers, and hikers have for years been accustomed to having the run of much of the forest. This has been with the tacit permission of the local timber companies, many of which had long and historic ties to woodland communities; but a lot has changed in recent years, especially during the 1980s.

The New England economic boom drove up land values throughout the region, which made lakefront and riverside property traditionally prized by outdoor recreationists far more valuable as second-home properties than as standing timber. A number of parcels were sold off, and some formerly open land was closed to visitors. What's more, the wild and undeveloped nature of the forest was compromised in many areas (such as along southern Moosehead and Mooselook-meguntic shores), and the handwriting seemed to be on the wall for much of the rest of Maine. At the same time, corporate turnovers in the paper industry led to increased debt loads, followed by greater pressure from shareholders to produce more from their woodlands, which led to accelerated timber harvesting and quickened land sales. Some 15 percent of the state changed hands in major land transactions in 1999.

Environmentalists maintain that the situation in Maine is a disaster in the making. They insist that the forest won't provide jobs in the timber industry or remain a recreational destination if the state continues on its present course. Timber companies deny this, and insist that they're practicing responsible forestry.

A number of proposals to restore and conserve the forest are circulating. These range from sweeping steps like establishing a new 2.6-million acre national park, to more modest notions like encouraging timber companies to practice sustainable forestry and keep access open for recreation through tax incentives. Statewide referendums in 1996 and 1997 calling for a ban on clear-cutting and sweeping new timber harvesting regulations were defeated narrowly, but the land-use issue has a long ways to go in sorting itself out. The debate over the future of the forest isn't as volatile here as in the Pacific Northwest, where public lands are involved, but few residents of the North Woods lack strong opinions on the matter.

carpeted and have wingback chairs for comfortable reading or watching television in the evening. Ask for one of the brighter, quieter corner rooms in the back.

## MOOSEHEAD LAKE REGION

Thirty-two miles long and 5 miles across at its widest point, Moosehead Lake is Maine's largest lake, and it's a great destination for hikers, boaters, and canoeists. The lake was historically the center of the region's logging activity; that history preserved the lake and kept it largely unspoiled by development. Timber companies still own much of the lakeside property (although the state has acquired a significant amount in the last few years), and the 350-mile shoreline is mostly unbroken second- or third-growth forest. The second-home building frenzy of the 1980s had an impact on the southern reaches of the lake, but the woody shoreline has absorbed most of the boom rather gracefully.

The first thing to know about the lake is that it's not meant to be seen by car. There are some great views from a handful of roads—especially from Route 6/15 as you near Rockwood and from the high elevations on the way to Lily Bay—but for the most part the roads are a distance from the shores and offer rather dull driving. To see the lake at its best, you should plan to get out on the water by steamship or canoe, or fly above it on a charter float-plane (see below).

Greenville is the de facto capital of Moosehead Lake, scenically situated at the southern tip. Change is creeping in to the North Woods—what was until recently a rugged outpost town is now orienting itself toward the tourist trade with boutiques and souvenir shops. Most shops now seem to stock a full line of T-shirts featuring moose. But the town's still a good place to base yourself for outdoor day excursions.

## ESSENTIALS

**GETTING THERE**   Greenville is 158 miles from Portland. Take the turnpike to the Newport exit (Exit 39) and head north on Route 7/11 to Route 23 in Dexter, following that northward to Route 6/15 near Sangerville. Follow this to Greenville.

**VISITOR INFORMATION**   The **Moosehead Lake Chamber of Commerce,** P.O. Box 581, Greenville, ME 04441 (☎ **207/695-2702**), maintains a very informative information center that's a strongly recommended first stop. Not only will you find a good selection of the usual brochures, but the center maintains files and bookshelves full of maps, trail information, and wildlife guidebooks and videos that visitors are free to use. There's also a limited number of guidebooks for sale and free advice from the staff. Open daily Memorial Day to mid-October 10am to 4pm, it's located on your right as you come into Greenville, next to the Indian Hill Trading Post(closed Wednesday and Sunday in the off-season). Advance information is also available via e-mail: moose@moosehead.net.

## OUTDOOR PURSUITS

**BOATING**   **Northwood Outfitters** on Main Street in Greenville (☎ 207/695-3288) is open daily and can help with planning a trip up the lake or into the woods, as well as load you up with enough equipment to stay out for weeks. They rent complete adventure equipment sets, which include canoe, paddles, life jacket, tent, sleeping bag, pad, camp stove, axe, cook kit, and more. The full kits start at $97 per person for 2 days, up to $272 per person for a week. Shuttle service and individual pieces of equipment are also available for rent, with canoes running $20 a day, and mountain bikes from $20 to $30 a day. The shop's Web site is www.maineoutfitter.com.

In Rockwood, **Moose River Landing** (☎ 207/534-7577) has motor boats for rent to explore the lake. A 20-foot pontoon boat is $125 per day (gas extra); aluminum and fiberglass outboards are $45 to $65 per day, with the first tank of gas free. (Canoes are also available at $15 per day.) The proprietor can make suggestions for beaches and quiet coves to visit along the huge lakeshore.

**CANOEING**   Follow in Thoreau's footsteps into the Maine woods on a canoe excursion down the ✪ **West Branch of the Penobscot River.** This 44-mile trip is typically done in 3 days. Put in at Roll Dam, north of Moosehead Lake and east of Pittston Farm, and paddle northward on the generally smooth waters of the Penobscot. There are several campsites along the river; pick one and spend the night, watching for grazing moose as evening descends. On the second day, paddle to huge and wild

# Moosehead Lake Area

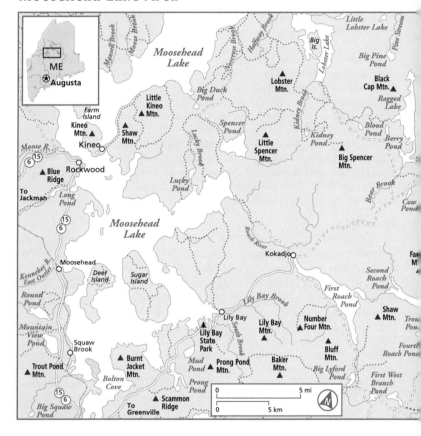

Chesuncook Lake. Near where the river enters the lake is the Chesuncook Lake House, a wonderfully remote farmhouse dating from 1864 and open to guests (see "Where to Stay," below). Spend the night here. The final day brings a paddle down Chesuncook Lake with its sweeping views of Mt. Katahdin to the east and the take-out near Ripogenus Dam.

**Allagash Canoe Trips,** P.O. 713, Greenville 04441 (☎ **207/695-3668;** e-mail: alcanoe@moosehead.net) has been offering guided canoe trips in the North Woods—including the Allagash, Moose, Penobscot and St. John's rivers—since 1953. A 5-day trip guided camping trip down the West Branch—including all equipment, meals, and transportation—costs $475 for adults, $350 for children.

If you'd prefer to go on your own, shuttling your car from Roll Dam to Ripogenus Dam is easily arranged. **Allagash Wilderness Outfitters** (☎ **207/695-2821**) charges around $50 to drive a vehicle from one end to the other so it will be waiting when you finish up.

If you're looking for less hassle and more drama, for about $275, two paddlers could depart from Greenville by seaplane (with your canoe lashed to the floats and your gear in the cargo bin) and be dropped off at Lobster Lake; 4 days later you'll be picked up at Chesuncook Dam and flown back to Greenville. Call Folsom's Air Service (see below) for details.

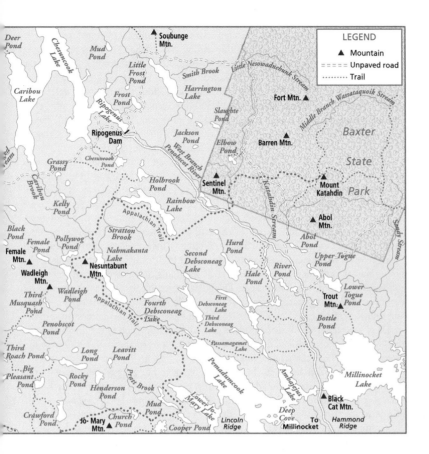

**HIKING**  A good destination for a day hike, and especially for families, is **Borestone Mountain Wildlife Sanctuary** (☎ 207/564-7946), located south of Greenville and north of the town of Monson. The mountain, which has not been cut for timber in more than a century, is today owned by the Maine Audubon Society. It's about 3 miles to the top of this gentle prominence; a booklet helps explain some of the natural attractions along the way. About halfway up, there's a staffed visitor center at Sunrise Pond that features natural history exhibits and displays of historical artifacts.

To find the mountain, drive 10 miles north of Monson on Route 6/15 (en route to Greenville) and look for the sign for Eliotsville Road on your right; turn here and continue until you cross a bridge over a river; turn left and head uphill for ³/₄ mile until you see signs for the sanctuary. Admission is $3 adult, $2 students, and children under 6 free. No pets.

Closer to Greenville, 3,196-foot **Big Squaw Mountain** (home to a ski area of the same name) offers superb views of Moosehead Lake and the surrounding area from its summit. The hike requires about 4 hours and departs about 5 miles northwest of Greenville on Routes 6/15 (turn west on the gravel paper company road and continue for 1 mile to the trailhead). Ask for more detailed directions at the vistior information center in Greenville.

One of my favorite hikes in the region is **Mount Kineo,** marked by a massive, broad cliff that rises from the shores of Moosehead. This hike is accessible via water;

near the town of Rockwood look for signs advertising shuttles across the lake to Kineo from the town landing (folks offering this service seem to change from year to year, so ask around; it usually costs about $5 round-trip). Once on the other side, you can explore the grounds of the famed old Kineo Mountain House (alas, the grand, 500-guest-room hotel was demolished in 1938), then cut across the golf course and follow the shoreline to the trail that leads to the 1,800-foot summit. The views from the cliffs are dazzling; one hiker I know says he has no problems on any mountain except Kineo, which afflicts him each time with vertigo. Be sure to continue on the trail to the old fire tower, which you can ascend for a hawk's-eye view of the region.

The famed **"100-Mile Wilderness"** of the Appalachian Trail begins at Monson, south of Greenville, and runs northeast to Abol Bridge near Baxter State Park. This is a spectacularly remote part of the state and offers some of the best deep-woods hiking in Maine. This trip is primarily for independent and experienced backpackers—there are no points along the route to resupply—although day trips in and out are a possibility.

One especially beautiful stretch of the trail passes along **Gulf Hagas,** sometimes called "Maine's Grand Canyon" (a description that's a bit grandiose, to my mind). The Pleasant River has carved a canyon as deep as 400 feet through the bedrock slate; the hiking trail runs along its lip, with side trails extending down to the river, where you can swim in the eddies and cascades. The gulf is accessible as a day hike if you enter the forest via logging roads. Drive north from Milo on Route 11 (east of Greenville) and follow signs to the Katahdin Iron Works (an intriguing historic site worth exploring). Pay your fee at the timber company gate, and ask directions to the gulf. Also near the Gulf is **The Hermitage,** a Nature Conservancy–owned stand of 120-foot white pines that have been spared the woodsman's axe.

A number of other hikes can be found in the area, but get good guidance as the trails generally aren't as well-marked here as in the White Mountains or Baxter State Park. Ask at the visitor information center, or pick up a copy of *50 Hikes in Northern Maine,* which contains good descriptions of several area hikes. Also, several local hikes are outlined on the Internet at www.maineguide.com/moosehead/mooshike.html.

**SNOWMOBILING** Greenville has become a snowmobilers' mecca in recent years, with hundreds of sledders descending on the town during good winter weather and then striking out into the remote woods. Along the Moosehead Trail, a 170-mile route that runs around the perimeter of the lake, you'll find lodging and meals at various stops along the way. If you're looking to rent a snowmobile, a recommended base is the modern **Evergreen Lodge** (Rte. 15, Greenville; ☎ **888/624-3993** or 207/695-3241; www.mainelodge.com), which has six comfortable guest rooms ($65 to $90 per night). The lodge has snowmobiles renting for $165 per day; a sledding package costs $475 double, which includes 2 nights of lodging, a 2-day snowmobile rental, and breakfasts both mornings.

For more information on snowmobile rentals and tours, contact **Sled Maine,** a consortium of white-water outfitters who switch to snow tours come winter. Call ☎ **877/275-3363,** e-mail info@sledme.com, or visit their Web site at www.sledme.com.

**WHITE-WATER RAFTING** Big waves and boiling drops await rafters on the heart-thumping run through Kennebec Gorge at the headwaters of the Kennebec River, located southwest of Greenville. Dozens of rafters line up along the churning river below the dam, then await the siren that signals the release. Your guide will signal you to hop in, and you're off, heading off through huge, roiling waves and down precipitous drops with names like Whitewasher and Magic Falls. Most of the excitement is over in the first hour; after that, it's a lazy trip down the river, interrupted only by lunch and the occasional water fight with other rafts. Also nearby is the less

# Moose-Watching

In the past 5 years a number of outfitters have sprouted up that offer to lead visitors along lakeshores and forest trails to view and photograph the wily moose, the region's most noted woodland resident. While you can see moose almost anywhere (keep a sharp eye out when driving!), a guided excursion will usually get you into some of the most beautiful spots in the region, hidden places you might not see otherwise. The moose-spotting batting average is quite high among all outfitters. Advance reservations are recommended, since guides often don't make plans to go out unless they have advance registrations. The friendly folks at the visitor information center can provide more information about these tours and help make arrangements.

Pontoon boats are perhaps the most comfortable vehicles to search for moose—it's like sitting in an outdoor living room that floats. **The Moose Cruise** at The Birches Resort in Rockwood (☎ **207/534-7305**) offers three excursions daily, each lasting a bit over 2 hours.

Those offering longer moose-watching excursions (4 to 5 hours) by canoe include the **Maine Guide Fly Shop** in Greenville (☎ **207/695-2266**) and **Ed Mathieu,** (☎ **207/876-4907**). Prices for the shorter tours run about $25, up to $95 for a 5-hour excursion (lunch or snacks included).

---

thrilling but more technical Dead River, which offers about a half-dozen release dates, mostly during early summer.

Commercial white-water outfitters offer trips throughout the summer at a cost of about $85 to $115 per person (usually at the higher end on weekends). **Northern Outdoors,** P.O. Box 100, The Forks, ME 04985 (☎ **800/765-7238;** www.northernoutdoors.com) is the oldest of the bunch, and offers rock-climbing, mountain-biking, and fishing expeditions as well, plus snowmobiling in winter. Other reputable rafting companies to check with include **Wilderness Expeditions,** P.O. Box 41, Rockwood, ME 04478, (☎ **800/825-9453**), which is affiliated with the rustic Birches Resort, and the **New England Outdoor Center,** P.O. Box 669, Millinocket, ME 04462 (☎ **800/766-7238**).

## DOWNHILL & CROSS-COUNTRY SKIING

**Big Squaw Mountain Resort** (☎ **207/695-1000**), located just outside of Greenville, fought an on-again-off-again battle with insolvency for years, but it's finally turned the corner. Founded by a paper company in 1963, the state took it over for a spell in the 1970s, and it's been owned by several private owners since. Most recently, it was acquired in late 1995 by Karen and James Confalone, who plan to expand the base lodge by 2001 to include a heated pool, spa, sauna, and hot tubs. More interestingly they purchased a Florida-based airline with 32 amphibious planes, with the idea of offering year-round service to the resort. Call for more information.

The ski mountain as yet hasn't been modernized and still features wonderful, winding old-fashioned runs (of the sort that the bigger mountains are now scrambling to re-create), and the views northward across frozen Moosehead Lake and Mt. Katahdin are terrific. The 18 slopes are served by two chairlifts and two surface lifts. Limited services, including ski rentals and a small cafeteria and restaurant, are located at the base. There are also 60 guest rooms on the mountain. Lift tickets are bargain-priced at $15

Monday through Thursday, and $24 Friday through Sunday. Expect to find old-fashioned New England skiing at its best-preserved here.

Cross-country skiing is available at **The Birches** (☎ **800/825-9453**), a rustic resort on the shores of Moosehead north of Rockwood. The resort offers 15 log cabins along with limited lodge accommodations. Some 24 miles of rolling backcountry trails are groomed daily.

## MOOSEHEAD BY STEAMSHIP & FLOAT PLANE

During the lake's golden days of tourism in the late 19th century, visitors could come to the lake by train from New York or Washington, then connect with steamship to the resorts and boarding houses around the lake. A vestige of that era is found at the **Moosehead Marine Museum** (☎ **207/695-2716**) in Greenville. A handful of displays in the small museum suggest the grandeur of life at Kineo Mountain House, a sprawling Victorian lake resort that once defined elegance; but the museum's showpiece is the *S.S. Katahdin,* a 115-foot steamship that's been cruising Moosehead's waters since 1914. The two-deck ship (it's now run by diesel rather than steam) offers a variety of sightseeing tours, including a twice-a-week excursion up the lake to the site of the former Kineo Mountain House. Fares vary depending on the length of the trip, and range from $12 to $25 for adults, and $6 to $13 for children 6 and over.

Moosehead from the air is a memorable sight. Stop by **Folsom's Air Service** (☎ **207/695-2821**) on the shores of the lake in Greenville just north of the village center on Lily Bay Road. Folsom's has been serving the North Woods since 1946 and has a fleet of five float planes, including a vintage canary yellow DeHavilland Beaver. A 15-minute tour of the southern reaches of the lake costs $20 per person; longer flights over the region run up to $60. A great adventure is the canoe-and-fly package. For $95 per person, Folsom's will drop you and a canoe off at remote river location; you then paddle to Lobster Lake, where you'll get picked up and returned to Greenville later that day.

## WHERE TO STAY & DINE

**Blair Hill Inn.** Lily Bay Rd. (P.O. Box 1288), Greenville, ME 04441. ☎ **207/695-0224.** www.blairhill.com. 8 units. $175–$265 double, including full breakfast. 2-night minimum on weekends. DISC, MC, V. Children over 12 are welcome. Closed Nov and Apr.

The Blair Hill Inn occupies an 1891 Queen Anne mansion that sits atop a hill with dazzling views of Moosehead Lake and the surrounding hills. It's been sparely and elegantly appointed with a mix of rustic and classic, like Oriental carpets on the white maple floors, and deer antler lamps. The bright first floor common rooms, the drop-dead-gorgeous porch, and the handsome guest rooms invite loafing. A pleasant afternoon spent here with a book in one hand and refreshing beverage in the other will not be considered a wasted afternoon. All guest rooms feature terry-cloth robes, spring water, and locally made soaps. Room #1 is the old master bedroom, featuring a panoramic sunset view, fireplace, a great old wardrobe and a classic bathroom. Room #5 is the smallest but still very bright with a large bathroom and two-person soaking tub. The rooms on the third floor (no elevator) have lower ceilings but are still quite spacious. All guests have access to the eight-person outdoor Jacuzzi, Adirondack chairs on the expansive lawn, and a small catch-and-release trout pond (ask about fly-fishing workshops).

**Dining:** The Fiddlehead Grille and features creative dinners, with entrees like penne with lobster and tarragon cream, and grilled beef tenderloin with a blue cheese crust ($13.95 to $20.95).

**Chesuncook Lake House.** P.O. Box 656, Greenville, ME 04441. ☎ **207/745-5330.** 4 units (all share 2 bathrooms), 3 cottages. $220 double, including all meals. Boat shuttle from dam: $110 per group each way. No credit cards. Open year-round. Pets allowed; $10 per day extra.

This 1864 farmhouse, located on the shores of remote Chesuncook Lake, is accessible only via seaplane, 4-mile hike, or 18-mile boat shuttle from Chesuncook Dam (details on reaching the hotel will be provided when booking your room, or see "Canoeing," above, for information on getting here by canoe.) During the day, guests can explore the remnants of Chesuncook Village, where Thoreau passed through in the mid-19th century, rent a canoe and explore 3,000-acre Gero Island, or just pass the time on the porch enjoying the views of Mt. Katahdin 35 miles to the east.

**Greenville Inn.** Norris St., Greenville, ME 04441. ☎ **888/695-6000** or 207/695-2206. www.greenvilleinn.com. E-mail: gvlinn@moosehead.net. 6 units, 6 cottages. Summer $135–$155 double, $165 cottage, $225 suite; off-season $125–$145 double, $155 cottage, $195 suite. All rates include continental breakfast buffet. 2-night minimum on holiday weekends. DISC, MC, V. No children under 8.

This handsome 1895 Queen Anne–lumber baron's home sits regally on a hilly side street in a residential neighborhood a short walk from Greenville's commercial district. The interiors are manly and sumptuous, with wonderful cherry and mahogany woodworking and a lovely stained-glass window of a pine tree over the stairwell. There's a handsome small bar, where you can order up a cocktail or Maine beer, then sit in front of the fire or retreat to the front porch to watch the evening sun slip over Squaw Mountain and the lake. The rooms vary in size (the new master suite with lake views is the best—and most expensive), but all are richly appointed. The trim cottages are furnished in a light summer-cottage style and have views of the lake. A European-style breakfast buffet includes homemade breads and pastries.

**Dining:** The dinners served in the elegant dining room are delicious. The menu features continental fare with a regional twist, with entrees of grilled lobster with lobster sauce and fresh corn couscous, and beef fillet with green peppercorn sauce and mushrooms duxelle. The restaurant is open for dinner daily late May through October; entrees range from $20 to $28.

**The Lodge at Moosehead Lake.** Lily Bay Rd. (P.O. Box 1167), Greenville, ME 04441. ☎ **207/695-4400.** Fax 207/695-2281. www.lodgeatmooseheadlake.com. E-mail: innkeeper@ lodgeatmooseheadlake.com. 8 units. A/C TV. $175–$395 double, including full breakfast. 2-night minimum. DISC, MC, V. Located $2^1/2$ miles north of Greenville on Lily Bay Rd. (head north through blinker). Children 16 and older are welcome.

The Lodge at Moosehead is housed in a regal 1917 home constructed on a hillside outside of town for a wealthy summer rusticator. The inn offers a mix of woodsy and modern; think Disneyland does the North Woods. The guest rooms are all carpeted, but there's Adirondack-style stick furnishings mixed in with wingback chairs and antique English end tables. The dining room, where a full breakfast is served year-round, has a brisk, modern feel in contrast to much of the rest of the inn. The hosts are especially proud of the beds they offer guests. Those in the main lodge are hand-carved by local artist Joe Bolf; the suites in the carriage house feature unique swinging beds, suspended from the ceiling by old logging chains.

**Little Lyford Pond Camps.** P.O. Box 340, Greenville, ME 04441. ☎ **207/280-0016** (cell phone). www.littlelyford.com. E-mail: info@littlelyford.com. 8 log cabins (each with private outhouse). $170 double. Rates include all meals. Accessible by logging road in summer; by snowmobile or ski-plane in winter. 2-night minimum on weekends and holidays. No credit cards. Pets allowed; $5 per day extra fee.

This venerable backwoods logging camp is one of the most welcoming and comfortable spots in the North Woods. Guests stay in cozy log cabins originally built to house loggers in the 1870s, each with a small woodstove, propane lantern, cold running water, a private outhouse, and plenty of rustic charm. The more spacious main lodge has books to browse and board games for the evening, and is where guests gather to eat. During the day, activities aren't hard to find, from fishing for native brook trout (fly-fishing lessons are available), canoeing at the two ponds situated down a short trail, or hiking the Appalachian Trail to Gulf Hagas, an appealing gorge 2 miles away. In winter, the cross-country skiing on the lodging's private network is superb, and time in the lodge sauna will make you forget the cold weather outside.

**Maynard's-in-Maine.** Rockwood, ME 04478. ☎ **207/534-7703.** www.maynardsinmaine. com. 14 units. $100 double, including 3 meals (bag lunch). AE, DISC, MC, V. Pets allowed. Closed late-Nov–May. Directions: Cross bridge over Moose River in Rockwood, make first left, continue to lodge.

Maynard's has long been one of my favorite places in the North Woods. This is the real thing—there's nothing the least faux, cute, or neo-rustic about it. It sits at the edge of Rockwood on the Moose River. While the sound of logging trucks across the way can be a bit jarring at times, the more memorable sounds are those of wooden screen doors slamming and the clank of horseshoes. Chickens wander through the grounds, and guests idle on birch and hickory chairs on cedar-post porches. Photos suggest that nothing has even moved, much less been replaced, in the main lodge over the past 50 years. The compound consists of a handful of rustic cabins edging a lawn, most furnished eclectically with some classic camp furniture, as well as cheesey flea-market finds. Wildwood Cottage has three bedrooms, all sharing a bathroom, woodstove and a large screened porch; Birch Cottage is smaller and appropriate for a couple, and has been less modernzied than others. The place is more *Field and Stream* than *House and Garden,* and if you're willing to abide by a sometimes funky aesthetic, it offers more than a glimpse of Maine the way it used to be. Note that not only are there no in-room phones, there's not even a pay phone on the premises.

**Dining:** The dining room is equally classic and unchanged. Coffee is offered before dinner, which is the old-school way. Two or more entrees are offered daily, usually New England favorites like pot roast, along with fruit juice, soup, salad, relish tray, beverages, and dessert. (No alcohol is served, but feel free to BYOB.) Outside guests are welcome to call ahead to see if there's room in the dining room; dinner is $12.95, and that includes everything but tax and tip.

## BAXTER STATE PARK & ENVIRONS

Baxter State Park is Maine's crown jewel, even more spectacular in its way than Acadia National Park. This 204,000-acre state park in the remote north-central part of the state is unlike more elaborate state parks you might be accustomed to elsewhere—don't look for fancy bathhouses or groomed picnic areas. When you enter Baxter State Park, you enter near-wilderness.

The park was single-handedly created by former Maine governor and philanthropist Percival Baxter, who used his inheritance and investment profits to buy the property and donate it to the state starting in 1930. Baxter stipulated that it remain "forever wild," and caretakers have done a good job fulfilling his wishes.

You won't find paved roads, RVs, or hook-ups at the eight drive-in campgrounds. (Size restrictions keep RVs out.) Even cell phones are banned. You will find rugged backcountry and remote lakes. You'll also find Mt. Katahdin, a lone and melancholy granite monolith that rises above the sparkling lakes and severe boreal forest of northern Maine.

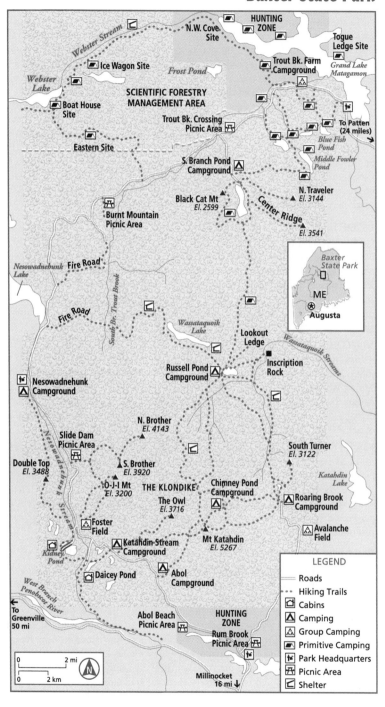

# Baxter State Park

HUNTING ZONE

N.W. Cove Site

Togue Ledge Site

Webster Stream

Ice Wagon Site

Frost Pond

Trout Bk. Farm Campground

Grand Lake Matagamon

Webster Lake

Boat House Site

SCIENTIFIC FORESTRY MANAGEMENT AREA

To Patten (24 miles)

Trout Bk. Crossing Picnic Area

Blue Fish Pond

Eastern Site

Middle Fowler Pond

S. Branch Pond Campground

Black Cat Mt El. 2599

N. Traveler El. 3144

Center Ridge

Burnt Mountain Picnic Area

El. 3541

Nesowadnehunk Lake

Fire Road

South Br. Trout Brook

Fire Road

Wassataquoik Lake

Lookout Ledge

Wassataquoik Streams

Russell Pond Campground

Inscription Rock

Baxter State Park

ME

Augusta

Nesowadnehunk Campground

N. Brother El. 4143

South Turner El. 3122

Slide Dam Picnic Area

S. Brother El. 3920

Double Top El. 3488

O-J-I Mt El. 3200

THE KLONDIKE

The Owl El. 3716

Chimney Pond Campground

Katahdin Lake

Roaring Brook Campground

Foster Field

Avalanche Field

Katahdin Stream Campground

Mt Katahdin El. 5267

Kidney Pond

Daicey Pond

Abol Campground

West Branch Penobscot River

To Greenville 50 mi

Abol Beach Picnic Area

HUNTING ZONE

Rum Brook Picnic Area

0     2 mi
0     2 km

N

Millinocket 16 mi ↓

LEGEND

Roads
Hiking Trails
Cabins
Camping
Group Camping
Primitive Camping
Park Headquarters
Picnic Area
Shelter

To the north and west of Baxter State Park are several million acres of forestland owned by timber companies and managed for timber production. Twenty-one of the largest timber companies collectively own much of the land and manage recreational access through a consortium called North Maine Woods, Inc. If you drive on a logging road far enough, expect to run into a North Maine Woods checkpoint, where you'll be asked to pay a fee for day use or overnight camping on their lands.

One bit of advice: Don't attempt to tour the timberlands by car. Industrial forestland is boring at its best, and downright depressing at its overcut worst. A better strategy is to select a pond or river for camping or fishing, and spend a couple of days getting to know a small area. Buffer strips have been left around all ponds, streams, and rivers, and it can often feel like you're getting away from it all as you paddle along, even if the forest sometimes has a Hollywood facade feel to it. Be aware that, outside of Baxter State Park, no matter how deep you get into these woods, you may well hear machinery and chainsaws in the distance.

## ESSENTIALS

**GETTING THERE**    Baxter State Park is 86 miles north of Bangor. Take I-95 to Medway (Exit 56), and head west 11 miles on Route 11/157 to the mill town of Millinocket, the last major stop for supplies. Head northwest through town and follow signs to Baxter State Park. The less-used entrance is near the park's northeast corner. Take I-95 to the exit for Route 11, drive north through Patten then head west on Route 159 to the park. The speed limit within the park is 20 m.p.h. Motorcycles and ATVs are not allowed within park boundaries.

**VISITOR INFORMATION**    Baxter State Park offers maps and information from its **headquarters,** 64 Balsam Dr., Millinocket, ME 04462 (☎ **207/723-5140**). For information on canoeing and camping outside of Baxter State Park, contact **North Maine Woods, Inc.,** P.O. Box 421, Ashland, ME 04732 (☎ **207/435-6213**). Information may also be found on the Web: www.northmainewoods.org. Help finding cottages and outfitters is available through the **Katahdin Area Chamber of Commerce,** 1029 Central St., Millinocket, ME 04462 (☎ **207/723-4443**).

**FEES**    Baxter State Park visitors with out-of-state license plates are charged a per day fee of $8 per car. (It's free to Maine residents). The day-use fee is charged only once per stay for those camping overnight. Camping reservations are by mail or in person only (see below).

The private timberlands managed by North Maine Woods levy a per-day fee of $4 per person for Maine residents, $7 per person for non-residents. Camping fees are additional (see below).

## OUTDOOR PURSUITS

**BACKPACKING    Baxter State Park** maintains about 180 miles of backcountry hiking trails and more than 25 backcountry sites, some accessible only by canoe. Most hikers coming to the park are intent on ascending 5,267-foot Mount Katahdin; but dozens of other peaks are well worth scaling, and just traveling through the deep woods hereabouts is a sublime experience. Reservations are required for backcountry camping, and many of the best spots fill up shortly after the first of the year. Reservations can be made by mail or in person, but not by phone.

En route to Mt. Katahdin, the Appalachian Trail winds through the "100-Mile Wilderness," a remote and bosky stretch where the trail crosses few roads and passes no settlements. It's the quiet habitat of loons and moose. Trail descriptions are available from the **Appalachian Trail Conference,** P.O. Box 807, Harpers Ferry, WV 25425 (☎ **304/535-6331;** www.atconf.org).

**CAMPING**   Baxter State Park has eight campgrounds accessible by car and two backcountry camping areas, but don't count on finding anything available if you show up without reservations. Park headquarters starts taking reservations in January, and dozens of die-hard campers traditionally spend a cold night outside headquarters the night before the first business day in January to secure the best spots. Many of the most desirable sites sell out well before the snow melts from Katahdin. The park is stubbornly old-fashioned about its reservations, which must be made either in person or by mail, with full payment in advance. No phone reservations are accepted. Don't even mention e-mail. The park starts processing summer camping mail requests on a first-come, first-served basis the first week in January; call well in advance for reservations forms. Camping at Baxter State Park costs $6 per person ($12 minimum per tent site), with cabins and bunkhouses available for $7 to $17 per person per night.

North Maine Woods, Inc. (see above) maintains dozens of primitive campsites on private forestland throughout its 2 million-acre holdings. While you may have to drive through massive clear-cuts to reach the campsites, many are located on secluded coves or picturesque points. A map showing logging road access and campsite locations is $3 plus $1 postage from North Maine Woods headquarters (see "Visitor Information," above). Camping fees are $5 per person in addition to the day use fee outlined above.

**CANOEING**   The state's premier canoe trip is the Allagash River, which starts just west of Baxter State Park and runs northward for nearly 100 miles to finish at the village of Allagash. The **Allagash Wilderness Waterway** (☎ 207/941-4014), was the first state-designated wild and scenic river in the country, and was protected from development in 1970. The river runs through heavily harvested timberlands, but a buffer strip of at least 500 feet of trees preserves the forest views along the entire route. The trip begins along a chain of lakes involving light portaging. At Churchill Dam, there's a wonderful stretch of Class I–II white-water for about 9 miles, then it's back to lakes and a mix of flatwater and mild rapids. Toward the end, there's a longish portage (about 150 yards) around picturesque Allagash Falls before finishing up above the village of Allagash. (Leave enough time for a swim at the base of the falls.) Most paddlers spend between 7 and 10 days making the trip from Chamberlain Lake to Allagash. Eighty campsites are maintained along the route; most have outhouses, fire rings, and picnic tables. The camping fee is $4 per night per person for Maine residents, $5 for non-residents.

Several outfitters offer Allagash River packages, including canoes, camping equipment, and transportation. **Allagash Wilderness Outfitters,** Box 620, Star Rte. 76, Greenville, ME 04441 (they don't have a direct phone line in summer; call Folsom's Air Service at ☎ 207/695-2821, and an operator will relay messages/requests via shortwave radio), rents a complete outfit (including canoe, life vests, sleeping bags, tent, saw, axe, shovel, cooking gear, first-aid kit, and so on) for $23 per person per day. **Allagash Canoe Trips** (☎ 207/695-3668; e-mail: alcanoe@moosehead.net) in Greenville offers 7-day guided descents of the river, including all equipment and meals, for $625 adult, $475 children under 18. On the Web, visit www.allagashcanoetrips.com.

**HIKING**   With 180 miles of maintained backcountry trails and 46 peaks (including 18 over 3,000 feet), Baxter State Park is the destination of choice for serious hikers in Maine.

The most imposing peak is 5,267-foot ✪ **Mount Katahdin**—the northern terminus of the Appalachian Trail. An ascent up this rugged, glacially scoured mountain is a trip you'll not soon forget. Never mind that it's not even a mile high (although a tall cairn on the summit claims to make it so). The raw drama and grandeur of the rocky,

# The North Woods & Allagash Wilderness Waterway

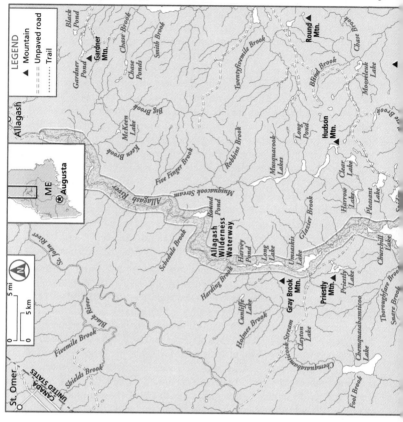

windswept summit is equal to anything you'll find in the White Mountains of New Hampshire.

Allow at least 8 hours for the round-trip, and be prepared to abandon your plans for another day if the weather takes a turn for the worse while you're en route. The most popular route leaves and returns from Roaring Brook Campground. In fact, it's popular enough that it's often closed to day hikers—when the parking lot fills, hikers are shunted to other trails. You ascend first to dramatic Chimney Pond, which is set like a jewel in a glacial cirque, then continue to Katahdin's summit via one of two trails. (The Saddle Trail is the most forgiving; the Cathedral Trail most dramatic.) From here, the descent begins along the aptly named "Knife's Edge," a narrow, rocky spine between Baxter Peak and Pamola Peak. This is not for acrophobes or the squeamish: In places, the trail narrows to 2 or 3 feet with a drop of hundreds of feet on either side. It's also not a place to be if high winds or thunderstorms threaten. From here, the trail follows a long and gentle ridge back down to Roaring Brook.

Katahdin draws the largest crowds, but the park maintains numerous other trails where you'll find more solitude and wildlife. A pleasant day hike is to the summit of South Turner Mountain, which offers wonderful views of Mt. Katahdin and blueberries for the picking in late summer. The trail also departs from Roaring Brook Campground and requires about 3 to 4 hours for a round-trip. To the north, there are several decent hikes out of the South Branch Pond Campground. You can solicit

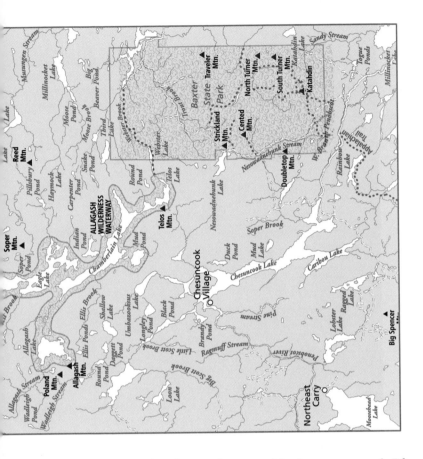

advice from the rangers and purchase a trail map at park headquarters, or consult *Fifty Hikes in Northern Maine.*

**SNOWMOBILING** Northern Maine is laced with an extensive network of snowmobile trails. If the conditions are right, you can even cross over into Canada and make tracks for Quebec. Although a handful of maps and guides outline the network, the trails are still largely a matter of local knowledge. Don't be afraid to ask around. A good place to start is **Shin Pond Village,** RR#1, Box 280, Patten, ME 04765 (☎ 207/528-2900; www.shinpond.com). Six cottages and five guest rooms are available, and snowmobile rentals are $125 to $150 per day. Three-day packages that include accommodations, two snowmobile rentals, most meals, and snowmobiling outfits are $749 double. Shin Pond is located within a ¼ mile of two ITS trails (the chief snowmobile routes).

**WHITE-WATER RAFTING** A unique way to view Mt. Katahdin is by rafting the West Branch of the Penobscot River. Flowing along the park's southern border, this wild river offers some of the most technically challenging white-water in the East. Along the upper stretches it passes through a harrowing gorge that appears to be designed by Cubists dabbling in massive blocks of granite. The river widens after this, interspersing sleepy flatwater (with views of Katahdin) with several challenging falls and runs through turbulent rapids. At least a dozen rafting companies offer trips on the Penobscot, with prices around $75 to $100 per person, including a lunch along the way.

Among the better-run outfitters in the region is **New England Outdoor Center** (☎ **800/766-7238;** www.neoc.com), located on the river southeast of Millinocket. **The River Driver Restaurant** is among the best in Millinocket; the owners also operate nearby **Twin Pine Camps,** a rustic lodge on the shores of Millinocket Lake with stellar views of Mt. Katahdin (cabins for two start at $105).

For other rafting options, contact **Raft Maine** (☎ **800/723-8633** or 207/824-3694), and they'll connect you to one of their member outfitters. You can also learn more about Maine rafting at the organization's Web site, located at www.raftmaine.com.

# Appendix A:
# Northern New England
# in Depth

Getting to know Vermont, New Hampshire, and Maine requires healthy amounts of both patience and persistence. None of these three states wear their attractions on their sleeve, waving them around for everyone to notice. They keep their best spots hidden in valleys and on side streets of small villages. Your most memorable experience might come in cracking open a boiled lobster at a lobster pound at the end of a dirt lane, or enjoying a million-dollar view from a low-rent hill in Vermont's Green Mountains. There's no Disneyland, Space Needle, or Grand Canyon here. Northern New England is the sum of dozens of smaller pleasures. Which isn't to say that northern New England lacks attractions.

It has the Green Mountains of Vermont, the White Mountains of New Hampshire, and Acadia National Park on the Maine Coast. It has wonderful, lost-in-time towns like Woodstock, Vermont and Hancock, New Hampshire; but attempting to explore this part of New England as a connect-the-dots endeavor, linking a few sights with long drives, is a recipe for disappointment. It's better to plan a slower itinerary that allows you to enjoy desultory trips between destinations, with enough time to explore sleepy villages and quiet byways, to turn down lanes you might otherwise speed by.

In the hills and along the region's waters, you'll find pristine landscapes, opportunities for outdoor adventure, and remnants of a rich past. Unlike Massachusetts or Virginia, northern New England wasn't a hub of colonial civilization.; but this region of rounded hills and fertile river valleys did attract early settlers, and thriving farms and villages dotted the countryside. Over the last century or so, northern New England suffered from an extended economic malaise, which incidentally helped preserve many of the old villages. Farm fields that would have sprouted neighborhoods of suburban tract homes in a more robust region remained farm fields here, and many villages are still dominated by churches and white-clapboard homes, and remain a long drive from the nearest mall. In parts of Maine, it's possible to live on the ocean and still be an hour's drive from the nearest traffic light.

Some commentators insist that New England's character is still informed by a grim Calvinist doctrine, which decrees that nothing will change one's fate and that hard work is a moral virtue. (New Englanders' dull acceptance that the Boston Red Sox will never be victorious is often trotted out as evidence of the region's enduring Calvinism.) One certainly can find healthy strains of Calvinism in certain popular New

England activities, such as hiking the severe, demanding paths of the White Mountains, swimming in the near-Arctic waters of Maine, or patiently waiting for fish to strike a fly while slowly being consumed by blackflies along a northern Vermont river. Don't expect posh resorts on sandy beaches where personal valets bring you fresh towels and Evian.

That's not to say a trip here means lumpy mattresses and inedible food. On the contrary, in the past 2 decades luxurious country inns and restaurants serving food to rival what you'll find in Boston have become part of the landscape. Enjoy these places, but to get the most out of your trip, be sure to leave sufficient time to rock idly on a porch, or to strike out on foot along an abandoned county road.

"There's nothing to do here," an inn manager in Vermont once explained to me. "Our product is indolence," and that's an increasingly rare commodity these days. Take the time to savor it.

## 1 A Look at the Past

Viewed from a distance, New England's history mirrors that of its namesake, England. The region rose from nowhere to gain tremendous historical prominence, captured a good deal of overseas trade, and became an industrial powerhouse and center for creative thought; and then the party ended relatively abruptly, as commerce and culture sought more fertile grounds to the west and south.

New England refuses to divorce its past. While cars, shopping malls, and condominiums have shaped recent culture here just as they have elsewhere in the U.S., these new interlopers have yet to overwhelm the region's profound sense of history. That's especially true in northern New England. Visitors to Maine, New Hampshire, and Vermont will find clues to the region's rich past everywhere they turn, from stone walls running through now-dense woods, to spectacular Federal-style homes standing alone in the countryside. Like the earlier glaciers, powerful economic trends moved across the region, then retreated, often leaving ample evidence of their presence in their wake.

Here's a quick look at some historical episodes and trends that shaped these northern states:

**INDIGENOUS CULTURE**   Native Americans have inhabited northern New England since about 7,000 B.C. While New York's Iroquois Indians had a presence in Vermont, northern New England was inhabited mostly by Algonquin Indians known as Abenakis ("people of the dawn"), who lived a nomadic life, moving with the seasons and traveling to areas where food was abundant. After the arrival of the Europeans, French Catholic missionaries succeeded in converting many of the Native Americans, and most of them sided with the French in the French and Indian Wars of the 18th century. Afterwards, the Indians fared poorly at the hands of the British, and never regained their stature in the region. Today, Indians are found in greatest concentration at several major reservations in Maine, including Indian Island in the Penobscot River, and two near the Canadian border in Washington County. Other than that, the few clues left behind by Indian cultures have been pretty much obliterated by later settlers.

**EUROPEAN SETTLEMENT**   Vikings are believed to have visited New England's shores 1,000 years ago, although they left little evidence of having done so. In 1604, some 80 French colonists spent a miserable winter at St. Croix Island at the mouth of the St. Croix River on the Maine–New Brunswick border. They did not care for their new home, and left in spring to resettle in what's now Nova Scotia. In 1607, 3 months after the celebrated Jamestown, Virginia, colony was founded, a group of 100 English settlers established a community at Popham Beach, Maine. The Maine winter demoralized the would-be colonists, and they returned to England the following year, leaving virtually no trace of their sojourn here.

Settlement of the region began in earnest in the later 17th and early 18th centuries as colonists from Massachusetts pushed northward and arriving Europeans settled along the south coast. The first areas to be settled were lands near protected harbors on the coast (such as Portsmouth, New Hampshire) and along waterways (like Brattleboro, Vermont).

**FARMING & TRADE**   During the 18th and early 19th centuries, the region followed two tracks. Residents of inland communities survived by clearing the land for farming and trading in furs. Vermont in particular has always been an agrarian state and remains prominent in dairy products to this day. (It's no coincidence that the Ben & Jerry's ice-cream company started here.)

Meanwhile, along the coast, the region prospered as boatyards were built in Maine's coves, and ship captains made tidy fortunes trading lumber for sugar and rum in the Caribbean. Even ice became a valued commodity, with Maine shipping tons of ice in insulated ships around the world—to the Caribbean, Brazil, and even India. More adventurous traders made the hazardous voyage to the Orient, bringing back lacquered furniture and Chinese paintings, which today still turn up in country auctions.

The pushing of the railroad into northern New England in the mid-19th century was another boon. The train opened up much of the interior, and some small towns sprung up overnight. The rail lines allowed local resources—such as the fine marbles and granites from Vermont—to be easily shipped to markets to the south.

**INDUSTRY**   New England's industrial revolution took root at the time of the Embargo Act of 1807. Barred from importing English fabrics, Americans had to build their own textile mills to obtain cloth. Other common household products were soon manufactured here, in particular shoes, which became an industrial mainstay for decades. Towns like Lewiston and Biddeford, Maine and Manchester, New Hampshire became centers of industrial production. The spread of rail encouraged the growth of industry, as products could be shipped more easily to lucrative markets. There was another effect: In the mid-19th century, the composition of much of the local population began to change as French-Canadians immigrated to work in the factories. Today, one can still detect a strong French-Canadian influence in Manchester, Biddeford, and Lewiston, a legacy of manufacturing days.

As with farming before it, manufacturing headed south, drawn by cheaper labor and closer access to raw materials like cotton and leather. Northern New England's industry began to die off slowly. Today, paper manufacturing and electronics account for much manufacturing, but far more residents are employed by service providers and government than by manufacturers.

**TOURISM**   In the mid- and late 19th century, northern New Englanders discovered a new cash crop: the tourist. All along the eastern seaboard it became fashionable for the gentry and eventually the middle class to set out for excursions to the mountains and the shore. The White Mountains of New Hampshire were among the first regions to benefit from this boom. By the mid-19th century, farmhouses were being converted to inns to accommodate those seeking inspiration in the crisp mountain air. Later in the century, tourists began to venture throughout the region in search of the picturesque and sublime. "Summer" became a verb.

# A Literary Legacy

Northern New England's role in the national literary tradition may best be symbolized by the poet, Robert Frost (1874–1963). This exceptionally gifted poet, who many believe was the greatest of the last century, was born in California but lived his life in Massachusetts, New Hampshire, and Vermont. In the New England landscape and community, he found a lasting grace and rich metaphors for life. ("Two roads diverged in a wood, and I— / I took the one less traveled by, / And that has made all the difference.")

Other writers from the region have also made their mark. Poet Henry Wadsworth Longfellow (1807–82) was born in Portland, lived much of his life in Boston, and was widely famed for his narrative poems. Sarah Orne Jewett of Maine has gained a following among scholars in recent years for her gentle stories of early life along the coast. Dorothy Canfield Fisher and Kenneth Roberts have done much to educate their readers about the history of Vermont and Maine, respectively. Edna St. Vincent Millay and Edwin Arlington Robinson both hailed from Maine; and Maine resident May Sarton, who died in 1995, was highly respected for her journals as well as her fiction.

Northern New England's influence is more subtle than the output of its authors. Travels through the region greatly influenced the work of Henry David Thoreau and Nathaniel Hawthorne. Artemus Ward, a comic performer who hailed from Waterford, Maine, was a national sensation as a comic backwoods philosopher in the mid-19th century, and humorist Mark Twain widely credited Ward as an inspiration for his own style of humor.

Contemporary writers seem to be attracted to northern New England not so much for its community of writers, but for the privacy the region affords. In Vermont, this includes novelist Howard Frank Mosher, whose works invest the Northeast Kingdom with mystical qualities, and Jamaica Kincaid and John Irving, who have adopted southwestern Vermont as their home. New Hampshire seems to have attracted more than its share of popular writers, including poet Donald Hall, essayist Noel Perrin, travel writer Bill Bryson, naturalist Sy Montgomery, and noted crank

---

The 19th-century tourism wave crested in the 1890s in Bar Harbor, Maine, which was flooded by the affluent, who spent time in their extravagant "cottages," and by the less prosperous, who occupied boarding homes and the lesser hotels. Several resort hotels from tourism's golden era still flourish in each of the three states.

**SLUMBER** While the railways allowed northern New England to thrive in the mid-19th century, they also played a central role in undermining this new-found prosperity. The driving of the Golden Spike in 1869 in Utah, linking America's Atlantic and Pacific coasts by rail, was heard loud and clear in New England—and it had a discordant ring. Transcontinental rail meant farmers and manufacturers could easily ship goods from the fertile Great Plains and California to faraway markets, making it even harder for New England's hardscrabble farmers to survive. Likewise, the coastal shipping trade, already in difficult straits, was dealt a fatal blow by this new transportation network; and

P. J. O'Rourke. Maine is summer home to a number of notable authors, including Anne Tyler and Christopher Buckley; and is the year-round home of native son Stephen King, considered not so much a novelist as Maine's Leading Industry.

Those looking for reading to broaden their understanding of the region need not look much further than the many excellent bookstores (both new and used) you'll find scattered throughout the region. Among my favorite books:

*In the Memory House* by Howard Mansfield (1993). This finely written book by a New Hampshire author provides a penetrating look at New England's sometimes estranged relationship with its own past.

*Inventing New England* by Dona Brown (1995). A University of Vermont professor tells the epic tale of the rise of 19th-century tourism in New England in this uncommonly well-written study.

*Lobster Gangs of Maine* by James M. Acheson (1988). This exhaustively researched book answers every question you'll have about the lobsterman's life, and then some.

*Northern Borders* by Howard Frank Mosher (1994). This magical novel is ostensibly about a young boy living with his taciturn grandparents in northern Vermont, but the book's central character is really Vermont's Northeast Kingdom.

*One Man's Meat* by E. B. White. White was a sometime resident of a saltwater farm on the Maine Coast and frequent contributor to *The New Yorker*. His essays, composed in the late 1930s and early 1940s, are only incidentally about Maine, but you get a superb sense of place by observing the shadows. Still in print in paperback.

*Serious Pig* by John Thorne with Matt Lewis Thorne (1996). The way to a region's character is through its stomach. The Thornes' finely crafted essays on Maine regional cooking are exhaustive in their coverage of chowder, beans, pie, and more.

*Vermont Traditions* by Dorothy Canfield Fisher. Written in that somewhat overwrought style popular in the 1950s, this still remains the best survey of the Vermont character.

the tourists found they could venture easily to the Rockies and other stirring western sites.

Beginning in the late 19th century and accelerating through much of the early 20th, New England lapsed into an extended economic slumber. As early as the 1870s, families commonly walked away from their farmhouses (there was no market for resale), and set off for regions with more promising opportunities. The abandoned, decaying farmhouse became an icon for New England, and open farmland that overspread much of northern New England was reclaimed by forest. With the rise of the automobile and the decline of the extended vacation, the grand resorts continued to languish. Many closed their doors as inexpensive motels siphoned off their business.

During the Great Depression, historian Bernard DeVoto toured New England. Of the depressed mill town of Fall River, Massachusetts, he wrote, "To spend a day in Fall River is to realize how limited were the imaginations of the poets who have described hell."

**BOOM**  Toward the end of the 20th century, much of northern New England has ridden an unexpected wave of prosperity. In the 1980s, a serious real estate boom shook the region, driving land prices sky high as prosperous buyers from Boston and beyond acquired vacation homes or retired to the more alluring areas, like the Maine Coast and regions near ski mountains in Vermont. Tourism seems also to be rebounding as well as urbanites of the Eastern seaboard opt for shorter, more frequent vacations closer to home.

Yet many communities have yet to benefit from the boom; they're still waiting to rebound from economic downturn of the 1930s. Especially hard-hit have been places like northeastern Vermont and far Downeast Maine, where residents still depend on dwindling local resources—timber, fisheries, and farmland—to eke out a living. For these folks, prosperity remains elusive.

## 2 The Natural Landscape

The natural history of northern New England is, quite literally, carved in stone.

The craggy White Mountains of New Hampshire, the famed rocky Maine coast, and the stony riverbeds that wind their way through pastoral Vermont are all evidence of the region's bedrock heritage. Visitors passing through much of northern New England will come away with impressions of brooding gray rock standing in only slight contrast to the dark spruce and fir nearby. Even in those softer-edged parts of the region—where green farmland and leafy hills predominate—the muscular, undulating ridges suggest that one needn't dig too deep before hitting unyielding rock.

Complex geological events millions of years ago laid the foundation for New England's terrain, but it was the massive and powerful glaciers that left the most readily identifiable fingerprints on the landscape. All three states were overspread with thick glaciers during several epochs, with the first glaciers forming as long as 1 million years ago. The last of the mile-thick glaciers melted away and retreated from northern New England relatively recently—some only 12,000 to 13,000 years ago.

Glaciers had an outsized hand in shaping the landscape. The sheer force and pressure of these massive ice sheets literally moved mountains and reconfigured valleys. As you travel, notice that many mountains are gently sloping on one side (usually the north), but fractured and craggy on the other. This resulted from glaciers grinding down the near side of the mountains as they moved through an area, then cracking and "plucking" mountainsides as they came over the crest. This is most plainly seen on "The Porcupines," a group of islands off Bar Harbor near Acadia National Park in Maine. The forceful action of glaciers also created dramatic, rocky bowls, called cirques, high in the mountains—spectacular Tuckerman Ravine on Mt. Washington is the most stunning example of this. Also notice the shape of the mountain valleys as you travel. Very few are V-shaped and steep-sided, as you find in the West; they're more often U-shaped, gouged out by slow-moving rivers of ice.

The glaciers took a sledgehammer to New England's landscape, but they also employed a more delicate hand. The northern woods are littered with "glacial erratics," boulders that were wrested from mountains (sometimes far away) and deposited by the melting ice in random, sometimes precarious spots. Geological gumshoes will find plenty more evidence of the glaciers as they travel, with landforms tagged with names seemingly from *The Hobbit*—kettles, eskers, drumlins, and kames. For more details on the glacial landscape, read the excellent introduction, *Glaciers & Granite: A Guide to Maine's Landscape and Geology* by David L. Kendall (Down East Books). Greenfield State Park in southern New Hampshire boasts several glacial landforms and is well worth visiting if you're curious about New England's glacial past.

Atop northern New England's bedrock foundation is a relatively thin veneer of mixed forest, home to a range of wildlife well adapted to the northern climate and terrain.

You'll discover two general types of forest in the region. In southern Vermont and New Hampshire, and from southwest Maine along the coast to near Acadia National Park, the landscape is blanketed with a leafy forest dominated by northern hardwoods, such as **maple** and **beech,** mixed with gracious **white pines** and **hemlocks.** This is the classic New England forest that, in autumn, attracts throngs to see the brilliant displays of fall foliage. In the northern reaches of the region, the forest is more stern and severe, dominated by the sharp, humorless spires of spruce and fir, the mood lightened here and there by thickets of birch. This is the forest explored by Thoreau in the mid-19th century, and one now prized by timber companies for its softwoods, which provide the raw material for paper mills and lumber.

When traveling in the mountains, notice also the changes in the forest landscape as you rise in elevation. This is especially notable in the White Mountains. You might hike through a leafy hardwood forest at the beginning of an ascent, then pass through spruce and fir forests before coming onto an Arctic landscape. As early as 1839, Thoreau determined that every 400-foot gain in elevation was equivalent to traveling 70 miles north. The scientist C. H. Hitchcock confirmed this observation, noting that the summit of Mt. Washington corresponded with Labrador and Greenland. "It is an arctic island in the temperate zone," he wrote. The Maine Coast shares some similarities. The cool summer temperatures (resulting in part from the offshoots of the Labrador current that sweep along the shores) create an ecosystem that one would expect to find at a more northerly latitude.

A rule of thumb in biology is that diversity diminishes as you head farther north, but abundance increases. That's true here with wildlife, which doesn't offer quite the range of the near-tropics, but what it has exists in quantity. Watch for **Eastern coyotes, fox, wild turkeys,** and **beavers.** Deer aren't as common as in the Mid-Atlantic states (although they're abundant enough to cause garden headaches on Maine's islands), but you may see **moose** and **black bear** at the edge of the denser forests. (Good places for moose-spotting are northernmost New Hampshire, and in Maine's Rangeley and Moosehead lakes region.) Along the coast, keep an eye peeled for **herons, ospreys,** and **bald eagles;** in the higher mountains, listen for the melancholy "quork-quork-quork" of the ravens. On the lakes throughout the region, watch for the beautiful, black-headed **loons,** and listen for their raucous whooping in the evening.

Keep an alert eye also for the hand of man in the natural landscape—we have long influenced the look of the land. With the decline of agriculture early in the 20th century, the forest has steadily reasserted itself, reclaiming fields and farmhouses. Today, it's not uncommon to come across stone walls in the midst of dense woods (built by farmers clearing rocks from their fields), or old cellar holes of farmhouses that once dotted remote valleys and high hillsides.

One final note: It would be almost criminally negligent to write of the region's outdoors without mentioning insects. You will experience them if you come here for camping, canoeing, or hiking, especially in early summer. Of particular note are mosquitoes and blackflies. Mosquitoes will be familiar to most visitors. The blackfly may not.

You will hear locals often speak of dreaded blackflies, and you may see them commemorated on T-shirts (One popular slogan puts it succinctly: "Blackflies don't just bite, they suck.") Blackflies are far smaller and nastier than common houseflies, and many visitors confuse them with gnats. Blackflies like to buzz jerkily around your eyes and nose, occasionally making kamikaze dives into an unprotected orifice. They'll rarely land and bite on your open skin; while some are distracting you with cunning nostril sorties, others will stealthily slip into cuffs and collars, tap you for a small donation of blood, then fly off and leave an itchy welt. Needless to say, this can be rather irritating.

A simple if slightly dorky defense is to button your cuffs and top shirt button, and tuck your cuffs into your socks. Most insect repellents also work decently against blackflies—lather it on your wrists, ankles, and neck; but there's only one foolproof solution: Explore the woods in late summer or fall, after the insect population has greatly diminished.

## 3 A Taste of Northern New England

The quintessential New England meal is the **clambake.** If you're adventurous, here's how it's done: Start by digging a deep pit at the beach. Build a roaring fire of driftwood and throw in some stones to absorb the heat. Cover the hot ashes and stone with a layer of seaweed, then throw in live lobsters. Add more seaweed, then unhusked corn on the cob, then another layer of seaweed followed by clams and a final topping of seaweed. Let sit. When the clams have opened, dig everything up and serve with lots of fresh butter. (A less gritty, easier version can be made in a large stockpot on your stove, or easier still, ask around in your travels—some restaurants and inns feature clambakes during the summer.)

All along northern New England's coast, you'll be tempted by seafood in its various forms. Live **lobster** can be had fresh from the boat at lobster shacks all along the Maine coast. The setting is usually rustic—maybe a couple of picnic tables and a shed where huge vats of water are kept at a low boil. A lobster dinner might include corn on the cob or some seafood chowder, and it isn't likely to cost more than $12 or $14 per person. Just ask if your lobster includes melted butter—not margarine, which does little to enhance the lobster's flavor, at least in my opinion.

Other seafood places near the ocean includes the ubiquitous fried fish joints, where you can get everything from cod to clams deep-fried with a breaded crust and served with a wedge of lemon or tartar sauce. Tasty, but not very wholesome if you're watching your waistline or nutritional intake. (A friend of mine once likened eating a bucket of fried claims to consuming a container of grout followed by a shot of Mazola.) The more upscale seafood restaurants offer fresh fish cooked over a grill or gently sautéed.

Inland, take time to sample the local products. This includes delectable **maple syrup,** which is sold at farmhouses and farm stands throughout the region. (Look for the no-frills signs tacked to a tree at the end of a driveway.) Check the label for Grade A syrup certification—it's lighter and sweeter than the heavier, more tart Grade B. (Many natives, however, prefer the stronger flavor of the lower grades.) **Cheese** is a Vermont specialty, especially the strong cheddar produced in cheese houses throughout the state. Look also for New England's famed **apple cider** and Maine's deliciously sweet and small wild **blueberries.**

Later in the summer, small farmers across the region set up stands at the end of their driveways offering fresh produce straight from the garden. Don't pass these by. You can usually find fresh berries, delicious fruits, and sometimes home-cooked breads. These stands are rarely tended; just leave your money in the coffee can, and make your own change if you need to.

Restaurateurs haven't overlooked New England's native bounty. Many fine restaurants throughout the region serve up delicious meals consisting of local ingredients—some places even tend their own gardens for the freshest greens and herbs. Some of the best restaurants are set well outside of the cities, borrowing from the French tradition of classic country inns serving superior food in pastoral settings. Talented chefs have taken basic ingredients that would have been familiar to the Pilgrims and adapted them to more adventurous palates. I'm thinking of some of the fine meals I've enjoyed while researching this guide, such as curried pumpkin soup, venison medaillons with shiitake mushrooms, and wild boar with juniper berries; but you needn't have a hefty budget to enjoy local fare. A number of regional classics fall under the "roadfood" category. Here's an abbreviated field guide:

**BEANS**   Boston is forever linked with baked beans (hence the nickname "Beantown"), but the sweet, earthy beans are popular throughout the region. Saturday night supper traditionally consists of baked beans prepared with molasses, salt pork, and dry mustard; whether or not to include an onion is often a matter of heated debate. Beans are served with sweet, heavy brown bread on the side. Some diners still offer up beans with breakfast. (Try it!) B&M Baked Beans are canned in a hulking old plant overlooking the water in Portland, but for more local flavor watch for community bean suppers that are frequently held on weekends.

**MOXIE**   Early in the last century, Moxie was a better-selling soft drink than Coca-Cola. Part of its allure was the fanciful story behind its 1885 creation: A traveler named Lieutenant Moxie was reputed to have observed South American Indians consuming the sap of a native plant, which gave them extraordinary strength. The drink was "re-created" by Maine native Dr. Augustin Thompson, who marketed it nationwide. It's still a popular drink in parts of New England (it's now manufactured by Coca-Cola), although some liken its taste to a combination of medicine and topsoil.

**LOBSTER ROLLS**   Lobster rolls consist of lobster meat plucked from the shell, mixed with just enough mayonnaise to hold it all together, then served on a hot-dog bun. I'll admit to being a heretic when it comes to lobster rolls— I've never really mustered much enthusiasm for them (a boiled lobster served with butter seems a much better use of the crustacean), but others rave about them. (I prefer crab rolls.) They're available at roadside stands and restaurants throughout Maine—even McDonald's in Maine offers a seasonal lobster roll that aficionados say is pretty good.

**CLAM CHOWDER**   Although clams are growing more scarce along the New England coast, a steaming bowl of clam chowder remains the preferred way to take the chill out of a drizzly, foggy day. In northern New England, you'll invariably find milk-based white chowder, in contrast to the much-disparaged tomato-based red chowder found farther south, in Rhode Island and New York. "Tomato-hating may seem a paltry thing on which to erect the foundations of a regional difference," writes food columnist John Thorne, but "the topic 'tomatoes and clams' has become a mainstay of Yankee identity, or at least the curmudgeonly, self-congratulatory kind."

**MUFFINS & PIES**   Muffins have long been a New England institution. A blueberry muffin is the classic choice, but a wide variety of fresh-baked muffins is available at bakeries, restaurants, and even convenience stores throughout the region. At a handful of traditional spots, blueberry muffins are still served with dinner. New Englanders are also serious about their pies, and it remains the dessert of choice throughout the region. Apple, blueberry, and mincemeat are the traditional favorites, but you can usually find a good selection of cream pies as well.

**INDIAN PUDDING**   Another traditional favorite throughout New England, Indian pudding is a baked pudding of cornmeal and molasses, often made with apples. If spiced just right, it can't be beat as a conclusion to a New England dinner. It's still served in many diners and old-fashioned restaurants. Ask for extra whipped cream.

**RED DOGS**   These garish red hot dogs are a perennial favorite among kids and a lot of older New Englanders as well. While there's no real difference in taste or content from the regular dogs, there's something unique—and somehow tastier—about eating a hot dog the color of a maraschino cherry.

**BEER**   Finally, I should mention beer. New England has more microbreweries than any other region outside of the Pacific Northwest—Maine alone has about two dozen craft breweries. Based on my own extensive and selfless research, Vermont's brews tend to excel with the lighter beers, including a number of fine lagers; breweries in Maine and New Hampshire tend to prefer the more robust brown and red ales, stouts, and porters.

Among my favorite brew pubs are the Portsmouth Brewery, Stonecoast Brewery (Portland), Federal Jack's Brew Pub (Kennebunkport), Sea Dog Brewery (Camden), Vermont Pub & Brewery (Burlington), and the Jasper Murdoch's Ale House (Norwich, Vermont). If you're buying beer for the road, I'd recommend the excellent Smuttynose Brown Dog Ale, Geary's Hampshire Ale, or the Carrabassett India Pale Ale; for dark beer, try Sea Dog's Hazelnut Porter, it has a wonderfully sort of burnt taste, a bit like Starbucks Coffee. Have fun discovering your own favorites.

## 4  Northern New England Style

When folks talk of northern New England "style," the conversation often veers toward church steeples and white clapboard, but New England style transcends those simple objects. Spend enough time here, and you'll realize New England style is defined by its *scale*, which is at once very grand and very human.

The scale can be seen in the way man's creations—whether public institutions, humble homes, or vessels on the water—relate to the landscape. You'll see it in the way a slender church spire rises from a wooded valley floor, or a silo from a hilltop farm. You'll find it in the way handsome homes cluster around a village green, or a low block of brick row houses curves toward the waterfront in a coastal city. You'll see it in the perfect lines of a lobster boat bobbing in a rocky cove, in the dimensions of an austere Federal house, and in the occasional surviving elm tree that perfectly frames a village street.

The building blocks of New England style, of course, are its early homes. You can often trace the history of a town by its architecture, as styles evolve from simple box-like homes to elaborate Victorian mansions. This primer should aid with basic identifications:

**COLONIAL** (1600–1700)   The New England house of the 17th century was a simple, boxy affair, often covered in shingles or rough clapboards. Don't look for ornamentation; these homes were designed for basic shelter from the elements and are often marked by prominent stone chimneys. Architecture of this early style is rather rare in northern New England, which was generally settled quite a bit later than Massachusetts. One good example is the Sherburne House (ca. 1695), at Strawbery Banke in Portsmouth, New Hampshire.

**GEORGIAN** (1700–1800)   Ornamentation comes into play in the Georgian style, which draws heavily on classical symmetry. Georgian buildings were in vogue in England at the time and were embraced by affluent colonists. Look for Palladian windows, formal pilasters, and elaborate projecting pediments over the main doorway. Some homes like Portsmouth's impressive Wentworth-Gardner House were made of wood but designed to look like masonry. Portsmouth is the best destination for viewing Georgian homes.

**FEDERAL** (1780–1820)   Federal homes may best represent the New England ideal. Spacious yet somehow austere, Federal homes are often rectangular or square, with low-pitched roofs and little ornamentation on the front (although carved swags or other embellishments might be seen near the roof line). Look for fan windows and chimneys bracketing the building. Excellent Federal-style homes are found throughout the region, many of which were built during the period of exceptional prosperity here prior to the Embargo of 1807. Kennebunkport, Maine, is rich with Federal homes set in tranquil neighborhoods.

**GREEK REVIVAL** (1820–60)   The easiest-to-identify Greek Revival homes feature a bold projecting portico with massive columns, like a part of the Parthenon grafted onto an existing home. The less dramatic homes may have subtle pilasters, or simply be oriented such that the gable faces the street, lending the impression that it has a triangular pediment. Greek Revival didn't catch on in New England quite the way it did elsewhere in the country, but some fine examples exist, notably in Newfane, Vermont, which is virtually a museum of Greek Revival architecture.

**VICTORIAN** (1860–1900)   This is a catch-all term for the jumble of late–19th century architectural styles that emphasized complexity and opulence. The best known Victorian style is the tall and narrow house with mansard roof and prickly-looking roof cresting. A wonderful example of this is author Stephen King's spooky house in Bangor, Maine, but the style also includes squarish Italianate homes with wide eaves; one of the best examples in the nation is the huge brownstone Victoria Mansion in Portland. Stretching the definition a bit, Victorian can also include the Richardsonian-Romanesque style, which was popular for railroad stations and public buildings. A superb Richardsonian building is the red sandstone Fairbanks Museum in St. Johnsbury, Vermont, built in 1889.

**SHINGLE STYLE** (1880–1900)   This uniquely New England style arose in the late 19th century and quickly became the preferred style for vacation homes among the very rich. These homes are marked by a profusion of gables, roofs, and porches, and were typically covered with shingles from roofline to foundation. Shingle-style homes project a sense of leisure and wealth. A number of the great "cottages" of Bar Harbor and Kennebunkport were constructed in this fashionable style.

**MODERN** (1900–present)   Quite frankly, the three states have produced little in the way of notable modern architecture. (One significant exception: Frank Lloyd Wright's Zimmerman House, in Manchester, New Hampshire.) This is even true in commercial architecture, a field in which much of the nation saw unsurpassed creativity in the mid-20th century. Remember that northern New England peaked economically in the mid-19th century. The subsequent lull did much to preserve the older architecture that lends the region its character, but little to produce modern buildings worthy of note. During the boom of the 1980s, a number of huge, ostentatious vacation homes sprouted, especially high on mountains near resorts and on rocky coastal promontories. My hunch is that architectural historians will in the future judge most of these homes rather unfavorably.

An excellent resource to have handy during a trip is *A Field Guide to American Houses,* by Virginia and Lee McAlester (Knopf, $21.95.)

Among idiosyncratic architectural styles to watch for is the "classic" New England farmhouse. These are huge and rambling, with the old barn connected to the main house with one or two intermediary buildings. This setup allowed the farmer to perform his barn chores in winter without having to brave the frigid winds. This style—locally called "big house, little house, back house, barn"—not only describes a building style, but was part of a well-known jump-rope rhyme. (Say it out loud.) These farmhouses are relatively common throughout the region.

Also very common is the simple Cape Cod–style home, the most austere and perhaps the most emblematic of New England architectural styles. These basic homes, built by farmers and fishermen, were designed to withstand severe winters, and typically consist of a door in the center flanked by two pairs of windows. Sometimes the chimney is in the center, sometimes on the end. Unlike Greek Revival homes, which turned the gable toward the road to affect a pedimented look, Capes expose the long roof to the road, and the fronts of these houses often seem to regard the landscape meekly. The style has endured for 3 centuries and never really went out of fashion. Even today, you'll often find new "capes" for sale in as-yet unlandscaped subdivisions, and even on the lots of modular home dealerships.

Where to go to discover the New England style? Northern New England is unusually blessed with perfect and near-perfect villages. Architecture buffs should head to Orford, New Hampshire; Castine and Kennebunkport, Maine; or Woodstock, Vermont. Aficionados of village greens will like Newfane, Vermont; Whitefield, New Hampshire; and Bethel, Maine. If it's that ineffable small-town feel you're looking for, set your sights on Grafton or Dorset, Vermont; Waterford, Maine; or Hancock, New Hampshire.

Keep in mind that New England is best appreciated when you're out of your car. Driving through a wonderful village, circling the green twice before heading onward, seems somehow inappropriate and unclean, like showing up at a wedding in gym clothes. You need to get out and stretch your legs, if just for a few minutes, to really appreciate the extraordinary scale of many of these towns. Take the time to walk the tree-lined streets or wander into a venerable church. These minor adventures often seem comforting and serene, like coming home after a long journey.

# Appendix B:
# Useful Toll-Free Numbers
# & Web Sites

## AIRLINES

**Aer Lingus**
☎ 800/474-7424 in the U.S.
☎ 01/886-8888 in Ireland
www.aerlingus.ie

**Air Canada**
☎ 800/776-3000
www.aircanada.ca

**Air New Zealand**
☎ 800/262-2468 in the U.S.
☎ 800/663-5494 in Canada
☎ 0800/737-767 in
     New Zealand

**Alaska Airlines**
☎ 800/426-0333
www.alaskaair.com

**American Airlines**
☎ 800/433-7300
www.americanair.com

**American Trans Air**
☎ 800/435-9282
www.ata.com

**America West Airlines**
☎ 800/235-9292
www.americawest.com

**British Airways**
☎ 800/247-9297
☎ 0345/222-111 in Britain
www.british-airways.com

**Canadian Airlines International**
☎ 800/426-7000
www.cdnair.ca

**Continental Airlines**
☎ 800/525-0280
www.continental.com

**Delta Air Lines**
☎ 800/221-1212
www.delta-air.com

**Hawaiian Airlines**
☎ 800/367-5320
www.hawaiianair.com

**Midway Airlines**
☎ 800/446-4392
www.midwayair.com

**Midwest Express**
☎ 800/452-2022
www.midwestexpress.com

**Northwest Airlines**
☎ 800/225-2525
www.nwa.com

**Qantas**
☎ 800/474-7424 in the U.S.
☎ 612/9691-3636 in Australia
www.qantas.com

**Southwest Airlines**
☎ 800/435-9792
www.iflyswa.com

**Tower Air**
☎ 800/34-TOWER
     (800/348-6937) outside
     New York
☎ 718/553-8500
www.towerair.com

**Trans World Airlines (TWA)**
☎ 800/221-2000
www.twa.com

**United Airlines**
☎ 800/241-6522
www.ual.com

**US Airways**
☎800/428-4322
www.usairways.com

**Virgin Atlantic Airways**
☎800/862-8621 in
   Continental U.S.
☎0293/747-747 in Britain
www.fly.virgin.com

## CAR-RENTAL AGENCIES

**Advantage**
☎800/777-5500
www.arac.com

**Alamo**
☎800/327-9633
www.goalamo.com

**Auto Europe**
☎800/223-5555
www.autoeurope.com

**Avis**
☎800/331-1212 in
   Continental U.S.
☎800/TRY-AVIS in Canada
www.avis.com

**Budget**
☎800/527-0700
www.budgetrentacar.com

**Dollar**
☎800/800-4000
www.dollarcar.com

**Enterprise**
☎800/325-8007
www.pickenterprise.com

**Hertz**
☎800/654-3131
www.hertz.com

**Kemwel Holiday Auto (KHA)**
☎800/678-0678
www.kemwel.com

**National**
☎800/CAR-RENT
www.nationalcar.com

**Payless**
☎800/PAYLESS
www.paylesscar.com

**Rent-A-Wreck**
☎800/535-1391
rent-a-wreck.com

**Thrifty**
☎800/367-2277
www.thrifty.com

## MAJOR HOTEL & MOTEL CHAINS

**Baymont Inns & Suites**
☎800/301-0200
www.baymontinns.com

**Best Western International**
☎800/528-1234
www.bestwestern.com

**Clarion Hotels**
☎800/CLARION
www.hotelchoice.com

**Comfort Inns**
☎800/228-5150
www.hotelchoice.com

**Courtyard by Marriott**
☎800/321-2211
www.courtyard.com

**Days Inn**
☎800/325-2525
www.daysinn.com

**Doubletree Hotels**
☎800/222-TREE
www.doubletreehotels.com

**Econo Lodges**
☎800/55-ECONO
www.hotelchoice.com

**Fairfield Inn by Marriott**
☎800/228-2800
www.fairfieldinn.com

**Hampton Inn**
☎800/HAMPTON
www.hampton-inn.com

**Hilton Hotels**
☎ 800/HILTONS
www.hilton.com

**Holiday Inn**
☎ 800/HOLIDAY
www.basshotels.com

**Howard Johnson**
☎ 800/654-2000
www.hojo.com

**Hyatt Hotels & Resorts**
☎ 800/228-9000
www.hyatt.com

**ITT Sheraton**
☎ 800/325-3535
www.sheraton.com

**La Quinta Motor Inns**
☎ 800/531-5900
www.laquinta.com

**Marriott Hotels**
☎ 800/228-9290
www.marriott.com

**Motel 6**
☎ 800/4-MOTEL6 (800/466-8536)
www.motel6.com

**Quality Inns**
☎ 800/228-5151
www.hotelchoice.com

**Radisson Hotels International**
☎ 800/333-3333
www.radisson.com

**Ramada Inns**
☎ 800/2-RAMADA
www.ramada.com

**Red Carpet Inns**
☎ 800/251-1962
www.reservahost.com

**Red Lion Hotels & Inns**
☎ 800/547-8010
www.redlion.com

**Red Roof Inns**
☎ 800/843-7663
www.redroof.com

**Residence Inn by Marriott**
☎ 800/331-3131
www.residenceinn.com

**Rodeway Inns**
☎ 800/228-2000
www.hotelchoice.com

**Super 8 Motels**
☎ 800/800-8000
www.super8motels.com

**Travelodge**
☎ 800/255-3050
www.travelodge.com

**Vagabond Inns**
☎ 800/522-1555
www.vagabondinns.com

**Wyndham Hotels and Resorts**
☎ 800/822-4200 in Continental
U.S. and Canada
www.wyndham.com

**Toll-Free Numbers & Web Sites**

# Index

**Index**

## FROMMER'S® COMPLETE TRAVEL GUIDES

Alaska
Amsterdam
Arizona
Atlanta
Australia
Austria
Bahamas
Barcelona, Madrid &
  Seville
Beijing
Belgium, Holland &
  Luxembourg
Bermuda
Boston
British Columbia & the
  Canadian Rockies
Budapest & the Best of
  Hungary
California
Canada
Cancún, Cozumel &
  the Yucatán
Cape Cod, Nantucket &
  Martha's Vineyard
Caribbean
Caribbean Cruises & Ports
  of Call
Caribbean Ports of Call
Carolinas & Georgia
Chicago
China
Colorado
Costa Rica
Denmark
Denver, Boulder & Colorado
  Springs
England
Europe

European Cruises & Ports
  of Call
Florida
France
Germany
Greece
Greek Islands
Hawaii
Hong Kong
Honolulu, Waikiki &
  Oahu
Ireland
Israel
Italy
Jamaica
Japan
Las Vegas
London
Los Angeles
Maryland & Delaware
Maui
Mexico
Miami & the Keys
Montana & Wyoming
Montréal & Québec City
Munich & the Bavarian
  Alps
Nashville & Memphis
Nepal
New England
New Mexico
New Orleans
New York City
New Zealand
Nova Scotia, New Brunswick
  & Prince Edward Island
Oregon
Paris

Philadelphia & the
  Amish Country
Portugal
Prague & the Best of the
  Czech Republic
Provence & the Riviera
Puerto Rico
Rome
San Antonio & Austin
San Diego
San Francisco
Santa Fe, Taos & Albuquerque
Scandinavia
Scotland
Seattle & Portland
Singapore & Malaysia
South Africa
Southeast Asia
South Pacific
Spain
Sweden
Switzerland
Thailand
Tokyo
Toronto
Tuscany & Umbria
USA
Utah
Vancouver & Victoria
Vermont, New Hampshire
  & Maine
Vienna & the Danube Valley
Virgin Islands
Virginia
Walt Disney World &
  Orlando
Washington, D.C.
Washington State

## FROMMER'S® DOLLAR-A-DAY GUIDES

Australia from $50 a Day
California from $60 a Day
Caribbean from $70 a Day
England from $70 a Day
Europe from $60 a Day

Florida from $60 a Day
Hawaii from $70 a Day
Ireland from $60 a Day
Italy from $70 a Day
London from $85 a Day

New York from $80 a Day
Paris from $85 a Day
San Francisco from $60 a Day
Washington, D.C.,
  from $60 a Day

## FROMMER'S® PORTABLE GUIDES

Acapulco, Ixtapa &
  Zihuatanejo
Alaska Cruises & Ports of Call
Bahamas
Baja & Los Cabos
Berlin
California Wine Country
Charleston & Savannah
Chicago

Dublin
Hawaii: The Big Island
Las Vegas
London
Maine Coast
Maui
New Orleans
New York City
Paris

Puerto Vallarta, Manzanillo
  & Guadalajara
San Diego
San Francisco
Sydney
Tampa & St. Petersburg
Venice
Washington, D.C.

## FROMMER'S® NATIONAL PARK GUIDES

Family Vacations in the
  National Parks
Grand Canyon

National Parks of the
  American West
Rocky Mountain

Yellowstone & Grand Teton
Yosemite & Sequoia/
  Kings Canyon
Zion & Bryce Canyon

## FROMMER'S® MEMORABLE WALKS

Chicago
London

New York
Paris

San Francisco
Washington D.C.

## FROMMER'S® GREAT OUTDOOR GUIDES

New England
Northern California

Southern California & Baja
Southern New England

Washington & Oregon

## FROMMER'S® BORN TO SHOP GUIDES

Born to Shop: China
Born to Shop: France

Born to Shop: Italy
Born to Shop: London

Born to Shop: New York
Born to Shop: Paris

## FROMMER'S® IRREVERENT GUIDES

Amsterdam
Boston
Chicago
Las Vegas

London
Los Angeles
Manhattan
New Orleans

Paris
San Francisco
Seattle & Portland
Vancouver

Walt Disney World
Washington, D.C.

## FROMMER'S® BEST-LOVED DRIVING TOURS

America
Britain
California

Florida
France
Germany

Ireland
Italy
New England

Scotland
Spain
Western Europe

## THE UNOFFICIAL GUIDES®

Bed & Breakfasts in
  California
  Bed & Breakfasts in
  New England
Bed & Breakfasts in
  the Northwest
Beyond Disney
Branson, Missouri
California with Kids
Chicago

Cruises
Disneyland
Florida with Kids
Golf Vacations in the
  Eastern U.S.
The Great Smoky &
  Blue Ridge
  Mountains
Inside Disney

Hawaii
Las Vegas
London
Miami & the Keys
Mini Las Vegas
Mini-Mickey
New Orleans
New York City
Paris

Safaris
San Francisco
Skiing in the West
Walt Disney World
Walt Disney World
  for Grown-ups
Walt Disney World
  for Kids
Washington, D.C.

## SPECIAL-INTEREST TITLES

Frommer's Britain's Best Bed & Breakfasts and
  Country Inns
Frommer's Britain's Best Bike Rides
The Civil War Trust's Official Guide
  to the Civil War Discovery Trail
Frommer's Caribbean Hideaways
Frommer's Food Lover's Companion to France
Frommer's Food Lover's Companion to Italy
Frommer's Gay & Lesbian Europe
Frommer's Exploring America by RV
Hanging Out in Europe
Israel Past & Present

Mad Monks' Guide to California
Mad Monks' Guide to New York City
Frommer's The Moon
Frommer's New York City with Kids
The New York Times' Unforgettable
  Weekends
Places Rated Almanac
Retirement Places Rated
Frommer's Road Atlas Britain
Frommer's Road Atlas Europe
Frommer's Washington, D.C., with Kids
Frommer's What the Airlines Never Tell You